Part II, "Mid-Passage," describes Flaubert's middle years as a noted author. He took an apartment in Paris, where he came to know the prominent artists and intellectuals of the time, among them George Sand, Emile Zola, Ivan Turgenev, and Guy de Maupassant. He continued to write: *Salammbô*, a tale of ancient Carthage; and *A Sentimental Education*, a picture of life among French dilettantes and intellectuals during the Revolution of 1848.

Part III, "Tribulation," reveals the aging Flaubert, beset with financial worries, problems with his publishers, and frustrations in his work. Still he continued to create—a new version of his early *Temptation of Saint Anthony; Bouvard and Pécuchet*, a satire of the bourgeoisie he hated; and the *Three Tales*.

Carefully and sympathetically—but never pedantically—Professor Bart has dealt with Flaubert's agony of creation, his family, his romantic and literary relationships, and with the final anguished years.

This volume, incorporating the results of other recent Flaubert scholarship as well as Professor Bart's own extensive research, also contains more than three dozen pages of illustrations and provides full source references.

Flaubert

Benjamin F. Bart, now professor of French in the University of Pittsburgh, has formerly held teaching positions in Harvard University, Syracuse University, Pomona College, and the University of Michigan. He holds the A.B., M.A., and Ph.D. degrees from Harvard and has done other work in New York University, Columbia University, and the Sorbonne.

Professor Bart is the author of two other books—*Flaubert's Landscape Descriptions* (1956) and *Madame Bovary and the Critics* (1966)—and editor of a French reader and a collection of Camus's short stories. He has had articles published in all the major periodicals in the field of French literature.

BENJAMIN F. BART

Flaubert

SYRACUSE UNIVERSITY PRESS

Manufactured in the United States of America

Preface

> Writing a book creates an eternal family for you in humanity. All those who later live upon your thought are like children seated at table about your hearth. How grateful I am to those wonderful, old authors whom you devour in huge mouthfuls, whom it seems you must have known, and of whom you dream as you do of dead friends.
>
> From a letter written while drafting *Madame Bovary*, 1854

It is time to prepare a new biography of Gustave Flaubert. Since the last general studies appeared, Flaubert's place in literature has undergone considerable revaluation, and he is firmly established as one of the principal sources from which the novel has been derived in the last hundred years. In addition, scholars have become aware of the tens of thousands of sheets of manuscript materials available to them for the establishing of a new biography. All earlier ones prove, in the light of these new materials, to be seriously inadequate, weakened by important misinterpretation of hitherto incomplete data, and based in considerable measure upon legend rather than fact. For this reason alone a restatement is in order.

Flaubert had little use for critics and less for biographers. Literary criticism he ranked below the writing of doggerel or the solving of acrostics, both of which he felt required more invention. The critic was the delight of the bourgeois, he felt; he added that mules admire geldings. And he was sure that there had not been one good critic since the beginning of time. Moreover, the better the work, the more the critics leap upon it, just as white linen attracts fleas. Critics are an eternal mediocrity living at the expense of genius either to belittle it or to exploit it, a race of insects happily eating away at the beautiful foliage of art.

It requires some courage, in the face of these warnings, to undertake a critical study of Flaubert; it is even more hazardous to undertake what is also a critical biography, because he felt that this was precisely to falsify the entire enterprise. In the first place,

Flaubert was sure that he had no biography (except a nonsense one which he offered to anyone who cared to use it and which rapidly degenerated into enormities and obscenities). Why should grocers and customs officials learn that you tended to drink too much or liked to play the harmonica? It was none of their business and would stand between them and your work of art. The biography of an artist was to Flaubert an enterprise infuriating, ill conceived, and immoral.

Nonetheless I have ventured to prepare a general study of the life and works of Gustave Flaubert, conscious that the master would have roared in pain and rage, hurled invective, and condemned me happily to an outer reach of hell no properly turned sentence ever reached. It requires justification, which may perhaps even win Flaubert's pardon.

Flaubert is, so far as I am aware, a unique case. He is a creative artist of considerable stature in whose life and works it is possible to study the creative process more adequately than perhaps has ever been possible or ever can again be possible with any other figure. While he is not among the score or two of the most gifted men and women in the history of the world, still his achievements, which include *Madame Bovary*, *A Sentimental Education*, *Three Tales*, and a body of theoretical statements on esthetics, rank him very high and give intense interest to the process by which he reached and formulated them. But, alone among major creative people up to his day, he carried the preservation of documents about himself to the point of mania, the word he himself applied to it. No paper with words on it was too trivial to be kept over the decades; no draft, however crossed out, did he ever deliberately throw away. In addition, as he himself said, he was a man of the pen, and thoughts were incomplete to him until he had written them down. Even passing feelings merited ink and paper: "My dog died last night; I am feeling more and more despondent." Hence this man's spiritual, mental, and emotional autobiography is all recorded, in an unimaginable chaos, to be sure; but it is there, and his concerns, his joys, his anxieties and his fears, his casual daily events and his psychological depths he recorded on paper and then kept. Many thousands of these documents have been preserved.

In addition, a would-be writer from childhood, he constantly wrote: letters to friends, short stories, plays, and other pieces, auto-biography and philosophy, anything and everything. What he sent to others, they tended to keep; the rest he preserved patiently. It all lies waiting to be interpreted.

It is in the matter of interpretation that the final unique element enters for Flaubert. So far as I know, no other creative man of his own day or earlier carried this mania to this extent; but others of a later day have done so, with solemnity or with glee. They, how-ever, can never offer the reader the raw, unconscious revelations which he does; for within a very short time after Flaubert's death in 1880, Sigmund Freud had eliminated for all time the possibility that an educated man would commit to paper indicative remarks about his psyche without knowing he was doing it. And that self-con-sciousness alone means tampering with the entire record. Flaubert died just in time to avoid this.

Out of thousands of letters, tens of thousands of sheets of drafts for his novels, and uncounted private papers in Paris, in Rouen where he lived, and in Chantilly where many of his letters are stored, I have sought to establish a coherent account of how he came to create what he did. I do not know what genius is, of course. But the record does illuminate certain sensitivities and certain ob-sessions, certain gifts of easy response and curses of disease, some fleeting but momentous occurrences and other long-sustained as-pirations; these gave to Flaubert's life and his picture of it a particu-lar cast. Since he happened to be able to learn to write, these led him to write as he did.

The mystery of creation is neither unveiled nor deflowered in these pages; but one may, with a kind of tender respect, watch a tortured man move from anguish to a written page. If the reader finds in it something of the awe that creation should always inspire, he and I shall have been lucky. If that is too much to hope for, then at any rate he will find here the record from which he may himself piece together some notion of how it takes place. For that record Flaubert did write, and its outlines I have reproduced here.

I have preferred to tell the story, as much as possible, in Flau-bert's own terms. Where I could be sure of my ground and know precisely what personal situation he was describing, I have let his own words, translated into English, bear the burden of what he felt occurred. Moreover, I have at no time attributed to him a thought or emotion which he does not somewhere specifically say he had, and if the lapse of time between the event and his statement could be crucial, I have let the reader know it.

I have attempted to write this study as Flaubert wrote his novels, without overtly intervening myself. He once said that the novelist should imitate the procedures of God in His creation: although present everywhere, he should be visible nowhere. I have tried to transfer this canon to the writing of a biography. While no biography can be objective, its presentation may at any rate be made to appear so. From the millions of items available, I have had to select those which were to me significant and representative. I have sought to keep the selection from being arbitrary, but the objective reality, Flaubert, is no more attainable—or "real"—than a friend whom one knows. Any two people describing him would work from the same data but produce two different portraits. Many years of research do mean that the data about Flaubert which are available to me are more extensive and more reliable than those available to earlier biographers of him. But the determination of which are significant and the emphases and filiations which are inevitable and indispensable in the writing of any biography make it a personal, not a scientific, work.

This book presents what Flaubert is to me. But I have preferred to leave it at that. I have lived—spiritually at least—with Flaubert for some twenty years; I hope that my readers will grow to share my fondness for him. But I have refrained from stating within the book either my approval or my disapproval of what I have to tell. Understanding of Flaubert has seemed to me more to be sought than praise or blame for him. Hence, following his own model in his novels, my effort has been to let the reader understand the man. Flaubert would have felt that, from such an understanding, admiration and affection, sympathy or compassion, will arise more surely and more lastingly than from the author's interjecting his own judgments in these matters. These judgments, Flaubert felt, can only come between the reader and the subject of the book, to the loss of both. I concur.

The specialist in Flaubert, unless he has worked in the manuscript sources, will be puzzled sometimes at the picture I present.

Unfortunately almost all the published texts of Flaubert's private papers have been heavily censored, usually without any indication that suppressions have been made. These have provided most interesting insights: editors do not suppress and censor the trivial. In bibliographical endnotes I have indicated where the supporting data are to be found.

There remains only the pleasant task of stating my debts, which are many and heavy. The bibliography of Flaubert runs into thousands of items; I have sought to read all the important ones, and I realize how entirely my study is a prolongation of these, a dwarf perhaps, but standing on their giant shoulders, to borrow the pleasant medieval image. Readers familiar with them will recognize how constantly I have drawn upon the studies of Descharmes, Seznec, Dumesnil, Gérard-Gailly, Pommier, Leleu, Thibaudet, Bruneau, and Levin, to name only the more obvious. Less obvious and therefore needing more careful statement, is my tremendous debt to several librarians, without whose assistance I could never have carried out my research, for it is of the nature of French libraries that only personal guidance suffices to thread the maze. Let me particularly thank Mademoiselle Madeleine Cottin, of the Department of Manuscripts in the Paris Bibliothèque nationale; her unfailing helpfulness when I was stopped by difficulties, her ingenuity in solving problems of reading or interpretation, and her wide knowledge of Flaubert himself were responsible for unraveling many of my tangles. In addition, Monsieur de Saint-Remy, of the Bibliothèque historique of the City of Paris, Mademoiselle Dupic, of the Rouen Bibliothèque municipale, and Mademoiselle Lapadu-Hargues, of the Library of the Musée des Arts et Traditions populaires in Paris, provided kindly and expert help, without which I could not have made the use I did of their admirable collections. Further, Mrs. Ruth Bandy, administrative assistant in the Syracuse University Graduate School, who typed the final manuscript, made many excellent suggestions, general or detailed, which I gratefully accepted.

To Professor Jean Pommier I am deeply indebted. His kindness in giving me access to the extraordinarily rich Flaubert collections of which he is curator in the Bibliothèque Lovenjoul at Chantilly was only the passport to many hours of helpful advice, penetrating interpretations, and the skills and insights which have put all students of French letters in his debt. His detailed knowledge of Flaubert, his skill in deciphering handwritings which puzzled me, and his inventive sensitivity in seeking meaningful interpretations to be placed upon the creative act have informed innumerable pages of this study.

Jean Seznec, Maréchal Foch professor of French literature at All Souls College, Oxford, was my master at Harvard twenty years ago and has been my mentor ever since. He taught me most of what I know of the goals and methods of the study of literature. I should have dedicated this work to him in very humble acknowledgment of my debt to him had it not seemed presumptuous. I can therefore only thank *il Maestro di color che sanno*.

The American Council of Learned Societies has on three occasions supported my work, the Ford Foundation on another occasion. The American scholar who works in Europe soon discovers how fortunate he is that such largesse is placed at his disposal. I am also most grateful to Syracuse University, which has been most generous with its time, its funds, and its patience, while it waited for this book to materialize.

Syracuse, New York   BENJAMIN F. BART
Summer, 1967

Contents

Preface   v

PART I—To *Madame Bovary*

1. Growing Up in the Hôtel-Dieu (1821-35)   3
2. Adolescence under Romanticism (1836-37)   23
3. Maturing (1838-39)   39
4. False Starts (1840-44)   63
5. Illness and Withdrawal (1844-45)   89
6. The Road Back (1845-46)   122
7. Louise Colet (1846-47)   141
8. Brittany (1847-48)   158
9. *The Temptation of Saint Anthony* (1849)   172
10. Around the Eastern Mediterranean (1849-51)   184
11. The Years of the *Bovary* (1851-56)   240
12. The Story Evolves   266
13. The Significance of Emma   315
14. The Novel as Art   328
15. The Trial of *Madame Bovary* (1856-57)   354

PART II—Mid-Passage

16. A Noted Author (1857-62)   369
17. *Salammbô* (1862)   396
18. Facing the Mid-Forties (1863-69)   437
19. *A Sentimental Education*   474

PART III—Tribulation

20. The Old Order Passes (1869-72) 543

21. *The Temptation of Saint Anthony* (1874) 573

22. *Bouvard and Pécuchet* 587

23. Old Age Begins (1872-77) 621

24. *Three Tales* (1877) 670

25. The Final Years (1877-80) 705

A Note on Sources 745

Notes 749

Index 775

Illustrations

Dr. Achille Flaubert
Madame Flaubert
Gustave's Brother Achille
Rouen in Flaubert's Youth
The Bureau des Finances in Rouen
A Street Scene in Nineteenth-Century Rouen
Gustave Flaubert as a Boy
Gustave Flaubert as a Young Man

following page 176

Gustave Flaubert, by His Brother Achille
Elisa Schlésinger, by Devéria
Gustave Flaubert
Trouville
Croisset
"Psyche," by Pradier
"Cupid and Psyche," by Canova
Louise Colet, by Winterhalter

following page 192

Colossus at Aswan
Tostes as Emma Bovary Knew It
Remains of the Swan Pond on the Chateau du Héron
Flaubert, Cartoon of 1857
Louis Bouilhet in the Last Decade of His Life
Flaubert, by Nadar
Maxime Du Camp, by Nadar
Suzanne Lagier, by Nadar

following page 384

Jeanne de Tourbey
Princess Mathilde, by Giraud
George Sand, by Nadar
Maxime Du Camp, Caricature by Giraud
Flaubert, Caricature by Giraud
Turgenev, by Nadar
Sainte-Beuve, Caricature by Giraud
The Pavilion in the Garden at Croisset

following page 400

Guy de Maupassant, by Nadar
Victor Hugo, by Bonnat
Madame Pasca, by Nadar
Madame Brainne
Madame Lapierre
Flaubert's Niece Caroline
Madame Flaubert in Advanced Years
Sketch of the Dead Flaubert

following page 664

Flaubert

PART I

To *Madame Bovary*

———

Growing Up in the Hôtel-Dieu (1821-35)

ROUEN, FAMILY, AND FRIENDS

Nothing can really let us know the gestation of an idea or
the first tremors which great works as yet unborn impart to
those who bear them; but it is moving to see the sites where
we know they were conceived, where they were lived, as if
these places kept something of the yet unknown ideal which
first quickened there.

Flaubert, writing of seeing Chateaubriand's boyhood
room, in *Across Field and Strand* (1848)

Busy commercial and industrial Rouen, capital of the ancient
French province of Normandy, was the birthplace of Gustave
Flaubert and the city in which he spent most of his life. As the
nineteenth-century traveler approached it along the road from the
north and the Channel port of Le Havre, the city remained long
concealed, only to come suddenly into view below. Flaubert once
placed Emma Bovary here[1] and had her notice how the city
dropped away in the shape of a great amphitheater, often veiled in
a light fog; its churches, houses, and other buildings spread from
the circling hills down to the low, flat land along the Seine and the
quays. Here bridges spanned the river and led to the rapidly developing industrial suburbs on the far side. Beyond them, the open
country stretched monotonously away to meet the hazy horizon
and the pale sky. Looking down from above, Emma saw the
whole panorama: ships lying at anchor crowded into one corner
in the port; the river curved along at the foot of green hills, and
the islands, oblong in shape, looked like great black fish pausing at
the surface of the water. The factory chimneys poured forth immense brown plumes whose far edges kept slipping away in the
soft breeze. She could hear the muffled roar of the foundries and

the clear carillon from the church towers rising out of the mist. The rooftops, wet and shining from the frequent rains, glistened as they reflected the light unevenly from the different quarters of the city. At intervals a gust of wind would carry the cloud layers over toward Saint Catherine's Hill, making them look like waves of air breaking noiselessly against a cliff.

Flaubert was born here on December 12, 1821; he grew up in Rouen and always maintained a home there or in nearby Croisset. Most of the days of his life he passed here, hating Rouen and his fellow citizens with all the romantic artist's frustrated fury against his chosen enemy, the bourgeois. But Rouen formed him, over the years it nurtured him, and he was never able to stand being long away from it. He hated its complacent, bustling provincialism, but during the 1820's and 1830's, as he went from boyhood to youth, and later as he became a man, its sights and its sounds, its people and their pursuits, were his life.

When Emma's coach reached the city, she left it and hurried to meet her lover; hence her mind was not on her surroundings. It was just as well, for the magnificent spectacle from afar roused expectations which the interior of the city was sure to disappoint.[2] By mid-century Rouen had some one hundred thousand inhabitants; its streets were narrow, winding, and badly constructed, and only along the quays beside the Seine was there any suggestion of elegance. Rouen's tremendous animation—which Flaubert so detested—struck all who visited the city. Its china had long been famous, and the colored cotton cloth made there is still today termed "rouennerie" by the French. These two local industries provided great wealth to their owners, but in these early days of the Industrial Revolution they also transformed the humbler citizens from a population of artisans and craftsmen into a hopeless proletariat, crushed in bottomless degradation and misery.

As a boy will, Flaubert roamed the streets of Rouen. It was a city of contrasts, its different quarters seeming to belong to different climates, even different worlds. The lower sections, down near the river and behind the elegant quays, were perpetually damp; rain water rushed or seeped in, and the Seine flooded over them; they gave off the peculiar, fetid smell of streets into whose narrow passages the sun never fully penetrates. The houses, still largely medieval, were dilapidated and frighteningly overcrowded with a growing population of workers whose health, precarious at best, was further weakened by the climate, which was cold and given to sudden, violent changes. Their lot, already poor at the time of Flaubert's birth in 1821, worsened rapidly as the textile industry was among the first to feel the inexorable, depressing effect of the Industrial Revolution. The plight of the Rouen workers was soon desperate, and their appearance must have seemed monstrous to the curious boy. Although they were humans, they must have appeared to share none of his sensitivities. He felt as distant from them as from the Chinese—or as close, he would phrase it, if you preferred.

Medieval Rouen, however, had bequeathed to its nineteenth-century descendants more than housing ill suited to an industrial age. The cathedral, the churches of Saint-Ouen and Saint-Maclou, and the Palace of Justice embodied in their delicate tracery the lush fantasy of the waning Middle Ages. Through the convolutions of their intricate lines they opened a boy's imagination to a world he would depict at the end of his life in the *Legend of Saint Julian*. The saint's story he first came to know in a stained-glass window in the Rouen cathedral. Then, too, the famous and popular Big Clock, or *Gros Horloge*, exemplified for him the more exuberant world of the Renaissance as it met his eye, framed in a great arch spreading across the narrow street like a bridge. Passing under it, he must have chuckled as do little boys today at the small gilded rat on the end of its single hand pointing to the hour.

The upper part of the city, along the slopes of the amphitheater, was drier and more open; what sun Normandy vouchsafed shone freely, and the air was well thought of for its health-giving qualities. Here was located the Hôtel-Dieu, or Hospital, of Rouen, presided over by Dr. Achille-Cléophas Flaubert, Gustave's father. It was housed in a grim, gray building of symmetrical, mid-eighteenth-century style; the doctor and his family lived in a wing forming part of the entrance court. The hospital lay in one of the suburbs which already in the eighteenth century had begun to creep up the slopes beyond the walls of the medieval city. It was, and it remains today, a gloomy building. In Flaubert's time, its fifteen wards contained over six hundred beds filled with the poor, the wretched, and the dying. The hospital with its sickrooms and its operating table was the home and the macabre haunt of the young Gustave.

Many were the occasions when he and his younger sister clambered up forbidden walls to peer furtively through the high windows at the operating table as Dr. Flaubert amputated a leg or casually brushed away a fly from the cadaver he was dissecting before his students. Years later Flaubert was still to recall his strange—and eventually calloused—reactions to his vicarious contacts with death when the flies buzzed over to light upon his own living flesh.[3]

As Flaubert in late adolescence came to the fateful years when a boy must judge his father, it was not an easy task.[4] On the one hand there were temperamental differences, and the boy longed for an approval he rarely was able to win. But on the other hand he admired and loved his father for his great and good heart. Ten years after the doctor died, Flaubert paid him his full measure of tribute in a loving portrait in *Madame Bovary*.[5] His father had been, he wrote, one of that group of great surgeons of the previous generation, now largely disappeared, who were men of thought as well as doctors and saw in their calling an art which they cherished with a fanatical devotion, carrying out their practice with exaltation and wisdom. Everything trembled in his father's hospital when Doctor Flaubert grew angry, but his pupils so worshiped him that they set about imitating his manner as soon as they were established in their own practices. In all the neighboring towns and cities one could thus see, reappearing on their backs, his long, padded wool overcoat and his black suit whose sleeves, ending in the lace cuffs of the period, extended down over his powerful, really very beautiful hands, which were always gloveless as though to be more ready for work.

Dr. Flaubert cared little for titles and decorations, was paternal with the poor, and, said his son, practiced virtue without believing in it. He would have been considered a saint, had it not been for the bite of his wit and the keenness of his mind, which made him feared as a devil. His look, sharper than even his scalpel, cut to the heart of the person before him, laying bare the truth beneath embarrassment and distortion. His easy assurance and majesty bespoke a man conscious of his great skill and of a lifetime of blameless hard work.

Achille-Cléophas Flaubert, born the son of a veterinary in 1784 in the nearby province of Champagne, had made an excellent start as a medical student in Paris. In 1818, some three years before Gustave was born, he settled in Rouen at the Hôtel-Dieu with his wife and a first child, also named Achille. Two further children died soon after birth; Gustave in 1821 was the fourth. Another infant, following Gustave, lived only a few months, to be followed in 1824 by a sister Caroline, the family's last child. Dr. Flaubert rose rapidly to the post of chief surgeon and head of this provincial hospital, where he remained for the twenty-five years until his death in 1846. His was a career which failed to fulfill its early promise: he would have been justified in hoping to move up, in early maturity, to a major Paris hospital. But he followed, to his loss, a declining group in the medical practice of his day and still looked to bloodletting as the sovereign remedy.[6] He was, moreover, a difficult man, nervous and irritable, and he was probably best off as the head of the Rouen hospital rather than fighting with his superiors in a Paris establishment. And so he remained a provincial, as his son would be after him. But he prospered, bought property and more property, and was able to leave to Gustave the comfortable income which kept him from having to try to earn his living by his pen.

Dr. Flaubert was a very good man.[7] On summer Sundays he would tell his wife that he was going for a walk in the country but would instead go to the operating room to perfect his art by dissecting. Flaubert could remember, too, long, expensive trips by coach to carry out an operation on a fishwife only because the case was of interest to science. His reward would be a dozen herring. When Gustave was still young enough, he could take pleasure in going out in snowy weather with his father to make the rounds of patients through the chilly countryside. And he never ceased to be warmed by a deep, recurrent pride in his father's achievements.

Unfortunately for family peace, the boy and his father differed in temperament, however much Gustave admired the doctor. His father was positive, incisive, and practical. The doctor used to speak enviously of his elder son Achille, who followed him into medicine: how much easier his own career might have been had he inherited the name and the fortune which came to Achille as part of his birthright. As Flaubert grew to be a man, he and his father could always be set at each other's throats. Loud, noisy, brutal discussions followed, and discourteous bickering became normal family life.[8] With his father as with the common citizens of Rouen, young Gustave too often felt distant and alien.

Since Flaubert did not himself marry, his participation in family life came solely from his childhood. This family and not one of his own creation had to serve as the refuge and the responsibility, the source of strength and the occasion to grow and to mature, which most men seek and find in two families, one of which they have established and in which they may often find their fullest stature, as husband, as father, and as head of a household. This aspect of family life, the grown man's relationship to it, Flaubert never knew. Indeed he came to suspect its existence only very late in life, for over the years it was his mother who kept house for him and his sister whom he was to remember as the only woman with whom he was ever wholly happy. His brother was eight years older and counted in Gustave's childhood only as a rival whom he could never match. It was to his mother and to his sister, his Carolo, his Caro, his "Bon Rat," that he gave all the tenderness of his profoundly emotional nature. Their roles were doubly important in his life, for in addition to mother and sister, they were also in some part object of devotion, wife, and child to this bachelor.

His mother was the most important single figure in his life.[9] She taught her children at home until it was time for the boys to go off to school, but she seems to have had little influence on Gustave's intellectual development. Ever present in his life (she lived with him until her death in 1872), she is a shadowy figure moving impassively in the background, ruling her son through a total dependence on him and through the unremitting threat of the pain it would cause her were he ever to make her less than the center of his life. She was as dark as a gypsy, with melancholy black eyes and glossy black hair to set off a face which was perfectly colorless. She struck others as being grand and solemn, looking as though she had never smiled. Her air and expression suggested some great sorrow in her past and the anticipation of more to come.[10] Born in 1793, Madame Flaubert was a few years younger than her husband and a vigorous twenty-eight when Gustave was born. She was from Pont-l'Evêque, near Rouen, the setting for most of Flaubert's later tale, *A Simple Heart*. Her family was comfortably off, and she brought her husband a fair dowry and later a good inheritance. To her Gustave used all the affectionate terms a man can find for a woman: she was mother, older confidante, mistress, wife, a tender and delicate charge who must be protected at all costs. Her strength was of that indomitable sort which comes from ruthlessly using alleged weakness to get one's way, always.

One day Dr. Flaubert tried to surprise his wife by giving her a most expensive new carriage which he had ordered specially from Paris for her. Alas, a glance sufficed to turn her against it: she found it ugly, uncomfortable, and too small for their large family. But it was not her way to say so to her husband, and she held her peace. Her habitual migraines and insomnias, however, redoubled —until her eldest son, now mature enough to intervene, explained matters tactfully to his father. The first carriage was sold, a second was purchased more to her taste, and Madame Flaubert's migraines and insomnias subsided to their normal levels.[11]

Throughout her life, Flaubert's letters to his mother show a constant terror of offending her: many things were irrevocably denied him because they would arouse her tremendous nervous irritability. He was always helpless against her because he could not face her sad expression and the tears in her eyes. Affection and deprecation, dependence and frustrated longings for freedom, hatred and desperate ill-understood desires he felt for his mother. His relations to all other women, and to men, too, sprang ultimately from this primal relationship.

His sister Caroline alone seemed to offer perfect happiness to her brother. She followed him about, did what he told her to do, acted in his plays, listened to his projects, and adored everything he did. He was her principal companion; she was his indispensable admirer. For her he thought up jokes, made faces, played tricks, acted the buffoon. As he approached manhood and she entered

her teens, he guided her reading, developed study plans, and began
to form her mind and spirit into the image of his own desires for a
woman. With the heroic and obedient devotion of a younger sister, she complied and basked in the sunshine of his approval. His
mother and his sister constituted for him, as for so many young
men, the composite picture of what he would meet and love. Naturally, what he feared he could always find; and what he sought
no mistress or wife could ever be. He and the women he loved
were all to pay cruelly for his early family life.

Across from the Hôtel-Dieu in Rouen lived *père* Mignot
(Flaubert was fond of giving this title to intimates), whom the
little boy loved to visit because Mignot would tell him stories or
read aloud to him from *Don Quixote*. While Gustave was thus
absorbing the adventures of the Melancholy Knight, he was also
learning, almost unbeknownst to himself, to look at life as an
inevitable, satiric clash between ideals, which alone he found
worth cherishing, and reality, which, with a few exceptions, he
found grotesque. While still very young, Gustave had already
memorized whole episodes of the *Quixote* and was attuning his
mind and his eye to this book and its world. They were a breviary
to a whole generation of writers for whom life made sense only
when viewed with an irony which was sadder but wiser than the
romantic idealism in the midst of which they were growing up.

Mignot's nephew, Ernest Chevalier, played a more immediately important role. Born a year or so before Flaubert, he was a
pupil with him at school. Gustave had almost no friends of his
own age; those he had were the more precious thereby. Ernest
must have been able to share his passionate devotion to all matters
literary, for this was all that concerned Gustave, and the two boys
were always together. Gustave was composing plays almost as
soon as he could write. Madame Chevalier directed them; Ernest,
one or two other friends, Caroline, and Gustave played all the
roles. They prepared programs and tickets and set up their scenery in the billiard room in the hospital.[12] Thursday afternoons
when they were free from school, Sundays, during vacations, the
boys sought always to be together. Ernest would sleep in Gustave's room, and the talk would range on into the night. He was
full of life and good spirits and must have helped to lighten or

dissipate the gloom and melancholy which were almost constant in young Gustave. When Ernest left for Paris in 1839 to take up the study of law, Gustave was plunged into deep melancholy by bleak premonitions. Later events bore him out, for he was never again to be really intimate and close to his childhood friend Ernest.

Alfred Le Poittevin completes the narrow circle of affections within which Flaubert moved.[13] A girlhood friend of Madame Flaubert's had married an important cotton manufacturer, Paul Le Poittevin. The two Rouen families remained closely linked over the years and over the generations. Dr. Flaubert stood godfather to young Alfred. Le Poittevin was godfather to Gustave. Alfred was Gustave's closest friend, closer than Ernest, and Alfred's sister Laure Le Poittevin was very dear to Caroline Flaubert. The four children (and Ernest) were constant companions and were really brought up together. Although in the Le Poittevin and Flaubert families only Laure and Gustave lived much beyond their twenties, neither ever forgot the childhood group. When Flaubert was fifty, Laure sent him her son so that he might make a man of him: his name was Guy de Maupassant. He gave to the aging Flaubert a filial devotion and became his most fervent disciple. Thus the bond moved down another generation, dying only when there were no more children to bear it forward.

Alfred was like an older brother to Flaubert, fulfilling a role that his real brother Achille was too much his senior to play. He was only five years older than Gustave, close enough to be an intimate, yet enough in advance to explore for Gustave each new choice which adolescence and then early manhood would offer. The Le Poittevin family was more cultured and had more feeling for form and tradition than did the family of Dr. Flaubert, who was after all only the son of a veterinary. This as well as his greater age designated Alfred as Flaubert's guide. He was so similar to what Flaubert became that it is hard to know whether he bent young Gustave to his will or only lent authority and weight to tendencies already there.

Alfred was very mild and of timid appearance, a restless, tormented person eaten with vague desires and gnawed by ill-contained ambitions. Introspective and full of pride, he was early disgusted with life, unremittingly pessimistic, filled with melan-

choly, and lacking in energy. His life as the son of a rich industrialist was in fact easy, but his temperament inclined him to be
sad. His intelligence was keen; well read and quick, he was attracted to metaphysical problems. But complex, abnormal sensations and impressions held a morbid fascination for him; he dabbled in spiritualism and liked to think of himself as the reincarnation of an Alexandrian Greek of the Late Empire, when decadence was a virtue and refined sensuality a refuge against all-
pervading ennui. Very early in life he sought release for his temperament and an outlet for his intelligence in writing, which was
his chief solace. Here, putting aside his personal anguish, he wrote
impersonally and impassively and put tremendous pains into correcting and reworking his manuscripts.

Flaubert turned always to his mentor in the early days, learning from him what to consider important and what to think. Le
Poittevin studied Goethe and Spinoza: Flaubert studied them. Le
Poittevin published five poems in a Rouen paper in 1836: Flaubert
soon sent in a manuscript. Le Poittevin longed for the role of a
great satirist: *Madame Bovary* and *A Sentimental Education* are
extended satires in new forms of the novel, which in some measure
Flaubert invented to contain his critiques. Le Poittevin decided
eventually to set his face resolutely against living a solid and practical bourgeois existence and instead sought to be an artist: Flaubert would be miserable until he, too, could turn solely to writing.
To succeed in this rigorous course, Le Poittevin found all human
attachment, except the affection he bore his friend, a weakness
fatal to attaining his goal: Flaubert, facing oncoming madness,
sought refuge in a similar insulation from the world. Rarely have
older and younger friend seemed so nearly alike in tastes, in
dreams, and in actions; hence it is not possible now to know how
much is the influence of older on younger, how much a coincidence of temperament.[14]

In only one way did Gustave determinedly avoid the path of
his older friend: Alfred lacked all will power. He knew his defect,
and, too late, knew that it had been fatal to him as man and as
artist. To Flaubert, the conquest of will was an arduous struggle;
he had to learn what to will and likewise what to will to do
without; but when he had learned his goals and his limits, nothing

could swerve him from his chosen path. Perhaps even in his weakness, Alfred was a lesson to Gustave by contrary example.

Enclosed within this provincial atmosphere and this narrow perimeter of affections Gustave Flaubert was to pass his childhood: a father toward whom his feelings were ambivalent, an older brother dimly sensed and felt largely as a rival, a mother and sister to whom he was an idol and on whom he was dependent; one friend who was vivacious, healthy, and normal, and another who was a guide and model in his sensitivity, which was refined to the point of decadence, and in his philosophy, which was blackest pessimism and total determinism. It was not to be an easy childhood, for the boy was sensitive and could not readily stifle affections in order to avoid being hurt. He might have come forth from it calloused, indifferent, and splendidly normal: he would then have had a solid career as a Rouen or Paris lawyer. He could, equally, have succumbed to all the unhealthy temptations of neurosis: he might then have been an interesting minor romantic failure. In fact, he had the courage to stand by his sensitivities and his ideals, though often he must have felt that he was almost alone in revering them. In addition he had the unknowable gift which neither he who possesses it nor he who does not has ever been able to describe; it serves only to mask our ignorance when we call it genius. This gift Flaubert had; and so he wrote *Madame Bovary*.

CHILDHOOD

> Those earliest impressions do not disappear, you know. We bear within ourselves all our past throughout our whole life; we are already marked by our first nurse. When I analyze myself, I can find within me, still fresh and with their influences undimmed (though modified by their crosscurrents), the place of . . . *père* Mignot, of *Don Quixote*, and of my childhood dreaming, beside the window of the operating theater.
>
> Letter to his mother, November 14, 1850

For the first fifteen years of his life a growing boy is primarily in and of his family. When, in later years, memory ranges back over childhood and picks out ever earlier events, it slips imperceptibly behind episodes actually remembered to those known only through later being told of them, but told so often and so early that one seems often almost to remember living them. This was the character of Flaubert's first knowledge of himself, a moment when his father had taken him down to the quays along the Seine to watch the Duchess de Berry pass by in her carriage. The child was so lovely to look at that the duchess paused, took him up into her carriage, and delighted in caressing him. The good doctor was triumphant on his return to the hospital and, after his death, his son liked to remember that at least on this occasion his father had been proud of him.[15] His oldest direct recollection was of spending the summer months when he was two and one-half years old in a nearby chateau. He could always recall the round plot of grass in front, the butler in his black coat, the great trees, and a long corridor which led down to his room on the left at the end.[16]

Childhood was not easy, and happy moments with Ernest, Caroline, Alfred, and Laure he later remembered because they stood out against the rest. He had a terrible fear of heights and of the dark which he overcame only in his teens.[17] And he had an innocent naïveté which proved irresistibly tempting to those about him. An old servant, Pierre, to rid himself of the six-year-old, would send him off to the garden or kitchen "to say Pierre wanted to know if he were there." The laughs with which cook or gardener met his query puzzled and hurt the child.[18] The naïveté continued undiminished over the years. At eleven, falling, as he thought, in love, he wished to give his heart to the child who had caught his fancy. For a long time he considered asking his father to operate—the idea was after all a commonplace in family conversation—and remove his heart so that he might send it in a basket to her. It would be placed, he felt, on the sideboard. Oddly, this hospital-bred child had no thought of incision or blood, but only of the gift.[19]

Gustave grew up under the watchful eyes of Julie, the family servant who joined the household in 1825, when he was three years old.[20] She was a reliable companion for the child, to whom he soon learned to turn when time needed to be whiled away with a tale. A bad knee had kept her in bed for a year and had enabled this very simple woman to read more than would have been her normal lot. Thus her stories sprang not only from her native village, but also from books. Julie never left Flaubert's service, caring for him as child, man, and crotchety old bachelor. She did not know till near the end that he was a famous author, but she loved him because he was her life. Julie was the model for Félicité, the servant whose story he told in *A Simple Heart*. She survived him by only three years.

Julie used to take Gustave and his sister Caroline by the hand to make the solemn and festive New Year's Day visits, which always ended at the home of the Le Poittevin family, with Alfred and Laure. Fifty years later an aging Flaubert still looked back nostalgically to these calls: the two children, their little bottoms pinched by the cold, would go from house to house to embrace all the members of the families, the women's bonnets engulfing the small heads each time. Even over the years the memory of those long boulevards could tire him. But it was good to remember the huge pieces of apple candy—Normandy is apple country—in which a child's teeth stuck until he wondered if he could ever pull them out. The day was also a momentous one back in the Flaubert household, with the big front doors standing open from seven in the morning to receive the flood of visitors who would fill a whole salad bowl with their calling cards, bearing witness to the respect, gratitude, and affection Rouen felt for Dr. Flaubert.[21]

The little boy needed moments like these to build the warmth and security to withstand much of the rest of his life as a child. Through the windows of the doctor's apartment in the Hôtel-Dieu, he could look out over the gardens of the hospital and see the convalescents and the attending nuns. Across the court were the windows of the wards and, inside, the long rows of beds. The surroundings were sad and, though sensitivity seems soon dulled by the constant presence of the familiar, these gloomy walls and their inmates played their part in the terrible nightmares of his childhood.[22]

He was of a meditative character, frequently totally lost in his childish thoughts and dreams. For hours at a time, he would sit, finger in mouth, absorbed. He was even more withdrawn when reading, as he played with a lock of hair and bit quietly on his tongue until, slipping farther and farther toward the edge of his chair, he would finally fall from it with a start.[23] The external world he would escape, when it was too much with him, by living instead in his own fantasies. Sometimes his imaginings ran a satiric, symbolic parallel to the world about him, but he would also depart from it to more alluring scenes. Very early he learned two divergent ways of living: he could analyze and dissect life until he felt himself its master and able to satirize it, or he could create a world of his own. It would take many years for him to learn to bridge this dichotomy and find, if not joy, at any rate peace in recreating a world which would be based on his analysis.

Many withdrawn children find adequate release in their dreams: Flaubert's childish tensions demanded explosions in addition. He was alternately meditative and expansive, analyst and actor. His anxieties and his tensions, his anger and his mockery, found oddly patterned outlets in his intermittent but irruptive humor—if the word may be stretched to include his incessant and unending repetition of the same jokes, slowly and lovingly elaborated over the years. One of the earliest formulations was an imaginary character, *Le Garçon*, The Old Boy, an incarnation of all the idiocies Flaubert detested.[24] Gustave's creative vein was satiric from the start. Le Garçon was full of little manias complicated by the added weight of all the bourgeois stupidities that Gustave and his friends observed or read of. He had his special shout and gestures, which were like those of an automaton; his laugh was a shrill cackle; he was immensely strong. His reactions were always the same, consecrated and inevitable. Whenever any two of the coterie who created him passed Rouen's cathedral, one of them would trigger the performance by observing: "Isn't Gothic architecture beautiful! How it elevates the soul!" This allowed the other one to adopt the role of Le Garçon and reply: "Yes, beautiful! And all the persecutions of the Protestants were beautiful, too: the Saint Bartholomew Massacres, the dragonnades, the Edict of Nantes!"

A sense of humor more delicate than Gustave's might have been content with a single performance of this duet: with Flaubert it became, instead, reassuringly habitual. Le Garçon had a whole repertory of speeches. He was given to pleading burlesque legal cases in the billiard room where Flaubert's plays were put on, or he pronounced heavy-handed funeral orations of living people who seemed to the children more suited to being dead. These lasted for hours, as each in turn added to the composite character. Thereafter Le Garçon took to writing poetry, and he ended by running the Hôtel des Farces, whose most magnificent moment, commemorated in endless performances, was the *Fête de la Vidange*, the Celebration of the Cleaning . . . of those places which served our forebears prior to the invention of the flush toilet.

Le Garçon never directly enters Flaubert's novels, but echoes of him reverberate here and there in them when particularly tiresome bores occupy our attention. The pharmacist Homais in *Madame Bovary* is surely quoting Le Garçon at times. Moreover, Le Garçon early underwent a strange, Protean change which but foreshadowed the odd destiny of many of those created characters with whom Flaubert's life was long intertwined. Le Garçon was born originally to incarnate bourgeois stupidity and to serve as a butt for shafts of satire. Over the years, however, he grew and became more lovable until he was not only his original self but, at one and the same time, his own opposite, a bourgeois and an anti-bourgeois.[25] He was both what Flaubert hated and in the same breath an incarnation of Flaubert himself. It was often to be thus: Emma Bovary started in satire and became, in part at least, Flaubert. And in Flaubert's last, uncompleted work the process was still continuing as Bouvard and Pécuchet became their creator. To some extent it makes for contradiction; far more, it helps to produce the rich texture of Flaubert's novels.

In general, as child and as man Flaubert lacked the release of spontaneous humor. Wit he never possessed, and his seriousness, often ponderous, prevented any but the heaviest of pleasantries, which were frequently overtly biting rather than funny. To appear to laugh but to do so bitterly leaves an acrid taste in the mouth which demands a repetition of the draught. Even his sister Caroline had to admit that the family sometimes found his games unbearable, although she added—typically—that, for her own part, she never never could have enough of them.[26] But Caroline loved him as no one else ever did. Serious he would always be and therefore never able to solace pain or rage with the tempering effect of self-sufficing humor. Baudelaire, too, suffered the same lack and paid an even crueler price.

The stupidity he constantly found in life oppressed Flaubert even as a child. He could almost never find the present pleasing. All too frequently it was only in retrospect, when it was irretrievably gone, that he could see how deeply good an experience had been. The rare moments which he did enjoy, he cherished; but their bright hues were too scattered to relieve the monotonous pallor of the stupidity he normally found about him. Even New Year's Day, whose memory he was so to treasure later, he bitterly proclaimed to be stupid when he was nine.[27] In such colossal proportions either this stupidity would defeat him or he had to best it: a lifetime of raging impotently at it was not possible. Therefore through his writing he waged war on it, each successive book constituting a new try for victory as this satirist sought to show his fellow man the ills he saw.

Le Garçon was only the first of a succession of efforts to master living with stupidity. He was followed by the Sheik, a similar creation, and then by vast compilations, whole cartons filled with careful annotations of idiocies.[28] He was still at it when death overtook him. His posthumous *Bouvard and Pécuchet* would have been its monument, had he lived to complete the book.

Consecrated, repetitive humor was only a partial release for tensions and an inadequate solution to the intermittent problems of social intercourse for an unsure boy: writing was his true and constant outlet. Before he was ten, he was already drafting comedies and projecting a literary association with Ernest Chevalier; Gustave would write plays while Ernest wrote his fantasies. The mocking Flaubert had also noted a lady who came often to visit his family and who always told stupid stories: he would write them up, too.[29] Somehow he also found time to write political and constitutional speeches of a liberal color, and shortly, when he had discovered Cervantes, he began writing material drawn from him.[30] Soon the scope widened to include subjects from the classical repertory, such as "The Miserly Lover," and historical ones such as *The Death of Louis XI*, a play. By the time he was fifteen, writing was already a long-established habit with him; into it he poured his enthusiasms and his hates, his broadening interests and his growing observations. It was, of course, a release, but it was far more a refuge, and above all it was his supreme joy.

What a boy, or a man, writes is in some measure a function of what he reads. A growing boy in France in the 1830's was almost sure to read certain of the great classics—Homer, Shakespeare, or Montaigne, to name but a few. These young Gustave did read, and eventually he learned much from them; but at the start he was more interested in the new productions of the high-water mark of romanticism in France. Hence his first experience of literature was produced by the generation before his. It was a great one.

During the course of the first decades of the nineteenth century there grew to manhood in France a generation of authors who carried out from 1820 to 1840 a revolution which they themselves called romantic and felt would lay for ever the ghost of a dead classicism. The poets Lamartine, Vigny, Musset, and above all Hugo exploited a lyric vein long unworked in France. An earlier world, Voltaire's for instance, had assumed that this was an orderly universe in which the right was knowable, and usually even rather smugly known. Reason prevailed, or at any rate ought to prevail, and so, given time, one could determine correctly the answer to any question. The way was clear, the goals defined; man could step boldly forward to claim his known heritage. If he stumbled—and Voltaire frequently found his fellow-man a stumbler—this was inexcusable, and a rational man would make a rational protest. This was, for instance, the age of Adam Smith and Economic Man. It was also the age when highly intelligent men could declare to be self-evident a group of truths over which mankind has been fighting since the beginning of history.

The romantic's world was quite other, replacing the rational and unique truth of the eighteenth century, knowable and definable, with a new emphasis on the individual seeking his own development and fruition. Individual needs and intuitions became more important than general truths; and the individual had to seek and find an individual truth, his own alone. There is no body of dogma, no coherent framework of doctrine, which may be deemed romanticism; it is, rather, an attitude. Faced with the great problems which involve man, God, and the universe, the romantic tends to start from himself, his own feelings, and intuitions, and he frequently feels no need to move beyond his own unique personality, his own unique experience. It is enough that he has wept, or loved, or hated.

Romanticism is the attitude Flaubert found in the authors who were of note in his growing years. Heroes felt violently; heroines loved passionately. Despair beckoned down into suicide; joy—oddly enough—never amounted to much, except as a subject for nostalgic regret when irretrievably lost. Chateaubriand wept his personal losses and found religion; Lamartine wept his deceased mistress and found a new elegiac note in poetry. If Vigny wept, he kept it to himself; but he found that the genius was, by virtue of being different and superior, necessarily alone, and he sought a stoic's answer in a Christian's world. Hugo, too, eschewed weeping romanticism and exploited instead his reactions to innumerable exciting subjects: the adventurous Middle Ages, the exotic Near East, the growing Napoleonic legend, his own growing family. His onetime friend, the critic and author Sainte-Beuve, delicately phrased an intimate aura in works which were to affect deeply both Flaubert and Baudelaire. These authors Flaubert read; he was delighted to discover that he, too, was unique—and so could write of what every one else was writing. He, too, was medieval and Spanish and exotic in his juvenile works, just like every other boy who wrote during this decade.

Before Flaubert was fifteen, two new figures had appeared, giants each. Balzac began to publish the novels which were to dominate much of the writing during the rest of the century. *Le Père Goriot* and *Eugénie Grandet* had both appeared by 1834. Close observation of modern society coupled with visionary powers was here establishing a new subject for prose fiction. Slowly the young Flaubert tried turning his attention in his writing, occasionally, from the romantically exotic in space and time back to something like the world he knew. It infuriated him in later years that his name was always linked with Balzac's, for he felt, and rightly, that he had moved a great step beyond his predecessor. But without Balzac to point the way Flaubert might never have written as he did.

The other great figure is the historian Michelet, who brought to the medieval period of France and to ancient Rome the same passionate fervor and flaming imagination which others applied to recounting love affairs. To Michelet, history was evocation, and for none of his readers was the evocation more effective than for the young Flaubert. Michelet and Balzac were impelling him in the same direction: it is not coincidence that the one was a professional historian and the other styled himself the social historian of his own age.

A budding playwright himself, Gustave also read plays and saw a considerable number on stage, as the Rouen of his day boasted two active theaters.[31] Moreover, whenever the boy went with his parents to visit their relatives in Nogent, they passed through Paris and frequently stayed long enough for an evening at the theater. He delighted in the mystery and excitement of the stage. On his return to Rouen he could mingle the pleasures of recollecting these moments with the more earthly joys of impressing his friends with gossip of the plays, the actors, and the actresses of the capital. None of this was wasted, for it is the essence of the theater that it does not talk about action, it displays it; the playwright does not comment, he shows. Flaubert's earliest writing and his strongest early excitement were in this genre, so many of whose approaches he would later transform into techniques of the novel.

He read the romantics and, as young boys have been doing ever since, he became one of them himself. Hugo and Dumas, Goethe and Byron, Michelet and Balzac, he devoured and made his own. But towering over all of French romanticism rises the great figure of Chateaubriand, as goal to be aimed at, as model to imitate, or as pervasive influence which could not be shaken off. Flaubert was no exception. He gave himself—and most of his heroes—the darkly melancholic air of Chateaubriand's ill-fated hero, René. Born listless yet sensitive, the Chateaubrianesque hero learns of the emotions before he has experienced them, and hence is already old in heart, bored and blasé, before he has yet felt anything. As with love, so with all else: friendship, politics, ambition, and religion pale or lose their savor to his tired palate. Too sensitive for crass pleasures, too intelligent for facile answers,

René wearily drags out a blighted existence made intolerable by ennui. Chateaubriand's ennui is the haunting ghost of this period, and none who lived romanticism escaped it, not even those of the next generation, which sought to revolt and move beyond it: Flaubert joins Baudelaire in proclaiming this.

Romantic ennui is at the core of the romantic's concept of love. To escape ennui is his constant preoccupation; his greatest gratitude to his beloved is for release from it: hence the passionate love affairs of the romantic hero. Since such passion withers under the ennui of humdrum, daily repetition, the romantic author almost always recounts the piteous overthrow and death-marked love of star-crossed lovers such as Romeo and Juliet, whom Frenchmen now discovered for the first time. The romantic hero spends his days seeking his true love; he finds her; and fate intervenes. But he and she each know what his own heart demands; each seeks relief from his own ennui. Conveniently, they are irrevocably separated before either they or their authors can discover the price for such self-seeking. Gustave was naturally fascinated by such themes, and surely a boy may be excused for taking them seriously, the more so because the grown man would write *Madame Bovary* to explore what happened if the lovers did live on together. But for the moment he knew only the passionate aspiration.

In the summer of 1836, Flaubert was fourteen and a half. His milieu and his adjustment to it had long been fixed. His friends Ernest Chevalier and Alfred Le Poittevin were known and reliable quantities upon which he could solidly count. His view of the world was romantic; he thought of himself as a budding genius; and he lived for art. Like René, he had read about love. Now he was ready for it. It came that summer, at Trouville, then a little fishing village on the Channel coast.

2

Adolescence under Romanticism (1836-37)

TROUVILLE AND ELISA

> . . . that beach at Trouville where I first met you and which, for me, always bears the imprint of your steps.
>
> Letter to Madame Schlésinger, September 6, 1871

IT HAPPENED one noontime so naturally that it must have had that air of fate which the romantically inclined have always delighted in attaching to the onset of their passions ever since Beatrice first appeared to Dante or Laura to Petrarch.

For half a dozen years or more the Flaubert family had spent alternate summers in what was then the fishing village of Trouville. Madame Flaubert had been born at Pont-l'Evêque, little more than fifteen miles away, and both she and her intimate friend Madame Le Poittevin had childhood ties to the village. When Flaubert was young, Trouville numbered only a scant thousand inhabitants; its larger neighbor of our day, Deauville, did not even exist; and the Flaubert family, eager for a quiet and peaceful vacation after the rigors and demands of a Rouen winter, could be assured of complete tranquility.

Gustave himself tried a few years later to put down on paper what Trouville had been like in the summer of 1836 before it was spoiled by becoming fashionable: a charming village with its houses piled one against the other, some black, some gray, others red or white, facing in every direction like a heap of shells and pebbles thrown up along the shore by the waves. A mile and a half of beach and a lovely site against sharply rising hills and cliffs were soon to bring renown to the village and destroy its naturalness with liveried servants and obligatory yellow gloves for the men. But in the summer of 1836, it was simple and untamed, with only its native inhabitants and a few artists and writers and its immense, unencumbered beach whose gray sand glinted under the sun, while off to one side the lazy waves beat sleepily against the rocks.[1]

Here, one morning as Gustave was walking alone on the beach, he noticed a red cloak with black stripes, which the rising tide was threatening to overrun.[2] It was a natural gesture, accomplished almost without thought, to move it farther up the beach out of reach of the waves. The light material was soft and cushioned to the touch. At lunch that day in the dining room of the inn he heard a voice saying: "Thank you so much for your kindness." He turned around to face a young woman seated with her husband at a neighboring table. A few more words and Gustave's preoccupied air gave way to embarrassment. She looked full at him; the boy dropped his eyes and blushed.

Flaubert never forgot her look. As he remembered it, her eyes seemed to burn out at him like the sun under her arched black eyebrows. He stood there immobile, as though stupefied, and felt something new and mystical and strange inside him like a new sense. She was taller than most women, with magnificent black hair tumbling down over her shoulders. Her skin was luminous and covered with a golden down which he noticed particularly on her upper lip, for it added a slightly darker tint there, giving to her whole face a vigorous and energetic expression, almost mannish. In contrast her figure was slight and delicate and, as she was nursing her three- or four-month-old daughter, her bosom was maternally large and full. Flaubert noticed the veins weaving in violet lines across it. Her voice was musical, modulated, gentle. The contours of her arms, which could be guessed at beneath her light muslin sleeves, suggested the soft, yielding flesh. She stood up, tied the pink ribbons of her bonnet, and was gone, leaving young Gustave to dream of her hands, slim yet just rounded enough to tantalize. Young romantic that he was, he longed to burn them with his kisses.

There is something peculiarly innocent and naïvely pure about a boy's first awakening to desire. He seemed to have grown taller and prouder in his bearing. The slightest thing about her, a fold of her dress, her smile, her foot, the most insignificant comment from her seemed of almost supernatural importance. He would follow her down the street; the rustle of her dress made his heart beat faster. He was drunk; he proclaimed that it was a state of blessed madness.

It was some days before he was to feel what he called the frantic and somber ardor of the flesh and of the soul, an ardor which would devour both. Meanwhile, each morning, he went to watch her swim, slowly learning to imagine voluptuously the soft and peaceful waves gently stroking her thighs or covering her breast with their foam. Her soaked garments clung to her body; he could sense the beating of her heart and watch the swelling of her bosom. When she passed him on the beach, he could hear the drops of water as they fell from her wet clothes, the rustling as she walked. He would drop his eyes; his ears would ring, he felt stifled. Even had he been deaf and blind, he was sure that he would have sensed the presence of her woman's body, almost nude, as she passed. For each time she did so, something sweet and soft within him relaxed into ecstasy and filled him with gracious images.

It marked the boy so that he could never wholly forget it. How could it be otherwise? It may be that at the first moment he did not consciously capture all of the experience, for this account he wrote only after a lapse of two years.[3] But this is the way he remembered it, described it, and experienced it anew. At the turn of the next century Proust was to illumine the sense in which an experience is not an isolated event but rather, over the years, an initial occurrence to which is added all the web of additional meanings spun by successive rememberings under steadily renewed circumstances. This Flaubert was now living.

By the time Flaubert wrote these words, he had already been introduced to sex by his mother's chambermaid and had discovered that prostitution could alleviate the momentary sting of desire;[4] but this had only served to etch more clearly what it was that bound him to this woman and which he could always recapture through the passing years. He was to love many other women, to know by direct experience the manifold expressions of carnal and of spiritual desire; but the impact of this first experience was such that he could always relive it in his imagination.

Again and again he told this momentous meeting in fictional form. Later versions lack the adolescent passion, the easy romanticism, the total absorption; but they still recount the same event. Thus the opening of *A Sentimental Education*, written almost thirty years afterwards, has the same shock of the first encounter: "It was like an apparition." Madame Arnoux's eyes are what the hero, Frédéric, notices first; her hat has the same pink ribbons, and her hair is abundant and black; she is wearing light muslin. Her skin has the same splendor; her fingers are so delicate that the light seems to shine through them, and he finds even her workbasket startling, extraordinary. Her scarf—it is not a cloak this time —slips almost into the water, when the young man leaps to save it. And again, desire for physical possession comes only later.[5]

The days passed that first summer, and the acquaintance grew. Elisa and her husband became his friends, and a bond was formed that lasted over the years. As Flaubert knew her, she was—or appeared to be—Madame Elisa Schlésinger, wife of a growing figure in the world of Parisian music, Maurice Schlésinger. He was a Prussian Jew who had been converted to Catholicism. For ten years he had been an active figure in the French music trade and had soon developed an unsavory reputation for exploiting talent; nevertheless, his sure sense for publicity made him sought out by musicians. His was an oddly improbable nature, by turns despicable and lovable, coupling in a single personality a conniving, fraudulent business man and a patron of the arts. He stole Rossini's *Stabat Mater*, yet he was one of the main supports of Richard Wagner for two years during the latter's youth—while baldly taking advantage of him at the same time. "Père Maurice," as Flaubert called him, was loud, vulgar, and showy; he used his friends shamelessly and they knew it. All his life he ran after pretty women. But he loved his wife, both her body and her soul; and countless people, including Flaubert, were deeply fond of him because he was warm and open in his affections and because his verve and impetuosity made him always an exciting companion.

Two years before the momentous meeting on the beach in 1836, Schlésinger had founded the *Gazette musicale*, a clever device which gave him a forum in which to laud the works of the composers whom he published, Meyerbeer, Halévy, and Berlioz, among others. In 1836 he was brought to Trouville by the elder Dumas, whose writings he published at intervals in the *Gazette*. Schlésinger was at the height of his success and looking for profitable investments. Being quite canny enough to see the possibilities of the future resort, he bought a hotel there as a speculation. Hence he and his wife returned to Trouville and continued their acquaintance with young Flaubert. Without this there would have been no *Sentimental Education*, for its basic fabric is the story of Gustave's love for Madame Schlésinger, the principal source for Madame Arnoux. Her husband, Jacques Arnoux, is patterned after Maurice, the shoddy hustler who, in Flaubert's fiction and in real life, too, was to drag her down in the ruin he was eventually to bring upon himself. All of this, however, was years away.

Elisa Schlésinger was a reserved and enigmatic figure, whose story Flaubert probably never knew: it was ferreted out only a generation ago. All those who describe her comment on the sad look in her eyes, and Flaubert's portraits of her suggest it. But none of her friends seems to have divined her secret. She was a Norman like Flaubert and was born in 1810, which made her eleven years his senior and able to fulfill the maternal role he always needed in women. In 1829, as she was approaching twenty, she married a second lieutenant in the army, with whom she left for five years in Africa, where France was at this time carving out her colonial Empire. Elisa returned in 1835, a year before her meeting with Flaubert. At some time during these years away, she ceased to live the role of wife to her husband. She came back to France alone and lived with Maurice Schlésinger, so far as the world knew as man and wife. When her husband did return, she was six months pregnant with Maurice's child, whom Flaubert later supposed to be her legal offspring.

Elisa's real husband did nothing about her actions; hence they must have had his consent. As no divorce laws existed, no legal means were available to break the marriage. The child, when she was born, was listed as the daughter of Maurice and an unnamed mother, and the date was falsified to suggest a birth at a more convenient moment to fit the fiction the pair established.

It is almost certain that no one in their circle, not even Flaubert, who was very intimate with both Maurice and Elisa, ever knew or guessed the secret. Elisa, quiet, solid, deeply religious, spoke always with fervent gratitude of how good Maurice was to her; but no one today knows why she accepted her role.

With her strong and reliant face and her full bosom, Elisa seemed a protective mother to young Gustave. Her marriage appeared to provide the safe and secure base to a relationship which might otherwise have frightened the boy back into his reserve. He came to know desire; his imagination tortured him with visions of Elisa in her husband's arms. But Gustave also imagined himself giving her almost filial caresses.

The youth did all the foolish things young lovers are supposed to do. He scrambled up a precipitous cliff one day to catch Elisa's Newfoundland and kiss him as she was wont to do.[6] And the three of them, Gustave, Elisa, and Maurice, went boating together or listened to music. Maurice even went to Honfleur nine miles away and walked back carrying a huge melon so that they might all enjoy it.[7] Gustave delighted that summer, as he would over the years, in being off alone with Maurice, and they spent long hours together smoking cigars or galloping their horses along the beach.[8]

The romantic notion of love held that true passion conquered everything; all obstacles should fall before it, be they the indifference of the lady or the narrow suspicions of her jealous husband. Alas, in Flaubert's case, this did not happen: Elisa remained a wife devoted chastely to her husband. Little by little the cruel truth became inescapable: romanticism had lied. An individual's passion did not alter the situation about him. The external world remained stubbornly unmoved by the young Flaubert. To come to know this was painful to Gustave; it was the first great crisis of his life. It was also the first great step away from romanticism. He proclaimed his anguish and his doubt in desperate cries, but other crises and other resolutions would be needed before he could oppose to romanticism anything but a shriller romanticism.

Rouen and Writing

Let us always busy ourselves with Art which, greater than nations or crowns or kings, is always there high above us in enthusiasm, with its royal diadem.

Letter to Ernest Chevalier, August 14, 1835

The summer passed, autumn came as usual, and Gustave returned to school. He had entered it as a little boy of ten in the autumn of 1832. Now four years later he was going on fifteen, he was in love, and he felt himself already a man. He grew to be very tall for a Frenchman of his days or ours, for he was only three-quarters of an inch short of six feet. In addition to his size, he had also startling good looks, as he soon began to realize. One evening at the theater he suddenly became aware that all glances were turned toward him admiringly; it was a delicious moment.[9]

Gustave's eyes were large and immensely gentle, the forehead above them was broad and high. His nose was straight and regular, but what one noticed after his eyes was his mouth. The lips were a little full, just enough to suggest his passionate nature. They were very well formed, almost feminine; the lower lip and jaw seemed to suggest reticence and withdrawal at the same time that his heavy jowl and strong chin hinted at belligerence. The contradictory adolescent within could be divined by all who looked at him.

School, for sensitive boys, is not a happy experience.[10] The building which housed Rouen's Collège royal was a former Jesuit construction in the quiet and rational style of the seventeenth century, dull and uninspiring as is often the case in school architecture. The classrooms were huge, and most of the pupils sat on oak benches along the walls without desks or tables on which to write. They let their easily distracted attention wander gladly to the melody of the organ grinder in the street outside or to the noise of the donkeys customarily tied near the school by milkmaids as they made their rounds. When a recitation was interrupted by a braying beast, it was a standard joke for the teacher to observe: "You had better wait for the other donkey to finish."

Gustave had the typical experience of the introvert at school. His mother had taught him to read, but only with great exertions. His younger sister Caroline had learned much more rapidly than he, a humiliation which made him burst into tears and led to his declaring that there was no need for him to master the art since *père* Mignot already knew how and could read to him whatever he wished. Now in school he found matters no better. He disliked the military atmosphere, the roll on the drums to announce the change of classes, the lines of boys marching from one room to another or the solemn files in which they went for walks on Thursdays.[11]

The boy's pride was already apparent, and he was, inevitably, to be made to pay for it. He felt superior to those around him because he knew he understood them, and he felt sure that they did not understand him. Time was proved that he was right to feel his powers thus, but it was cold comfort to the grown man, and the young boy had no defense at all. He was unpopular; he made no friends. He sat on the same benches for half a decade with another student, Louis Bouilhet, who was later to become his closest friend and confidant, but they struck up no acquaintance in school. His work suffered, of course; even some of the subjects he would most love later he neglected in school. He had not yet found himself, except to know that he was in revolt.

His performance was uneven. The cast of his adult mind was already taking form, suggesting where the material could profitably be worked and where, on the contrary, it had best be left alone. Mathematics he never really grasped, and as a grown man he still had to write out in full twenty times fifty, with all the zeros, to discover that it made a thousand. In history and philosophy, however, he had good teachers fully able to exercise and develop his inborn aptitudes. Of the two it was history which first appealed to him. He studied under a young teacher, Chéruel, who had just returned to his native Rouen at the age of twenty-four in 1835. He had vivacity, energy, and that stage presence which alone makes it possible for a teacher of young boys to inspire them. Chéruel had studied under the romantic historian Michelet in Paris and came to his own Rouen classes full of the excitement of his master's new *History of Rome*. Moreover, Chéruel was a remarkably erudite man for such a provincial post: his *Dictionary of French Institutions* is still today a useful reference tool for historians. He aroused Gustave's enthusiasm and with another teacher, Gourgaud, started the boy writing short stories on historical subjects. Writing was, even more than it had been before, an outlet and an escape. But this precocious child also showed a refreshingly human failing, for in one of his early works he wrote a story which is copied directly in its theme, its development, and even its climax line from Chateaubriand![12]

The annual Saint Romain Fair during the last two weeks of October was a major event in Flaubert's school year. Its principal attraction was a marionette show. Each year since early childhood Gustave had gone to see the performance; it was always the same, "The Temptation of Saint Anthony." No single work of Flaubert's so occupied him as did his effort to write his own account of the Temptation of this desert saint. A first attempt at it precedes *Madame Bovary;* a second follows it. And the third version, the only one he published, occupied two or three more years late in his life. His hopes and his disillusionment, his anguish and ultimate, tolerant calm, all of his desires and most of his answers Flaubert poured into these three versions of one book, which was in germ as he sat watching the marionettes. Many years later, when George Sand was visiting him at the time of the Fair and they attended the performance together, a charming but improbable legend holds that someone told the puppeteer that the author of his play was in the audience. He could hardly be restrained—so goes the tale—from presenting Flaubert to the other spectators. And Flaubert began the manuscript of his own first version with a four-line epigraph from the marionette play:

> *Messieurs les démons,*
> *Laissez-moi donc!*
> *Messieurs les démons,*
> *Laissez-moi donc!*

More than most, the boy Gustave was inexorably father to the man through the formative years of his adolescence. His world of escape and illusions, pieced together out of his fears, his inadequacies, and his loneliness, had now to confront the imperturbable indifference of a world made up of other people. This is a common problem, and for common people there is a common solution. One learns to match indifference with indifference; one calls childishness the dreams of youth, which are now firmly put aside, and another practical man is born. But if these dreams were the stuff of greatness, then it is sad to contemplate, for to have followed them might have meant to stand one day upon a hilltop where the common man will never tread. Many of Flaubert's generation, as they grew older, did put aside their dreams in bitter disillusionment and banded together to form what they were pleased to call the School of Common Sense. Flaubert wrote in *Madame Bovary* that in every law clerk there lies the debris of a poet.

Provincial Rouen was remarkably in step with the capital, and each development of romanticism in Paris had its immediate repercussions in Normandy.[13] Gustave and his young companions were wild in their extravagance as each sought to discover himself by patterning his dreams and his actions on the great romantic models who seemed to have incarnated untrammeled individualism. Goethe's Werther, Chateaubriand's René, Byron's Don Juan, Dumas' Antony sounded a clarion call to these youths, to which they responded with shout or sigh depending upon their mood of heroism or despair. Vogue succeeded vogue: one was troubadour yesterday, insurrectionary today, Bedouin tomorrow. An ill-digested potpourri of readings and imaginings bubbled mightily and gave off fumes sufficient to addle older pates. Like Antony, the youngsters carried daggers in their pockets to be the more prepared; Gustave even slept with one beneath his pillow. But sometimes impassioned acting revealed in a terrifying flash the dangerous reality beneath the grandiloquent surface. Romanticism is not nonsense: it is a very real and ever-present temptation. Some of Flaubert's friends imagined despair so potently that histrionics gave way to madness: one youth put a bullet through his brain; another hanged himself with his necktie.[14]

Already in school days Gustave had been sad, he remembered later. As he moved toward late adolescence, he was bored, and yet also eaten with desires, consumed with burning aspirations toward a mad and action-filled existence. Beyond the still uncrossed barrier of the age of twenty, he thought he sensed an incandescent, perfumed world of distant splendor and the noise of triumphs, a living fairy-tale life through which he would stroll along great galleries with streams of diamonds glistening under the light falling from fiery tapers in the golden chandeliers. Enchanted doors would open, he imagined, of their own accord before the magic of a name, and as one stepped forward, ever forward, dazzling perspectives would stretch away to the far horizon. A smile would cross the boy's lips as he thought of all of this, and he would close his eyes.[15] One has to dream this richly for the disillusionment to be anything more than another tired growing-up.

The problem of romanticism in France during the 1830's was to learn how to live with it. A belief in the importance of the individual had led to emphasis upon emotion; now this was running wild, for the romantic attitude provides no check or balance. But from his youthful experiencing of romanticism stemmed so much that was good in Flaubert: his hatred of the platitude because in it convention stifled individual discovery, his immense surge of enthusiasm in the presence of greatness, his passionate, sustaining love of literature.

Some of his romanticism made him smile in later years: he kept a skull in his bedroom on which he had written, "Poor empty shell, what are you trying to tell me by your grimace?" But the dreams were also majestic and more splendidly robed than cardinals in their purple; in these imaginings he lived a life where nothing but beauty entered.[16] Ridiculous though the posturing was, still he knew always, even as a grown man, that whatever he amounted to had this as its indispensable core.

The dreams of these boys came in large measure from their reading. When the day's assignments were finished, they turned to the new works of romanticism, devouring them far into the night by the flickering lights of stolen bits of candle.[17] Here they found their models. Following a luminous example, young Flaubert sought to reincarnate René, Chateaubriand's melancholy hero who helped so much to body forth the imaginings of young French romantics. Gustave memorized whole pages and forty years later would still be moved almost to tears as he recited them.

So omnipresent were these reincarnations of René by the 1830's that Chateaubriand himself became alarmed and vowed that, could he but withdraw the book, he would hasten to do so. Lamentable and disconnected sentences burst upon the air, and stormy winds howled on every page. To Chateaubriand's dismay every callow schoolboy deemed himself the most unhappy of men; at sixteen each felt he had drained the cup of life, each had been tormented by his genius and had given himself over to that vague misery which comes of knowing of passions one has not yet felt. Each saw his fate symbolized in the melancholy dance of the fallen autumn leaf; each grew sad as distant bells, preferably from a Gothic spire, brought black thoughts of eternity and nothingness; each besought a look, if only of compassion, from a pure woman. Chateaubriand was right: René's progeny were a sorry spectacle.[18] But in his secret heart the older writer was also glad to have given a generation a mode in which to phrase desire, longing, even aspiration and idealism. No generation which is going to be great can be great without them.

This romanticism young Flaubert wrote in story after story to fill a thousand longhand pages in the few years from fourteen to eighteen. Under the lash of Byron's irony he turned to revolt and to atheism; Goethe's Faust pushed him toward a defense of man and a vision of the universal striving of the cosmos toward a more perfect form. Hugo and Dumas taught flamboyant passion and color at all costs; Michelet allied poetry and reality, color and modeling, facts and dreams, a whole world of history. These, the staples of his readings, he prepared in recurring dishes for himself as much as for his few indulgent readers.

The scrupulous stylist of the later novels is nowhere to be found in these first works. A facile, almost oratorical style sweeps all before it in the easy flow of emotion; if the author seems to drown his sorrows in these flooding waves, that is what he sought, rather than to save them, through his style, for our perusing eye. The later man was much too wise ever to think of publishing what the boy had written and put away. And yet his development is clear enough in retrospect in these works.[19]

Albert Camus has suggested that the true novelist, the one whose concern is his fellow man and who seeks communion with him through the novel, is always writing the same book, in one guise after another, as experience of living teaches him more of what to say and experience of writing teaches more of how to say it. In Flaubert's case the experience of living appeared to be teaching important but disparate truths: he had first to learn how they were one. Only then could the craftsman's question of formulating it be reasonably met and answered. A number of diverse facets proved, eventually, to be defining the shape of a single crystal: for the moment the fact that they lay on different planes was all that he knew.

The winter of 1836-37, following the meeting with Elisa, was a momentous one for a budding author: his first work appeared in print in *Le Colibri*, a biweekly Rouen journal in which Alfred Le Poittevin had already published. It was not a very good story, filled as it was with abuse of epithets and enumerations and with exaggeration doing duty for feeling, but it was in print. Six weeks later a second piece appeared, a satirical parody of the office clerk, devoutly attached to his enormous overcoat and boots, his visored cap, his vest, and his frequent pinches of tobacco. When Flaubert died forty-five years later, he was again at work on a tale of clerks: there were two of them now, Bouvard and Pécuchet, and they gave their names to the book he never finished. Overcoat and boots, cap, vest, and tobacco all recurred in the same satiric guise.

While only two articles ended in print, Flaubert was writing constantly and voluminously. Two main themes recur. Both were compounded of demoniac tensions of opposing forces, each demanding outlet. One such pair was the boy's need to love (and be loved), coupled now, each time it leaped to life, with a desiccating irony, a sneer which killed all gentler feeling before it could be wounded. These stories depict a contemporary world and show its fruitless attempts at love. Most of the scenes are painted in such violent tones as to achieve monotony by dulling sensitivities, but occasionally the author's eye has caught the pose and deftly rendered it in quick, sure strokes.

Each scene seemed an end in itself at the time, its purpose fully served when its last word had been set down on paper. But a common need to love and yet to mock underlay them all, and it grew stronger with the years and demanded larger canvases. Here the earlier, smaller scenes could be fitted in; they found their purpose and turned out, unwittingly, to have been sketches for these later, greater works. These observations, scenes, or characters prepare the way for *Madame Bovary*.

Flaubert's second pair of counteracting tensions were religious belief and doubt, his despairing longing for some certainty in the universe, some assurance that God was, and as a counter the satiric laughter, the scorning mockery which rose in him at the sorry state of a universe which made doubt inescapable. Tales of this lineage depict and analyze this doubt in all its protean forms: the fleshly pleasures and their challenge to morality, of course, but far more the anguish of the mind which knows no certainty and finds in the past only the debris of man's rejected certainties, old religions now long forgotten and crude or laughable to the God-slaughtering wisdom of an arrogant teenage boy.

In stories of this type Satan usually conducts one or another of his willing or complaining victims about the universe to observe its miseries and contradictions, its fugitive joys and abiding sorrows, its false truths and eternal doubt. The tales are bitter, poisoning the sweetness youth should have for the young. They grow longer with the passing years; they encompass more doubt and more anguish; and they culminate in *The Temptation of Saint Anthony*, who will be led by just such a devil over just these paths in 1849.

Gustave would write that one should never believe people who say that they are atheists, but in almost the same breath, he, too, sought to deny God.[20] With Elisa he had met desire and unsatisfied passion; he now also knew belief and doubt. Both tensions brought frustration and pain, and therefore both matured him. In a succession of tremendous combats, he sought to still the conflicts within himself in each arena, realizing only after many years that the two terrains must be made one. But this he did not yet divine. Theology and horror, orgies and questioning, alternated as tale piled upon tale in the boy's folders. But the two themes which in a decade or two would make up the great novels were already beginning to dominate.

Madame Bovary in particular was being put together in bits and pieces over these years as various scenes turned up in scattered works. In one tale a young man went to a priest to assuage his doubts; he met only callous incomprehension.[21] Emma Bovary sought out her village priest on just such an errand and with just this result. In another story Flaubert made his first use of a ball he attended during these years at the nearby Chateau du Héron.[22] He had arrived by lamplight; he entered and listened to the scraps of conversation; as the dancing began, Flaubert, who never learned to dance, listened to the noise of the shoes as they slid over the waxed floor; he looked up to see the local peasants gathered at a window. At three in the morning there was a cotillion and then the older ladies went up to their rooms. Eventually, miserable and angry, the boy himself took his candle and went to bed, the music ringing in his ears and desire for one of the ladies coursing through his body. He got up and looked out the window; eventually he dressed again and went for a walk in the park, his shoes rustling amongst the leaves. Reaching the lake, he sat down in a boat, paddled idly about looking at the swans, and at last returned. In the autumn of 1837 Flaubert had the hero of the story he was writing attend this same ball. He, too, saw the lamps and the peasants and listened to the conversation and the music because he could not dance; he walked in the park and made the leaves rustle; he, too, saw the swans.

Fifteen years later Flaubert's concern was Emma Bovary, who needed to experience for one brief moment a reality which she would mistake for her romantic dreams. What more bitter irony than to send her, too, to this ball where an adolescent boy had eaten out his heart over his failure? And so, as in a dream, the scene moves forward, unchanged through the years, and Emma is one of the women Flaubert watched.[23] She will see the same sights and hear the same sounds. But where he had experienced frustration and could not sleep, Emma was happy and did not take the early morning walk or see the swans from the boat.

It is, however, in *Passion and Virtue*, again of 1837, that for the first time the story of Madame Bovary begins to take its future shape.[24] The heroine, like the later Emma, was filled with boundless desires and dreamed of infinite loves. Gradually she came to hate her unfeeling husband and sought infatuation with a lover. When her possessive, romantic notions drove him from her, hatred ensued, hatred for everyone, but particularly for her husband. The rest of the tale diverged sharply from Emma's fate, but this much existed already when Flaubert was not yet sixteen. When the man of thirty sat down to write Madame Bovary's fate, this tale and all the others had been maturing for nearly fifteen years awaiting this moment.

By 1837 the roads toward *The Temptation of Saint Anthony* and *Madame Bovary* had already been discerned, and Flaubert would follow them. For to write, he exulted, was to seize possession of the whole world and condense it into a book. It was to feel one's own thought being born, growing, and rising to its pedestal, there to remain forever. How could one voluntarily live in any other way?

3

Maturing (1838-39)

1838

I was seeking for beauty in the Infinite and found there only doubt.

From *The Memoirs of a Madman* (1838)

IIe had been launched upon his youth by love; he ended it in despair.

From the first version (1843-45)
of *A Sentimental Education*

AROUND the age of sixteen a boy begins to grapple in earnest with the problems which will surround the man he is to become. At this age he sounds like a man and he is beginning to look like one; but in fact his sensitivities, like his size, have outrun his strength, and he faces many of a man's combats with no more than a boy's force. For Flaubert's generation, moreover, romanticism, by promising new emotional heights, had opened new depths of despair as well and had intensified all the problems to which adolescence is heir.

Never again was Gustave to be so strikingly handsome as over the next three years.[1] In the autumn of 1838 his period as a boarder in the school ended: he had now the coveted role of day student, a prisoner perhaps during school hours, but a free man at other times. By leaving the Hôtel-Dieu a few moments earlier in the morning and crossing the heart of the city quickly, he could stop to take his coffee and smoke his cigar at the Café national across from the Church of Saint-Ouen. For a few moments the master of his fate, he could survey the bustling scene (fairs were frequent on this little square) and with his smoke breathe in a heady satisfaction over the figure he imagined he cut at his table.

But then the bell would ring at the school; he would pay for his coffee, snatch up his books and notes, and hurry off to the restrictions of the world of children again.

Flaubert's mood was often melancholy and pessimistic during 1838 and 1839. Vice and virtue seemed equally dull in prospect. To Alfred and to Ernest he confided that his habit of analysis was his undoing: he dissected himself and all he met. It was a morbid habit which the reading of Sainte-Beuve's analytical work, *Volupté*, fostered.[2] It amused him to behave thus, he said, but the smile can have been no more than a thin, worn cover over shivering misery, for the dissection always revealed gangrene within the fairest flesh. When he had found corruption in what had seemed pure, he boasted, then he would raise his head and laugh.[3]

This dismal cast of mind led to an unhappy agnosticism and corroding doubt. Pascal seeks to console the agnostic with the comforting reminder that he would not be searching for God had he not found Him; but the proffered paradox proves cold in the face of anguished doubt. Young Flaubert could no more put his doubt behind him than he could deny the God he sensed. Religion as he knew it could not help him. His family lived entirely outside of any formalized religion; they were neither anticlerical nor devout, being perhaps more deist than otherwise, and more concerned than committed to any position. Through his reading, however, and through his youthful friends, Gustave came to know the romantic form of esthetic Christianity which had been given vogue a generation before by Chateaubriand. He relaxed briefly into the facile notion that Christianity is beautiful and hence must be true. In church he listened, enthralled, to the solemn, sonorous tones of the organ rising majestically in the nave. In the distance he heard a frail and gracious child's voice which was married (in his miserable metaphor) with the aroma of incense, like two perfumes. The sunlight, piercing gilded windows, sent a mystic, azure light over the church and filled the youth with a gentle revery of love and faith. God became his new passion. But, he added, it passed, just as others do.[4] Such moments, however, kept recurring.

Despairing skepticism became his fixed obsession. His was the romantic revolt, the outraged cry of the supreme individualist against a God who would not bend His will to man's. The eternal Why of life and death, of despair, joy, and unhappiness, tormented him. Was death then the only reality and annihilation the only truth? It had been so with his dreams and hopes. The thought of death began to haunt him.[5]

Meanwhile he had discovered sex and sexuality. Industrial Rouen provided easy access to prostitution, and during these years of adolescence he sought to prove himself a man here. Was it an autobiographical twist which, forty years later, he gave to the end of *A Sentimental Education*, perhaps the lingering memory of a boyhood escapade? The hero Frédéric and a friend reminisce, recollecting a summer's eve of 1837 when, taking their courage in their hands, they picked two bouquets of flowers and slipped off to a brothel. Stepping inside, Frédéric stood transfixed, holding out his bouquet as a lover would to his fiancée. The warmth of the evening, the apprehension of the unknown, a sort of remorse, and, coupled with it, the sight of so many women at his disposal, so upset him that he paled and stood stock still. The girls all laughed, delighted at his confusion: he turned and fled. Since it was he who had the money, his friend was forced to follow.[6] The episode has a wry, autobiographical ring. In any event, it was in approximately 1837 or 1838 that Gustave discovered prostitution.

His experience was both a lure and a disappointment to him. Was that all it amounted to, he wondered?[7] Steadily over the years he was to turn to it as a convenient, animal satisfaction which in no wise engaged his spirit. Quiet and detached, he could observe the ironic, bitter poetry he found in it. For many years it remained an obsessive necessity. It is the paradox of virility that it demands to be constantly proved when it is in doubt, either overtly or from hidden, unphrased implications barely whispered to the conscious mind.

Meanwhile sexuality had taken the other form that it always does among adolescent boys: he had discovered masturbation. There is nothing startling about this; but in Gustave's case, as not infrequently occurs, it was accompanied not only by rising tension and release but also by deep-seated feelings of misery and guilt. It is, in addition, a habit so easily gratified that abuse is an ever-present temptation. And Gustave did abuse it. A hearty and strong constitution and what our grandparents termed a sanguine temperament helped him for some years to withstand the nervous debilitation that too frequent masturbation may bring in its train. At sixteen, however, one feels one's strength eternal, and excess is delightful in itself. The school lavatories were ever after associated in his mind with these moments. A part of his childhood was destroyed when they were torn down many years later and, grown man that he was, he lamented their disappearance.[8]

The expanding world of sex compounded Flaubert's problems. But he was a reader and hence he took his problems to his books (whence many had come) and there he sought his answers. From Chateaubriand's René he had learned skepticism and pessimism. Now the Montaigne of the "Apology for Raimond Sebonde" taught him radical doubt, a skepticism over the poor, puny powers of man's reason, which led his own doubt even further. He soon made Montaigne almost his only reading.[9]

Equally, perhaps even more, he was excited by the now wholly forgotten *Ahasvérus* of Edgar Quinet,[10] the story of the cursed and wandering Jew overwhelmed by the indefinite sadness which comes from knowing nothing and being unable to love anyone, while having an immense need for knowledge, for tenderness, and for affection. These may be great concerns, as in the problems to which existentialism has currently given vogue. In the tawdry robes which Quinet gave them, however, they appear the tired garb of a ranting romantic actor and not the sober dress of a truly pessimistic philosopher of despair. But motley though they were, they served to clothe Flaubert's despair in raiment he found beautiful.

Flaubert turned now to the longest fictional work he had yet undertaken, fifteen thousand words filling today sixty pages of printed text. He put the last touches to the story a month after he was seventeen, and he called it, with little exaggeration, *The Memoirs of a Madman*. They told his state and his story.[11]

He was evolving with his period in thus turning, around 1838, from historical works, which had made up the bulk of his production until then, to autobiography. His *Memoirs of a Madman* he intended to reflect the workings of his mind, the random flow of his thoughts. They were therefore unlike his earlier works in being formless and planless. They would be unreadable, were it not for the depth of his hurt sensitivities. Moreover, his experiences frequently paralleled his readings and he could and did lean heavily on his favorite authors. Rousseau, in his *Confessions*, had lamented his misfortunes in a tone which had suggested, erroneously, that anyone could imitate it. Too many had, but this was no deterrent, and Flaubert tried his hand. René and Goethe's Werther may have posed, too, for some of the sadder moments, but the guiding influence on the boy was the outlook of Montaigne, who led him to ever sharper doubts. Where Rousseau had seemed to suggest the hope of being loved and of rebuilding, young Gustave turned to radical pessimism, finding nothing but mockery and hollowness on every hand. Waning romanticism was turning in this direction, and Gustave would have felt authorized in his views, particularly as he read the works of Théophile Gautier, the painter turned poet, novelist, and critic. Gautier brought to romanticism a note of bitterness sharper than ever before; it matched Gustave's temperament.

Flaubert was also deeply marked by Gautier's proclamation that art was its own end. Insofar as an object was useful, it served man's needs, and these were ugly. Flaubert, seeking to justify his own revolt and longing to underpin his response to art with a doctrine as well, aligned himself with Gautier. The lines which open the *Memoirs* cried aloud his defiance: the book was good for no useful purpose. Did he dream, as adolescents will, that he would one day meet the great man and by some clever move attract his attention, perhaps even impress him? Within half a dozen years it was to happen, and Flaubert was to enroll himself in what he would term the School of Gautier. Gautier was a man of but secondary rank as poet, and as critic, too, he was less than great. But he influenced Flaubert; and Baudelaire dedicated his *Flowers of Evil* to him, calling him magician of French letters, friend, and master.

René had explored the delicious miasmas which surround and isolate the genius even when he is with his fellow man. The world had nothing to say to him. How could it understand him? How could he shrink his giant's life to the level of their society? Gustave wrote of sitting on his school bench, absorbed in his dreams of the future, his imagination sublimely uplifted to the highest reaches a child can master, while the pedagogue (the boy's own sneering word) presumed to mock his Latin verses and his comrades looked on contemptuously. The fools, he cried! How did they, who were so weak and common and limited, dare to laugh at him, whose mind was soaring at the outer bounds of creation, lost in the world of poetry. He knew that he was greater than them all and could feel infinite joys and celestial ecstasies before the intimate revelations of his soul.[12] The influence of René was not toward modesty.

Giant that he felt himself to be, he was nonetheless crippled, and he knew it. Love, he said, he had tasted and found flat; like Chateaubriand he proposed, in one mood, to yawn his life away.[13] But then up would surge his vague aspirations, his desire to escape beyond confining reality to an infinity where he might find the truth and beauty of which Plato spoke. Yet all a romantic youth in 1838 could find was doubt. The tolling church bells had brought serenity to Chateaubriand's René. When Gustave heard them, he wrote, he, too, wished to see the world in beauty, to hear the cries of triumph and glimpse eternal majesty. He would cross the fields to the hilltop overlooking the ripe, golden wheat to listen to the frail sound of the village church bells singing in the midst of the countryside while insects buzzed in the grass and birds murmured among the leaves. But the bells, he knew, would toll one day to announce his death and the next minute would ring out for a baptism: they were a derision, like all the rest.[14]

How could he descend from his infinite atmosphere of love and ecstasy to this frigid earth where all fire had died, all energy disappeared? Analysis had destroyed belief in the goodness of life and men. It was wiser, following Rabelais, to be a man of sense, a skeptic, and a good drinker. But skeptical doubt led only toward measureless abyss.[15]

Into the midst of these adolescent outbursts Flaubert thrust an account of his meeting with Elisa.[16] Two and one-half years had passed since that day on the beach at Trouville, yet he found that he could imagine her presence so strongly that he would look around, half-expecting to see her. It had the force of a hallucination, and he began to write it down, reliving it as he discovered the extraordinary world of his imagination. He could see and hear the trembling of the leaves; the slightest fold of her dress seemed there before him; the tone of her voice sounded in his ear.[17]

To relive was, for Flaubert, in some sense to live for the first time. Reactions with him were habitually delayed until these moments of recreating events and scenes when, for the first time, their full power would evolve under his scrutiny. His immediate reactions to Elisa had been shock and numbness. Over the following months his senses had revived and he had begun to have the normal reactions of a boy (or a man) who is in love with another man's wife. His writing had showed the effect and had become more carnal. It was only now, however, that the tone acquired the violence one might have expected earlier. He recalled watching Elisa nurse her child, and his imaginings became more cruel. The Marquis de Sade he now discovered and made a favorite author.

Blocked in what he wanted, Flaubert turned against mankind, which set up these barriers. He longed to hurt men and then to laugh in derision.[18] As it was love itself which he most desired, this he hated most. Armed with a knowledge he was not yet wise enough to wield, he lunged out foolishly, seeking to wound when all he could do was to expose his own heart. Beneath the affected worldly wisdom there was a suffering boy; Gustave described a couple panting for each other and driven together by an ardor without equal, for these two souls—the irony is childish but betrays the hurt—have their organs violently excited. Then he depicted them grotesquely coupled with grunts and sighs, both bent only on reproducing one more imbecile on earth, a poor wretch who would imitate them.[19] The effort to be bitter was no more than sad.

He had thought a woman was an angel, he confessed; now he agreed with Molière that she was more like a soup. The need to dissect himself was leading him to probe too deeply: his ideals were being torn apart; next it would be himself. The disquieting note returned as he began to think of his own birth, and beyond that to his conception. For many boys of seventeen, this is a difficult thought, better banished with a laugh until it no longer seems important. To Flaubert it became an obsession which he sought to

kill by rending himself and it apart. He envisioned his father returning drunk from an orgy, his mother attracting him. The language bears the imprint of the youth's powerless rage.[20] Words
were all he could hurl.

What could this young man do? His emotions were violent,
his sensitivities tender. His affectionate nature would always froth
over, the bubbles evidencing the turmoil beneath. If some of the
froth this time was muddied, the waters beneath were as capable
of limpidity as ever and, his rage calmed by his writing, he closed
his *Memoirs* with a tender farewell to Elisa. He was wise enough
to know that other passions would entrance him, that he would
perhaps forget her. But he also knew that she would always remain in the bottom of his heart. The heart, he wrote, is a terrain
which each new passion upsets and plows over, but the ruins of
the earlier passions are still there beneath the turned furrows.[21]
And so he bade her and his childhood adieu.

QUANDARY

> Now I am at the bottom of the abyss . . . unless there be
> hells below hell and another despair beyond despair.
> But can I go on living when life is always thus?
>
> From *Smarh* (1839)

To say farewell to childhood is not, unfortunately, to step into
manhood, and young Flaubert had years of turmoil ahead as he
struggled in a tangled underbrush of unfulfilled desires.[22] Childhood was ending for him in 1839: Ernest Chevalier, who was a
year older, left for Paris to begin his studies for a law career; a
few months later Achille was married. A kind of security within
the comfortable circle of family and childhood friends was being
burst apart: in the endless process of growing up which marks the
passage of the years, those who stood ahead of Flaubert in the line
were stepping forth to take their places. That he was in no way
ready for their departures could in no way delay them.

Where could he turn? He could only wait. Meanwhile his
imagination balked at producing the gaudy images he had earlier

enjoyed so much. Rather, what he put on paper he now found dry, forced, and torn from him with real pain. He knew so well where his problem lay: he had modestly promised himself in advance everything most beautiful in the world. Now only the irony of it remained. Each contact with living led to a recoil into satire. From this he took refuge in his imagination, which depicted a richer, fuller life. In turn, the clash between this and the real world led him to create his own world, in art. The satirist, the man of imagination, the artist—the three stages led inexorably forward. Satire was too bitter to be a way of life; imagination demanded expansion, not frustration. Living must then be within the framework of the paradox that henceforth he would live best only within his imagined world of art. To discover and learn to live this paradox was in itself a major task; it filled his early manhood.

In *The Memoirs of a Madman* the satirist was already observing the world and himself and sharpening his scalpel against the day when he must dissect Emma, who would portray the errors in romanticism, the fatal flaw within René. Flaubert had of course described his meeting with Elisa in the consecrated phrasing of romanticism; but he had gone beyond this to mock the emotionalism such moments seemed to require, the laments over a stupid world, one's admiration for a sunset, a meadow. He wrote too much, and he lacked the precision which alone can make a dart a deadly weapon; but the target he had already found.

Flaubert's romantic satire of a hated modern world invited an equally romantic picture of prior ages, especially Rome of the decadence. The boy's undiscriminating desire for release from the tedium and convention about him made captivating a vision of antiquity seen as the age of orgies. Nero's unabashed sensualism led Flaubert to describe Rome as a beautiful queen rolling deliciously in orgy and soiling her robes in the wine of debauchery, prouder of her vices than she had been of her virtues. Above it all stood Nero, with his diamond-studded chariots flying across the arena, his tiger-like loves, his immense, voluptuous nights, and his bloody illuminations of Rome. How the boy longed to return to it! So seldom did the modern, bourgeois world permit itself thus really to live![23]

He would have liked to hear bones shatter in the crackling

fires and to gallop over whole peoples bowed before him. At the peak of his vision he was Nero, terrifying the world by the raising of an eyebrow. He would ultimately learn to salvage much for art from these sublimations of his inhibited sensualism and even his sadism; but until he could elaborate an esthetic which would control them, they remained only the lucubrations of a man possessed.

To an escape into past ages romanticism had added a parallel escape to other, better climes. The Greek War of Independence, fought during Flaubert's childhood, had generated the Philhellenism of Byron and then of Victor Hugo in France. Byron, who had died at Missolonghi fighting for the cause, had been able to make his world adopt the impress of his poet's vision. The poet—Flaubert meant Byron, of course—was the soul which resounded to the echoes of all the sorrows about him and gave words to all these ill-formed voices, which now came forth to mark eternally in history the place of a society or an epoch and the poet's role within it. That was why, young Flaubert felt, poetic truth was truer than historic truth. The few moments of enthusiasm to which he admitted, he had owed to art. But perhaps it, too, was largely a vain hope, for it demanded an expression and form which seemed to the boy to be unattainable.[24]

Flaubert needed to underpin his romantic intuitions concerning art with a philosophic base which would withstand the assaults of his analyses and his desiccating doubt. Through his philosophy teacher Mallet, he began to investigate Victor Cousin's eclecticism, which was an attempt to draw together into a coherent doctrine the more valid insights from a number of earlier philosophies.[25] From Spinoza, from Hegel, and from Plato, Cousin elaborated a concept of a universe harmoniously one, in which, perhaps most important for Flaubert's development, the true and the good were but two ways of looking at a single harmony, the cosmos. Moreover—and here the Platonic element was strongest—the beautiful in Cousin's view was the resplendent aspect of the true. Thus, albeit indirectly, young Flaubert was being led back at the start of his training as thinker to Plato and to his fundamental intuition that the good, the true, and the beautiful are one and the same: they are equivalent ways of observing and understanding a single, harmoniously ordered universe. This would remain the foundation of his esthetics.

For Cousin ideal beauty was a Platonic idea, distinct from real beauty, through which alone, however, one might approach it. But here, abandoning Plato, Cousin affirmed that as one approached the ideal it receded unceasingly; the last term of this retreat was the infinite. If this mystic leap seems hard to reconcile with logic, it had for Flaubert the advantage of concording with his own vague aspirations and providing, in its climax, a ground for hope that thus the ideal might be approached, for Cousin held that the work of art threw the soul into a revery which lifted it toward the infinite. This notion, powerful because ill defined in the young man's mind, brought a beginning of solace, even though all too frequently it ended in doubt.

Cousin's eclecticism, setting art outside of life, was a philosophy particularly necessary to the rising generation of Flaubert, Baudelaire, and others born around 1820. Their predecessors had turned from a concept of pure art to doctrines holding that the artist was a sort of sage or prophet destined to lead his blinder fellows forward toward a world of progress and out of the morass which rising industrialism was creating about them. George Sand was using the novel to depict a new world in which women would take their rightful places beside men. Lamartine followed Chateaubriand's lead into politics, and Hugo began to turn this way, too. From the older generation only Gautier and Cousin still seemed exalted by beauty and art.

Now, in 1839, Flaubert was seventeen, and the doubts seemed clearer than his dim, vague goals; hence doubt was what he sought to phrase. To put such questioning into fiction he had for many years used a wild, satanic vision of a flight through space in which the confused and doubting soul had the Devil for his guide This line of tales begins with his *Journey to Hell* of four years earlier and culminates in *The Temptation of Saint Anthony* in 1849. *Smarh*, as he called his new work, was both his most ambitious attempt yet in the vein and the last one before *The Temptation*.[26] It has nearly twenty-five thousand words. Chateaubriand's ennui, Byronic satanism, and the universal desire which spurred on

Goethe's Faust combined here with lesser models like the Wandering Jew, Ahasvérus. Smarh, the tempted hermit, foreshadows Anthony, and the tale's scenes of bloody carnage give uncomfortable premonitions of the death and destruction in *Salammbô*, Flaubert's novel of 1862 concerning the War of the Mercenaries in ancient Carthage.

After a rapid prologue, the scene opens in Asia Minor with the hermit Smarh on stage and Satan in the guise of a learned doctor to tempt him: the opening for the later *Temptations* has been found. Much of the first half of *Smarh* has the form of a dialogue, deriving from Flaubert's plays for the Billiard Room of the Hôtel-Dieu. It gives way only toward the very end, when the personal element comes to dominate the work and it returns to the style of *The Memoirs of a Madman*. *Smarh* established the form which all the later *Temptations* would adopt, a fluid, dramatic dialogue alternating with a supple, unobtrusive narrative flow when the author, chorus-like, intervenes to move events more rapidly.

Satan has no difficulty in tempting Smarh by proving that the world is ruled by doubt, violence, and pride, and by showing him how little he understands of God or man. While Satan promises to dispel this ignorance, his servant Yuk (the origin of his name, as of Smarh's, is obscure) tempts a woman who has come to consult the naïve hermit. As she leaves, frenzied with desire, Yuk laughs a mad, obstreperous laugh of victory. It first resounded in the *Journey into Hell*; its last echo will rebound on the final page of *The Temptation*. Transparently the hermit is young Flaubert as he confides that what he needs is a divine knowledge, something to raise him above the level of common man and draw him closer to his God. Now, knowing that this knowledge exists, he further learns the law of human nature that a little is always enough to arouse a ferocious taste for more, that as desire grows by what it feeds on, so knowledge leads to doubt.

The notion of a God perceived in nature will no longer do; Satan takes Smarh high into the atmosphere to let him observe for himself. All creation cries aloud in pain over a universe foredoomed to misery by a God who is imprisoned in the fatality of his own work. Smarh thus meets the inexorable and terrifying fatality which dogged Flaubert through all his years. It is the curse Smarh rails at; it is Rodolphe's excuse when he abandons Emma Bovary; it is her husband Charles' explanation for why her sad life turned out as it did.

The truth is unattainable, and Satan calls it a shadow which flees as man runs ever after it: Cousin's doctrines had reduced Flaubert's Smarh to despair. The hermit is now under the domination of Yuk, God of the Grotesque, the True and Eternal Buffoon, the Ugly, the only ever-present force in the universe. The word "grotesque" is one of the keys to Flaubert's vocabulary and thought. Le Garçon had incarnated it earlier; in Yuk it is now more philosophical. It was a word which Flaubert liked to use for all he hated; but he did not yet fully perceive what it was he loathed, and Yuk remains less than precise; he does not survive in later formulations of Flaubert's concept.

Smarh's loose structure now seemed to Flaubert to permit a digression in the form of a playlet, a "Little Bourgeois Comedy," written as a draft indicating what the stage action would be. It deals with a young pair who are in love, then marry, and start domestic life. The girl, full of romantic notions, discovers that her husband's tastes do not extend beyond money and geometry; his interest in her is only that he possesses what others covet. When childbearing destroys her figure, he returns to his bachelor ways. The husband appears with no redeeming traits; the girl, for all her nonsense, is a sad portrayal and seeks to evoke our pity. Her flaw is that she believes in romanticism, just as Emma Bovary will. But Emma, vigorous and determined, will seek to live her dreams as this girl does not. And the reader of *Madame Bovary* is not invited to sympathize with the tinsel of Emma's imagined world as he is here. Young Gustave had to be a romantic before learning to castigate romantic yearnings.

Flaubert's private papers bulge with scenarios (as he called them) like this, story lines more or less fully evolved into plays. Elaborating such dramatic presentations was an exercise he enjoyed; it came in unbroken sequence from the days of his childhood, and he kept on writing them even for his later works. By envisaging living humans moving through the action of his story, he could ensure that the abstractions of his initial concept had the warmth and direct appeal of human contact.

The playlet had constituted a digression. When Flaubert returned to Smarh, he abandoned the effort to give his hermit a character of his own: henceforth he incarnates only the unhappy, libidinous fantasies of Flaubert himself. To his chagrin, Flaubert now found that when he sought to describe sensualism (or the infinite, for that matter), his command of style failed him. For days he lingered lovingly, evoking scenes of exquisite sensualism, unbridled license, garlanded nymphs, and lubricious women. But, perhaps under the influence of the delicate, allusive intimacy of Sainte-Beuve's novel *Volupté*, he conceived of voluptuousness as so transparent and bodiless that it was a vapor impossible to seize. Only a clearer concept of it would allow him a clearer description. When he had it, he boasted, whole cities would rush to brothels on reading his page. He was still an adolescent.

Eventually sated beyond desire, the hermit feels only ennui, which hangs deadly round his neck. With Yuk obscenely desecrating all Smarh had once desired, sadism and destructive fantasies seize the hermit as they had Flaubert in *The Memoirs of a Madman*. Only Death seems momentarily to offer eternity, but even it bows before Yuk. The grotesque alone survives. In an epilogue, Flaubert bade farewell for the second time in six months to the beautiful days which a lying dawn had promised him so resplendent and so pure. Smarh (and the young man, too), separated forever from their dreams by grotesque reality, whirl off through endless, empty space, as Yuk's laughter trails them down.

The months slipped by and almost nothing went on paper. One year later he brought out the manuscript and, rereading it, added a brief note that it was permissible to write works which were pitiably bad, but not this bad. He had thought himself a young Goethe, but a story depended on ideas and this one had none. Sadly he foretold a life of enthusiasm over dreams and disgust each time he sought to realize them. The wisest counsel he could offer was not to write. And for a year or so, he did just that. An ending had been reached.

TRANSITION

I do feel, but in a confused way, that something is taking place inside me; I am in a transition stage and I am curious to see what will come out of it. This is my moulting stage (in the intellectual sense). Will I end it with all my plumage lost, or superb?

Letter to Ernest Chevalier, February 24, 1839

By the summer of 1839 Flaubert was seventeen and a half, *Smarh* was written and put away, and all his hopes and illusions lay in ruins about him. He was working at the preparation of the examinations which in France mark the end of the lycée and open the professional schools to a youth. He spent another year at it and wrote but little, having no heart for anything at all. What he did put down on paper recorded his despair at his loss of Christianity.[27] Christ's Passion was the most beautiful concept he knew, and he longed to be able to prostrate himself before a God in Whom he could believe; but he found only emptiness within himself. When he looked about him, the modern, bourgeois world offered him its railroads and its factories, its chemists and its mathematicians. Only the thought of orgy could rouse him; the stories written this summer were the last of his childish attempts to shock his reader by the display of horror. If only he could find a way to be either more stupid or more intelligent, a total atheist or a confirmed mystic, but something at any rate which was complete and entire; if only he could find his identity![28]

At this juncture Flaubert had his first brush with adult justice.[29] In December of 1839 Gustave and several others created an uproar in a class; soon it became general. The headmaster, who was new, threatened the original three or four with dismissal. Gustave's name headed the list of signatures on a letter which the boys drafted and sent to him protesting what seemed to them an injustice. They wrote: "We have been told that we were children and that we were acting like children; we are going to try, by our restraint and by our integrity, to convince you that this is not so." Children can be naïvely concerned with justice; schoolmasters must deal with practical problems of the maintenance of order and authority. Gustave was dismissed from school on December 14, two days after his eighteenth birthday, as the result of what he must have considered a necessary and righteous defense of justice. It was an inauspicious entry into the world of adults.

To break from the circle of hope, disappointment, and frustration a new track had to be found. Romanticism had consistently encouraged illusions it could not satisfy, and as the 1830's waned, the latter-day converts to the school could offer nothing but louder moans, wilder shrieks, and more horrible predicaments. Romanticism, visibly, was dying, and a new ideal needed to be found: Flaubert, in coming to silence himself, was responding to the dilemma of his age.

Romanticism had been a passing affair in France, decried even by many of its proponents, like Chateaubriand, who sought above all to rejuvenate a classicism which continued to be his closest allegiance. Victor Hugo himself, seeking a convenient poetic alter ego to serve as mouthpiece, selected the classical name Olympio, and many of his lines resound with the vigorous imagery of the hundreds of lines of Virgil which he knew by heart. The French romantic screamed aloud his defiance of a dead classicism, but he never moved far from a living classicism on which he was nurtured. The schoolboy Flaubert, outdoing René in his writing, was still engaged as French children always have been in reading the classics of Greece and Rome. When, with his generation, he turned back to classicism to reconsider it, it was no unknown terrain he was reconnoitering.

Flaubert's intense, enthusiastic reading of Plutarch's stories of ancient grandeur stirred him as deeply as did *René* or *Hernani*. Moreover, the examinations to be prepared sent him on wider excursions, and he began his study of Greek, reading Aeschylus, Demosthenes, and above all Homer. But when he had written *The Memoirs of a Madman* (1838) or *Smarh* (1839), classicism had seemed lost in its sumptuous dignity and unaware of the echoes of romanticism, or at best only a treasure house to be pillaged for Nero and his debauchery or Alexander and his dreams of world conquest. No deeply, surely moored truth seemed anchored here.

The change in Flaubert's attitude toward classicism came quite suddenly when it did appear. It was peculiarly suited to his temperament, and to the underlying bases of French culture as well, that the revolution should have come from the theater. Almost always, as much yesterday as today, the theater is the great bastion around which French literary battles swirl and in the taking of which true victory is signalized. Sartrean existentialism had to win the stage and romanticism had ridden to victory in what was at once baptized the "Battle of *Hernani*," fought over Hugo's play. It was the theater, too, which would now sound the death knell of romanticism, through the genius of a great actress. The tragedienne Rachel came at the right moment: the cultivated public in France was ready for a revival of classicism. The battle was hard fought and proved, eventually, not to have been a total victory; but in 1840 it seemed secure. It was then that Flaubert first saw her.

In June of that year Rachel played an engagement in Rouen. The year before, Flaubert's sister Caroline, in Paris for a quick visit, had arranged to stay over an extra night to see the actress who was already being proclaimed as the greatest of her generation.[30] When Rachel played in Rouen, the whole family must have gone together to see her. To Flaubert it was a tremendous esthetic experience: to him, as to many in his generation, Rachel was a reincarnation of Greek art, a form of beauty he had not heretofore suspected. He sought to put it down on paper the next day; her performance was cause enough to return to writing.[31]

He wrote that he would long remember her. It had been as though a Greek statue, amply draped, had opened its mouth to speak lines of Euripides. She had revealed the purity and simplicity of classic art by her forceful poses, her overpowering gestures, and her careful diction. But above all it was the spirit animating her which had moved him, a controlled inspiration beating in her heart but not displayed before the public, so that all her emotions could be fused in a harmonious interplay, complex and captivating. She had shown that within the strict esthetic of classicism there could be an art more moving than all the explosions of romanticism.

Her acting brought to his mind images of ancient Greeks waiting through the long winter months for spring and the appearance of the sparrow in the greening fields, for this meant the return of the rhapsode, the wandering poet, to sing to them from Homer. They greeted him with flowers and fruit; as he departed, they accompanied him to the village fountain, where they blessed his lyre, wished him godspeed and above all a swift return. In these words Flaubert closed his account.

Shortly after seeing Mademoiselle Rachel, Flaubert passed the examinations for which he had been preparing: to celebrate, the family rewarded him with a trip to the Pyrenees and Corsica.[32] Travel literature, that is, an account of a journey, played a crucial role in developing the new form of writing which was going to be called realism. The great American realist, William Dean Howells, began his career by writing precisely such accounts; from them he advanced hesitatingly to a closer consideration of the people making the journey; finally the journey could be abandoned completely, and Howells would be writing the first American realistic novels. In Flaubert's case the transition is less clearly marked out, and the role of his travel notes—he always made voluminous ones —is more tenuous; it is nonetheless real.

Flaubert and several older friends of the family left in late August, returning to Rouen ten weeks later. If one is nearing twenty, good-looking and vigorous, and with an eye disposed to light up at the sight of a pretty woman, a leisurely trip may be brightened by a chance encounter almost anywhere. For Flaubert it happened at Marseilles, where three French women just back from Peru caught his eye.[33] They lived in the Hôtel Richelieu on the gay Rue de la Darse close to the Old Port and the sailors' quarter. One day as he was returning from a dip in the Mediterranean, one of them, Eulalie Foucaud, looked temptingly at him; he threw her a kiss—and that night she came to his hotel room. There, with the fountain in the courtyard outside splashing in their ears, they made love. She was voluptuous and thirty-five, like Elisa old enough to play a maternal role while still being flattering to his virility. Poor Eulalie was completely overwhelmed; for six months she and Flaubert exchanged burning letters. Her misspellings were fascinating, "ottomatic" in particular.

As Flaubert journeyed southward with his party in that summer of 1840, his father sent him a letter of wise advice on how to travel, reminding him of Montaigne's counsel that a trip should be an occasion to observe and carry back impressions of how other people live and to "rub and polish our brains against those of others." He urged his son to look closely and take notes; he was not to journey like a bourgeois grocer or a traveling salesman.[34] Early in the trip, therefore, Gustave started to fill idle moments by making occasional notes which he twice paused to work up into more careful form during the trip. He completed them on his return to Rouen.

The early pages are steadily and systematically self-conscious as Flaubert apologizes to himself for his return to writing. But write he did, and he strove not unsuccessfully to avoid the older romantic notion of a travel book: with mock regret he averred that he was in despair at having no fantasies to offer from his meditations. But he was, he said, above all a man of caprice, who needed to tempt his muse. He was determined to make no effort at style, nor was his to be an erudite journey with inkwell prepared, learning duly catalogued, and emotions well stocked beforehand. Unfortunately, he stated his intended simplicity in as complex and contorted an image as he had yet written: his sentences were to smell of the leather of his traveling boots; they should not be decked out with spats or waistcoats, nor should they have pomade dripping in fat periods, or cosmetics to stiffen them into hard expressions. In point of fact by thus complexly insisting that he would write a simple, intimate, and personal account, he was following the developing vogue of the romantic travel book, which had now reached just this stage.

Slow and painful efforts to find and manipulate images gradually taught Flaubert to see the wind at low tide fretfully dragging a trivial wave hither and thither over the pebbles as though it were an old rag. He was learning to allow what was before him to penetrate into him, rather than seeking in romantic fashion to project his mood onto it. He found he could now remain motionless for half an hour at a time looking steadfastly—like an idiot, he called it—at the white line of a horizon. On the long rides through an unfamiliar nature he was discovering a new joy in laying aside his burdens as he became absorbed in the world around him.

Corsica was even more strikingly different from Normandy

than the Pyrenees had been. Flaubert and his party rode along the shore one day; the sea was calm and threw a light spray up over the rocks, making them scintillate like diamonds. The sea air was scented, and he breathed deeply, drawing in the sun, the breeze, the very sight of the horizon and the perfume of the myrtles. These were, he wrote, happy days, during which the spirit was open to the sun like the countryside and, like it, bathed in the aroma of hidden flowers. He found himself smiling at the noise of the wind moving the treetops or the murmur of the tide along the strand; his spirit rushed over the waves with the breeze; something ethereal, great, even tender, hovered in the very light of the sun and lost itself in the radiant immensity with the pink mists of the morning. For the first time in nearly twenty years of living Flaubert had stepped outside of himself. It had brought peace and had given his pen a sweep and a power it had never had before.

His new attitude on this trip brought new problems, which a glimpse of Spain brought vividly before him. He knew already her tinseled form from Victor Hugo's verse and plays, a brightly colored backdrop for French romantic visions, their essential hollowness in some part masked by being placed far away. Now this country of which he had dreamed lay on the far side of the river; his heart beat faster and he felt foolish for it. But when he crossed over and was actually in it, the reality proved more stimulating than his imaginings had been. Also as he became aware of the shortcomings of his knowledge, his self-assurance collapsed into irony. How embarrassing it would be, were he to acquire enough learning to judge his ignorant reactions to the Spanish churches before him! He was, as he put it, elaborating a philosophy of art before he knew the alphabet. But now that he understood something of his limitations, he could strive to overcome his ignorance and could seek knowledge as the basis for a new esthetic. The staggering foundation of erudition which would underlie his later novels had its origin in these Spanish churches whose sculpture he could not understand.

At this turning point in art, so Flaubert wrote, none knew which way to seek for beauty; but as he moved away from romanticism, he was being steadily impelled toward classicism. He found it everywhere in Corsica, where it was a way of life based on simplicity and directness, a world in which, as Baudelaire would later put it, action was the sister of one's dreams, and thought and deed had the same splendor. What he saw led him to reconsider classicism in literature, where he found it more complex. His closest acquaintance with it at this time was in terms of France's seventeenth century, with Corneille, Racine, and Molière. Examining their styles, he observed that they sought precision of concepts and tight, clear sentences so that the idea within was like a lamp in a crystal globe, whose light was so pure and brilliant that the crystal disappeared. The strength of this style lay in form.

Scattered over the south of France and particularly in Provence, the *Provincia* of the Romans, are a considerable number of Roman monuments: arenas at Arles and Nîmes, theaters, the aqueduct of the Pont-du-Gard rising one hundred fifty feet above the river bed, and then the Mediterranean, the classic sea. Flaubert's excitement mounted as he entered Provence: he was living in the midst of antiquity. He reached Nîmes as sunset neared, and the great arena projected its shadow far across the ground. The night wind was rising and whistled through the wild fig trees growing high up along the arcades. It was the time of day when the Roman spectacles would have been drawing to a close after the lions and gladiators had struggled long and hard. Flaubert walked along the galleries, thinking of all the feet that had trod these stones and had now left forever. The benches were all in place; he could pick out the emperor's box and the seats for the knights below; the Vestal Virgins were over there, the gladiators and the animals down below. If the dead returned, they would find their places intact, left empty these two thousand years. The arena seemed to be waiting for its departed guests.

The site took hold of Flaubert, and he peopled it with what he could remember of Tacitus, Suetonius, and Michelet. How much these bare stones knew!—ferocious cries, stamps of impatience, sad and gay things, atrocious or foolish ones. There had been a time when all this arena was full of sonorous voices. The cloaks were of violet or purple; the blood flowed hot onto the sand yellow with saffron. What did the crowd talk of? Did the senators laugh to see all the knights' places filled to overflow? Why did the freedmen standing at the top of the arena shout so loudly that everyone turned in their direction? And then at dusk, when all was over and the emperor rose from his box as the heavy smoke climbed skyward warm with blood and breath, the sun would set as it was doing this day in its blue sky and the noise would die bit by bit. They would come and carry off the dead; the courtesan would get into her litter to go to the baths before dinner, and Gito would hurry quickly to the barber to have his nails cleaned and his cheeks shaved, for night was coming and so many women waited.

The vision had been more real than the stones themselves, shadowy in the gathering darkness. It began as an evocation called to life by the site around him; it ended by taking on a life of its own. The lively crowd owed its existence to the amphitheater; but the courtesan and Gito came into being only to keep the dream from fading. Flaubert found it delicious to circulate thus in a world one had created for oneself.

Spurred by the site and by his dreams, he began to see ancient Rome all about him. The common people of Nîmes recalled the lower classes of a bygone age—the freedmen, the barbers, the pimps, and the valets of Plautus, the Roman comic author. Then there was the Mediterranean, changeless and still as Virgil or Homer had seen it. It had something grave and tender which recalled Greece. Brought up in cloudy Rouen amidst the rain and fog, Flaubert came to life under the Provençal sun as it sparkled on this sea. Had Xenophon's Ten Thousand come back down to a northern sea, green and furious, he wrote, instead of the Mediterranean, they would never have given their great shout of hope. But beside the Mediterranean, with its azure water surging up into the sun between the cracks in the rocks, his heart seemed to leap up and race along the crests of the waves toward those fabled shores where the ancient poets placed all beauty and to those suave lands where the sea foam, one morning, brought the sleeping Venus upon a great sea shell. What Rachel had taught him to look for, he found here.

The joy of travel he had come to know, the blind, unreasoning wanderlust which drives some men to go to places they have never been because they sense an untasted beauty or joy or wonder hidden there. From now until his death he would steadily and

unremittingly dream of travel; and he became one of the most
widely traveled men of his day, certainly the most widely traveled
French author of note. From Corsica he had seen Italy, a thin line
along the horizon. The Mediterranean, for all its Greek quality,
also had something immense and voluptuous which brought the
Near East to mind, as though he were in the Levant with a warm
sun and all nature rejoicing and entering his pores to fill his heart.
In Marseilles he lingered in the shops filled with Turkish pipes,
strange sandals, woods he did not know, and endless trinkets from
Smyrna, Alexandria, or Constantinople. They carried the perfume
of the Near East and images of harems, caravans creeping across
the desert, and ancient cities buried underneath the sand or moonlight on the Bosphorus. He would go, he vowed, to see them all
and stand upon these dead sites where humanity had first nursed
its dreams of grandeur.

Homeward bound, he took his leave of the Mediterranean. It
was cold and raining in Paris as he passed through, but his heart
was still back in the warm and sunny climate he had left.[35] He
imagined himself already in Greece, his copy of Homer in his
hand, or in Constantinople where one slept on rugs, breathed perfumes, and saw slaves and harems and mosques paved with por-
phyry. It was too bright a dream to let it go, so he set aside ten
notebooks for his next trip.

Autumn came, and winter. On the night of January 2, 1841,
Flaubert returned late from a ball which had prodigiously bored
him: its alleged joys he had found even more stupid than sad. Nice
little girls had worn white or blue dresses whose décolleté revealed only their shoulder blades, which stuck out and were covered with pimples. Their faces reminded him of rabbits or weasels,
martins, cats or dogs: imbeciles, at any rate. The whole mass of
them chattered and prattled, danced and sweated, and worst of all,
forced Flaubert to be one of them with the same words in his
mouth, the same sort of garb, the same foolish questions and inane
answers. They even sought to make him dance, he recorded in
horror!

As he had done when he returned from the earlier ball at the
Marquis de Pomereu's, he remained awake reminiscing. Five
months had passed since he had ended his schooling. His trip to

Corsica seemed almost to have happened to another man. His mind wandered back to the first night with Eulalie: it had been in a room like his, low and with a red-tile pavement, and it had been two-thirty in the morning then as now. After his return from the trip, he had wanted to work and he had not; he had longed to travel, and there were no prospects of it now to console him; he had read of the desert and dreamed of a Bedouin's life, but he could not have it. If only he could be free, really free![36]

So the months passed, while Flaubert was allowed by his family to idle his time away and try to find himself. Little Caroline was growing up, and she became his pupil as he taught her history or helped her with her English. Flaubert himself worked, but not hard, at Greek and Latin, for he had come to suspect that in the classical ages lay what he most wanted.

Principally, however, Flaubert was digesting his bitterness. Whatever leanings toward religion he may have had a year before had now left him, and he felt that he was rather more a materialist than anything else. School was behind, and nothing definite seemed to lie ahead. Passing fancies abounded—to master Greek or take flight to exotic climes—but what he was really seeking was to escape from himself and be as unencumbered as the smoke from his chimney or the leaves falling from the trees outside his windows.[37] In the spring there was a brief reunion with Ernest, but the dead pall of the future lay heavily over the two young men: their ways were now separate, and each knew it. As summer neared, there was the drawing for military service. Young Flaubert was lucky: he drew a number which exempted him. Time slipped noiselessly by, and still he sought to find out who he was; summer, autumn, and winter came and went. But as New Year's Day of 1842 approached, he ended his idleness and prepared for the move to Paris to begin the study of law.

4

False Starts (1840-44)

A YOUNG MAN'S FANCY (1840-42)

I am in a bad way. . . . I have bought my law books and will eventually get to work on them . . . but what is always in the forefront of my mind and makes me drop the book on which I am trying to take notes . . . is my old love, the same old *idée fixe*, writing.

Letter to his former teacher, Gourgaud-Dugazon,
January 22, 1842

RARELY has a young man's career begun under poorer auspices than did Flaubert's. He contented himself with registering for his law courses (all that was required of him), after which he spent a few busy days and gay nights in Paris and then returned to Rouen, ostensibly to study law but in fact to read, though not in the law, to write, and to idle away his time. He had still not found himself.

Christmas was a particularly difficult moment, for already Flaubert was beginning to look back to earlier years, imagining them more splendid than he had felt when he lived them. His philosophy was one of fatalistic despair during these years when in fact his life was no more than unhappy. His sensitivity made of it, however, a strangely hard training ground whose rigors were born more from inner necessity and imagined turmoil than from external, catastrophic fate. But only a few years away, destiny was waiting to torture him beyond the strength that most men have: this intervening period was an apprenticeship in disappointment and unhappiness. Now the holiday season reminded him of bygone years when he and Ernest Chevalier stayed awake to see the New Year in, each in bed in the dark puffing importantly on his pipe. Flaubert sincerely thought he recollected how much they had loved the day.

All was changed now. It would be only another day to him this time. He would rise at four in the morning as he always did these days to read his daily pages of Homer, smoke his cigarette at the window, and watch the moon shine on the roofs across the street. He would make no visits and instead would remain bearishly at home in his cavern and see no one.

Flaubert was studiously neglecting his law books in favor of Tacitus and Homer. He had matured and, in his reading, had found something of his way; but he was as much at odds with his environment as ever, for he should have been working at his new career. Moreover, he had found, with maturing, a firmer love for writing. He would go through the motions of getting his degree— but his thoughts, his admiration, and his enthusiasm entirely went to literature.

He had three separate plans for literary works, each a problem to be solved, for each required its own special style. Writing them would show, he hoped, whether he had it in him to be an author. But this was to underestimate the matter. Dimly he did glimpse what would much later be basic to his writing, the concept of the importance of form; and his next work was better, it is true, but only here and there. Proving himself an author would require many more years.

Although he did not yet have an apartment in Paris, Flaubert did make trips to the capital every few months to renew his registration at the law school. In November, in January, and again in April he was in the city for a week or so and was able to live the life of which he had dreamed. He visited Ernest Chevalier, who had set himself up with a mistress in the Latin Quarter. Flaubert enjoyed astounding her by his observations; and the three would go off together to gay and inexpensive dance halls, where they quaffed great goblets of white wine and felt very free and wicked.[1] Soon the handsome young man came to know a number of Paris brothels and could mention with elaborate casualness the streets and quarters of the city most likely to yield interesting women. In retrospect he would later insist that his attitude toward sex during this time was more an obsession that the attraction of pleasure.[2] But in the 1840's the *Jeunesse dorée*, or Gilded Youth, of the Bourgeois Monarchy under Louis-Philippe joined with the prostitutes created by the Industrial Revolution to establish in Paris some of the most lascivious haunts this capital of gaiety has ever known. Flaubert dreamed of it as he sat in his room in Rouen. A fine afternoon would make him picture how Paris would look that evening as the prostitutes, in low-necked dresses, would stroll on the Rue de Richelieu. This was Paris at her supreme moment, and eight o'clock in the evening made him think of antiquity in its licentious splendor.

Finally, in July, 1842, Flaubert moved into the capital for a month of steady work before taking the law examinations in August. This was to be his pattern: months of almost total neglect would be followed by a few weeks of frantic study attempting against hopeless odds to recover lost time. His heart was never in it. The more he matured, the more loath he became to draw conclusions and to come to final answers. Hence the whole notion of justice and judging seemed absurd.

Flaubert felt instead that truth was to be found in everything and that his role was to understand, not to censure. With such an attitude knowledge would become possible, and he might even learn to live serenely. This he knew was almost to be happy. Instead he was being made to study the law, ostensibly so that he might later earn his living. But his father had amassed a considerable fortune: why then, Flaubert asked, should his son work? He would always have a sufficient income. He wanted to write, and his only other concern was with the unhealthy and utterly charming life of the carefree and lusty youth that he was. The law was a distasteful distraction from both occupations.

To make matters worse, when he was in Paris Flaubert discovered he was homesick as he toiled over his law books. He lent some of these feelings a year or so later to the hero of the book he was then writing. Bewildered by the noises of the streets, Flaubert wrote, and by all this mass of people milling around him and with whom he had no connection, his hero was suddenly overcome by a desire for peace and quiet and a life away from all of this in some forgotten village on the slope of a hill in the shade of its oak trees.[3]

The studying was itself bad, but in addition Flaubert never felt fully at home in the capital. Throughout his life he loved Paris, but Parisians never mistook him for one of their own. His unhappiness there was not feigned, a garment to be slipped off when it was not appropriate. So really miserable was he in his student days that in a moment of acute masochism he was tempted to castrate himself.[4]

Part of Flaubert's difficulty was that he never learned to master the light banter which is the basis of Parisian chatter. Gallic wit has varied in its forms over the ages, but it has always been light and swift. In Flaubert's day the current vogue was for *la blague*, which was dependent upon refusing to take seriously anything of importance; instead one elevated to importance what was in reality totally futile. Well handled, it delights even those who take important things seriously, and Flaubert constantly rejoiced in it. But he sensed that he was not really capable of it himself, and from the first was anxious never to be long in the capital. Even years later when he was accepted as a famous author and sought out by many, he found it imperative not to be in Paris more than a few months at a time. Longer stays would dry up whatever wellsprings he had as he splashed away his reserves in a vain effort to make his presence sparkling. Understatement or the suggestion barely intimated were not his forte, and rapidity was absolutely denied him. Even Emile Zola, funny, provincial Zola, who loved him, knew Flaubert was no Parisian.

In August, 1842, Flaubert took his law examinations, the first of a succession of them; and he failed. It was exasperating and humiliating: how could a man of his gifts, he had to ask himself, fail at so absurd and menial a matter as this. It was an ugly question, to which he had to address himself. He left the city to rejoin his family, who had preceded him to Trouville. It was to be a momentous vacation.

Trouville embodied many of the best of Flaubert's childhood memories. Even his arrival there this time was spectacular and stood out in his memory over the years. He was alone and had left the public carriage at Pont-l'Evêque to walk the remaining ten miles to Trouville. It was the middle of the night; the moon shone clearly as he trudged gaily along, dressed in a cloth jacket and carrying his white walking stick. A decade later he could still conjure up the mystery and majesty of the scene. After a while he began to catch the scent of salt in the air: the sea must be near.[5]

Flaubert was returning to his family from a Paris life he had come to loathe; he was about to experience his first adult affection and, for the only time in his life, to consider marriage. Caroline had already written her brother of the delightful new English family, the Colliers, who were summering at Trouville.[6] One of the daughters, Harriet, had a severe spine ailment which kept her an invalid most of the time. Her sister, Gertrude, Caroline found very pretty; she spoke excellent French, adored Mademoiselle Rachel, and knew all of Shakespeare by heart. Caroline was sure Gustave would like her. There was also a brother, Herbert, and, of course, their parents. Captain Collier, of the British Navy, had lost much of his fortune through the irregular dealings of his banker and had come to the continent many years before, in part for relief from his creditors, in part because living was cheaper there. His was the traditional British contempt for the French. He went from shop to shop giving his orders to his daughters, who would then translate for him: "Tell that damn fellow that I am an Englishman and that one Englishman could knock out four Frenchmen and they must now send what I am going to order." The arrangement worked surprisingly well.

At Trouville the Colliers soon met Flaubert's family, for each day Harriet was carried outside to sit for hours enjoying the sea air in a little park beside the Flaubert's house. The doctor's family kindly offered her a chair and cushion, and acquaintance began. Through Caroline, the Collier sisters and Gustave met as Harriet lay stretched out on her large chair with a coat of white ermine thrown over her legs to keep her warm.[7] Flaubert was a figure to catch a young girl's eye: tall, slender, and graceful, he wore a red flannel shirt and rough blue cloth trousers with a blue scarf tightly bound around his waist. His head was usually bare, though sometimes he wore a sort of soft sombrero. It was inevitable that both girls should fall in love with him. Gertrude confessed as much in her memoirs many years later.

With Harriet, matters were more complicated because Flaubert fell in love with her in return. He tried to write a story about it.

Noble Arthur, a youth whose rough garments but ill conceal the fine lace of his cuffs beneath the coarser cloth of his jacket, is seated by a windswept coast when he notices the beautiful Henriette (the French form Flaubert almost always used in addressing Harriet). Flaubert wrote an opening paragraph that was not very good. He rewrote it, trying for more inspiration, but this, too, was miserable. Decidedly, he was in no mood for literature. So he set his two sheets of paper aside, adding only a note to himself that he must, after all, change the girl's name. He never touched the sheets again, but he never destroyed them either, and they lie today among his papers in Rouen.[8]

Flaubert's state of mind was deeply confused. The girl loved him; he was obviously much interested in her. Yet he was not prepared to give up the delightful orgies he had been having in Paris and which he had found ways to continue at Trouville, so vigorously in fact that on one occasion to his humiliation he found that he had presumed beyond his strength. A hurried letter to Alfred brought reassurance that there were many possible causes for this and no need for alarm.[9] Harriet, moreover, presented a further, special difficulty. Her father appeared to consider Flaubert an honorable man, but no power on earth would induce him to allow his daughter to marry a Frenchman. Flaubert decided to say nothing of Harriet to Alfred for the moment.

November (1842)

The beginning of *November* is a work he could still sign today.

Goncourt *Journal* for November 1, 1863

Lying on the beach at Trouville where he had met Harriet Collier and where he could hope to see her, Flaubert had been mulling over the story on which he had been working for some time. He called it *November* and he put the last touches to the manuscript on October 25 before he returned to Paris.[10] It is the first of his early works that he himself ever mentioned in later years. He never consented to publish it (quite rightly, because much of it is sentimental and declamatory), but he was willing to show it to a few people, and their enthusiasm for it pleased him. It is more readable than the earlier writings because for the first time style was his conscious preoccupation and, now and again, the later stylist shows vaguely through the clumsiness.

Flaubert was acquiring the observant writer's eye.[11] Already he was accustoming himself to consider people he met as characters to remold into books. Each one should be studied, compared to others, and allowed to melt into the syntheses which an artist needs. He tried to imagine the lives of people he noticed on the street, or he would look only at their feet and then would try to foretell the rest. Balzac liked similar exercises; he boasted once that he could reconstruct an entire man by studying one of his gloves. The new form of novel which was coming into being over these decades was based on this sort of observation. Balzac, and after him Flaubert, saw things in this way—minutely, to be sure, but only in order to be able to see the whole more clearly, all the parts being significant because they all signified the same man.

Flaubert was also beginning to want more freedom in his choice of subject matter. The whole world should be the keyboard; the writer would delight or terrify by the notes he selected to play. But all the notes should be used; there was to be none of the restraint which decadent classicism had imposed through its concept of the noble subject. High and low society were equally good, for the truth lay equally in all. The romantic revolution of a decade before had won for authors the right to depict the grotesque as well as the sublime, and Victor Hugo had placed beside the gypsy beauty Esmeralda the hunchback of Notre-Dame, Quasimodo. Toward 1840 the lesser romantics had begun to find that to attract attention it was no longer possible merely to depict the grotesque; if one felt it necessary (and what romantic did not?) to shock the bourgeois, then the horrible and the hideous were indispensable. Almost with tongue in cheek, they turned to more and more horrendous topics. Flaubert was moving with his generation when he chose for his heroine not a courtesan (even the word has a glamorous, exotic ring) but a prostitute, and for the setting not an alcove but her bedroom with its worn rug and curtains.

Flaubert shared the romantics' hatred of the bourgeois, and he was delighted to turn bourgeois stomachs when the opportunity offered itself. But in seeking to move his complacent enemy Flaubert always ended by overwhelming himself. It was his naïve hope that the study of everything and the tolerant effort to understand would lead to a calm and serene state of mind. But the youth of twenty-one mistook emotion for understanding and supposed that to weep was to comprehend. It was the general failing of French romanticism to imagine that one could move others by being moved oneself.

Although *November* was completed during the early weeks of his acquaintance with the Colliers, it shows no trace of Flaubert's new preoccupations; but it is a highly personal book. Like the hero of the earlier *Memoirs of a Madman*, the new hero, again a thinly disguised Flaubert, had had exaggerated imaginings of what life would bring him. The heroine, the prostitute Marie, is also autobiographical, a character readily created by a simple transposition of sex, as the heroine of *Passion and Virtue* had been and as Emma Bovary would be. Marie had Flaubert's erotic desires, his morbid curiosity about sex, his need to find the infinite fully realized in his passions—and his irritation and disgust when the universe refused to oblige.

The young hero, like Flaubert, owed much to René: like him, he had read of love for so long that he knew each move beforehand. Youthful though he was, he solemnly deplored the vast solitudes of his heart, into whose immensity, he proclaimed, none could ever fully penetrate; still it was the theater upon which lay scattered the debris of a thousand existences he had already lived. Baudelaire would later begin a deeply moving poem by saying that he had more recollections than if he were a thousand years old:

J'ai plus de souvenirs que si j'avais mille ans.

But he did not then attempt to tell them until his patience ran out. Flaubert did.

He would always think of himself as old, and in a sense he was right, because he had lived so much and so rapidly in imagination. This imagined living was so gripping that it surpassed the real event. It had been so for him with friendship, with love, with sexual intercourse, with writing. Chateaubriand, from whom he copied the pose, had found it splendid and exciting to mourn this early aging. Flaubert, though imitating, took himself more seriously and found it neither splendid nor exciting.

In almost every case, Flaubert overshot his mark. Chateaubriand had observed with melancholy eye the autumn leaf flying before the wind and had likened his storm-tossed soul to the buffeted leaf. Flaubert borrowed the image, but where Chateaubriand had given it a pensive, saddened quality, his young imitator used it only to express disgust and satiety. When would something carry him from the loathsome sights and scenes he knew?

"Woe unto those who do not understand exaggeration!" Flaubert would later exclaim. His very exaggeration of ennui let him turn it into durable art upon occasion, even in this early work, as his exaggerated position became a vantage point from which new vistas might be seen. Thus the hero of *November* calls ennui a terrible habit, because he finds that he is beginning to take a certain pleasure in it and in the befuddled state it engenders. When exaggeration has pushed so far beyond the bounds that an artist can separate himself from it and observe, coolly, the monster he has created, a new art can be born which will have not involvement but impassivity as its basis. It will be antiromantic, though stemming out of the romantic.

The time for weaning was at hand. He could write that his was not the sorrow of René and the heaven-filling immensity of his ennui, more lovely and more silvered than the rays of moonlight; nor had he been chaste like Goethe's Werther or debauched like Byron's Don Juan. He had been neither pure enough for the one nor strong enough for the other; he had, instead, been himself. But when a man feels that he is most consciously himself, it is possible that he has only found a new model for his conduct and does not yet recognize it. Flaubert, by being more bitter, more shocking, and more deliberately carnal in *November*, was following a new path but recently traced out by Gautier and the lesser romantics of the end of the 1830's. Gautier was much on the young author's mind: he was a striking figure to all young writers as he upheld the banner of a truculent devotion to art. Moreover, Alfred Le Poittevin had offered to introduce his young friend to the critic and novelist and in letter after letter he urged him to go to Gautier's apartment and present himself: he would have a warm welcome. There is much of Gautier in *November,* when Flaubert turns to direct portrayal of voluptuousness and sensual gratification. Gautier had dwelt on these moments in *Mademoiselle de Maupin;* Flaubert sought to go further in his burning descriptions of carnal love as his prostitute mistress lies nude across his body. The writing stems from experiences in Paris brothels.

The book opens with some of its best pages, which even many years later he was still willing to read to others, including Baudelaire and the Goncourt brothers, critics and novelists in their own right. The two brothers agreed that these pages in no way belied their author's genius and stature.[12] The opening paragraphs describe his love for autumn, the melancholy season which so suits memories.* When the trees had no more leaves and the sky at dusk still kept the ruddy tint which cast a golden light over

---

*"J'aime l'automne, cette triste saison va bien aux souvenirs. Quand les arbres n'ont plus de feuilles, quand le ciel conserve encore au crépuscule la teinte rousse qui dore l'herbe fanée, il est doux de regarder s'éteindre tout ce qui naguère encore brûlait en vous.

"Je viens de rentrer de ma promenade dans les prairies vides, au bord des fossés froids où les saules se mirent; le vent faisait siffler leurs branches dépouillées, quelquefois il se taisait, et puis recommençait tout à coup; alors les petites feuilles qui restent attachées aux broussailles tremblaient de nouveau, l'herbe frissonnait en se penchant sur terre, tout semblait devenir plus pâle et plus glacé ... .

"... comme j'étais là, assis par terre, ne pensant à rien et regardant au loin la fumée qui sortait des chaumes, ma vie entière s'est placée devant moi comme un fantôme, et l'amer parfum des jours qui ne sont plus m'est revenu avec l'odeur de l'herbe séchée et des bois morts; mes pauvres années ont repassé devant moi, comme emportées par l'hiver dans une tourmente lamentable; quelque chose de terrible les roulait dans mon souvenir, avec plus de furie que la brise ne faisait courir les feuilles dans les sentiers paisibles; une ironie étrange les frôlait et les retournait pour mon spectacle, et puis toutes s'envolaient ensemble et se perdaient dans un ciel morne" (*ODJ*, II, 162-63).

withered fields, his hero found it sweet and soothing to look upon the dead embers of what had heretofore burned within him.

Flaubert had his hero go for a walk and observe the empty fields and cold ditches where the willows grew, the wind whistling through their stripped branches. The tiny leaves on the bushes were set trembling, the long grasses shivered as they were bent to earth, and the whole world seemed pale and frozen. He sat down and watched the smoke rise from the peasants' cottages; his life, he said, passed before him like a phantom, and the bitter perfume of days gone by came back with the scents of the dried grass and the dead wood. His melancholy years returned to his mind and seemed gripped by winter in a lamentable torment; something terrible appeared to roll them hither and thither in his memory, with more fury than the breeze which was rushing the leaves along the peaceful paths before him. A strange irony brushed against them and turned them over for his gaze; then suddenly all were caught up together and lost themselves in the mournful sky. This was not bad writing; Emma Bovary would have a similar moment.[13]

The hero, who is so pathetically the young Flaubert, looked back to his school days when, through the long hours of study hall, he would promise himself the delights of revery to come in the evening as he dozed off. Boundless flights of imagination would then be his as he imagined what it would be like to be a grown man, when his future had arrived. Soon he was seized with the desire to love; he coveted not a woman but love itself, for, as he put it, the puberty of the heart precedes that of the body: he had much more need for love than for physical possession.

Flaubert's pain led him now to extend his fatalism to the entire world. It seemed to him to manifest itself as universally as did the sun, and he delighted in his sorrow over it, he said, savoring the despairing joy of the patient who madly scratches his wound and laughs insanely when he finds blood on his nails. In morbid mood, his hero recalled an orgy of sensuous imagining as he stood before the window of a Paris shoemaker and let his wanton fancy toy with the tiny ladies' slippers in the window. Much of this is pathological. Paris brothels had served only to destroy the illusion that in prostitution lay the ideal communion he demanded. Now despair was leading to distorted desire. His sensitivity was slipping over the tenous line into abnormality; but for some types of writing only an excess of sensibility is enough.

Such tensions, if long continued and reveled in, can bring to the surface the latent death-wish in any man. Flaubert now had his hero write that he had been born with the desire to die, that life was stupid and that it was shameful to cling to it. All children were so, Flaubert affirmed; man loves death with a devouring love, and he had known these self-torturing, distorted moments himself. He gave such an experience to his hero and had him stand on the Pont-Neuf, the quiet, solid, old bridge which spans the arm of the Seine from the Left Bank over to the tip of the Island, where Henry the Fourth's Square lies, and which goes on from there to the Right Bank a little upstream from the Louvre. It was winter; the Seine had cakes of ice in it which slipped slowly along with the current and shattered against the piles of the bridge. The greenish water prompted thoughts of those who had come there before him to put an end to things. He considered them: they must have passed the spot many times, hurrying to love affairs or business; now he could see them advancing slowly, their hearts beating. The vision began to grip him in the fatal, inexorable grasp of the suicide urge, as it becomes easier to let the fascination replace the unbearable load of taking a decision oneself. He saw these other people make the moves he would make: they approached the parapet, they climbed up onto it, they leaped off. It was the end. The frigid, wet tomb opened for another body. How many there must be, at the bottom, rolling slowly with the current, their faces distorted, their legs and arms blue with the cold. And each cake of ice would push them forward in their long sleep, nudging them gently toward the sea.

It is not easy to break the hold of such a vision. But break it Flaubert did, and he lived to write of it, giving it here to himself as hero of *November* and returning to live it through again with other heroes of other books. But he had come too close to madness for his comfort.

Such moments of abysmal depression were the fee Flaubert had to pay for other times of unbounded joy and serene concord. One such day he had had in Corsica, riding along by the seashore. He now recounted another one, in Normandy and again along the coast. The quiet, reassuring beat of gentle waves upon a sunlit shore could prove as all-encompassing in its way as had the frozen Seine. His hero went out alone on a long walk near the shore. To get a moment's rest, he lay down under the hot sun in a plowed field and listened to the intermittent waves. In the quiet between waves, while the swollen ocean sat silent, he would listen for an instant to the call of the quails. Then the wave would sound again, and then the birds.

Standing up, he raced down to the edge of the sea, leaping over furrows, his head high with pride. The spirit of God seemed to fill his soul. His heart was bigger; he adored something unknown. He longed to be absorbed into the light of the sun, to lose himself in the immensity of the dark blue sky along with the scent of the seaweed rising from the surface of the waves.

He seemed to understand the happiness of creation and all the joy God had placed there for man. Nature was beautiful in her complete harmony, and only ecstasy could comprehend it. All that was disparate and evil disappeared from the face of the earth, and he loved even the rocks whose sharp edges cut his feet, all of insensible nature, which he felt loving and hearing him. He longed to be these objects about him and could equally imagine the ineffable joy of singing canticles at eventide at the foot of a madonna lit by candles, of the Virgin Mary as she appears to sailors in a corner of the stormy sky holding the gentle Christ Child in her arms. Then it was over, and the curse upon him resumed its weight. He was again within humanity, and he fell into a nameless discouragement. He hastily completed his walk.

These desires remained with Flaubert over the years. They are what lead to his close, loving observation of nature and are the base on which he builds his later, intimate depictions of her, minute down to the veins in leaves or the individual hairs of a sheep's woolly coat. The desires which underlie this will plague Anthony, the desert saint; and the longing to become one with inanimate nature will be his final and supreme temptation.

Neither nature nor religion can always appease such longings, and Flaubert knew it. In *November*, his hero came one day to realize that all nature was at peace, its desire satisfied; he alone violated its law and cramped his desire within unnatural bounds: he must put an end to these restrictions. He recalled the magic he attached to one talisman word, adultery. In adultery it seemed possible to imagine the excitement of love without responsibility or venality. An exquisite sweetness seemed to hover over the word and make it stand out among all other ones. Everything the boy did or read or thought seemed a comment upon it. It was, to him, a supreme poetry, a mingling of malediction with voluptuousness.

His hero now remembered a particular house in town. He had passed it so many times that he knew just what it looked like, with its three steps leading up to the door and the green curtains at the window. It seemed to take him a hundred years to reach the street; he could hardly find his breath. At last he was there; he climbed the stairs; he was in her room. The description which follows, going beyond Gautier, foreshadows some of the audacities not tried in printed works until the twentieth century.

When it was over, the hero of *November* found himself overwhelmed with an indefinable sadness; he was sated, tired. So that was all there was to love! He left the girl shortly. Her name was Marie; it was the name of Elisa's daughter. The day passed slowly for him, filled with nervous irritability. Gradually he found that his prior imaginings of lovemaking were fusing with the actual experience and coloring it with their more enticing hues. Desire rose within him again, and he returned to Marie.

At this point in *November,* romantic fantasy takes over and autobiography perhaps ceases, for Flaubert has the prostitute fall in love with his hero. She tells him the story of her endless, frustrated efforts to find love as mistress and as prostitute. Now she has at last found the man for whom she has been searching. She offers him a heart which, she avers, is still virgin; she cuts off a lock of his hair; she makes love to him. The theme of Don Juan (with the sexes reversed) here joins another popular theme of the romantics, the courtesan rehabilitated by her love. But in this version of these themes, no satisfaction results, and the young hero prepares to leave. There is, Flaubert wrote, an instant in a departure when, as one anticipates the pain of separation, the loved one, though still present, is no longer with you. Whom did Flaubert have in mind? Eulalie Foucard of Marseilles? Elisa? His own family in a chaster departure? At any rate, it was an experience he remembered, for he repeated the observation in a later work.

Now a strange transition takes place. Fiction had displaced

autobiography. In turn Elisa Schlésinger displaced the fiction, as the act of writing brought nearer the surface of consciousness the old love and the old longing. The hero is nearly dismissed (he will leave entirely shortly), and Flaubert himself takes command, to offer his thoughts directly in the last of his unabashedly autobiographical writing. The second woman a man loves, he stated, almost always resembles the first; it would take a really corrupt heart, he thought, to love all sorts of women. No doubt this is why he gave to the prostitute Marie large, arched eyebrows, an aquiline nose, and high nostrils which moved as she breathed; her upper lip, full and warm, was sharply divided and had a bluish down on it; her throat was soft and white and round; the form of her breasts, firm and full, was apparent under her light robe; her hips were generous. It could be a portrait of Elisa. Flaubert's hero was making love to Madame Schlésinger in a new incarnation.

Twenty years later a tired and blasé Flaubert would write with more experience that in adolescence it was true one loved other women because they resembled the first one more or less, but afterwards one loved women for the differences between them. It is the comment of an older but a sadder man.[14] Now, instead, he could note quite casually that he "had a friend" who had fallen in love at fifteen with a young mother who was nursing her child and that because of this for years he had felt nothing but contempt for slim figures.

The memory had been evoked: Flaubert's hero recalled the odd sensation of walking through a field and being so sure that Marie was behind him that he turned about suddenly, expecting to see her. The feeling recurs in *Salammbô*. Long concentration on Flaubert's part often led to such hallucinatory experiences, and years later he used to find that after an extended session of writing at his desk he would look up and suddenly be overcome with the terrified feeling that someone was standing close behind him.[15] There was also a further experience relating presumably to Elisa which he recorded now in *November* and which he repeated in later works: he was watching a carriage as it disappeared around a corner, when it seemed to him that a white veil was thrust out a window and shaken to attract his attention. It twisted and appeared almost to call to him . . . but it disappeared and he was more alone than ever.

Writing of these moments had been an odd experience. He had put them on paper just as Proust would later in an effort to give permanence to transitory time; he was *à la recherche du temps perdu,* in search of time past, as Proust would later call his series of novels. Flaubert had not succeeded this time, he admitted, for he knew far more than he had been able to say. Proust would succeed in making permanent for himself the beauty of hawthorns or the view of the church towers of Martinville, but he had to spend years in perfecting a form adequate to the task. Flaubert was still a beginner.

The hero, finding the whole idea of intercourse revolting, now sought escape in dreams of travel and imagined feeling a camel's back bending under him as the sky reddened from the sun setting over the brown sand of the desert; or he saw himself standing in the immobile shadow of destroyed temples as goats browsed on the plants growing in the cracks where the marble had broken. If only he were a muleteer in Andalusia and could watch the moon mirror herself in the pool of the Alhambra, where in ancient times the sultanas bathed. His hero let himself go in what were Flaubert's own lascivious dreams, for the notion of water where voluptuous women had swum always excited Flaubert, perhaps because of his first encounters with Elisa on the beach at Trouville.

Flaubert's hero now dies; a friend finds his manuscript and adds a few pages of commentary. How the dead author had loathed the idea of having a child! You would be responsible for all the tears he shed. Without you the child would never have been born; and you had conceived him solely for your own amusement. The lines breathe Flaubert's hatred for his father and his undue attachment to his mother. It was not a favorable augury to thoughts of marriage with Harriet Collier.

At the very end of *November,* the friend recalls the hero's returning to the shore to take again the long walk which had earlier brought him such peace. None of it was the same; at the inn, no one remembered him; his favorite spots along the beach now held the debris of other people's picnics. Nature herself had forgotten him. He meditated on death; the thought of suicide returned. But quite suddenly his Paris life looked good again; he set aside his resolve to kill himself and returned to the capital.

That December he died. It would be like Flaubert's private irony to have thus named the month of his own suicide attempt on the Pont-Neuf.

PARISIAN INTERLUDE (1842-43)

The joys he had promised himself did not materialize; and when he had exhausted a lending library, gone through the collections in the Louvre, and had been several times in a row to the theater, he fell into total idleness.

Of Frédéric Moreau's studies for the law in Paris
in *A Sentimental Education* (1869)

On October 25, 1842, Flaubert finished *November* at Trouville with his family and the Colliers. Harriet had by now been placed under the care of Dr. Flaubert, and the Colliers accompanied the Flaubert family back to Rouen[16] when the doctor's duties again demanded his presence there. Shortly it was time for Flaubert and the English family to return to Paris, he to his law studies, they for the season which would soon be opening.[17]

Upon his arrival in Paris, Flaubert began looking for an apartment. A young friend, Hamard, helped him. Their intimacy dates from this period; later Hamard married Caroline, Flaubert's sister. Now, for the first time Flaubert had his own place. It was on the Rue de l'Est, a street near the Luxembourg Gardens, which disappeared at the time that the Boulevard Saint-Michel was constructed during the Second Empire. His windows opened pleasantly onto the greenhouses and nurseries of the Luxembourg, but for years after he had abandoned these lodgings he avoided walking along the Rue de l'Est so as not to be reminded of how atrociously bored he had been there.[18] He felt deprived in not having been able to afford an armchair and was out of money within days; he wrote asking his sister to use her good offices with Dr. Flaubert. He did have three straight chairs and an odd sort of divan which, he said, could serve as chest, bed, bookshelf, and shoe rack, as well as doghouse or pony stable. He also suggested that this was where he would have his parents sleep; but this was perhaps before he quite realized what he was saying.

Flaubert hated studying for his law examination; moreover, he was being tortured by toothaches. To save money he was dining in student restaurants on tough beef and bitter wine tempered with water which had warmed as it sat all day in its glass carafe in the sun. Thoughts of meals at home only made it worse. Within two weeks he felt he had been at this for twenty years or that it had never had a beginning and would never have an end either. His sole distraction, so he told his sister, was to rearrange his boots at intervals.

Some days were worse than others. A sudden mild spell in the midst of winter brought on wretched homesickness as he thought of how nice it would be to visit one of the country places his father had bought. A light rain was falling, and he imagined going into the carriage house with his dog to wait it out. As so often, the vision took on its own imperious life: he saw himself standing there watching the rain fall and puffing quietly on his pipe. Yet here he sat in his Paris room like an imbecile with his elbows on his table not knowing what on earth to do.

His sister's laugh, gentle and sonorous, he particularly remembered and loved: he could hear it ring in his ears and would leap to his feet to go over to the mirror and make the faces he used to make for her. On his visits to Rouen, she would come into his room each afternoon at two under the pretext of doing history or English with him; but soon they would drop all serious matters and laugh and joke the whole afternoon away. Both were supremely happy, for the situation seemed to make no demands which they could not easily meet.

Caroline was no longer a child. She was eighteen this autumn and, though sickly and hence slow to develop, she was becoming a young lady. Flaubert missed being able to hug her whenever he wished. His affection bothered even her at times. His clumsy, awkward kisses were so rough and noisy that their mother had to intervene and even an adoring sister had to tell him to stop. Caroline's engagement to Hamard was a blow to Flaubert when it came some little time later; her marriage was even harder for him.

This man, already tied to his mother, had now to wrestle blindly with a further bond which could not lead to marriage.

It was natural that he should think of the Colliers. He called on them in Paris soon after his arrival. Herbert, who now called Flaubert "Papa," threw his arms about the tall Frenchman, and the whole family was most cordial, insisting he remain for dinner. At Trouville, Flaubert had seen the Colliers away from their own home and in temporary surroundings. Here they were in their own apartment at the Rond-Point of the Champs Elysées, where they had long lived. He was surprised at how well off they were.[19] With time Captain Collier had been able to make good the breach in his fortune. Flaubert had been promising himself that, this year, he would pay proper attention to his law studies, but it was not going to be easy.

Gustave wrote to Alfred confessing the whole matter. Le Poittevin replied that he had never supposed Flaubert incapable of falling in love and that time alone would tell what the outcome would be. Flaubert determined to be punctilious about his work schedule: he would rise at eight, go to his lectures, have a frugal lunch, and work steadily until five in the evening, when he would go out for dinner. By six he would be back at work again, and it would last until midnight or later. It was a heroic program, and, briefly, he followed it. Only once a week would he allow himself to leave the Left Bank, cross the river, and visit the Colliers, where he could sit with Harriet, who was now constantly confined to her couch by the trouble in her spine.

Flaubert also renewed his acquaintance with the Schlésingers, on whom he had called the previous April only to learn that they were not to be in France for the next few months. Now they were back, and he could see them at their regular Wednesday evening receptions. He went to their house for their annual dinner on New Year's Eve, and he called frequently at Maurice's office, where Schlésinger edited the *Gazette musicale:* one could always count on good conversation there.[20] Flaubert's *"père* Maurice" was at the height of his glory in these years. His wife, too, was freer now than she had been when she first met young Flaubert. In 1839 her real husband had died; a year later she and Maurice

were married. Schlésinger, already the owner of a hotel in Trouville, was giving the future resort constant publicity in his
Gazette, and a common interest in Trouville as well as in art drew
them all together.[21]

The art studio of James Pradier, easy in its casual familiarity of
tone, Flaubert also frequented. Pradier, now a forgotten neoclassic
sculptor with a feel for sensuous volumes, formed Flaubert's taste
in sculpture and very nearly falsified it for him. It was said of
Pradier that each morning he set out for Athens but never got
beyond the gayer quarters of Paris bordering on Montmartre.[22]
His muse was sensuous, frequently sensual; and so·was the tone of
his studio. Here one afternoon Flaubert met Victor Hugo, for he,
too, appreciated the atmosphere of the studio and its models. He
spoke but little and seemed to be watching every gesture. Flaubert
sat beside him and looked at him as one would at a case of diamonds; he thought of all that had come from this man, as Hugo
sat quietly looking at his hand, which had written so many beautiful things.

It was soon a delightfully debauched life that the young man
was leading, the more so as he passed his first law examinations in
December, 1842. Strikingly good looking, he had white skin
slightly pink over the cheeks and long, floating hair whose individual strands were fine and delicate like a girl's. But his tall stature and broad shoulders, his heavy beard of a golden blond, his
very large, sea-green eyes, black eyebrows and resounding voice,
his exaggerated gestures and uproarious laughter all suggested to
his friends a Gallic chieftain of long ago; his bearing, too, was
reminiscent of theirs, impetuous, impatient of restraints, and both
dominating and charming as he deployed his endless reserves of
energy.[23]

Sexual outlets were easy now that Flaubert was resident in the
capital; he gave free rein to his thoroughly lusty temperament and
became the sort of man to whom friends write for addresses. In all
of this he was urged on by letters from Alfred Le Poittevin, who
sought to make up for not being in Paris by taking a vicarious
pleasure in what Gustave was doing. Alfred's obsession with sexuality was pathological; he was contemptuous of women, who were
to him only machines for intercourse, and he found his own pleas-

ure more and more exclusively in torturing his sexual partner. Approaching impotence alone lessened this anguish and turned him from any desire for women at all. Meanwhile his affection for Flaubert grew stronger by virtue of their very separation, and he could write that he thirsted for him.

Not only was Flaubert leading a sexual life which would have debilitated anyone; he was also exasperated by his studies when he turned to them. Each new examination and the struggle to prepare for it constituted a new and dangerous crisis, as fear and frustration combined in pathological tension. His sister, his closest confidante, knew nothing of his night life. His companions in Paris, who did, knew too little of his childhood and his nervous susceptibility. No one could guess that his system would not indefinitely tolerate the life he was leading. He was living on coffee and smoking thirty pipes a day; he also stuffed on good food and drink whenever he could get it. Moreover, he had been accustomed in Rouen to a considerable amount of exercise; in Paris he was deprived of this, and he began to put on weight. Shortly he had to confess that, had his boots had laces, he would not have been able to tie them.

With so many distractions on every hand, and continuing as he was to haunt the Parisian brothels, it was not easy for Flaubert to make up his mind about marriage. He preferred not to. He kept calling at the Colliers' apartment over the winter, but Harriet was getting worse. She was still in bed as spring began to appear. Flaubert took to reading aloud to her from his favorite authors. She would lie stretched out on a small iron bed near the window, her head reclining on a pink pillow while Gustave sat on a chair beside her; she would turn her back to the room and watch the carriages passing by on the Rond-Point of the Champs Elysées.[24] He introduced her to René's silvered melancholy and went on to *Atala*, Chateaubriand's tale of love among the Indians of North America. Flaubert led Harriet, too, to Hugo, reading *Hernani* to pass the time away in sharing what he most loved. Then, to console her for having missed Hugo's newest play, the first in five years, he read *Les Burgraves* to her. *Hernani*, thirteen years before, had signaled the triumph of French romanticism. Now all was changed: the new play was a terrible failure. As Flaubert read aloud in his sonorous voice the rolling alexandrines of Hugo's verse, he may have known that he was burying French romanticism and, in part, his own.

Spring in Paris is legendary; Harriet hoped it would lead Gustave to ask for her hand. A letter to Caroline had suggested that she hoped Gustave would read *Les Burgraves* to her. Caroline had transmitted the message, adding how much she preferred the invalid sister to the older one, Gertrude, who seemed frivolous, lacking in culture, and too eager to capture Gustave. As the spring months passed, the young man was a constant visitor at the Colliers', despite his disclaimers in letters intended to pacify a family nervous about his forthcoming law examinations. (There were new ones to be taken in August.) Unfortunately, Harriet grew sicker as the summer passed; Gertrude, meanwhile, pursued Flaubert more and more and even made him play the role of suitor to her in public.

One cannot forever love an invalid, when one is but twenty-one and eager to experiment with all of life. The Colliers moved to the suburb of Chaillot, even further from Gustave, and the summer of 1843 saw an end to what the summer of 1842 had so romantically begun. Flaubert failed his examinations that August, repeating the defeat of the previous year. Did Harriet's father become even more alarmed? Gustave was not only a Frenchman, but also perhaps incapable of supporting his daughter. Did Flaubert's failure and ensuing despair turn him from Harriet? Or did the affair simply die? In any event, for the next two years there seems to have been no communication. Harriet Collier is the only woman Flaubert ever considered marrying: solitude was soon to be his lot, though he could not now imagine it.

Meanwhile Flaubert had met the man who was to be his closest friend, his mentor in some ways and his pupil in others, and his constant companion for much of the next decade. He was the Baron Maxime Du Camp, two months younger than Flaubert, and like him passionately absorbed in literature. His father and mother had both died when he was still young, leaving him a modest but adequate fortune. His guardian had just consented to his following a career as a writer when he met Flaubert. The friendship was instantaneous: each recognized himself in the other. Both had had ideals; both were disillusioned. Both longed to travel to far places; both were ferociously eager to assert independence while, in reality, needing desperately to love. Both had known the life of the Gilded Youth of the period. Like two fiancés they soon exchanged rings with the Latin inscription *Solus ad solum*, which is most dubious Latin for what they intended: "From the only one to the only one." They became inseparable.

Du Camp was the more sophisticated of the pair, Flaubert the more profound. Gustave's pessimism was deeper and of a firmer alloy than the more superficial blend of Maxime's. Although both wished to write, Du Camp would constantly have a public in mind and would always trim his writing to the prevailing wind. Flaubert was handsome, but in a slightly dreamy, somewhat heavy way. Du Camp was an extraordinarily good-looking young man. He wore his hair rather long; it was dark and had just enough waviness to look soft. A close-cropped beard and mustache concealed a good part of his cheeks and jaw but allowed his full, slightly pouting, lower lip to appear and suggest the sensual egotist that he was. His eyebrows, without being unduly dark, seemed to crowd down toward his eyelids and partly obscure them above his burning eyes, which were what one first noticed. They were medium to small in size and not particularly wide-set, but their gaze was of extraordinary intensity. Coupled with his slightly petulant mouth, they gave his face the air of one used to having his own way and quite prepared to claw if he were denied it. He looked straight at people with whom he was talking, fixing them with these remarkable eyes and giving an impression of total absorption in what they were saying. If one eyebrow lifted slightly, the sensitive mouth seemed to deny the possibility that Du Camp was a cynic; indeed, it was not easy for him to decide which he was, the man of feeling, emotion, and integrity, or the successful schemer calculating his poses. Only with women was he perfectly sure of what he wanted, and equally sure of getting it. His ardent eyes suggested total captivation; a faint suggestion of a light laugh carried promise of entertainment; the sensual lips suggested his temperament; and an air of assurance carried every defense before it. He was a handsome, successful lover, and he knew it. So did every woman he met.

Like Flaubert, Du Camp was, as he put it, torn between a desire for things he did not have and sorrow over things he no longer had. Both young men were in revolt against contemporary society without being entirely clear about what they were revolting for, except that society should be freer, more inclined toward the arts, and more deferent toward them. Gustave loved Max and thought of him as a brother. He called him a good, even a great person, to whom he had riveted himself from the first meeting. He found his exquisite manners (which Flaubert knew he himself lacked) an echo of his exquisite character and heart. And Du Camp was his first literary disciple. Maxime had been writing trivial and ephemeral pieces which Flaubert persuaded him to abandon in the name of a higher concept of art as something sacred.[25]

The two young men had in common their three strongest passions: writing, art, and women.[26] Du Camp had an avid, facile taste in painting and sculpture, which matched a growing one in his friend. Maxime, able to travel sooner and more freely than Gustave, wrote close descriptions of the works of art he saw. Art moved him more by successful eroticism than by beauty; he scorned Michelangelo and Donatello when once he had seen some of the later, more provocative works of lesser men. In addition, when traveling or when in Paris, Du Camp was never long without women and, with his friend's hearty approval, always sought out first a good brothel in any city he was to be in more than a single night. The letters the young men exchanged reveal not only their vigor, which was impressive, but also their obsession and their constant need to experiment, to reaffirm, and indeed to reassure themselves and each other. The character of their relationship soon led Maxime to hate and despise Alfred Le Poittevin, whom he called a decadent Greek of the Late Empire and from whom he sought to wean Flaubert.

August and the return of the law examinations were upon Flaubert almost before he realized it. He had spent his days and nights on everything but the law. Hours had gone into work on a novel; days had passed in delightful companionship with Du Camp, to whom—as a mark of special trust—he had read *November*. There had been ritual evenings in the apartment of the Rue de l'Est, where, surrounded by coffee and tobacco, with a choice friend or two Flaubert would while away the night, his store of candles illuminating the display of his splendidly shining boots. These and other follies took his time and his money; he had to write again to his father in traditional student fashion to beg more funds.

Even so, his studies were more than he could stand, and he began to cast about for ways to shorten them. A first idea was to limit them by not pursuing an advanced degree in the law; he set about persuading his father. This, however, was not enough and, consciously and subconsciously, he continued to search for means to put an end to this hated perusal of law books and the dread specter of ever-recurring examinations. He was treading on dangerous ground.

His family came down to Paris to celebrate with their son the triumph they expected in the examinations that August. The railroad linking Paris and Rouen had been completed the previous spring and could have brought them to the capital in a few hours; but Gustave so violently opposed the risks he felt it entailed that they were forced to come by carriage and take several days. Gustave had good reason to suspect what the result of the examination would be, but he vowed even before failing it that he would prepare the next one no more fully and would present himself again and again until finally someone let him pass.

Flaubert did set to work, but not on the law. He turned instead to the classics and began close analyses of the comedies of Plautus, the Roman playwright who so well understood the dramatic needs of the theater and how to conduct a scene to keep it moving and constructive. He was also reading Renaissance poetry, particularly Ronsard. Here again the schooling was excellent, for Ronsard speaks with simplicity, with limpid images, and with chaste precision based on a careful use of language. Such perfection could be achieved only by control and by total, constant preoccupation with form. It was a revelation to Flaubert to see old familiar images—the rose, the bee, and others—so garbed in French verse that they became new creations.

In September, 1843, Flaubert was with relatives in Nogent, on the other side of Paris from Rouen; he and his family were not infrequent visitors here, and Nogent would be the family home of Frédéric Moreau. Both Frédéric and Gustave hated this city and life in it. Shortly, however, he was back in Rouen at work on his long novel, and in November he returned, this time by train, to Paris. Here he managed to push beneath the surface all the tensions under which he was living. He wrote a number of letters to his sister in Rouen, all full of good spirits and suggesting a happy, well-adjusted young man about to take his law examinations in quiet, normal fashion.

This was in fact the dead calm before catastrophe struck. Flaubert was now to suffer the penalty for straining a system beyond its breaking point. There was no hint of trouble, no wild outburst to indicate the turmoil within. On December 20, 1843, Flaubert wrote to his sister confirming his plan to be home in ten days or so to spend almost two weeks with his family in Rouen. He expected to return for the month of March and would be back again in July. He made no mention of the law examination of a few days away, but his sister knew the date. He also commented—though he could not then know its significance—on the fact that he was glad the plans had fallen through for some rebuilding on property his father owned at Deauville: he had not thought well of them.

His last days in Paris were busy ones. Christmas night he spent with the Colliers, reading Hugo's *Hernani* to Harriet once again. Here in the quiet happiness of the family celebration, he enjoyed the atmosphere and shared in the Christmas pudding. During the next days, along with the examination, which he failed, he had to undertake a number of errands for his family. Then, on December 31, he set out for Rouen, stopping on the way at Vernon, the home of Madame Schlésinger; he was expected for supper and spent the night. On New Year's Day, he reached home, hurried upstairs, and was reunited with his family.

His father and mother, brother and sister, were deep in discussions of the Deauville property and the chalet they wished to build. A trip had to be made there, and Gustave and his brother undertook to make it at once. It was on the way to Deauville, somewhere near Pont-l'Evêque, around nine in the evening, that the disaster Flaubert had been courting for years caught up with him and, strong man that he was, it nearly killed him. He had an attack of epilepsy.

5

Illness and Withdrawal (1844-45)

EPILEPSY (1844)

When an event is destined to take place, there is prepared in advance a sort of greased plank down which it rolls.

First version of *A Sentimental Education* (1843-45)

Borderland insanity, crankiness, insane temperament, loss of mental balance, psychopathic degeneration . . . has certain peculiarities and liabilities which, when combined with a superior quality of intellect in an individual, make it more probable that he will make his mark and affect his age, than if his temperament were less neurotic. . . . The psychopathic temperament . . . often brings with it ardor and excitability of character. The cranky person has extraordinary emotional susceptibility. He is liable to fixed ideas and obsessions. His conceptions tend to pass immediately into belief and action; and when he gets a new idea, he has no rest till he proclaims it, or in some way "works it off." "What shall I think of it?" a common person says to himself about a vexed question; but in a "cranky" mind "What must I do about it?" is the form the question tends to take. . . . What, then, is more natural than that this temperament should introduce one to regions of religious truth, to corners of the universe, which your robust Philistine type of nervous system, forever offering its biceps to be felt, thumping its breast, and thanking Heaven that it hasn't a single morbid fibre in its composition, would be sure to hide forever from its self-satisfied possessors?

William James, *Varieties of Religious Experience*

IT HAPPENS by great good fortune to some men that, when in the normal course of human life disaster strikes them, it seems suddenly to give meaning to what had before seemed but fortuitous, and all their life up to that moment seems now to have been a preparation for it. It may be only an appearance, and prior events may have in reality been only fortuitously arranged; or in some sense these men may have shaped their own disaster; or, if life has meaning, this is perhaps part of its form. In any event, Flaubert's was such a life.

The blows of fortune and, indeed, disaster, Flaubert had always been preparing for. Yet until January, 1844, he had in fact had a reasonably happy existence. Difficulties and disappointments he had known, but they were as often as not of his own making, and in general they were not crippling. Despite this (and he was not wholly unaware of the paradox), his had been a philosophy of total despair. He had been unconsolable and had had to discover how to live with it. Now for the first time real disaster and real unhappiness were to be his lot: not something dark and fearsome in his imagination but rather something outside and tangible, something he could not create or dispel at his pleasure.

It happened without warning.[1] Achille and Gustave were driving in the family cabriolet toward Deauville, where they intended to investigate the problems of the chalet to be built there. Shortly before nine in the evening they passed through Pont-l'Evêque and turned north toward the coast through the darkness of the night; Gustave had the reins. It was so black that he could not even see the ears of his horse before him. A carter's wagon approached from the opposite direction, and Gustave suddenly fell to the floor of the cabriolet as if struck by apoplexy and feeling that he was being carried off in a torrent of flames. Doctor that he was, Achille for some ten minutes thought his brother beyond hope. He struggled to get the senseless form into a nearby house where he could try to relieve whatever had struck Gustave down. A proper pupil of his father, Achille knew only bloodletting as the remedy for all ills, and so he bled Gustave. When one incision proved unavailing, he made two more, and the blood poured from the opened veins. Finally Gustave opened his eyes; he was not going to die. The opposite side of the road was lined with trees: he could still recognize them ten years later.

As soon as he thought it safe, Achille returned to Rouen, where in his father's house Gustave could be given all the medical care that his period knew of. But he was never to be fully cured.

Month after weary month he had to bide his time in patience, waiting for some relief from the attacks which, at first, were almost daily; then they spaced out slowly, and eventually seemed so to have abated as almost to have disappeared. But tension could always bring them back, and Flaubert could never again risk being alone frequently or for long periods. The young man of heroic stature who enjoyed the outdoors, rowing and swimming, was now an invalid and would never be entirely hale and hearty again. Disaster had begun.

The trouble lay in the brain, his father thought; it was some sort of congestion, an apoplectic attack in miniature perhaps. Gustave was fed pills and asked to down infusions; he was purged and he was bled, and a wick and stiff collar were used for drainage in his neck. His beloved pipe he was forbidden to smoke, and his nerves were terribly on edge; at the slightest noise they vibrated like taut violin strings, and his knees, shoulders, and belly would tremble like aspen leaves.

After ten days he seemed a little better, and his father risked sending him back to Paris. Here, however, the first serious nervous tension brought on trouble again; and the law and any thought of living in Paris had to be abandoned. Flaubert returned to Rouen, a very sick man whose whole attention would have to go to striving for some sort of recovery. To make matters worse, his father's carelessness now complicated the cure. One day, as he was about to bleed his son, he poured water over the young man's arm, only to discover too late that it was boiling hot. It took months for the skin on his right hand to recover somewhat, and it always remained scarred.[2]

Under a regimen of absolute calm the major attacks began slowly to lessen in frequency, but six months later minor moments of discomfort were still normal every day, as streamers of light flashed before his eyes, looking like gleaming hair or brilliant fireworks. He felt he was reliving the torrents of flame which had first struck him down.

On and off over the years the attacks kept returning, each time accompanied by a feeling of abject terror as Flaubert feared that his very personality was slipping away from him, that he was in the act of dying. It seemed as though there were an involuntary downward rush of ideas and images. Full consciousness would disappear, along with any feeling that he was alive. He could feel his soul escaping from him as clearly as he felt the blood flowing out through the incision when he was being bled: it was, in fact, just like a hemorrhage of the nervous system, if that could exist, a hundred thousand pictured images leaping about at once like fireworks. What made the attacks most unbearable was that his reason remained lucid to the end, so that he was able to suffer throughout it. He often reached a state in which he could not speak, but awareness he still had. His soul was turned in upon itself, like a porcupine jabbing itself with its own quills.

Flaubert could describe the precise course of an attack in close and agonized detail. It would begin with a vague, indeterminate discomfort (the "aura") which grew slowly into anguish, a feeling of waiting painfully for something which you are sure is going to happen. Then, with the suddenness of a bolt of lightning, there would come an instantaneous irruption of the memory into his consciousness, for that is what the greater attacks were for Flaubert, an illness of his memory in which all that it held was suddenly poured out and burst forth in his skull like an explosion. Sometimes a mad procession of images would follow one upon another too quickly to be observed. At other times it would be a single image which would grow and finally cover all of objective reality—a spark, for instance, which might flutter about and then grow to become a roaring fire. When this happened, he could watch the mirage and at the same time think about other things.

The role of Flaubert's will in all this bewildered him. He had often tried to bring on hallucinations in the years before these crises began but had never quite succeeded. On the other hand, he learned with time to dispel these new epileptic hallucinations by will power, or so he felt. It was sometimes, however, too fine a line to try to draw between what took place because he wanted it to and what happened without the intervention of his conscious will. He remembered from his childhood a feeling he frequently had at the theater, that instead of spectators the hall was full of skeletons! And yet, had he conjured up this vision by thinking about it? Or had it thrust itself upon him? He could no longer tell.

Memory was for Flaubert the seat of his trouble. He was sure that even conscious imitation of others was dependent upon a recall so clear that it was like a hallucinatory memory. When his attacks came and he was living through a hallucination, it was his memory at work, he was sure. One eye would see the false and deceptive image, so to speak, and the other would see what was really about him. The shock of comparing was what caused the anguish: a memory broken loose from its anchorage, its moorings slipped in a mad world which lacked compass or map and filled with all the nameless terrors of the night, but always over and against it the knowledge that reality was there outside of you and unattainable. Perhaps you were seeing it, slowly, for the last time.

What Flaubert was suffering from it was impossible to diagnose in his period—the beginnings of a diagnosis began only a decade or so ago—and this was part of his problem. His brother used the word "epileptiform" to describe the ailment;[3] Gustave himself tended to use euphemisms like "nervous malady," or at worst a phrase on the order of "something like apoplexy." Epilepsy itself was still looked upon, as it has been until very recently, as a sign of a divine curse, a hated, feared, and mysterious illness which reduced man to a frothing beast: the word could never be used lightly. During Flaubert's lifetime almost no one ever used it of him in public, but shortly after his death Maxime Du Camp, who had been estranged from him during many of his last years, published a full exposé of it. There were protests and unavailing attempts to deny it; but at least one man who knew Flaubert intimately wrote to Du Camp to congratulate him for telling the truth.[4] The form of epilepsy from which Flaubert suffered, however, was one which the nineteenth century did not even know existed.

His father and brother recognized it only broadly and gave him the standard treatment in the period for epilepsy: bloodletting, leeches, drainage wicks applied to the neck, infusions of orange blossoms, valerian, and others, hot baths, calm and quiet in his daily life, abstention from tobacco, alcohol, and women.[5] With more knowledge today than was then available, a doctor would now point to other symptoms which the electroencephalograph has indicated to be related to epilepsy and to a hereditary disposition toward it. Madame Flaubert and, after her, her granddaughter Caroline suffered atrociously from migraines.[6] If these were, as seems likely, the true migraine headache, they were of the family of epileptic ills. And Flaubert himself had shown symptoms which would have alarmed a modern neurologist. As a child he could become so lost in his reading, as he played with a lock of hair and bit at his tongue, that he would eventually fall from his chair:[7] a passing moment of epilepsy could have produced this, especially if Gustave's forearm passed back and forth before his eyes and produced the effect of a flickering light—a common way for a neurologist to induce an attack in an epileptic patient.

Epilepsy, modern medicine has shown, is a simple name for a complex of symptoms whose origins are still not understood. It is always accompanied by a break in the normal rhythm of brain waves, a dysrhythmia or abnormality in the discharges of potential from one area or another of the brain. When this occurs, depending upon the character of the alteration in the rhythm and its location, the patient falls into the unconscious fit of "grand mal" epilepsy or has the passing discomfort of "petit mal" epilepsy or has one or another of various symptoms, for instance a migraine headache or an abnormal sensory experience (in Flaubert's case, a visual one). What is common to them all, however, whether the patient knows he is having an attack or not, is that the brain waves abandon their normal pattern and adopt instead a characteristic, abnormal one.

The cause or causes of the dysrhythmia are unknown, beyond a few factors. To begin with, there is often a strong hereditary disposition to epilepsy. Further, the attack is frequently triggered by a specific event or events. A number of these stimuli are now known. A photic seizure, one induced by sudden light, is among the most common: in Flaubert's case it was the light on the oncoming wagon. It is significant that—apparently—this first attack was the only one that progressed to full loss of consciousness. Thereafter, he had the classic form of focal epileptic sensory seizure, in that the later seizures were simple paroxysmal flashes of light, alone or accompanied by memory disturbances and fear: that is, all his later attacks were, in this sense, abortive.

Where did Flaubert's epileptic discharges take place within his brain? The presence of visual phenomena in his hallucinations show that the optic radiation was being affected by the discharges, so that he thought he was seeing flashes of light which in reality were not there. The further fact that he felt himself to be suffering from a sudden discharge of memory shows that the abnormal discharges were occurring near the memory centers of the brain. These and the terrible fear suggest to a neurologist what is now known to be the commonest form of epilepsy in adults, temporal lobe epilepsy, in which the discharges arise in the lobe of the brain behind the right or left temple. If it were clear in which lateral half of the visual field his flashes of fire occurred, then one could even state which temporal lobe was involved. But it is essential to recall that in the present state of medical knowledge one can be reasonably sure only that it was temporal lobe epilepsy. And it may have had a hereditary base. When the cause of such a scar can be determined, it is most commonly an injury at birth or in early life, a disease of infancy or childhood, a high fever, or a congenital abnormality.

Anxiety or fear, visual hallucinations, the feeling that one has already experienced what is presently going on (the *déjà vu* phenomenon), the sudden influx of remembered events, an abnormal increase or decrease in awareness of what is transpiring about one, are all characteristic of a temporal lobe epileptic seizure. In addition, some who suffer from it also suffer from psychiatric abnormalities, neuroses, and disturbances of interpersonal relations.

Coincidentally with the onset of this temporal lobe epilepsy, Flaubert appears to have lost the easy flow of words which had up to now delighted him in his writing. Du Camp so reports it, and others confirm his statement.[8] Very soon what had been a joyous and facile productivity was to become a slow and tortured wringing out of words, one at a time, from an unwilling brain: the agonies of producing good style, to which he often referred. It is possible that some earlier brain damage caused both the epilepsy and the loss of rapid creative facility with words, especially as neither showed any increase with the passage of time. The impairment of abstract thinking (in this case the slowing of the creative process with words) is the essential behavioral impairment which results from brain damage. One may conjecture—but that is all— that this and the epilepsy had a single cause.

Flaubert had done what he could to bring on these attacks. He had long had what he termed "absences," moments when he was no longer with those about him;[9] a modern diagnostician would have thought of mild epilepsy, but in Flaubert's day this form, like migraine, was not understood in its true light. He had overindulged in alcohol and hearty eating; he had endlessly lived under intense emotional strain; high living had been his goal. And all of these dispose the body to attacks.

Much of his treatment was either useful or at worst harmless. The relief from tensions and the restraints on his eating and his drinking of alcohol were valuable. The drainage wick in his neck, while a nuisance, did no harm. The bleedings were, however, harmful, as were the quiet imposed on him and the frustrations it entailed. The various infusions, too, were perhaps harmful, as limiting the liquid intake of the epileptic will often reduce his seizures.

Much more important was what Flaubert and those about him thought of his having what was regarded as a shameful disease. For many epileptics the syndrome is deeply painful and a serious impairment. Yet on the other hand, the list of great epileptics is long, from Julius Caesar and Saint Paul to Flaubert and Dostoevski. In fact, for Paul and Pascal, an epileptic attack was the mode through which they had their visions.[10] For any epileptic, the problem is brutally direct: will the disorder dominate his life; or will he—if it can be controlled—learn to master it? It can even happen that, through successfully rising above it, epileptics may reach heights which they might not otherwise have dreamed of attaining. In Flaubert's case, the anguish and the heightened perceptions were integral to his writing. He saw what nonepileptics do not see, and he gave some of his experiences to his characters. But most significant is the fact that his best work, his only great writing, lies after, not before the onset of his epilepsy. He did succeed in rising above it. As he came over the years to understand the insights these seizures had given him, it is not clear that he regretted experiencing them.

Flaubert had perhaps unconsciously sought illness as a relief from a life he loathed being forced to live; and he sensed that his malady had been occasioned in some way by the frustrations of his enforced studies of the law; but he did not consciously find in this an excuse for having succumbed to it. He felt he had allowed what was a phenomenon of the mind to become one of the body; for an artist this was to allow an idea to pass from the mind, where it is fertile, to the body, where it is sterile. It had been a detour or deviation, and neither genius nor health had profited.[11] And so he fought his attacks by trying to understand them scientifically through cool observation and above all by an act of will as each attack began. He could feel his mind escaping his control and his consciousness being overwhelmed like a ship in a storm; he fought it moment by moment by clinging to his conscious reason until finally, after a decade, he could boldly play at bringing on an attack, so sure was he of dominating it. Then he could look back and feel his nervous ailment had cleared his head by transferring to his body all the foolish, romantic nonsense which had so plagued his youthful dreams. It had been a deflection of vital energy which he had now mastered. He was the better for it, for he had now, in a sense voluntarily, moved his own inner world outside.[12]

The practical problem was how to live with this ailment. Many years before, Flaubert had abandoned any thought that life would be pleasant or that it would provide fulfillment of his dreams. The attacks at least solved the problem he had found insoluble, the demand that he study law. But the impairment, the limitation, and the frustration reinforced his fundamental pessimism and despair.

The first step was to control or diminish the frequently recurring seizures so as to direct as much as possible of his energy and reserve it for his life as a writer. It was a matter of pulling back within his shell, of trying to live as little outside of himself as possible. Thereby what energy was his, apart from the seizures, could be devoted to his art. He saw few people, and the circumstances of his life at the start were such that any sexual contact with women was impossible: in fact, for a year and a half he lived a monastic life, entirely eschewing intercourse even when women were again available. During the first few months he sought relief in masturbation; by springtime he abandoned even that and lived in complete chastity for twelve more months, a course of conduct which he wryly observed some attributed to impotence, others to homosexuality.[13] The violence of the change from debauchery to asceticism, its absolute quality, could not fail to accentuate a number of his attitudes toward sex: his obsession with it, his latent contempt for women, his gloomy forebodings about the whole matter. He was a recluse, and he snarled that he was happy to be one.

Flaubert now separated existence into two clear-cut parts as a result of the experience of the illness. On the one side there was the external world, and this he wanted varied, multicolored, harmonious, immense. Of it he accepted nothing but the spectacle; he would stay apart from it to enjoy it at a distance. On the other side there was his inner self, which now experienced an almost mystical existence as he concentrated it to make it more dense. Keeping the external world of things and emotions outside himself made it only the easier to be open and receptive to the floodtide of the inner life. While he had to refuse to participate with his heart, he could make up for it by an all-embracing understanding.[14] He would know consciously what others merely felt unreflectingly. And hence he was ready for an art based not on being emotionally overwrought in romantic fashion but rather on watching or remembering perceptively and sympathetically, while others poured out the substance of their lives in living. He believed—wrongly as it turned out—that he could never again live that way himself; but then others could not write as he could, for they would not be seeking to understand. The essence of it all was that he rejected nothing but his own overinvolvement. Love, friendship, everything was to be observed, to be understood, to be accepted. It was to become, after much turmoil, strife, and pain, a very beautiful way of life.

Flaubert's pessimism changed character, for his sadness was no longer the result of the excessive demands he had been making on life. External reality was, quite simply, bad; and he had to learn to live with the fact that in certain ways he was less a man than he had been and that he was an object of pity to those about him. His earlier misanthropy, based on a conflict between an imagined and a real world, was now reinforced by a convergence of the two.

Romantic pessimism had rejoiced in the concept of the hero (invariably the self) as the chosen victim of malicious fate. This had been, in part, Flaubert's position. Now, however, in the same way that he had pushed sometimes beyond romanticism to antiromanticism in his writing, particularly in parts of *November,* so in his living he turned to an antiromantic view of life. Where the romantic had seen a personal fate, Flaubert instead proclaimed that it was a law of nature, not the sad privilege of a few elite souls. And here he could draw on long preparation, for this view was already incipient in *The Memoirs of a Madman.*

His greatest immediate problem was companionship: not the casual presence of loved ones, of which he now had plenty, but rather the sharp and stimulating give-and-take of his intellectual peers. His sister continued to be very close to him, coming in each morning from eleven to twelve to sit on his bed and listen while he explained Shakespeare to her. In his more tired and infantile moods, she would fit in by the hour with his little games, as she pretended for his amusement to be his little dog; he would miss her cruelly later.[15] But there are presences, he wrote, which make one feel more alone than does loneliness. While his sister's companionship satisfied some of his longings, it was not mental companionship, and he continued to need this as he had before.

His parents, too, were of course there. His mother offered him the silent, tenacious devotion she had always shown; and, no doubt, in part he owed his recovery to her. But his spirit contained whole regions in which she had never traveled. As for his father, Gustave's illness marked the end of any hope the doctor may have retained for his son's future; it must have been a terrible blow. Nor can Gustave have been ignorant of how his father felt. But these three were the only people whom he saw, aside from servants, as lengthy day succeeded lengthy day.

His ennui and loneliness exceeded any bounds he had ever imagined. As he was later to phrase it for Emma Bovary, the future was now a long corridor absolutely dark, and the door at the end of it was locked shut. Nor did it occur to him that the corridor could be far bleaker or the way far lonelier.

Of Flaubert's close friends only Du Camp was free to come to his bedside. Toward the end of April, Flaubert's state was judged satisfactory for having Du Camp with him; he came for several days. It was good that Maxime could do so, for on the fourth of May he set out on a long trip through the Near East. He was going to be accomplishing one of Gustave's dearest dreams, and Flaubert must have been envious of his friend's good fortune.

Maxime was gone for nearly a year.[16] When he reached Arles, it was as though Flaubert himself were returning there. Maxime, too, imagined a combat of gladiators taking place before his eyes; but the very first thing he had done was to find himself a pretty Arlésienne to while away the time. From Turkey he wrote of the carnal effects of a Turkish bath and the massage which regularly terminated the ritual: despite yourself you found it physically exciting. And here, as everywhere, there were women who could be bought and whom he had.

Flaubert wrote to Du Camp his gloomy thoughts on the future before him. Maxime did what he could, at a distance, to cheer his friend by pointing out sounder perspectives for him than the hermit's life he was envisaging. After all, he had twice been in love, and it would happen again and would make him grow in stature more than he could now imagine. He must keep an open mind about the future; only thus would he be ready when the opportunity came.

A few days after Maxime left him, Gustave and his family went to the Channel Coast to try the effect of sea air on the patient: it must have helped him, for in a few days he returned to writing once again. The new spurt of writing, begun in May and carried on rather steadily until the following January (1845), sufficed to finish the book-length novel, *A Sentimental Education*, which had occupied him at intervals since 1843.

In June Flaubert returned to Rouen, considerably improved by his stay at the shore. But would his illness, which was slowly easing, ever let him return enough toward a normal life? He did not wish to have to take up the law again, yet could he not envisage a new life in Paris with a small group dedicated to art? They would meet two or three times a week for a good dinner washed down with a fine wine, and the conversation would be of poetry. This dream he thought not too ambitious.

If only there were someone with whom to talk of literature and life! His notions of style were clarifying, and he needed someone with whom to share them. Reading Plutarch was precipitating his thinking as he compared the debauched and effeminate Heliogabalus to the calmer, more haughty Nero. Heliogabalus was Asiatic, fevered, uncontrolled; this was the delirium of romanticism. If only in this contrast, Nero, more assured and controlled, seemed more classical. As Flaubert realized, it was this latter attitude he needed in his own life as a counter to romanticism.

Flaubert was also reading the French and Latin authors most calculated to strengthen his own prose style: as he put it, he preferred male sentences to female ones. He wanted them strong, substantial, clear, and with the muscles standing out under bronzed skin. His bedside reading was the skeptic Montaigne, who liked and wrote such sentences, pithy, filled with marrow, and able to follow every twist and turn of thought, as Flaubert described them. He also continued to enjoy Rabelais, a heartier fare, whose words came tumbling out in unordered profusion and who never stopped for fear of having said too much. Flaubert rejoiced in the energy and uninhibited prose of this man of the Renaissance who loved life without reservations. Then there was the satiric poet, Régnier, an ardent individualist and biting critic, a contemporary of Montaigne, who insisted on the freedom to say in his verses what he pleased and to find the way to say it that suited him best, without regard to so-called rule or precept.

The eighteenth century, too, provided models. There was La Bruyère, whose *Characters*, thumbnail sketches of humanity, showed how much could be delineated in a few words, providing one was sparing of line and kept to clean, muscled prose which never wasted words in fatty digression. And there was Le Sage, whose picaresque novel *Gil Blas* owed so much to *Don Quixote* and showed in French the literary possibilities to be gleaned from all sorts of milieus and characters, if one could learn to look clearly and sketch rapidly. A content succulent and full of boiling, bubbling life; a style lean, strong, and direct: these were what he sought in his favorite authors and what he would strive to write himself. But above all other authors he placed Voltaire, and particularly his *Candide*. Here he found the idea and the form wholly at one; no word was wasted, no shaft missed its mark. And man is faced fully in all his weakness and his folly. It was Flaubert's constant breviary.

In mid-June the whole family moved into the new country house which Dr. Flaubert had purchased at Croisset, some three or four miles from the heart of Rouen along the Seine and downriver from the city.[17] It consisted of several acres along the river bank with a comfortable eighteenth-century house which had been built as a dependency of the Benedictine abbey of Saint-Ouen in Rouen. There is a legend—not really very probable—that Prévost wrote *Manon Lescaut* in this house. It is too bad it is not more likely, for there would have been poetic irony in one single site for the creation of lovely, romantic Manon and provincial Emma, who lost so much for having tried too hard to imitate Manon!

The long, white house had an ugly façade toward the river but a more interesting courtyard within. The rooms were few in number but large. Upstairs the one which Flaubert used over the years as his study was big, though low ceilinged; three windows opened onto the garden with its walks and terraces, while the other two looked past a splendid tulip tree to the Seine beyond.

Today the house is no longer there: it was destroyed to make room for a distillery which in turn gave way to a paper factory. Progress is said to demand such sacrifices. But the river is still there, though its bank has been moved a little farther from the property it once almost bathed. The garden rose slightly toward the house, which backed against a considerable rise. A walk bordered by lindens rose up this hill to the top and gave a splendid view over the valley. At one corner of the garden, down by the river, there was a small pavilion which is today the only remnant. The quiet walks, the peaceful view out over the Seine and beyond to the plains across the river, and the solemn, slow parade of boats constituted the haven where Flaubert this summer sought to recover his health, where over the years he would live most of his days, and where one day he would die.

In the summer of 1844 the family shared the property with the

masons and carpenters who were remodeling it for its new owners; in November it was finally necessary to abandon it to them so
they might work in peace to complete it over the winter months.
In the meantime Flaubert had the best of it. The water was beside
him for swimming and canoeing; these were his only pleasures,
and he was in or on the water almost daily, either vigorously
swimming about or paddling up and down as he circled about the
two ferries which crossed the river near his house.

As summer came on, Gustave was able to give up, one after
another, the various treatments, although his skin was still covered
with some sort of outbreak, and he could neither sit nor walk with
comfort. The drainage wick was removed from his neck, the mercury frictions were no longer deemed necessary, and he could
begin to look forward to smoking again before very long. There
were, however, clear suggestions that he also contracted syphilis.[18]
He said so himself, and mercury frictions were a standard treatment for this ailment (as for several others) at this time. All this was
puzzling to his doctors and deeply discouraging to the patient. Under such confusing circumstances, what hopes could one entertain?

Flaubert had to experiment to find his way. At first bitterness
seemed justified and wise; he would meet his crisis by consciously
evolving a completely self-centered life. Any other notion was
foolish, and he wrote to Maxime Du Camp, taking him to task for
naïvely hoping to find happiness in marriage and children. Only
art was sure and worthy of trust. He would build his life around
it. It was a natural reaction for a man in his distraught condition
and tried by grievous blows; but it was dangerous.

Du Camp undertook to help Flaubert to sounder understandings. It was not easy and it had to be done by letter, but he was
deeply fond of Gustave. He began by agreeing that a brief fling
of independence was a joyous thing, but he warned that if Gustave persisted in it, then he would know the long solitudes that
can be avoided only by having a family. It alarmed Du Camp to
have him thus seek out so blithely the very solitude which, as an
orphan, Maxime knew all too intimately. He urged that if Gustave
could live for just six months the solitary life that he had known
from childhood, he would gratefully return, calm and collected,
to the loved ones of whose company he now complained. More-

over, he reminded Flaubert that he had a devoted circle of friends, himself and Hamard at their head: they would never abandon him.

Then Maxime turned to Gustave's feeling that he could substitute art for life. He agreed that art satisfied the mind and the spirit. But—and he must have weighed each word, for it was dangerous to say this to Gustave—never had art been able to satisfy the heart, and it was by the heart and not by the head that one must live.

Gustave, he said, had been misled and accepted as true many ideas which were false. His nature was admirably sensitive and ready for everything great of the mind and the spirit, but the easy attraction of surface impressions had led him astray. He had thought he had seen the beautiful in places where it was not; he had become enthusiastic over harmful works and doctrines whose artistic excellence should not have clouded their basic horror and foolishness. Flaubert had an intelligence, his friend wrote, which placed him among the elite, and instead of following where it should have led him, he had aped a corrupt being, Alfred Le Poittevin, who did not believe a word of all the corroding things he told Gustave and which Gustave so readily accepted. Maxime dared him to show Alfred his letter.

Maxime's warm affection and his concern were in every word. But what of his comments on the role of art? No doubt for the generality of men he was right: art could not satisfy the heart. But the generality of men do not write great novels, and Flaubert never long doubted that he had it within his power to write them. Was it perhaps true that artists had to deny life or else deny their art? Was this not the terrible failing of the romantics, that they had sought to fuse the two? In any event, right or wrong, he had no choice, for each new tremor of his emotions meant a new tremor in his nerves and more flashing lights before his eyes and more terror. And what should Gustave think when Maxime attacked Alfred Le Poittevin? Du Camp was probably right that a great deal in Flaubert which was false was a response to Alfred and had probably been nurtured by the older man until it was second nature in his pupil. But Flaubert could hardly find it so. Maxime, too, seems to have realized that he had done all he could.

Du Camp had mentioned Hamard and how close he felt to Gustave. This had not been so over most of the four years that Flaubert had known him. He had indeed helped him to find an apartment in Paris; he had courted Flaubert's sister Caroline for years and so had been much in and out of the family. Now, as autumn came on, Caroline and Hamard announced their engagement. The blow had struck; the real solitude Du Camp had spoken of was about to descend. His sister, his pupil, his friend, in some sense his creation, was about to take her leave of him and go build her own life apart. When they told him the news, he said only "Ah!" Flaubert wrote of it to the absent Du Camp, who was delighted. He knew Hamard well and wrote immediately to Gustave with congratulations and reassurances: had Caroline been his own daughter, he would not have chosen another man for her. And then, with a sensitivity rare among men, he added that he would hasten his return to France, for he knew what the separation from Caroline would mean to his friend.

The First *Sentimental Education* (1843-45)

By writing of his personal sorrows he made them go away; from his heart they overflowed into nature and became more general, more universal, gentler.

Of Jules in *A Sentimental Education*

In May, 1844, Flaubert had been well enough to begin writing once more on the book which his studies and then his illness had forced him to abandon the previous autumn; during the night of January 7, 1845, as he noted on the manuscript, he wrote the last words at one o'clock in the morning. Such solemn moments he liked to record, sometimes even to the minute, so as to give to their fleeting presence something more of permanence. It was a strange book, disjointed, its composition broken in two by his nervous attack, ill conceived in its basic structure, and its parts largely unrelated. For these reasons Flaubert never consented to publish it; but despite its defects, it embodies in its themes, its situations, and its ideas the prototypes of much of *Madame Bovary*. It was a major milestone.

Flaubert called the new work *L'Education sentimentale*,[19] a title he used again twenty years later for a different work. The title is probably patterned on Sterne's *Sentimental Journey*, but the resultant translation is not entirely meaningful in French. "Love's Apprenticeship" or "The Education of the Feelings" might suggest what it connotes to a Frenchman.

The plot is complicated, so complicated in fact that Flaubert loses track of it, and his chronology is not always consistent. Young Henry Gosselin is a student in Paris living at the combined school and boardinghouse of Monsieur Renaud, with whose wife Emilie he soon begins a love affair. The happy pair enter upon the brief, roseate period of romantic love. When it wanes, they become convinced, following the romantic clichés, that they will be happier elsewhere. Hence they flee to America, where soon they run out of money. Their bright passion is finally extinguished in the total ennui of impoverished life in New York. They then come back to France, where Henry abandons his mistress and she returns to her husband. Henry settles down to a life of steady self-seeking, makes numerous conquests, and learns to avoid disillusionment by refusing ever to hope. He is a success in the eyes of the world and has completed his education in love.

Henry's character, as it evolved, proved unable to bear the load of more than the negative side of the argument. Jules, his friend, was invented to express the other elements. Like Henry, he had to learn that romanticism could not be lived; but he would also reject the practical world of successful men. When he becomes infatuated with the actress Lucinde and lends her money, she leaves town without repaying; she had been duping him from the start. With heavy irony, Flaubert has this occur during the time when Henry and Emilie are enjoying their first blissful days together. Jules now knows that romanticism is a lie. Completely divorced from all contemporary events, he lives a life of meditation, study, and art. As the book closes, he is on his way to the Hellespont with a copy of Homer under his arm. His education in love has led him to seek an artistic and intellectual fusion, purged of romanticism and guided by a newly conceived religion of art which will complete and mature what he has glimpsed by the end of the book.

To clear away an underbrush of error, Flaubert turned to satire in this book. Such an extended use of it was a new and difficult apprenticeship for him, as it required that he lay aside and actually mock much of what had made the excellence of his own earlier, romantic works. He evolved instead what would be the basic structure of his later novels, which are made up in large measure of a succession of "scenes," many of them autobiographical. Here, recounting dryly and from the outside, he held up to ridicule the weaknesses he sought to satirize. Many of these scenes recur in the later novels. The device slows the pace of the work so that its time can, if need be, approximate that of the reader, who may thus live more intimately with the characters. Moreover, at least in theory, all phases of a novel—dialogue and analysis, action and description, narration and psychology—can be advanced simultaneously.

For the first time in a long work in novel form Flaubert was not writing in the first person. How then could he make observations? Romantic literature, conveniently, permitted the author to intervene at will; Flaubert, ever present, took center stage and drove his actor from public view in many scenes. Even when presenting a character, he cheerily took his reader to task: "But you have not noticed her striking, polished teeth?" On one occasion he even engagingly mocked the clumsiness of one of his own tired images.

A further problem of writing in the third person was to get the characters in the book to take on the tremendous immediacy which Flaubert himself felt in their presence. He must have remembered the decade before, when he had been writing plays to be put on in the billiard room: the shock and sparkle of speech itself sufficed to give this living quality. And so direct dialogue bulks large here. At one point, with only three characters to handle in a little genre scene, the conversation is scarcely broken by the alternating "he said" or "she said." Soon even this disappears and the content of the rapid comment alone makes clear who is the speaker. Then, caught up in the excitement of the scene and

the technique, Flaubert started to write it in the form of stage
dialogue, with the name of the character in small capital letters
and the speech following it. Even stage directions, in italics, crept
in to complete the illusion. It was an exciting and pliable technique
which Théophile Gautier had already used and Flaubert easily
adapted to his needs.

Flaubert's cast of characters he drew largely from his own
experience. Jules, in considerable measure Flaubert himself, was
credulous and loving, and had a facile enthusiasm. His was a sensitive and almost feminine temperament, readily hurt and readily
joyous. In Madame Renaud Flaubert created a new embodiment
of Elisa Schlésinger. Her manner was maternal; she had beautiful
black eyes and sharply marked eyebrows, her bosom was full. Her
look was languorous, Andalusian, motherly, and lascivious. Thinking, no doubt, of Maurice Schlésinger, Flaubert added that Henry
hated Emilie's husband whenever he came up to plant two resounding kisses, one on each of her cheeks; Flaubert termed them
those insolent kisses that legitimate husbands give to their wives
with so much naïveté that one should laugh at them rather than
vomit.

A great many details and scenes come directly from Flaubert's
life. When Lucinde abandoned Jules, he, too, considered suicide,
and once again it was from a bridge, although the time was summer and the stream carried bits of grass, not cakes of ice. Jules
thought often of death—as Flaubert must have done, especially
after his attacks began. Like Flaubert, Jules worked at his Greek
and enjoyed Plutarch for his tales of war and heroes. More scabrous details, too, slip in. One of Henry's fellow students came
down with venereal disease and had to submit to daily attentions
from his doctor, who brought potions and pills, pastilles and infusions.

There is even a ball at the Renaud's house, and Henry, of
course, attends it. Naturally he could not in these surroundings
drive up a long driveway as Flaubert had done, but he could feel
the loneliness which Flaubert had felt nearly ten years before as
the dancing went on and on. In fact, Flaubert so much substituted
himself for Henry that, as before, he wrote that the older ladies
retired at three in the morning—even though no older ladies were

present at this party! When all had left, Henry went upstairs, and the reader has the strange, dreamlike foreknowledge that the young man will walk over, open the window for a breath of fresh air, and watch the dawn rise. But he cannot then go out and observe the lake and swans; instead, as in *November*, he relives his past life, whose events blow before him like leaves in the wind, precisely as they had in the earlier story, although the image is not now so crisply handled.

Flaubert later pillaged this work, not only its title but many scenes, for the novels which he did publish. Emilie pushed Henry into leaving for America: Emma Bovary would try to drive her lover Rodolphe into such a departure. Similarly, a well-handled moonlight scene in the *Education* constituted a distant first draft for the later novel. Emilie and Henry, while their affair was still a chaste one, dreamed of galloping off into the woods together. Emma would ride off in just such fashion, and there give herself to Rodolphe for the first time. Henry and Emilie took a ride in a hackney cab, the forerunner of the more famous one which Emma would take with her second lover, Léon. And finally, one of Flaubert's minor characters actually lives in abridged form the career of Emma Bovary.[20]

Much which Flaubert found he could incorporate in this first *Sentimental Education* he could embody in more durable form in *Madame Bovary;* but the later novel was to be much more tightly constructed and much more uniform in tone. It forced Flaubert despairingly to leave out whole facets of his flamboyant nature. He was less sure in his taste when he was in his early twenties, and he included in the *Education* elements which he wisely rejected in the *Bovary* and instead reserved for other and later works like the exotic Carthaginian novel, *Salammbô*. In the bourgeois surroundings of the *Education*, these longings could enter only as ill-assorted dreams of frustrated young men and women imagining earlier ages. They were out of place, but even so, writing them served to sharpen Flaubert's perceptions and to tighten his grasp on his pen for the later novels.

Emma Bovary, like Lucinde, was a provincial French girl: neither could readily be described as reminding the reader of those daughters of Eve who come to earth to destroy the sons of men or—like the fantasies of Marie in *November*—as being one of those women who play with serpents, coil them about their bodies, and charm them by their voices. Neither Emma nor Lucinde nor Marie should be so described; but Lucinde is. Emma is not, and hence, all through the long years of writing her story, Flaubert yearned for the wild, sensual glories of such other women; and Salammbô, daughter of Hamilcar Barca and wise in the ways of the Moon Goddess, will play in this fashion with her sacred serpent before going out to give herself to her lover Mâtho.

An apprenticeship is important for what it leads into. Flaubert was beginning to sense that the novelist creates more than his characters and their world of people and physical surroundings and events: he also creates the relationships between these characters and their world. The author may, if he wishes, break their customary links and enter a strange, dislocated void beyond time and in dissociated space. In the world of fantasy literature this was commonplace, and many tales by the young Flaubert stem, in imitation of *Faust*, directly from this easy source. But what if one lets normal people have this abnormal experience of dislocation and dissociation? In the seduction scene Flaubert wrote of Henry that slowly, without his thinking about it and "with the supernatural facility which we experience in dreams," he raised his arm, extended it, and put it around Emilie's waist. It is only a phrase here, but such departures from normality were to be the bases for vast and lonely experiences in Flaubert's later works, in which his characters could enter a frightening world dissociated from the normal one. Saint Anthony struggles with the three states of consciousness: normality, fantasy, and dissociation. Emma Bovary lives a platitude, imagines a dream world, and sinks into the dark, hostile world beyond time and space. Even the phrase itself, "the supernatural facility we experience in dreams," recurs in *Salammbô* and many of his other works.

The first *Education* derives from a number of literary currents. When Flaubert opposes to the romantic notion of total bliss the more limited concept that happiness is relative, how one feels and not how things are absolutely, he is echoing his master Montaigne. He also writes Byronic moments of religious skepticism and pens Balzacian boardinghouse scenes; he mentions Chateaubriand's *René* and Goethe's *Werther*, "those books which take away one's taste for living." But more important, perhaps, were other works of Goethe's, his *Truth and Poetry* and especially his *Apprenticeship of Wilhelm Meister*, the *Lehrjahre* or "Years of Learning," as Goethe had named his work.[21] Flaubert's own title perhaps echoes Goethe's. The German work must have seemed to him to recount so much of his own background. Like young Gustave, Wilhelm had lived only for his dreams of the stage and had had his imagination kindled by puppets, just as Flaubert had at the Saint Romain Fair in Rouen. Perhaps this is why, when Flaubert added Jules to his book, he found it easy to model him on Goethe's hero. *Wilhelm Meister* is also endlessly digressive, which may have led Flaubert to feel more justified in pouring out his own thoughts and feelings in page after page.

The education of which Flaubert wrote was predicated upon clearing away false notions by unsparing satire. Henry's father is the butt of many easy shafts of tired wit. Flaubert presents a list of his idiotic remarks, but it is too wooden a device; it palls, where it should provide malicious delight. His satire is more effectively aimed at Madame Renaud's certainty that in some vague "otherwhere," a place different from Paris, she and Henry will be happy. They also lament the loss of the past. Who will give me back, Flaubert cried out, the sound of the bell which pealed yesterday at dusk and the twittering of the birds this morning in the oak tree! But—and it is here that the satire he learned from Gautier enters—he was bored when the sun was in fact setting, and yawning with fatigue when it had risen. Similarly Jules's trouble, Flaubert wrote in a sentence which equally describes Emma Bovary, was that he confused what really was with what he felt ought to be. He had many of the dreams Emma Bovary would dream later: the magic effect of bygone costumes with high boots and purple cloaks, Venice, tempests, lakes with moonlight and fragile barks, ruins, innocent virgins and Alpine shepherdesses, troubadour poetry, and all the rest.

As the love affair between Henry and Emilie descended in Paris from the early excitement of a dream realized to the doldrums normal to such attachments, each discovered that the other was in fact no more than a simple, ordinary sort of person, much like most of the rest of the world. Hence began their foredoomed quest for something new and marvelous to sustain a flame which had never really burned except in their own separate imaginations. Flaubert's irony becomes bitter and personal when he describes the nadir of Henry's affection for Emilie in New York as Henry returns day after miserable day to her eternal, stupid smile of affection. It is the end of Henry's passion, the first great step in his sentimental education.

The story of Henry and Emilie in New York and the analysis of their slow tiring of one another was a chapter of which Flaubert was proud,[22] his account of what love in the romantic vein must always be. Emilie proved jealous, moody, and exacting. Henry learned, slowly, to abandon his wilder hopes and to feel for Emilie more of respect as he turned to her for consolation and strength. But his poverty stood between him and carrying out his dreams for her, a devastating experience Flaubert had already sketched in *November:* Henry came to doubt what he had believed in and loved. He became aware that no two lovers are ever at the same stage in their affair: one is always deeper in love than the other at any given moment, and hence the ideal of romantic communion can never be fulfilled in practice. The problem was not, as Gautier and his generation had imagined, to learn to substitute real women, those of one's own time and culture, for impossible, romantic ones; the difficulty lay in accepting the fact that no such dreams could ever be fulfilled with anyone.

Henry in New York was making the dread discovery which Emma would later make in provincial Normandy: adultery has all the platitudes of marriage. Flaubert must have thought back to his own purple mirages when he was eighteen and had found in this word "adultery" all the poetry of which his imagination was capable. Now, sadly but firmly, he had to dismiss it, for it was no solution to any problem. Henry was completely alone with his mistress and she lived only for him. But women, wrote Flaubert, cannot follow their lovers when they seek to generalize their thoughts and to move beyond the particular. He must have been thinking of Caroline or, more probably, Harriet Collier. The sad judgment would recur.

The unhappy pair turned to their last possible refuge, seeking to substitute orgies of the flesh for what their spirits could no longer furnish forth. Emilie's vigorous waist suggested sudden convulsive or elastic movements; her full, rounded hips and firm breasts promised languor and voluptuousness. Here, too, however, the education of the couple could lead only to the sad awareness that voluptuousness cannot replace love and that only confusion, misery, and regret for the lost past can come from it. Henry did enjoy occasional lascivious moments with Emilie—the flesh is part of man—but he found his peace in settling down to the not disagreeable life one can lead with a beautiful woman when she has a sociable character and is not too dull during what Flaubert called the chaster hours of the day. It was a view to which his friend Du Camp would come twenty years later.

Love is a garment of many colors and cast upon many shoulders in this long and rambling work. Jules sought to break from the prison of self by imagining an active life full of sexual delights and with a huge fortune which would put them all at his disposal. Borrowing Flaubert's dreams, he imagined living in the orgiastic, pleasure-seeking antiquity of Caligula and Nero, with its mad joys and insensate spasms of pride and blood always mingled with its roses. But this was a dream that could never be realized in the gray modern world.

Flaubert told the story of a Negro on the ship which took Henry and Emilie to America. His father had sold him for a package of nails; he had come to France as a servant and had stolen a scarf for a chambermaid with whom he was in love. He spent five years at forced labor for it, and had just walked the whole length of France to get back to his mistress, who was no longer there. Now he was returning to his native land across the sea. He, too, Flaubert concluded, had completed his sentimental education. In a bitter postscript at the end of the book Flaubert termed this Negro perhaps the happiest of all his cast of characters, for he had died the day before he returned to his native land.

The last third or so of the work is dedicated to an exploration of how Jules substituted scholarly and esthetic pleasures for those emotions which had led him only to disaster. For the first time Flaubert found himself capable of frequent ironic detachment from his characters and able also to criticize himself. He had Jules come to understand that what he knew of wisdom derived from having learned to sever with his irony the ties which bound him to what he had once cared for. He could now recognize the past as his poetic period, a sort of Golden Age of his heart, acceptable in itself—when once past—and now to be valued for the artistic uses to which it could be put. This was Flaubert's solution, and it is the last word of the later *Sentimental Education*, of 1869.

Each of Jules's feelings melted into an idea. Thus he learned to extract theories from the feelings of voluptuousness which no longer besieged him. To live became, for him, to learn more and hence to improve his art. Experience added accretions of fact; art, using them, could reach in one bound to the final perfection, which life itself could never vouchsafe. It was a way to know, and Flaubert was approaching the doctrine of the creative imagination as Baudelaire was evolving it over this same decade and separated from him by only a mile or so during his long stays in Paris.

The new element in Flaubert's life, impassivity, is the new basis for his esthetic. The artist must be insensitive to the passions of which he writes, an observer and not their servant, for it is impossible to see the passions whole if one is deeply engaged within them. Thus all that Flaubert had lived could now take on meaning and seem to have come about for a real, albeit an unperceived, reason. In the earlier part of the book he had written impertinently that lovers should not take up the pen to write of love: their hands should be otherwise occupied. He had thought of life as a masked ball and of himself as condemned to sit to one side in boredom, for he had believed that one had to join in the dance to enjoy it. Now he perceived that writing about his sadness with a calm perspective had, itself, relieved his sadness, for he had learned to generalize it.

Flaubert and Jules had based their spiritual recovery upon becoming objective. Jules, with the easy privilege of the fictional character, could in one leap fly over the thorny hedges which set barriers to Flaubert's own ambitions toward serenity: it was far easier to write of a stoic ideal than to live it. With a becoming honesty Flaubert, who was but twenty-two, realized that such knowledge usually comes later and aged his hero to twenty-six.

Flaubert elaborated his new objective esthetic around the idea of a historical novel which Jules wanted to write. The hero of *November* had visited museums and imagined displaying certain historical epochs in a new light. He dreamed—rather idly—of all of this and saw himself learning all the languages he would need to know, traveling through distant lands, reading inscriptions and deciphering obelisks. But then his hero had decided it was all silly and had leaned back in his chair and folded his arms.[23] It had been no more than a passing and foolish fantasy. Flaubert now addressed himself to what he termed a task of reconstruction which would give to the past a real life based on the close uniting of learning and inspiration. The two together would raise history to the level of art and philosophy because, as Flaubert put it, history needed analytic experimentation to be true and the clever manipulations of perspective to appear so.

Jules began from the facts of costume, period, and country. Behind this, he sought the man, and within the man, what it was that made him what he was. He strove for a humble, uncomplaining acceptance, since any effort to reject would dwarf nature. Epic poems he began to find less poetic than history, and prior historical novels had been only attempts to lodge somewhere in the past a set of preconceived notions. Their falsifications history crushed with the majesty of its own proportions. Art must, instead, accept the exigencies of history and seek as its proper function to complete what history said, to express what it did not get around to saying. Flaubert put into Jules's mouth his own cry of anguish, however, as he contemplated the vast stores of erudition he must accumulate, the sagacity required to apply it, and the keenness of vision he would need to see things as they really had been. The doctrine has frequently been called realism for reasons largely of historical accident; but the name is deceptive and blinding, for it refers, in Flaubert's case, to only half the approach, to the effort "to see things as they really had been." This he looked upon as the erudite part of his task, indispensable but in no way art, and "realism" was a word which always appeared to him so partial as to be foolish.

There is a bland optimism, for a later age, in the expectation that one could ever, by any amount of labor, come to know things as they really were or are; but this was not a difficulty over which young men in the 1840's were likely to trouble themselves. Positivism was on the rise, and things "as they really are" seemed reassuringly fixed and knowable. Scientism, the belief in the unlimited possibilities of science, was widely dominant. In some of Goethe's reflections, already available to Flaubert in translation, the German poet and thinker had cautioned the writer never to seek beyond the phenomenon for some further, added lesson; in the arts, in science, and in daily life, what is important is the ability to see objects as they are and to treat them according to their nature. This was Flaubert's goal now, for he was learning to strive for that suspending of judgment which, with Montaigne, he felt to be the only source of wisdom: *ne pas conclure*, do not seek to come to conclusions, was his oft-repeated maxim.

Jules was slowly adopting this broad tolerance which could lead to understanding. He admired Shakespeare and Homer for having achieved a natural and complete harmony which linked art and passion. And it seemed so calm. Hence Jules came to feel inspiration must be self-contained: it was denatured or destroyed by external excitements. One must be sober to sing of the bottle and in no wise angry when depicting wrath. That way Homer and Shakespeare had been able to include everything so that their creations became like those of God. They were the conscience and the consciousness of the world, for all its elements were assembled within their works and could be grasped there and understood.

These notions of the role of passion in the arts were in the air of Paris during the early 1840's.[24] Balzac had expressed some of them, when he suggested that it was part of Rabelais' excellence that he drank water while singing his praises of the vine. The great romantic critic Sainte-Beuve accepted and thereby consecrated the new antipersonalism of these years. Flaubert was in the capital and in touch with the new developments in art through Maurice Schlésinger; he had been prepared for them by some of his readings, and his friend Alfred Le Poittevin had already helped him toward their acceptance.

Flaubert would use his art to display the beauty, harmony, and symmetry of the world. By synthesizing life, he wanted to reduce it to absolute principles that would thus—so wrote this agnostic— reflect the face of God. Art should raise life to a higher beauty, to the ideal from which it came, so that it could arouse that admiration which he called the prayer of man's intelligence.before the staggering manifestation of the infinite intelligence. It should arouse enthusiasm, which is the supreme grasping and understanding of beautiful things.

The wellsprings of these doctrines are numerous and deep. There is an underlying assumption that the true and the beautiful are one, which has its origin in Plato; and neoplatonic ideas were not uncommon in France in the 1840's, where Baudelaire was acquiring them, too. Moreover, Flaubert's enthusiasm for Plato went back to his school days under Mallet and to his reading of Victor Cousin. A current of German mysticism or idealism also enters here, as well as ideas flowing from Spinoza as the Germans understood him.[25] For Spinoza the universe is a total harmony which may be perceived as truth or as beauty; since it is a single harmony which is being perceived, the two ways of viewing it are concordant. For the thinker, whom Spinoza had seen as living apart from life but understanding it and explaining it to his fellows, Flaubert substitutes the writer, and has Jules look forward to fulfilling the role. Like Spinoza, Jules will not seek the beautiful directly but will rather strive to reproduce the harmony of the universe, which will therefore contain beauty. Form and content, then, as correlative intuitions of the same basic harmony, will be one. It seems probable that Flaubert's immediate source was, however, Hegel, who provided the basis for so much of romantic thinking in France. He denied, as Flaubert would, any valid distinction between form and content and held that ultimately, the world of art was truer even than the world of nature and of history, because it depended more exclusively on the world of ideas.

Quite late in the book, as Jules was about to launch his lengthy disquisitions on art and life, he came upon a mangy dog, which refused to leave him despite the stones he threw at it. It followed him and then led him along the riverbank to the bridge near which he had sought to commit suicide. A strange fascination with the animal gripped him. The incident is perhaps based on the poodle episode in *Faust* and imitates some of the mysterious aspects of *Wilhelm Meister*. Jules returned home, deeply troubled, and shortly stepped out again to see if the dog were there: he was. But with that the chapter ends, and the next one begins with Jules's rejection of the whole episode.

This tale of the mangy dog is a peculiar affair. In part it reflects the fact, of which he was immensely proud, that Flaubert felt animals were always especially attracted to him. More significant, though, are Jules's reflections. While he looks at the dog in the dim moonlight, the beast's eyes grow larger and larger, and he appears accursed: Jules is completely caught up in the specter before him. The episode has been thought to have symbolic overtones.[26] It can, however, be understood directly and in its own terms. It was totally unreal, entirely the product of his overwrought imagination. But it had, for him, a hyperreality: it was more intimate and more profound, he wrote, than external events and had a reality of its own, of another sort but as real as the normal one, even while it seemed to deny the validity of the real world. The figment of the imagination had superseded mere external event: so could well-conceived fiction, if its form were right.

Readers accustomed to literature written in English are frequently puzzled when they first meet French insistence upon the importance of form. La Fontaine is a writer in whom they have rejoiced as children; it had not occurred to them that French adults would treat him seriously, calling him a master of form and one of the great stylists of the language. The excellence informing the even perfection of a line by Racine excites the Frenchman's ear and delights his mind in a way bewildering to habitual readers of English. And yet it is an old notion in France, first born perhaps with the poets of the middle of the sixteenth century and rising to total domination of all great French literature by the time of Louis XIV and the age of classicism at the end of the seventeenth century.

This abiding importance of form is probably the basic concept demarcating the bounds of what the Frenchman would call his classicism. When an author gives first importance to form, sacrificing to it, where need be, other elements (color, spontaneity, or lyricism, for instance), then the Frenchman accepts that author into the select company of the classicists.

To the classicist each idea has its perfect form, the right way and the only way to clothe it. This must be sought and found, for it (and it alone) will determine the broad structure of the work, be it sonnet or full-length novel. It will also preside over the innumerable lesser choices which go to make up the style of the work. Until the present century, England and America have had few such authors and they are in general far distant from the present scene: some of the poets around the first Elizabeth, for instance, or Dryden or Pope, all of whom readily understood the notion. France, however, numbers such men by the score, albeit never in the novel before Flaubert.

Romanticism had felt freer about form; it had insisted on freedom for the author to violate any prescription in the name of expressing what was on his mind, or, more likely, in his heart. Flaubert's generation, the men born around 1820, grew up enthusiastic over such romantic works. Flaubert's own earlier productions had wandered at will about his fancy. Even his current novel, this *Sentimental Education*, had abandoned considerations of form for its whole last third as he detailed the thoughts and concepts of Jules. And yet it was in this work that Flaubert first began to show an understanding of the importance he would later always attribute to form and to style. It would long be thus: he would discover principles to which he gave hearty allegiance and which he loudly proclaimed, but it would be years before he could put them into practice. Here, in his discovery of form and style, he was enunciating doctrines and maxims which he would not himself fully follow for half a dozen years.

Jules, said Flaubert, set about the great study of style. Thus he could learn how to write the sort of fiction that would have that hyperreality he had discovered in the episode of the mangy dog. He observed closely the birth of the idea at the precise moment when the form was being born and into which it melted at once. He studied their mysterious developments, parallel and each adequate to the other, and sensed that he was here in the presence of the mystery of the creation of beauty, which he always felt to be akin to the processes of the deity.

With the innovations of Gautier in the 1830's the doctrine of art for art's sake, *l'art pour l'art*, had been launched. With Flaubert there begins a new understanding, life for art's sake. It was a practical problem, a constantly renewed struggle so to live that his art might always benefit. Unable fully to persuade himself of the validity of any religion, he sought instead to understand his universe in terms of beauty. Art was, thus, a means of knowing and understanding. Jules, like his creator, lived less and less in the midst of men. It was a complex attitude, only in part the result of a consciously made decision. Experience suggested it was good; Flaubert's pride had been hurt, and chance circumstances had led to it. Moreover, communication with others was becoming so much harder now; trivial contact was too futile and distracting, and really to convey to another what one felt or thought was nearly impossible. On those occasions when one's writing achieved the level of art, then communication was so perfect that all casual conversation seemed idle beside it.

Jules sought that intimate fusion which Flaubert termed the emotions of the intelligence, that radiance which came from the beauty he dreamed of within himself. Penetrating below surface appearances to essences and overleaping the accidents of external existence, Jules, through art, was saved for the marvelous observation of the self, for the proper study of mankind, which is man. Montaigne had led Flaubert to this; now he would turn the study to the profit of fiction.

The convalescent Flaubert appeared to be leading a life of tedium and monotony; so did Jules. Actually, it was a life of infinite dimensions, formed of living the life of everything about him. Artistic beauty was to be found everywhere, as flowers grow equally in gardens and on tombs, and art was a method for extracting it. Jules tensed in excitement at the thought of braving unnecessary dangers; he came to rejoice in the medieval period, the ancient world, the stormy sea. He learned to walk in a cathedral and respond to its stained glass. His was not a life of amusement, as was Henry's, but there were days when he could delight in this total observation of his own spirit and soar in it like an eagle in the clouds. This was Jules's, and Flaubert's, reward for a life lived for art's sake.

Jules's greatest joys were a sunset, the noise of the wind in the trees or the song of a lark at dusk, the turn of a phrase or a sonorous rhyme, or an old statue. These, and only matters like these, plunged him into the long ecstasies which were the reason for his way of life. He stopped at its inception the emotion which would upset his calm and sought instead to bring to life that sensitivity which alone was creative. Life furnished him with the transitory example, and he strove to return to it art, which is external. Through his vocation, Flaubert wrote of Jules, he succeeded in giving concrete form to his own sensations; it was a mission, the way of life for which his genius fatally destined him, as did his own labors. Through it, he partook of the immense pantheism of the universe, which passed through him to reappear as art. This was Flaubert's life for art, his religion of art, the reason for his withdrawal.

6

The Road Back (1845-46)

THE RETURN TO LIFE (1845)

I have weaned myself of my own volition from so many
things that I can be rich in the midst of absolute poverty.
But I still have a way to go.

Letter to Alfred Le Poittevin, July, 1845

THE YEAR 1845 opened for Flaubert with the writing of the last
pages of his *Sentimental Education:* the year was to mark an important transition for him as he moved away from the sheltered
existence he had led for the twelve months since his first epileptic
attack. He was still forced to follow a quiet way of life, but he
was free now to read or write as he pleased: the illness, while a
serious hindrance, was still better than Paris and law studies. And
so he read and studied Greek and observed himself tentatively to
find out what he could risk doing in the external world.

His family's life was soon filled to the brim with the forthcoming marriage of his sister Caroline to Hamard. It took place on
March 3; the young couple lived with the elder Flauberts for a
month before going on their honeymoon. Even a walk through
Rouen with Caroline was now saddened by memories of the days
when he had been everything to her. Soon the honeymoon journey was to take place, but the whole family planned to accompany the bride and groom down the Rhône to Marseilles and Flaubert's old haunts and then into Italy, which he was most eager to
see.

Like many sick people, Flaubert found change frightening and
distasteful: this was his reaction to leaving Rouen. The grip of
habit he readily accepted, and any departure now always impressed him more with what he was abandoning than with what

he would find ahead. He dreaded forsaking the long conversations
—sometimes five or six hours without interruption—which he had
been having with Alfred Le Poittevin over the previous three
months. Seated across the hearth from each other, they had explored the wildest flights of mind and imagination. Gustave
looked to Alfred to guide him in finding what his new life should
be. In neither mind nor body was Le Poittevin a wise choice, but
his influence, mystic, introverted, and masochistic though it was,
nevertheless was necessary to Flaubert.[1.]

Le Poittevin's state in this spring of 1845 was very serious.[2] He
was leading a debauched life, in part to conceal from himself his
own futility and lack of will. He was quite ill, probably from
syphilis, and he was turning against all healthy forms of life.
Women attracted him only in painting or sculpture, an observation which was to leave a deep trace on his friend. Life itself, so
beautiful in other forms, he found not so in man. And woman
disgusted him even more; he seemed to hate her for the illusions
she had occasioned in him. He wrote at one point to Flaubert of a
plan he had conceived: he would return to the places where he
had been as a child, but now he would go in the company of a
common prostitute chosen for the purpose. They would spend a
few days there: he would find joy in taking her about this region
where he had first dreamed of being in love. Then, on their return
to Rouen, he would send her packing. Flaubert wrote back that
the plan was worthy of a great man like Alfred.

Flaubert's trip started off in Nogent with relatives.[3] He was
glad to escape briefly from here for a quick trip to Paris, his first
in a year, though it seemed more like a century. He wrote that at
the start he felt as though he were going back up the stream of his
past like a man struggling against a torrent. Later he felt more at
ease, but still alone in the midst of the crowd. It reminded him of
himself three years before in the autumn of 1842, coming to begin
his study of the law.[4]

Flaubert called on the Colliers.[5] It was strange to sit with Gertrude and Harriet again and to recall long afternoons spent in
reading *Hernani* or *René* to them. He knew that now he would
no longer do that. But Harriet was still there in her chair with the
same smile and the same voice, and all the furniture was the same.

To complete the illusion there was even the sound of a barrel organ rising from the street as there had been formerly. It was good to be out in the world again and Flaubert savored it, he said, as a sentinel would rejoice in a soft bed after a night on duty. Yet, though Harriet had not changed and did not seem to know he had, still he was now so distant from her that only pain could ensue. But for today only the organ player's melody seemed bitter.

After a fruitless call at the Schlésinger's—Maurice was away—he went to call on Louise Pradier, the wife of the sculptor. "Ludovica," as her friends termed her, was separated from her husband as the result of a scandalous affair she had carried on under his nose with a young man. She was living in relative poverty in furnished rooms, and the police were watching her moves, set onto it by the youth's parents. Flaubert termed the scene moving and ironic. But in fact she stirred him deeply, and his veiled comments in letters to Alfred led the latter to suggest that on his return he must try to make her his mistress.

On April 3, 1845, the family set out for the south, and Flaubert rejoiced in a feeling of new-found freedom and basked in the comfortable welcome relatives gave them in Dijon.[6] Goethe's Wilhelm Meister had learned from writing a travel diary (albeit imaginary) to observe the world about him more closely. Flaubert kept a real one, as he had before. Sometimes foolishly, frequently sententiously, at intervals perceptively, he wrote and wrote. On the opening page of his Notebook, he inscribed the Greek verb *psalo*, to indicate that he would pluck his lyre and he added "$x=x$," with the explanatory comment "epigraph." Self-consciousness could still make him ponderous.

Flaubert was returning to the classical world. The Rhone was to him the river of Hannibal and of Marius, at once ancient and barbarian, its waters yellow with the soil it carried and the sky blue above, as he and his family took the riverboat south from Lyon and the young man sat on deck reading Horace. At Nîmes the Maison Carrée again taught him the serenity of classical art, unknown to northern Gothic. In the Arena, he remembered his fig tree from the time before, but now it was leafless, dried up, and silent. He began to conjure up the roaring of the excited, clapping crowd of Roman days, but then, suddenly, he had to leave, for the family had finished its sightseeing for that day.

Love of antiquity was a part of him, and the Mediterranean again revived it, reaching to his depths as he thought of Roman keels splitting the eternally undulating waves of this ever-young sea. He sailed about one afternoon in a small craft, and as the water lapped against the sides of the boat, the realization stole over him that Cleopatra or, later, Nero had heard the same sea and the same murmuring. The ocean was more romantic and nearer the nature of modern man, but it was thereby less beautiful perhaps. The Mediterranean was at its best when it was calm: serenity suited it.

Marseilles, he had promised himself, would be a particularly apt, ironic experience, for it meant a return to Eulalie Foucaud and a love now dead five years.[7] He felt a modicum of smugness and expected her to have grown ugly; he prided himself on the ease with which he thus saved himself from disillusion. Not wholly logically, he noted also that disillusionment is itself a poetic state and not to be scorned.

The family reached Marseilles in a dulling rainstorm. As soon as he could, that very evening, he hurried down to her hotel. He could hardly find it. All was dark; the shutters were closed, the hotel abandoned. He asked a few questions, but the answers were so inconclusive that he gave up seeking her out, contenting himself with the sententious observations that his heart, too, was like an abandoned hotel now long past its moments of tumult and that one writes recollections only in order to mingle them with other recollections.

The oriental look of Genoa delighted Flaubert, making him think of Constantinople, and his journey began to look up. He was, as always, miserable at leaving, but shortly an entire day on horseback reassured him about his health. Como and the Italian Alps affected him deeply: nature began to give him voluptuous sensations. When he looked closely, he could participate in its life. The pantheistic joy he had known in Corsica and described in *November* welled up within him.

Strange bubblings were going on. The Colliers and then the possibility of seeing Eulalie had, in fact, moved him. But his surface feeling was largely (in imitation, perhaps) that of Alfred toward women. He felt distant from them and sated as are those who have been too much loved. Had he perhaps given of himself too much and brought on impotence by rejoicing in the seething emotions inside to the point where he could no longer bear to let them pour out? His sexual activity had ceased for over a year; a passing skirt now aroused not even a faint curiosity toward the unknown.[8]

The sap was, however, rising with the spring. A coquettish maid in a hotel one night started a train of lubricious thoughts.[9] He did observe a brothel he had earlier patronized at Arles, but with only a distant, ironic view. In a museum stirrings went further, and he imagined handling the soft belly of a Silenus. In a church he watched the bent necks and pure profiles of the girls, and his mind slipped back to Don Juan as he would have observed them. Soon he was really noticing the women and no longer in such detached fashion. In a later church, he imagined the delight of making love there as evening came on and the candles were lit. He turned the thought aside at once; men of his sort were meant to feel such things and to write of them but not to experience them. Art alone was sure. And safe. The Italian mistress of friends, a brunette of forty, plump but with delicate hands, did excite him; but his principal thought was that the woman of forty had not yet been introduced into literature; she could be an interesting topic.[10.]

In an Italian art gallery he came suddenly upon Canova's "Cupid and Psyche," the delicate and refined marble statue of the sensuous Italian master who had died in 1822. Letting his family go ahead at their own pace, he returned several times to contemplate the work and, the last time, he bent over and kissed the armpit of the swooning Psyche. It was the first sensual kiss that he had given in many months, and it was excusable, he urged, because it was beauty itself that he was kissing, a tribute which he was paying to genius. In burning enthusiasm he had thrown himself upon pure form—almost, he felt, without thought of what it said. He was returning cautiously toward life. Emma Bovary will have a Canova, probably a plaster reproduction, in her house at Yonville.[11] In a not unrelated mood in the church at Monza a day or so before, after viewing Charlemagne's iron crown and running an ancient Lombard comb through his hair, Flaubert was standing silently by as a priest lit the candles and the incense. The majesty of the long ages all meeting here led him to slip quietly to his knees for a moment.

Flaubert's Notebook contains, almost from the start, casual notes on paintings he saw and references to ones viewed earlier. Soon he was reacting very strongly, imagining a whole life for the sitter or responding to the erotic suggestions of a Titian "Magdalene," "embellished by her prostitution, spiced by her repentance."[12] A depiction of "Judith and Holofernes" reminded him that it was a subject he had wanted to write of. He would treat the theme later in *Salammbô*.

Switzerland was full of literary memories for him: at Coppet he meditated on Madame de Staël, wondering if her romanticism were not perhaps, like that of the painter Girodet, somewhat less than pure, too declamatory and intentional, not as people now wished it to be. He looked so intently at her portrait that two years later he could still describe it in some detail.[13] At Chillon, Byron's name carved on the wall all but effaced any memory of the prisoner he had written of. Putting his hand on his heart, Flaubert found that it was beating faster.

He had anticipated a slow, careful visit to each place of interest and had studied the history of each region. But he had two of his nervous attacks on the trip, and his father became a poor traveling companion, for Dr. Flaubert rapidly contracted an eye ailment which confined him to his room in each city and which he threw off only when the trip was nearly over. He constantly missed the presence of his older son Achille, whom he had left behind to take care of the hospital and who complained steadily in his letters about the amount of work he faced. Even the daily round in the hospital now seemed appealing to Dr. Flaubert. Moreover, Caroline, who had felt well for the first few days but who was already pregnant, soon began to be ill and to have sharp pains in the small of her back. By the time the family group had reached Genoa, life together had become impossible. Caroline and her husband agreed to go on to Naples alone and the remaining members of the party returned to France via the Simplon pass. It was better thus, Flaubert knew, for Naples in this company would have been only frustration. Alfred understood him, as Flaubert was sure he would.

The honeymoon trip displayed clearly to Flaubert his need for some inner refuge. Sometimes, when he could be alone, an exquisite calm would descend upon him and he could, even in advance, sense the joyous emotions of the next moment already coming to birth. More frequently, though, he was interrupted. A night walk with the moon shedding a grave and peaceful light on the abandoned streets had to be cut short before he had been able to ruminate over its calm. His family was all the world he had, but they were unbearable to him.

To Alfred Le Poittevin he poured out his irritation in letters. On his next trip he must be free so that he could let his eye be absorbed in what it saw, uninterrupted and undivided in its love. Involuntarily his family was aborting each new experience by tearing it from him before it was really his. He savored the bittersweet charm and melancholy of remembering the joy of his previous trip. As with the Colliers in Paris, he found the trees and waterfalls, the streets and shorefronts all the same; he alone had changed, and only working at his art could offer salvation. All he wanted now was the tranquil solitude of his room, with a big fire in winter and two fresh candles each evening.

In Paris rough and painful shocks awaited him once again, as he sought to preserve the chaste security of such distilled emotions. It was quite otherwise with Harriet Collier. Three times Flaubert called on her and, as he put it, he found the chink in his armor: eighteen months later he could still be shaken by recalling it.[14] Harriet was charming and admirably beautiful, in a Christian, almost Gothic fashion. She was direct and simple, easily moved, and passed readily from tears to laughter. She lay stretched upon her couch watching Gustave, her blue eyes on him.

One afternoon they were alone and seated on a sofa; she took his hand and passed her fingers between his. Flaubert, really very pure despite his poses, let her continue without any thought on his part till suddenly he looked up and caught her expression. At that instant her mother entered, understood, and smiled indulgently as though to her future son-in-law, her look a strange, sublime mixture of benign indulgence and superior cunning. And now Flaubert realized what had happened: Harriet had given in to a mood of uncontrollable tenderness, one of those moments, he noted, when everything in one seems liquid and dissolving and which would be delicious were it not that one is about to burst into tears.

Flaubert's reaction was blank terror at this emotion which he had provoked and to which he could not respond. He returned to his hotel overcome, reproaching himself for being alive. Apparently it was not enough to keep himself from feeling; he must also learn not to let others have feelings toward him. It was the end of his relationship with Harriet Collier.[15] She left France the following year and he did not see her again for five years. A water color of Gertrude's, however, a safer memory, he kept in his study over the decades.

During the trip Alfred's letters had urged Flaubert to visit Ludovica at once upon his return to Paris. Now that she was no longer living with her husband, she was fair prey, and her lascivious tastes were notorious. Flaubert replied that he would dine with her, but that it would go no further unless she were most insistent: intercourse had nothing further to teach him, and his desire was now universal, not particular. He did in fact see her momentarily, but the visit had no immediate sequel.[16]

Once back in his own room in Croisset, he resolutely put the past behind him and sensed instead of its dead hand rather the vague hope of a more perfumed breeze ahead. The trip had been upsetting and disappointing, but it had brought renewed contact with a world which again tempted him from a distance. He had now to find that state of relative serenity which would prove fruitful to art. He looked forward to a calm, quiet monotony in his existence and was far less bitter on his return this time than he had been in 1840.

His sentimental education was not yet complete, however. Disgusted though he was with the idea of a love affair, still there came moments of aspiration toward one. Pradier, whom he had seen in Paris, had told him that he needed a mistress. Flaubert was tempted but declined: he was sure that he would be unable to keep it within bounds. It would plunge him back into the active, physical life which his sanity required him to avoid. Fatalist that he was, he added that if it were supposed to be, it would be. Friends all about him were marrying, but this earned only his contempt as he imagined the ensuing children dressed in the idiot fashion of the day as little sailors or artillerymen and reciting La Fontaine's fables in the living room after dinner. He even paraded the foppish pet names which would be used for them.

He noticed that he seemed to have given up laughter. But just as quiet ponds do not suffer from tempests, so he wanted his heart to stagnate. If he no longer laughed, neither did he weep. He had reached, at long last, a state of equilibrium which he called maturity, and he could continue his slow, steady progress at his art in the unspectacular fashion of the good worker he longed to be. At a certain point of mental development, he observed, everything tended toward pride: it would be easier to teach geometry to an oyster than to explain an idea to three-quarters of the people he knew. At a similar point of spiritual development, everything tended toward pity. Paradoxically, at this stage, both presumptuousness and compassion disappeared, while sensitivity was more delicate and one's internal isolation was more total.[17]

His equilibrium that summer of 1845 made it one of the most fruitful periods of his life. His reading was again voluminous: Herodotus in Greek, Quintus Curtius, the plays of Voltaire, Shakespeare, Stendhal, Chinese philosophy, and the critic Saint-Marc Girardin. He also began writing once again and was learning to look about him so closely that the simplest and most natural gestures and the most banal phrases now astonished him; anything did, in fact, provided he looked at it carefully enough.

He had plans for half a dozen works he wished to write: they were, in fact, to constitute the themes of more than half of the books he would later write, and he had so many ideas that it was hard to know where to begin. The history of Genoa suggested a tale which he rapidly sketched and for which he did some reading. While in Genoa he heard of a subject which he thought would make a good opera. Observing Italian women kneeling in the churches had suggested Don Juan, whose story he would later try to elaborate. A further idea, which he put aside only many years later, began also to take shape: a Near Eastern Tale involving a father and several sons, whose various lives could be interwoven or separated so as to allow a multicolored tone.[18] But the great works were other than these.

In Genoa, Flaubert recorded that he saw the Breughel "Temptation of Saint Anthony" and that it made him think of arranging it for the theater. It was only a passing notion and would require, he felt, another sort of talent than his. Meanwhile, he would have given huge sums to own the picture. The dutiful expression of a lady and gentleman who had passed through the room while he was there delighted him. As the days went by and he moved on to Milan, he found the picture haunting him and in retrospect gradually effacing all the rest of the gallery. He wrote, from memory, [19] a close and startlingly accurate description of the painting crawling with life on every side, leering in grotesque uncontrol underneath the apparently quiet surface. While at first it had appeared only confused, gradually it became strange and then something more. He was never wholly to throw off the macabre fascination of this subject: within a year he was at work on his own *Temptation of Saint Anthony*, which he rewrote in 1856 and again around 1870; he finally published it in 1874, and it remained close to his heart till his death.

Beneath the surface of his mind still other themes were stirring. *Madame Bovary* was inherent in his interest in Don Juan, to whom she is in some ways a female counterpart; and a Madame Delamare stopped to call on his mother that summer, perhaps the lady whose son Eugene was a doctor in the little town of Ry. The sad escapades of his wife a few years later would provide the story line for *Madame Bovary*. In addition, a weird dream so bothered Flaubert that he wrote it down during the trip, some three weeks after it came to him. He saw himself walking in a forest with his mother, surrounded by monkeys, which soon became menacing. When one tried to stroke him, Flaubert shot him, only to have his mother ask why he had wounded his friend who so loved him and who so resembled him. With a feeling of anguish he had awakened, sensing a close communion with all of the animals and fraternizing with them in a tender, pantheistic communion.[20] The pantheism would tempt Saint Anthony. The animals crowding in threatening fashion about Flaubert and then being killed eventually found their place in his *Legend of Saint Julian*.

Flaubert could properly write to a disillusioned Alfred, as September came on: "Work, work, write, write as much as you can, as long as your Muse will carry you. She is the best courser, the best carriage to get one through life. Being tired of living does not bear down upon our shoulders while we are writing. To be sure, the moments of fatigue and lassitude which follow are the more terrible, but never mind. Two glasses of vinegar followed by one of wine are better than one glass of reddened water."

DEATHS (1846)

> When I had a family, I often wished to be rid of them in order to be freer, to be able to go live in China or among the savages. Now that I no longer have them, I miss them and cling to the walls where their shadows seem still to linger.
>
> Letter to Louise Colet, August 8, 1846

The summer of 1845 had seen the family happily reunited at Croisset. It seemed a good and full life; Flaubert's nervous attacks were waning, and in the autumn he had the last one for many months. At the same time, however, Dr. Flaubert developed a severe cellular inflammation which led rapidly to a deep abscess in his thigh. Eventually his son Achille performed a radical operation, hoping to arrest the course of the infection, but to no avail: on January 15, 1846, Dr. Flaubert died. The terrible cry his mother uttered as she reached for her dead husband's hand Flaubert never forgot; the experience turned her from deist to atheist.[21]

Flaubert had loved and admired his father, however different their temperaments. He now observed, over the years, that his father seemed to grow in stature in his recollection. Innumerable events brought back memory and Flaubert found himself mentally asking counsel of him or seeking his approbation. The feeling, painful at first, took on with time a gentle gravity, a sort of religious accompaniment to his daily life.[22]

Caroline had returned home to help care for her father, but

she was far along in her first pregnancy. A few days after Dr. Flaubert's death, the saddened household was the scene of a new birth, a daughter called Caroline after her mother. To Flaubert the significance of the event can hardly have been clear: he hated children and was deeply engaged in maneuvers to win his father's post at the Rouen hospital for his brother Achille. He probably paid little or no attention to his sister's condition after the birth: mothers did not rapidly leave their beds in those days. But Caroline was not making a proper recovery; shortly there was considerable alarm, which was then allayed by the end of the month. As February drew on, however, there could be no further doubt: Caroline was ill with the dread puerperal fever for which there was then no remedy. No doubt she contracted it because of the hospital contacts of her family. Flaubert watched in anguish as his sister slipped slowly from him into the grip of the inexorable malady.

The sweet, gentle companion, the only woman with whom he had always been able to share his dreams and his joys and sorrows, grew steadily worse.[23] Her husband, Hamard, could only stand helplessly by. Flaubert's mother seemed more like a weeping statue than a human. Only Caroline talked and smiled, gently patting her grieving family and finding tender, affectionate words for each. But her mind was becoming confused; she wondered why her father seemed to have deserted her. There was a strange grace about her movements as she lay in her bed, sometimes holding her baby as she nursed her and the little one cried. Poor Achille, who could no more save his sister than his father, watched silently, unable to speak.

As the end drew near, Caroline remembered her childhood and talked affectionately of Ernest Chevalier, convinced that he was in the house somewhere. Her father came more frequently into her conversation. Then the suffering became unbearable, and she could only alternate between heartrending cries and softer murmurs of pain. During the morning of March 20, a merciful death put an end to her anguish.

Flaubert had her face and hands molded in plaster to aid his friend Pradier in making a marble bust for him, though he resented the touch of the coarse workers on his sister's skin. For himself he kept a lock of her hair and a shawl she had especially prized because Harriet Collier had given it to her; her desk and table, too, were to be his. It was all that was left. But he found these, his relics, far more moving and meaningful to him over the years than were the tombs of his father and sister. Their real life lay in his memory.[24]

He kept vigil over his sister's body that night as she lay robed in her wedding gown and holding her white bouquet.[25] He remembered when she and he as children had climbed up to the window of the operating theater to watch their father dissecting cadavers. Now both father and daughter were corpses, too. Alternately Flaubert looked at her and at the book he was reading; her husband was moaning in his sleep; the priest was snoring.

It was Montaigne's *Essays* that Flaubert read, so full of suggestions of death and how to meet it. His first position is the stoic one, which urges man to make all life a preparation for death; in later skeptical passages he casts doubt on the value of any human endeavor. But the final Montaigne, the calm philosopher, gently suggests we abandon metaphysical inquiry and turn only within ourselves for the simple assurances we need.

After midnight Flaubert's mood changed, and he brought out the packet of letters, misspelled and naïve, which he had received six years earlier from Eulalie Foucaud.[26] Was it his fruitless effort to find her house a year before in Caroline's company that made him think of Eulalie now? At any rate he opened the packet and read the letters with a strange feeling of regret. Had she perhaps really loved him? At this moment he may have realized more fully how little he could afford so cavalierly to dismiss affection. At a quarter to two he had finished; he made a few notes on the outside of the package and set it aside.

As he contemplated the room and his sister, he kept telling himself that forms pass and that the idea alone remains; and he would quicken with enthusiasm over phrases in Montaigne. Then he reflected that Montaigne, too, would pass. It was freezing cold; the window was open because of the odor from the body, and from time to time he would get up to look at the stars, calm, radiant, and eternal. He realized that when they, too, paled forever, all would be over and it would be even more beautiful. Peace would have been attained.

Caroline was buried the following morning at eleven, still in her wedding gown and holding a fresh bouquet. As Flaubert took his last look at her in her long white veil, she seemed taller and more lovely than she had been in life. He leaned down to give her a final embrace and felt the lead of the coffin bend under his hand.

At the cemetery the ceremony was atrocious. The grave had been dug too narrow, and the coffin would not fit. The workmen pushed and pulled; they brought spades and levers and turned the coffin in every direction. Finally one of the gravediggers stood upon the coffin at its head to force it down into the earth. Only then did Flaubert cry out in rage and protest.

He returned alone with his mother and the baby to Croisset and its cold, empty rooms. Madame Flaubert's calm was terrifying: she busied herself trying to become a mother once again for her grandchild, whom she had sleep in her room so that she could rock and care for the child herself. Flaubert knew that the reaction must come; he dreaded it in advance and rightly so for her despair, when it came, was frightening and lasted for months.

At first Flaubert feared to have his friends about him lest their gentleness and concern break down his reserve. He had believed that, by voluntarily renouncing ordinary ambitions and vanities, by abandoning even any hope of happiness, he could have repose. He had been wrong. Man's very entrails tie him to humanity, and none, he now knew, could escape sorrow. Caroline's death had been even more horrible than his father's, as it seemed so unexpected. To watch a young woman in the full force of her beauty and her intelligence die thus seemed outrageous injustice. He almost never spoke of her again.[27] Only slowly could he come back to his calm serenity. How he longed to return to his quiet life of art and meditation as he had come to know it over the autumn.

He sought peace. The baptism of his small niece showed him that religion could not offer it to him. The priest galloped through a Latin service he did not understand; those present were not listening. The child held her head under the holy water; the tapers burned; the beadle responded "Amen." Flaubert felt that only the ancient stones of the church really took part; formerly perhaps they had understood all of this and might have retained some of it. The satiric portrait of the curate Bournisien in *Madame Bovary* was taking form in Flaubert's helpless rage.

Flaubert's health through all of this continued to be good so that, without physical ailments to contend with, he could strive to put these painful bereavements into perspective with the rest of his life. A further retreat into self seemed the only safe answer. One should seek to stay as one was, avoid marriage and children, flee the ties of affections, and offer as little hold to envious fate as possible. The younger, romantic Flaubert had chased after his dreams even while proclaiming that he could not catch them; now, frightened, he sought not even to dream. Hurt more than he could admit, he wrote that he would furl his sails and, back to the wind and chin on chest, await the worst.

Flaubert had been reading Buddhist works and was coming to a belief in an overall harmony into which he could return as to nothingness. In this, quite as much as in a monastic faith, peace could be found; in fact, Cleopatra had died as serenely as Saint Francis, he noted. His new serenity meant that he had been far more to be pitied earlier than he was at present. Now, with the dispassionate eye of the artist he sought to relive his sorrow within himself so that he might analyze it for his work. The saddest mournings, he observed, are not those for which a black ribbon may be worn.

He felt himself suddenly very aged, older than an obelisk, and he sought refuge in recreating that inner life in which he had rejoiced before. He wished to make himself inaccessible to any outside contact. As a sense of security slowly supervened, he came to imagine that the rest of his life would be lived according to the quiet train of ordinary daily living which he was now establishing, a life drenched in the habit of work. Only thus could he avoid revery, the siren whose song he feared led on and on to new desire. Tranquility alone was real, and he cautioned Du Camp against taking too seriously the love affair he was engaged in, for it would lead to dreams of felicity, a gorgeous purple garment but whose lining was in tatters and which would be swept away by the wind when one sought warmth within it. For himself he strove more than ever to evade reality in the idea, to be reabsorbed through work into nothingness.

Flaubert imagined a writer who would spend his whole life at his desk and then, in one grandiose gesture, publish his complete works. One must write for the sole pleasure of writing. He began to wonder if he would ever print a line himself. In point of fact, he was doing far more reading than writing now and hardly planning any new work that spring. Preparations for the "Near Eastern Tale" were requiring much research; and in any case to read was to forget the world. It was an opiate he needed now; later it would be an addiction. To complicate matters, his critical sense was growing rapidly and he was becoming ever more aware that what he did jot down failed to meet the exacting criteria he had established for himself in *A Sentimental Education* a year and more ago.

Reading and some writing were filling a long day, eight hours at the least, often much more, and habit was becoming his rod and his staff. If he were disturbed even for a moment, he was almost sick with nervous irritation. Frequently days would pass without his stirring even to the foot of the terrace to look out over the Seine. The future monk of letters—and the confirmed, fussy bachelor—were coming into being as he allowed the lulling effect of ingrained custom to soothe his hurt spirit. He was working hard to try to learn Greek, he was struggling to overcome the ignorance he suddenly found within himself. To be sure, more learning would impede the free flow of inspiration and passion, but he could no longer allow himself to know so little.

He read the classics, he browsed in Buddhism, he sought to drown his memories in history, above all the ancient world. He went back to Michelet's *History of Rome* and was almost drunk with it. He must have lived in an earlier age, he was sure, under Caesar or, better, under Nero. He would drift off into an imagined evening when the emperor returned to Rome in triumph at the head of his legions, perfumes burning about his chariot and captive kings walking behind. These orgies of the imagination would lead to *Salammbô*.

Flaubert lived the life of a recluse at Croisset, seeing only his aging mother and taking care of her as she, in turn, took care of him and her grandchild. In later years, when his health permitted him to go out in the evenings again, he would never return and go to bed without first tiptoeing into her room to give her his good-night kiss and hear her murmur a good-night to him in her sleep.[28] She was in no sense his intellectual companion; they never talked of art and literature; but she sacrificed her whole life to him and to her granddaughter and made possible the novels which were to come. On the other hand, she needed him so constantly because of her bereavement that her need became his tyrant.

Few people were allowed to approach Croisset uninvited. Le Poittevin would have been welcome, but he was occupied else-where. Only the discovery of a new friendship broke the monot-ony of Flaubert's long days. Louis Bouilhet now suddenly became his fast and constant friend. Their close union, never broken or even strained over nearly twenty-five years, was one of the few solid points in Flaubert's existence henceforth. Bouilhet, some five months younger than Flaubert, had sat with him in the same class-rooms year after year in school, but neither seems to have paid much attention to the other.[29] After both had graduated, their paths diverged as Flaubert left school and soon went off to Paris. In 1842 Bouilhet, who had remained in Rouen, became a medical student under Dr. Flaubert; to make enough money to live on, he gave lessons in Latin and French composition. Meanwhile, all his free time went to composing poetry. In school he had already shown some talent—he had for instance won a first prize in rheto-ric in a year when Flaubert took a second—and now it was the only part of his life in which he really delighted. During the years before Dr. Flaubert's death the two young men had some con-tacts, but not enough for either to discover how nearly identical their tastes and aims were. Early in 1846, Bouilhet abandoned the study of medicine entirely in order to spend more time writing, but he had to continue to give lessons as it was many years before he could make a living from his pen. Perhaps it was the death of Flaubert's father which brought the two men together. In Febru-ary, 1846, they were already showing each other their work, and Flaubert, away briefly in Paris, wrote to Le Poittevin to ask how a play of Bouilhet's was progressing.

From 1846 until Bouilhet's death in 1869 no single line of Flaubert's was ever prepared for publication that did not pass under the scrutiny of Monsignor, as Flaubert affectionately called him. Eventually Bouilhet moved from the role of critic to that of occasional initiator, when Flaubert's flow of thought would run dry, for Flaubert's confidence in Bouilhet's literary taste was reinforced by the deep sympathy between the two men.[30] They thought alike; they laughed alike and hated alike; in due course they even looked alike. Henceforth each wrote, first and foremost, for the other. When they were living in the same city, Paris or Rouen, they saw each other at least weekly, when they were apart, the Sunday letter to the other was a sacred duty.

In May, 1846, Flaubert began to be enough recovered from the first impact of his sister's death to wish for closeness and consolation from his friends. Du Camp came quickly from Paris, and Bouilhet joined them for frequent literary sessions. Soon Bouilhet and Flaubert were collaborating in writing a verse tragedy together. The circumstances were not conducive to writing a lofty work, and the choice fell upon a parody or satire to be entitled, "Jenner, or the Discovery of Vaccine."[31] It was their intention that no object should ever be named directly: the noble neoclassic paraphrase should stand in its stead. Preferably every object should be described metaphorically. And what metaphors! In the opening lines a severely pockmarked face is likened to a sieve. But the sieve, naturally, can be described only indirectly, so that it becomes the humble household object, pierced in a thousand places, which the matron uses in her anxious zeal when, against the unctuous sides of the foam-covered earthenware, the marrow of meat bones trembles in a boiling froth. The character of the verse was in no way superior to the level of the metaphors and the tragedy was never really carried beyond the first act. But it served its immediate purpose of distracting Flaubert, and years later he still loved to declaim passages from it.

The friendship with Bouilhet began only just in time, for Alfred Le Poittevin was about to leave Flaubert to be married and go live in Paris. To one less violent and extreme than Flaubert, such a step might not have meant the end of a friendship, but to Gustave, still quivering from recent family losses, the idea of freely founding a new family could mean only apostasy. Alfred, realizing what Gustave's view would be, had kept the plans from him: Gustave learned of them only one month before the marriage, which took place in early July. He wrote as mildly as he could, but even so the tone strained the friendship. Alfred was, Flaubert wrote to him, the victim of an illusion; he was making a mistake, an enormous one, as Flaubert now felt man always did whenever he voluntarily committed himself. Was his friend, O Great Man, not about to become a bourgeois? In all Flaubert's thoughts of art, he had always united Alfred to himself. It was this, he said, that made him suffer; but in fact he was jealous. Alfred would always find him ready and waiting if he called, he said. What he doubted was whether Alfred would be there when he needed him. For Flaubert it was like another death.[32]

Alfred's place in Flaubert's empty life was fortunately already being filled by Bouilhet and Du Camp. Gustave imagined that his life had now settled into its definitive plan, whose shape would never change. He was determined that it should not.

7

Louise Colet (1846-47)

An Interlude

Everything had settled down. . . . You came along and with
the tip of your finger you stirred it all up. The old sediment
boiled to the top again, and the lake of my heart shuddered.

Letter to Louise Colet, August 9, 1846

In February, 1846, Flaubert perforce began making trips to Paris
on business arising from his father's death. In April he was in the
capital again, despite the further shock of his sister's death. And
during the summer he seemed sufficiently well to make frequent
trips there to see Pradier about the monument which was to be
erected to his father and also the bust he wished of his sister.

On July 28, amidst Pradier's marble sculptures and plaster
casts, Flaubert first saw Louise Colet, the famous, successful, and
beautiful romantic poetess.[1] The passing of time has made her
verse today seem shoddy, but her extraordinary beauty easily concealed this from those who knew her and led them with one accord to call her The Muse. Pradier's studio had been the scene for
the meeting, a decade before, between Victor Hugo and the actress Juliette Drouet, who soon became his mistress. The sculptor
had long urged upon Flaubert that what he needed to restore his
health was a love affair. Louise Colet was in the studio daily in
July, since Pradier was working on a bust of her. He urged her to
strike up an acquaintance with the big blond fellow whom she
first saw across the room. He, too, had noticed her; but he felt too
unsure of himself to approach her. When they were introduced,
he was still too upset to try to make an impression upon her, but
he must have succeeded in spite of himself. Paris was beginning
the annual celebration of the "Three Glorious Days," which had

marked the advent of the Bourgeois Monarchy sixteen years before. There were to be fireworks that night, and it was the provincial newcomer, Flaubert, who captured the successful poetess and was her escort for the evening. As they watched the display from one of the heights about Paris, their conversation became more intimate and sentimental. Although it was to be some days before her timid lover finally conquered Louise, the pair always treated this moment as the start of their love. The courtship lasted a week. Its various phases constituted thereafter the models he used in his novels for the slow psychological elaboration of a love affair when the lover was as fainthearted as Flaubert proved to be. His heroes frequently had other reasons than his for their timidity, but his sympathy for it sprang from personal experience in this week.

Born in 1810, Louise was eleven years older than Gustave.[2] Now as always, he was seeking as much a mother as a mistress. Louise was from Aix-en-Provence, and in France southern women traditionally are believed to have a more fiery, Latin temperament; she did not belie the tradition. As a child her studies had been hasty and casual, but compared to the nullity of the education given most young ladies in her day hers was surprisingly good and explains in some measure the ease with which she could later talk with some of the most brilliant men of the age. She married a not very successful music professor and in 1835 moved to Paris. The following year she was already publishing verses and beginning to make a reputation as a poetess; soon she was receiving a literary pension from the government.

This was not enough, however, for the ambitious Louise, and she had another resource in her quite striking beauty. The powerful Victor Cousin, whose works Flaubert had read as a boy and who had acquired a considerable voice in official France, arranged to have the French Academy award her verses a prize and opened the influential periodical, the *Revue des Deux Mondes*, to her work. In return she became his mistress; her husband was discreetly cooperative.

The liaison was soon widely known. Parisian gossip whispered that Cousin was the father of her child, and the satiric journalist Alphonse Karr alluded to the tale in print. Real scandal burst full-blown when Louise, in fury, tried to knife her accuser in the back. Karr, unscathed, hung the weapon in his living-room above a malicious card: "The Gift of Madame Colet, offered while my back was turned." Cousin is said to have muttered wryly a neatly turned Latin pun on his mistress: *Maxime mulier sum, sed virago.* The first half is a flattering compliment, "I am tremendously a woman"; but the latter half hesitates between "virago" and *vir ago,* "like a man I act." The relationship ultimately proved satisfactory to neither, and Cousin suffered at not being able to see his daughter as frequently as he wished.[3]

In the half-dozen years preceding her meeting with Gustave in 1846, Louise was climbing to the height of her power. The king himself sent her a medal for her verses; the Minister of Education, perhaps urged on by Cousin, was supporting her requests for money; she was received even in the elite circle about Madame Récamier, the aging inspiration of Chateaubriand. Cousin, tired of her violences, was now no more than a tender friend, undemanding but useful, and Louise received much of literary and artistic Paris in her salon. Her complaisant husband offered no difficulties and eventually preferred to drop out of sight.

Louise was a stunning creature in 1846. The minor poet Banville, who knew her then, has described her high forehead and eyes more alert than a morning churchbell, her small nose slightly turned up at the tip—the sort of nose that changes the course of empire—pretty lips with a charming bow, pink cheeks and masses of blond hair falling in a profusion of curls down over a bust whose striking, superb, white riches—so Banville lyrically proclaimed—sang exultantly, wildly, the glory of a Rubens drunk with pink. The poet phrased in painter's terms Louise's most noticeable traits, her hair and her very full bosom. The latter, as with every woman Flaubert loved, suggested the mother; but her blue eyes, which Banville skipped too lightly over, deserved comment, too. Large and slightly prominent, they stared boldly at you with a faint suggestion of impudence, seconded by the hint of an impertinent smile lurking at the corners of her provocative mouth. Louise made any man's breath come faster; she knew it, and it delighted her. Maxime Du Camp, who did not like her, reported that she used to ask, "Have you heard they have found the arms of the Venus de Milo?" When her listener asked "Where?" she would reply "In the sleeves of my dress."

Gustave's powerful stature, good looks, and youth appealed to Louise. His long-enforced chastity, his reviving health, and the calm which he had recovered after the deaths of his father and sister all prepared him to notice The Muse. On July 28 he had already escorted her once to watch the fireworks. The following evening he was again with her, and now the exploding rockets seemed to provide what Gustave would later call the flaming inauguration of their love. That night he timidly found courage to kiss her hands when they parted. The evening of July 30 was the last of the fireworks celebrations, and again the two were together, this time in an open carriage with Louise's daughter, little Henriette, who went with them to enjoy the displays. As the carriage swung from the Place de la Concorde into the long rise of the Champs Elysées, the two looked deeply into each other's eyes; neither spoke but Louise's gaze seemed somber yet tender. Her eyes gleamed in the dark. With the gentle movement of the springs to lull them, their hands met: Henriette had fallen asleep. Gustave, feeling an ecstasy he had never known, drank in the long, slow waves of love that seemed to be coming from Louise's glance.

This was exactly what Flaubert had promised himself never to do again: he was allowing himself to base his happiness on another person. Frightened and yet invincibly attracted, he sought desperately some way to hold himself back. He knew that Louise would be at the studio the following day and that she would be expecting him. Summoning all his strength, he stayed away.

It was a heroic gesture and completely in vain. Louise was hurt and annoyed and reproached him for his conduct when, as was inevitable, he arranged to meet her after another twenty-four hours. His return was, of course, a capitulation, and both took it that way. To rediscover the earlier mood, they again went out driving; this time Henriette remained at home. There were flashes of lightning and the lanterns in the Bois de Boulogne cast a strange color upon the trunks of the trees. They were alone and happy; that evening it was her forehead he kissed as they bade each other good night.

How could he resist? Each day's concessions were so slight in comparison to the temptation before him. It was obvious that she loved him; he was flattered and attracted. Moreover, in the easy confusion made by all who knew her, he thought her a great poetess and an impressive mind. Was she then, perhaps, the exception among women, the only sort of mistress it would be possible for him to have? To ask the question was to answer it, and the even tenor of his days was now broken.

The next day was Sunday, and Louise was having dinner guests that evening. Flaubert joined the group and waited impatiently for the others to leave. At last they did, and he and she were alone together. Timidity again overcame the seemingly brash giant, who finally had to agree with himself that, when the oil in a particular lamp ran out, he would ask Louise to become his mistress. Poor man, when the oil did run out, they did have their first kisses and then, to his chagrin, too taut and overtired by the three previous days, he was humiliatingly unable to satisfy her. Only her gentleness and understanding came to his rescue.

Gustave felt infinite incredulity after Louise had given herself to him. A year or so later he put it into the scenario of a play he prepared: the hero, serious, tender, timid—and hence given to mockery—loves a coquettish widow who has had an unhappy first marriage.[4] At their first kiss, he trembles like a thief. She has sworn to make him fall in love with her and has succeeded. But in the end she marries him, and he stands dumbfounded, unable to believe that so much happiness could come to him.

Louise was the first passion of Gustave's mature life: neither the affair with Eulalie nor his deep affection for Harriet Collier had been like this. He was grateful to Louise, and he said so repeatedly. Monday he gave her a bracelet as a remembrance of their first night. They spent the day together; in his hotel room he read her some of his writings and, sitting on his bed, Louise recited one of her poems to him. That evening Pradier had dinner with them at Louise's. The couple enjoyed all the little games of younger lovers, allowing their feet to touch as they turned to talk and sharing all the secret gestures which give such charm to beginning love. Surprised and entranced, he spent the evening in her boudoir watching her face, pale and trembling under his kisses.

Already the artist was detaching himself to become the observer. The next day, Tuesday, around noon a weeping Louise saw him off on the train for Rouen, where normal, daily life, and with it his mother, awaited him. She, too, was weeping. He wondered if it might be an omen, but he resolutely put such thoughts aside.

Louise had given him a sachet, her handkerchief, a lock of hair, and a pair of bedroom slippers. He set aside his black-bordered mourning stationery, for everything about the new love was to sing of joy and not of death. It seemed impossible that the grass should be of the same green, the trees of the same size, the water flowing as before. The sound of her voice, violent yet gentle, accompanied him; he could imagine her lips moving, full of grace and appeal, irresistible, provocative. All that he had so sedulously repressed during the long months now flooded over him: he wanted her there to bite.

Work was impossible, but he did not care. How had he thought he did not need this sort of life? At every moment he envisioned her, especially as she had been when he first saw her in Pradier's studio, her ringlets gently moving over her white shoulders. He no longer wished to worry about the future or anything else. He would let himself drift with the winds of this new passion; shoals and reefs could be considered when they appeared.

Between Croisset and Paris there now began a tremendous correspondence. Flaubert told his mistress of his adolescent infatuation for Elisa. Reminiscing as he wrote, he suggested to her that some day a child would fall in love with her. He would find her beautiful, as the child who had been Gustave had found Elisa. He would be timid, gentle, and trembling, yet he would keep searching her out. Gustave urged her to be kind to him and to let him take her hand: it would make him drunk with happiness. She should lose her handkerchief so that he might find it; he would drift off to sleep with it, his eyes wet with tears.

Then Flaubert recounted to Louise his long period away from all women, which she alone had been able to break. He acknowledged his deeply rooted timidity and confessed the ironic view he had of himself whenever he tried to say to women the sorts of things they wish to hear and which he wished to say. He explained his need to keep his intimate life guarded from all outer contact. But all of this was only to declare his love for her: she had come to awaken in him all this side of his nature, which had been slumbering. And he blessed her for it.

Then her first letter came, sad and offering to try to forget Gustave if he preferred it that way. She seemed sublime in her sacrifice. He began to read her poems; they moved him deeply, and some seemed so fully to express his own thoughts that it was as though he had written them himself. Shortly, when Du Camp came up from Paris for a visit, he brought Louise's engraved portrait. Flaubert could congratulate himself on his extraordinary good fortune: his mistress was stunningly beautiful and a unique woman. His mother, who was supposed to know nothing of what was going on, said the sitter must be pretty, animated, open, even good.

There were suggestions of trouble almost at once. Louise's first letter already contained reproaches and harsh replies to things he had said, but Gustave could blame himself for these, while wondering that she should so easily turn to reprisals. Then there was the extraordinary suggestion from one so intelligent as Louise that he should teach her Latin by letter. More important, although Louise had so attracted him that he had broken his reserve, he had not for all that abandoned his fundamental fear of any attachment.

Before they had been apart a week, Gustave was already writing letters whose tone forced Louise either into a defensive position or, worse, into counter attacking, a role which her imperious character and long success made only too natural. Where she looked for the tender words and blinded idealism of a new lover, Flaubert wrote to her that he was broken, bewildered, with emptiness in his heart. She had made his work impossible and he told her he wished they had never met. To be sure, he hastily explained that he meant this in large measure for her sake: she was suffering and would suffer more. But she would have noticed that it was his suffering and not hers which had first led him to the notion. When he added that it would have been far better to stop with the first ride in the carriage, the one with Henriette along which closed with his kissing her hands, and when he also said that he had realized this at the time, it made her furious.

Relentlessly, Gustave drove his mistress into an impossible position for a woman. He would make her unhappy, despite himself, he said. He was not constituted so that he could be happy, he wrote, when she would have preferred to hear how happy she had made him. He had intended to live wholly apart from women and have only men for friends. But Louise was a poetess, thought Gustave, a creator of ideas and of beauty; her mind and her spirit, then, must be strong, firm, and virile. She had a stunning woman's body, and Flaubert rejoiced in this, but he wanted all the rest of her to be a man. She could thus be a friend like Du Camp with her mind, and a mistress with her body. He wrote to her that she was too superior a person for him to lie to her about their love. When they were together, he had refused to say he would love her forever, and he now steadfastly refused to say it in his letters. Louise was woman enough and foolish and vain enough to prod him. He replied, significantly, that he had addressed himself to her virile intelligence and had thought she would understand him without mixing her heart into it. Alas, he said, he should not have been so honest: he had told her what he was really like, and now she was not grateful for his frankness. Women insist on being deceived, he complained; they force men into it and resent it bitterly if men resist.

The difficulty was that, in love, Flaubert really wanted a man. Over and over the note recurs: he was addressing himself to the man in her. Like George Sand, Mme de Sévigné or Mme de Staël, Louise was, he hoped, a woman who was half-man. These women, he once noted, even shared a physical type: a bit plump but with a virile waist, from the eyes up they were men. Femininity began below.[5] There is a sense in which any woman is flattered to be told that she has virile qualities, but the traits must be selected with great tact and, while she may be praised for having them, she will never consent to be upbraided for lacking them.

Gustave now portrayed himself much as he had his hero in *November*. He was, he told his mistress, old and contradictory in spirit. Desiccating analysis had driven him to doubt of everything. He assured her that he would have liked to come to Paris, but he asserted without adequate explanation that it was impossible. Had he been able, he said, to live there and see her daily, then he could have let himself go; but separated they must be, and the prospect was hideous. He was torn in two: he could not bring himself to leave her, and yet he wrote to urge her to break things off while they still had time. He enjoyed writing to her, but the fact that she wanted a letter a day was enough to make it almost impossible for him to write at all. Then he said she should live for art and not for him: the dreadful truth had slipped out.

Louise wanted desperately to see her lover again. Her senses demanded it and instinctively she knew that her physical presence was the only weapon with which she could fight against the incomprehensible situation into which she was rapidly being thrust. Like anyone in love, she began immediately to write of the next time they would be together. Flaubert's reply was categoric: it could not be. He could not come to Paris, he was not free, his mother needed him: he wished he lived where no one loved him. Relenting a bit, however, he suggested that within a few weeks a convenient excuse would present itself and he could come to Paris; it would be before the month was out and they would have all of a full day together. To Gustave it represented a triumph of clever planning; to Louise it was a niggardly and paltry affair made little better by the promise that there would be one day in September as well. Before the appointed day in August had had time to arrive, however, Flaubert was rendered hideous by an attack of boils as was his wont in the presence of frustration or tension. Even in this pre-Freudian age it was not unknown that such maladies had a nervous or psychological origin, and Louise may have been puzzled. Moreover, in noting his joyous anticipation, Flaubert was coupling it with the regret they would feel over the ensuing separation.

On August 19, some two weeks since he had last seen Louise, Gustave came to Paris. In the evening they sentimentally went for another ride in the Bois de Boulogne; Louise came to his hotel room; there was peace between them—so much so, indeed, that Flaubert later told his mistress someone should really write the history of a bed, a project realized only nearly a half-century later by his disciple Maupassant. But then it came time to separate. Reflecting on the whole visit, Gustave wrote to Louise of his amazement: never before had he ever made a trip for any woman!

He wrote of his returning serenity as he resumed the deliberate regularity of his days. At intervals they would meet again, briefly, he said. Anything else would naturally be an interruption to his work and to hers. As a poetess she would understand; in fact, at the start, he assumed that she, too, would wish it thus. But when he asked what was more important than art, Louise replied unhesitatingly that love was, and she asked in turn whether true love could possibly be so tranquil, so resigned, and so exempt from all desire as his was. It seemed absurd to her that, if he were really in love, he could become impetuous only on certain days of the year when his work permitted it.[6]

Flaubert continued to make a virtue of refusing to varnish the truth for his mistress. Within a week he was already objecting to her letters, which were filled with the easy chit chat of Parisian small talk. From the very first she had been writing to him of emotional patriotism, the noble flow of generosity, the splendor of courage, all of which she found fully exemplified in the daily newspaper. These emotions she portrayed with a verbose and abundant facility, but poetry to her would never be more than a pale copy of what she felt in her lover's arms. Her approach to writing—spontaneous, emotional, and personal—stood at the opposite pole from his; hence he was driven to write to her paragraphs of exposition, cajolery, and command. She, on the other hand, had always to oppose his views of the primacy of art; for, by definition, this gave her second place. She vented her irritation by complaining of his harshness and doubting the sincerity of his sadness. To Gustave this was inexplicable; in a tone of injured innocence (which he honestly felt) he asked if she were expressly seeking to be bitter.

It was against his better judgment that Flaubert had given in to the folly of imagining that love provided happiness. But now he had aroused Louise's temper. Moreover, with a carelessness which seemed unbelievable to him, the last time they had been together he had in some way erred, and now they could not be sure she was not pregnant.[7] Louise rejoiced in the idea and innocently told her lover so. His reply must have cut to the heart of her womanhood. She was at peace, he wrote, in the sublime egoism of her love, over the possibility of a child to be born. He asked her to confess to wanting it as a sort of fatal bond which would rivet their destinies together. He called it a tribute to her power over him that he was not wild with fury.

Flaubert was in terror for his own future happiness. That Louise might be frightened for her own safety as much as she was happy for the two of them, or that she might even feel a woman's pride in conceiving and wish reassurance and communion from her lover, seems not to have occurred to him. He saw only that he, who had foresworn all attachments to others, had now perhaps become a father. He would not complain, he assured her, if it did happen; he would love the child; he would even raise it if Louise were to die. But it was all terrifying. He would willingly kill himself at once if it would do any good. It was all his fault. He would never again be guilty of such idiocy. And then, when he had received Louise's wild letter of reply, he insisted—and he surely thought he had always meant it—that his regret for the child to come had been solely for her sake. Flaubert's niece, in publishing these letters many decades later, tactfully suppressed the passages necessary to a full understanding of his actions.

Nor was this the only problem Louise had to face: there was also Flaubert's mother. His life, he wrote to Louise, was riveted (the same word!) to his mother's, and it would be so long as she lived. What his life might be when, later, he would be free to be driven hither and thither like a rootless plant, he did not know; for now, he must remain with her. When a servant wakened him by bringing in a letter of Louise's, it was, he wrote, like one of those beloved kisses with which mothers waken their children, a morning caress whose benediction lasts throughout the day. It must have infuriated Louise thus to have her affection compared to his mother's, for she early suspected that her greatest rival was Madame Flaubert.

Gustave lived in mortal fear that his mother might learn of his love affair. She cannot, in fact, not have known of it: there were the constant letters, if nothing else. But he and she pretended she did not know anything, and Flaubert refused even to discuss having Louise come to Croisset. When pushed, he admitted this was because his mother would be jealous of her, an emotion he said his mistress would understand when her own daughter was eighteen.

Finally exasperated by Gustave's excuses, Louise taunted him that "they keep as close watch over you there as though you were a marriageable daughter!" Imperturbable because he had to be, Flaubert changed the line of discussion and spoke, truthfully, of the constant pall of sorrow by means of which his mother held him.

Everything about the house, Gustave wrote his mistress, was sad and somber. He knew that she, too, had difficulties, and he sympathized with them, he assured her. Beside him, though, he saw another sorrowing woman, but who never complained, who even smiled. Louise's pain, however great, set against this was a pinprick compared to a burn. He was caught, he pleaded, between his love for her and his compassion for his mother. It was all unconscious, but he had deftly managed to extricate himself and to put both women in the wrong.

Flaubert was acting from compulsion. With one part of himself he longed to love as Louise did, but he could not, for his love had to fit within the restrictions of the other parts of his personality. He wrote to her that, with any other but a mistress, he had succeeded by separating his internal from his external life; from the former he barred all but Du Camp and Bouilhet. With a mistress, could it not be much the same? As bodies, the two would share an external life, rich and voluptuous; but then, still sharing, they would move as it were from one water tight compartment to another and would transfer their communion from the sexual to the spiritual sphere of literature.

Slowly Gustave sought to educate Louise to his vision of what love might be. First, she must understand that the body and the spirit were separate. Even if he were sleeping with another woman or regularly frequenting prostitutes, he assured her, it would have no effect upon his love for her. How odd it was, he averred, that women, who place so much emphasis on things spiritual, should be so obsessed with the body. The next step was to persuade her to accept the supremacy of art over life and, therefore, over love. What they should look forward to, he urged, was writing to each other, thinking of each other, but above all working. Louise should undertake some great poem into which she would pour all that she was learning from their love. It was rich and vibrant today, but could either be sure he would not some day be unable even to remember the other's face? Art alone was eternal. And so, as the supreme compliment to her mind and soul, he asked her about her poetry and what she was reading and thinking; and he wrote of his own work. But it was to no avail. She was hurt and bewildered; there were even the marks of tears on her letters.

Louise allowed her irritation to show in a succession of letters in early September charging him with cold heartlessness. Since in his own mind his sole effort was to raise her to the exhilarating heights of art toward which he was himself striving, her complaints bewildered him. He replied with becoming patience, explicitly accepting her reproaches and her claim that she was better than he. His position seemed unassailable to him, and must often have seemed exasperatingly so to Louise.

September, Flaubert had promised, would see another meeting, but it was proving more difficult to arrange than he had at first thought. After an elaborate series of lies to his mother, he wrote proudly to Louise that they could have a few hours together if she would come to Mantes, half-way between Paris and Rouen, on the ninth. Louise was heartsick and protested violently at so short a visit. But she came; and never had they been so at one. At the station the attendant was kindly and understanding.[8] The Grand Cerf—the old hotel across the street from the present building—was charming. In the best romantic fashion they went boating, but were soaked by a sudden downpour. Even lovemaking seemed to have new depths. Flaubert, who knew he should have left, yielded to Louise's prayer that he stay the night with her. Next morning again, a despairing Louise begged him to remain. But Gustave pleaded an anguished mother, and Louise had to accept the martyr's role: let his mother never have to blame their love for having made her unhappy. If his mother had all his life and she only one day, at least hers was his tenderest and most perfect one. At the station she wanted her lover to leap the barrier and come steal a last kiss, but embarrassment overwhelmed him and he contented himself with waving her off.

Meanwhile Madame Flaubert had been deeply anxious. Gustave had had no attacks for nearly two years, but a nervous mother knew her hold on her son and never let him forget the possibility of a recurrence. At eleven in the evening she had gone to the station to see what could have happened; she spent a sleepless night and was on the platform to meet the train which brought him to Rouen. Somehow, while telling her son all of this, she managed to give him the impression that she was in no way complaining. Gustave wrote of her with admiration to Louise. A woman too, she no doubt understood the maneuver.

The reunion at Mantes gave the lovers new hope. Louise had worn a sprig of greenery in her hat; she gave it to Gustave, and he kept it as a memento and an augury.[9] He inferred that now it would be easier to be apart for long periods without danger to their relationship; Louise inferred the opposite; and each in his own way was right. Gustave, however, insisted on his view; but it cannot have been easy, and as more time passed, Louise, thoroughly frightened, began to consider abortion rather than bearing a child to this man who was so anxious not to have one.

Inexorably the cleavage between the two lovers reappeared. The separations were frustrating, Gustave agreed; but in any other way they would soon tire of each other, he suggested, not very gallantly. But she kept up her constant complaints at not seeing him. Then at last Gustave was freed of his worries: she was not pregnant. Maxime Du Camp, who had by now met her, congratulated Gustave. It would have been, he pointed out, an unbearable burden to both of them for the rest of their lives, and with no compensations.[10] Flaubert agreed.

Bickering and pained reproaches could now flow unrestrained, and the two drifted steadily apart as autumn moved into winter. At Christmas he confessed to her that he was thoroughly tired of the idea of great passions and exalted sentiments. Love, he now clearly saw, was something other than the romantics had conceived it to be. It was something independent even of the person who inspired it: neither outrage nor ten years of separation could touch it. A baffled Louise wrote in the margin: "What can one reply to this?" He now began to cast about for ways to end the liaison, a problem he would face with Rodolphe and Emma in *Madame Bovary*. Fate seemed the only safe culprit to blame and so, having asked rhetorically whose fault it was, he replied in a letter to Louise that she should blame no one, or God, or life itself. Angered, he also noted that she had needed either a child or a hypocrite as a lover, and that he was neither.

In January Du Camp, to whom Flaubert had written frankly, most unwisely showed the letter to Louise. Furious and hurt, Louise wrote Gustave directly and compared her love for him to that which his mother bore him. The unbridled violence of his answer must have frightened her and prepared her for the break.[11] Louise had asked if he mocked his mother's love for him as he did hers. In a growing paroxysm of fury Flaubert raged that you could not make fun of those things which were driving you out of your mind, as was his mother's affection. He wrote of his annoyance at the way she tied him down; and then suddenly the flood gates opened and out poured what had almost always lain barely concealed beneath the surface. As he had once before, in *November*, so again here his blind hatred for the moment of his conception erupted. Those who had given him birth and who now, by their presence and their love, forced him to continue to live, he cursed. His conception, he threw at Louise, had been love, too, like what she was so constantly speaking of. And a pretty business, at that! For their own private satisfaction and surely not for his, they had created him one night, while each told the other of his love. He prayed that the monstrous wretchedness, the colossal, gluttonous, devouring misery which gnaws at every child might be, for his father, so great a source of remorse that he, too, would regret having lived. For some weeks thereafter there was silence.

Flaubert would not have sent his letter to Louise had he understood how monstrous it was. He had written it in pain and in anguish, and he had sent it because it was honest. Louise refused all further contact for the moment, and Gustave only hesitatingly resumed the relationship in mid-February when he was again in Paris.

He reached the city on a Wednesday.[12] That day and much of the next he was busy with details concerning Pradier's statues of his family. When he was free—after all, she had broken with him—he went to see her, late on Thursday. With a certain inconsequence which any lover will recognize, Louise was annoyed and showed it. On Friday they met again, but by now she knew that Flaubert was seeing another woman. With what he would have termed its habitual irony, fate was at work; Louise Colet, in caricature, would be one of the principal models for Emma Bovary. Now, as her hold on Flaubert was weakening, it was to Louise Pradier, to "Ludovica," that he seemed to be turning: and she is the other great model for Emma. Louise Colet, furious, made a scene in Du Camp's apartment. An impenitent Gustave slipped away as quickly as he could, promising to see her again on the morrow. Saturday, however, Louise, still outraged, was so foolish as to vent her annoyance in a letter delivered to Gustave's hotel and written in the third person: it was Emma commenting on Emma. Twice during the day Louise, now full of regrets, had herself driven to his hotel to ask his forgiveness; twice he refused to see her. In the evening, furious himself at last, he departed for Croisset.

On March 7, nearly three weeks later, he wrote to his erstwhile mistress, now that he was calmer and more able to find his words. Louise wrote across the top of it in her spidery hand "last letter," before she filed it away with the others. Gently, Gustave confessed that he understood why she no longer considered him as her lover; but she was wrong not to understand that he was still her friend. The meetings in Paris had driven him to fury: how could Louise have misunderstood about Ludovica, for whom he felt only a vague friendship and with whom he enjoyed only a rather amusing familiarity? Did Louise not understand that actually he had to keep Ludovica at a distance so as to miss nothing and thus be able to analyze her? Had he, as Louise put it, "pressed her in his arms," he would no longer have been able to judge her. To Louise, whom he reminded of her role as writer, he added prophetically: "This woman seems to me to be the very type and model of woman with all her instincts, an orchestra of female sentiments."

Then he turned to Louise herself and, from the bottom of his heart, offered her his gentle benediction. He knew that she would have done anything for him, that she still would, he wrote; he realized that her love would have merited an angel, and it broke his heart that he had not been able to respond. But was it his fault? Was it his fault? In vain he had fought against the fatality of his nature, but to no avail. Her taste for the petty and the attenuating sentimentality in which she drowned everything fatally opposed his own heroic enthusiasm for bygone ages. She had never understood his concept of love. And then he closed with shorter sentences, a return to the serenity he longed for: "You ask that our memories at least mean something to me. So, as on the first evening, I give you a chaste kiss on the forehead. Adieu, imagine that I have left for a long trip. Adieu again. May you meet some one more worthy of you. To give him to you I would go seek him out at the ends of the earth. May you be happy." There was no signature.

Gustave and Louise did not see each other again for many months, and the few letters they did exchange only covered again the now familiar grounds for their disagreement. Six months later Louise would renew the affair, this time on Gustave's terms, but for the nonce it appeared to have ended. Flaubert could now honestly write to old friends that he was leading a monotonously regular life, just as he had before. Ten years from then, he noted proudly and sadly, they could return to find him as before at the same writing table in the same posture, leaning over the same books or toasting himself in his armchair before his fire, smoking his pipe, as always. Louise had been an interlude; it was now over.

8

Brittany (1847-48)

THE HIKING TRIP (1847)

Dear Old Friend, It was very moving to think once again
about our good trip through Brittany. Yes, I agree, it isn't
likely we'll ever make another like it. You can't do that sort
of thing twice . . . and still, what a beautiful succession of
pictures in my memory just now: dust in the air, curves in
the road, hills to climb in the hot sun, or just the two of us
sitting by the edge of the ditch!

Letter to Maxime Du Camp, May, 1848

THE Louise Colet affair comfortably behind him, Flaubert was
readying himself for a hiking trip through Brittany with Du
Camp.[1] It fell at a favorable moment in his development as
thinker, as writer, and as man, so that it crystallized several years
of preparation and launched his first attempt at *The Temptation
of Saint Anthony*. A Shakespeare, he felt, could safely ignore
questions of form and impassivity, but a lesser man could not.
Only through these could he hope to reach beauty and truth (he
used the beautiful and the idea interchangeably now). A Byron
had only to portray his pain to be a poet, but a Shakespeare was
so universal that he made his reader feel greater and more intelligent for having read him. And a Flaubert? Perhaps all he could
strive for was to avoid errors, to understand the negative aspects,
that is, to be impassive and impersonal. It was discouraging, but at
least it was better than being an unfeeling bourgeois: how did
these people who did not spend their days writing ever manage to
make them pass?

His melancholy took on a new cast. The serious and the
absurd, heretofore differentiated as in Smarh and Yuk, seemed
now to fuse: pathos invaded all gaiety, and irony all seriousness.

He was drawn to Callot's engraving after Breughel's *Temptation of Saint Anthony* for its sadly grotesque quality; it was both bitter and facetious, like his own nature. It was only a step to the decision to write the story himself. The trip through Brittany led him to take that step.

On April 29, 1847, Flaubert left Croisset to begin the three-month walking trip with Maxime Du Camp. On April 30 he was in Paris. As Louise Colet refused to see him, he spent the time with friends and, on the first of May, set out on the trip he and Du Camp had long been anticipating.

For the sedentary recluse Flaubert, fantasies of travel were a natural release. The previous autumn he and Maxime had spent three days discussing a vast Asiatic trip to last six years and cost some four million francs (Flaubert's annual income was some six or seven thousand); they had established the itinerary and planned where they would buy horses, what the wages would be for armed escorts in dangerous terrain, even their purchases of guns and clothes. Gustave was wild with excitement, Maxime had a fever, and Louise was furious that her lover had not spent the time with her.[2]

The Breton tour was a lesser but more practicable substitute for the Asiatic trip. It was to be made on foot for the most part, and Madame Flaubert, who did not wish Gustave that long out of her sight, was to join them at Brest and do some of the trip by carriage. By February all details were in order, and each had marked out blocks of studying for himself, for this was to be no casual, vulgar, bourgeois outing like the honeymoon journey to Italy. They would go first to the Touraine and its chateaus and then hike around the whole periphery of the Breton peninsula to Mont-Saint-Michel and on to Trouville before returning to Rouen. It was to be three months of freedom and independence.

Traveling, when it was done properly, opened for Flaubert a new life. Thirty years later his enthusiasm was undiminished, and he still reveled in the thought of how easily one breathed in foreign parts and how one admired and loved everything.[3] The short Breton trip, moreover, did not mean abandoning the nook by his fireplace for long enough to allow homesickness to develop. Hence, proud of their vagabond appearance, the two young men set off. It was the moment Maxime would always recall as their best together. Flaubert felt released from himself for the first time since the onset of his epilepsy, because so many of the frustrations which made him unhappy at Croisset were no longer present and he was thus free to turn outward and observe people, buildings, nature, or whatever else was before him. His natural exuberance, too, began to return. As his imagination filled with exciting new sights and scenes, the historical past, the insistent present, the problems of all men, there was no longer time for obsessive private problems. He was delighted.

In Brittany the romantic past was rapidly being eroded by a voracious, positivist present, which, Flaubert wrote, had the past polish its boots and did not even thank it. He and Maxime avoided such modern miracles as model penal colonies. When they were forced to observe progress, they sharpened their wits upon it: a semaphore telegraph they described as sending through the pure air where bells ring and birds fly the news that stocks were falling or the queen of England had given birth to still another child. Brittany, like Paris and Rouen earlier, seemed to confirm the comfortable romantic clichés which had surrounded Flaubert's youth. A tawdry, bourgeois civilization was invading and destroying the integrity of Breton life and making it, here as everywhere, a crime to follow one's instinct.

Chateaubriand, a Breton himself, had written a romantic epic, *The Martyrs*, situated in part in Brittany and portraying the druidesses. Flaubert, who knew passages from it by heart, tried his hand at the theme. At night, he wrote,* when the moon was rolling through the clouds over the great Celtic site at Carnac and the sea was lowing on the sand, the druidesses wandered amongst these stones holding their golden sickles and wearing their crowns of vervain and their trailing white robes reddened with the blood of men. Like long shadows pale beneath the pallor of the moon, they walked without touching the ground, their hair awry.

---

*"La nuit, quand la lune roulait dans les nuages et que la mer mugissait sur le sable, les druidesses errantes parmi ces pierres ... devaient être belles ... avec leur faucille d'or, leur couronne de verveine et leur traînante robe blanche rougie du sang des hommes. Longues comme des ombres, elles marchaient sans toucher terre, les cheveux épars, pâles sous la pâleur de la lune" (*PLC*, p. 103).

At Saint-Malo, Flaubert and Du Camp visited the yet unoccupied tomb of Chateaubriand, set upon a little island in the har-
bor and awaiting the old man's death. The two young men went
there one evening as the tide was low and the sun setting. The
water was still flowing rapidly down the sands, and the dripping
seaweed spread about like a woman's hair streaming over an ancient tomb. Flaubert lengthened his periods in the rolling style of
Chateaubriand to describe it:* the spiritual father of all the
French romantics would one day sleep here, his head turned toward the sea; in this sepulcher built on a reef his immortality
would be as his life, far from the rest of men and surrounded by
the storms. The waves, with the ages, Flaubert wrote, will murmur for long around this great memory; in tempests they will
bound up to his feet, or on summer mornings when the white sails
are spread and the lark arrives from beyond the seas, the long,
gentle waves will bring him the melancholy voluptuousness of
distant horizons and the caress of wide-ranging breezes. As the
waves from the shore of his birthplace go on endlessly swinging
back and forth between his cradle and his tomb, the heart of
René, now cold, will be scattered into nothingness, to the endless
rhythm of this eternal music.

A few days later at Combourg, Chateaubriand's boyhood
home, late at night Flaubert rose, sleepless, to muse on him. Rereading *René* the evening before as the shadows began to fall on
the pages, the bittersweet sentences had filtered into his heart melting it deliciously into Chateaubriand's strange, gentle melancholy.
Written works like these were what posterity would remember of
him and not the futile occupations of foreign affairs and domestic

---

*"Il dormira là-dessous, la tête tournée vers la mer; dans ce sépulcre bâti
sur un écueil, son immortalité sera comme fut sa vie, déserte des autres et
tout entourée d'orages. Les vagues avec les siècles murmureront longtemps
autour de ce grand souvenir; dans les tempêtes elles bondiront jusqu'à ses
pieds, ou les matins d'été, quand les voiles blanches se déploient et que
l'hirondelle arrive d'au-delà des mers, longues et douces, elles lui apporteront
la volupté mélancolique des horizons et la caresse des larges brises. Et les
jours ainsi s'écoulant, pendant que les flots de la grève natale iront se balan-
çant toujours entre son berceau et son tombeau, le coeur de René devenu
froid, lentement, s'éparpillera dans le néant, au rythme sans fin de cette
musique éternelle" (*PLC*, p. 295).

politics which had filled so many of his days. It was a mistake Flaubert's generation was determined not to make.

The way home to Rouen led through Trouville; the two travelers arrived very late at night. Five years before, in 1842, a healthier, more ebullient Flaubert had also arrived there on foot and at the same hour: he remembered it sadly, for that time he had met the Colliers, fallen in love with Harriet, and almost married; now he could find only memories and would take away only a deep distaste. As the two hiked along through the evening, Flaubert, without actually recognizing the places, sensed that he was approaching Trouville and the memories began to flow over him. The moon rose above the ocean; the lighthouse at Le Havre beckoned. The long shadows of the two men stretched away beside them on the beach and the phosphorescent water sparkled. They fell silent and let the somber night take hold of them; it was almost frightening. At two o'clock only a marsh separated them from Trouville, and shortly they were there! But in the old inn of his childhood the proprietors had completely forgotten him; he had to give his name just as he had imagined it in *November*. He began to wonder if one could even count on recognizing oneself.

In the morning, wandering about, Flaubert rediscovered some of the sights and sounds he had known. The trees were the same; the pillars of the church were as they had formerly been; but for the most part Trouville had changed over these years, and what he had clung to in his memory was no longer there. The soil, the houses, even the pavement had altered. At the neighboring village of Toucques, he did recognize the village priest, and they lunched together. Flaubert ate and drank enough to be ready to fall under the table, but the good priest was still undaunted when the champagne was served. Poor Flaubert had to refuse, only to have the priest mock young Parisians like Flaubert who swilled champagne at their midnight suppers! When they came to the provinces, they tried to pretend to be such delicate people. Flaubert was enchanted at the picture the priest had of his orgies. How little the priest knew of the chaste and limited life he now lived.

The trip, begun so joyously, was ending sadly; the last page of the Notebook Flaubert carried with him he covered with melancholy adages.[4] Happiness, he wrote, is a dinner of which you never eat more than the first course. This is why wise people leap upon it so avidly. When you reach a certain age, he noted too, the arms of a chair tempt you more than those of a woman. They may embrace you less strongly, but they are more capacious for, while the woman's contain only the voluptuousness of the body, the chair's give all the voluptuousness of the mind.

Pressed on by Madame Flaubert, who feared for her grandchild in a local epidemic, the two friends hurried to Croisset and then out to a small nearby village where the air was reputed to be more healthful. Life here, dull and gray at best, was rendered worse for Flaubert by Maxime's departure and by confused relations with Louise Colet. After her refusal to see Gustave in Paris, she had also refused to write to him on the trip. Far from seeming pleased to be rid of her, he had instead written warm pleas and earnest entreaties, to which, gradually, she had responded. His hasty return to Croisset disarranged his plans, however, and on the anniversary of his meeting with Louise, the night of July 28, he was alone and writing the last notes of his travel diary, recalling the Trouville arrival, and remembering the events of a year before. He was in a sad and gentle mood, prepared to be warm toward Louise. Du Camp, however, on reaching Paris found an infuriated Louise storming over being left alone during the anniversary week. Gustave owed it to her to be with her. The prudent and cynical Maxime offered palliatives and excuses and concealed Gustave's address from her.[5] It was consonant with an observation he had made in Brittany: the first reaction of a man who has just slept with a woman, even when the pursuit has been long and arduous, is to wonder how he is going to get rid of her.[6] Louise did not know this, nor did she suspect that Gustave so approved the remark that he had recorded it in his notebook and would use it in the second *Sentimental Education*.

Flaubert, while anxious to see The Muse again, was adamant about not entangling himself with her. No woman was to hold him exclusively, and all were of interest. He had again gone to a brothel during the Breton trip, and in his diary he had noted that a man may readily love two mistresses at the same time, just as he may love both his dog and his horse, that which adores you and that which serves you.[7] Now Gustave was pursuing Ludovica, just as Louise had earlier been sure he was. He hoped to see her in Paris, unbeknownst to her husband Pradier or to Louise. Maxime, unfortunately, had to report that Ludovica was too busy with moving to a new apartment: she would have no time for him. Louise, on the other hand, wrote him a warm, tender love letter: it opened up the possibility of having two mistresses at once. Flaubert congratulated himself and settled into what was to be the pattern of his sexual life for the next two decades and more, all the years of his vigorous manhood.

Across Field and Strand

> The difficulty in this book consisted in the transitions, in the effort to make a single whole out of the disparate elements. It gave me a great deal of trouble and is the first work I wrote with difficulty.
>
> Letter to Louise Colet, April 8, 1852

From quite early in the planning of the Breton trip, it had been the intention of Flaubert and Du Camp to write an account of it. The "picturesque journey" with or without illustrations was a standard romantic book, and the idea of a collaboration appealed to the two friends. Shortly after the trip Maxime rejoined Gustave at Croisset to write it.

In between bouts of translating Aristophanes and Plautus the two men began drafting *Across Field and Strand,* as they decided to call their work; each wrote alternate chapters.[8] Shortly they abandoned the idea of publishing the book so as to have greater freedom for digressions and for what they deemed humor, of a less delicate sort. Flaubert's chapters evoke the gaiety and contentment he felt on the trip and the varying complexity of his personality, now dreamy and speculative, now observant, now lyrically romantic, now savagely ironic.

For the first time Flaubert was having acute difficulty in writing, although it still seemed almost an animal function, as natural as sleeping or smoking. In September, 1847, Maxime had joined him for what they expected to be a month of work. In October they realized that another month would be needed; in December they were hoping to end by New Year's. Spring was upon them before it was finished. Flaubert had occasionally had trouble in writing back in his school days, sometimes writing easily,· sometimes seeming to run dry, but only with the "Near Eastern Tale" of the previous winter had he become afraid to write. With the Breton account, major trouble began; it never left him. He was uneasy by day and sleepless by night; one whole day went to the correcting of five pages. Later, with *Madame Bovary*, sometimes only one corrected page would come from such a day of labor. As his taste became more refined, he found constant new difficulties and derived less satisfaction from a good page than irritation from a single wrong word. Adjectives put him through humiliations, and the omnipresent French *que* (with so many meanings and uses)· seemed to work outrages upon him. Perhaps he would end by being unable to write a line!

Some pages were excellent—those on Chateaubriand, for instance. Earlier he described the view from the chateau at Amboise* out over the surrounding countryside, which was of a tender green. The lines of the poplars stretched along the banks of the rivers, the meadows advanced to the water, their distant limits gray and blurred in the bluish, hazy atmosphere vaguely encompassed by the contour of the hills. The Loire flowed through the middle, bathing its islands, soaking the edges of the fields, passing under the bridges, turning the mills, and letting the boats glide over its silvered meanders; they were tied together and moved peacefully, side by side and half asleep, to the creaking of the great rudders which guided them. In the distance were two large sails brilliant with white in the sunlight. It was the sort of descrip-

---

*"Elle [la campagne] était d'un vert tendre; les lignes de peupliers s'étendaient sur les rives du fleuve; les prairies s'avançaient au bord, estompant au loin leurs limites grises dans un horizon bleuâtre et vaporeux qu'enfermait vaguement le contour des collines. La Loire coulait au milieu, baignant ses îles, mouillant la bordure des prés, passant sous les ponts, faisant tourner les moulins, laissant glisser sur sa sinuosité argentée les grands bateaux attachés ensemble qui cheminaient, paisibles, côte à côte, à demi endormis au craquement lent du large gouvernail qui les remue, et au fond il y avait deux grandes voiles éclatantes de blancheur au soleil" (*PLC*, p. 23).

tion he enjoyed, at which he would become one of the great masters, and which he was already learning to end with a little touch which would serve as an accent point.

He was also learning to depict light. On another day he noticed that the sky was pale. A delicate rain, wetting the air, cast a sort of uniform veil which enveloped the landscape in a gray tint. The light, stopped by the foliage overhead, was greenish and weak as on a winter's evening. Ahead, however, there was a stronger illumination playing on the edges of the leaves and lighting their jagged indentations.

Flaubert's thinking as well as his handling of style was growing firmer during these months of freedom. In Brittany, ancient and little changed by the passing years, older ways were still dominant, especially the constant presence of religion, simple and direct, a way of living a faith which had been new to him. Before the end of the trip he had already determined that his next work would be *Saint Anthony*, so that he might have an opportunity to write about it. Brittany had served to provoke the subject, nearly dormant since Italy two years before.

On occasion Flaubert found that out of doors in the sunshine under the open sky he seemed closer to God; in general, in Brittany, however, it was in the churches that he felt it and most strongly in the simple, older, romanesque ones. These less pretentious Carolingian churches seemed more Latin and of a simpler, more primitive theology; the religion itself appeared more valid. Each day as the people came in, they were surrounded by the tombs of those who had come before them and who, never completely absent, now joined with them in their prayers. In quiet harmony the Breton peasant thus lived out his life between his baptistry and his cemetery, unlike modern man who relegated eternity to the suburb and put the dead out amongst the factories.

The people, too—grave, rough, and heavy-chested—were powerful yet gently graceful as they knelt in prayer. They were the remnants of a race now disappearing, but they seemed so real and full that each appeared to contain more within himself than it is the normal lot of man to bear. Their faith made their truth.

The cult of the Virgin was at the core of this fullness. Her chapels, shining and spotless, were everywhere with their fresh flowers and lighted candles. The Breton might be poor, but his Virgin was rich. Always beautiful, she smiled for all, and souls in travail came to warm their tired spirits at her feet as at a hearth which never cooled. Returning to a thesis which he had first broached in *November*, Flaubert pondered the voluptuous delights the Breton derived from this cult, as the prostitute Marie had lusted for the body of Christ on the Cross. Asceticism, he noted, is related to epicureanism, and dieting can be a refined form of gluttony. Religion contained carnal feelings, prayer had its debauchery, and mortification its intoxicating moments.

The men who came each evening to kneel before these statues felt their hearts beat faster and vague delights swept over them. Out in the streets, children returning from school stopped dreamily before the Virgin in the stained glass, this ardent woman smiling sweetly, almost invitingly—and Flaubert had already glimpsed the first of Anthony's temptations, as the saint would, later, bend over the illustrations in his prayer book. Flaubert wrote in Brittany that this was the eternal religion, the religion of man's own entrails, which underlies all the others, sometimes covert but never perishing. It is the cult of his own being, for it is the worship of life in the life-giving principle. Long before Freud made it explicit, Flaubert was moving with his period to discover how deeply religion is rooted in sexuality. But this in no way diminished its validity: rather in Brittany he had experienced for himself its simple nobility and its rightness.

Among his other adages at the end of his Notebook he observed that God is a word so great that man cannot understand its meaning and it is his greatest glory to have succeeded in using words to build something inexplicable. What most gives him an understanding of his humility is also what most shows his strength. But religions, he sadly noted too, are in the life of humanity what love affairs are in the life of individuals: the present one is the best; the one which is just beginning will never end; and the most beautiful was the last one. For his own part he was continuing to find that only the religion of art endured; the only way of life was the writer's.

THE HERMIT OF CROISSET

The history of the arts is a long tale of martyrdom.
Letter to his niece Caroline, December 4, 1877

In late July, 1847, Flaubert established himself, hermit-like, at Croisset for nearly two years of writing, the even tenor of the days broken only by occasional visits from Du Camp or quick trips to Paris. Three evenings a week Louis Bouilhet would call, and together he and Flaubert analyzed the plays of Voltaire scene by scene, a dull apprenticeship but invaluable training in moving plot forward through dialogue.[9] Chateaubriand, forty years before, had predicted that the destruction of the monasteries by the French Revolution would lead certain Frenchmen to live thus as secular hermits. They would be, he suggested, odd combinations of passion and philosophy, unable either wholly to abandon the vices of the age or wholly to love the age. They would mistake their hatred of men for genius and would renounce all duty, human or divine. Living apart, they would cherish the wildest fantasies and plunge deeper and deeper into a proud misanthropy which would lead to madness or death.

Flaubert's health declined seriously over these two years as his nervous attacks recurred. He may have had one during the Breton trip.[10] In September there was a bad seizure, and the autumn was rendered miserable by continuous minor onsets and by rheumatic pains in his neck which added to his discomfort. The hallucinations seemed to start within his head, but then they appeared to move out in front of his eyes: the fantastic seemed to be taking on body. Death, he suspected, must be like this, if it came when one was conscious of it.

In addition to his illnesses, his life within his family was nearly unbearable. When he came downstairs after eight hours of work at his desk, his head full of his writing, preoccupied, and often with his nerves on edge, he would sit at table opposite his mother, and she would look significantly at the empty places and sigh. Little Caroline would begin to weep and then, to her uncle's terror, she would have hallucinations like his. To add complications, her father, Hamard, had lost his sanity and was beginning to cause serious legal troubles. Flaubert found man a sorry machine of which he was heartily tired.

There were other causes for melancholy: Alfred Le Poittevin, mentor and friend, had been spiritually apart from Flaubert since his marriage. A long honeymoon trip and then the concerns and interests proper to marriage had had the effect Gustave feared of estranging Alfred from his belligerently bachelor friend. Now they were drawn together again, but only because Alfred was dying and it was Flaubert's sad privilege to be his companion over the final weeks and days: the end came in April, 1848. Alfred was conscious up to the last moments and suffered acutely; Flaubert was with him.[11] For two nights thereafter he kept vigil beside the body, reading a study of ancient religions in preparation for his *Saint Anthony*, which Alfred would now never see. The window was open onto the night and the sound of cocks could be heard; a moth fluttered in; at midnight there came the sound of a distant hunter's horn. The second night he read Hugo and kept coming upon the poems Alfred liked best. From time to time he would step over to the corpse and raise the veil which had been placed over the face; he was himself wearing a coat which had belonged to his father and which the doctor had worn only once, at Caroline's wedding. Gustave's whole life was gathering here beside the dead body of his friend.

Wrapping Alfred in his shroud was a strange sensation of cold and stiffness; it remained in his fingertips all day. When the task was completed, he was suddenly overwhelmed with a feeling of joy and liberation for his friend, and throughout the ceremonies of burial he kept repeating to himself—or rather it was as though Alfred's voice kept repeating it to him—a line of Alfred's: "He will go, like a joyous bird, amongst the pines to greet the rising sun."* Bouilhet was with Flaubert at the cemetery, where it rained hard. On the way back they both sat on the outside seat and shouted to urge on the galloping horses. Gustave wrote to Maxime that he had had unheard-of apperceptions and been daz-

---

*"Il ira, joyeux oiseau, saluer dans les pins, le soleil naissant."

zled by the splendor of untranslatable ideas. It was his past which filed before him to the accompaniment of choirs of music and gusts of perfume. Ten years later when he was signing a copy of the newly published *Madame Bovary* for Alfred's sister Laure, he wrote on its flyleaf that he sent it in memory of their common past. If Alfred had lived, he said, the book would have been dedicated to him, for Alfred's place had never been filled in his heart.[12] The final version of *The Temptation of Saint Anthony* in 1874 was, in fact, dedicated to him.

Alfred was gone; there remained Du Camp and Bouilhet and, of course, Louise Colet and Louise Pradier. For The Muse's love, when he had it, Gustave felt deeply grateful. But the liaison was now almost entirely taken up with quarrels, coldness, and disagreements. It dragged out its tiresome course until Christmas Day, 1848, when through the agency of Du Camp, whom Louise hated, the end came once again. Maxime was pleased: life with Louise, he wrote, would have been a continual nuisance.

"Ludovica" was another matter entirely. She, Maxime, and Gustave had an odd three-way relationship. They would all dine together, or Ludovica would write to Flaubert proposing that she come live beside him in Rouen or Du Camp would regret not having enough money to support the three of them. She continued as shameless as ever, but in a strange gesture of loyalty she and Maxime resisted temptation one evening, persuaded that it would hurt Gustave if they did not.[13] Thus, from close-up Flaubert was having the opportunity to study this "orchestra of female sentiments."

Meanwhile France had had her Revolution of 1848. There had been Reform Banquets before it, and Flaubert attended one in December, 1847. Nothing, he reported, could have given him a more complete disgust with political success than such an opportunity to see the price one had to pay: in the midst of the wild enthusiasm of his fellow citizens he remained cold and nauseated. He was part of the National Guard and began even to imagine that he would enjoy being sent off for duty in case of war: it would mean a change from living with his family. In June he was in Paris when the mob broke loose. He had observed the various scenes of the Revolution of 1848 which he would later satirize in *A Sentimental Education.*

In May, 1849, the state of his health had become so serious that he had to go to Paris to consult several doctors. The verdict: chronic syphilis of long standing. The symptoms, presumably chancres or rash, kept reappearing despite treatment over the years. The doctors wondered if this were perhaps the cause of his nervous ailment, a not unnatural query before the invention of electroencephalograms to confirm epilepsy. Flaubert, on the other hand, was more suspicious of the strained life he was leading, probably a better guess. He was strongly urged—almost ordered —to seek warmer climes as soon as possible.[14] He waited only until the following October in order to finish *The Temptation of Saint Anthony,* the book on which he was working, and then left at once for long months of travel in the Eastern Mediterranean.

9

The Temptation of Saint Anthony (1849)

I shall spend my life watching the Ocean of Art on which others sail or fight, and I shall occasionally take pleasure in diving to the bottom to find yellow or green shells, which no one else will want; and so I shall keep them to decorate my cabin.

Letter to Louise Colet, October 4, 1846

THE three versions of *The Temptation of Saint Anthony*, which stretch out over most of Flaubert's lifetime, are at the center of his philosophic and artistic life.[1] Numerous works from his adolescence foreshadow it, and its conception goes back to the Balbi Palace in Genoa with its Breughel painting, which he saw during the honeymoon trip of 1845. But the real birth of the book was during the trip through Brittany, where many of his earlier preoccupations were revived in this first long, connected contact with the outside world after the onset of his epileptic attacks.

Many of Flaubert's early works are involved in the complex genealogy of *The Temptation*.[2] The playlets which he, the Le Poittevin children, and Ernest Chevalier presented on the billiard table in the Hôtel-Dieu mark the start of the dramatic form Flaubert used here. The marionette shows depicting Saint Anthony at the Rouen Fairs fascinated him throughout his life. Goethe's *Faust*, dramatic in form and emphasizing the desire for learning and the tortures of doubt, Byron, Gautier, and Quinet's *Ahasvérus* suggested further possibilities. Each year of Flaubert's adolescent writings had showed new attempts to manage the theme, culminating in *Smarh* in 1839. Later, some of the temptations suffered by Jules in the first *Sentimental Education* served as models for Anthony.

Other roads also led here. Because Brittany remained profoundly and overtly pious, the whole question of religion rose to the forefront of Flaubert's consciousness: Anthony's temptations were a natural and easy mode for such a discussion. But religion and sexuality meet deep in man's psyche, and to contemplate the one is to arouse the other. Louise Colet and then Flaubert's return to prostitutes had revived the problem of sex in his own life, too: the whole matter of carnal joy was easy to fit into the temptations of the saint, and Flaubert did so. In several places in Brittany there were sculptures depicting Anthony; certain paintings, too, by their colors recalled the tonality of the Breughel work. Hence every now and again Flaubert found himself seeking ways to use the saint.

The Seven Deadly Sins were by tradition the principal basis for Anthony's temptations, and much could easily be included through them. But a viable story, capable of interesting generations of artists and writers as Anthony's had, must be susceptible of expansion to allow for the introduction of new emphases or new elements as later ages change their center of attention from one area of man to another. Flaubert felt, not always wisely, that he could so enlarge the scope of Anthony's experience.

One of Flaubert's concerns was pantheism. In his metaphysical studies he had been meeting this as the formal doctrine that the whole universe is God; he had also been experiencing it personally and emotionally in those moments when nature seemed to him alive and he was able to feel himself one with it. Le Poittevin believed in pantheism; Spinoza, who had influenced Flaubert's esthetics in *A Sentimental Education,* demonstrated it philosophically, and the studies in Near Eastern religions which he undertook for his "Near Eastern Tale" gave it mythic formulation. More important was the ready response he found within himself, overshadowing any other joy he knew. Hence the really dangerous temptations for Anthony are the metaphysical ones like pantheism and not the physical ones like lust, which had been the principal concern of so many of the earlier artists who had treated the subject.

Pantheistic feelings swept over Du Camp and Flaubert many times during their Breton trip. *Across Field and Strand* describes an evening walk* as the two men strolled along the seashore splen-

*"Aspirant l'odeur des flots, nous humions, nous évoquions à nous tout ce qu'il y avait de couleurs, de rayons, de murmures: le dessin des varechs, la douceur des grains de sable, la dureté du roc qui sonnait sous nos pieds, les altitudes de la falaise, la frange des vagues, les découpures du rivage, la voix

did for the scent of salt, the colors, the slanting rays of the sun, and the murmur of the waves.³ Each of their senses was drunk: the seaweed took on endless shapes, the sand was soft underfoot, the firm rock resounded under the metal cleats of their boots. Gently the evening breeze flowed over their faces, and overhead swift clouds rolled powdered gold across the sky. The moon was rising and stars were beginning to appear.

Through every pore the two men were partaking of the scene, their minds enmeshed in the profusion of these splendors. Their nostrils opened wider, they listened more attentively as something emanating from all these elements assimilated itself into their being and let them in turn penetrate into nature. Their tremendous joy was like the ecstasy of love: one wanted more hands for caressing, more lips for kissing, more soul for loving: "Spreading ourselves out upon nature, rejoicing, delirious, we were sorry that our eyes could not penetrate to the heart of the rocks, to the bottom of the

---

de l'horizon; et puis c'était la brise qui passait, comme d'invisibles baisers qui nous coulaient sur la figure, c'était le ciel où il y avait des nuages allant vite, roulant une poudre d'or, la lune qui se levait, les étoiles qui se montraient. Nous nous roulions l'esprit dans la profusion de ces splendeurs, nous en repaissions nos yeux; nous en écartions les narines, nous en ouvrions les oreilles; quelque chose de la vie des éléments émanant d'eux-mêmes, sous l'attraction de nos regards, arrivait jusqu'à nous, s'y assimilant, faisait que nous les comprenions dans un rapport moins éloigné, que nous les sentions plus avant, grâce à cette union plus complexe. A force de nous en pénétrer, d'y entrer, nous devenions nature aussi, nous sentions qu'elle gagnait sur nous et nous en avions une joie démesurée; nous aurions voulu nous y perdre, être pris par elle ou l'emporter en nous. Ainsi que dans les transports de l'amour, on souhaite plus de mains pour palper, plus de lèvres pour baiser, plus d'yeux pour voir, plus d'âme pour aimer, nous étalant sur la nature dans un ébattement plein de délire et de joies, nous regrettions que nos yeux ne pussent aller jusqu'au sein des rochers, jusqu'au fond des mers, jusqu'au bout du ciel, pour voir comment poussent les pierres, se font les flots, s'allument les étoiles; que nos oreilles ne pussent entendre graviter dans la terre la formation du granit, la sève pousser dans les plantes, les coraux rouler dans les solitudes de l'océan et, dans la sympathie de cette effusion contemplative, nous eussions voulu que notre âme, s'irradiant partout, allât vivre dans toute cette vie pour revêtir toutes ses formes, durer comme elles, et se variant toujours, toujours pousser au soleil de l'éternité ses métamorphoses" (*PLC*, pp. 130-31).

sea and the outermost bounds of heaven to see how stones grow, how waves are made, and stars light up. We longed for ears which might hear granite being formed within the earth or sap rising in plants and coral flowing in the solitudes of ocean; in the communion of this contemplative effusion, each of us yearned to have his soul radiate throughout all creation, live in all of this life, and clothe itself with all possible forms, to last as they do, endlessly varying and producing their metamorphoses under the warming sun of eternity."

This overwhelming, pantheistic vision had its roots in Flaubert's experience along the seashore in Corsica; he had described the sensation anew in *November*. It was akin to what he felt as he kept vigil beside the body of his sister or visited the tomb of Chateaubriand and meditated on the long future.[4] Now again it engulfed him. Naturally it constitutes one of the principal and most dangerous of the temptations of Saint Anthony.

Upon his return from Brittany most of Flaubert's days went to the writing of *Across Field and Strand*, but he fitted in the reading he knew to be necessary for *Saint Anthony*. He began with the mystics; theology and the Bible followed; and before he had written the last lines of *The Temptation*, he had read almost all the relevant authors, ancient and modern. In April, 1848, as Alfred lay dying, the Breton trip was finished, and Flaubert turned resolutely to the last of his readings in preparation for the work. At a quarter past three on the afternoon of May 24, 1848, as he noted on the manuscript, he began to write *The Temptation of Saint Anthony:* it would occupy him until twenty past three on the afternoon of September 12, 1849, a year and a half away.

In the first *Sentimental Education* Jules had indicated the proper method for historical evocations: a close study of all the erudite material in order to understand the past so as to be able to complete its statements. Now, plunging into fourth-century Egypt, Flaubert began with the best secondary studies in order to familiarize himself with the general aspects of his material and then turned to the primary sources, seeking directly the color which the desert hermit had had. Only then could he proceed. His imagination, so fertile for the production of imagery, was timid in developing historical context, the facts, so to speak, of the situation. Where his sources failed him, for instance in the appearance of Egyptian cities, he did not dare to invent but preferred to leave all such urban settings imprecise; only after long months in Egypt and Palestine did he bring in the evocative details which would make such pages alive in the later versions.[5] While this was perhaps no more than prudence and scruple here, it would, in later works, turn out to be a weakness which would increase with the years.

Where he could find adequate sources, Flaubert reinforced, condensed, or amalgamated them to produce an accurate mosaic as the basis for a passage; only thereafter would he go beyond his historical sources to literary considerations. His effort, as he had insisted from the beginning, was to complete history, to formulate its implications and achieve its intentions; it was not to be a new start, much less a romantic and personal overlay or substitution. His erudition was to keep him from lyrical surges of personalism. Or so, at least, he hoped. In fact, however, these surges proved irresistible and, as he came to realize soon after he had finished the book, its fundamental flaw was that he had allowed himself to take the place of Anthony. His temptations, and not those of the simple fourth-century hermit, had filled the long night of anguish.[6]

The form Flaubert selected and developed for his *Temptation* was a fluid adaptation of a play to depict in a single night all the sufferings of the saint. The work opens with a description of the setting (the platform before the hermit's cell), after which the saint speaks, moves about, and speaks again. Soon other characters enter, in a reversal of the *Faust* technique, where Faust journeys, often miraculously, from one scene to another to produce in the spectator a kaleidoscopic view of the world. Here Anthony does not move, but an unending variety of visitors besiege the saint and reproduce for the reader the effect of *Faust*. Usually Flaubert provides a full description of each new character and supplies stage directions for managing his entrance, actions, and exit. On rare occasions, however, description alone appears, and frequently the long monologues of the saint are quite unsuited to actual staging. The device is an adaptation of stage presentation, not directly theater.

It was only the previous winter that Flaubert and Bouilhet had

DR. ACHILLE FLAUBERT

The career of Gustave's father, Dr. Flaubert, had not fulfilled its early promise. The tilt of the physician's head and a tired skeptical sadness in his penetrating eyes reflect his frustration, while his mouth, a little full but drawn taut even in repose, seems to suggest the sardonic comments for which he was known and feared.

MADAME FLAUBERT

This pencil drawing of Gustave's mother was copied by her granddaughter Caroline from a sketch made by an old family friend, Ernest
Langlois, whose volume on stained-glass windows Flaubert later used
for his tale *A Simple Heart*.

GUSTAVE'S BROTHER ACHILLE

Older than Gustave by several years, Achille had a handsome appearance and assured air that made him a rival Gustave could not challenge
during his younger years.

ROUEN IN FLAUBERT'S YOUTH

The amphitheater in which the city lies is partially hidden by the near hill. The church towers rise high above the other buildings, and bridges span the river, joining the city to the industrial suburbs on the left. Croisset can be seen dimly on the far bank where the river makes a definite bend to the left. Musée des Arts et Traditions populaires, Paris.

THE BUREAU DES FINANCES IN ROUEN

This elegant building of 1610 is one of the few remaining older structures in the city. From a nineteenth-century lithograph.

A Street Scene in Nineteenth-Century Rouen

One of the cathedral towers is in the background, and in the foreground vendors cluster in the streets. The bustling people and the blacks of the lithograph conceal the somber melancholy of the humid shadows.

GUSTAVE FLAUBERT AS A BOY

In this portrait by Ernest Langlois, made when Gustave was ten years old, the diffident youth, his hair characteristically unruly, stares out defensively at a world he already suspects he will never love.

GUSTAVE FLAUBERT AS A YOUNG MAN

Gustave's increasing good looks and bemused air in this portrait by an unknown artist veil but do not hide his gentleness and timidity.

studied and analyzed Voltaire's plays and outlined a number of their own. The final form of these plays was in general not written: it was enough to sketch exactly how the entire action could be shown on stage. Flaubert's interest lay in inventing situations which would permit the display of action, the essence of the theater, so as not in his novels to have to fall back on narration, a technique which he felt destroyed their impact. The nearly dramatic form of *The Temptation* was to guarantee this predominance of action over narration. Moreover, the theater has its own special optics: exaggerations, gestures, and strong phrasings are normal. And, too, it permitted here showing the settings, the strange costumes, the color, and the plastic values of the Egyptian subject.

Of character there is perhaps too little in *The Temptation*. There is only one continuously present actor, Anthony. While he is remarkably tenacious in the face of temptation, he is almost never sufficiently organized to fight back and is lost in an immense universe over which he has little or no control. Neither his senses nor his intelligence nor his emotions seem adequate to cope with the mad night he is spending: it all passes before him in a wild phantasmagoria. The tortured saint, perhaps because Flaubert was seeking to preserve his own impassivity, remains too passive.

The Temptation is divided into three Parts. In the first, at the end of day the saint is about to begin evening prayers, when he is overcome with distaste and exacerbation over his miserable life. As he opens his prayer book, the image of the Virgin appears to come to life, and he finds sexual excitement in her glance. At once the Devil, the Seven Capital Sins, and a new creation, Logic, arrive to tempt him. Most are traditional, except for one of Pride's temptations, a vision of the vast succession of heresies. It is of no avail; the saint holds fast.

In Part Two, after resisting Pride and Lust, Anthony all but succumbs to the insidious temptations of the fantastic and the monstrous presented in a powerful pantheistic vision.

Part Three is theological. Anthony is tempted further with pantheism; then Lust and Death vie for his choice. At last, in a final assault, Death and the Devil show him the despairing parade of all the religions which have come and gone. Anthony, though sorely distressed, remains steadfast and kneels in prayer as the sun rises: he is saved. In sum, Part One is the temptation by all the Seven Sins, culminating in the procession of the heresies; Part Two is the further attack of Lust, Logic, and Pride, culminating in the procession of the fantastic monsters and the appeal of pantheism; Part Three continues the temptations of pantheism and Lust and adds that of Death, culminating in the procession of the dead gods.

In Brittany, Flaubert had made many critical observations which he now embodied in *Saint Anthony*. Prayer itself, the direct communion with the Deity, could be, he had noted, a source of intimate delectation.[7] It was one of Anthony's first temptations as he discovered within himself the abysses of pride which made him a fair mark for the Devil. Immediately thereafter—again it is a Breton observation coupled with a note to include it for Anthony—he found the Virgin not merely beautiful but actually seductive. A tempting voice whispered to Anthony that she was, after all, a woman like others and, like them, felt lust herself, perhaps for him.[8] Not even the blows of his whip could appease the fire within him, for he found perverse delight in the stinging lashes. He was ripe for the Seven Sins.

The Deadly Sins were the traditional basis for Anthony's temptations and by using them Flaubert could easily avoid personalism in his presentation. But by the same token they offered a narrow terrain on which to parade the inner problems which, ultimately, were impelling Flaubert to write his book as he and Du Camp hiked through Brittany. Chief among these was ennui, the great romantic vice and Flaubert's own most deadly problem. Most unwisely—and in defiance of his stated canons—he attributed the vice to his desert ascetic. The Devil tempted Anthony with the assurance that the ennui of doubt was universal: all the other hermits felt it, too. Even the Deadly Sins, in imitation of Flaubert, proclaimed their ennui: they were bored with themselves! Elsewhere Anthony, like Flaubert, bemoaned his anguish at not knowing what he wanted, at not even having the will to desire to want something.

It was all so very complex and so typical of the nineteenth century. Anthony lamented that if he were a tree or a pebble or even his pig, then he would know exactly and fully what he should be. But as a man he did not know why he was himself or why he was not other or why anything was; and yet, as a man he needed to know. He became more and more the youthful Flaubert as the pages filled: he even regretted the death and disappearance of the courtesan, beginning with Helen of Troy.[9]

The Temptation is constantly personal, despite Flaubert's professed theories. The long and monotonous parade of most of the classical heresies at the end of Part One fascinated Flaubert, if not his saint or readers. In the vision presented by Lust, it was particularly personal to Flaubert to offer Anthony a vision of a Greek courtesan whose function it was to enhance and not debase life by adding the joy of sensuality to all other pleasures. Demonassa, the Athenian courtesan, is no common prostitute but rather the embodiment of Flaubert's dreams. Her servant, regretting Demonassa's forthcoming departure, recalls how the courtesan used to wander among the guests at noble feasts, delighting each by a word. Philosophers, aroused by her presence, discussed the beautiful, painters, their arms sweeping in flowing gestures, spoke with amazement of her profile; and poets, paling, trembled. Athens would suffer at her loss, but she, too, would suffer, for nowhere else in the world was beauty so appreciated. It is Flaubert's lament, not Anthony's.

Learning is a further personal temptation of Flaubert and his generation, the men whom knowledge, particularly science, drove from religion. Before Saint Anthony's terrified gaze Knowledge attacks Faith. The Devil warns his young child, Learning, that he can have peace only after he has killed Faith, and Learning himself warns her that a time will come when the world will be washed of the maledictions Faith has hurled at it; what is obscure will be clear, what now seems monstrous will be superb. Learning promises to unravel the enigmas of body and soul, and good and evil. Moreover, he will become ever younger while Faith totters toward her grave. Not even the Ideal will be able to save Faith, for (and again it is Flaubert, not Anthony, who is involved) Art itself will be detached from her and will stand alone with Learning.

Anthony's role in the presence of Flaubert's temptation is ambivalent. He suffers Flaubert's temptations, but he clings tenaciously to his beliefs. And he is not made to seem foolish for doing so. Flaubert, like Renan at this period, was quite unable to imagine accepting Faith, but in Brittany as elsewhere he had observed that Faith could have purity, dignity, and truth. Saint Anthony, too, knows this. Unlike him, however, Saint Flaubert, whose temptations we are really witnessing, knows full well what other and irreconcilable possibilities there appear to be. Logic, Learning, and finally Art for him must all stand opposed to Faith. And yet Faith, in Brittany, was true. He longed for it.

When Learning was apostrophizing Faith, he had threatened her that ultimately he would be able to explain how the monstrous was natural. This was what had first intrigued Flaubert in the Breughel and Callot works, what he called the sadly grotesque. In the first *Sentimental Education*, he had declared it foolish to invent impossible monsters, winged horses, and others. The fantastic as an excuse or cover for weakness of imagination was to be avoided; it had its proper place only as a development of the intimate essence of our own nature.[10] Only as such would it prove tempting to a desert saint or to Flaubert.

Looking at a collection of monsters during the Breton trip, Flaubert had been led to wonder whether this apparently unnatural world, which obviously had its laws, might not also have its beauty. Was not classical mythology precisely this, with its satyrs, its sirens, its chimeras?[11] In his *Temptation*, Flaubert amused himself by writing a dialogue between the Sphinx and a Chimera, making it into a representation of the eternal opposition between logic and fantasy, caprice and reason. The procession of the monsters followed.

The temptation of the monstrous could become dangerous. In his Breton Notebook, Flaubert jotted down further ideas for his saint. On first seeing the Devil in his true form, Anthony was to be frightened by his ugliness, but the more he looked the more he was to admire him! This was the temptation, Flaubert wrote, of ugliness for its own sake, an attraction similar to that which one feels for offending smells or for the voluptuousness of fear.[12] This pathological reaction Anthony experienced as the parade of monsters moved before him. To look into the eyes of one of the animals, the Catoblepas, was instant death, and Anthony had been warned. He averted his eyes—and then began to wonder what looking might be like. Insensibly he shifted from considering the possibility to actual wanting of the fearsome event. Pathology was leading Flaubert to explore domains for which a later age would coin the term subconscious.

Now the full temptation of the fantastic was upon Anthony. Completely surrounded by monsters, he hardly dared breathe for fear of inhaling poisonous elements; his ears rang with the buzzing of these ill-shaped forms; he was afraid of crushing them underfoot. At first they were like the simpler forms the Flemish had invented, the composite monsters of a Bosch: alligator heads walking on duck feet, owls with serpent's tails, winged bellies flying like mosquitos. But then Flaubert moved nearer to the disquieting monsters such as Breughel was perhaps the first to depict, in which animal and vegetable fuse. In Flaubert women have lotuses for faces, and aloes are covered with pink pustules like human flesh, while polyps have eyes and threaten to engulf everything into their swelling, dilating selves. But he did not, however, adopt the ultimate Breughel horror, in which animation is lent to the inanimate so that it may become actively hostile.

As the monsters menace the poor saint, he reaches madness and thinks himself animal, then vegetable; then he longs to emanate like an aroma, enter into each atom, circulate in matter, finally be matter itself so as to know what it thinks. With this the Devil seizes the saint and whirls him into the upper airs so that he may learn; the Second Part ends and the theological discussions of Part Three begin for a change of emphasis at the end. This change will not occur in 1874: at that time the final temptation and the final vision will be pantheism.

Personal elements continue to dominate all of this phase of the saint's temptations. Flaubert tended to feel that metaphysics, on which he had worked rather hard, was a waste of time; hence the Devil's exposition of logical paradoxes to confuse Anthony is somewhat dry and unconvincing. It is quite otherwise with pantheism. Satan reminds Anthony of moments when he and the object began to become one, each sending emanations which penetrated so into the other that they were on the verge of uniting. Anthony's excited assent to the Devil is the measure of Flaubert's, not his own, temptation.

Late in the book came the great parade of the ancient gods,

urged on by Death's pitiless whip. Flaubert's developing method reached its climax in these scenes: from secondary sources back to original documents he pursued the basic color for each of the gods he displayed, deliberately exploiting the dramatic and plastic possibilities inherent for the artist in the growing studies of the history of religions.

The panoply of the Greek and Roman gods benefits from a kindliness which reflects Flaubert's own reactions whenever he thought of living in these ages when action followed instinct, when reason and thought had not yet intervened to sickly o'er the world of action. These lost ages, Satan proclaimed, would never recur. Idea, order, and the notion of the great had been the heart of Jupiter's world: as he left the stage he offered Flaubert the hope that those who cherished these values could yet be his children, under whatever skies. The real Anthony would have found little meaning here, but Flaubert had often longed that it might be so. The Muses, though, were perhaps his most personal lapse, for they lamented future ages when people would write books without paying attention to the sentences! But they did not leave without their hymn of praise to this juvenile age of the world with its sublime art ennobling life, when there were women whose equals the world would not see again, and whole mountains of marble awaited the sculptor.

The last great apparition was preceded by a clap of thunder. Death dropped her whip; even the Devil stepped back, and Anthony prostrated himself on the ground as a voice proclaimed: "I was the God of Hosts, the Lord, the Lord God." Now alone, displaced, without temples, all worship transferred to His Son, to that Son's mother, to His friends and disciples, even to His saints and martyrs, the reign of the Lord God, too, had passed. He ended with the same grim words with which he had begun.

The closing pages have that ambiguity which alone concorded with Flaubert's refusal to come to conclusions and which has seemed the essential meaning of life to the twentieth century. To have ended the book with faith easily dominant would have denied the experience of life as Flaubert knew it; to have denied the longing for Faith would have been equally opposed to his experiences in Brittany. He sought to fuse the two. After the

Lord left, there was a brief interlude, and then the atmosphere changed. Anthony realized that something immense and infinite, turbulent yet suave, was spreading its wings to raise his soul toward God; already his head was calmer, and Hell seemed more distant. The Lord was smiling upon him in His mercy. Night slipped away, and the morning light reached him as the sun came through the clouds. The Devil departed, but with a mocking laugh as he told the saint that Hell was really within him: there was a curse upon his nature. It was twenty past three in the afternoon of September 12, 1849; the sun was shining and there was a wind as Flaubert wrote the last line.

At once Flaubert asked his two closest friends, Maxime Du Camp and Louis Bouilhet, to hear the new work and give an opinion.[13] Alas, it could not be favorable. While there were many well-written sections, and the underlying conceptions for many scenes were good, the abounding personalism of the work limited its appeal for any but its author. Moreover, Flaubert had observed no sense of measure; ideas good in themselves, such as the three processions, became intolerable through sheer weight of words. He had evolved a most interesting esthetic of impersonalism and impassivity, but he was as yet quite unable to resist the temptation to intervene in his work. Hence, with anguish and pain he was forced to accept the verdict of his friends: as a totality, the new work must be adjudged a failure.

Flaubert set *The Temptation* aside, but the blow to his hopes, his pride, and his cherished projects for the future was incalculable. It made him sick for months. Was he, perhaps, not a writer after all? Fortunately, the long-delayed trip through the Eastern Mediterranean, so needed for his health, had already been delayed far too long; it was time to make final preparations at once. Within a month he and Maxime were under way.

10

Around the Eastern Mediterranean (1849-51)

Departure

If it weren't for my mother back in France and her affectionate need for me, I really would keep right on going until I reached China.

Letter to Flaubert's doctor from Damascus,
September 7, 1850

You can see that everything is going very well. . . . Maxime is keeping an eye on me constantly and takes care of me as though I were a child. I think he'd like to put me under glass, if he could, to keep anything from happening to me.

Letter to his mother from Alexandria, November 22, 1849

A FULL CENTURY before the jet plane, travel was a meditative affair, a time in which to collect the soul and to examine it.[1] Through months of doubt and despair on his Mediterranean trip there slowly emerged for Flaubert the certainty that he did know how to write and, equally slowly, there was born the determination to write of the nature of love, to anatomize it for a post-romantic world made foolish or fatalistic by its misconceptions of it. Within sixty days of his return to Croisset, Flaubert had adopted the subject of *Madame Bovary* and was beginning to sketch out his plot line. The story of his journey through the Near East is the story of his discovery and ultimate conquest of himself.

Parting is not always such sweet sorrow. Gustave's mother had consented to the trip only because she felt her son's life threatened. After the deaths of her husband and daughter, he and little Caroline constituted her sole reasons for existence. Living apart from her son Achille, she had only Gustave for adult companionship, and now he was planning to be away for nearly two years. She was quite brave enough to consent to a necessary plan, but her anguish was limitless and, not unnaturally, she could not find the strength to conceal it.

In *A Sentimental Education* Henry had found that his long trip to New York seemed unbearable as the day of departure approached. He would have liked to see it slip away into an indefinite future, or else come upon him suddenly and without warning. Gustave and his mother now experienced just this pain.[2] On Monday, October 22, he and she went together for a last few days in Paris. On Tuesday evening Flaubert attended the opera with Maurice Schlésinger, to whom he remained devoted long after ceasing to covet his wife. On Wednesday Gustave and his mother left Paris for Nogent and her family there: the parting would thus be easier. But the next day, Thursday, proved atrocious, the worst that Flaubert could remember having lived, as the minutes ticked by, omnipresent and full of grief. Up and down the small garden he and his mother walked, this mother against whom he had so many times hurled imprecations in the silence of his room or whose tyranny he had so frequently cursed in his letters to Louise Colet. Now he found his own anguish so impossible to bear that he resolved to leave that day, forty-eight hours early. He fixed the moment as five o'clock. His hat was ready, his trunk at the station: the clock hand seemed to have stopped as his leaden heart showed him the weight of his attachment to his mother.

She was seated in an armchair when the moment came; he caressed her cheek, spoke with her, kissed her on the forehead, and then rushed from the room closing the door as quickly as he could, but not before her cry rang in his ears to echo there, reminding him of the one she uttered when she first touched the hand of her dead husband. Overcome with emotion, his immediate reaction was to shut out his feelings. Dry-eyed and tearless he left, accompanied by the suggestion of his relatives that he really ought to draw up a will: fury momentarily displaced pain.

As one sets out on a long journey, it may happen that the full realization of the meaning of solitude comes upon the traveler only after he has left. It was so with Flaubert, who now had the train ride from Nogent to Paris in which to face his act and discover its meaning for him. To leave a mother is a normal action for an almost thirty-year-old son; to Flaubert it was nearly without precedent. To a normal son it brings a momentary pang of regret, perhaps; but to Flaubert it was an almost insurmountable catastrophe. To him and to most of the artists of the romantic and postromantic world the artist is not, in his person, everyman: he is above, beyond, below—whatever the nonartist wishes. But he is exaggerated. When one has within oneself the scale of a Flaubert, it is easy to find therein the full compass of normal man at the very top (or bottom) of his bent. Anything less would constitute a lack. Flaubert, leaving his mother, felt not merely normal regret but an abject, all-encompassing despair. It must have been exasperating for his friends to have him so demean himself. But it is far more important that he now knew the full range which the pangs of departure can encompass, for he would one day have to dissect it in *Madame Bovary:* Emma's anguish when Rodolphe abandons her could not have been written without Flaubert's odd, exaggerated reaction to leaving his mother. The nonartist frequently protests, but this is possibly unjust, probably blind, and quite certainly futile.

Alone in the carriage Flaubert put his handkerchief to his face and wept. Sobs shook his frame, and he heard them as though they came from someone else; he even noticed, dispassionately, that they sounded like those of the great romantic actress, Marie Dorval. Again and again his solitude swept over him and set his head to whirling. Frightened, he opened the window to let the cold air on his cheek revive him. But then his mother's face, contracted with pain, appeared before his eyes, the corners of her mouth turned down.

Stopping at a station bar, he had three or four quick glasses of rum, and his sadness took another turn: should he perhaps return to her? He could almost hear the sound of the servant's voice as she shouted "Madame, it is Monsieur Gustave!" He imagined his mother's pleasure: it lay in his power to give it to her, now or at any moment in the next days. He lulled himself with the thought, his strength and will broken: it tempted and comforted him.

Decision could not be long postponed. Crossing Paris from the railroad station, he promised himself that he would make up his mind before he reached Maxime's apartment off the Place Royale; but when he got there, he found that he could not yet bear to face the decision. Maxime was out and his servant prepared a warm fire; Flaubert turned this way and that until midnight when his companion returned. Now the die had to be cast: he found the strength to go. By one o'clock he was able to write to his mother. She must be asleep now, he thought, and he wrote of his tears and those she must have shed; he promised to write and begged her to send him volumes, to unload her grief into them. The decision was made.

Never again could he explain to a mistress that it was his mother's fault that he was not able to leave her; never again could he imagine, himself, that he was free. As he set out upon his twenty months of finding himself, this was his first and most painful discovery. Tied for life to his mother, he would never be able to love a woman his own age in any way which could give his mother a rival—the phrase is his own to her. Women would be only sex to him, and this prostitutes could satisfy. The gay decades of the unhindered bachelor were thus assured him, but the miserable, lonely solitude of his last decade was also being prepared here. He had, however, no choice.

The final days in Paris were a whirl of activities, seeing friends, making last visits, drinking, eating, wenching, whatever would fill the hours and keep the mind from thinking. The physical senses, Flaubert wrote, are never far from the psyche; his nerves, cruelly twisted, needed to unwind. Music, often meaningful to him, was a help as he listened to Meyerbeer's newly written *Prophet;* he would have liked to embrace Mme Viardot for her performance in the leading role. He had noted her name carved at Chillon four years earlier, but many more years would pass before he would come to know her.[3] Meanwhile, she had done him good and brought relief. Ludovica, too, had to be bade adieu, fondly, on her staircase; and her husband, the sculptor Pradier, kept bobbing up here and there to wish Maxime and Gustave well.

Sunday Flaubert spent in company with Louis Bouilhet, who had come in for the final hours. Together the two friends went to the Louvre to delight in the Assyrian sculptures like those Flaubert expected to be seeing in Asia Minor. Next, because they knew the artist,[4] they went across the river to Saint-Germain-des-Prés, where they looked at Flandrin's mediocre fresco of Christ's

Entry into Jerusalem: it would come back to Flaubert as he stood outside the Holy City. Then on to dinner at a famous restaurant in the Palais-Royal, the Trois-Frères-Provençaux, where the hero of the second *Sentimental Education* (1869) would later enjoy eating. Théophile Gautier joined them to talk of art and literature and antiquity.

On Monday, October 29, Flaubert and Du Camp left the latter's apartment, where all the servants wept, to go down to the coach station. It was the same courtyard from which Flaubert had departed for Corsica nearly a decade before. That had been a good trip; perhaps it meant this one would be, too. All their friends assured them it would be so, and they were off!

The itinerary was enormous, taking the two men through most of the Near East and lasting twenty months. In all, the trip cost Flaubert over thirty thousand francs or, to put it another way, nearly as much as he earned from all his writing throughout his life. The journey began down the Rhone to Marseilles; then by ship to Egypt; months in Cairo and a boat trip up the Nile to the Second Cataract with a side journey to the Red Sea; a lengthy circuit in Syria and Palestine from Beirut to Jerusalem, Damascus, and Baalbek; the island of Rhodes and the Turkish mainland to Constantinople; Greece, including several weeks in Athens and long trips through the countryside; months in Italy, especially at Naples and Rome but with more casual stays in the cities of Umbria and Tuscany; and a return home via Venice.

Stupendous as this itinerary is, however, the projected journey was even longer as they first conceived it. It was their hope, as they left Paris, to make a protracted expedition from Syria through Persia to the Caspian Sea with a return to the west through Georgia and Asia Minor. Fron the start, though, this plan was dubious, and the whole Persian part of the itinerary was abandoned; it would have been very expensive and dangerous because of uprisings there. Moreover, as they reached Syria and had to make the final decision, homesickness was probably overtaking Flaubert.[5] By the time the two men reached Rhodes, money, too, was a major problem. They went almost directly to Constantinople, which they could not leave until additional funds reached them from France. Greece had then to become a matter of weeks.

Once in Rome, where his mother joined Gustave and from which Maxime left for Paris, Flaubert was forced to curtail the remainder of his plans still further because of illness and had to hurry home under the care of his mother. Even reduced in this fashion, however, it was a tremendous journey and left Flaubert one of the most widely traveled writers of his century.

Almost all of the trip was an extraordinary success. On the way down to Marseilles, Flaubert and Du Camp stopped in Lyon with the painter Gleyre, a friend of Pradier's who had spent long years in the Near East. On his advice they prepared to spend more time in Egypt and to cut down on their Caucasian expedition. At Avignon, Flaubert remembered with melancholy his serenity—albeit cut short—alone in the museum four years before, when he had traveled this way with his family. In Marseilles there was nothing left to recall Eulalie Foucaud. On board ship to Alexandria, Flaubert was heroic while poor Maxime suffered below decks with seasickness. Not even a considerable tempest could quell Gustave's good humor for long; he reported that he was the delight of passengers and crew. It was a good omen for the entire journey.

EGYPT

> Here we are in Egypt, *land of the Pharaohs and Ptolomies, country of Cleopatra* (as they say in literary style). Our heads are shaved as bald as kneecaps, and we are smoking our tobacco in long pipes, and drinking coffee as we recline on divans. . . . I am just barely getting over my initial bewilderment. It is as though you had been thrown sound asleep into the midst of a Beethoven symphony and had wakened as the brasses were tearing your eardrums apart, the basses were thundering, and the flutes sighing.
>
> Letter to Flaubert's doctor from Cairo, January 15, 1850

Arriving in Egypt was a momentous occasion. When the ship was still two hours out of Alexandria, Flaubert went to the bow and could make out the black dome of the harem of the Pasha of

Egypt under the blinding silver light which melted down over the blue sea. Soon there was all the chaos of the Near East before them: Arabs, Negroes, camels, turbans, beatings administered to right and to left, and guttural cries on every hand. It was a solemn and tense moment as he set foot on Egyptian soil.

Flaubert and Du Camp spent six weeks in Cairo. As each had an official mission—Flaubert was to report on agricultural statistics—they were well received and given semiofficial privileges, including an escort of soldiers, which delighted Flaubert. The mission itself he rapidly decided to ignore.

On the other hand, he could not so easily extricate himself from the complications involved in a radical idea of Du Camp's: his friend had decided to be among the first men to take the newly invented camera into the Near East. In these early days such an undertaking involved long hours of work and cumbersome equipment, but Du Camp had the perceptiveness to understand the importance of the venture and the patience to carry it out. Flaubert could be patient about literature but about little else, and soon Du Camp's photography proved a trial. Flaubert tried to take himself off or read or sleep or write letters. But at best the photography was vastly time-consuming and bored him prodigiously.

To give some measure of permanence and to keep up his practice at writing, Flaubert steadily maintained a record of his trip. He had had some thought of publishing a travel book on his return, and some parts of his Notes, particularly those on Egypt, he reworked while en route. Eventually, however, he found it wiser to content himself on the journey with being an all-seeing eye rather than taking time to seek for literary effects or even literary excellence and a polished form. To say, as he once did, that the Notes were only a direct transcription of what was in front of him was perhaps inexact, but they were not another of the "Picturesque Journeys" so popular in his day.

It was Maxime Du Camp's task to watch over Flaubert throughout these long months. He had charge of a patient ill with chronic syphilis and subject, without real warning, to epileptic attacks. Flaubert was, moreover, deeply moody, very self-centered, and accustomed to having his own way. It was a difficult, almost impossible task, but one which Maxime accomplished with heroic selflessness, keeping constant and careful watch over his friend, assuming most of the responsibilities for the material aspects of the journey (if only because chaos resulted each time he was forced to leave Flaubert in charge), and relieving Gustave of every form of dangerous fatigue. Oftentimes for days on end they had only each other to talk to, and in circumstances which would have destroyed a lesser friendship. In twenty months there were, of course, moments of strain; but on the whole Flaubert could and often did note how deeply he was attached to Maxime and how much he relied on him. More experienced as a traveler, Du Camp already knew something of the areas they were in and carried his responsibilities calmly. Flaubert could constantly reassure his mother of Maxime's solicitude and of his watchfulness in enforcing the regimen prescribed by Flaubert's doctors.

The two men had so much in common: a love of antiquity, a quick response to art, a delight in their physical prowess, an enjoyment of evenings in brothels. Particularly they shared an almost idiotic sense of humor. Maxime had been introduced to Le Garçon, The Old Boy, that childhood creation of Flaubert and his friends in the Hôtel-Dieu back in Rouen. Maxime and Gustave felt that they had found him alive and breathing in the person of the consul at Rhodes.[6] Meanwhile in Egypt there came a new satiric creation, The Sheik, the aging, imbecile traveler who incarnates all the idiocies of the day. He would inquire in each new city if there were literary circles and whether the railroad had yet been introduced; he spoke in a trembling voice, and soon there were dialogues. Then The Sheik, now played regularly by Maxime, acquired a nephew, a servant, and even a friend, Quarafon, played by Flaubert.

Over and over the same jokes recurred in the same playlets. In Greece The Sheik was still very active, although other dialogues had been invented for other characters; when Maxime left Gustave in Rome, Gustave missed all of this sorely. He wrote Maxime that Le Garçon thought Parmesan cheese had painted all the canvases attributed to Il Parmigiano (in French, le Parmesan): at table The Old Boy always complimented the cheese on his work and sought to engage him in conversations on esthetics.

Thanks to their missions, their photographing, and their

youth, the two men were well received everywhere. In Egypt, Flaubert was nicknamed Abou-Scheneb, "Father of the Mustache." Here and there he met men who had known and respected his father. At one moment on the upper Nile he and Maxime were admired for resetting a broken leg for a member of their crew. There had been a sickening noise as the bone snapped, but the two novices were proud that their man was walking steadily again in forty-five days, a success which was to be exactly duplicated by Dr. Charles Bovary with the leg of his future father-in-law, Old Man Rouault.

Egypt had long been an obsession with Flaubert and especially in recent years because of Saint Anthony, whose hermitage was on the Nile near Thebes. Hence many aspects were rediscoveries, a matter of actually seeing what in fact he already knew to be there. In Alexandria, he saw live before him the models for ancient Egyptian sculpture with their high shoulders, long torsos, and thin legs. It was as though he were suddenly rediscovering old, forgotten dreams. In a Pasha's garden he could imagine the sultana watching in the distance for a dromedary at full gallop as she sadly scanned the limitless horizons. All of the Egyptian and Syrian countrysides were thus: only the cities were unexpected.

Everything he saw fascinated him. For days he tried to find a way to bring a gazelle back to little Caroline, but it proved impossible; the best he could do was, years later, to put one in the courtyard of Salammbô's palace, where its hooves made a charming sound on the marble.[7] He even hoped that it might be possible to get a mummy past the Egyptian border guards, but this, too, proved unfeasible.

Flaubert could be a remarkably observant traveler, delighting in what he found and displaying often an alert, penetrating curiosity.[8] Soon the two men discovered what later archeology would confirm, that seeing Egypt would require not months but years. It was a strange, incongruous country: even after three months it seemed odd to sit in a fashionable Cairo café with a donkey in one corner relieving himself and a man in another doing the same. No one else found it strange or even spoke of it.

Camels crossing the bazaars, mosques with their fountains, cafés smelling of Near Eastern tobacco, public squares with mimes

GUSTAVE FLAUBERT, BY HIS BROTHER ACHILLE

The uncharitable portrayal of Gustave's full lips and unmanageable hair
suggests a not entirely sympathetic older brother.

ELISA SCHLÉSINGER, BY DEVÉRIA

Since Elisa's infant seems to stand only with his mother's help, this portrait must have been done about the time Flaubert met her. Gustave particularly noticed her large eyes, full lips, and maternal bosom.

GUSTAVE FLAUBERT

On the threshold of manhood Gustave could not help but know his
startling good looks. The pipe in his mouth is by a later hand, perhaps
by Gustave himself, for the young man prided himself on his smoking.

Trouville

This engraving shows Trouville as it appeared when it began to acquire fame. The hotels and some suggestions of private houses appear, with cabins for changing clothes along the sandy beach. From a contemporary guidebook in the Musée des Arts et Traditions populaires, Paris.

CROISSET

This pencil sketch is by an unknown artist, perhaps by Flaubert's niece Caroline. Flaubert's room was on the second floor at the left corner. The property extended some distance to the left, with a pavilion at the far end of the garden.

"Psyche," by Pradier

The sensuality of Pradier's nudes, a quality which excluded almost all others, formed Flaubert's taste in sculpture. Photo Giraudon.

"CUPID AND PSYCHE," BY CANOVA

Flaubert, already prepared by Pradier to respond to sensuality in sculpture, saw this statue in an Italian gallery in 1845. After he and his party had passed on to other rooms in the gallery, he returned to view it alone.

LOUISE COLET, BY WINTERHALTER

"The Muse," as Madame Colet was known, became Flaubert's mistress in 1846. Winterhalter, a popular German portraitist of the day, caught her bold eyes and inviting lips and emphasized the softness of her skin and bosom.

and jugglers, these were the real Egypt, much more moving than the romantic fantasy. On the desert in a sandstorm a caravan passed them, barely glimpsed the murky light, the women heavily veiled, the men with their robes wound around their heads and leaning over the necks of the dromedaries. They passed close beside Flaubert and his party, but no one spoke; the members of the caravan were like phantoms in a cloud. A chill went down Flaubert's spine, a feeling of terror mingled with wild admiration; he laughed nervously and realized that he must be very pale. The dromedaries seemed hardly to touch the dimly perceived ground as though they had sunk into a cloud to their chests. The vision passed and was gone: this was the desert as it really was.

To Flaubert the landscape of Egypt was color and monumental grandeur, regular and pitiless. The architecture, the lines and volumes of the land, and the people seemed all made by the same hand. Even the palm seemed an architectural tree. The landscape could be totally silent, not a sound emanating from it. Experienced thus, it was terrifying like the Sphinx: a silent immobility, grandeur absolutely motionless.

Egypt could also be color and light as Flaubert's pen became more practiced. Thus he described gray mountains covered with a blue tone and with sheets of purple atmosphere spreading out from them over the Nile; gradually this color whitened and night fell. The light in Egypt was a recurrent delight to him: it was a liquid flooding over everything, filling the transparency of the atmosphere, drowning the pyramids and Sphinx, seeming to penetrate the very surfaces and enter into what it shone upon.

One sunrise found the whole Nile Valley bathed in mist resembling a motionless white sea. The desert behind it with its mounds of sand looked like a second ocean, each of whose waves had been turned to stone and tinted dark purple. Meanwhile, however, the sun had been rising; the mist was torn apart into light gauze; the meadows cut by canals were like green carpets. The colors, the light, the rising sun and the moving fog all converged in the description to evoke the feeling of present immediacy. Two or three years later as Flaubert worked on *Madame Bovary*, when Emma rode off in the early morning to be seduced by Rodolphe, this was the view which she was to discover; but it would be her little village of Yonville which would appear as the mists separated. And half a dozen years after that, other parts of the scene found their way into *Salammbô*.

The landscape descriptions are the great pages of Flaubert's Notes. The twenty-month journey gave him an opportunity vouchsafed to few writers of his day to observe and record scenes from Egypt and Syria, Greece and Italy, as the landscapes ranged from the varicolored desert to verdant river valleys and snow-capped mountains. Colors he came to analyze very closely, rarely contenting himself with simple hues but preferring rather to distinguish the exact nuance. He also noted the tint of the light playing over a countryside as he grew more conscious that the color and mood of the landscape itself are established by it. His sensitivity here foreshadowed the Impressionists, but, unlike them, he remained constantly sensitive to the plastic shapes before him. Finally, he now began to show a responsiveness to the dynamic quality of clouds, of the light, and even of the landscape itself; these sensitivities infuse his vision and give it a personal excitement which adds a dramatic time element to what are often, in other writers, static portrayals.

Flaubert's was also an immensely scholarly trip. With the exception of learned expeditions to Egypt no travelers had been so scrupulous as he and Du Camp. They spent eight months; they provided themselves with a small library including Homer, Herodotus, the Bible, dictionaries, Müller's erudite *Manual of Archeology*, and several specialized works as well.[9] Flaubert took minute care to draw up lists of perfumes and spices; they made notes on folklore; they informed themselves in detail about ancient and modern religions.[10] For Flaubert this was all a delight as the learning he had acquired for *Saint Anthony* came to life. He talked with Coptic bishops and made arrangements to see Armenians and Greeks. His notes recorded theological points, and he constantly stood off to observe himself, to realize consciously that he was enjoying it all. This experience, too, sent shivers down his spine.

He and Du Camp made an expedition out from Cairo to see the pyramids and the Sphinx. Around half past three in the afternoon, as they reached the desert, the tension began to increase. Half an hour later they were at the base of the hill, and Flaubert could contain himself no longer. Putting his horse into a full gallop he dashed forward towards the Sphinx; it grew and grew as he approached, rising out of the desert like a dog. At last he was beneath it, joined a moment later by Maxime, whose face was as white as a sheet of paper. Flaubert's head was spinning. No picture he had seen gave any idea of the monster, especially its eyes, expressive and terrifying. At dusk the pink light of the setting sun bathed it.

The baggage was delayed, night was coming on. At last their men arrived, and Du Camp and Flaubert could inaugurate their tent: all night the wind beat upon it. At two they awakened and stepped out a moment to look at the brilliant stars of the clear, dry evening: a jackal whined behind the Second Pyramid. The Arabs, lying in holes they had scooped out of the desert, were lit by the remains of their fires. A few, seated in a circle, smoked their pipes and listened to the monotonous singing of an older man. A few hours later it was time to bestir themselves if they were to see the sun rise from the top of the pyramids. Maxime hastened easily to the top, but it took two Arabs behind and two in front of Flaubert to hoist his bulky frame up by pushing and pulling, groaning and puffing. The sun rose and completed what Flaubert called one of the most voluptuous and dizzying times of his life.

All was not happiness in Egypt for Flaubert, however. He was miserable over the failure of his *Temptation of Saint Anthony;* there was Max's photography, and above all Gustave missed his mother. For some time after leaving her in Nogent he had written almost daily, gauging her pain by his own and trying to relieve it, promising even to come back at once if it were necessary. The second day was easier than the first; he comforted her that the third would be still better. How he longed for her first letter! A lover could not have been more attentive as he conjured up for her visions of his return when they would sit beside the hearth and speak of the desert; he would describe his nights under the tent, and they would both recall how sad they had been over the separation and their common anguish. He assured her that he would come back well, that she alone was what he missed, that their friends would help ease her loneliness.

Again and again Gustave wrote from the Near East to those about his mother, asking them to tend and care for her, to cherish her as best they could in his absence. He imagined her by his side rejoicing with him in what he saw, and he asked his brother Achille to try to offer her something of that daily ration of affection to which her husband and then her younger son had accustomed her. When, going up the Nile, he was perforce without letters for weeks at a time, his anxiety to reach places where mail might be waiting was all-consuming and kept him from sleep the night before; when there was no word from her, his disappointments were devastating. As he longed for her, it was like a physical cramp; tears would fill his eyes, and he could see her wrinkled face and her glasses on her nose, as she leaned out the window to watch for the postman.

Early in February, with a total disregard for expense, the two men chartered a boat for the long trip up the Nile to the Second Cataract: the expedition lasted almost five months. The first night on board was a lyric moment. Flaubert, deeply moved, recited some of Bouilhet's poetry; he could not bring himself to go to sleep; thoughts of Cleopatra obsessed him. On the trip south at any rate (though less so on the return north) he and Maxime led a serene, happy life marred only by the absence of letters from France. They lay on deck dozing or idly watching the passing scene and the simple, childlike sailors. Flaubert worked at deciphering the *Odyssey* in preparation for his trip to Ionia and Greece; later he would study the *Iliad*.

Soon the boat was in the region of Saint Anthony, the Thebaid or region about Thebes, and Flaubert could talk of the desert saint with learned men still living there. He even saw the holes in the cliffs where the desert hermits had dwelled. The pyramids and Sphinx had earlier recalled lines from *Saint Anthony* to both men. Now the crocodiles suggested the parade of the monsters: it seemed an animal evil for the pleasure of being evil. Everywhere his *Temptation* came to life for him. In Syria, prostitutes dancing for Greek sailors recalled a scene from it, and at Corinth he thought of his episode of Demonassa, the Corinthian courtesan.

The trip up the Nile was an almost unqualified success; the trip back north, dreadfully slowed by Maxime's photography and note-taking, was nearly unrelieved boredom. One temple was like another, and Du Camp insisted on wearisome hours of archeological work. Finally Flaubert came to feel that the Nile itself was bored: that was why, like a sated monarch, it would change beds.[11] Still, when once he had returned to Cairo, he missed the boat and wondered whose feet now trod it! The rhythmic beat of the oars pounded in his head and made his melancholy even more excruciating.

Thebes and Karnak the Frenchmen saw both coming and going on the Nile. They were even more striking than the pyramids and the Sphinx. Archeological study the two men put off to the return trip down the Nile, but on the way up their boat pulled in for a few moments. Flaubert was watching the three waves which made up the wake and felt a solemn happiness rising within himself to meet the spectacle before him. He paused, grateful for being capable of such a conscious enjoyment of the intimate voluptuousness penetrating his being. When they returned three months later, it was nine in the evening as they approached, and a brilliant moon illuminated the columns; the dogs were barking and the huge white ruins were like phantoms; the moon, full and round and just above the horizon, appeared motionless and there only for their pleasure. The great palace seemed the home of giants where, on golden plates, they served whole men on spits like larks.

A side trip to the Red Sea gave Flaubert and Du Camp a taste of the real desert.[12] After the long camel ride Flaubert was wildly anxious to reach his goal, hurrying ahead on foot and scrambling up hillocks in his desire to get a first glimpse of the Red Sea; when at last he did, his excitement was tremendous. He shortly went bathing in it, rolling voluptuously through the water, acutely and overtly conscious of its sexual implications. Later he went by himself to look at the varied range of colors of the sea. Its surface ranged from chocolate to amethyst, from pink to lapislazuli to pale green. Observing it Flaubert found as moving as an adventure, and again he stood off to observe himself experiencing it.

His departure from the Red Sea was one of the most painful of the trip for Flaubert. He had an oddly affectionate nature, always apprehensive of change, regretting the old and usually suspicious of the new. Each new departure throughout the trip was anguish. Leaving Cairo meant seeing no more fellahin. Going away from Syria was adieu to the desert, the camels, and the Bedouins; boarding the ship from Constantinople to Athens signified the end of the Turkish world with its veiled women, its mosques, and its cafés. Athens, too, was another heartbreak when it came time to leave, and the departure from Greece marked the real end of the Near Eastern trip: Italy, after all, was Europe. But then Italy became his home, and leaving Rome was a new pang. Wherever he was was good; wherever he was going was lesser; and he repeated this for twenty months. Finally he came to understand it as human nature to avoid flying to evils whose nature we know not of. When it came time to leave the Red Sea, Flaubert and his host for these few days had tears in their eyes, as both knew they would not meet again. They embraced, and Flaubert, his heart filled with a bitter melancholy, climbed up onto his camel and leaned down to take his friend's hand in a final clasp. It was an experience whose depths of feeling were repeated only as he left Athens. But typically, he wrote of the departure from the Red Sea that it was one of those experiences of melancholy which are perhaps among the most profitable things a trip can afford. The writer who was being formed over these months was learning that he must experience all human emotions if he wished to be able to write.

After eight months full of sights and sounds and smells which would give texture to many of his later works—*Salammbô*, *The Temptation*, and *Hérodias* directly, and the others indirectly—Flaubert left Egypt by ship for Syria.

SYRIA AND TURKEY

The Arab proverb is right: "Beware of the pilgrim." Anyone would return from Jerusalem less devout than he set out.

They have done everything they could to make the Holy Places ridiculous. . . . I am furious with these scoundrels for making it impossible for me to be moved, and I wanted nothing so much as that, as you know.

Letters to his mother and to Louis Bouilhet
from Jerusalem, August 20, 1850

It was mid-July, 1850, when the two Frenchmen landed in Beirut. They made a long circular trip to Jerusalem, Damascus, and Lebanon before returning to Beirut in September, two and one-half months later, to sail for the island of Rhodes. Beirut, built of stone and reminiscent of the crusaders, was a striking change from Egypt. The reddish ruins, many of them Norman, would have seemed more at home in a misty northern land.

Syria marked the beginning of easier traveling. They were very pleased at the size of their outfit, ten animals and eight men. All day long the mule bells tinkled steadily as a background to Flaubert's meditations and conscious delight in the sky, the stones, the sea, and the ruins. Syria was as beautiful and wild in its contrasts and colors as Egypt had been calm, monotonous, and pitilessly regular. For hours at a time the two men would ride side by side without opening their mouths, only suddenly to burst forth into one of their periods of joking or playing The Sheik. On several occasions, to spice their days, there were attacks or threats of attacks from roving, robbing bands ferocious and presistent enough to add the penetrating charm of danger. One time, with bullets whistling by them, only a wild gallop saved the party as they took cover behind a turn in the curving road. Flaubert's sole concern was to keep from falling from his madly racing horse, and he delighted in his fearlessness under fire.

Egypt had been the land of the pharaohs and of Cleopatra;

Syria was the land of ancient religions and the Bible. At the cedars of Lebanon Flaubert found people worshiping them as in the time of the Prophets; he felt he was in the midst of all the heresies he had studied for *Saint Anthony*. At Carmel the olive trees began; they were enormous and often hollow, symbols of the Holy Land, as the palm trees had been of Egypt. The Bible was all about him: old engravings from it flooded back into his mind. He thought, too, of Chateaubriand, who had written warm pages about his journey here, and of Jesus, who had walked barefooted over these roads. The landscapes, the costumes, even the look of the far horizon seemed familiar. The women grouped about the fountains were just as they had been in the time of Jacob, no more changed than the blue sky above. He told his mother that if she wished to know what he was seeing, she should read Genesis or Kings. It was a rough, powerful country, grandiose and haughty, the right background for the Bible.

In his Notebooks he sought to capture the quality of these landscapes and expecially the hallucinatory consistency of the light, which he rendered in ever bolder images to try to suggest its liquid quality. He described the night sky growing blue and passing over the trees and between the abandoned houses of a village. Elsewhere a fog seemed to drown a whole plain and looked like a great lake of fluid milk between two mountains; little by little it divided into long vapors which gradually lowered, leaving more of the mountain top visible until, dropping all the way to the ground, this white smoke disappeared in separate, gauzelike strips.

To Flaubert the Holy Land and especially Jerusalem were touchstones by which he hoped to find and test his own faith. The yearnings and doubts of adolescence, the hopes and gentle ending he had written into his *Temptation*, were now to be tried. The living land of the Bible about him allowed the hope that the road to Jerusalem might be, as Paul's journey to Damascus, a moment of revelation. The night before his arrival at the Holy City he was unable to sleep. When he knew he was drawing near to it the next day, his exitement mounted. As with the Sphinx, here again he put his horse into a gallop and dashed ahead of the others until Jerusalem came in sight, and he paused, astonished to have it before him.

Its walls were better preserved than he had expected; it seemed very neat.

Then this agnostic had a vision of Jesus Christ at His entry into Jerusalem surrounded by the cries of the crowd and the palms, just as he and Bouilhet had seen it depicted in Flandrin's fresco at the Church of Saint-Germain-des-Prés nearly a year before. He seemed to leave the city to climb the Mount of Olives; His robe was blue, and there were beads of perspiration on His brow. Mount Hebron rose behind in a misty, transparent light; all the foreground was dry, harsh, and gray under the crude, white, wintry light. A moment later Maxime rejoined him; he recorded, perhaps because it displeased him, that Du Camp was smoking a cigarette.[13] At four-thirty they entered the city.

Had Jerusalem been what he hoped for, Flaubert's religious life might have been different. Had it incarnated Christianity as adequately as Athens later incarnated Hellenism, he might perhaps have been able to appease that longing for faith which had led him for weary months to work at *The Temptation of Saint Anthony* and which had kept him awake through the long hours of the night before his arrival at the Holy City. It was not to be so. Jerusalem seemed a charnel house in which dead dogs rotted in the streets and dead religions rotted in the churches; the curse of God seemed to hover over it and its ruins. It was immensely sad, for Flaubert had gone there, he knew, very humbly and naturally, without striving for anything and with all the simplicity of a heart at peace. He envied those—rare indeed—who could weep celestial tears in Jerusalem, and his heart went out to the patient medieval pilgrims. He knew the bitterness they would feel upon their return when people asked them to speak of Jerusalem and were envious of them.

The whole city was a hypocritical prostitution based on cupidity, falsification, and the hope for material gain. There was no trace of sanctity anywhere. Flaubert longed, and deeply, for the simple churches of his homeland with their lichen-covered walls. Jerusalem was not of his northern world, and he remembered Luther returning a Protestant from the Italy of Leo X. Every spot was identified and ticketed for the tourist, even the places where

the blood of Christ had fallen; the guides wished to make everything precise, to hold God cupped within their grasping hands.
On the Mount of Olives three Capuchin monks were caressing the
soft white breasts of complaisant girls.

Flaubert made a first visit to the Holy Sepulcher and was
revolted. The Pasha had the keys: otherwise the various Christian
sects would have been at each other's throats. Mutual hatreds
dominated the scene, except for a full-length portrait of Louis-
Philippe, the Bourgeois Monarch. Flaubert left, all emotion dashed
to the ground and only a feeling of irony left. The reign of the
grotesque dominated the world, apparently: its realm extended
even to the tomb of Jesus.

Profoundly sad, Flaubert returned to his hotel room to read
the Passion story in the Gospels. It was the fact, he wrote, that a
dog would have been more moved that morning at the Holy Sepulcher. Now, tired to the very marrow, he read on in the Gospel
according to Matthew, his heart opening up in total purity as he
came to the Sermon on the Mount. It brought calm to replace the
cold bitterness of the morning. The Christians had done all they
could to make the Holy Places ridiculous. Whose fault was it,
then, that he could feel nothing? Theirs? The Lord's? His own?
All three, he felt, but particularly the Lord's. It was the falseness
which made it unbearable, the fact that it all had a commercial
end. He was furious with the priests for having defrauded him of
the emotion he had longed for. He would never again hope that
organized religion could be anything but a travesty of genuine
religion.

Flaubert returned later and was approached by a priest who
opened a cupboard, took out a rose, and handed it to him. Following the traditional ceremony, he then poured orange-blossom
water over Flaubert's hands, took back the flower, placed it upon
an altar, blessed it, and returned it. The moment was profoundly
bitter for Flaubert as he thought of how many faithful souls
would have wished to be in his place. It was a strange reversal of
the usual romantic longing to be, oneself, in someone else's place.
The occasion was, he knew, wasted on him. He felt all its emptiness and the uselessness of the ceremony, its grotesqueness. And
yet he sensed its perfume; he kept the rose. He did not weep for

his lack of emotion; he regretted nothing, but felt rather the strange sort of emotion, as he wrote to Bouilhet, which the two of them had, sitting by the fireside, when they tried to imagine what sort of abyss was really represented by the word "love." For the emotion he could not feel here was also, as he knew, a form of love.

The Grotto of the Nativity at Bethlehem was better. The lamps hanging there reminded him of the Magi, and he described them minutely in his Notes.[14] There was for him a mystic suavity and a gentle splendor at the Manger, which soothed him. At Gethsemane he dismounted for a moment of silence alone and then, remounting, returned to Jerusalem. After a month they left.

In Lebanon, Baalbek brought Flaubert his first contact with classical antiquity in the Near East. The great Roman colonnade looked like chiseled vermillion under the sunlight; a piece of frieze seemed cut from gold ingot. Imperial Rome stood forth here in her majesty, even in these thistle-covered ruins. Seventy feet up a great bird of prey with reddish plumage poised motionless on a column, like Jupiter's eagle. The shadows of other birds in flight would now and then fleck across the pavement. Then there would be nothing, only wind and silence. The second day the sun, alternately hidden and exposed by passing clouds, would suddenly light up the ruins: it was, Flaubert noted, like the smile of a sleeping god opening and closing his eyes. He wondered if one could fall in love with a colonnade.

The island of Rhodes brought the classical world even nearer. The bazaars were sunlit and began to suggest the Greek merchant. The ancient Greek walls, admirably built, were a foretaste of Greece itself. The mainland of Turkey, to which the travelers soon sailed, continued the change. The landscape was more European than Syria had been, but it somehow seemed older, more distant and Asiatic. The Turkish khans or inns set his imagination to work: they were what one wanted for the end of the long overland route, where merchants in furs arrived with distant treasures. The profiles of the Greek women, too, now and then suggested the ancient Hellenic world they came from. The camel seemed an intruder from the desert.

The Levant was in a process of decay before the all-invading

Europeanization. It dismayed Flaubert thus to observe the rotting of a civilization he had dreamed of and its conquest by a world he had fled. Even in Damascus he had watched Turks in the cafes in European dress avidly following the billiard games. Only the Bedouin seemed virile enough to regenerate this world. In Constantinople the European quarter was peopled by Turks in patent leather shoes and white gloves and Turkish women drove about in coupés. The two worlds were hopelessly mixed: one passed whirling dervishes on one's way to the opera; there were lending libraries and hat shops in Constantinople. The women's veils were becoming slighter and slighter; soon the veil and the harem, too, would go. A whole world was disappearing, and Flaubert found it sad. The idea of a novel on the Europeanization of the Near East and the barbarizing of Europe began to take form in his mind. Had he written it, it would have been a bitter satire of both worlds.[15]

In mid-November when Flaubert and Du Camp reached Constantinople, they had been away from France more than one year; they waited here a month for additional funds from home. The city offered all the pleasures of a cosmopolitan center. Here Flaubert went to hear the opera *Lucia*, which he had first heard in Rouen in 1840 and which would start Emma Bovary on her final downfall. At the embassy they were delighted with the warm reception given them by the jovial, informal ambassador—General Aupick, the stepfather, ultimately hated and despised, of a poet they would come to know, Charles Baudelaire. They also met a fellow French traveler, Edward Delessert. From this contact Maxime would derive a mistress and Flaubert some character traits for personages in his later *Sentimental Education*. Everything was grist to the mill of the writer he was rapidly preparing to be.

The incredible size of Constantinople and its milling population from all over the globe gave one a feeling of being crushed. But it seemed indeed the city where one would live with the ravished odalisque. The crowds of veiled, silent women looking out with their large eyes, this world of unknown faces, so foreign, led to sad reveries which gripped Flaubert strangely. About to leave the Near East, he found how much he had learned to love it; it would haunt him and his writing.

GREECE

I was really happy, way deep down, yesterday as I first saw the Acropolis brilliant white in the sunlight under a sky laden with clouds. Up in the bow of the ship . . . looking ahead I let myself go in "solemn thoughts." . . . I was more moved than at Jerusalem. . . . This was closer to me, more part of my nature.

Letter to Louis Bouilhet from Athens, December 19, 1850

In the middle of December, their funds seriously depleted, the two friends set sail from Constantinople for Athens to remain in Greece some seven weeks, too short a time but all their resources would permit. About half of these weeks went to exploring Athens and making one-day excursions to Marathon and Eleusis, whose mysteries had occupied Flaubert in his studies for *The Temptation*. Two long trips took them out of the city, one to Delphi and Thermopylae, the other down through much of the Peloponnesus.[16]

The sight of Athens stirred Flaubert profoundly as he gazed at the Acropolis before him in the sun with the Island of Aegina to the left and Salamis ahead. He was more moved than he had been on reaching Jerusalem, for there the anticipation and the hope had been alloyed with doubt; at Athens there was only serene expectation, and he caught himself beginning the eternal monologue of all travelers to Greece, full of admiration and amazement on considering this tiny corner of ground in the middle of the mountains dominating it. He felt Olympian and was filling his lungs and his mind with classical antiquity.

The peaceful beauty of the countryside concorded with his picture of Greek culture. His spirit responded when gentle, harmonious mountain views opened out in grandiose serenity at Eleusis or later at Olympia, a landscape to Flaubert typically classic in its simplicity and charm. Its tranquility seemed to infiltrate his muscles; the blue of the sky descended into his spirit and, like the ancient Greeks, he could live its peace. Long before, he had written to Louise Colet that happiness was a lie, the search for which had been the source of most of life's calamities. He had affirmed that there were serene moments of peace which imitated happiness and were perhaps its superior.[17] And he had tried to teach her to seek these moments in art. Now he was discovering, as others had before him, that the Greek countryside could offer this peace and that it was deeply consonant with the Greek spirit.

Flaubert felt that literary masterpieces and great natural scenery had much in common: both were totally simple and had a quiet, peaceful air, that serenity which, in antiquity, was the hallmark of the divine. Marcel Proust once suggested that Flaubert's talent for description lay in his ability to fuse himself with the object he was describing. The true miracle—the word is Proust's —comes only when the artist disappears or becomes one with his material.[18] Such a fusion occurred when Flaubert essayed a description of Mount Parnassus at dawn. His description penetrates intimately its essential shape and suggests a sculptor's feeling for three dimensions in the treatment of the plastic values. These, the nuances of color, and the dramatic changing of the light, he recorded with such brilliance and imagery as to rival Chateaubriand and Hugo, the other great French masters of this art in the nineteenth century.

The Parnassus was before him as the sun rose, showing all its snow, he wrote;* it was formed of two sharp slices which rose far above the wide bases on which they rested and which, for the eye, made the transition between them. The summit, flattened and thin, was of a brilliant white like varnished mother-of-pearl; the light, circulating above it, seemed like a potter's glaze of liquid steel. Soon a pink tint appeared, then disappeared, and the summit became white again, with black patches of vegetation where the snow had not fallen. Behind him a part of the sky was all red,

*"Le Parnasse, au soleil levant, montrait toutes ses neiges; il était taillé en deux tranches aiguës, proéminentes, appuyées sur des bases très larges qui en faisaient, à l'oeil, la transition. Sommet épaté, mince, d'un blanc brillant comme de la nacre vernie; la lumière, qui circulait dessus, semblait un glacis d'acier fluide. Bientôt une teinte rose est venue, puis s'en est allée, et il est redevenu blanc, avec ses filets noirs placés où la verdure paraît, où la neige n'est pas tombée. Derrière nous, une partie du ciel toute rouge, roulée en grosses volutes, avec des moires en bosses, et entre elles des places brunes de cendre" (*NDV*, II, 89).

rolling upward in huge volutes, with brilliant areas standing out and, between them, areas of ash brown. Gautier could have been proud of his disciple: art for art's sake had not often had this dynamic brilliance.

Athens, too, moved Flaubert, but in two contrary ways. On the one hand it gave play to a minute sort of observation, the counting of columns or close study of hair arrangements, which almost at once led him to total sterility by absorbing his attention in details which could not be, for him, evocative. When, however, he resisted these temptations, then the extraordinary richness of Greek art aroused his reverence for its purity and its vibrant life or excited his relish for its sensuality. The "Victory Adjusting Her Sandal" at the Temple of Nike Apteros, by her graceful movement and thinly draped form, appealed to his sense of dynamism. It also showed him what Pradier could not: supple harmony of body and garb, and elegance and virtuosity in rendering of pose could be exciting but chaste; indeed the chastity would heighten the excitement.

The Parthenon was like the Red Sea in providing one of the deepest emotions of his life; it repeatedly evoked his tremendous enthusiasm. The stupendous naturalism and dynamic vigor of the frieze of Phidias suggested bases for art which ran deeper than romanticism and could be used as counters to it. Moreover, however simple the general tone of the Parthenon might be, the sculptures were rich. Classicism, as he had suspected, did not need to be emaciated, cold, or bare. Rather, in the hands of the Athenians, it was vigorous and natural, and rich in detail but simple in effect. Flaubert dreamed of a form of writing which would have the same qualities.

Greek art, he discovered, required perfection of technique. The wall of the Propylaea was, in fact, so well put together by Greek masons that one could hardly distinguish the joints. His respect for this wall, bare and unadorned but perfect, was the craftsman speaking. Twenty-five years later it would still be a touchstone to him, a way to suggest to others what made his concept of the writer different from that of even a Zola.[19]

Flaubert's two trips through the Greek countryside brought archeology to life for him. Names long familiar came to have plastic, three-dimensional meaning as his route took him up Mount Helicon and Mount Parnassus. The Valley of the Muses he traversed with a warm sun bringing relaxed ease; the noise of streams muted consciousness; the colors of rock and foliage delighted his eye. He responded with a smile and a sense of well-being so impossible in Paris or even Croisset and so normal here. The grace and majesty of the ravine provided an intimate charm and rustic seductions on every hand. The knotty oak trunks blown down by winds seemed natural seats for the Muses, and the goats and goatherds recalled ancient pastorals and idylls. The Age of Hesiod was all about him.

His wide and excited readings came to life. At Marathon he heard for himself the whinnying of horses just as Pausanias had; sheep reminded him of Polyphemus; Greek glades seemed made for nymphs. The landscapes in particular seemed dimly to recall old engravings or blackened pictures hung in odd corners of apartments. He was haunted by the feeling of having seen some of them before. He came upon a huge greenish rock marked with longitudinal squares like marqueterie in the midst of a grove of olives dominated by the high slopes of a mountain. It seemed to him, in his phrase (which is today the psychologist's term), *déjà vu*, already seen. The *déjà vu*, while by no means confined to epileptics, is more than usually common among them and was recurrent for Flaubert in Greece. He wondered, of this rock and olive grove, if he were recalling very old memories, perhaps of pictures seen in childhood and whose titles now escaped him. Or had he lived there before? He could not answer. But he readily peopled the scene with a priest in white robes and maidens with long hair walking by over there behind the dry wall. It was like a snatch from a dream passing through the waking mind. It seemed so real, so true. He began to wonder where it had all happened. And then suddenly the charm was broken, and all that was left was the chill running down his spine again, as when the caravan had passed him in the desert storm in Egypt.

Alternatively and more commonly, Flaubert's mood was heroic. In general the weather was bad, sometimes dangerously so. In later years recurrent rheumatism was to remind him painfully of these weeks. He was wont to blame it on the endless rain, the snows of Mount Parnassus, and all the wet hours he spent in Greece.[20] Fording rivers, he and Du Camp were frequently up to the saddle in water. During the lonely days they would meet only sheep and their shepherds or the wild dogs of Greece, rushing to snap at the horses' legs.

Lodging for the night was often an anxious question. Sometimes they slept in stables, men and horses crowding about the small fire as in ages long past. But the khans scattered along the routes afforded the most common stopping places. Usually only a single room, the khan required all to sleep together amidst wine bags, piles of wheat, cheeses, onions on strings, and other provisions. In a corner an old woman would rock a child in a hollowed trunk which also served as kneading trough and laundry tub. Smoked out regularly, robbed by the owners, spending sleepless nights because of the fleas, shivering in drafts which made his candle run like a rheumy nose, he was experiencing the pain and the joy of living in ancient heroic ages. Slowly there began to evolve the project which would excite him particularly in his last years, a tale based on the defense of Greece against the Persians: The Battle of Thermopylae.

Several places aroused Flaubert. Livadia, changed beyond recognition by earthquakes, held somewhere the site of the grotto of Trophonius, familiar to him through his studies of Apollonius for *The Temptation.* Delphi was a lyric site, a landscape of religious terrors, the right background for the soothsaying of the Pythian Sibyl. Circling the base of Mount Parnassus, he and Du Camp thought with amusement of the rage it would have occasioned in the hearts of the anticlassical romantic rebels who had made the Battle of *Hernani.* And Thermopylae, site of Leonidas' last stand, bewildered them as they sought to identify the Pass in a geographical puzzle made baffling by silting which had altered the shoreline. The Mount Cithaeron Range was a wild, midnight ride through snow and a desperate effort to find their way again before cold closed in upon them or robber bands attacked.[21]

Their northern trip completed and Athens having absorbed all the time Du Camp and Flaubert could give to her, the two men set out by a circuitous route for the western coast of Greece, Patras, and the ship for Italy. The last day in Athens was a solemn and momentous time for Flaubert. He went up to the Acropolis to bid it adieu, noticing in the Parthenon the broken remains of a femur, gray from exposure. The wind was high; it was sundown, and the sky was red out over the island of Aegina; behind the columns of the Propylaea the clouds spread out, egg-yellow in hue. As he started back across the Acropolis to come down into the city again, two great birds took flight from the Temple of Neptune and headed east in the direction of Smyrna, of Asia, where he had been. To try to hold the sense of the scene, its special poignancy, he added in his Notebook the smaller details which held a sort of cameo quality for him in retrospect, giving validity to the whole by their chiseled relief. He left the Acropolis and noticed that the hinges squeaked; in a moment a soldier came up to him to try to sell a little figurine. A woman in rags was climbing slowly up toward the top; a donkey brayed. And, a final note, for a long time he paused to look at what had been for him one of the two or three greatest Greek works, a minor fragment of a woman's torso whose breasts so excited him as to overshadow almost everything but the greatest works of Phidias and Praxiteles. He wrote of it as one would of a mistress in orgiastic frenzy, and carried away with him in his memory a vision of an art which, chaste in itself, could be for the viewer a tremendous erotic experience. He would strive to find its equivalent in his writing.

The route which Flaubert and Du Camp followed on the first day out from Athens led along the Skironian Cliffs to Corinth. The landscape aroused in Flaubert that sense of classical antiquity which brought on at once, for him, a feeling of intimate happiness and intense well-being. His direct physiological responses to sense impressions were in themselves stronger than those of most travelers: he saw and smelled and felt more than they. In addition, he had long cultivated his psychological responses to these stimuli. His tremendous reactions during this day in Greece—which had little effect on Du Camp—suggest the potentials of sensitivities and emotions he could draw on as a writer.

Flaubert's notes became lyric as he described the sun, the feeling of liberty, the view with its broad horizons, and the odor of the seaweed. The whole landscape seemed calm and full of gracious dignity, a summation of all that the classical had meant to

him from that day in 1840 when he had first seen the actress
Rachel perform. He felt as though he were in love; he wanted to
burst into tears and roll upon the ground in order to give vent to
his feelings. He wanted to pray, but he knew neither formula nor
language adequate to his needs. Five years before in Italy, he had
at least been able to fall on his knees in a church.[22] Now, after
Jerusalem, this was no longer possible. He was in Corinth that
night, but it was the courtesan Laïs and not Paul's Epistles to the
Corinthians which came to his mind to close this lyric day.

Over the long months of travel, Flaubert developed what he
later called his myopic vision, the ability which short-sighted people have to see things very minutely and hence very well because
they must pore over them.[23] He noted autumn leaves of an oak
tree, ruddy blond in color, twisted and curly at the ends, with the
blue of the unrelieved sky passing through this gilded foliage; the
leaves were paler on their outer edges. Bats seen against the light
seemed to have the blue air passing through their thin, gray wings.
Such details could be used for powerful effect at the end of longer
descriptions to give a final, sharp point to them, a device he would
constantly use. Near Athens he watched a flock of sheep with the
shepherds carrying in their arms the little ones who could not yet
walk. The men wore great leather coats still retaining the long,
white wool, and in their hands they carried crooks. Their hair,
full and curly, fell at random on their shoulders. The wool of the
sheep, he noticed, was very white and fine.

In opposite fashion Flaubert was also sensitive to broad, over-
all effects, especially light, which he had already begun to notice
in Egypt and Syria. In Greece the rain of light—to use Chateaubriand's term—which often envelops the mountains impressed him
as it has so many others who traveled there. In one view he noted
the gray mountains, spotted here and there with pale green and
having a pink glaze, very light, which trembled over their surface.
In another, perhaps the most startling of the trip, he turned to a
direct painting of the light alone; later he would use parts of the
description for the opening and the close of his *Temptation*. He
dealt with the sun, the clouds, and the sky, before returning to
earth to observe their effect upon the objects below. In a bold
inversion, it was not they he painted but the light, using the tech-

nique of Rembrandt revived by the painters of his own generation. He first noted* the sun piercing the clouds, which then withdrew on both sides leaving the sun covered with a white transparency which dulled and blurred its edges. The sky, black to the
left, gradually became ultramarine of a very tender hue, with
darker, thick places here and there. The blue had a pearl-gray
tone melted over it. Then the masses dissipated, the blue remained
bordered with little white clouds unrolled along its edges; to the
right was a small cloud of ashen hue near to him and hanging over
the hill. The light, falling from his right and almost vertically, cast
a strange light on Du Camp to Flaubert's left: he stood out against
a black background, and each small detail of his face could be
picked out clearly. The light fell upon the green grass and seemed
to spread about over it a restful, gentle fluid of a distilled blue
color.

Such hyperacute vision, not uncommon among epileptics,
Flaubert could put to gripping use in his writing. The extraordinary light of this scene he allowed to play over the surroundings
of the desert saint when he came to rewrite the opening scene of
The Temptation. It made everything seem as hard as bronze, while
the pearly gray and blue colors spread over the sky above. The
sudden withdrawal of the clouds Flaubert used for the final
vision: here, as they drew back—like the curtains of a tabernacle,
he wrote—they revealed the disc of the sun and, in its very middle, the face of Christ appeared to the beleaguered saint. It was the
majestic and tender ending Flaubert wanted, replacing with its
gentleness and power the earlier strident laugh of the Devil. The
rain of light in Greece had provided it.

*"Le soleil perce les nuages, ils se retirent des deux côtés et le laissent
couvert d'un transparent blanc qui l'estompe: le ciel, noir sur la gauche,
devient bleu outremer très tendre, avec des épaisseurs plus foncées dans
certains endroits; le bleu a un ton gris perle fondu sur lui. Les massse se
dissipent, le bleu reste bordé de petits nuages blancs déroulés; derrière
l'acropole d'Argos, à notre droite, près de nous et sur elle, un petit nuage
blanc, cendré. La lumière, tombant de ma droite et presque d'aplomb, éclaire
étrangement François et Max à ma gauche, qui se détachent sur un fond
noir, je vois chaque petit détail de leur figure très nettement; elle tombe sur
l'herbe verte et a l'air d'épancher sur elle un fluide doux et reposé, de
couleur bleue distillée" (*NDV*, II, 143).

Down through the Peloponnesus and interminable rains Flaubert and Du Camp made their way to Patras. They were in pitiful condition at the end of the long horseback journey. Secretly, of course, the two were proud of looking like Cossacks, and Flaubert delighted in his heavy beard, his stockings which had no heels left, his tattered shirts and patched boots. All this obvious virility helped to compensate for the premature loss of his hair, which was going rapidly and made him fear that soon he might be completely bald. It was true, also, that he was acquiring a paunch. Maxime made fun of paunch and baldness, but to Flaubert they were the first signs of senility and decadence, a deeply shameful and humiliating state. At best he could smile wryly and observe that shortly he would be one of those men with whom prostitutes would prefer not to sleep.[24] In Italy, returning to more civilized lands, he even shaved off his beard, which, as he wrote to his mother, he had bathed in the Nile and through which the wind of the desert had blown. Beneath it were revealed the heavy jowls and general physiognomy which went with his increased girth. It was a difficult discovery for a man of only twenty-nine.

ITALY

In four days we are embarking for Brindisi. There we return to the status of ordinary tourists. The real trip is over.

Letter to his mother from Patras, February 9, 1851

Italy was in every way a return to more civilized living.[25] Arriving at Naples in the rain and watching the Neapolitan women trotting along on the pavements recalled his return to Paris in November, 1840, when he had just been in the wilds of Corsica. The museums in Naples were the most exciting he had seen yet; day after day he and Maxime passed in them every hour that they were open, studying the great Greek, Roman, and Etruscan works.

Rome at the start was a tremendous disappointment. Flaubert had sought the world of Nero and, of course, none of it remained.

Little by little, however, he began to find ancient Rome, at first in the countryside, the *campagna romana* Chateaubriand had glowingly described for Flaubert's generation. Now he saw it for himself—uncultivated, empty, accursed like the desert, with its remains of aqueducts and its herds of cattle. This was the Rome of which he had dreamed—magnificent, deserted, and wasted; here he was happy. Within the city, at least in the obvious places, ancient Rome lay hidden. At the Coliseum he found a cross in the center and a dozen chapels about the arena; one may hardly blame him for his irritation. But as he came to know the city better he found that there were quarters such as he had imagined, especially down along the banks of the Tiber, odd, deserted corners full of dung and reminiscent of an older age. Here, too, he was happy. But Greece had made him hard to please in architecture, and the Parthenon spoiled whatever pleasure he might have had from Roman buildings. They seemed somehow false or trivial.

Christian Rome, too, at first irritated Flaubert much as Jerusalem had. The robe of the Jesuit, as he phrased it, covered everything with the dull tonality of the seminary: the city of the Caesars suffered from the miasma of the priests. Endless churches succeeded one another; convents and monasteries were everywhere; the long streets were neither sufficiently noisy with people nor sufficiently empty as Baalbek had been. It was not the romantic Rome of his imaginings.

Slowly, however, the observer in Flaubert discovered a new Rome, one he had not been looking for in his fantasies and his desires; this was Renaissance and baroque Rome. Saint Peter's, it is true, bored him, seeming glacial and pompous beside the giant work of antiquity. But the paintings and statues of this age were a succession of revelations. He had known the Louvre and had seen some Italian galleries during the honeymoon trip of 1845, so that the world of painting was not new to him. During the trip he had often noted that certain scenes looked as though they should be painted or engraved because of their colors or composition, and he had frequently observed that certain sights were as one pictured them from having seen them in works of art. But the actual experience of the stores of art in Italy was beyond anything he had expected.

One could, he wrote, spend a lifetime contemplating them in a completely ideal atmosphere, untouched by mundane affairs. He could imagine, now, living there in some side street in a populous quarter. By dint of solitude and meditation one could mount high in understanding the melancholy of history. In *Salammbô* and in two revisions of *The Temptation*, Flaubert would try this, and the last work he completed was the melancholy story of John the Baptist and Herodias.

His mother joined Gustave in Rome, and Maxime, turning his charge over to her, left for France. The reunion had been arranged six months before, when Flaubert had been separated from his mother for a year and neither could stand it any longer. They agreed she would come to Italy to meet him. Now after almost a year and a half they were together in Rome, never to be separated again for more than a month or so until Madame Flaubert's death some two decades later. Her love, seemingly selfless but in reality all consuming, was the only abiding tenderness he ever knew. Her companionship was what made up the daily routine of his life and the color of his days. She was his strength and, ultimately, perhaps his greatest limitation. It was well that she and he came to know it during this period of self-discovery for Flaubert.

Gustave had longed for the moment of reunion with his mother. But she told him almost at once that his manner had changed. For all his yearning for family and friends, to her he seemed brutal, perhaps because he was now more independent. It puzzled Gustave, who felt that he was being particularly kindly toward her and easy to live with. It was part of his reaching maturity that he had, thus, to acquire the right to be himself. To some extent his mother had kept him from normal marriage; he defended himself by living a life which was, ultimately, as much centered about himself as his mother's was about herself.

Despite his mother's presence Flaubert continued his long museum days. For nearly four months in all he looked at the galleries and churches and museums of Italy, forming his taste and extending his knowledge. Of classical works he particularly admired the great Vatican "Torso," "a back with all its muscles." Work of such intense observation he had already learned to admire in Greece, and the basic esthetic could readily be transferred to literature.

Classical busts so excited him that they pursued him even as he tried to fall asleep at night. In them he sought portrayal of character and the suggestion of the ideal. But when he attempted to understand the technique and made notes for himself on it, he could only record the number of curls in beards or hair; Pradier had been unable to teach him the inner nature of sculpture.

As in Greece, he rejoiced in the later work, that of Lysippus and others, for its charm; but his real delight went rather to Roman animal depiction for its verity and intensity. Lack of accuracy, however, bothered him: the fact that sculptors failed to make the second and third toes alike or that they attached the tails of fauns at impossible places on the spine. "Realism," if the word has any meaning in Flaubert's esthetic, is a negative matter only. One may not be inaccurate; one must not violate the natural. Flaubert was no more than amused by the realistic triumphs of *trompe-l'oeil* painting at Pompeii, but he was immensely moved by what he termed the prodigious Byzantine mosaics of Rome: their highly stylized renderings led him to remark dejectedly that no one had studied the Byzantine yet.

Flaubert had a modest competence as a critic of painting. At Cana he knew enough to recall Veronese's painting in the Louvre; the aspect of Mount Lebanon, and particularly its rocks, was in the style of Poussin; elsewhere the works of minor artists whom he had seen in the Salons of his day would come to mind. In Italy, Fra Angelico became for him, as for much of his century, the supreme painter of faith and gentle religious emotions: he would later consider using him as a means of suggesting certain parts of Emma Bovary's religious feelings. Botticelli and Raphael he enjoyed, but Michelangelo's "Last Judgment" was, with the Vatican "Torso," the supreme monument of Rome to him, the realization of an immense concept, like the art of Goethe but more passionate. Michelangelo seemed more than human, a Shakespearean Homer, mingling antiquity and Dante. Complex and unique, "The Last Judgment" satisfied him completely while terrifying him by its grandeur.

The Venetians he rightly looked forward to coming to know in Venice, finding their work the most immediately satisfying, a judgment which would still find acceptance with Berenson fifty years later. They were perhaps materialists; this he did not deny or particularly mind. What he liked was their color and their poetry. He would himself be open to the charge of materialism in his later works, but he hoped to have done with his materials something akin to what the best of the Venetians had done with theirs.

As always with Flaubert and works of art, there was the question of sex. There had been the undraped torso on the Acropolis at Athens. In Italy a Parmigiano pleased him, depicting an adorable little woman to be kept in a nest; a Rubens Bacchanalia he found impossible to take his eyes from. Even lesser works, sculpture or painting, could become fascinating on this account; thus one piece delighted him because, while it avoided frank obscenity, it had a sort of internal corruption.

Two paintings, neither obviously erotic, surpassed all the others in their obsessive power over him. Other canvases he knew to be artistically superior; but these he could not drive out of his mind. The first, the Murillo "Virgin and Child" from the Palazzo Corsini, once seen, pursued him like a perpetual hallucination; the Virgin's dark, staring eyes passed again and again before his imagination like dancing lanterns, a sort of waking and delightful parallel to the mad lanterns of his epileptic seizures. He was once again living the sort of experience he had had in Brittany and which he had imagined the Breton peasant as having. Carnal love and religious fervor were so commingled as to be hard to distinguish, as he had portrayed them in Saint Anthony. It is perhaps significant that the face of Murillo's Virgin bears a distant resemblance to Elisa Schlésinger. Several works of art or actual experiences thus stimulated him sexually to begin living within the hallucinations his imagination produced, the sort of self-induced madness which he could learn to control for his writing. Titian's "Assumption of the Virgin" in Venice literally frightened him, so gripping was his reaction: to have stayed longer in the city would have risked his sanity, he felt, for he would have fallen in love with her. Religion, sexuality, and art were intimately allied in Flaubert's enjoyment of painting. They had been joined in parts of his *Temptation of Saint Anthony;* the relationship was to become an obsession in the writing he was planning.

After four and one-half days in Venice, Flaubert had to leave. Earlier he had envisaged a roundabout route back to France including Vienna, Prague, Dresden, Cologne, and Brussels;[26] but now illness, which had been dogging him since Rhodes, forced radical changes in the itinerary, and he hurried home to Croisset with his mother.

SEX AND SEXUALITY

I suspect a Maronite girl of having made me this present. But it may have been a little Turkish one. Was it the Turk or the Christian? Which one of the two? What a problem! What a thought!!!

Letter to Louis Bouilhet from Constantinople,
November 14, 1850

Flaubert's illness, which thus curtailed the end of his trip, was the paradoxical result of the return to good health, which had been the purpose of the long period in warmer climates. Renewed vigor had meant, of course, a renewed interest in sex. It was a major attack of venereal disease which precipitated his hurried retreat to Croisset.[27]

In the reasonably healthy man which Flaubert rapidly became during the trip, sexuality occupied a normally prominent place. Sometimes it was no more than idle fantasy as when, at Corinth, he thought of her courtesans of bygone days bathing their bodies and their hair in the waves he was looking at. Or it could take the sublimated form of excitement over art works, Murillo's or Titian's "Virgin." Recalling the bit of sculpture at Athens representing a woman's torso evoked in him responses normally reserved for actual sexual experiences. His reaction to its undraped right breast was almost orgiastic: it was made to drive one mad, he proclaimed. It was round like an apple, full and abundant; it was widely separated from the left one and would be heavy in one's hand. There were in it fertile maternities or delights of lovemaking which would make a man die. The rain and sun had given the marble a tawny color almost like flesh. The torso seemed so peaceful and so noble; it looked as though the chest would swell and the lungs fill with air. How one would have rolled over it weeping or fallen on one's knees before it, hands crossed. He almost wanted to pray.

Flaubert's prayer would surely not have been Renan's "Prayer on the Acropolis," a hymn to the wisdom of Athena and the impossibility for northern races of totally accepting her; but Flaubert might have borrowed the words he had put in the mouth of Venus when she tempted Saint Anthony: it was her paean to her own role in Greece. "I was free, I was pure; . . . when I crossed the oceans, the waves trembled with pleasure at the touch of my feet. . . . I was Beauty, I was Form! The gods fainted with desire at the sight of me; I vibrated endlessly over the primitive world and the benumbed matter, drying under my glance, grew firm and took onto itself precise contours. . . . Slowly I dreamed of poses and harmonies of line and the secret rhythms of splendid bodies. The artist, in anguish, invoked me in his work, the young man in his desire."[28]* Now Flaubert invoked the torso. It has never been identified since then, but perhaps it is better not to be able to look at a battered fragment through other eyes than his.

Living women, too, he noticed. Egyptian women, modestly covering their faces with the garment which normally covered their torsos, led him to observe that the shape of their breasts did not excite him. At Nazareth, however, he found the women unchanged since Old Testament days, and he noticed that their robes, which were gathered about the waist by a sash, gave what he called a Biblical movement to their bodies. Years before, as a student in Paris he used to sit at Tortoni's and watch the prostitutes stroll by. He was devoured, he said, with the poetry of the Bible at such moments, with the Song of Songs or the maledictions

---

*"J'étais libre, j'étais pure ...; quand je parcourais les océans, les vagues frissonnaient de plaisir au contact de mes talons roses ... J'étais la Beauté! j'étais la Forme! Les dieux à ma vue se pâmaient d'amour, je vibrais incessamment sur le monde engourdi, et la matière humide, se séchant sous mon regard, s'affermissait de soi-même en contours précis ... j'avais rêvé avec lenteur des attitudes d'existence, des harmonies de ligne, et tout ce rythme secret des splendides anatomies. L'artiste, plein d'angoisses, m'invoquait dans son travail, le jeune homme dans son désir" (*TENT*, p. 479).

of the Prophets against fornication in high places.[29] Now at Nazareth he saw it again as the women passed royally by, hips and buttocks prominent as they walked.[30]

How different from European women! He could burst out in invective against the narrow, hypocritical life women were prepared for in France, an apprenticeship in dishonesty from first to last, which left them in the end bigoted, limited, and denatured. Society made it its aim to destroy in the bud one of the most charming of God's creations. What he feared, he said, was the moral corset in which they were brought up.

Since that was the way women were, and long experience assured Flaubert that in his society it was so, then only cynical disregard was reasonable and love must be considered only a physical need to be relieved in whatever receptacle could be found, vase of gold or pot of clay.[31] Only chance made the difference. And so he took once again to frequenting prostitutes. In Alexandria, up the Nile and back down again, in Jerusalem, in Damascus, in Constantinople, he and Maxime paused briefly in one brothel after another, finding it strange in Egypt not even to be able to exchange a few words with the girl, or in Damascus rushing off at eleven in the morning to spend a few quick moments with a seventeen-year-old before setting out for a week or so of enforced chastity in the desert. And, as was almost inevitable, Flaubert, Du Camp, and their servant as well, all came down with various venereal diseases.

In Flaubert's case painful irony was involved. After leading a lusty sexual life in Egypt and in the early part of the journey through Syria, he had settled down to a more chaste existence after leaving Damascus in September, 1850, impelled by a sudden fear of infection. Unfortunately this wise moderation he abandoned, and by the end of the month, in Beirut, he contracted a venereal disease. As he had earlier had what was diagnosed as syphilis, and since this cannot be contracted twice, the new infection was perhaps chancroids. Heroic efforts to control the progress of the disease by mercury dressings seemed of no avail. Horseback riding in Rhodes and in Asia Minor was excruciating. This was an aspect of travel in the Near East not mentioned in the nicer literary magazines.[32]

Painful and seemingly never-ending chancres developed and led to his having to beat an embarrassed retreat from a brothel in Constantinople. He did not try again, waiting for healing to be complete. The loss of his hair, which began now, may have been a further symptom and, while he retained considerable physical vigor when it was needed, he was clearly not well. Maxime agreed not to leave him until his mother, hastily summoned from France, could join them in Rome. Finally, as Flaubert left Greece, the sores had healed over leaving only the induration to disappear.

In Italy the secondary stage of his malady made its appearance. He reached Naples considerably indisposed: he was debilitated and constantly felt weak. He had at all times a slight fever which, while it did not keep him in bed, still accounted for his fatigue. Across the lower belly there were small red spots, presumably the rash of venereal disease but perhaps—Gustave was not sure—a touch of typhoid fever. He was forced to leave the insistent Neapolitan prostitutes untouched. By the time he reached Rome and the illness was six months old, one testicle was seriously involved, and a facial neuralgia was causing pain: Du Camp wrote again to hasten Madame Flaubert's arrival. Poor Madame Flaubert came and took charge. Thenceforth in Rome and in Venice her son lived very chastely. Had they been able to go to Brussels, he was preparing himself for an orgy to make up for lost time, but even that was denied him as he hurried home.[33] He probably never was cured of the infection. He dosed himself on mercury and ever more mercury over the years, for this was the only cure available, although it is more likely to kill the patient than to arrest the microbe.

In Egypt, prostitution also gave to Flaubert two memorable experiences. On the way up the Nile on one occasion he refused the proffered embraces of the women in an odd, dispassionate mood which seemed to him akin to that which a writer must have. He was walking through the prostitutes' quarter of a city in which they had stopped. There were five or six curved streets with little huts along them in front of which the women stood or were seated. Their clothes were a riot of colors; their skins, white or black, added accents. The loose garments floated in the wind, the smell of spice was everywhere. Their drawling voices kept calling to him. He walked slowly back and forth, distributing money as he went and refusing them all deliberately, so that the melancholy of the picture might more readily be kept intact. He left, stirred and even dazzled by it all. Had he given in and participated in it, he would, he knew, have added another image which would have effaced this one, as he had claimed to Louise Colet in the case of Ludovica. Impassivity, a certain cool detachment, was necessary to any esthetic pleasure.

Shortly before at Isna in the villa of the celebrated courtesan Kuchiuk-Hânem, he had been less distant.[34] It was an evening with dancers. He told his mother only that their dances alone were worth the trip up the Nile. But the facts were more intoxicating. As their Nile boat pulled ashore they were met by Bambeh, a sort of servant and fellow courtesan with Kuchiuk; she was followed by a tame sheep and escorted the two foreigners to her mistress' house. On their arrival Kuchiuk met them, standing at the head of her staircase, the light from behind surrounding her and silhouetting her figure. She wore pink trousers and had only the lightest of gauze, dark violet in color, over her torso. She was fresh from her bath and her breasts smelled of oil of roses. She perfumed her guests' hands with it in a gesture of welcome. She was a splendid, a royal creature, whiter than an Arab and from Damascus originally. All her flesh was firm and hard; walking or seated she was desirable.

For hours the party lasted, dancing alternating with love making. Kuchiuk and Bambeh danced, and a third woman joined them. While Flaubert and Du Camp had seen better dancing earlier in Cairo, this was still magnificent and, as a prelude to love making, superb. Flaubert felt like a tiger. Nearly thirty years later he would have Salomé dance one of Kuchiuk's first dances to win the head of John the Baptist from Herod. Later Kuchiuk danced the famous "Bee," in which one garment after another is discarded until only a piece of gauze is left to protect the dancer from the bee. Finally even it is thrown away. Flaubert noted each move in the dance with minute care and began, almost dispassionately, to observe himself as he enjoyed the courtesan. He could even notice and record that the shape of her knee cap as she squatted on the floor was magnificent, absolutely sculptural. She came over, tired, lay down beside him on the couch, and went to sleep as he threw his coat over her. The dances continued and, later, Kuchiuk wakened to dance again.

During the evening Flaubert stepped out of the house into the street beside it. A star shone very brightly in the sky over a building to the left. Only Kuchiuk's window was lighted and, except for the sound of music and the voices of the women, there was complete silence. With his face turned away from the street and without moving more than necessary, he amused himself by killing insects on the wall. The vermin, the stars, and Kuchiuk were all, equally, parts of Egypt.

Flaubert and Kuchiuk passed the night together, she asleep and he watching through the long hours by the light of an ancient lamp whose wick rested in an oval bowl. His mind wandered down long corridors in a searching intensity of meditation and revery. That was what he had stayed for, although, in fact, they did make love again. But it was more to watch this beautiful creature sleep, her hand held in his, most of her face in the shadow and her body pressed close against him. At one point he dozed off, his fingers passed through her necklace as if to retain her. Later he wakened and again stepped into the street. She wakened and went for a pot of coals to warm herself, for she was chilled and coughing. Flaubert thought of Judith and Holofernes lying side by side.

Quietly in the morning Du Camp and Flaubert left Kuchiuk's house. How sweet it would be, he thought, for one's pride, if one could be sure of leaving a memory there, or know that Kuchiuk would think of him more than of the others, as he had had Marie do in *November*. It had been a stupendous evening: this, too, was a part of woman and hence of love. Man would always aspire to it and dream that it could be; but only with a prostitute could such physical joys be tasted, and with her there would then be the lingering regret that it had been only physical and mercenary. Kuchiuk's dance weaves its way behind later enchantresses in Flaubert's works, but she is much more important for showing him the limitations of physical love. Ever greater aspirations would always be awakened by it, and love as aspiration would become the central theme of most of his works.

He came out into the morning air and went hunting with

Maxime, his mind wandering back, as it had during the night, over the long years of pleasure that he had known, gay nights in Paris, other nights still earlier. And finally his memory settled on the painful morning so long ago when he was fifteen after he had spent the evening at the ball in the Chateau du Héron and been miserable and stayed up the whole night to go walking in the park all alone in his schoolboy clothes to think over the evening. Then his aspirations had been toward the sort of night he had just had; now he knew too much and aspired higher to something else beyond the reach of men.

On the way back down the Nile Flaubert and Du Camp stopped again with Kuchiuk, but such nights cannot be relived. It was very sad: she had been sick, the weather was heavy. They promised to return in the morning, but they did not do so. Flaubert sensed the bitterness of the moment: being aware was the important thing, and he had felt it to his core. Months later he still longed to return once more though he knew it could never be. But he knew that he had spent an evening few of which are vouchsafed in one lifetime. And he had realized it as it passed. Sexuality here joined art in cool observation and the consciousness of the performer.

Kuchiuk-Hânem's dance Flaubert could observe with a practiced eye—sensually aroused but still expertly critical—because he had seen a number of Egyptian dancers already and understood something of the possibilities of erotic dancing.[35] He early recognized the ancient, hieratic character of much of what he saw: the Bible, he reported, was in Egypt an account of contemporary life, always young because nothing ever changed there. Again and again he recorded in detail the steps and poses and gestures he saw: some were even strong echoes of the ancient dramatic pantomime, which would recur when Salammbô or Salomé danced. But in general he found borne out what he was told from the start: beautiful women dance badly. At the cataract at Aswan, however, he did see a beautiful Nubian woman, Azizeh, who danced superbly; but here it was no longer, as in Cairo, Arab dancing: it was more ferocious and more abandoned, suggesting the Equator and Black Africa. Twenty-five years later Azizeh dancing the Bee at Aswan would lie behind the change in Salomé who, after gentler pantomimes, turns fully to the seduction of Herod and dances

"like the Nubians of the cataracts."[36] It was a private memory of
his, slipped into the middle of a sentence, a tribute to a time long
past.

Their guide and interpreter assured Flaubert and Du Camp
that the Bee had become almost a myth, a lost dance of which
only the name really remained. He had seen it danced correctly
only once, and then by a male dancer. From the start the male
dancers had excited Flaubert and Du Camp. In Cairo, where prostitutes were forbidden, such male dancers dressed as women were
very common: Flaubert and Du Camp arranged for a demonstration. Totally impassive, the dancer watched himself constantly in
a mirror, his face expressionless beneath its perspiration and make-
up. His head remained grave while his body performed the lascivious movements, more erotic for his garb which left the belly and
lower back covered only by gauze. His dance, endlessly varied,
was like that of the women but far superior. It was, Flaubert
wrote, too beautiful to be exciting; it gave him a migraine for the
rest of the day. Despite his statement, he was nervously aroused.

Homosexuality, open and frank, was all about them.[37] At table
after a few denials and affable chaffing, everyone admitted it. His
curiosity aroused, Flaubert determined to try it himself. Normally
such affairs took place in the public bath. Many of the masseurs
were young boys and homosexuality was common. One reserved a
private bath and masseur, but when Flaubert did so the boy he
wanted was absent for the day. He lay there in the hot water
watching the light filter into the chamber and let his thoughts
flow in idle revery while his body relaxed. It was voluptuous and
melancholy, alone thus in the semidark of these cavernous places
where the slightest sound reverberated and the masseurs worked
over one's body as if they were embalmers. If sex were only a
physical sensation, why hesitate? He returned to the baths on
another day.[38]

There had long been some element of ambiguity in Flaubert's
sex life. In *November* he had been quite content to adopt from
Théophile Gautier the notion of wishing to be a woman. It was
complex, however, as his hero would then have wanted to disrobe,
let his long hair fall to his heels, and gaze upon himself. In Brittany he had observed with almost loving care the long blond hair
of a young man as it unrolled when he removed his cap on enter-

ing a church: Flaubert felt, and strongly, the charm there would be in passing his hands through it. Joking about homosexuality was common among him and his friends. Moreover, as the years went by he became increasingly suspicious of women: all alliances with them were dangerous. Later on he himself wondered, almost idly, if he were bisexual; and discussions of the mechanics of pederasty were entertaining to him. In fact throughout his life he always preferred the company of men to that of women. While (as Louise Colet evidences) he was quite capable of an affair with a woman, particularly a somewhat distant one, his real interest, his affection and, one may even say, his real love went to Le Poittevin, to Du Camp, and to Bouilhet. Women, Zola once said, sensed that he was a feminine type, more like them than like a man.[39]

Flaubert's was an ambivalent state, as was Du Camp's also; the Near East brought it into the forefront of their consciousness. The beauty of men frequently attracted Flaubert's notice. In Greece particularly, the male children and adolescents were striking. In Damascus he thought of the success these youths of eighteen to twenty would have had in Paris, and he added that, were he a European woman, he would make a pleasure trip to Damascus. Obscenity in the Near East was as often homosexual as heterosexual, and he was constantly surrounded by reminders of it. Even eunuchs, strangely tempting and strangely repulsive, caused a nervous, irritating reaction. Du Camp, moreover, was of a very similar temperament. Immediately upon landing at Alexandria, Maxime had been excited by a Negro woman and then by little colored boys; in fact, queried Flaubert, was there anything which did not excite him? Later, as Flaubert wrote secretly to Bouilhet, Maxime on one occasion himself sought to seduce a homosexual in a deserted spot.[40] Eventually even the games Du Camp and Flaubert played took on a more clearly sexual character, and Gustave would play the little mincing mistress to Maxime's feigned advances. It was all a pleasantry and overtly innocent, but it allowed their deeper natures to rise nearer to the surface. Sexuality of every sort was part of a whole broad way of life and, in the Near East at least, Flaubert gave freer rein to it.

THE DEVELOPMENT OF THE WRITER

Am I perhaps coming back to life again?
> Letter to Louis Bouilhet from Damascus,
> September 4, 1850

Flaubert had begun his long trip embittered at the failure of *Saint Anthony* and crippled by doubts of his own abilities. All he could find within himself was the sort of irresolution which had characterized him since adolescence, and he wondered if he would die at sixty without ever having made up his mind about himself or ever having written a work which would show his stature. Like most reflective people since the advent of romanticism, he needed to find out who and what he was. The only peace he could find was to live like a plant, soak up the warm Egyptian sun, and gorge himself with light and colors. He was, he put it, only eating: digestion must come later, if at all.

Egypt had been very good for him: the pitiless grandeur of the country reduced individual vanities to their proper proportions. His initial reaction was to push aside any thought of ever achieving success, and to content himself with the good fortune he had: enough money to live on, two hundred sharpened goose quills, and the knowledge of how to use them. To his mother's reiterated queries in her letters about a post he might hold on his return, he replied brutally that there really was none he was competent to fill and that any job would infringe upon his writing. Moreover, no post could let him be so constantly with her. This last shaft hit too close to home; she abandoned the attack, and Gustave was free to relax into what he termed the most delicious of contemplative idlenesses. Seated in the front of their boat Flaubert spent hours ruminating upon his past life, seeking to make some sort of meaning from forgotten moments now returning like old childhood airs, of which bits come slipping back. Was he, he wondered, on the threshold of a new life? Or of a complete decadence? How could he dare to begin a new work? Could he face still another unsuccessful attempt?

At the pyramids Flaubert had been struck by a story told by Herodotus concerning Mycerinus, king of Egypt and builder of the Third Pyramid, who had become enamored of his daughter, so Herodotus reported, and had raped her. The girl had hanged herself for grief, and the father had entombed her embalmed body in a hollow statue of a cow. Flaubert imagined the king riding in a chariot about Lake Moeris, a priest beside him on the seat. The king is confiding his love; it is an evening in harvest time; the water buffaloes are coming in.[41] But it was too facile romantic exoticism and promised little more; Flaubert abandoned it.

He took to making brief jottings in his travel notebooks: a reminder to compare the shape of a ravine to. that of a coffin or the noise of gnats to the sharp music which accompanies burials. Often, he wrote, he would move apart from his companions and lie down in the middle of the day, stretched out at the feet of the motionless camels. His face turned toward his own country, he would weep and talk aloud. Flaubert added—the one original note —that he must bring out the intercommunication between the man's eye and the hair of the camel or the grain of the rocks. Or he would talk directly of himself, imagining that he was addressing the river: O Nile, he had himself say, my sorrow overflows as do your waters and no one can tell its source. My flooding came in the midst of my summer, but nothing will grow on the soil it deposits. In a final note he affirmed that, when night came, he breathed more easily and, lying on his back and raising his two arms toward the stars, he looked upon them as he would have upon women.[42] Thus far he was dealing only in clichés.

The problem was to begin the effort to see things as they were and not as they affected him. Here the landscape descriptions were helpful. He had come to Egypt full of the Byronian picture of the passionate and violent Near East replete with curved scimitars and dancing girls. What he learned to see for himself and to prefer was a grandeur unaware of itself, a harmony of disparate elements, the Near East of the Bedouin and the desert, of the crocodile, the camel, and the giraffe.[43]

In any seeing there is the viewer with all that he brings to the act, and then an unknown and somewhat unknowable object being partially perceived. All of this one may seek to report to a reader. The report or description may emphasize what the viewer sees and what he finds his experience to have been. This will be termed subjective: much of romanticism was of this character, and Byron's report of the Near East was typical. Alternatively, a description may strive to discover something of the unknowable object before the viewer and may thus make an effort at an objective presentation. The two accounts differ in emphasis. The objective one is validly so termed because it seeks to reduce the role of the subjective, personal viewer; the subjective one, on the other hand, may go so far as almost to eliminate the object in the course of exalting the reaction of the viewer. This complex matter Flaubert was slowly elucidating for himself as he moved from romanticism toward an antiromantic literature, from the Byronian vision to the Near East he could observe.

Flaubert's return to Cairo marked—and he was clearly aware of it—a sudden return to intellectual vigor and a need to write after eight months of near sterility. This period even provided Madame Bovary with a name, for hers is derived from Monsieur Bouvaret, Flaubert's hotelkeeper in Cairo, a former French provincial actor who hung Gavarni lithographs in his hotel for the delight of his guests. In addition, far up the Nile Flaubert had received a copy of Augier's *Gabrielle*, a miserable play dealing with a simple husband and a wife with romantic notions. In Augier's play, at the end the wife discovers the true poetry of a hard-working husband and returns happily to her conjugal duties; but this could only have persuaded Flaubert that more could be said on this subject. His Emma would not end her version of these problems this way.

Perhaps the most important change in Flaubert was that, for the first time in his life, he was becoming emotional. As an adolescent he had had no more than the facile sentimentalism of his years and perhaps even not much of that. As a young man he had been too self-absorbed ever to wonder about the feelings of those about him. With illness and acquaintance with death he had deliberately sought to insulate himself entirely. As the summer wore on in 1850 and he and Du Camp slowly traveled through Palestine and Lebanon, he found new sensitivities arising and a new emotionalism. Many things could bring tears to his eyes and insignificant moments gripped him deeply. His pity could now be aroused for little Negro slave girls being mistreated or for a small Arab boy playing with tobacco stalks, his legs sticking delightfully out from his filthy rags.

Flaubert's problem was to come to grips with this new emotionalism and to master it without stifling it. Otherwise he would be no more than a latter-day romantic, the very sort of writer he had come to detest. He had now, in his powerful reactions, the stuff of which literature could be made, where Saint Anthony had been resolutely denied this inner drive and this readiness to mingle with life and be moved by it. Such a giving of himself Flaubert was now frequently experiencing. At Aden he sat up with a Carmelite father caring for the servant he and Maxime had with them, who was very ill. The moon was startling, lighting up the whole valley. The plain disappeared out into the depths of somber blue, where silence lay. The priest reminisced, telling of when he had left his mother for the last time and of all those near him who had since died. It was one of the gravest and most profoundly poetic moments of Flaubert's life. He would remember the priest's long black robe silhouetted against the moonlight as he kneeled to pray, or his maternal care of the sick servant and his angelic patience in boiling tea over a fire made of bits of straw.

Now Flaubert was ready for more. He could think back to Chateaubriand, however, and realize that he must seek for something other than the preordained emotionalism of this father of all the romantics. Chateaubriand became for him the symbol of a ready sentimentalism which must be countered by reverence for the strength and integrity of antiquity. There were moments— Smyrna was one of them, as he wrestled with the onset of his venereal disease—when he was profoundly discouraged and as gloomy as the approaching winter. He felt old and disabused; but now, as opposed to when he was eighteen, he really understood his state. He was doing less meditating; for the most part he was observing humanity about him, learning what he would one day write. He had not foreseen this psychological, human, comic aspect of travel. The basic evil of mankind showed up so clearly, immutable and eternal, mingling filth and braided stripes, rags and laces, and forever reminding the traveler of his own basic humanity. He found it made him very humble.

Only writing could tell Flaubert what his measure was. He was worried that his introspection, the clarity with which he viewed himself, might keep him from being able to create. But he knew that now he must overcome his terrors and write despite them. The time had come to learn what the quality of his land was and what its limits were in preparation for plowing it. He must now settle down and establish himself in the life of the writer. He needed to talk of these matters, but at the same time he found it impossibly frustrating, especially with Du Camp.

Maxime's views of literature were undergoing radical change. Both men had had many long talks in Cairo with Charles Lambert, prophet of the mystical Saint-Simonian doctrines of the sort which Karl Marx dubbed "Utopian Socialism." Flaubert was only excited, but Du Camp was converted and accepted the notion that art must have a social and utilitarian aim. Science and industry were accomplishing prodigious feats, while the artist was standing by, a contemptible figure scratching at the tired strings of his lyre. Poetry must instead popularize and give direction to modern industry, the scientific movement and the new socialistic, humanitarian movement.[44] The ideas had already begun to occupy Maxime early in their Near Eastern trip, but Flaubert, watching an incubator in Egypt, far from finding it a miracle of the modern world, termed it strangely corrupt, the artificial replacing the organic. He was, of course, limited and stubborn in his view, but it is more important that he was now deprived of a trusted companion with whom to explore his new ideas of literature. He imagined with joy a return to the quiet life of writing which he had known, a vision which revolted Maxime, who was already filled with noisy projects for making a success in Paris. The long trip was a slow and affectionate parting of the ways for the two men. After it their friendship cooled for nearly a decade, but it endured and was to tide Flaubert over difficult moments in later years.

In the new socialism Flaubert found only matter for satire. He had read Auguste Comte and found him incredibly dull. The immense seriousness of the work revealed untapped mines for

comedy, Californias of the grotesque, as he termed them. His satire began to take shape: he would write a play, impartial in tone
but brutal and farcical underneath: he was impatient to be at it.
Much of this found its final form in the second *Sentimental Education* of 1869.

Flaubert suspected that a new literary public was perhaps coming into being. France's revolution in 1848 the bourgeoisie had
stolen once again, as they had the previous ones. There had been
the election of a president, Louis-Napoléon Bonaparte, a man
with a prestigious name. In 1852 there would be new elections and
a climactic moment. It seemed entirely possible to Flaubert that a
new bourgeois triumph then—which is what actually occurred in
the *coup d'état* Louis-Napoléon engineered—would establish a new
social system. The public, tired of politics, would perhaps wish
literary distractions; a new reaction would take place against the
positive and the active and toward the world of the imagination.
That would be the moment for writers to seize. Both modern
literature and the modern public needed, he said, a new Christ to
heal their leprous condition.

Meanwhile Flaubert was worried about the state of society
and its writers. They had style, talent, and widely varied resources; they knew all the tricks and devices. But they lacked the
basic principle, the soul of a book: the Idea. They were scholarly,
they were archeologists, historians, doctors, men of taste; but did
they have anything to say? Were they writers? Was a ferocious
originality (which Flaubert knew to be indispensable) compatible
with so much eclecticism, such ready acceptance of so many disparate esthetics? Perhaps his generation must resign itself to being
precursors broadening the field of vision for a later generation,
which would once again have the verve and dash of the romantics,
so lacking today.

Flaubert's quandaries were at an irritating stage as he reached
Beirut in July, 1850. His critical sense was parrying each reviving
thrust of his intense desire to write descriptions of what he saw or
to make reflections on its meaning. To an old friend in Rouen he
sketched his view of Mount Lebanon wearing a necktie of clouds
and a wig of snow, but at once he noted the impertinence of
trying to describe it. The effect of his trip would be to keep him

from ever publishing a line on the Near East! And yet he could ill resist the temptation: he slipped into a comment on the blue of the water which made a swimmer's arms seem tinted with emerald and his feet appear whiter than ivory. How totally Nature ignored man and remained insensible of his presence and his views.[45]

As he explored this dilemma over the next months, Flaubert began to sense what his choices would be. In Greece he saw the classical resolutions of his problems and prepared to adopt modern equivalents of them. Then, to counter excessive critical faculties, he became aware that the artist must cultivate exaggeration. He was not yet sure, but either it was indispensable to beauty or, at the very least, it was sufficient to produce it. At its best this intuition underlies the creation of Homais, the pharmacist, or the death agony of Emma Bovary. But in both these cases limiting factors did exist, despite Flaubert. In *Salammbô*, chosen to eliminate all restraints, the full force of his doctrine of exaggeration could be brought to bear: its fundamental unsoundness destroyed the novel.

In opposite fashion Flaubert also became deeply aware, during these months, of the recurrent serenity of nature in contrast to all the febrile agitation of man. Art, even when portraying that agitation, must remain serene. A leper colony suggested what he had in mind. Near a fountain a man was seated; all about him the site was charming, full of shade in the noonday sun, silent, and cool; the trees trembled with life and youth; two or three hens were pecking at invisible grain on the ground. But the leper held out his arms and called to Flaubert in Arabic. His lips were eaten by the disease and revealed his mouth back to the throat; he was atrocious with his infected sores and disfigured hands which looked almost like rags extending from his sleeves. Nearby, the leper colony was neat and clean and in good condition. In such contrasts of man and nature Flaubert began to see the role of art. Like the serene Greek landscapes, whatever it portrayed and however it might exaggerate, it must remain imbued with that tranquility, harmony, and peace which he had found in Athens and the countryside of Hellas.

What could one write of? The problem demanded resolution. The return to antiquity had already been accomplished; the medieval period had been overworked by romanticism. That left only the present, but Flaubert detested it. It was unstable: how could one draw conclusions about it? Only by dealing with it, however, could one have vitality and write for the enduring future. Balzac had; his death, of which Flaubert learned during this summer of 1850, moved him deeply, for he felt that Balzac had been a writer who had understood his time.

In these months of enormous artistic fertility for Flaubert the answer became clear. To be sure, his age was confusing, but to object to this was to fail to enjoy dusk or dawn and to insist on living only at noon or midnight. What tomorrow might look like was, in fact, irrelevant to the artist: he had today, and it was full of those grimaces which the postromantic generation needed for its materials. The problem, and it was idiotic, arose because Flaubert had been seeking to draw conclusions and come to firm resolutions of the dilemmas. He had only to realize, he now saw, that he was no more than a thread in the whole cloth and could not expect to see the pattern. What great artist, beginning with Homer, had attempted to offer conclusions? Instead one should be content with producing the picture.

Was this the personal renaissance he hoped for? Or would it all come to naught? This summer and autumn of 1850 were to be the crucial moments. The failure of *Saint Anthony*, while it could still bother him on occasion, no longer had the power to make him almost ill, as it had for the first four months of the journey. Now, instead, as he traveled through Syria, he was full of projects. There was the possibility of the play satirizing the socialists. When, he asked, had the bourgeoisie been more staggering than now? In Molière's day, the bourgeois whom he satirized was negligible compared to the modern one. Also in satiric vein were new ideas he began to have for his *Dictionary of Accepted Ideas*, that compilation of all the clichés of his age put together in serious fashion and with, now, a preface to be written to show that the book was offered to the public as an aid to maintaining order and sound traditions.

Much more important, however, were three allied subjects which Flaubert was considering.[46] One was to be *A Night of Don Juan;* it occurred to him in Rhodes during the days when he was coming down with his venereal attack. The second was to be called "Anubis" and would tell the story of a woman who mistakenly thought she was having intercourse with a god. The third was to deal with a mystical Flemish virgin living out her life in the provinces. Flaubert was fascinated and worried by the evident relationship between the three stories; they were in reality three story lines to carry the same subject, aspiration toward love. Don Juan would sleep with the dead nun Anna Maria, who would return to life for him. His would have been the endless search for something beyond physical love, hers the search for a solid underpinning to religious exaltation. Each would complete the other. The story line would follow the unappeased aspiration through to its ultimate satisfaction in the linking of terrestrial and mystic love. In "Anubis" he would again have a woman seeking to link the two loves, religious and terrestrial, but being deceived by the priests so that, in fact, she would know only physical love. Flaubert would show that this was less exalted because it was more precise. In the third story, the novel about the Flemish virgin, he boldly envisaged showing her seeking solitary satisfaction for her physical desires and then, in parallel fashion, seeking self-induced mystic exaltation. She would live quietly in a small provincial town with her father and mother. Flaubert already envisaged the garden, set along the edge of a little river: it would have cabbages and carefully clipped trees. She would die of her religious esctasies. In all three cases, love would be an aspiration which remained unsatisfied or led to the grave. He was worried at his ability thus to dissect his story lines: Was this an excess of the critical faculty?

The three outlines all concerned women tormented with sensual dreams of the unrealizable. "Anubis" would eventually lead to Salammbô, who, desiring to preserve the moon goddess Tanit, would sleep with Mâtho, whom she deemed to incarnate Moloch, the sun god. Neither of the other two stories was ever directly and fully worked out, but both find their way, fused, into *Madame Bovary*. The story of the Flemish virgin, her house so well evolved in Flaubert's mind, is the more complex and goes back at least to Flaubert's Breton trip when, at Blois, he had sensed how the lives of the inhabitants would pass here day after day absolutely unchanged. He had let his fancy create behind the peaceful facade of one of these houses a sickly passion, the unending love of a spinster, devout and bigoted, which would last until her death.[47] This story he mulled over carefully: it would provide much of Emma Bovary's life.

Don Juan, much worked on but ultimately set aside, would provide the basic psychology and character oppositions of *Madame Bovary*. The subject had long intrigued Flaubert, as it had most of his contemporaries and the preceding generation as well.[48] The legend had appeared here and there throughout Flaubert's juvenile works. *November* had been in part the story of the prostitute who longed for a real passion which would go beyond the senses and who, essentially, seduces the virginal narrator. The roles in the story had been reversed, and the endless aspiration of Don Juan had been transferred to the prostitute, Marie. The Don Juan theme deeply attracted the romantics. Mozart's *Don Giovanni* was a favorite at this time and, for Flaubert, one of the supreme creations of all art. The elder Dumas, Gautier, Musset, Byron, and Mérimée, to mention only a few among Flaubert's preferred authors, handled the theme, too.

The precise derivation of *Madame Bovary* from the Don Juan theme Flaubert would work out only upon his return to France. In the meantime, however, his *Night* took precedence over the other two story lines. As Flaubert jogged along over the roads of Greece he kept turning it over in his mind. This was December, 1850; now the fears which he had had in the summer concerning critical sterility came back to plague him. His concept of the Spanish don seemed common; it had been handled too many times. Hence it would require a tremendously strong style: not a line could be weak. In this realization lay Flaubert's final discovery: a great work of art is always, in some sense, a stylistic *tour de force*. Every one of his works from then until his death would be a wager, established against all probability, that he could find and master the new style required by the subject he was about to undertake. In Italy, sick and occupied for most of the day in museums, he nevertheless found time to make a few jottings for his *Don Juan*. Guy de Maupassant owned and published these pages after Flaubert's death.[49]

This was that renaissance Flaubert had hoped for, that second maturation he had sensed was taking place in Constantinople, and which Greece completed. He wondered if he would find again the reserves of strength and vitality which he had squandered so lavishly on *Saint Anthony.* Slowly he went back over his past; he was haunted by memories of his sister. He would look out from a perfumed torpor, upon landscapes or remains of columns; but his mood remained reserved, melancholy, a somnolent state in which the settings changed before his eyes and sudden melodies came to his ears, the noise of the wind, the rush of torrents, the bells of the sheep. Everything disposed one to silence and to thought. It ripened and aged one; would it, as he hoped, prove fertile, too? There were moments, especially in Greece in the countryside or in Italy in the museums, when he knew it would, when he was totally at peace with himself. He no longer needed to torture himself over what he would do on his return. It would, he now knew, take care of itself. All that was needed was another six or eight months.

Flaubert's way was set, after all the doubts and turmoil of Egypt and the searching in the Levant. His mother's reiterated urgings that he marry forced him to explain to her how totally settled he was. He knew that, for himself at least, he had passed the age of change. He knew every minor turn and twist of his make-up and had examined it again and again. Marriage could only interfere now; it would be a sort of apostasy, a scandalous matter like the marriage of Le Poittevin, which Flaubert had never forgiven him. His way must be to remain outside of life, a monstrosity probably. Mingled with life, forgetting that cool detachment which was indispensable, the artist was destroyed. As he had learned to enjoy Baalbek or the Parthenon or Kuchiuk-Hânem's dancing as a detached observer, so he must also write his books, not entangled with life. He must be able, as in the night at Isna, to step outside to smoke his cigarette, look at the stars, and meditate.

It was in reality more complex, for there was always his mother. The anguish of his departure from Paris in the autumn of 1849 was now matched by his anxiety to be with her again; he wrote letters to her such as he might have written to a wife. He told her of his deep satisfaction with the life he lived with her, full of serenity and such a grave charm; he knew—as he had told her—that he would never love another woman as he loved her. She need have no fear: she would never have a rival. Passing fancies there might be, but they would never take the place of what was enclosed in his heart as in a triple sanctuary. Others might step upon the threshold; they would never enter. When she joined him in Rome, she had a particular fan with her. He kept it ever after until his death: it was one of his treasured relics.[50]

The marriage of Ernest Chevalier, his childhood friend, which occurred now, seemed a case in point. Dispersed forever were any hopes that Ernest might one day accomplish the bold dreams of the bygone days. It was atrocious to think of, and Flaubert determined to banish Ernest from his mind. Only when he wrote to congratulate his old friend did he perhaps glimpse the lonely abyss to which he was condemning himself or, as he put it, to which he was condemned. Ernest had, he confessed, taken the right path; the wrong one he himself had taken or been taken by. Ernest would taste joys Gustave could never know, and he agreed that happiness did lie in living with a good wife. But how could one meet her, and how could one be a good man oneself? It was a double and frightening requirement. Now he lacked the courage, and 1870 came and went before he knew fully what he here set aside; then it would be irrevocably too late. The hermit's life for art was to be his chosen way of sacrifice and salvation.

Italy put the finishing touches upon his mood. There the melancholy of the now irretrievable past he enjoyed almost deliciously. Naples, sun filled, gay, and easy, revived his flagging spirits brought low by illness. Even the horses had bouquets of peacock feathers attached to their ears. For a week Flaubert had a passing passion for an actress he yearned to come to know. But he no longer had the money to try to captivate her, so he contented himself with watching her perform each day and thus, as he said, he wore out his temptation.[51]

Outside Rome one day in April, visiting the great basilica of San Paolo fuori le Mura, Flaubert was suddenly attracted by a woman before him. Such passing fancies any man has had, but not to the degree that this experience held for Flaubert. The hallucinatory power of his imagination gave it an irresistible grip on all his perceptions: without warning he found himself intrigued, then absorbed, and finally madly taken with her. She walked slowly and leaned on the arm of an older woman; an old man followed. Unable to resist, Flaubert put his glass to his eye and walked toward her. She was pale with dark eyebrows; he studied her walk, watching her waist twist slightly. Barely able to control himself, he put his hat before his eyes to keep from leaping on her. Then an overpowering sensation of sweetness came over him. She seemed to be from another world and totally, entirely calm. She was perhaps convalescent; this might be the first time out of her house? He longed to throw himself at her feet, to kiss the hem of her dress, to ask her hand in marriage! If only he had the money to have one of the great painters of the day, perhaps Ingres, come to paint her portrait! Or could he present himself as a doctor and offer to cure her? He would have given anything to hold her head in his hand and to kiss her on the forehead. Instead he and Du Camp had to return quietly to the hotel. By four o'clock already her features were beginning to fade from his memory. He bade them a fond adieu.

It was time for Flaubert to go back to France. He had returned, fully, to life. Madame Bovary, already taking shape in the Flemish virgin and in Don Juan and his nun, was almost ready to be born. Flaubert did not yet know that he knew her name, but the lineaments of her story were already visible. Now he needed to get to his writing table to discover her.

11

The Years of the *Bovary* (1851-56)

THE MONTHS OF DECISION: 1851

Something is going on inside me. This is a critical time in my life. I'll be thirty very soon; it is time to make a decision and to stick to it.

Letter to Louise Colet, November, 1851

SHORTLY after mid-June, 1851, Flaubert was back in France. His health soon improved, and a momentous summer began: mistresses, writing, and more travels clamored for his attention. Maxime, who had returned earlier, had already renewed casual relations with Ludovica and had written of it to Flaubert in Italy, enclosing a letter to him from this always receptive woman. She had grown heavier, he said, but was as magnificent and free in her morals and language as she had always been. She alone had been able to provide the address Flaubert wanted of a particular brothel in Brussels when he still hoped to return slowly and in licentious fashion from Italy; she could even tell him what room to ask for. Maxime and Gustave had spoken of her at intervals during the long trip; Flaubert now determinedly sought to make her his mistress, and Du Camp stepped aside in his favor.[1]

Meanwhile there was Louise Colet. Flaubert's liaison with The Muse had been completely broken before his departure, and he had hardly given her a thought since then. Briefly her husband had returned to live with her, but he had died during the spring. She had then taken up with a leftist deputy. This, however, came to an end in July, leaving this passionate woman sick with disillusionment and wholly without emotional ties except to her daughter. She was in difficult financial straits as well, and desperately lonely. Slowly and very tentatively she and Flaubert moved toward a resumption of their liaison, but this time Gustave knew that the love of which he had once dreamed he could not have with her. Cautiously he kept her at a distance and insisted on his own terms. He would not come to Paris to live near her, and they would found their renewal on the search for serenity; it was a return to the first days of the liaison. He did not mention Ludovica to her; in fact he several times denied the existence of other women in whom he was interested. But then, she was never quite open with him either over passing fancies which she, too, had in the next years; in fairness and because he did not really mind, he never protested.

Louise's circle of friends appealed to Flaubert. Lively and not always decorous women were always on hand; writers, painters, musicians, and critics crowded her salon. While the very great were absent or infrequent, one could at least meet Hugo's two sons or the aging Musset, Pradier, the newspaper publisher Girardin, and the admiring Cousin and Villemain from the ministerial world. Champfleury, the champion of realism, and the future Parnassian poet, Leconte de Lisle, were often there.[2] It was the sort of gathering Flaubert had enjoyed in Pradier's studio.

But Croisset was his real home and writing his real occupation once more. After nearly two years of living the life of a traveler as other men lived it, he was now returning to his old life and to his protective shell. He began almost at once to recopy and rework his travel notes. It was an oddly nostalgic moment when he transcribed the description of initiating the tent that night two years before as he and Maxime had camped beside the Sphinx: he had folded the tent away for the last time and stored it only the day before at Croisset. The trip was really over and, slowly revisiting these old notes and reliving, among others, the moment of departure from Paris with all his anguish at abandoning his mother, he felt as though the Flaubert he was describing was no more than a cadaver on whom the new one was performing an autopsy.

Almost at once he abandoned the futile idea of writing a travel book. There were more live subjects to tempt him, those he had envisaged as the trip was nearing its end. And so, seeking to live largely the life of a hermit of letters, he drew to himself from the outside world what it had that was best for the solitary and introverted world of Croisset: its dreams and aspirations. These he would make into literature, for all else was transitory or illusory.

Don Juan still intrigued him, and he wrestled with it for a few months, only gradually discarding it in favor of another story into which he could introduce many of its elements. A young man, Eugène Delamare, whom Flaubert knew at least slightly, had been a medical student of Dr. Flaubert's and had gone out to a country practice as health officer.[3] Here, after a first marriage to an older widow, he had married an ambitious farm girl, Delphine Couturier, whose escapades with other men soon became notorious. First there was a law clerk; then there was a neighboring squire. Moreover she had fallen heavily into debt. Ultimately, when the financial chaos became too great, she had committed suicide. This was the story which Flaubert decided to write: Delphine, after all, could be envisaged as a modern, female Don Juan. It was not really a change of theme, but only of time, sex, and locale. Shortly he decided to call his heroine Emma Bovary. *Madame Bovary* had now been born; the date was September 19, 1851. Thirty years of living thus acquired meaning, and untold scores of occurrences and reflections thereby became preparations for this novel. Du Camp wrote enthusiastically and promised to provide personal experiences and insights to help fill out the story.

To turn to a modern, provincial French subject after writing *Saint Anthony* was a major and exciting decision. So long as romanticism tended to feel that literature must idealize or be heroic in order to display passionate individualism, then simple present-day subjects were impossible. Chateaubriand had categorically proscribed them, and most French romantics had concurred.[4] But already during the Mediterranean trip it had seemed to Flaubert that, despite the gigantic presence of Balzac's novels, there still remained esthetic and stylistic innovations to be carried out within the framework of the modern novel. Flaubert's first *Sentimental Education* had dealt, albeit weakly, with this modern world, and Jules had seen the interest of such subjects after having supposed that only the ancient world was a fit topic for a sensitive man. Just as in his daily living Flaubert had returned to the concepts he had held in 1845 before Louise Colet had led him to abandon them, so now he was returning to his esthetic of those days, too. After six years of a mistress and travel and upset, he wanted peace; after the orgies of Saint Anthony he would seek the solid reality of the contemporary, bourgeois world.

There were further reasons for choosing to write *Madame Bovary*. Flaubert did not like the modern world, but he felt that he had excellent reasons for his distaste and his alarm. These he wished to put into a novel upon which his generation might meditate. Moreover, the discipline of such a quiet, down-to-earth subject would be helpful in itself by curbing his literary tendency toward hyperbole and exuberance, which had so harmed him in handling Saint Anthony.[5]

Almost at once he was interrupted: he had long been promising his mother that he would visit the great London Exposition with her.[6] Little Caroline accompanied them. At the Exposition the physical presence of the displays from India and China let him see elephants and pagoda ornaments from these countries which had so often filled his dreams. He regretted the interruption to his writing, but the Exposition was a reward, and he needed the time to sort out the decisions he had just made.

It was Flaubert's intention to be chaste in London. He helped his mother in the selection of a governess for his niece, the first of a succession of young English women who would live in the Croisset house, some of whom would tempt him sorely. But this was for later. Meanwhile, however, London was and had been for some years Harriet Collier's home, and Maxime, leering, had written that he should try to seduce her, her sister Gertrude, and any other females who came handy. Flaubert's intentions, however, were far purer. It was strange to see Harriet again. Her health was markedly improved. Her mother had died the year before, and her father, now very lonely, needed her with him constantly. It was a tender and nostalgic reunion. The Sunday afternoon when Flaubert was leaving, he went out for a walk with her through Hyde Park, and the heavy fog over the city reflected the feeling within him. How annoying it was that her cousin insisted on going with them.[7]

Back in France he kept remembering the renewed contact with Harriet, and he wrote fond letters telling her how much he wished that she were again living in Paris so that he might come to read to her as he had so many years ago, while she lay resting on her bed by the window looking out on the Champs Elysées. He would talk to her of all he had seen in his travels, but it would not be as it had been before, when he had been so easily able to make her laugh. Now he knew that he was less gay, but he would love her none the less for that, he wrote affectionately. Over the months, in fact, he continued to write to her in a warm, comradely tone, fondly recalling old times and hoping that she, too, recalled them thus. She knitted for him, and he wrote to thank her; she begged him to say nothing of it to her sister Gertrude. With returning spring his tone became more tender still; she replied by sending her portrait, a more intimate gift than Gertrude's earlier water color. He placed it close to the bust of his sister, and Harriet thus became one of the few silent guests whom he admitted to his hearth. Soon he hoped to be back in Trouville again, so filled with memories of her. How long ago all that seemed, however, and by autumn, somehow, it was no more than another dream, a charming illusion, fondly cherished but never intended for reality. Slowly it had evaporated in the desiccating air of a life from which Flaubert resolutely excluded the personal involvement of passion. The letters grew fewer; when Harriet married some three years later, Flaubert learned of it only after the event; her portrait, sitting there all the time, had told him nothing of it, he complained in sad surprise.[8]

Even during the first winter after his return, when he was writing warmly affectionate letters to Harriet, Flaubert was not really thinking of marriage. In fact, he was happy in his liaison with Louise Colet and stretching the truth to deny flatly to her that there was any other woman of whom he was even fond. Du Camp had seen Louise while Flaubert was still in London and had noted that she was really a good soul.[9] Gustave's way of loving her was not good, and he knew it; but in his way he loved her, and he saw in the affair the same ironic fatality he found everywhere and which would be the key to Emma Bovary's sad destiny. Fate might always couple things for the greater harmony of the whole, but it was surely always to the detriment of the parts. It was fated, he wrote, that the liaison should continue, and so it did.

As Flaubert was leaving for England, Du Camp had been completing arrangements to take over a famous periodical, the *Revue de Paris;* he was going to edit it in association with Théophile Gautier and another friend. Du Camp displayed that feverish activity which, during the trip throughout the Near East, he had been so keenly anticipating. It posed a problem for Flaubert: should he, too, be showing such activity? Or was Du Camp's desire to achieve rapid success a mistake, even perhaps immoral?

Gustave wrote at length to his old friend.[10] He was torn, he confessed, between his dislike, on the one hand, of actually doing things and his temptations, on the other hand, now that his friend was in control of a periodical. He asked Max whether he should seek to publish something, perhaps some extracts from *Saint Anthony?* He and Bouilhet had been unable to come to a decision. That was the trouble with life; it was forever forcing you to think about foolish things such as eating or dressing or publishing, in fact about everything except what mattered, art. It had always been thus, he realized; he had found life equally hateful in school, in Rouen or Paris, or on the Nile. Maxime, Flaubert reminded him, had the opposite sort of nature, clearheaded and precise, and he had always objected violently to Gustave's lack of these qualities, even to the point of hurting his friend seriously.

The problem was, Flaubert admitted as the flow of ink through the pen seemed to make confession easier, that he had had no choice. If he preached chastity, it was because he knew he looked foolish in the posture of a lover. It was his nature to be passive; it had to be that way. He was perhaps even wrong now in his writing to be countering his natural bent, which was to give way to howls and shouts and philosophico-fantastical eccentricities. With *Madame Bovary*, instead, he was undertaking a solid and reasonable book. It seemed somehow not his own at all. And now he had another choice to make: should he publish? It would change the purity of his work, which had heretofore been written only to be beautiful. Now he might be seeking to please, and it would be a loss. He would have to do all the dreadful things people did to acquire and retain popularity. These were matters he was proud to know nothing about and to see Du Camp weighing corrections in the light of what others would think had already hurt Flaubert.

He had told his friend all and held back nothing of what was torturing him. Now he counted on him, on his instinctive sense for the good life, which seemed sound to Gustave, and on his intelligence, which was keen. He would do, he said, whatever Maxime told him to do, for he was tired of making up his own mind. He had not really intended getting into all of this, but now that he had, he was glad. So he mailed the letter.

It was, of course, an impossible letter to answer, and Maxime wisely realized it. Patiently he explained to Gustave that success required careful cultivation.[11] There was a literary revival coming upon them, and in the battles which were going to ensue, he wished to be a captain and not a private. Gustave's trouble was that he knew nothing of this sort of matter; he had already paid heavily for this ignorance, and he would continue to seem inferior to people of far less than his worth unless he changed his ways. But this he must do himself, for no one else could undertake it for him. If he wished to publish, and when he felt himself ready, then Maxime would have the place waiting for him. But what could he publish? And here the burgeoning editor could ill resist the opportunity to be patronizing. *Saint Anthony*, except for extracts, would bore the public, and this would be ruinous to a new author. When Flaubert had something good, let him send it to the *Revue:* Maxime would arrange to have it accepted.

But then Du Camp turned to the graver matter of Flaubert's way of life: was it really, as Flaubert had claimed, fated and wise, given the hateful character of life itself? This was nonsense. Gustave had not chosen this life; he had passively accepted it and had allowed it to become second nature to him. It had begun, to be sure, with his illness and had been necessary then. Thereafter, facing the deaths of his father and sister, it had been his duty to be beside his mother to help her through the crises. But to continue it beyond that time had been no more than his fear of her unspoken reproaches and the timorous hatred of change which he brought to everything he did. In fact, Gustave was not the recluse he claimed to be: the proof lay in the delight he felt every time he broke away from his mother's bonds. He really enjoyed himself then and should give over deceiving himself in this fashion.

His solitude and his way of life entirely centered in himself had been devastating, Maxime continued. Not only had it made him the helpless prisoner of his mother; it had also accustomed him to think solely of himself and of what suited him. He was enclosed within the narrow walls of his own personality so that, while he knew well enough how he lived and what his life was, he had no idea at all of what the life of others might be, of what life itself was. When he thought he was looking about him at other people, he was mistaken: he saw only himself and had depicted only himself in his books.

With a better chance to succeed than any of his friends, he had done nothing at all. If it were to go on another two years, Du Camp said, he could not predict whether Flaubert could ever break out of his closed circle. And so Maxime insisted that he could give Gustave no advice: the matter was too grave for him to have the right to do so, for it might lead his friend into paths which were not rightly his and Maxime could not risk having thus tempted him. He contented himself with renewing his offers to help with publishing.

Du Camp closed with a sharp but honest jab: he had come to love Flaubert in a form which Flaubert no longer had. When he had seen the change, he had pulled back and had changed the form of his own friendship. Since much of the new Flaubert Du Camp did not like, he occasionally spoke bitterly. Flaubert must understand.

It was a terrible letter which Du Camp had written, but much of it he had had to say. Any real friend had to pick up the gauntlet Flaubert had thrown down when he declared that life was hateful, but it cost Maxime Gustave's friendship for several years to come, the more so in that the letter was, of course, wrong in part, too. Du Camp was urging that Flaubert adopt the unsavory life of the man out to make a rapid success without regard to the cost in personal integrity. Flaubert seized upon these errors and wilfully blinded himself to the insights offered him. He had chosen his way so many years before that the idea of abandoning it seemed inconceivable.

Flaubert felt, in these last months of 1851, that the solemn change he had so long announced was finally maturing within him. It was a change, but it was largely that he was now really to do what heretofore he could only imagine. He would be writing the books he had conceived during the time of writing the first *Sentimental Education,* and he would be mastering the esthetic and the style he had called for then. Until 1851 it had been only a dream, a wild hope steadily dashed to the ground by uncontrolled lyric impulses. Instead, as he worked through the plans and early drafts for *Madame Bovary,* he sensed that he was at last on the right track to attain it. It was a solemn moment, and it was indeed time for it to manifest itself. That December, he was thirty.

A WRITER'S LIFE

> It was the more triumph for his morale; for the truth was that they [his works] were heaped up to greatness in layer after layer, in long days of work, out of hundreds and hundreds of single inspirations; they owed their excellence, both of mass and detail, to one thing and one alone; that their creator could hold out for years under the strain of the same piece of work.
>
> Thomas Mann, writing of Aschenbach in *Death in Venice*

In the years of writing *Madame Bovary,* from 1851 to 1856, Flaubert at last found the patterns for his life. For the first several years he lived for the most part in Croisset and spent his time in writing. But in 1854 he initiated the practice of moving to Paris for the winter months and thus achieved fully the life he wanted, essentially that of the Hermit of Croisset, but with just enough gay diversion and important contact with friends in Paris to relieve loneliness and make him glad to resume once again his life in the country.

His health, which had dictated or served as an excuse for the Near Eastern trip, continued to be in a most grave state. His teeth were decaying and his hair was falling out; he had painful aches in his shoulders and neck, which he attributed to the freezing rains of Greece, and serious headaches sometimes made work or even sleep nearly impossible for weeks at a time. It seemed to a gloomy

Flaubert that major physical decadence was already setting in. Perhaps some of the virulence he showed toward Homais was that, like Molière with his pharmacists, he was seeking revenge for the inability of medicine to help him.

In August, 1854, he had a grave attack of mercury poisoning resulting from his dosing with the drug to counteract his syphilis.[12] His tongue was so swollen that he could no longer contain it within his mouth; speech was impossible, as was eating. Ice, laxatives, and leeches slowly reduced the swelling; or perhaps it was the change from mercury to iodides. After three weeks his tongue returned to normal, and the discoloration of his genitals subsided. He returned at once to the late hours and heavy smoking and drinking which were his normal regimen. He put off the visit he had been promising himself to make to Dr. Ricord, the great Paris specialist.

Even without the syphilitic attacks, Flaubert was always under painful nervous tension. The squeak of a door hinge or the appearance of a bourgeois or a stupid remark could make his heart pound and upset his day. It was worst when his writing was going badly: he became more irritable or felt like bursting into tears. In contrary fashion, a high wind could so lull and charm him that, intoxicated with work, he became wholly unaware of the outside world. He was terribly frightened on one occasion when he suddenly came to himself again and discovered his mother already in his room; fifteen minutes later his heart was only just beginning to return to normal. These hypersensitivities, transferred to Emma, give to her nervous make-up its lived reality. More personally and more profoundly, these sensitivities helped to produce the violent reactions to living and to life which made it imperative for Flaubert to write.

He suspected that genius and folly were closely akin. He knew that the artist had to see things differently from other men and that art was a special atmosphere, but he was also sure that he was now beyond any danger of insanity. While there were moments when extreme tensions and anxieties could once again put flashing lights before his eyes, these symptoms of his epilepsy were so rare as to be no longer alarming, and he could begin to look forward to writing of the curious psychological phenomena he had experienced. He realized that he must wait longer, however, until he was so far cured that he could risk voluntarily inducing crises in order to study them. The moment never came, though, when soundness of mind, time for experimentation, and freedom to write this book coincided. And so he confined himself to giving Emma Bovary and others of his characters some of the terrors he had experienced.

During these years of writing, although Flaubert was for the most part in Croisset and having little to do with the outside world, much was going on in Paris and he could not remain wholly indifferent to it. Louis-Napoléon Bonaparte, who had been elected president of the Second Republic, through two *coups d'état* made himself Emperor of the French; fairly rapidly the nobility, the upper bourgeoisie, and the conservative elements in the Church gained control. The tight censorship imposed on the press precluded discussion of most political and religious issues and turned writers perforce to studies of the individual or of social mores. The climate was ripe for Flaubert's novel, as he had foreseen that it would be while he was still on his Mediterranean trip. He worked almost uninterruptedly at it and found little in the daily life of the capital to lure him from his retreat at Croisset.

The idea of living in Paris still seemed impossible to Flaubert in 1851; he would inevitably slip into its machinations and intrigues. But he did at intervals make trips there either for a few days or, more rarely, for two or three weeks at a time. Thus it happened that he was in Paris at the time of the first *coup d'état* in December, 1851. It was an exciting moment, as there was firing in several parts of the city. But the stupidity of it all and the intriguing behind the scenes did not increase Flaubert's respect for the mob or for the bourgeoisie. As the Empire became firmly seated, he found that ennui was overwhelming France: wherever he looked, he saw either tears, misfortune, and wretchedness, or else stupidity, cowardice, and viciousness.

Nor was Flaubert alone in his attitude. A considerable number of the more sensitive of his contemporaries elected to withdraw from any participation in public life. Hugo, exiled, fled to the Channel Islands and hurled invective at the regime for two decades. The poets Leconte de Lisle and Baudelaire found in the events of the day reason to lose any interest in such matters and turned to a life devoted exclusively to art. There were others, too, who decided to pay no further attention to such degrading events. The painters Manet and Degas and the scientists Pasteur and Claude Bernard, to name but a few of the extraordinary men of the Second Empire, elected to live outside the scope of its social and political life. Flaubert was convinced, perhaps without adequate proof, that he could have been a remarkable diplomat; but now, in the presence of the Second Empire, he deliberately withdrew to his ivory tower, to use a phrase which the critic Sainte-Beuve coined in this period.

Safely removed to Croisset, Flaubert could reasonably hope for a peaceful existence there: it was not, he felt, too much to ask. Little Caroline, who was six before the new novel was much more than launched, brought an element of gaiety into the household; soon Flaubert was giving her lessons in history and geography and, before the novel was completed, he was rereading Herodotus so as to be able to tell her more fully about the Battle of Thermopylae, which had excited him when he was twelve and whose site puzzled him in Greece.

She later recalled how fully the daily order of events was subordinated to her uncle's tastes.[13] In the early morning total silence reigned until around ten, when there would come a violent ring from his bell, to signify his awakening. After breakfast and a look at the mail—Caroline was too young to understand the importance of Louise's letters—he dressed and around eleven came down to lunch. Afterwards, a long-stemmed clay pipe in his teeth, he would go out for a walk with his mother and his niece along the terrace bordering on the Seine. At one, the whistle of the passenger boat going between Rouen and the villages along the river would sound; it was the signal for the start of Caroline's lesson. After it Flaubert would settle in to work steadily at *Madame Bovary*, pausing only for occasional breaths of air at the window or brief walks on the terrace to relax while hunting for a phrase. This continued until seven, when dinner was announced. After it and another walk, the little group would often pause in the small pavilion which was then at the water's edge. Here, for an hour or so, Flaubert would rest and talk until, around nine, he would say that it was time to return to the *Bovary*, this mysterious word which seemed to his small niece to be some sort of synonym for work.

Several months at a time would go by this way, broken only by the Sunday visits of Louis Bouilhet, who would spend the night at Croisset so that he and Flaubert could each read to the other what he had written during the week. Shouts, exclamations, and endless controversies would ensue over rejecting or maintaining an adjective. The only other breaks in the routine were visits, three or four times a year, to Paris.

Flaubert's mother, who in fact lived another two decades, was aging markedly. She had too little to do and even so was worn down by insomnias, in this being perhaps a model for a part of Emma. At intervals she would invade Flaubert's sacred work room to complain of domestic problems which really existed only in her own mind, and he would have to interrupt his writing to make peace with the servants. It infuriated him, but he was now too wise to suppose that he could live without her. His mother and he had worries real enough, however, over little Caroline's father, Hamard. Flaubert never spoke of his dead sister, but in his heart he kept a special place for her, the soundest and most charming woman he had ever known. Now her husband, "vulgarity incarnate" Flaubert termed him, was causing serious alarm by his habitual drunkenness and incipient insanity. In 1854 a legal guardianship had to be established for him.[14]

The family seemed to Flaubert a dubious institution. Dinners with his brother Achille's household, full of bourgeois pomp and ceremony, were a dull duty at best. And, renewing contact with Ernest Chevalier, whose marriage had seemed to forebode little good, he now learned that his friend was deeply concerned about his wife and finding in his marriage only sources of additional cares. When Madame Flaubert told her son he was growing unpleasant and irritable, in his heart Gustave felt he had good reason to be.

Du Camp's handling of his *Revue de Paris* showed that he no longer shared the views of Bouilhet and Flaubert on art. Gustave found his old friend pitiable. Then Du Camp, who had refused to give advice to Flaubert nine months before, in July, 1852, sent him a letter of paternal counsel: Flaubert should come ·to Paris to take up the place which was rightly his in the vanguard of the younger men who would lead the future literary battles. Flaubert, furious, replied bitterly that he found no meaning in this silly and ill-conceived chase after glory: if what you wrote was good, it would achieve its place in six months or six years or after your death. He was, he assured his erstwhile friend, in no hurry, and Maxime would be far better advised quietly to let the water flow as it wished. Du Camp, unable to understand any of this, replied more sharply, suggesting that Flaubert must be suffering from a softening of the brain. Flaubert answered even more bitterly, and the gap between the two men widened beyond hope of bridging until time could fill in some of it. On Flaubert's part it was both a revenge for his earlier humiliation when Du Camp had refused to counsel him and also a question of integrity: he could not accept the role of successful man of letters which Du Camp now urged, for it meant compromises with everything in which he believed. The first six months of writing *Madame Bovary* had shown him his path and made it a moral obligation to continue in it: Du Camp's advice came too late to be adopted.

For some few years the two men were widely separated. Flaubert felt that Maxime's further progress bore out the gloomy predictions he had made for him. And Du Camp, who made one or two gestures in Flaubert's direction, must have felt equally confirmed in his dire forebodings as the *Bovary* dragged on for years without ever being finished; moreover, he, too, must have been hurt that his friend could so treat him. But when *Madame Bovary* was finally completed, it appeared first serially in Du Camp's *Revue de Paris:* Maxime was helping his old friend as he had promised he would, if ever the moment came.

Louis Bouilhet's Sunday visits and the pitiless critiques which the two authors gave each other eventuated, for Bouilhet, in a long poem, *Mélaenis*, which brought him some little fame despite unkind words from Sainte-Beuve. Flaubert at last introduced Bouilhet to Louise Colet, and she arranged a reading of part of the new work in her salon. Flaubert was overjoyed; so was Bouilhet, especially as his verses were read by the attractive Madame Edma Roger des Genettes. Flaubert rightly guessed that poet and reader would soon be lover and mistress. Bouilhet and Louise Colet, too, established a warm and pleasant relationship based on their common fondness for Gustave.

The success of Bouilhet's poetry, however modest, slowly brought the beginning of a new life for the two friends: Bouilhet's presence now became indispensable in Paris, and in the autumn of 1853 he prepared to leave Rouen. Flaubert was desperately sad, while loyally insisting that his friend must depart. As he put it, the only ear to which he could really speak was now to be absent. It was the end of an epoch for him: henceforth he would experience that solitude he had proclaimed he wanted. He was hurt and humiliated at dreading it. On the third of November he and Bouilhet dined together and, for the last time, attended the Saint Romain Fair to admire the marionettes; three days later they had their final Sunday at Croisset, and then Bouilhet left, never again to be a regular weekly visitor, although he eased the blow by returning for a few days almost at once.

There now began a real literary correspondence between the two men.[15] Since they could not be together each weekend, they made it an invariable practice to send each other a letter on Sunday, often only a quick note but sometimes an extended, detailed discussion of their literary problems of the week. Bouilhet perhaps asked more advice than he gave and relied more broadly on his friend than Flaubert did on him, but on several occasions it was Bouilhet who rescued Flaubert from difficulties he seemed unable to resolve. He also provided technical information Flaubert lacked, for instance medical notions about the climate at Yonville or the infection in the Blind Man's eye. These were particularly useful because they came from a fellow craftsman who understood the problems, and Bouilhet often accompanied them with wise counsel on how best to make use of the information.

The Sunday letters were a help, but neither man was happy about the long separations. For Bouilhet, black melancholy was a constant enemy to keep at bay. Unlike Flaubert, he had no private income; hence literary success was indispensable. The alternative was a humiliating return to giving private lessons in Rouen. But success was so slow in coming! After the long winter apart, both were delighted when it was possible to be together again, first in

Paris where Flaubert made an extended stay and then in Rouen when summer relieved Bouilhet of any need to be in the city. They began to envisage collaborating on various books as soon as Flaubert had finished *Madame Bovary*.

Gradually it became the agreement that Flaubert would spend the winter in Paris; a separation of one year had already been quite enough, too much in fact. And so Flaubert's complete claustration at Croisset came to an end with the summer of 1854, and he began to get to know the capital from more than the viewpoint of an impecunious student: only thus could he ten years later write the second *Sentimental Education*, which deals so much with Parisian life. Together once again and now sure that separations would be only for months and not constant, the two men settled happily into their roles of intimate and mutual counselors, a joint life which continued fifteen more years till Bouilhet's death. *Madame Bovary* was dedicated to Bouilhet, and after his death Flaubert wrote that he had lost his literary compass, the man for whom he really wrote his works.[16]

Louise Colet had resumed her role as Flaubert's mistress within a few months of his return from the Near East and largely on his terms. Despite several violent disagreements by letter, they saw each other at intervals, and for the first time he sent her sizable packets of his earlier writings, the first *Sentimental Education*, his notes from the honeymoon trip to Italy, and above all *Saint Anthony*. His feelings for her were a complex mixture in which friendship, physical attraction, esteem, and tenderness all played parts. He assured her, perhaps not very tactfully, that if he were to love others, it would not touch his feelings for her, for it would involve only his physical senses or be a matter of a passing caprice.

There were many sources of strain: Louise was having money troubles, and Flaubert's efforts to help only irritated her. He and Bouilhet were correcting her verse. It was peculiarly unfortunate that the first poem was a sentimental piece on a penal reform colony which had so little interested Flaubert and Du Camp that they had not even bothered to go slightly out of their way to visit it during their trip through Brittany.[17] As spring came on in 1852, Flaubert's tone in his corrections of her poetry became as harsh as that which he was accustomed to using with Bouilhet. To have her work called "atrocious" made Louise furious. Still another area caused friction: she was steadily insistent that she meet Gustave's mother. He was ferocious in his constant refusals, fearing probably that his mother would not like Louise and knowing, in any case, that her glacial demeanor would not please his mistress. But forty-eight hours together in their old hotel at Mantes brought the two lovers closer together. He wrote after it that he felt as though he had oceans of cream in his soul, and he longed for the moment when he could finally bring a large section of the *Bovary* to read to her.

Flaubert's absence from Paris and from his passionate mistress had a further and wholly natural consequence: Louise became interested in other men, in particular the aging, debauched, and sick poet Alfred de Musset. Flaubert's was not a jealous temperament, and Musset, by now an alcoholic and physically repulsive in his drunkenness, was not a rival he needed seriously fear.[18] But when his mistress took to going on moonlit rides with the poet, he cautioned her against appearing a coquette. One time Musset became violent in pressing his suit; Louise slapped him and jumped from the moving carriage. It enraged Flaubert, but he was wise enough to understand both sides and gently reproved his mistress for having led Musset on. He wondered if he had been jealous, but it seemed to him rather that he had been overcome with a feeling of his own powerlessness to help: he was so rarely with her; he was not really a lovable man. But it was perhaps better not to think of it any more. He told her how proud he was that she had written the whole thing to him.

Matters did not go very well between them in the winter of 1852. Gustave kept refusing to see her because—he now admitted it—it interrupted his work. For a few weeks she thought that she was pregnant.[19] While his corrections of her poetry infuriated her, her refusal to adopt them was driving him into almost insane rages when he wanted to throw up the whole affair. Then, against his better judgment, he acceded to her request and sent her the notes he had made during his Near Eastern trip: perhaps he foresaw what her fury would be when she came to the passages on Kuchiuk-Hânem. His efforts to explain how little all of this meant to him were belied by what he had written and by Louise's intuition. His attempts to persuade her that they should share something higher than love, something above the physical aspects of most relationships, were not entirely convincing against this background, however much he may have hoped that they could enjoy a Don Juan-Anna Maria relationship.

A reunion at Mantes in the spring of 1853 was again deeply good. Flaubert realized he was very much in love with her and saw anew what an unusual woman she was to put up with his manias. Next year he hoped to finish *Madame Bovary* and be free to take an apartment in Paris. He would be there three or four months each winter, but she must not press him on this matter. It was bad enough that, like Léon, he was wasting so much time imagining what his apartment would be like. But quarrels and reconciliations kept alternating.

Flaubert's attitude toward women was slowly crystallizing, as he faced the realization that neither his adolescent dreams nor the more mature ones which had underlain his *Don Juan* were possible for him. Fundamental to it all was his basic inability to be successful with women. He knew that he was always going to be embarrassed, even prevented from paying compliments to them. In the very moment when he was tempted to try, he found himself fearing that the woman would be thinking to herself: "What a charlatan!" And the phrases would freeze on his lips. In self-defense and in revenge he reacted with contempt for women. Every man, he opined, discovered before adolescence was over that they accorded their favors to the least meritorious. And so men responded by treating them with great exterior deference and a total contempt inside. As a matter of fact, he suspected that success with women was a radical mark of inferiority; yet he knew that this was something every man envied. This led intelligent men, he said, to the wholly erroneous conclusion that women were stupid, which was not true. Women judged from their point of view, men from theirs; physical attractiveness did not mean the same thing to the two sexes, and there was no possible way to come to agreement.

When Louise replied to Flaubert's objections by saying that women were not really free, he agreed at once. This was what his *Bovary* was discussing. No one in modern society was in a position to tell women the truth, and he underlined the whole sentence. To make it worse, when men did speak honestly to them, they became exasperated over such strange conduct. What most annoyed him in their behavior was their insistence on poetizing everything: if a man loved his laundress, he would still know she was a fool, whereas a woman in love with a lout would find him an unrecognized genius. This was the way he was displaying Emma in relation to Rodolphe and, above all, to Léon. From the point of view of love itself, this blindness was an undoubted superiority; objectively it was an inferiority. Trying to get oranges from apple trees was a malady women all suffered from.

And so Flaubert was led to offer poor Louise a series of maxims about women. They were never frank with themselves, because they would never admit the purely physical aspects of attraction and must always deny the existence of evil or vice in their loved ones. Its ironic acceptance, which he defined as cynicism, was closed to them. Their hearts were a keyboard upon which man the egotist produced brilliant airs, to which women gave themselves entirely. In reality they longed in everything for the eternal spouse and always dreamed of the great love of a lifetime. What they wanted was not an idea, but a man, a child, a lover. Their most ethereal dreams were based upon the most material of appetites. This was Emma's confusion and his difficulty with Louise.

Flaubert's situation was, however, more complex than he was willing to confess to Louise, however much he felt she might be told more than most women. Du Camp was, for instance, keeping him informed about Elisa Schlésinger and her husband, who now left France definitively for Baden.[20] Flaubert wrote to Maurice that he never passed through Vernon, their old home, on his route between Rouen and Paris, without leaning out of the railway carriage half-expecting to see him on the platform. More important, however, was Ludovica, for Flaubert's long campaign to become her lover was now successful and he could salaciously urge Bouilhet to profit by her easy morals: she was better in bed than Louise. Flaubert's first occasion, in the summer of 1853, had been a failure, as had the first time with Louise Colet; but he soon made up for his deficiencies.[21] Louise he wished to occupy a position above and beyond all of this; he was quite honest with her. And if he tolerated easily her excursions with Musset, it was in part because he was sure that only the senses were involved, as they were for him with Ludovica.

Shortly after his first and unsuccessful assignation with Ludovica and immediately after visiting Louise in the summer of 1853, Flaubert made a momentous visit to Trouville. The previous summer, when he had thought he could take the time for the trip and while the correspondence with Harriet Collier had not yet died, he had written to her of what it would mean to him to see her house once again and the place where she used to lie in the sun with her white ermine cloak over her feet. A year later he was able to make the trip. It was a good moment for it: the lingering affection he had felt for Harriet Collier had now subsided into memory; Ludovica had given herself to him, and he was, like Charles, full of the felicities of his recent visit with Louise, for he went directly from Paris to Trouville. In fact the whole summer had been full of revived memories. He had been rereading children's books for his *Bovary* in an edition which he had colored as a child. A minor incident had brought back to memory a visit to an insane asylum with his father, and pictures of his life with Caroline had flooded back unbidden. He was tense and showed it in a sudden revival of heavy smoking and obsession with his pipe.

He felt that the trip would do him good, and he was anticipating it: it had been two years since he had been in the country and six since he had seen Trouville. Moreover, he foresaw what memories would surface once he was there. He traveled most of the day and arrived at seven-thirty in the evening. The following evening he wrote to Louise of the thirty-six hours of memories he had just experienced. They went back to his earliest days, and he was almost physically tired from reliving them. He had arrived as the sun was setting in the sea, its great disc the color of a red currant. It had reminded him of the last time in the small hours of the morning with Du Camp and also, though he did not tell her why, of the occasion five years earlier when he had come to Trouville to meet Harriet and fall in love with her. Fate took a hand, and he was lodged in the house of a pharmacist whose kitchen was filled with the bottles of seltzer he was producing.

The son, the future hope of pharmacy, was a child of ten who practiced raising weights with his teeth. Homais had come to life.

The bathers were an incredible sight, and he spent a whole hour on the beach one afternoon watching the ladies go for their swim. Formerly this had been a simple bit of exercise. Now the sexes were separated by a net, and there was an inspector to insure decency, for Trouville was on its way to becoming a major resort. Flaubert wondered how the human race could have become so idiotic and have so lost all sense of elegance. Nothing could be more hideous than the sacks the ladies consented to wear and the waxed-cloth headgear they adopted. And their feet, reddened, skinny, with corns and calluses, deformed by their boots, were long as weavers' shuttles or as broad as the boards laundresses used to beat their wash! Amidst the ladies were little children who were chilly, weeping, and screaming. Farther off were the grandmothers knitting and gentlemen wearing gold-rimmed spectacles as they read their newspapers, looking up between articles to savor infinity with an air of approval. It made the satirist in Flaubert satisfied that he had been right in *Madame Bovary*, while it also made him want to flee to some uncivilized place where the beaches were not soiled by such ugly feet and the atmosphere was not tainted by such fetid individuals.

As he walked about in the old familiar places he came to a spot he had loved, only to find there the remains of a party with bits of pâté and cigar ends. He had written of just such a discovery in *November*, ten or more years before, and the event confirmed his intuition that well-imagined scenes always corresponded to reality: Emma Bovary was no doubt weeping in twenty French villages at that very moment.

Trouville, except for the smells of the sea, seemed changed. But on closer examination he found that the people he had known in prior years were still here, aged a bit but essentially as he had remembered them. Their immobility in the face of so much alteration stupefied him. And then the memories began to rush over him. Elisa's house brought her back with her husband, with whom Flaubert had enjoyed so many horseback rides along the beach. Or a nearby village recalled an occasion when he and a group of others had ridden over one evening during the summer when he

had met Harriet. It seemed all the same, and Nature was so insolent to lend herself now to others: he was still a romantic remembering a poem of Hugo's. He realized how much he himself had
changed, though, when he recalled how his heart had beaten many
years before at this spot, over Harriet.

There was no other refuge from all of this but his familiar
withdrawal. He would put his loves and his hatreds into his books.
Happiness and beauty must be kept separate: he could always
write the *Bovary*, and he could never count on happiness. One
should live like a bourgeois and think like a demigod. It was better
to nourish posterity with one's dreams than to try to actualize
them. Art demanded sacrifice and patience, but it would fill a
man: it was the only way. This Emma would never know.

Now, far from Louise and any physical attraction, he could
meditate on what she meant to him. Ludovica or other women he
would no doubt continue to see and to pursue; but Louise was
something different. She would always be a special sort of affection for him, beyond comparison with any other woman. He
wrote it to her, and he meant it. He did not think of her as a
mistress: there was a pact between them, almost independent of
them. And he loved her, not wildly and romantically as Emma
dreamed of being loved, but with his mind and his spirit. He felt
closer to her than ever before. Unfortunately, Louise, being a
woman, wanted to be loved as Emma did. That was part of why
Flaubert knew so well what his heroine longed for.

The rain was falling, and the sails of the fishing boats were
black against the sea; peasant women passed carrying their umbrel-
las, and sailors called to one another. Ennui came over him, and it
seemed ten years since he had left Louise. His whole life these
days was so quiet, so much a dormant pool, that the slightest event
falling into it, like a pebble, caused ever-widening circles on its
smooth surface and troubled it for long hours before it recovered
its serenity. The mud from the bottom was disturbed, and all sorts
of melancholies, like frogs, interrupted their sleep and put their
heads out of the water to make their strange music. He felt old, so
very old.

The memories, he wrote in an image he tried to lend to Emma,
were crying aloud beneath his steps like the broken shells on the

beach, as each wave aroused long echoes in his memory. He remembered the spasms of hope he had had, his sadnesses or the women he had coveted; the recollections whistled through him like the wind in the rigging, and a great, vague, longing whirled about in the blackness surrounding him, like a flock of wild gulls in the storm clouds. He was reviewing the whole course of his intimate, personal history on this beach which had been the theater of so many of his passions and to which he was bidding a final farewell. He had reached the midpoint of life; he had been shocked at the number of white hairs on his chest. The sorrows of his youth were now over and, like Candide, he was ready to "cultivate his garden," to turn to the daily tasks and to accomplish them without a glance to one side or the other. The *Bovary* was drawing to its close; the age of reason should begin. With time—though it took a year—he could write that all the sites of Rouen, which used so to sadden or infuriate him, he could now look upon with quiet indifference. Peace had been achieved; at Trouville he had had done with his past.

It had been three weeks of summation for Flaubert. He no longer wanted to write his memoirs; nothing so personal tempted him now. Let it all be dead, in order that everything might be absorbed into his writing as the dew rises to form in the skies the gigantic volutes of the clouds, all radiant with the sunlight.

He was eager to be back at his writing so that he might turn to transposing and embroidering all of this for literature. He longed to have done with essentially critical works such as the *Bovary* in order to write an epic in which all of this might shine forth in flaming colors.[22] The milieu and the character of his novel disgusted him more than ever and required still greater efforts of imagination to envisage. How pleasant it would be to write directly! But then he realized this was precisely why the *Bovary* was good for him: it had curbed this direct lyricism and forced him to derive everything from his concept of the subject. It was really better and could lead to serenity of writing. Great art should neither make one weep nor laugh, but rather should act as nature does. Serene of aspect, incomprehensible, it should set one to meditating. He yearned thus to turn from the personal, which disgusted him, to the idea, to which he clung desperately.

One day earlier than he had planned, he returned to Croisset. At Pont-l'Evêque he had been reminded of his January ride with his brother, when his epilepsy had first struck. On the boat from Honfleur to Rouen he recalled traveling that way with Maxime on the return from Brittany and, ten years before that, with Alfred Le Poittevin. Memories were still about him and would recur when he returned to Trouville two years later, but now he was determined to transpose them into art.

Louise Colet, unfortunately, was ill-satisfied with all of this. She was no more inclined than before to accept the rather odd role he proposed to assign her in their liaison. He wrote again from Trouville that she was more man than woman, a compliment which was neither correct nor as flattering as he thought. On his return he refused to travel all day in the train to spend two hours with her at a town half-way to Paris. And he began once more to show irritation over her continued efforts to meet his mother; but his partial excuses based on the condition of his nerves were less than adequate palliatives to Louise, who had been waiting for nearly seven years. At last the timid Gustave did manage to persuade his mother to meet her, but it was a terrible and frightening scene in which Flaubert's harshness appalled even his mother.[23]

Flaubert was by now sure, and he wrote of it to Bouilhet, that Louise was tiring of him and what she called his sepulchral detachment from everything. He did not blame her, or himself, for that matter: the fault lay with fate, a familiar word. Louise then foolishly tried to separate Gustave from Louis Bouilhet. This was to misunderstand the relationship of the two men, and it produced only an exchange of letters between them in which Flaubert vented his irritation secretly to Bouilhet and suggested that Louise should keep her nose out of affairs where it did not belong.[24]

The rest of the winter and the early spring of 1854 went on in the same fashion, with the same recriminations and the same refusals on Flaubert's part.[25] In mid-April in a long letter he restated all of his positions on their relationship, on the importance of the idea in it and the hermaphrodite role he wished she would play, on her defects of personalism in her art, and on the higher ideal of love he wished she shared. A few days later, the end came, unexpected in the sense that neither knew beforehand that it was imminent but so long in preparation that it could be no surprise to either. They had rejoiced in each other's bodies and, more than most lovers, they had been the sort of soulmates Flaubert had hoped for. But few women if any could have been expected to play the role Flaubert wished in a mistress, and he knew it; so he accepted the end gracefully and was glad to regain his freedom. With Louise, who had probably loved more and was certainly more hurt, it was otherwise.

In the summer of 1854 Flaubert came to Paris but carefully kept word of it from Louise, for he and Bouilhet were delighting in the theatrical world which Bouilhet was just coming to know. Each had his actress, and Louise may well have seen them all together without their knowing it. She was licking her wounds and biding her time. That winter, adding the ultimate blow to her unhappiness, Flaubert moved to Paris as he had kept saying he would. They did not meet, but Louise knew he was there, and one day in March she tried on three separate occasions to see him at his hotel. He wrote a curt note, informing her that he would never be in to her. It was the final end, his last communication with her.

Louise tried to renew the relationship through Bouilhet, who contented himself with telling Flaubert that she was inundating him with letters.[26] In April, 1855, Flaubert had already left Paris, and Louise learned of it only through friends. It was a sad way to have the liaison terminate, and a new one with the novelist Champfleury was poor compensation for her. Unfortunately, she had always been vindictive with her pen, and she now told the story of their love, thinly disguised, in a novel. Flaubert was nastily treated, but he was wise enough not to reply; moreover, he was busy with the last details for his own novel, which would be a far greater vindication. In 1857 unpleasant rumors of her irritation reached Flaubert, and in 1858 they met; but in 1859 she published another novel attacking him, and further jibes followed. Perhaps the last time she saw him was in 1863, when she was walking with her daughter and saw him in the distance. She exclaimed, "How ugly he looks! How ugly!"

When Flaubert and Louise broke off relations in April, 1854, he immediately took up with actresses, who for years to come would satisfy his physical needs.[27] By the summer, much of which he spent in Paris, he was more or less the official lover of the actress Beatrix Person; in August came the renewed syphilitic attack. He continued to amuse himself while in Paris, happy that this solution did not impinge on his solitude and his writing. When in Croisset, he put such matters out of his mind and returned to the solution of his youth, masturbation.[28] Meanwhile, for casual excitement, he had the succession of governesses who came from England to care for little Caroline; with Louise out of the way he even found he was having to restrain himself from grabbing one of them on the stairs.

It was an unusual, even a strange life, but to Flaubert a good one. It sufficed for the writing of *Madame Bovary*.

12

The Story Evolves

FROM FACT TO FICTION

I'm making very slow progress with my book and am
spoiling a considerable quantity of paper. There are so many
lines crossed out. . . . If you knew how much I am torturing myself, you would pity me.

Letter to Louise Colet, November, 1851

THE STORY of Delphine Delamare, which Flaubert had now determined to write, offered very little scope for a novelist: its bones
required fleshing out. A provincial health officer had twice married; a daughter was born of the second marriage; his second wife
was guilty of adultery on more than one occasion. Perhaps Madame Delamare had poisoned herself, although this may have been
only imaginative embroidering as the tale passed from teller to
teller.

A first problem was to introduce more scope into the narrative
by varying the character of the successive liaisons.[1] In the early
drafts Flaubert followed fact and had Emma give herself to her
first lover, the Léon of the novel (although that was not yet his
name).[2] This, however, made monotony difficult to avoid for the
second affair and, as plan succeeded plan, it occurred to Flaubert
that it would be more interesting to keep the first relationship
entirely chaste. So in the tale as he told it Léon and Emma longed
for each other, but in their provincial naïveté they did nothing
about it despite their common desires. After a while, miserable and
frustrated, the young man left for Paris, and Emma was in fact
first seduced by a second man, Rodolphe, a neighboring squire
who completely subjugated her. Eventually tiring of this too
facile conquest, he left her. When Léon returned, a second liaison
began, this time with Emma as the dominant partner. Several of

the faces of love are thus displayed: a naïve and unwilling chastity, submission, and domination. Already the emotional richness of the tale was developing.

A second and graver problem was to provide the psychological motivations. Why did Emma behave as she did and what led her to her final downfall, whether the suicide was an invention by Flaubert or a part of the original story? Here Flaubert had help from an unexpected source: Ludovica.[3] He obtained a lengthy memoir presumably written by a servant and confidante of hers, detailing the amours and financial problems of her mistress. Madame Pradier had married, the servant explained, to get away from the authority of her father. This first marriage was unsuccessful but was soon terminated by the death of her husband. She wept for him: after all, he had wished her only well. She was never able really to love; but equally, she was never able to abandon the hope. The fashionable sculptor Pradier became infatuated with her. For a brief moment she thought that she was in love with him: they were married. It was ill-fated from the start. Children came, some his, some not; but she was at least a very good mother. Meanwhile a succession of lovers, not even always one at a time, kept her heart busy.

Ludovica's debts, too, were accumulating. Since she took entire charge of all household bills, it was easy for her to start signing promissory notes and to keep putting off all but the most pressing creditors. But always and essentially she was searching for a lover who could satisfy her yearnings, and this was where her story joined that of Emma Bovary and Don Juan. Ludovica arranged to get a forged power of attorney, thus gaining control over her husband's income. She went deeper into debt until finally every resource was exhausted. Trapped, she turned to her lovers to rescue her, sending her servant with letters to one after another, but in vain. Flaubert marked with a cross the further statement that not one of them even bothered to be polite in his refusal. The end came when the property of the household was sold to cover the debts: then and then only did her husband discover the extent of the catastrophe. He sought and obtained a legal separation. Here the memoir ended.

Now Flaubert had the materials he needed to enrich the psychological fabric of his story. For Emma he borrowed Ludovica's "poetic need of luxury," as he phrased it. Emma would feel, as did Ludovica, that a full and happy love required material well-being for its surroundings. In the early moments of each of her passions she would be indifferent to money, but as the first bloom wore off, she would need to freshen its appeal by what money could buy, and as time passed she would, like Ludovica, borrow more and more until finally she, too, would be trapped. From the first Emma was to end her life by suicide: it is as good a way as any to bring a character to a final end. But only as he wove in the material from Ludovica did it occur to Flaubert to let the suicide come about as a result of financial entanglements and not her love affairs.

Lastly there were all his own earlier works for Flaubert to draw upon. As early as *Passion and Virtue* (1837) Flaubert had studied a woman striving to satisfy her longings through ever more violent voluptuous delights, only to find that each new discovery left only an acrid taste for further ones. He had depicted her rage at her husband's failure to understand her needs and his calm assurance as he embraced her each evening on returning home. She took a lover but, tiring of the affair, he gradually withdrew and finally sent a letter explaining that he was called away. In the end she poisoned herself for love of him.[4] Here was the basic theme of love as unsatisfied aspiration. It had recurred in *November*, where the chaste young hero had longed for a mistress and the prostitute heroine had sought a pure lover.

Above all, love as aspiration had been the common theme of the three tales Flaubert had considered toward the end of the Mediterranean trip. Of these, "Anubis" he set aside for the moment. From the tale of the Flemish virgin, he retained the surroundings of his heroine, the countryside, a cast of somber characters and the general gray, moldy color. To make his thoughts more comprehensible and, in fact, more acceptable, he adopted Delphine as being a more human woman, more like those one ordinarily met;[5] then he added to her the motivations he had gleaned from Ludovica.

There remained *Don Juan*, which he had almost written instead of the *Bovary*. He abandoned it only because, on examination, it turned out that much of what he had wanted to say in this guise could be equally well told in the form of a modern novel with a contemporary subject. *Don Juan* itself derived in part from an earlier tale to be called "Giaffar," in which Flaubert had intended to study how fear and ferocity combined, at the peak of love, to make tenderness complete, as when lovers feel the desire to bite welling up.[6] The tale was to show how love turns out not to be an end in itself but seems instead to require something beyond it for its own completion. "Giaffar" was conceived before the departure for the Near East; now he knew more of what it was that love aspired toward, and he had proposed to write it in *Don Juan*.

Don Juan, as Flaubert conceived him, is essentially the Emma of the late affair with Léon, the woman who dominated her lover and sought endlessly for something more in her passion.[7] The nature of Juan's desire was aspiration, a longing to possess everything, coupled with the feeling of ennui and fatigue which Musset had given to Juan, the infinite tedium, as Flaubert phrased it, of the woman already possessed. He had discovered, like Giaffar, that the excitement of physical desire leads only to more desire: any ultimate physical satisfaction is impossible. Hence, in the midst of the most licentious dreams and longings, Juan sensed vague, mystic aspirations toward a religious experience and culmination.

Anna Maria is the dead nun who mysteriously returns to life for a night of love with Juan. Her unsatisfied longings and aspirations were to know the fullness of life. Since as a nun she could not, she learned to love the confessional, approaching it with a feeling of voluptuous fear, for here she hoped that her heart would open its mystery and shadows. But she had no sins to recount! How she longed for them: there were, so people said, women who lived passionate lives and were happy. She also desired frequent communions so as to possess Christ in her body, as had the heroine of *November*. This was that intimate alliance of religion with sexuality which Flaubert had noticed in Brittany and which he had given to Anthony as his first temptation. But Christ had not replied to her love, despite her prayers. Why had He not listened? All of this Flaubert easily transferred to the young Emma being brought up in a convent. Her name, originally, was Marie.

The purpose of the story, Flaubert wrote, would be to display the union and the equality of this pairing, in which each term had been until now incomplete. They would fuse, and each form of love would be the greater thereby. Flaubert had earlier characterized Don Juan and Anna Maria as unappeasable love in its two forms, terrestrial and mystic, whereas in the story of the Flemish virgin the two forms of love would be united within the same person. The one would lead to the other, and his heroine would die of religious exaltation after knowing the exaltation of the senses.

In Emma Bovary, a poisoned compound of Don Juan, a Flemish virgin, and a Spanish nun, the two loves would still be united in a single person. But in Emma all would be negated. Where *Don Juan* had been intended to be the story of a consummation of love, *Madame Bovary* would recount its grim perversions. Emma would know religious exaltation only partially and always turned aside from its purity. And she would fix her eyes resolutely (at the end) upon the exaltation of the senses. She would thus never know true exaltation, the joy of Anna Maria's complete love, and she would pay with her death for this sin. Never could she know that peace and serenity which had led Flaubert to conclude one sketch for his *Night of Don Juan* with the observation that what Anna Maria had given to the Don did not perish when the statue of the Commander dragged him down to Hell. Emma, too, would be persuaded that she was being dragged there on her deathbed. But she would know that she was taking nothing with her.

THE STORY IS FLESHED OUT

I invented some things, I remembered others, and I put them all together.

Letter to Louise Colet, August 15, 1846

When a writer like Flaubert puts a story together—and it took him five years to write *Madame Bovary*—all his resources, conscious and unconscious, living or literary, come into play. Flaubert thought carefully about the structure of his successive scenes (for that is what *Madame Bovary* really consists of) and wittingly called up innumerable memories. While the creative act, even at the easy level of elaborating a plot line, is more complex than author or critic or reader can ever fully divine, still some of the hidden workings do occasionally come nearer to the surface and can be seized upon for what they may tell of the depths from which they arose.

Flaubert's story line is a congeries of inventions and discoveries, but he could discover only what lay within himself, and he could invent only what the person he had been and the life he had lived would allow him to imagine. His greatest single source was himself, and although he admitted it perhaps only three or four times in his life, he always knew that Emma Bovary was himself. Transposed in sex (which his own sexual ambivalence let him easily imagine), deprived of the only salvation he knew—love of art—and condemned to a milieu far less exciting than Flaubert's, still she was Gustave Flaubert with his anguish and his ennui, his dreams and his bitter disillusionments, his longing for life and his hatred of it. The story of *Madame Bovary* revolves around the life of Flaubert, flesh of his flesh, blood of his blood. On the other hand, no matter how many traits of physique or character or how many events from his own life or from those of intimate friends may underlie the story, its totality, its psychological unity and esthetic validity, so to speak, are his own creative concept, original with him. And that is what makes the novel.

Madame Bovary opens in a tone of easy and personal familiarity soon to be dropped: "We were in the study hall . . ." and Charles Bovary makes his gauche and painful entry into the Rouen school, a country boy alone and untutored, knowing nothing of the customs of this youthful jungle into which he is being thrust and quite incapable of coping with it. He has only his sweetness and his goodness to oppose to it and this is not enough to counterbalance his insensitivity and his stupidity; it never will be. He is at once the center of clamorous humiliations as he tries to find what to do with his hideous cap, reminiscent of odd ones Flaubert had noticed in Brittany and perhaps also owing something to a similar scene published during his adolescence in the humorous magazine, the *Charivari*.[8] Frightened and cringing, the new boy is unable to do more than mutter "Charbovari," as a frustrated proctor tries to elicit his name.

Charles's life was fated to be this way, and he was slowly to understand this fact. He was, at the start, a timid, proper, and punctilious student. Later, in medical school, however, he degenerated into the relatively poor scholar Flaubert became in Paris and, like his creator, he failed his first examinations dismally.

With diligence and enough time Charles eventually passed the relatively simple examinations which gave him the title of health officer. As Eugène Delamare and Ludovica had each had a first, unsuccessful marriage, so Charles, under the guidance of his mother, now marries an aging and querulous widow alleged to have money. The couple settled at Tostes, a little village near Rouen. (Thumbing through a seventeenth-century guidebook some four years earlier, Flaubert had noted with pleasure that around 1600 the coach from Rouen to Dieppe used to stop in this village thrice weekly for a luncheon and rest stop of three hours.[9]) Here Charles set up his practice.

Among his early patients was the wealthy farmer Rouault, who had broken his leg. As Flaubert had reset the sailor's leg on the Nile, so Charles took care of his operation: each required forty-five days to heal. It was during this time that Charles met and fell in love with the daughter of the house, Emma Rouault. Conveniently Charles's first wife died. Withered and harassing as she had been, he thought affectionately of her: after all, she had loved him. It was a parallel to what Ludovica had mused of her dead husband.

Charles was now free to pursue his love for Emma. With the timid young man, however, time dragged by, and finally, like Flaubert summoning his courage to ask Louise to sleep with him, he had to set himself a fixed moment a few hours ahead by which time he swore to make his request of her father. He did and was accepted. The couple was engaged and then married in an incredible peasant wedding scene over which Flaubert lavished his Rabelaisian taste for large eating and deeper drinking. Emma would have preferred to be married by torchlight at midnight, but her father forbade the notion. Forty-three people attended the ceremony and then sat at table sixteen hours.

Now Emma could settle into the bliss she supposed marriage would be. Charles was infinitely happy and would kiss her moistly on the cheeks at every turn, as Gustave had been wont to do with his sister Caroline. Emma would push him away, half smiling, half irritated, as with a child who hangs upon one too insistently. Was this all that love consisted of? She had thought that she was in love with Charles before her marriage, but the expected joys had never come. What was meant by these words, happiness, passion, ecstasy, which had seemed so lovely in her reading? Ludovica had spent her life chasing this dream, and as a young man Flaubert had, too.

Emma's marriage fully established and her problems emerging, it was time for Flaubert to go back into her earlier life to elucidate what had brought her to this situation, in which, as much fated as Charles, she would necessarily chase rainbows till the obscured sun made them fade into no more than somber rain clouds and soaking downpour. How had she reached this state? Where did the illusions of modern woman come from?

Flaubert had long proclaimed the source of the malady: it was the way girls were brought up. He had written a diatribe to his mother from the Near East protesting it, and now he could display it in detail. Emma had been sent, as nice girls were, to a convent to be properly trained. In this tepid atmosphere she had rapidly learned to distinguish beneath the decent veil of tired religiosity its warmer, fervent base in sexuality—which Flaubert had asserted in *November* and elucidated most recently in his studies of Anna Maria, Don Juan's nun. Gently relaxing into a mystic languor, Emma had caressed the notion of a Lamb, of little Jesus. The endless comparisons, too, which recurred in the sermons stirred her: fiancé, bridegroom, celestial lover, eternal marriage were words which brought unexpected feelings of warmth and sweetness deep within.

It was, surprisingly enough, around landscapes that Flaubert sought to portray precisely the temperament of Emma. He had taught himself the austere esthetic pleasure to be gained from being caught up in the scene before one; this pleasure he specifically denied her. She knew real nature too well, he wrote, to be excited by artistic renderings of it. She was accustomed to calm, natural scenes from childhood (and these were to Flaubert supreme, as serenity was in every respect), but it was her nature to revolt, and she longed for storms. In sum, he said, it was imperative for her to draw some personal profit from everything; she could not lose herself in what was before her. Hers was a sentimental, not an artistic, temperament; she was seeking not landscapes but emotions. Flaubert's own salvation he was expressly denying his heroine from her early youth. She was, he said, a somewhat perverse woman impregnated with false poetry and false feelings.

The most serious harm done to Emma was through her contact with shoddy romantic literature, the risk now many times compounded since Chateaubriand's *René*. By learning of imagined passions through books long before experiencing them in life, generations were now growing up, Chateaubriand had warned, who were blasé without having lived, tired and disabused before having illusions, and doomed to disappointment without ever having had a chance at happiness. Emma, like Flaubert before her, is a child of René.

Flaubert, as he wrote Louise Colet, had to try for days to enter into the vapid dreamings of young girls as they read the novels so expressly written for them. He had to navigate through what he termed milky oceans of castle literature, with troubadours wearing velvet toques and white plumes, and chatelaines awaiting their knights; he hoped Louise could give him precise details to fill

it out. In *Across Field and Strand* he had mocked the false poetry
of turrets, damsels, palfreys, lilies and oriflammes of Saint Louis,
the white plume of Henry IV, and all the other similar foolishness.[10] Now, in the convent, Emma avidly devoured this worthless
but entrancing sort of novel, and the familiar heroes and heroines
filed before her eyes in a justly famous paragraph in which Flaubert developed his earlier themes.

Everything about the atmosphere of the convent concurred in
developing false tastes. In the music class simpering romances told
of little angels, lagoons, gondoliers, and far-off places. Her companions had keepsakes, the popular romantic books with gauzelike
paper protecting sentimental engravings. Emma, perhaps already
predisposed, came to think of the future only in these terms. Flaubert's tone is satiric in describing these convent dreams, but they
are his own fancies he is deriding. In Cairo he had conjured up the
sultana watching her lover gallop toward her over the sands; he,
too, had imagined exotic voyages and impossible loves. The bitterness of the satire in these crucial pages is the self-castigation of a
man who loved these things too well.

When her mother died, Emma had an opportunity to play at
romantic despair. She wept copiously, was pleased to be the center
of attention, and gave herself over to philosophic meditations on
the transitory nature of life. She asked to be buried in the same
tomb with her mother and felt secretly pleased at having reached,
in her first attempt, the heights of the pale existence she had heretofore had to content herself with admiring in others. But with
time, unfortunately, she came to feel bored with life at the convent, and eventually, to the satisfaction of all, she left. Marriage to
Charles then became a means to escape from the monotony of
farm life into the excitement of love; like René, she had read
about it.

Now, at last, she would possess this marvelous thing, passion,
which until this moment had soared over her head like a great bird
with pink plumage out of reach in the splendor of poetic skies, as
Flaubert had seen them at Baalbek and Athens. It was, however,
impossible to suppose that the dead calm she now felt could be the
happiness of her dreams; the fatal grip of her illusions closed about
her. Like all the romantics, above all like Flaubert himself, she felt

sure that certain places—though not where one was oneself at the moment—necessarily produced happiness. Bliss was like a plant peculiar to their soil and unable to grow healthily elsewhere.

Nor is it hard to sympathize with Emma's feeling that provincial Normandy in the early nineteenth century was not such a soil. The bleak, blank houses crowd together even today down the single streets of these Norman villages and seem to stare in armored hostility at anything that moves. Their stern immobility harshly belies the possibility that they could be the setting for caprice or passion.

To make it worse and more infuriating, Emma's husband obviously thought her serenely happy and was so himself. His placid calm and his heavy satisfaction and blatant joy in her were insults to her frustration, a note Flaubert had already introduced in *Passion and Virtue* in 1837. At times, however, following her theories of the nature of love, passion, and happiness, she sought to arouse her own feelings by reciting poetry to him or singing the romances which, in the convent, had seemed to promise so much. Alas, she was as calm after it as before, and so was Charles. Hence, as Flaubert wrote, her life was as chill as an attic whose only window faces north, and ennui, the silent spider, wove its web in the shadows of all the recesses of her heart. The situation was very much that of Augier's *Gabrielle*, which Flaubert had read on the Nile: a young and vivacious wife full of romantic dreams and married to a good but prosaic husband. Flaubert, however, was too honest to end his novel as Augier had, with the wife's happy discovery of her husband's unsuspected values and her ecstatic exclamation to him: "Oh Poet!"

Emma was now the victim of the real romantic malady, ennui. It, too, had its roots in Chateaubriand and was the recurring problem Flaubert faced himself; his heroes were beset with ennui, from his earliest works to *The Temptation of Saint Anthony*; it had been his intent to make it the basis of Don Juan's difficulties. Now it would become Emma's life.

Only her greyhound Djali (named for one of Flaubert's dogs) provided interest in the worn monotony of the days until, quite unexpectedly, there came an invitation to a ball at the neighboring chateau of La Vaubyessard. Emma and Charles went, of course;

and of course it was the same ball to which Flaubert himself had gone in 1837 and to which he had been sending heroes and heroines for so many years. It was so long, he wrote to Louise Colet, since he had been to one that he had to make great efforts of imagination to fill in the details beyond those he remembered. Moreover he always found narration more annoying to write than its dramatic counterpart, dialogue. Finally, there had been so many scenes of balls in so many novels that it was difficult to maintain originality. He succeeded by an ingenious grafting of Emma and her life onto the ball which he had attended and had already practiced describing.

Charles and his wife arrived as the lamps were being lit. At dinner she sat beside a senile old marquis, who had to be helped with his food and who drooled the sauces down his grimy chin. But he had lived at court, they said, and slept in the beds of queens! Emma watched as if she were living a fairy tale. The evening wore on and the dancing began; it seemed to her in the flashing splendor of the present moment that her past life, hitherto so clear, was disappearing from sight until she almost doubted that she had ever lived it. Here, for the first time brushing against real wealth, she found that some of it rubbed off onto her heart and left a yearning which would never disappear. She would die because of it.

She danced, she even tried the waltz. She looked up at the windows and saw the peasants peering in—as they had been doing for fifteen or more years now, waiting for her. And then it was time, at last, to go to bed. Charles had spent the last five hours standing watching the whist players, without ever understanding anything of the game.

Going to the open window of their room with her shawl about her shoulders, Emma leaned her elbows on the ledge and looked out into the night, as Flaubert had before, seeking to prolong this moment of wonder and luxury as long as possible. Flaubert, the schoolboy, had done as much and realized his own miserable position. Emma knew her weakness, too, and her creator for the first time drew closer to her: for a moment the irony lifts and she crawls shivering to bed.

Flaubert, like Emma, had stayed up for the dawn, but he had

then gone walking and had boated on the swan pond. In the early drafts Emma went for such a walk, but on reflection Flaubert decided that this was improper for a young woman and so he eliminated it. It is typical of the early drafts thus to derive directly from memory but then to be transposed in later versions. Sometimes, however, as here, there is a lingering touch of the original event: after the breakfast at La Vaubyessard the crumbs were carefully gathered for the swans by one of the young ladies of the chateau.

It was time to ride back to Tostes. On the way a group from the chateau galloped by and, a little later when Charles stopped to fix a broken piece of harness, he found an embroidered cigar case on the ground. He took the cigars from it; Emma kept the case to represent for her the luxurious life of the chateau. To Flaubert it was a mixture of the presents women had given him—Harriet Collier, Louise Colet, and no doubt others.

Charles was happy to be home again; for Emma it was the beginning of unmitigated misery. Day by day, then week by week and month by month, she waited to be invited once again to the chateau. The invitation never came. When she was at last forced to admit it never would, then, wrote Flaubert, the future was a corridor, all black, which had at its end a door shut tight.

What was the rest of the world like? And Paris particularly? People were happy elsewhere. Tostes was an exception, a boring countryside, stupid, petty inhabitants, and an unrelievedly mediocre existence. But out beyond in the rest of the world there stretched limitlessly the immense domain of felicity and passion where, in her confused desire, the sensuality of riches and the joys of love, elegance of surroundings, and delicacy of feelings somehow meshed into one inextricable whole which she must have. Charles, moreover, was growing fat. He worked hard and had a good practice, but at night, sleepy like Dr. Flaubert before him, he would fall to drowsing while Emma, as exasperated as Flaubert himself had been, tried to talk to him.

Despairing, like the hero of *November* she took to waiting for an event, something to break the unending file of days, all alike, numberless, bringing nothing, stretching before her. Other women were luckier: they could hope for change. But for her there would never be anything. Hers was the sadness of an earlier Flaubert, and like his it was increased by little outside touches. An organ grinder, for instance, made her misery sharper by playing for her one day. Writing *Smarh*, in 1839, Flaubert had depicted such a woman forced to abandon her poetic visions, a prefiguration of Emma, but this first time portrayed sympathetically, for she was but Flaubert himself with sex transposed. Now, a decade and a half later, he remembered the dreams and the anguish of abandoning them, but he knew their flimsy hollowness and could no longer depict them as valid.

Emma knew she was the equal of those other women who had peopled her books and her dreams and who had such happy lives, for she had seen duchesses at the chateau, and they were less beautiful than she. She cursed the injustice of God and leaned her head against the wall to weep and envy the tumultuous lives, the masked balls, the insolent pleasures and unrestrained passions which such lives must of necessity provide.

For two long years she put up with this life at Tostes, and then, driven mad by it, she forced her husband to leave and take up a new practice at the larger village of Yonville. Part One ends with their departure for the new home as Emma became pregnant. Flaubert was afraid that it had taken too many pages. And yet so many important things had had to be established in it: psychological preparations, the various sites, the exposition of character. He could not cut it down, and so, wisely, he let it stand.

The departure from Tostes offered Flaubert the sort of occasion which he liked for the use of overt symbolism. The first example had been Charles's cap, symbolizing his ineptitude. Later Flaubert made similar use of wedding bouquets. Charles, somewhat insensitively, had neglected to remove his first wife's bouquet from a vase in the bedroom before Emma arrived; belatedly he took it to the attic, and Emma wondered what would be done to hers if she died. In point of fact now, as she was packing for the move to Yonville, she came upon it by pricking her finger on the wire. She tossed it into the fire.

On the same page with the discovery of the first wife's wedding bouquet Flaubert mentioned the plaster statue of a curate placed in the garden at the back of Charles' house. The garden in

Flaubert's story about the Flemish virgin was to have been like that of a curate and so was Charles's which derived from it. The statue was a sort of last bow in the direction of the original story and its garden. Toward the end of Emma's second year at Tostes, the surface of the plaster curate began to deteriorate badly; as the wagon with their goods lumbered along the road to Yonville it tumbled to the ground, crashing into a thousand pieces into which Yonville would break their lives.

Part Two opens as Flaubert takes his reader on a tour through Yonville, standing always at his elbow to single out and explain the points of interest. Cultivated lands to one side, pastures to the other, divided the surroundings of Yonville, a little town sleepily left behind the progress of the century because it was off the main road. The tour takes the visitor through the village and lets him see all the principal houses and the inn, the *Lion d'or*.

Yonville's single, long street and old houses evoke a mood, just as Blois had when Du Camp and Flaubert had walked through it on their way to Brittany. There Flaubert had written that it was inviting to meditate on the intimate and deeply moving stories which might have taken place behind these peaceful façades, perhaps a fatal passion lasting until death, the uninterrupted love of a devout old maid or virtuous woman. One almost imagined some pale beauty with long fingers and slender hands, an aristrocrat with cold manner, married to some ill-tempered, avaricious, jealous husband. She would be dying of consumption.[11] Now, however, five years later, Flaubert's mood was satire, and he dreamed of no such nonsense for his very positive little heroine whom he would place behind just such a peaceful façade.

The sources of Yonville are complex, with deep roots in Flaubert's past. His family owned property within the confines of a village called Yonville, which gave its name, but only its name, to Flaubert's imaginary village. His is so totally typical of Normandy that several villages have, as the Asian cities with Homer, vied unsuccessfully for the honor of giving birth to it. Forges-les-Eaux, where Flaubert spent a few months in 1848 during the Revolution, lent some of its features to it; and nearby Ry was for long so sure it was the source that, oddly, the book influenced the village, though the reverse may not be true, and plaques indicate the supposed location of the houses Flaubert mentions. Inhabitants of Ry took to remembering as part of their past people who would do as prototypes for figures in the novel. Historical research, less excitable that local pride, has made short shrift of all these prompted memories, and Flaubert's Yonville remains what he intended it to be, a summation of all Norman villages, containing the essence of them all and contained, itself, in none of them wholly. And so it would be with his characters, too, who would soon be meeting Charles and Emma. Bournisien, the curate, and Binet, the tax collector, bore ancient and typical Norman names common in the region, as did Lestiboudois, the sexton and gravedigger.[12].

Here, in this typical Norman village surrounded by typical Norman folk, Emma Bovary would play out her bold attempt to live her dreams. She now had to dream them because of what the convent had taught her to expect and what La Vaubyessard had once shown her to be possible, or so she imagined, little guessing the boredom behind the handsome façade. Now, here, and very precisely in these carefully delineated surroundings, Emma would be caught. She would be the helpless victim of her own acts, irrevocably damned because nothing in her environment could save her and she could not save herself. Her temperament, her desires, and the courage to try to realize them, she already had. It remained only for Flaubert to set the stage so as to remove paths of exit from her. Trap and victim would be ready, and it would then be time to spring the one to catch the other. The impending, fated doom of Greek tragedy has here been replaced by the faith of Flaubert, a faith not in the almighty gods nor indeed in a Divine Father, but rather, as he had endlessly repeated, in the Providence of Evil, determinism, that irony of fate which always combined things toward the undoing of man. Or, in this case, of woman.

To introduce the principal characters Flaubert evolved an ingenious presentation which allowed him to return to the impersonal tone which had prevailed before the tour of Yonville. Charles and Emma arrived there late in the day by the slow-moving stagecoach ironically called the *Hirondelle*, the Swallow. They are expected by everyone at the Inn, where they will take dinner. Here one of the great characters of the novel, Homais, the pharmacist, is waiting for them, busy and self-important as he will always be. The young law clerk Léon, handsome, idle, and bored, comes in for his meal: he will still be there when Emma arrives. The curate Bournisien, a rough country parish priest, has forgotten his umbrella and stops by. And the reader hears, if only for a moment, of the cloth merchant Lheureux and observes the limping, clubfooted stableboy, whom Charles will seek, disastrously, to cure. Léon will be Emma's lover, and she will use the *Hirondelle* to keep her assignations with him in Rouen. Lheureux will trap her financially; Bournisien will fail her in her need and will bury her. And through it all Homais will busily and complacently pursue his own successful career, incarnating every bourgeois virtue which Flaubert hated; and only he and the crafty merchant Lheureux, of all the characters in the book, will be triumphant at the end.

It was an extraordinarily difficult scene to write. Nearly all the characters have to appear, and most of them must talk at length. Yet Flaubert could not squander in this one scene all the typical words and gestures he had found for these people. Many touches which would have enlivened the scene had to be held back for later where they would be essential. Homais does most of the talking at the start, describing the medical situation in the area in a long and pompous speech based on information Bouilhet provided about the relations of climate and soil to health. The reader learns much about Yonville but even more about Homais, who adds all sorts of misinformation, corrects himself, uses Latin words for simple things, and rejoices throughout at having an audience capable of following him. Léon, too, talks in a long, foolish conversation with Emma, filled with all the romantic clichés, as each discovers a spiritual mate in the other. Flaubert first sketched the scene in his *Memoirs of a Madman* (1838). The conversation wandered at random while Léon and Emma explored each other's sensibilities and found them kindred as they talked of the world of their dreams, the world they would never know in reality. The satire is devastating, the caricature complete; but neither Emma nor Léon knew it. Where else, Flaubert wondered, had a novelist risked poking such fun at his hero and heroine?[13]

Emma went to sleep that first night convinced that life would now be better; different places always brought different ways of living, and what had gone before had been so bad that what would come now must be better. As for Léon, the evening at dinner was the first time in his life that he had talked for so long at one time to a lady. His head was awhirl. And he was the first thing Emma saw in the morning.

To be ready for plucking, Emma needed ripening. She needed to have all support removed from her and gradually increasing experiences to weaken her scruples and to arouse her imagination. At first there was the possibility that motherhood would provide a new and sounder outlet for her energies. Unfortunately there was not enough money for the layette of her dreams, and so, as Flaubert put it, she had none of the pleasure of those preparations which arouse a mother's tenderness in advance. Then Charles's father and mother paid a visit. The old gentleman had been a gay blade in his day and now enjoyed telling Emma tales of his travels and his mistresses. When he took to grabbing his daughter-in-law about the waist on staircases and calling to Charles to be careful, his wife took him away. But not before he had brought a breath of another world to Emma.

As Léon and Emma walked down a village path to visit the wet nurse who had her daughter, for the first time they became aware of the attraction they felt. Many villagers saw the walk, and it caused gossip, as well it might, for each felt a similar languor invading him. Totally innocent, though, they were separately astonished at the suavity of what they were feeling, but neither thought to tell the other or even to seek out what its cause might be. But each, irrevocably bored in the small village, was driven constantly to seek out the other's company. Indeed, as Homais and Charles would fall asleep over conversation at the pharmacist's or the doctor's, Léon, who lived with the Homais family, would settle into the charming intimacy of reading poetry to Emma in scenes which brought back to Flaubert's mind the long afternoons with Harriet Collier in Paris.

As Léon came to realize that he loved Emma and as he found that he was too timid to speak to her, more and more of Flaubert's own experiences crept into the book, for if he was Emma Bovary, he was also Léon. As Harriet Collier had knitted for him, so Emma knitted a rug for Léon. He took to seeking out excuses to talk of her, as Flaubert had sought occasions to discuss Louise Colet with anyone who would listen in the early days of their liaison; he was afraid and ashamed of his fear, as Flaubert had been. Indeed, Léon took to setting moments by which time he would have spoken, as Charles had done when it was a matter of asking for Emma's hand. Léon even began going off with Charles on his sick rounds thinking, as Flaubert had of Maurice Schlésinger, that her husband was, after all, some part of her.

The final catastrophe—still several hundred pages off—is the result of Emma's inescapable penchant for mixing love and money, passion and luxury. The two are constantly intertwined in the course of the novel so that the end may be no shock to the reader. Thus, at long last Emma does discover that Léon loves her, and she is charmed by it, charmed at the notion and also at the timidity which keeps him from mentioning it. The next day the merchant Lheureux calls to show her some particularly fine goods which have just come into his store and to offer her the possibility of buying on credit, even of making loans to her if she were to need ready cash. The temptation which had destroyed Ludovica was now before Emma, but at the start she refused it, feeling as virtuous about this as about Léon. Instead she turned to intensive care of her household and the little child Berthe.

Léon was sure he could not seduce Emma and, perhaps like young Gustave with Elisa, he came to a very pure feeling for her. Since he thought her beyond his reach, he also put her beyond desire. But Emma was in fact passionately in love with him, full of desires and of raging hatred for Charles, all of which she carefully hid. Desires of the flesh, desires for money, the melancholy of concealed and silent passion, all became a single, confused suffering within her. For all of this she now blamed her husband, whose placid obliviousness seemed a kind of ingratitude for her suffering and her sacrifices. Why was she, then, so pure in her conduct?

Emma and Léon each turned in his own direction. For Emma, the chance incident of hearing the ringing of Bournisien's church bell led her to long memories of her convent days: she went to the curate. As in the *Don Juan* sketches, Flaubert wished to discuss the dualism of love, its physical appetites and its spiritual hunger. But it was never Emma's temperament to ally the two. Instead she sought in her meeting with the priest to achieve some sort of spiritual devotion, a devotion of any sort, providing only that it would entirely absorb her soul and that her whole existence might be swept up into it, something like Anna Maria's life in the convent before she met Don Juan. Instead she found the stupid, unimaginative, and inept priest, Bournisien. He was surrounded and harassed by the rascally children present for their catechism; his robes were shiny with age, ragged at the edges, and spotted with grease and tobacco juice all down the front. The skin of his face and neck was reddened, and yellow spots marred it. He had just finished dinner and was breathing heavily.

How could a man like this understand Emma Bovary? Flaubert had first written of such a moment of incomprehension on the part of a priest in 1838 in his tale *Agonies*.[14] Now he expanded it. When Emma spoke of not feeling well, Bournisien referred to the warm weather and asked if her husband had not prescribed for her condition. When Emma said she needed other than earthly remedies, Bournisien was too busy chasing children to hear her. While she needed his help and attention, he spoke of the hard work he and Bovary had to accomplish and of the difficult life of the farmers; he picked at his teeth with a corner of his handkerchief. Emma suggested that there might be others needing his pity —and he agreed: city dwellers, too, had problems. Emma's head seemed to reel as he continued his grotesque misunderstandings. With his final suggestion that she try hot tea, a despairing Emma left the honest but uncomprehending priest. Motherhood, family, the church had proved of no avail.

The episode with Bournisien is the first occasion when the reader pities Emma. It is also the first occasion when he feels real distaste for another character, this time the priest. With time the reader's feelings for Emma become really confused, but the steadily increasing distaste for Bournisien and for Homais never wavers. The priest and the pharmacist, religion and the bourgeoisie, constituted the two poles of the Second Empire; Flaubert hated both and wanted his reader to share his hatred.

Léon, meanwhile, as frustrated as Emma, was seeking another outlet: he was dreaming of Paris as young Gustave had in his boyhood in Rouen. Léon shared Emma's illusions, for though neither had ever been to the capital, both were sure it was the scene of every delight, as Flaubert, too, had imagined it. At last

Léon found an opening for his slender talents as law clerk, and it was time for him to take his leave of Emma. Like Flaubert fondling Louise Colet's child when he could not kiss the mother, Léon embraced little Berthe and, in a moment, was gone. As Emma looked out at a stormy sky and rain began to fall, Homais and Charles discussed the licentious life they imagined Léon would soon be leading, and Flaubert lent to Homais the remark the curate at Touques had made to him about the gay nights, the masked balls, and the champagne which flowed so freely in student Paris. Then, without regard for consistency and borrowing from Flaubert's *Dictionary of Accepted Ideas,* Homais commiserated with Charles over the sad fate awaiting Léon. Where a moment before he had spoken of fashionable women falling in love with him, now it was instead the perils of a city full of pickpockets and confidence men and where no restaurant could offer the solid, healthful bourgeois cooking of the home. It was a mixture of the illusions and the miseries Flaubert himself had had and the ineptitudes and grotesque prejudices he had long castigated in the bourgeoisie.

The next day was, Flaubert wrote, funereal for Emma, like the days after the ball at La Vaubyessard. Ultimately she came to regretting not having given herself to Léon. Then, slowly—and it was perhaps worse—her desires calmed and her life became a total blank; a hideous chill cut through her, and the bad days of Tostes began again but blacker still, for now she knew this would never end. Sorrow settled into her spirit with the soft moanings the wind makes in winter in abandoned chateaus, the sort of revery one has over what will never return. Emma felt as Flaubert had at each stage on the Near Eastern trip: she succumbed to that lassitude which, he wrote, overcomes you at the end of each action, that pain which interruption of customary movements always brings, like the sudden cessation of a prolonged vibration. It was perhaps not precisely what Emma was feeling. (What customary movement had she ceased making?) But it was as good an account as Flaubert ever gave of his own feelings during the trip.

So much virtue must, after all, have its reward: Emma began to spend money, to allow herself to indulge small fantasies as repayment for such great sacrifices. Like Ludovica, she needed frantically to surround herself, with luxuries. Soon they were bigger ones, and Du Camp, who saw the manuscript later, accused Flaubert of exaggeration when Emma purchased lemons to use on her fingernails at a rate which worked out to one hundred a month! She took to buying from Lheureux objects she had earlier refused to consider.

Charles's mother, who came to visit, had no trouble diagnosing Emma's real ill: she needed work, hard manual work, and lots of it. Running her house would provide it. But who has ever listened to a mother-in-law's distasteful counsel? Another door was closed for Emma. Charles and his mother, did, however, succeed in cutting off the supply of wretched romantic novels Emma was having sent from Rouen. It did not really matter: for she was about to live her dreams and would no longer need these books.

It was time for Rodolphe, who would seduce Emma, to make his entrance. His name might have been other, his looks, age, or background somewhat different. But approximately a Rodolphe was now indicated, a man sufficiently young to be attractive, sufficiently old to be experienced: a man who would see and understand Emma at a glance and who would want her because she was pretty. Rodolphe was thirty-four, a man of many conquests, essentially brutal but with a discerning intelligence. He met her on the occasion of bringing a servant to be bled by Charles. When Homais' apprentice, Justin, fainted at the sight of the blood, Emma was called in to care for him. Little Justin—like Flaubert with Elisa—adored Emma from afar and all unbeknownst to her. He was the witness to this first meeting, while Rodolphe coolly considered Emma. She was, he saw at once, bored to death in Yonville and longing for a love affair, like a carp on a kitchen table gasping for water. He knew she would be tender to have, charming in fact. But how could one get rid of her when it had all begun to pall, he wondered in the cynical way Du Camp had during the Breton trip. It was an idea which fascinated Flaubert, and he would use it again. In imagination Rodolphe undressed her, and, pleased with what he divined, decided to have her. A bold frontal attack would be best, he decided.

It was at the Agricultural Fair of Yonville that Rodolphe began his campaign. The fair, one of the justly celebrated passages in the book, is an incredibly complex orchestration of many different themes, a symphony in prose, Flaubert rightfully termed it. To describe it requires untangling the threads, which falsifies what is essentially a totally integrated and woven tableau. Flaubert's labor was immense. The fair occupies some forty pages in the text and it took more than five months to write. Bouilhet felt it would be the best scene in the book, and perhaps it is. Some passages Flaubert rewrote as many as fifteen times before finding their final form. Even then two paragraphs written with this incredible labor had at the last moment to be struck from the printed version; they slowed the movement of the scene too much.

Flaubert found such fairs grotesque and almost nauseating; so did Rodolphe, and when he met Emma, he made fun of it to her. As the deputy prefect from Rouen began his speech, Rodolphe persuaded Emma to go upstairs in the municipal building to watch from an upper-story window. The stage now had, as it were, three decks. At the top were Emma and Rodolphe, about to begin the most banal of seductions; below them was the government official, equally banal in his ideas; at the lowest level were the prize animals and vegetables. While the poor official tangled his metaphors and lauded the monarch guiding the chariot of state through the stormy seas, and as the animals lowed and grunted and bleated, Rodolphe spoke of his tormented soul and proclaimed that beings destined for one another would always meet: it was the will of fate. This word—Flaubert's fundamental creed—Rodolphe used here for the first time in the novel. It would recur at later, equally crucial moments. Emma, much moved, recalled the viscount who had waltzed with her at La Vaubyessard: Rodolphe used the same perfume on his hair and beard. Then, glancing out the window, she saw the *Hirondelle*, the coach which had served to take Léon away from her; now she was feeling the same thing that she had felt for him. She let Rodolphe keep her hand. As he begged her to let him occupy some slight place in her thoughts, in her life, the authorities outside were awarding a prize for the largest pig in the fair, the sum to be divided equally between two farmers. Desire at its peak made their dry lips tremble and softly, effortlessly, their fingers intertwined. The first battle was over.

A few moments later, Emma, receptive and incapable of resistance, warmly clasped Rodolphe's fingers within her own; outside a prize was being given to a domestic for fifty years of faithful service. The smile of infinite and complacent self-satisfaction on the face of the official who presented the award to Catherine Leroux found its ironic counterpart in the yielding warmth in Emma's heart and body.

Events could now move more rapidly. The celebrations ended in a dinner, long, noisy, and badly served. All the local inhabitants ate too much, drank too much, and sweated copiously. The fireworks intended to enliven the occasion had become damp and refused to explode, and at last the drunken coachman reeled off with the deputy prefect. The report Homais prepared for the Rouen papers was, nonetheless, a panegyric. This was the milieu in which Emma had to seek the strength to resist temptation. Perhaps Rodolphe's word was right: fate was intervening.

There is a further theme present here. Just before Rodolphe and Emma met, the reader learned that Lheureux's machinations had been successful in winning control of a cafe which was a rival to the one which welcomed Emma and Charles; he had gained it by lending money to the owners. He will ruin Emma in the same fashion. Her growing debts to the canny merchant are in a minor and threatening key against the dominating crescendo of love and its major key.

The seduction scene came as an inevitable sequel to the fair. Flaubert had imagined it, at first, exactly like the moment when he had seduced Louise Colet. It was to take place in Emma's bedroom, beside her lamp, a successor to the one Flaubert had watched in Louise's apartment. The seduction was to come only after Emma's long struggle within herself and was to remain in her mind as the dominant sexual experience of her life, coloring all the later ones. But this was not really Emma's nature, and a new story line had to be evolved.

As Emma's health seemed less than good, Rodolphe suggested riding to improve it and offered an extra horse of his: he would accompany her. Charles urged his wife to accept; she demurred on the grounds that she had no riding habit. When Charles agreed to buy one, the temptation of the fashionable clothes decided her:

she would go. It was a foolish way to make a decision, but it was her way, and she would repeat it later with Léon.

Emma and Rodolphe rode off and came to a high point where they paused a moment. They began to talk; never had anyone said such ingratiating things to her. As Rodolphe began his attack of flattery, Flaubert wrote that her vanity, like a person in a steam bath, began to stretch softly, giving itself over entirely to the warmth of the words. They were high above the village, lost in a fog which suddenly broke under the sunlight, as a similar one had in Egypt. As she looked down upon the village, poor and small below her, it seemed mean and worthless. She consented to dismount from her horse. Rodolphe, touchingly attentive, helped her. She leaned her head against his shoulder, and the cloth of her robe caught on the velvet of his riding habit. She bent her head back, her throat swelled with a sigh and, almost fainting and in tears, with a long shudder and hiding her face, she gave herself to Rodolphe. Flaubert handled it as chastely as that, having wished (he wrote Louise Colet) to leave any physically exciting details of the scene to be provided by the reader, not by the text.

Flaubert had to find a way, without intervening himself, to tell his reader what went on in Emma's spirit at this moment. He did it through describing the scene about them, giving to it that yielding receptiveness which he felt literature should not paint directly in Emma, any more than Greek sculpture was directly erotic, however great the ultimate responses in the onlooker. The shadows of evening were falling, he wrote, and the rays of the horizontal sun, passing through the branches, blinded her eyes. Here and there among the leaves or on the ground, luminous spots trembled, as if hummingbirds, flying by, had scattered their plumes about. The bright colors and the evanescent lights were in Emma's heart and not on the leaves and ground, but to place them outside her let the reader see within, whereas a description such as D. H. Lawrence would later write of intercourse would risk so arousing the reader that he would only feel and no longer see and comprehend. Instead Flaubert continued, describing the silence everywhere. Something soft and sweet appeared to emanate from the very trees; Emma could once again feel her heart, whose beats seemed to begin anew. And she became at last aware of her blood as it circulated through her body with the suavity of a river of milk.

Such scenes, Flaubert felt, required some little, pointed touch at the end to give emphasis to all the rest. And so he had Emma hear, far off beyond the woods on the distant hills, a vague, prolonged, drawn-out cry, to which she listened silently as it mingled, like music, with the last vibrations of her relaxing nerves. Rodolphe, a cigar in his mouth, was repairing one of the bridles, which had broken, as Charles had repaired the harness on the return from La Vaubyessard. A more chaste description of lovemaking Flaubert would never write. But in what he said of nature, which the reader may transfer to Emma, he had suggested the transports of the senses which Emma now knew at the experienced hands of Rodolphe.

As Madame Bovary rode home that day nothing in nature had changed; and yet for her it was as though something more portentous had occurred than if mountains had, indeed, been moved. She returned to find—in irony and in pathos—that Charles, to surprise her, had bought a horse to be her very own.

As soon as she could rid herself of her husband, she went up alone to her room to exclaim to herself over and over that at last she had a lover. Now she would have those joys she had dreamed of, those feverish moments of which she had read so often. She remembered the long list of heroines whom she had so admired in her books in the convent: they were her sisters, now. Moreover, had she not suffered enough to merit this? With the satisfaction of a revenge she contemplated herself, without remorse, without worries, without doubt. All the devastating effects of romanticism, like the avenging Furies of ancient Greece, had swooped down upon her, and she headed gaily toward a disaster she had known of since childhood, without ever understanding it. But her ignorance would spare her from no slightest element of what she now so freely embraced.

For the first time in the book Emma was resplendently happy. Flaubert, oddly, found this honeymoon atmosphere most difficult to handle. He could not really imagine happiness, he said, and so tended to remain cold and stupid before his page. Moreover, the moment had come to move his reader insensibly from psychology and states of soul over to action: it was going to be difficult. He resolved it by having Emma live and say all the clichés of romantic ecstasy as he sought to phrase what was in her heart, moving from desire to word and deed and back again. Eventually it could be almost action alone.

Bit by bit Emma came to understand that Rodolphe had meant something else by their liaison, something very simple and very earthily sensual. As a matter of fact, now that he had possessed her, she was already less meaningful to him, and he was bored, incarnating an aspect of Don Juan which had interested Flaubert. Emma's despair he phrased with an image: this great love, into which she sought ever to be plunged, seemed to sink down under her like the waters of a river disappearing into its bed; now she could perceive the mud at the bottom. She sought frantically not to believe it and redoubled her tenderness, but Rodolphe, the charm of victory already withering from use, hid his indifference less and less until, completely subjugated by him, she was nearly afraid of her lover. Their adultery had become as calm and quiet as a marriage. The terrible punishment for her course of action was upon her.

This section is a major turning point in the novel. The psychological base was now complete, and the more entertaining part, the eventful and dramatic sections, could begin. The preparation, Flaubert feared, had been far too long: the active part was going to seem short in contrast. But these were, he felt, the natural, true proportions. One dreamed and longed for an event for years; its accomplishment sometimes filled only minutes. Was he, however, safe to follow this natural order of life? Or were esthetic proportions different? It was, however, too late to change.

Events now crowd in, the first an effort by Charles to carry out a major new operation. It had never been a part of Rodolphe's plans that he should submit to the demands of his mistresses as their husbands had to. Hence, when Emma sought to require things of him, he failed to keep several assignations. She attempted to counter his fascination by restoring the prestige of her husband; she would persuade him to operate on the limping stableboy at the inn. He had been there on their first evening; he was still there. Clubfoot that he was, he was remarkably agile. But a new operation was being discussed: could her husband perhaps carry it out and, a benefactor to mankind, stand forth a hero in her eyes? It would forever remove her from bondage to Rodolphe; after all, Charles was her husband.

Aided and abetted by Homais, Emma drove Charles to try an operation he could in no wise handle and which ended—how could it be otherwise?—with calling in another doctor to amputate the leg, now a gangrenous mass thanks to Charles's clumsy efforts. The poor man, turning to a refuge which would later be used against him, called it the fault of fate, the second time this powerful word is invoked in the book. But Emma felt personally humiliated: how could she ever have been so stupid as to believe he could succeed in anything?

Baudelaire well understood Flaubert's intentions. The episode served, he pointed out, to reveal Emma's character. It let her blind, long-concentrated hatred now burst out. She left the room, slamming the door, when her husband sought solace in her arms. Poor Charles, who had never been able to give his wife any spiritual sustenance, was relegated to his room to do penance for a crime he could not even suspect. And Emma, desperate, was like Lady Macbeth tied to an inadequate husband. Why could she not, Baudelaire had her ask herself, be married to a great scientist? Then at least she could be proud of him. But to be the spouse of this incompetent fool who could not even correct a club foot! Charles is to be pitied; but, as Baudelaire points out, Emma, in her paltry milieu and within her small horizon, is pitiable, too, as she reaches for what she conceives sublimity to be.[15] What Baudelaire does not say, however, is that she is also trapping herself and so, perhaps, is at best sublimely wrong. At any rate, consciously hating Charles, she turned again to Rodolphe. Never had she so worked to excite and charm him.

Emma was, as Baudelaire emphasizes, a determined woman, almost a virile one. If Charles would not do, then she must run off with Rodolphe. And poor deluded girl, she almost forced Rodolphe into it before his good sense intervened. Sitting on the floor between his knees, a pose Flaubert had associated with extreme license ever since his law-school days in the brothels of Paris, her braids undone, her look wild, she persuaded him—for

the nonce—that he wanted to run off with her. Only in running
away, so Emma thought, could she find unfettered and total devotion, but Flaubert knew better. Such devotion does not normally
arise except as a disguise for purposes of seduction. Yet he felt that
women are right to suppose that it can exist. He himself had felt it
and knew it could be: it was the worship he had paid to Elisa
Schlésinger.

Flaubert had placed beside Emma just this sort of silent and
undemanding devotion in the person of Homais's poor little clerk,
Justin. He adored Emma; he even put up with the horrid jokes of
Homais, who had noticed how he hung around her house and
supposed that he was courting the servant girl. But when he was
with her he could watch Emma's clothes being ironed and imagine
her in them, and he could clean her boots of the mud they had
acquired in her assignations with Rodolphe. He did not complain;
it was enough that he could adore her.

To attach Rodolphe the more closely Emma resorted to those
tricks which Harriet Collier and then Louise Colet had adopted,
essentially innocent gestures of love but intended, surely, to bind
the beloved the more. Poor Louise! She had given Flaubert a
jewel she had inherited from her mother, first having it set in a
cigar case with a motto around it: *Amor nel cor*, "With love in
my heart." What was her horror to discover on reading the published book—their liaison was now at an end—that the motto was
inscribed on the ring which Emma now gave Rodolphe. It was
not a very delicate gesture on Flaubert's part; and when the powerful critic Sainte-Beuve heard the details—he was shaving at the
time—it seemed so funny to him that he had to lay down his razor
to avoid cutting himself. Of course, he knew the lady and could
imagine her fury.[16]

Lheureux, who had guessed something of Emma's plans to run
off with Rodolphe, saw in them the possibility he had been waiting for. Emma needed money and needed it so badly that she
would not haggle over the notes she signed. At first Lheureux let
her borrow and borrow, asking only that she continue to sign
further notes for principal and accumulated interest. When finally
he announced that he must have his money, she discovered, as had
Ludovica before her, that she could intercept the payments made

to her husband and use these to cover the debts she had contracted. Lheureux was delighted to put off his final seizure while he made more money from his victim.

It was the essence of Flaubert's belief that a real love could and did exist, fulfilling both terrestrial and mystical aspirations as he understood them. It had been his initial purpose, in *Don Juan*, to portray it. With *Madame Bovary*, however, he had to content himself with a negative statement, an account of how not to go about it. Rodolphe, too, then had to be a portrayal of a man who would only defile Flaubert's sacrosanct picture of complete love, physical and mystical. He had to be so blasé as not to see what it was that Emma was offering him. She was not experiencing complete love as Flaubert understood it, yet terrestrial love at any rate she did feel, and madly, for Rodolphe. But, as Flaubert wrote, because lips that Rodolphe had bought had said these same things to him, he scarcely believed what Emma told him of her love. Exaggerated statements, he felt, could only conceal very moderate feelings. He was unable to understand what Flaubert had so often experienced himself, that when the heart and mind are full to the bursting point, they can only break forth into the most banal of metaphors. Since no one can give the real measure of a truly full heart, Flaubert sadly wrote, and human speech is no more than a broken kettle upon which we beat out melodies for dancing bears, Rodolphe failed totally to understand that what Emma stammered out was the truth. It was very sad. But, like the rest of the story, it was inevitable.

There was a time during which Emma actually succeeded in persuading hard-headed, practical-minded Rodolphe that he did wish to flee with his romantically-minded mistress. For days and weeks it was the constant subject of their conversations. Such dreams of a long journey away from the humdrum surroundings of everyday life were a constant fantasy with Flaubert; he could easily write Emma's. He had already tried his hand at the scene in his first *Sentimental Education*, when Emilie drove Henry into fleeing with her to New York. In 1846, however, when Louise Colet had written of the possibility of their running off together, her lover had replied that he knew all about these mad dreams of flight and the thought of living together somewhere else, somewhere romantic like Rhodes or Smyrna. He had, he wrote her, spent whole days at a time dreaming of blue seas, tents in the desert, tiger hunts, and the noise of bamboos being crushed under the feet of elephants. But did one forget what one had left behind on such trips? He was afraid not: one would no sooner reach these fairy-story lands than one would yearn to be back at home again.[17] Now in the 1850's and with a long trip behind him, he knew, alas, that what he had imagined was true. Even sailing up the Nile his thoughts had been of Croisset. And yet dreams continued; even as he wrote of Emma's foolish ideas, he was himself lost in mad longings to go to Constantinople again, or to China.

Emma found it worst at night. She would go to bed early and pretend to be sleeping when Charles came in. Flaubert's esthetic theories forbade his intervening to point the folly of her dreams. So he arranged to do it by contrast, depicting first the half-waking fantasies of Charles to serve as a foil to those of Emma. Her husband would come in quietly and notice the crib in which his daughter was sleeping. He would imagine the life she would soon be growing up into. Shortly she would be going off to day school, then to boarding school. This would take more money, but he would work harder. How pretty she would be at fifteen, dressed like her mother, so that they would look like two sisters. In the evenings, at home, she would embroider slippers for him and would fill the house with her gaiety and laughter. Then they would find her a good husband and she would settle down near them. It would last that way forever.

Now, none of Charles's dreams were going to work out, and in the light of Berthe's actual destiny they were of savage irony. But at least they stemmed from a goodness of heart too simple to imagine the catastrophic reality which lay ahead of him and which Emma, in her own fashion, was envisioning. Four galloping horses pulled the coach carrying her and her lover off into the bespangled lands of their dreams. As she lay in bed, she imagined it all. They had been gone a week; arms about each other, they hurried ever forward, not needing to speak. Suddenly a splendid city would appear below them as they looked down from a mountain-top: its domes and bridges, its ships and forests of lemon trees, its cathedral with white marble and pointed spires all seemed to live before her. They would reach it, and women would offer them flowers, as the Neapolitan prostitutes had offered them to Flaubert. They would settle in some fisher's cottage by the shore. This, too, in its vagueness, was to last forever. And Emma would drift off to sleep only when dawn came.

At last it was the day before their departure. All plans had been made and the itinerary had been established, first to Paris and then down to Marseilles and on to Genoa. It was the itinerary of Caroline's wedding trip in 1845. They met in the evening for a final embrace and, to set the mood, Flaubert depicted the moon rising on the far side of the river beyond the fields.* Full and almost blood-red, it rose swiftly through the branches of poplars which here and there hid it like a black curtain pierced with holes. Then, startling in its whiteness, it appeared in the clear sky above, filling it with light. Slowing its rapid rise, it let fall upon the surface of the river a great patch of light like a multitude of stars. This silvery glow seemed to twist its way to the bottom of the river, like a headless serpent covered with luminous scales. Or it was a monstrous candelabra from which there flowed like a stream drops of liquid diamonds. The sweet, soft night spread out about them and coverlets of shadow filled the branches. Emma,

---

*"La lune, toute ronde et couleur de pourpre, se levait à ras de terre, au fond de la prairie. Elle montait vite entre les branches des peupliers, qui la cachaient de place en place, comme un rideau noir, troué. Puis elle parut, éclatante de blancheur, dans le ciel vide qu'elle éclairait; et alors, se ralentissant, elle laissa tomber sur la rivière une grande tache, qui faisait une infinité d'étoiles; et cette lueur d'argent semblait s'y tordre jusqu'au fond, à la manière d'un serpent sans tête couvert d'écailles lumineuses. Cela ressemblait aussi à quelque monstrueux candélabre, d'où ruisselaient, tout du long, des gouttes de diamant en fusion. La nuit douce s'étalait autour d'eux; des nappes d'ombre emplissaient les feuillages. Emma, les yeux à demi clos, aspirait avec de grands soupirs le vent frais qui soufflait. Ils ne se parlaient pas, trop perdus qu'ils étaient dans l'envahissement de leur rêverie. La tendresse des anciens jours leur revenait au coeur, abondante et silencieuse comme la rivière qui coulait, avec autant de mollesse qu'en apportait le parfum des seringas, et projetait dans leurs souvenirs des ombres plus démesurées et plus mélancoliques que celles des saules immobiles qui s'allongeaient sur l'herbe. Souvent quelque bête nocturne, hérisson ou belette, se mettant en chasse, dérangeait les feuilles, ou bien on entendait par moments une pêche mûre qui tombait toute seule de l'espalier" (*BOV*, pp. 274-75).

her eyes half-closed, breathed in the cool air with long sighs. Neither spoke, as each was lost in invading revery, and the tenderness they had felt in bygone days swept over them again, abundant and as silent as the river flowing at their feet or with the same softness as the fragrance of the syringas which the breezes brought. The tenderness cast back over their memories shadows more immense and more melancholy than those of the motionless willows which stretched out over the banks. Often some prowling night animal, a hedgehog or weasel, would disturb the foliage; from time to time they would hear a ripe peach falling of its own weight from the tree.

Even Rodolphe was momentarily under the spell of the night; Flaubert had been for fifteen years, as it was a scene he had described over and over again. As far back as *Smarh*, in 1839, he had essayed this most romantic of themes; there, however, he had known only enough to list the physical details: the perfume of the flowers, the rays of the moon, and the overwhelming desire. Then in *A Sentimental Education* he had attempted the scene again, this time with the beginnings of the very metaphors he now re-used for Emma, but with none of the mastery over them which the intervening years procured for him.[18]

Rodolphe, however much entranced by the moonlight, shook off its spell once he was away from the scene and Emma's arms. On his way back to his chateau he began to think out a more reasonable course of action for himself. What a fool he had been! And he prepared to write a letter to bring the whole plan to a halt. Rodolphe was Flaubert himself as he now sat down to draft the paragraphs. Shortly before writing this scene Flaubert had had occasion to reread all the innumerable letters he had received from his many correspondents. For hours and hours he had gone through the boxes and cartons. There were so many people he had completely forgotten, an experience which, in anticipation, he had already noted for Don Juan. Now Rodolphe went over his letters, too, in an effort to rouse in himself something of what he had formerly felt for Emma. Some were badly spelled, as Eulalie Foucaud's had been; others brought back gestures or tones of voice; sometimes he remembered nothing.

Rodolphe finally set his letters aside and began to write to

Emma, the same message (except that Rodolphe was cynical) that Flaubert had written to Louise Colet in 1847 when he had broken off their affair. Was it his fault, Rodolphe asked her? And replying at once, he assured her that it had not been so, that she should accuse only fate. He added to himself, perhaps with satisfaction, that this was always a good word to bring in. Flaubert believed in it and Rodolphe did not, but both had used it, Flaubert in his letter, Rodolphe when first seducing Emma during the Agricultural Fair and now again. It would return. Rodolphe added a few drops of water to simulate tears—an act Flaubert may have considered but did not carry out in writing to Louise—and he dispatched the letter to Emma at the bottom of a basket of apricots he sent by his servant. The valet had instructions to say that his master had left for a long trip.

Emma, alarmed at receiving the letter, fled to the attic to read it. When she was done, her first reaction was fury, then she thought of suicide, but was prevented from it by her husband's calling to her. Half out of her mind, she turned and came down, leaving the letter behind in the attic. Dinner was almost unbearable, and she fainted as Rodolphe's carriage passed her window. It was the beginning of a long and serious illness. Her recovery took months and required expensive medications. Fortunately for Charles, Lheureux was always there, happy to take promissory notes in lieu of money for bills and glad even to add a bit of cash as an increase to the loan.

Emma had a new interest, religion. At one of her sickest moments she had sent for Bournisien to administer the last rites of the Church. Weakened by her illness and chastened by her experience with Rodolphe, she now turned to religion in a new way and, almost fainting with celestial joy, opened her lips to receive the consecrated wafer. Her head fell back upon the pillow, and she seemed to hear the tones of angels' harps and to see God the Father upon a throne of gold in the midst of his saints.

Flaubert himself had seen this vision in Florence as he admired the gently sentimental pictures of Fra Angelico; his notes for the passage refer to the Florentine painter.[19] Fra Angelico had seemed to him to inspire devoutness and make one long for heavenly joys in which to lose one's soul. Now Emma was perhaps feeling something of this religious aspiration which had been the basis for Anna Maria's whole life. But always self-centered, she began to imagine a pure love which would be above all earthly loves and a felicity beyond compare: she determined to become a saint and turned once again away from Flaubert's concept of a complete love.

Unfortunately, the Yonvilles of this earth and their good curates are ill-prepared to handle such aspirations. Bournisien mingled delight with apprehension as he watched his new lamb's fervor mount to the point of heresy, not to say folly. And, despairing of his own lights, he sent for religious pamphlets to aid his charge. The style of these pompous or sugary works and their tone of fabricated piety soon bored Emma, but she was never easily discouraged and would kneel in prayer despite her lassitude. The memory of Rodolphe, Flaubert wrote, recalling Egypt, was more solemn and more motionless than a mummy in its vault; but it remained at the bottom of her heart, its remembered perfume scenting the atmosphere of immaculate devotion in which she sought now to live. And so, kneeling to her God, she murmured to Him the same suave words she had formerly uttered to her lover in her moments of adultery. But it was of no avail; none of the delectations she had imagined seemed to materialize.

It was precisely to relieve her boredom and tedium that Homais suggested to Charles the idea of taking his wife to the opera at Rouen, where the great tenor Lagardy was to sing in *Lucia di Lammermoor*. It was to lead to Emma's final downfall. The opera, based as it is on Walter Scott, took her back to those romantic novels which, in the convent, had first fired her heart and imagination. Flaubert, who had seen it in Rouen a dozen years before as an adolescent, picked it for these qualities and also because it had for him the special memory that he and Du Camp had heard it together in Constantinople. If he could not return there in the flesh, at least he could allow his memories to color even so improbable a page of *Madame Bovary* as this. Not even Bournisien objected very much, and so the fateful journey was decided upon.

As a matter of fact, Emma was not eager to go, but Charles once again insisted, and Emma gave in. At the opera he was so unaccustomed to such matters that at every turn he made humiliating mistakes and got them to the performance hours before it began. He then totally misunderstood the story, which Emma recollected from the convent, and embarrassed her by asking questions in a loud voice during the singing.

Emma was hanging on every word of the opera. And then Lagardy appeared on stage: she felt as she had toward Rodolphe, but Rodolphe never talked as did Lagardy now. After a moment of resistance she longed to be swept up into his arms. Lagardy was, however, on stage and unavailable. Charles, who had been to get ices, now returned with the word that he had met Léon; the young man was on his way to greet her at the very moment. Charles, almost without being urged, suggested that his wife remain in Rouen another day or so. She agreed. On this decision Part Two ended.

Part Three is the affair with Léon, in which instead of being dominated Emma now dominates. And it ends in disaster. It occupies a third of the book, but, as Flaubert realized, it was in reality far more filled with events than the other two had been. He had to condense, to suggest, to eliminate. Moreover, the events he had to narrate were full of apparently grotesque, farcical elements, but he wished so to tell them that the reader would understand their real sadness and would weep, not laugh. The book would succeed or fail depending upon his ability to find the right tone; to a large extent he succeeded.

Léon, more mature now, determined to be bold. Despite his illusions of sophistication, he was in fact naïve and obvious, so much so that Emma smiled behind his back; but since she wanted to be seduced, Léon's task was not unduly difficult. They arranged to meet in front of the cathedral in the morning. He arrived first and spent what seemed an interminable time waiting for her. Then, in one of the very few humorous scenes of the novel, a guide pursued them until they consented to tour the church. It was infuriating to Léon, but Emma pretended to enjoy it until, finally, they managed to escape.

Once outside the cathedral and away from the clutches of the guide, Léon sent for a hackney cab. The ensuing episode was one of those which were later to bring Flaubert into trouble with the authorities. At first Emma demurred at the thought of entering the cab with Léon. But, just as the possibility of owning a fashionable riding habit had made her consent to go horseback riding with Rodolphe, so now Léon's assertion that this sort of thing was done in Paris led her to accept his suggestion. The heavy carriage set out on what was to be an all-day tour of the city, its shades drawn tight shut. Whenever the poor driver sought rest for himself or his beast, a voice from within would shout angrily to drive on. At last, as evening fell, the cab paused, and a veiled woman slipped out: the ride was over. Flaubert had enjoyed himself. Vicariously he, who was always timid with women, was himself seducing Emma, in mock and ironic fashion.

Emma, exhausted, slept all the way back to Yonville where a new drama awaited her. It, too, was ironic in ill-understood significance. On her return she went at first to Homais's pharmacy, where poor Justin was being scolded for daring to use druggist's equipment for household purposes. Homais wondered at his boldness in entering the room where the drugs were kept. Suppose he were inadvertently to get into the arsenic! And Homais described the color of the bottle, its location, its label. There would come a time when Emma would recollect it all; but now, back from her first tryst with Léon, she little dreamed of this.

Charles's father died at this juncture, and the crafty Lheureux foresaw the possibility of an inheritance; he was happy to extend further credit to Emma and even proposed that, again like Ludovica, she should extract from her husband a power of attorney so that she might the more readily handle his affairs to their mutual convenience. With the legal problems of this maneuver as an excuse, she returned to Rouen to consult Léon.

For three blissful days they were alone together. The hotel room was now a familiar place, "their room," as they liked to think of it, just as Flaubert and Louise Colet had treated the hotel room in Mantes and as Flaubert had long before described it in *November*.[20] They did all of the prescribed things, even to taking a ride on a lake, an experience romantics had been treating with reverence ever since Rousseau had described it glowingly in the middle of the eighteenth century. Lamartine had given it consecrated form in 1820 in a celebrated poem, and Flaubert himself had tried it long before in his *Memoirs of a Madman*. For Emma it was somewhat marred when the boatman indiscreetly revealed that Rodolphe had used the same boat only a few days before for the same purposes.

It was essential to be able to repeat this lovely time together, and Emma readily persuaded Charles that she needed music lessons in Rouen, as Ludovica had had no difficulty in deceiving Pradier. Now the trysts could become regular weekly affairs. But this involved Emma in more expenses; besides, it seemed indispensable to have many little luxuries when they were together. She happily paid for it all with funds uncomplainingly supplied by Lheureux.

At first all was harmony, even delirium. She would reach Rouen in the early morning and see the city before her in the mist. Their room, cozy and warm, was always ready for them, and Léon found Emma the heroine of all the romantic books he, too, had read. The only jarring element was the hideous blind man who always sought alms as the *Hirondelle* was ready to take her back to Yonville. His eyes were nauseatingly diseased, and he clung to the coach despite vicious whiplashes from the driver. He was destined, as the story matured in Flaubert's mind, for a major symbolic role in the book. For the moment he was a reminder of the decay and degeneration to which the flesh is heir.

On Emma's return from Rouen, Justin was there to wait upon her and ease the transition to life at Yonville by his silent devotion and attention to her needs. The shock was, however, too great and seemed to demand extravagant spending to compensate for it. Even so, her desires always exceeded her actions, and she was perpetually gnawed by frustration. Charles, on the other hand, was totally happy.

Emma, whose whole life was now a lie, refused to become alarmed even when Lheureux saw her with Léon in Rouen. He was so complaisant, so ready with financial expedients which never seemed to involve more than the signing of further papers in exchange for further ready cash. Eventually, however, unlike Ludovica, Emma became hopelessly confused and had no idea of the extent of her debts. It was enough that she had money.

Meanwhile Emma completely dominated Léon, whom she frequently called "mon enfant." He was so weak and easily led that the ennui Don Juan had felt for the woman possessed Emma began now to feel for him, and the inevitable cooling of the liaison began. Seeking to revive it, she turned to voluptuousness. Flaubert was discreet in his language but clear in his intentions in further passages which were to trouble the guardians of public morality when the book was published. Léon was annoyed at her dominance and anxious to be free of it, but he was completely helpless in her hands. Wondering if his cooling were because of another mistress, she considered having him followed by a detective, a course Ludovica had rejected. Her world was going slowly to pieces beneath her. Flaubert had experienced this with Louise Colet and, even before that, had described it at length in the first *Sentimental Education,* in a passage of which he was very proud, when Henry and Madame Renaud, tiring of each other in New York, discovered lassitude replacing their earlier transports.

One afternoon, having left Léon earlier than usual, Emma walked slowly toward the coach stop and paused on a bench beside her old convent, whose bell tinkled softly. It brought back her days as a young girl there; her early dreams about love flooded over her. Soon, tumbling pell-mell out of her memory, came all the other moments when she had thought she was glimpsing happiness: the ball at La Vaubyessard, her meeting with Rodolphe, the evening at the opera with the tenor Lagardy, and then Léon. It was a miserable, timeless moment, all of her past and her present fusing into quiet agony. Why had she never been happy? Why was she thus different, persecuted? And Flaubert gave to her that nameless anguish which he, too, suffered when, in his attacks, past and present were one and indistinguishable and time went adrift.

This was an indefinable torture, formless and impossible to grapple with; Lheureux was another matter entirely. He was almost ready to close in on his victim, persuaded that she had very little further money he could extort. Her attention, however, was not on this but on the anguish within her. Her disposition, sunny and shining at the start of the affair with Léon, was now seriously affected, and her husband feared a return of her nervous ailment.

It was difficult writing for Flaubert, as he tried to couple his own psychological experiences with the infinite complexities of Lheureux's financial dealings. He had to consult with lawyers to be sure he understood the arrangements himself, and then he had to write of them in such fashion that the reader would understand something of what was going on without being able to penetrate further into it than did Emma, who knew only that trouble lay ahead.

Emma's straits were soon desperate. In addition to the financial complications and her own anguish of soul, there was the fact that Léon was by now thoroughly tired of her. His liaison was widely known in Rouen and was leading to scenes with the notary for whom he worked. He was, moreover, humiliated at being sent by her to pawn her things. And he was about to be promoted to the position of head law clerk in his firm! He could no longer afford these compromising positions. As Flaubert wrote, there is in every notary the debris of the poet he once might have been. Léon had little but the debris left now.

It was a sad page for Flaubert to write, for he had in mind his childhood friend Ernest Chevalier, who had been his companion in literature and full of the fervor which had filled Flaubert himself. Now, as Flaubert had learned during his long trip, Ernest was married and rising rapidly in the legal profession. He was grave and serious and sought to conceal even little follies. He had, he said, given up imagination as too dangerous. It had been atrocious for Flaubert thus to watch the degeneration of his friend. Now he was writing it of Léon.

Emma had not learned from her liaison with Léon. She was finding in this adultery all the platitudes of marriage itself, a bitter phrase which Flaubert later softened for fear of the censor. Hence she supposed that Léon must be the wrong man. When she wrote to him, she now imagined another in his place, a fantasy composed of her most ardent memories, her most moving readings, her strongest desires. Then reality would return, and she would be more exhausted by these dreams than by debauchery. Real and tawdry debauchery, too, she was to know, for she went with Léon to a students' masked ball. Other students were there with prostitutes. In the gray hours of the morning when it was over, she was totally disgusted with herself, with life. She returned to find that Lheureux had now sprung his trap: her property had been seized, and there was to be a sale.

She had twenty-four hours in which to act. A visit to Lheureux proved fruitless, even when she tried putting her hand on his knee. He suggested that she appeal to her lovers. It was a hideous rush of visits based on Ludovica's. She hurried back to a frightened Léon, to whom she suggested that he steal from the notary for whom he worked. And then, despairingly, she stood in front of the cathedral awaiting the returning *Hirondelle*. The same guide who had shown her and Léon about was standing there, and the viscount drove by in his fashionable tilbury. As she was returning, she found herself in the company of Homais, who chose this moment for a lengthy explanation to the blind man of how he should treat his illness. Flaubert borrowed from Bouilhet the poignant suggestion that Homais tell the impoverished idiot beggar to eat nothing but good roast meats and to drink only the better sorts of wine.[21] Moments were slipping rapidly away from Emma. At last only Rodolphe remained. It was a cold, callous scene, when once he realized what she wanted. He, too, refused her.

As she was coming back across the fields from Rodolphe's chateau to Yonville, her misery reached its unbearable apex. Flaubert now gave to her one of his epileptic attacks in its full horror.[22] All her memories and all her ideas seemed to burst from her head at one moment, like the thousand parts of a huge fireworks display. She could see her father, Lheureux's office, the room in the hotel at Rouen, a different landscape from the one about her. She was going mad and was frightened, succeeding only partly in regaining control. She suffered now only in her desire for love, forgetting completely the questions of money which were pressing in upon her. Her very soul seemed to be escaping through this memory, as severely injured people, in their death agony, feel their existence slipping away through their wounds.

Night was falling; ravens flew about her. It suddenly seemed to her that fiery balls were bursting in the air about her and turning round and round to fall finally and melt upon the snow between the branches of the trees. In the center of each there appeared the face of Rodolphe. They multiplied in number, drew closer, penetrated her. And then everything disappeared and she recognized where she was, with the lights of Yonville shining in the distance through the fog. She decided on suicide, remembering with horrible clarity the location of Homais's arsenic, even the color of the bottle. Forcing Justin to open the locked doors for her, she rushed in, seized handfuls of the poison, and ate it in front of him. Only her death now remained.

At first Emma felt nothing, told no one of what she had done. Death seemed simple. Flaubert, carefully looking up the symptoms in a medical book, made a curious mistake, for he turned accidentally to the page on mercury poisoning, which happened to be next to the one on arsenic. He therefore erroneously had Emma first sense the inky taste in her mouth which is characteristic of mercury but not of arsenic. Irony then entered: Flaubert himself began to have the taste in his mouth! He believed it was his imaginative involvement with his heroine, whereas it was in fact no more than a physiological reaction to the mercury with which he was dosing himself against renewed bouts with syphilis. To compound the irony, mercury, the only drug then known against syphilis, would shortly be shown to be far less effective than arsenic. Had he fed the mercury to Emma and taken the arsenic himself, he would not have had the ink taste but he might have been cured of his syphilis; and Emma would have been equally dead.[23]

Madame Bovary had sinned, grievously. But the penalty she was now to pay, the torture of death by poisoning, constituted full amends for what she had done—if amends are possible. After becoming aware of the ink taste, she began to vomit and feel intense chills. Relentlessly, Flaubert followed her through each of the various stages recounted by his medical books. Poor Charles was helpless in the face of this inexplicable catastrophe; Emma spoke to him gently and asked to have little Berthe brought in. Her mother's state frightened the child. Charles had sent for the doctor who had stepped in when the gangrenous leg of the stableboy had to be amputated. He saw at once that the patient was too far gone to be helped, a diagnosis confirmed by the great Dr. Larivière, modeled on Dr. Flaubert, when he too arrived, summoned in all haste by his unfortunate confrere. Emma was beyond human help.

Bournisien arrived to administer the last rites of the Church.

Following the ritual closely, Flaubert had the priest present the crucifix to her. Suddenly peaceful, Emma raised her head and pressed her lips upon the image of the body of the Man-God, placing there the most passionate kiss that she had even given. It was an old scene to Flaubert. His prostitute in *November* had felt such desires for the image of Christ on the Cross; in Brittany he had observed its basis anew. In his *Saint Anthony* he had used it. But here, instead of a lascivious description, Flaubert contented himself with the simple statement, leaving it to his reader to supply the rest.

Then began the Extreme Unction. Here, too, the ritual provided what Flaubert needed, as the priest anointed her eyes, which had so coveted earthly goods; then her nostrils, so anxious for the perfumes of love; then her mouth, which had opened for the telling of lies and which had cried out in amorous transports; then her hands, which had rejoiced in suave sensations; and finally her feet, which had been so rapid in her haste to reach her assignations and which would now run no longer. The beautiful form of the ritual, with its constant consciousness of the presence of sin, served Flaubert well; it also protected him when the public prosecutor, not recognizing the source, blamed the passage.

Then the death agony began.[24] Flaubert was seeking now to give to his heroine a grandeur that would let the reader rediscover himself in her, a stature in which her petty escapades could become the sins of all mankind. The anguish of her moments up to this point were in some sense an atonement, giving the reader the feeling that she had paid enough. It now remained to try to leave the Norman peasant girl, Emma Bovary, and to become aware instead of man's fate, what happens to him when he dreams, not wisely, not well, but with his whole passionate soul. Emma was now to become a symbol.

Her breath began to come more rapidly, her tongue hung from her mouth, her eyes, losing their luster, seemed like lamps about to burn out. The priest prayed, the first doctor summoned looked vaguely out the window. Charles clasped her hands. The end was only seconds away. Suddenly outside the window came the raucous voice of the blind man from Rouen singing his cabaret song about seducing young girls when the heat of a beautiful day makes them think of love. With a scream Emma sat bolt upright and shouted: "The Blind Man!" And she burst into an atrocious laugh, frenzied and desperate as she thought she saw the hideous face of the wretched man rising amid the eternal shadows to terrify her. Another two lines of the song and she was dead.

It was a powerful ending of great stature. It sought for the dimensions of tragedy and it almost reached them. But two flaws deeply marked it. The first is a matter of the distance at which we stand to watch Emma on her deathbed. Flaubert had a difficult choice before him. By now, having lived with constant thoughts of Emma for almost five years he had become, in a sense, fond of her. She was no longer the silly fool of the start of the book: she had incarnated too many of his own dreams for that and had become in so many ways Flaubert himself. He felt a close and loving pity for her and wished to evoke about her death an aura of pathos which would equally move the reader. Yet at the same time his story cried out for something more than the clutching throat one feels when a beloved person dies. Emma needed the stature of a tragic heroine, someone as far removed as is Hamlet when Horatio addresses his dead friend with the tender farewell:

> *Goodnight, sweet prince,*
> *And flights of angels sing thee to thy rest!*

Here, to be sure, the tenderness does heighten the tragedy, but dignity and restraint mark Shakespeare's lines. Flaubert had to try to attain the same stature when Emma screamed out: "The Blind Man!" But on the way to that moment wholly other and irrelevant memories intervened. Flaubert had had to watch Alfred Le Poittevin die and also his sister, a young woman like Emma.[25] When he saw Emma upon her deathbed, it was Caroline who lay there before him. And he wrote of her as he had seen his sister. He described her head falling upon her breast, her eyelids drawn wildly open, and her poor hands dragging across the sheet with that hideous and gentle gesture of those who are on their deathbed and who seem to be trying to cover themselves already with their shroud.

The flaw in this passage, moving as it may be, is that it fits the death of his sister and the emotions appropriate to that, but not

Emma. The adjectives "poor" and "gentle" set a tone and draw the reader inevitably into the very scene, so closely that he can feel only the immediate emotion.

Flaubert had to depict the death of a young woman whose character and flaws he fully understood. And yet he needed to draw back from her to give her that awesome dignity of Man at grips with his Fate. Contrast the evenness of tone or distance in the handling of Anna Karenina, toward whom Tolstoi is far warmer than Flaubert is toward Emma, but where author and reader remain consistently on the outside of the character. In an effort to achieve dignity and symbolic stature Flaubert himself capitalized the words. It is a real woman dying (as it must be), but the tone has established a mood of pathos, of unconcealed tenderness which drives out the majesty of tragedy. Emma, however appealing she may have been, was paying the price attached in human life to violating its laws, as Caroline had not. And this, surely, is what Flaubert hoped to be saying. But instead he drowned awareness of the larger implications of her fate in overwhelming pity for Emma Bovary, suffering here so atrociously. The particular woman, Emma, the reader does suffer for, as her hands make this poor, gentle gesture. The symbol Woman has, however, been displaced. Other women, in other circumstances, might not end this way; and at any rate the reader feels, for the most part, only stabbing pangs of regret that Emma is having to suffer thus.

This is a first radical flaw: the ending clearly strives for the dimensions of tragedy as the symbol of the crucifix reminds us of Western man's aspirations, and the grandeur and beauty of the ritual join in. Emma's recognition of the symbol of the Blind Man is equally grandiose. But pathos was not permissible so close to the end: it could not be consonant with that final Satanic laugh, reminiscent of the laughter of the Devil that had closed *Saint Anthony* and had made a mockery of his hope for salvation with the returning sun. On the other hand, the grandiose and frightening symbol of the laugh is not consonant with the moment when Emma, so very much her own confused self, had given that passionate kiss to the crucifix.

One could phrase this first flaw as one of timing; it is more likely that it is one of consistency in the distance at which the reader stands to watch Emma. He alternately stands off and draws near, he is torn between sympathy and irony. He may have shared her physical anguish from the poison, but he does not identify himself with her mental anguish and so does not see her as symbolic of himself and of mankind until this last instant. The clash between points of view is resolved here, perhaps, but the reader is unprepared for his new attitude toward her. He has stood off to condemn her too often for it to be entirely satisfactory to accept her now as one with all men, and a book which might have pointed the way toward a form for tragedy in the modern novel closes instead without achieving quite that stature.

This first flaw reduces the scope of the book, but it still leaves it bulking large and does offer at any rate pathos if not full-scale grandeur. The second flaw nibbles away even at that. For this is not the end of the book: it continues for another thirty pages. Why? It is perhaps useful to remember that the book did not open with Emma but rather with Charles. Flaubert wished his heroine to be seen within the frame of her environment; in fact, the "Provincial Customs" which was his subtitle was as much the subject as was Emma, or, more properly, Emma's is the story of what happens to a young woman of unbridled temperament who is brought up according to provincial mores, which vitiate what is fine within her. (It was not Flaubert's belief that urban mores were any better, but this was not his topic in this book.) What had preceded Emma and what had surrounded her had already been portrayed, but the final side of the frame, what followed her, remained as yet unsaid. The dramatic finale had already come with Emma's death, but Flaubert's concept of the book required him to continue beyond it. Hence the remaining pages.

Flaubert had a number of further points which he wished to make, and these pages were the place in which to put them. Homais and Bournisien, the bourgeoisie and the church, kept vigil together over Emma's body. The passage is an acrid satire which leaves its bitter taste in the reader's mouth as Homais is idiotically rationalist and Bournisien stupidly devout in the argument which they pursue, shouting at each other their beliefs about the after-life. During the second night of vigil they both fall heavily to sleep, "facing each other, their bellies sticking out, their faces puffy and scowling and as motionless as the corpse beside them, which seemed to be asleep."* Charles, coming in, did not waken them. When, later, they did revive, they came to agreement on a common need for food and wine. The pages are Flaubert's bitter revenge on what they represent.

Charles, on the other hand, grows in stature in these last moments. He had come in to say his final adieus to his wife. It was Flaubert's intention that the body, which he described closely as decay set in, should haunt the reader. Now Charles was contemplating it for the last time. Sweet-smelling herbs were burning and giving off clouds of bluish smoke; a few stars remained and the night was gentle. Emma, in her satin wedding gown, seemed slowly to be being lost into the surroundings, into the silence, the night and the passing wind. And then, gradually, memories began to come back to Charles. He could see her in the garden at Tostes, or in Rouen, or at their marriage. The room was full of the perfume of her hair, and her dress trembled and crackled under his touch. Despair overcame him, and he fled, leaving orders, as had Flaubert concerning his sister, that he wished a lock of her hair.

A long two pages recount the arrival of Emma's father, and three further ones describe the death services and the procession to the cemetery. Then, gradually, all the other characters turn to thoughts of their own futures. Homais regrets that he did not seize the occasion to pronounce a funeral oration. Emma's father thinks of his own deprivation and leaves; Charles's mother is happy in the thought that she will come to keep house for her son. Rodolphe and Léon sleep soundly.

Charles remained awake, thinking of her, but he was not alone in this. And here Flaubert deployed the resources of the musical, rhythmic French prose he had imagined and learned to write, to describe Justin: "At the grave, among the pines, a child knelt and wept, and his chest, racked by sobs, panted in the shadows, under

*"Ils étaient en face l'un de l'autre, le ventre en avant, la figure bouffie, l'air renfrogné ... et ils ne bougeaient pas plus que le cadavre à côté d'eux qui avait l'air de dormir" (*BOV*, p. 458).

the weight of an immense sorrow, more gentle than the moonlight and more fathomless than the night."* Justin recalling Emma is Flaubert loving Elisa. And this love had already been tarnished by Homais's leering insistence that it was really lust for Emma's servant. Now it is the gravedigger who comes in and is sure that Justin has been stealing the potatoes he was improperly growing in the cemetery. Life, as Flaubert understood it, would always thus tarnish anything pure.

The end, filling the final ten pages, is rapid because so many events have to be recounted. Soon Charles and his mother fought and she left him. Everyone descended upon him to claim debts Emma was alleged to have owed them. The servant took to wearing her mistress' clothes, except for a few which Charles had set aside as Flaubert had kept his sister's shawl and as he would do again when his mother died. But shortly the servant left and took her mistress' clothes with her.

Léon married, and then Charles, rustling about the attic one day, found Rodolphe's letter to Emma, abandoned the day she had fled there to read it. He decided that the affair had been a platonic one: it seemed so natural that all men would have adored her. But then, later, he found the packets of letters from Léon and Rodolphe. It was anguish; for a moment he was no longer sane. It broke his spirit. One day, inevitably, he and Rodolphe met; to keep some sort of countenance, Rodolphe invited him to share a bottle of beer. Mastering the fury he felt at first, Charles managed to say that he was no longer angry with him. It had been, he said, the fault of fate, the fourth and last time the word appears in the book. Rodolphe, who had, as Flaubert put it, managed this fate, found Charles comic, even a bit vile.

In the remaining page of the book it is the next day, and again Flaubert turned to beauty of prose to give to Charles whatever of nobility might properly be his. Flaubert had earlier told Louise Colet how she should handle a death scene she needed to place in

---

*"Il y en avait un autre qui, à cette heure-là, ne dormait pas.

"Sur la fosse, entre les sapins, un enfant pleurait agenouillé, et sa poitrine, brisée par les sanglots, haletait dans l'ombre, sous la pression d'un regret immense, plus doux que la lune et plus insondable que la nuit" (*BOV*, p. 469).

Provence. There should be the noise of goat bells, the sound of the flowing Rhone river, the ruddy color of the brush, an immense and calm countryside, and in the midst of it Louise's poor old woman dying very gently.[26] Now, in his own description, the sentences begin to lengthen, the rhythm slows, and the peace of nature is allowed to surround the broken man.* He went to sit beneath the arbor where, unbeknownst to him, Emma and Rodolphe had held their trysts. Sunlight passed through the trellis; the vine leaves etched their shadows on the sand, the jasmine perfumed the air, and the sky was blue above; dragonflies hummed around the lilies, and Charles was suffocating like an adolescent under the vague outpourings of love which swelled his sorrowing heart. A few hours later, his child Berthe, coming to play with him, pushed him gently. He fell to the ground. He was dead.

This, too, might have been a fitting close to the book. But to have stopped here would not have phrased Flaubert's hatred of life. In a few words Berthe is sent to the cotton mills, but the last lines of the book are reserved for describing Homais's large clientele and noting that the authorities were being careful in their dealings with him, since public opinion protected him. Flaubert closes the book with: "He has just received the Cross of the Legion of Honor." Flaubert's bitterness, not the tragic grandeur of Emma or even the gently handled pathos of Charles, had the final word. The bare bones of the tale of Delphine Delamare and her adulterous loves in the village of Ry had been fleshed out with Flaubert's own flesh and infused with his own blood. But it was his bitterness which had given the last pages of the novel their ultimate appearance and significance.

---

*"Le lendemain, Charles alla s'asseoir sur le banc, dans la tonnelle. Des jours passaient par le treillis; les feuilles de vigne dessinaient leurs ombres sur le sable, le jasmin embaumait, le ciel était bleu, des cantharides bourdonnaient autour des lis en fleur, et Charles suffoquait comme un adolescent sous les vagues effluves amoureux qui gonflaient son coeur chagrin.

"A sept heures, la petite Berthe, qui ne l'avait pas vu de toute l'après-midi, vint le chercher pour dîner.

"... croyant qu'il voulait jouer, elle le poussa doucement. Il tomba par terre. Il était mort" (*BOV*, pp. 480-81).

13

The Significance of Emma

EMMA BOVARY

. . . no longer to be oneself, but to circulate all through the creation of which one is writing. Today, for instance, simultaneously man and woman, at once lover and mistress, I was on a horseback ride through a forest on an autumn afternoon under the yellow leaves; and I was the horses, the leaves, the wind, the words they exchanged, and the red sun which made them half-close their eyes, which were brimming with love. Is it pride or compassion? Is it the idiotic overflowing of exaggerated self-satisfaction? Or a vague and exalted religious instinct? I do not know, but when I meditate on delights like these, I should be tempted to address a prayer of thanks to God, if I knew he could hear me.

Letter to Louise Colet, December 23, 1853

FLAUBERT wrote the story of Emma Bovary because he had to.[1] His mind and his spirit were passionately absorbed in the problem of how to experience a complete love which would conciliate and fuse terrestrial and spiritual love; once he had envisaged the possibility of discussing this subject around Emma, his imagination became fired with her. She and her entourage, these particular people and particular events, constituted the center of attraction about which his more generalized concern could gravitate. The characters, then, starting as counters which could be moved through a logical sequence in an abstract analysis of love, became people living in emotionally charged situations. Emma had begun as a psychological equivalent for certain aspects of Don Juan and Anna Maria, which were now placed in a more convenient story line. She then took on life and grew into a particular person, a breathing creation of Flaubert himself. It was this which excited him in writing and made of it a way of life supreme.

Actually drafting the pages of the book was alternately a slow and painful anguish or a delicious and fulfilling triumph over difficulties. The materials for *Madame Bovary*, the notes, plans, and drafts, fill nearly four thousand manuscript pages; no doubt many more once existed, for endless and sometimes torturing efforts went into writing the book. Within a week or so of the start there began the difficulties which were to keep Flaubert chained to his desk for most of the next four and one-half years. His acute critical sense made any writing difficult, but the whole color of the book, provincial Norman, was so new for him that he had constant problems. At times hours would go by while he seemed able only to lie on his divan in a sort of idiotic stupor; or correcting a single line would take a whole day. Any interruption, a trip to Paris to see The Muse, or even going to Rouen, sufficed to break into the productive flow. And, as he often frankly admitted, there were many periods when the whole book profoundly irritated and bored him. It was true that his theme could be developed through it, but only in negative form and in a milieu which he frequently found fetid.

There were also what he called his Olympian times, when he could work all day and far into the night, lie down to sleep for an hour or so, and then return to his desk. At daybreak he would pause to go out for a turn around the garden. The dew would be on the grass, the birds would be starting to sing, and great slate-colored clouds would scud across the sky. These moments of serenity would give him strength to live through the others, when he would be experiencing infertility and impotence,—the tortures of art, as he termed them.

Part of Flaubert's pleasure in creating Emma Bovary came from giving form to his hallucinatory imagination. She was a convenient and continuing center for imaginings which otherwise were disconnected and random. Flaubert and Bouilhet both delighted in thus creating an imaginary world, about which they might then move. One Sunday evening they had begun to consider what their old age would be like: they saw themselves decrepit and poverty-stricken, either in the public hospital for incurable diseases or else out in the cold as street-cleaners. The session lasted four hours and, while it had been funny at the start, at the end the two men were so caught up by their game that they were almost in tears; but they had enjoyed both emotions. On another occasion, much as when he had imagined Christ at Jerusalem, Flaubert was standing beside a flowerbed which reminded him of a poem of Bouilhet's about his grandfather's tulips. Suddenly hallucination took over: the old gentleman, Bouilhet's grandfather, clad in eighteenth-century garb with knee-breeches and powdered wig, was standing there, and beside him was a child of four or five, whose breeches were buttoned to his coat. His cheeks were full and healthy, he was gazing, quiet and wide-eyed, at the flowers. It was, Flaubert knew at once, Bouilhet as a child; his clothes were a deep purple brown.[2] Such hallucinations were involuntary, to be sure, but different from those which accompanied his epileptic seizures, for here there was no terror.

Another form of hallucination, the creative one, was likewise without terror and in fact was usually accompanied by joy, even when the imagined event was unpleasant. Thus writing of Emma's poisoning brought on not only the ink taste, which may have been induced by his mercury treatment, but also acute physical nausea and vomiting as he came to describe these reactions in Emma. Out of these hallucinations as much as out of Flaubert's conscious thinking came the personality of Emma and her fascination for him.

Emma Bovary is a very ardent woman who knows passion briefly but who discovers that sensual pleasure alone (Flaubert's "terrestrial love") cannot produce a complete and durable love. She is Don Juan, but Don Juan transposed into the bitter, ironic key of the antiromantic. So long as, in romantic fashion, she seeks her own, individual satisfaction, she is necessarily doomed in Flaubert's eyes. Complete love he envisaged as aspiration, outgoing rather than self-centered. But he made Emma, from the very start, seek only a personal profit from any emotion, even from a landscape. This is what romanticism as she knew it in the convent invited her to desire. In facile, romantic novels the lover and his mistress are so much at one that all desires are held in common. Any romantic girl, Emma for instance, will then suppose that a lover is a man who wants what she wants, who exists for her. Nothing in Emma's character led her to doubt this, and nothing in her training could teach her otherwise. This, perhaps the most common and most serious of the romantic illusions, is at the core of *Madame Bovary* and helps to keep the book alive, for the succeeding years have not diminished the problem.

But Emma is more than that. Sensual, self-centered, vitiated by romanticism, she still carried to the grave some feeling of nobility and of grandeur. She has about her an aura of something extreme and rare. What she desires—furnishing her house, Léon, Rodolphe —may be petty, but her desire itself—to transcend Yonville—is neither tawdry nor wrong. The framework is akin to that of *Don Quixote*, in which Cervantes mocks the reality of what the knight wishes—the windmills, the real Dolores—but withholds his irony from the aspiration itself.[3]

Flaubert once said that everything he was had its origin in *Don Quixote*, in which he admired the perpetual fusion of reality and illusion. But Don Quixote is deluded by his imagination; with Emma it is in large part her feelings which invalidate her perceptions. To some extent there is here a contrast between ideals and sentiments. Hence it is that Quixote's illusions have attained immortal life while Emma's feelings are forever damned. Quixote has misconceived reality but not his ideals; in some senses Emma misconceives both. Her surroundings are petty, it is true, but neither Léon nor Rodolphe is her equal; hence the objects of her desire are grotesque. Still, with the courage and violence of a Nero she drives toward her goals and gives of herself with generosity and grandeur, as Baudelaire points out. Sinclair Lewis' Carol Kennicott will have the same problems later in Gopher Prairie.[4]

There is a further element to Emma, inherent in the determinism of Flaubert's philosophy. Since her specific fate is determined by her specific surroundings, it becomes possible to wonder whether other surroundings might not have let her have another fate. Contrast Don Quixote, who lives in a country with many windmills and no knights. Emma has no relatively harmless windmills against which to tilt and come out only bruised: she must confront Léon and Rodolphe and Lheureux. And Charles is so much of what she cannot stand: another husband might have alienated her less. Her child turns out to be a girl, when she longed for a boy. She could have had another priest than Bournisien.

Homais's wife might have been a different sort of woman, capable of guiding her.[5]

The issue the reader must decide is whether the determinism of *Madame Bovary*, the fated or inevitable quality the reader feels, depends in fact on a chance absence of anyone strong enough to break the chain of intellectual and moral conditioning. Flaubert was quite conscious of the problem and sought to transcend it by generalizing his portraits, by depicting not individuals but types. Bournisien is not a specific village parish priest, but the summation of all of them. Had he been more gifted, more sensitive, and hence more able to help Emma, his parish would no longer have been Yonville. Had he been less so, he would not have been in the priesthood. Similarly, Charles subsumes all possible husbands, Berthe all possible children. In each case the portrait is a type. For Flaubert the elements of Emma and Yonville were indispensable, but they had to be transcended. Emma is so real that she finally passes beyond immediate reality to become typical instead, and all specific examples of her type find themselves in her. And she is reacting to equally typical elements of provincial Normandy in her century. Finally, she reacts in a way which has thus far proved timeless.

The type Emma, as opposed to the person, is a strange one, relatively new in Flaubert's day and not to be confused with the woman whose problem is only that she has made the wrong marriage, a type common enough in all literature and especially frequent in Balzac and Mérimée in French fiction immediately preceding Flaubert.[6] New in this novel, she has become steadily more common, once Flaubert gave her her classic formulation. She has sensuality, which is perennial. She has romantic illusions, which have shown no sign of disappearing. But she also has an uncontrollable desire for things, for material luxuries. And, with the lessening of her passionate involvement with Rodolphe and then with Léon, she finds less and less reason to control this latter passion. It is this, not her adulterous love affairs, which brings about her downfall. She is, in fact, the victim of a moneylender, not of a lover or an irate husband. Her materialism, not her sensuality, causes her death, although she does not so understand it.

Flaubert here interweaves his threads to give to his tapestry that almost inextricable confusion which suggests reality. Emma is in fact hopelessly caught by Lheureux as she returns from her fruitless visit to Rodolphe: her household furniture is about to be sold, and her husband will be there either already knowing all about the financial catastrophe or sure to learn of it within hours. But this is not why Emma takes arsenic! Rather, hopelessly disillusioned by the discovery that neither of her lovers will save her, she measures the extent of their devotion more truly than she ever had before. In the face of this despairing calculation, she forgets the cause of her visit to Rodolphe; financial matters disappear from her ken, and she commits suicide because of a world in which it is no longer possible to love.

Emma defiantly faces her world of Yonville, proclaiming her values over against its conventions. So long as her fantasies are not fatal, she and not Yonville controls them. Even outside of herself she is so strong that, a giant in her surroundings, she can dare to pile Pelion and Ossa on Mount Olympus to scale her heaven, though it is the tragedy of the modern world that not Hercules but Lheureux brings this latter-day giant down. Before this, however, and for some little time it is she who is dominant, even illuminating those about her so that they take their color only in reference to her.

It is she and not Charles who makes him what he becomes. Charles is, as Emile Zola pointed out, an author's *tour de force*, a completely mediocre person whose presence is always there from start to finish. As Zola notes, in reality such men are gray or colorless, with nothing to bring them to one's attention; but Charles is constantly in our view.[7] Partly Flaubert makes him important by observing him closely. But to a far greater extent it is Emma who is responsible for Charles, his role, his importance, and his fate. In and of himself he is inoffensive at worst, and frequently he is very good. His regret for the death of his first wife showed sweetness; his present of a horse for his wife may have been disastrously blind, but it was, again, a gentle and loving gesture. The absolute confidence which he reposed in Emma made possible her adulteries; but it, too, was a virtue. Unfortunately, placed in the specific context of the husband of Emma all these pale to unimportance beside her need for flaming romanticism. That what she wanted does not exist is not quite the problem here: what matters is that Charles is totally unable to help her, and hence his very virtues become terrible weaknesses facilitating or even bringing on the destruction of his wife and hence his own. His was a limited world, all of which he could compass; hers was limitless, but she wished to experience at least more of it than Yonville and marriage to Charles could allow. And so she had, in the end, to shatter the bounds which limited Charles' world and let him see that more lay beyond. That view would ultimately break him.[8]

Rodolphe, too, is as flat and ordinary as Charles, but he is so in ways which Emma does not understand. Both men repair harnesses or bridles in her presence, and both think of cigars while doing so; but Rodolphe is smoking his own, which he carries in his own case; while Charles will keep his for a treat after dinner, and it came from someone else's lost case which he found lying in the middle of the road.

Rodolphe, who initiates an inexperienced Emma into adultery, does eventually dominate her, except for a momentary lapse during which he, too, envisages running away. Despite Emma's illusions, he is in fact the cold and calculating seducer, not the flaming visionary that Emma was. And this she will ultimately be unable to control. Like Leporello, Don Juan's uncomprehending servant, Rodolphe imagines that all women are alike and all loves the same. Flaubert had intended that the vulgarity of Leporello should display the superiority of Juan and his search for the ideal. When Rodolphe almost casually abandons Emma, he is bringing out the same contrast. His nature dominates, but when it has and he leaves Emma, he returns to his own tawdry and uninteresting self: his existence as an exhilarating and exciting personality is in Emma's mind and imagination alone.

Léon, too, comes to rich and full existence for a time, but only by virtue of a special relationship to Emma. Afterwards he will be no more interesting than Charles or Rodolphe. At the precise moments that he and Emma meet, particularly on the second occasion, he can appear to be the person she imagines. Hence she will lend to him the coloring he needs to play the role. It is only when familiarity has rubbed off these borrowed hues that Léon will revert to mediocrity.

What then is Emma, this ardent woman who is doomed herself yet who is able to give to her husband and her lovers a life which they hardly possess but which is wholly theirs so long as they are hers? Flaubert was conscious that he had something particular and special to say in the book, an account of the profoundly sad aspect of modern man. It was something he felt he had learned in his talks with Alfred Le Poittevin. That is why, had Alfred lived, the book would have been dedicated to him. Flaubert had had, he knew, a remarkably passionate youth, such as one could live only in the provinces. Here there was, as Balzac had noted, time for the condensing and distilling of emotions which were dissipated in Paris. And he knew what wounds this could leave, especially in an ardent, sensual woman. He wrote to Louise Colet that he had known the sorrows of such poor obscure women, whose hearts were as humid with shut-in melancholy as their provincial court-yards surrounded by high, moss-covered walls.

Emma dies, damned by Yonville. At the touch of reality her dreams must necessarily shatter. To be sure, she is wrong to dream them, and Flaubert castigates her for them. But what of this society which has brought her up this way? What of Yonville, which damns her? We cannot infer that it is right because she is wrong.[9] This is why Flaubert could not close his book on the death of Emma or even on the death of Charles. In Emma there was virile strength and the willingness to sacrifice for an ideal; in Charles there was simple goodness, too simple perhaps, but still goodness. Both had been destroyed. It remained for Flaubert to have his final say on the destroyers.

Madame Bovary is a tale of destruction. For when Emma and Charles have been destroyed by Yonville, that destruction means the triumph of people who had already destroyed everything fine and noble in themselves. *Madame Bovary* has in it the internal driving power of life itself: the reader can readily prolong it and imagine a sequel at will, which would display the triumphant success of Homais and of Lheureux.[10] On the debris of Emma and of Charles, even of Léon, Homais and Lheureux will build their structures—and this, to Flaubert, was even worse. That a living Emma Bovary was weeping in twenty villages of France distressed him, but it enraged him that uncounted men such as Homais were building futures that would give them the Legion of Honor. And this was Flaubert's ultimate message. It may have been unfortunate that his hatred of the bourgeoisie outweighed his affectionate understanding of Emma, for understanding is more important than hatred. But the Emmas and those associated with them all over the world have been grateful for the understanding and have, in general, been content to laugh off Homais, who does not read books anyway and whose triumph in the last pages disappears, somehow, from the memory of readers, who are overwhelmed by the grandeur of Emma's death or the pathos of Charles.

THE PHILOSOPHY OF AN ANTIROMANTIC

I am bored with great passions, exalted feelings, wild love affairs, and howling despair. I prize common sense above everything else, perhaps because I so lack it.

Letter to Louise Colet, December, 1846

Flaubert could depict the charmed world of Emma Bovary's romanticism while at the same time satirizing it more bitterly than had any of his predecessors because, although he had grown up a son of René, his cooler allegiance now went to dispassionate detachment. If his emotions threatened constantly to break loose along the paths Chateaubriand had indicated, it was nevertheless always his firm resolve to curb them under a sadder but wiser philosophy of antiromanticism.

Flaubert wrote novels in part as other men drink alcohol or take drugs, because it was intoxicating. He wrote a long letter to Louise Colet when he was writing the seduction scene in *Madame Bovary*. For twelve hours, broken only by twenty-five minutes for dinner, he had been living completely within the illusion of what he was writing. When he wrote the words "nervous attack" concerning Emma, he was so carried away, shouting out his words and feeling with his heroine what she felt, that he became frightened and feared for a moment that he would have one, too. He had to stand up and open his window to calm himself and stop his head from whirling. Now, after all these hours, his muscles ached, but he was filled with the total relaxation of fulfillment, an intoxicating lassitude. For a week it had been going that way and, while he feared that the pages might not stand up under examination, still it had been a wonderful period, and he thanked God for not having made him a cotton merchant or a vaudevillist or a man of wit. He would go on as he had begun.

He could have moments of anxiety, particularly when he realized that he had never yet given what he was sure was his full measure; and he must remain ill satisfied until that moment. The flesh itself, too, could rouse his ire. He remembered the time when, at the age of nineteen, he had almost castrated himself. Nowadays, at moments, he thought of entering a monastery, of giving vent to the need to make himself suffer, to externalize his hatred for the flesh and show how hideous it seemed to him. He knew that only his love of form separated him from the ascetics and the mystics.

And so, limiting himself to the gentle emotions of pity which he had learned to feel during the trip through the Near East, he sought tranquility and felt that his life was settling into a routine which he would still be pursuing at forty or fifty or sixty. As the polar bear lived among the ice-floes or the camel walked the desert sand, so he was a man of the pen; he felt through it, because of it, in relationship to it, and far more deeply with it in his hand. He had found his way.

He had his moments of romanticism, but he fought relentlessly to attain and to hold the higher ground of detachment. While he could still delight in the ruins of a cemetery, he preferred the calm Mediterranean to the tumultuous ocean. Yet he was conscious of the role of emotion and sentiment in his works: all the irony with which he attacked them was either the cry of a man they had vanquished or his shout of victory. But victory depended upon a daily, indeed an hourly, combat. Only through detachment could he learn to achieve that delicate balance of disdain and comprehension which could allow laughter; and laughter, Rabelais had taught him, was that which was proper to man. But though he did learn to stand off from Emma so as to comprehend her faults and to treat them with compassion, it was precisely because he could not do this with Homais or with Bournisien that he found it necessary to close his book not with grandeur but with a snarl.

Like his master Montaigne, one day in Rouen he saw a group of savages who were being displayed: they attracted him immensely, for it seemed as though they had stepped directly out of some distant time when all living beings crawled on their bellies: they were wholly natural. Humanity as he knew it was not so, but rather grotesque, and for this reason totally comtemptible. Men should be treated, without exception, as a vast association of cretins and rascals. Wherever one stepped, it was on filth, and Flaubert expected the world, for a long time, to go ever deeper into this latrine. He felt for his fellow man what he called a serene hatred or so inactive a pity that it amounted to the same thing. Aristotle's featherless biped seemed to him a cross between a turkey and a vulture, meriting only scorn and disdain. Man's limitless respect for himself, incarnate in Homais, seemed the real source of the trouble; it explains the irruption of Homais into the ending of *Madame Bovary*.

The masses disgusted Flaubert, and the bourgeoisie, tranquil in self-adulation, seemed even worse. Ernest Chevalier's apostasy, echoed in Léon, was so disturbing on this account. Flaubert found himself becoming violently aristocratic; the lice on a beggar seemed as akin to him as the beggar himself. Men were not brothers; they were merely victims who suffered together. The fact that an imbecile had two legs like Flaubert instead of four legs like a donkey seemed no very good reason to love him or to say one liked him and found him interesting. Flaubert preferred to a love of humanity a love of justice and beauty.

For all his loathsome weaknesses, man still remained the most fascinating of subjects, and Flaubert continued to seek to understand his fundamental make-up, even though he did not love him. At the base were sexuality and religion, closely related. Flaubert now understood the age-old fear of the ascetic, frightened lest this substratum overcome him. And he saw how his whole century was revolting against the notions of love it had inherited. There was a terrible reaction going on. It had begun by howls of irony and now continued in analysis and dissection. The pursuit of love, like that of religion, must for the moment be rejected; otherwise one went down the path Emma had followed to her grave. Romanticism had lied, and there was no other solution.

The whole matter of spirituality demanded reinvestigation. Materialists, who made man into a pig, were just as foolish as spiritualists who made him into an angel. He was neither the one nor the other and demanded to be studied according to whole new disciplines, whose first principles had not even been established yet. Flaubert longed for these new sciences and felt confident they would come. There must be a scientific study of instincts and the social forms which resulted from them. Similarly a new and generalized approach to religion must be found which would seek out the underlying feeling lurking below external differences. And finally, the laws of social development must be determined so that a Shakespeare or a new style of architecture could be predicted.

Flaubert's hopes for the future of science were part of the Age of Scientism, and many of his expectations would be realized. Charcot and Freud, Taine, the anthropologists, and the sociologists would later arise to study man's instincts and his society. Maury, Renan, and others would shortly be laying the bases for comparative religion. But Flaubert hoped for more: he longed for answers with the precision of mathematics, and he still retained a faith that science and art would one day fuse.

By pressing on unwarily Flaubert was falling into the trap of all his generation—the assumption that because science could do so much, it could do everything. He did not live long enough to see any of his sciences really develop, but he died soon enough to avoid having to live sadly through what would be called the "Bankruptcy of Science" at the end of the century, when it became apparent that science could not carry out all of these dreams.

Flaubert hoped to counter romanticism by his belief in science; here and only here could he imagine mooring an antiromanticism to something discernibly outside the personal. But for his religion, for his own source of ultimate answers and primary motivations, Flaubert turned now as before to a religion of art, to a Platonic reverence for the idea, which he continued to find higher than happiness, love, or the notion of God. His greatest communion with creation remained a pantheistic penetration into nature. Communications between humans were no more intense, he found. His religion, his antiromanticism, and his esthetics were here at one. In Emma he had phrased all their opposites, and that is what made her so significant.

This religion of art was the refuge to which Flaubert personally turned for relief from the austerities and disappointments of a philosophy of antiromanticism. He sought in *Madame Bovary* to write from such a vantage point of dispassionate observation. A state of Olympian serenity could at least be imagined in a life of writing: one could always seek to write coolly and oppose romantic inspiration. The imagination could produce a masked ball which was delightful, but it was a form of overintoxication to be avoided. Like Diderot and Wordsworth, Flaubert demanded for art only emotions recollected in tranquility. In this fashion, lamenting nothing, the artist would avoid the folly of complaining of existence and would content himself with describing it. Turning from its hideousness to an esthetic mysticism, a religion of art, one could always contemplate the great blue dome of poetry, as the gray wings of the Egyptian bats had let Flaubert see the azure of the sky beyond. From this could come detachment, the ability to stand off from one's own personality and attain the serenity of the comic view, that of Aristophanes or Shakespeare, which was the ultimate for Flaubert.

14

The Novel as Art

FLAUBERT'S ANTIROMANTIC ESTHETIC

It seems to me, in all conscience, that I am accomplishing a
duty and obeying a higher fate, that I am carrying out the
Good and living in Justice.

Letter to Louise Colet, April 13-14, 1853

No great work of genius has ever been founded on hatred
or contempt. In some corner of his heart, at some moment
of his history, the real creator always ends by reconciling.

Albert Camus, *The Artist in Prison*

FLAUBERT's antiromantic religion of art was the credo on which
he based his esthetics.[1] Belief in a life for art easily accommodated
the notion that all writing must have art as its goal, and not, for
instance, social betterment or philosophical exposition or entertainment alone. Hence by almost imperceptible steps Flaubert was
led away from the understanding of the novel which Balzac and
others had handed down to him. With a Platonic concept of the
novel instead, he saw it as one of the multiple ways of approaching the true through the beautiful, a belief which placed esthetics
at the center of his faith.

Flaubert's published novels, in which he sought to embody this
concept, and his statements on esthetics in his letters, when they
were published late in the century, engendered his tremendous
influence on American and English novelists and critics as they
discovered their own concordant beliefs and his phrasings and incarnations of them. First Walter Pater, then Henry James, and
later yet James Joyce and Ezra Pound would in the half-century
after Flaubert's death give to these doctrines the central place in

world literature which they had long occupied in Flaubert's personal beliefs. They also gave to Flaubert himself the place in world literature which the development away from his concepts and style in French letters was then denying him in his own land.

Antiromanticism, the origin of Flaubert's esthetic, demands impersonalism as the central canon to counteract the basis of romanticism. In an age when antiromanticism was so very new, any course other than impersonalism and impassivity risked tumbling the author into pathos and sentimentality.[2] Even in Emma's death scene there had been moments thus vitiated and turned to the false or the restricted. During these years of writing *Madame Bovary* Flaubert used in his letters a number of lapidary phrases to formulate the idea. One so delighted James Joyce that he transcribed it almost verbatim in his *Portrait of the Artist as a Young Man*, adding only the final touch to give it his own Joycean stamp: "The artist, like the God of the creation, remains invisible, refined out of existence, indifferent, paring his finger nails." He should, Flaubert held, so hide himself as to make posterity think he did not even live.[3] His art should be a second creation to be placed beside the original, and the artist, its creator, should show the same hidden and infinite impassivity, which would overwhelm the reader.

The innumerable areas where Flaubert drew on his own personal life in *Madame Bovary* have raised questions concerning the validity and sincerity of his assertions. If in fact he is so personal, then what is the sense that is to be attached to his proclamations against it? The question is based upon nothing more solid than a misunderstanding. Every novel is in some measure a confession; contrariwise, every confession contains fictional elements.[4] It is a matter of balance, of attitude, essentially of effect upon the reader. Flaubert's impersonalism is only a rejection of that personalism which would vitiate art. In general, he succeeded in appearing impersonal and impassive. When he is in fact not so, the reader, unless forearmed by literary research, is usually unable to detect it. More important from a theoretical point of view, where the reader does sense it on his own, he loses confidence and thereby proves the accuracy of Flaubert's thesis. The flaw, if flaw there be, is only that Flaubert, in the case in question, has inadvertently let the reader see the string moving the marionette. In the nature of literary creation, the string had to be there.

In the decade of the 1850's Flaubert was pushing his doctrines further than before or understanding better what they implied. Paradoxically, this led him in part back to doctrines elaborated in the preceding century by the philosopher and critic Diderot, whose ideas had been submerged under the countercurrent of romanticism. Impersonality, Flaubert now realized, allowed the author to relax before the object, to let it penetrate within him and circulate there until he had fully mastered it. When the model was thus clear before one's eyes, then one wrote well. The great artists were those into whom this penetration went deeper and even hurt more. Thus Molière's sorrow was the result of his discovering that all the idiocy and folly of mankind had penetrated within him. Genius, Flaubert could now state, was precisely this ability to work from an imaginary model which could be made to pose at will. This is Diderot's concept of the *modèle intérieur*, or model inside one's head, renewed nearly one hundred years after Diderot had enunciated it.

The soul, Flaubert now wrote, must withdraw into itself to create beauty. He recalled that it was in Holland and in Venice, two gray and foggy lands, that the great colorists in painting had developed. Artistic observation was different from scientific: it must be instinctive for the most part and depend upon the imagination. The artist starts from a subject or a color and only then looks outside himself for external support. The subjective, though not the personal, must be the starting point.

The endpoint, too, was now clearer in Flaubert's mind. The artist must not attempt to come to a conclusion, to prove something. God alone knows the beginning and the end; man sees only the middle, and he begins to lie the moment he pretends to more. Writing should not seek to be useful, which implies knowing the ends for which life was created. Such ethical preoccupations necessarily falsify the imagination. Man is, because he is. No great genius had ever sought to prove; Homer does not, nor does Shakespeare.[5] One should seek for endings like that of Voltaire's *Candide:* "Let us cultivate our garden." It was as quiet and as simple as life itself, commented Flaubert. But the reader is not apt to find the last line of *Madame Bovary* so peaceful.

Does this refusal to conclude mean that *Madame Bovary* is immoral or, at best, amoral? Baudelaire phrased the reply cogently. A real work of art, he pointed out in reviewing the book, needs no supporting moral structure. If it is truly beautiful, that is, if its style is adequate to its subject, then the logic of the work will supply the ethical framework, and the reader will have only to draw the conclusions implied by the ending of the book. Bouilhet and Flaubert agreed that the theater of the nineteenth century was weaker for having to conclude, particularly in front of the assembled spectators.[6] *Madame Bovary* would be stronger for not doing so.

But the values in *Madame Bovary* are by no means unclear: they are merely unrewarded. The stoic virtues of patience, hard work, and devotion are present in Dr. Larivière, in little Justin, in the servant who receives the medal. But Larivière's is a lonely life, Justin's is a sad fate, and Catherine Leroux's medal is a mockery. Nonetheless the reader understands their virtues as clearly as he understands the vices of Homais or Lheureux; he is merely unable to draw the comforting and false conclusion that virtue is always rewarded.[7] That does not make the book either immoral or amoral. Flaubert was persuaded that it made it more moral.

To Flaubert and the artists of his generation the problem was esthetics, not ethics. Anticipating Baudelaire's title, *Flowers of Evil*, Flaubert recalled the manure from which melons grow and from what depths of ignominy human grandeur springs: authors must draw from the putrefaction of humanity subjects for its delight and grow flowers of beauty on humanity's displayed miseries. Facts were distilled by entering a beautiful form as they rose to approach the ideal.

Could all subjects be made to produce the beautiful, Flaubert often wondered. They could be made interesting, if one's comprehension and penetration of them was adequate; of this he was sure. But metaphysics, for instance, which he had been unable to handle artistically in *Saint Anthony*, seemed perhaps so unclear as to be forever deficient for art.

Flaubert learned from Goethe to understand that everything

in a work of art depended upon the initial conception. Good or bad, well- or ill-understood, it controlled what the work would be. In Flaubert's case the conception would arise from one of two aspects of his temperament, where, as he was quite conscious, there lay two different people with two entirely opposed sets of conceptions. One was fond of shouting and loud noises, lyricism and wild flights of fancy, sonorous phrases and high ideas. The other part dug into the truth and examined it as closely as it lay in his power. With this side of his nature he studied the lesser, quieter aspects of reality quite as much as the flamboyant ones. It led him to want his reader to feel almost materially the objects he described, a concern which set *Madame Bovary* off from *The Temptation*. The story of Emma was a *tour de force* for him, requiring him to deny much of the other side of his nature and to create characters and situations frequently antipathetic to him. But this was a sound apprenticeship, and he knew it. *Madame Bovary* was in fact a temptation to disaster for both sides of Flaubert's nature, the flamboyant as much as the minute. Emma was a passionate, ardent woman; her milieu, in contrast, was irrevocably tawdry. On the one side lay unbridled lyricism and on the other, simple vulgarity. He had to fuse the two in an analysis which he could then display only by means of a narrative.

A philosophy of antiromanticism led Flaubert to fear this emotionalism and the uncontrolled imagination in life and hence in art. Emotion would always be inferior to the illusion art could produce, for tears could be aroused by any cheap melodrama, while Goethe had never cost him a single sob. Pursuit of such emotion in art was to confuse sensitive nerves with a valid feeling for beauty, and art as he conceived it was not such a weakness of nerves; on the contrary, weak nerves were a major disability. Only through calm domination of them could one achieve that serenity which was his goal in life and without which, in his art, the imaginary, internal model could never be made to pose.

The effect of the work of art should be total calmness: repose is the attitude of the Deity. The masterpiece should exude a feeling of tranquility, whatever the violence of its matter. Like great animals or mountain ranges, it should be serene. One must write with the head, he said, even if, secretly, it is warmed by the heart.

Even when he was deeply, lyrically, moved, Flaubert had learned as early as in Egypt to try to dissect what was going on, to achieve that detachment which had given its ultimate meanings to his night with Kuchiuk-Hânem. If it was the chill steel of the scalpel entering his flesh, still his own was the only heart he could really study. He wished, like the short-sighted, to see from close up and in detail right into the very pores of things. In this fashion he could hope to represent the true, without risking a personal interpretation.

In *Madame Bovary*, as he put it, Flaubert had gone at reality heroically, that is, minutely and accepting everything he found. This acceptance might well be ironic and lead to reshaping existence into artistic forms which could then be grasped by the reader; but it must be total, for art is acceptance, not rejection. On the other hand it was the error of the so-called realists that they failed to realize that the acceptance must be ironic and in this way lead to detachment: hence the execration which Baudelaire and Flaubert felt for them.

The Agricultural Fair was such an ironic acceptance of all the hideousness of this particular form of existence. Neither Rodolphe nor the government nor even the animals had been embellished or caricatured: they had instead been accepted. The ironic reshaping of existence entered when Flaubert elected to orchestrate the three themes simultaneously so that each would become a commentary upon the others. This was art as Flaubert understood it, for it depicted honestly man's inner being (or nullity) in its modern complexity, and it accepted his sorry lot. It was the hazardous enterprise, which only the very great could do well, of seeking to handle commonplaces. Average talents in general avoided them in favor of the ingenious or the unusual. He would audaciously seek, instead, to produce written reality.

It was in this highly special sense that Flaubert, living in the age of scientism, understood the place of science in art. The age of the purely beautiful had passed, he felt. Humanity would probably return to it one day, but for the moment art must become scientific as science was becoming artistic. The two methods started from separate bases but would join at the summit. Wide knowledge was now indispensable for the artist. His monstrous ignorance was a lack Flaubert could no longer allow himself. Homer and Rabelais, for instance, had been encyclopedias of their ages.

Literature in his day should become, Flaubert asserted, the scientific form of life through the precision of its observation. But—and here Flaubert opposes the so-called realists—the directly observed is of necessity accidental and merely individual. With this the artist has no concern, any more than the scientist does: both must rise to generalizations. To the scientist this is the norm of a large number of cases; to the artist it is intuitively obtained. Material reality is always truncated, and ever since the first *Sentimental Education* Flaubert had been insisting that the task of art was to complete what reality offered, which was necessarily incomplete. One needed documentation for this, of course, and Flaubert was to lean ever more heavily upon it; but the purpose of such knowledge, of such a scientific approach, was only to allow the writer to absorb the spirit of what he wished to depict. Without this absorption and mastery, documentation was a hindrance. The notes Flaubert had taken for *Saint Anthony* had kept him from seeing the saint:[8] art must be kept from archeology.

The scientist seeks a real truth; the writer deals with an ideal artistic one.[9] Artist and scientist must start from the real, the specific, the individual; but neither has succeeded unless he has ended with a type. The artistic type—or truth—is, however, special in that beauty must be inherent in it. It is not opposed to scientific truth but rather complementary to it. Following Plato, Flaubert used to enjoy repeating that beauty is the splendor of truth.[10] Thus and thus only could the artist deal with life and have his say about it.

The search for beauty within truth is not a matter of a selection of the ideal and a rejection of the ugly, as it had been in the narrow poetics of neoclassicism. Since it is instead a search for the typical, then the hideous, the monstrous, and the exaggerated are wholly compatible with art.[11] Flaubert observed Rabelais and came to suspect that for fantasy to be durable it must be specifically monstrous. If one could not produce the pure beauty of the Pantheon, then at least one must pile up the monstrous size of the pyramids. Indeed, over the years, he became ever more convinced that limitations were mistaken and that no good quality gained by being forbidden excess. This doctrine directly controverted the notions of restraint and tranquility which he derived from his antiromanticism. Whole books of his, *Salammbô* for instance, are vitiated by it. But the subject matter of *Madame Bovary* fortunately provided an adequate counter.

Flaubert's difficulty was in part that reality kept exceeding his wildest imaginings. He had the sad duty of attending the funeral of an older friend's beloved wife. He went, in part from affection, in part to observe how people conducted themselves. He expected to observe real sorrow, which he could use for the burial of Emma; but he hardly expected to have beside him a gentleman who interrupted at every turn to question him about Egypt and who was saddened to learn that the state of museums and public libraries there was lamentable. The gentleman was, however, glad that it was a Protestant burial ceremony so that the service was in French: thus the flowers of rhetoric, as he put it, could have their place. The grotesque, Flaubert confessed, always went beyond what one could imagine, and so one never needed to fear exaggeration. The argument, later readers noted, relates to the truth of reality, and not necessarily of esthetics.

Classicism is a considerable part of the positive side of Flaubert's antiromanticism. The realists later obscured not only his repeated and categoric statements opposing them but also his actual practice, which was always far broader in its approach than a mere reliance on documentation. Involuntary high priest of a cult of realism which he never espoused, he has been depicted by devoted followers as a traitor to classicism. This is belied by his attitude from as early as the first time he saw the actress Rachel give life to classical esthetics.

Flaubert's classicism had been a personal discovery. It was in no sense the neoclassicism of his day, which had become largely a tired insistence upon rigid rules whose inner vitality was no longer felt. This he continued to detest as vigorously as before. He strove to understand for himself, and day after day as he plunged deeper and deeper into the *Bovary* he worked at learning Greek. He returned to it almost immediately after starting to draft the novel, for to study Greek was to increase his ability to comprehend the nature of art. And he also came to a fuller understanding of his enjoyment of French seventeenth-century classicism, at least as Molière, Boileau, and La Fontaine practiced it: a quest for the perfect form. Boileau might in fact have little of poetry to say, but it was said in a form so suited to it that his verse would last as long as French literature. All of these writers had grasped the need for the right expressions. Theirs had been lives of close devotion to the harsh taskmistress art is to those who revere form. And the verses they wrote were full to the bursting point.

Art and the beautiful had been for Greece constituent elements of life. Ways had to be found in the modern world to make them so again. Everything surrounding a Greek served to train his developing esthetic sense. Even the mountains suggested tranquility by their shapes and were of marble for the sculptors. What must a courtesan have been like, who had been raised to contribute to all the pleasures of a Plato! From such an approach to life could come that Olympian serenity Flaubert longed for. In the modern world it would permit undertaking the difficult task of rebuilding art and science together so that they might, in some distant future, fuse and become the constituent base of life itself.

Classicism led Flaubert to an awareness that each new work of art is a new subject and a new form to be found; each requires its own poetics. He sought this for the *Bovary* and wished it specifically to have a classic air to it, haughty and perfect in its form. Its precision and its chasteness, too, would come from this same fount, as would its inclusiveness. He was working here in the great tradition and he knew it, beyond the confines of petty schools and seeking rather that understanding of art in which the beautiful is one and the same always, differing only in its aspects from author to author. In this sense Boileau and Hugo are admirable for the same things, as are Homer and Shakespeare.

Flaubert sought, consciously and deliberately, to be if necessary more classic than the classicists and to make the romantics pale with envy by going beyond what they had dreamed of. It would be folly to seek to be shod with Greek shoes. Modern man could envy the Greeks for their existence amidst beauty, and he could admire their works. He must try to be as artistic as they were, if he could; but he must be so in other ways. In a striking image Flaubert pointed out that the belly of Sancho Panza had burst asunder the girdle of Venus, and the modern world demanded new forms. From antiquity one could learn to depict everything calmly and beautifully; but one must learn to depict even what did not exist in antiquity. This he sought in *Madame Bovary*.

The calmness and beauty of antiquity Flaubert could not find in his own day except in a retreat from life into a religion of art. By denying this religion to the typical characters of *Madame Bovary* he damned them, as he did most of his characters, who are failures. But the books themselves are not failures, and thus Flaubert himself could escape what he felt was the normal condition of most of mankind, vowed to destruction by that Fate which four times he invoked in *Madame Bovary*.

In all honesty Flaubert believed that life was hideous and to be avoided by living in art, in the incessant search for the true perceived through the intermediary of the beautiful. This experience he found the greatest voluptuousness he knew. It let him be a priest of a special cult accomplishing a duty and obeying a higher fate; he was doing the good and living in justice. Thus he could always affirm with Baudelaire that the morality of art lay in its beauty and that what he valued above all else was style, for it permitted him to approach the truth.[12] This he explicitly denied to Emma Bovary and so, within what he knew of living, Emma was damned. Readers cannot all be artists; hence the dignity and meaning Flaubert at this stage did find in life were of little value to most readers.

Finding so little good in life and placing all his morality in art, Flaubert not unnaturally denied his main characters any valid moral sense. T. S. Eliot objected to this view of mankind. He explained that he could perfectly understand the Olympian elevation and superior indifference of the great artist who has detached himself from any moral attitude toward his characters. What he did object to, though, was that the characters themselves, allegedly human beings, show no respect for or even awareness of moral obligations. They have no conscience at all. And the objection may fairly be leveled at *Madame Bovary*, where the three or four virtuous people and moments can hardly count against the overwhelming mass of the rest of the novel.

Life may of course be viewed as having no more significance than Flaubert attached to it when he wrote *Madame Bovary;* and the doctrine of irony has been pervasive since his day. But the really great books of the Western tradition counsel the understanding of life and urge terms in which it may be accepted. They go beyond the bitter taste of irony to some form of love. The *Iliad* shows sure knowledge of how vicious man may be to man, but before it closes it shows the mastery of the vice it portrays, and it ends in serenity and acceptance. This pattern, it would appear, has been followed by all the later books which long agreement has placed on the shelf of truly universal literature. If *Madame Bovary*, now a century old, is placed on the shelf below, it is still put there with affection and with deep respect for its author, who had given to it so much—all he had, in fact.[13] There were left twenty-five further years for him to learn more to give to his art.

STYLE

> What a heavy oar the pen is when you must row with it up the swift stream of an idea.
>
> Letter to Louise Colet, October, 1851

When Flaubert put aside *Saint Anthony* as a failure, he knew that its principal defect lay in its style; this error he must not repeat. He continued to believe that he had real talent—innateness, he tended to call it—but he also knew that he was not one of the towering geniuses, a Shakespeare or a Sophocles. In such men the magnitude of their creations and their ability to generalize created new types and gave to humanity forms unknown before them. Creators of this stature did not need to worry about style: they would be great despite all their mistakes, in fact partly because of them. While Flaubert did not rank Balzac with these geniuses, it is probable that this is a fair description of his work and an account of the difference between it and Flaubert's.[14] Lesser people had instead to seek excellence through perfection of style. To try to imitate the great masters would be folly; in fact it would be disastrous, for their work lacked that very polish upon which he felt his own writing must depend. One should know the masters by heart, admire them, try to think like them—and then make one's own way.

Flaubert was deeply worried, as he had been on the Mediterranean trip, that the acute development of critical faculties which he shared with his generation might interfere with his newly developing notions of style. He felt, probably rightly, that no one had ever taken the pains with style which he was lavishing on *Madame Bovary*. But suppose this critical faculty were the antithesis of imagination, that in fact it stifled it! He recalled that Pradier had always been wholly unable to utter a word about the theory of his art. This made him a superior artist, one who worked from instinct. Now, when all Flaubert's words seemed to miss the mark of his thought, he was aghast that he might be incapable of writing the style he could now imagine.

To begin with, there was the matter of the over-all plan. Flaubert rightly attached great importance to this but usually ended up with a rather poor one: *Madame Bovary* was no exception, with its oblique beginning and less-than-perfect ending. It was in the nature of his attack that the difficulty lay. To be sure, his initial notions were very broad and general, but he passed rapidly through this phase to another which lasted for the duration of the writing and in which he elaborated separate scenes. He did not build his novels, as did Balzac, out of a dramatic and visionary experiencing of the material which lay before him. While Flaubert did, in fact, experience this himself, he distrusted it as an uncontrollable inspiration and sought always to discipline it by a controlled handling of each detail; every one of these he subjected to a sensitive and cultivated taste. Each word, literally, had to be scrutinized; paragraphs were already complex enough to be hard to grasp as totalities, and the scene was apt to be the largest unit he could comprehend as a whole. Hence the scene risked running away with the novel, as when Homais and Bournisien keep their vigil over the body of Emma. No wonder, then, that Flaubert longed constantly for a book which would write itself, in the sense that the sentences would flow along as easily as the air one breathed.

It was difficult, very difficult, for Flaubert to work with the length of the novel. He had begun his life writing short stories, and he would return to them in his last decade. The plan of the first *Sentimental Education*, which had the length of a novel, was a total failure. *The Temptation* and the "Near Eastern Tale" were both broken up either into extremely short scenes, as for the theater, or were almost frankly separate tales strung together. *Don Juan*, too, as Flaubert had envisaged it, would probably have been relatively brief. But now he was shackled to a long work which would in part depend upon his ability to master its very length. All through the years of composition he worried about the relative size of the various parts, and yet he felt helpless in the face of the difficulties he sensed so fully. He fought them doggedly.

The romantics had believed in styles, because they created them; the classicists, Flaubert among them, believed in a single style, eternal, and to be found, not created.[15] Style to him meant the rendering of "content" in a "form" completely consonant with it, so that form and content would be one. But Flaubert and his generation, like all those which had come before them, extended and gave new meaning to classicism. Particularly Flaubert sought for a mystical harmony between his initial concept and the prose which embodied it. The purpose of art is not to reproduce externality but to render its general truth through beauty so as to generate the good. Style, then, the means an author uses to render externality, is like a filter through which externality is passed and which, while admitting all of it, transfigures all of it. If one could learn to see the world solely through such a filter, then the world would be colored by its beauty, presiding at every phase of composition from the over-all plan down to the final search for the right word, *le mot juste*, to be fitted into an actual sentence.

In a flight of fancy Flaubert once imagined, but only as an ideal, a book in which the subject matter would disappear, if this were possible, into the internal force of the style. He felt that art was developing in this direction, and to clarify his meaning he noted that earlier ages had needed the epic, full of matter, while later ages turned to the sonnet, where the matter is almost negligible and the form, the fourteen lines of octet and sestet, becomes the poem. This is, however, but to restate his fundamental position that form and matter are inseparable: it was his aim to give to form its equal place with matter, whereupon the two would fuse wholly, and the matter would no longer be the essential basis of the book.

Style was to Flaubert an absolute way of looking at life, which would give its own excellence or defect to what it displayed. He therefore turned to style to solve the difficulties his initial concept presented. Primary among these was the vulgarity of his subject. He sought to handle it by writing simply and correctly. The scene in which Emma and Rodolphe met was a case in point. The spurting of the blood from Rodolphe's servant, the fainting adolescent Justin, Emma leaning over, and the lecherous onlooker had all to be rendered convincingly enough so that the reader would accept and understand. But, as Flaubert lamented, if he succeeded to perfection he would still not have a great scene, a beautiful work of art: the fundamental basis here precluded that and the whole scene would be no more than a *tour de force*. The reader would pass over it without even noticing. Nevertheless, it had to be written, rewritten, corrected and redrafted five times until it reached that perfection of which he was capable. Without the mention of the problem in a letter of his which happened to be kept and published, Flaubert would no doubt have been right: few readers would have noticed.

Another example of vulgarity, which Flaubert almost removed from the book, involved the effort to describe Charles' happiness in the early days of his marriage, when he would ride off in the morning after the felicities of the night. Flaubert wrote that he went away ruminating his happiness like a man after dinner who can still taste the truffles he is digesting. On rereading the passage after a lapse of time Flaubert found the image shocking and would have removed it if he had been able to find another.[16]

The issue in *Madame Bovary*, as Baudelaire outlined it, was whether Flaubert could analyze his essentially vulgar subject with sufficiently penetrating logic to master it. If he could, then the style would flow directly from this assured source and the result would be artistic. Flaubert's success in his endeavor, Baudelaire proclaimed, was exactly the demonstration his generation of artists needed, for it proved what they had all believed was true, namely that style was purely subjective, a way of looking. Later on Henry James would concur, agreeing that because *Madame Bovary* was ideally done, it showed that eternal beauty could be found in such vulgar elements.

Avoiding vulgarity through excellence of style in turn generated a new problem: the risk of falling into what Flaubert termed "Chateaubrianized Balzac," the writing of a novel on a bourgeois subject like those of Balzac but with the purple mantle of Chateaubriand's prose cast over it. Flaubert's concept of the relationship of form and content rejected such an artificial connection between the two. He sought rather an organic relationship, integral and generated from the outset, much as the American periodical, *The Dial*, would conceive it in the 1920's, when it served as a vehicle for the diffusion of the ideas and work of Joyce and Pound, which in part stem from Flaubert.[17]

The chaste phase of the liaison between Léon and Emma illustrates this problem. Flaubert could have written a Balzacian passage of dynamic imagination and have cast over it a Chateaubrianesque grandeur and the majesty of full-blown prose, but this would have been to deny the inherent triviality of the scene. He had instead to analyze its true amplitude and universality. Then he could begin to write the style he wanted. The opening dialogue between Emma and Léon in the inn, full of its clichés and shopworn poetry, resolved the problem for him: ironic detachment succeeded where lyric exaltation would have been a contradiction and a failure.

The task of resolving his difficulties through an organic concept of style confronted Flaubert at almost every line. His novel in its entirety took place in similar milieus and the subject was largely the same throughout. For instance, both Tostes and Yonville, two Norman villages only a short distance apart, had to be described in sufficient detail to convince the reader, and yet they must be distinct in his mind. As Flaubert put it, with the same ingredients to be served up endlessly, he had to vary the sauces. Tostes is, in fact, hardly described, except for its psychological aspects: its total ennui the reader fully understands, and this is enough. Yonville, instead, comes to life in its details: the reader knows its topography and that of the surrounding hills and plain; he knows enough of the inhabitants to carry the tale forward; and he understands its petty village life. More than that, he has a well-defined attitude of hostility toward it, a point of view that Sinclair Lewis would later induce in his readers toward Gopher Prairie.

The proper means of achieving style, the depiction of truth through beauty, must be found by an individual person, the author, and yet his personalism is always irrelevant to the search: hence the prominence in Flaubert's esthetics of the negative caution, impersonalism. He had to explore, develop, or invent a host of techniques to present his material in this fashion. Among the most useful was to vary the point of view from which he told the story. While an occasional minor author, perhaps more in England than in France, had tried this before Flaubert, he was the first to give it enormous, systematic development.[18] The novel opens with Charles' arrival at school as seen when "we were in the study hall." "We" disappear almost at once, and the omniscient author takes over, recounting rapidly what has occurred. At intervals he will return, as in the visit the reader makes to Yonville under his tutelage. But for most of the novel the point of view becomes that of one or another of the characters—Charles, then Emma, sometimes Léon or Rodolphe.[19] Much of what we know of the characters we learn not as something the author thinks (antiromanticism discouraged this) but as what one character thinks of another. Emma finds Charles stupid; Léon finds Emma a lady; Rodolphe finds her starved for love. Each time, without apparent intervention on Flaubert's part, the reader learns from these oblique points of view something of the character portrayed and, often, something of the person making the judgment.

There is a danger inherent in impersonal presentation: it can result in a chill, inhuman tone for the reader as he coolly observes specimens moving objectively before him. When the novel first appeared, some critics objected that this was the case; but later readers have tended to feel that Flaubert in fact largely overcame this difficulty. He realized that somehow the warmth of coursing human blood, so easy for the romantic with his personalism, had to be restored to the characters of the impersonal novel. So phrased, the problem defined itself for him and suggested where he might seek his answer: reader and character must be brought close together at suitable moments by narrowing the esthetic distance between them.

Flaubert's greatest single device for this is to report in indirect discourse and past tenses what is actually going on in the thought patterns and idle meanderings of the character.[20] Conveniently, this device can be shown in translation. Emma seated outside her convent late in the book and lost half in meditation, half in thought, could have been reported thus in direct discourse: "How calm things used to be! How I envy the ineffable feelings of love that I used to try to picture from my readings." So written, the passage would be absurd. Flaubert actually phrased it in what has come to be called free indirect discourse: ". . . she sat down on a bench in the shadow of the elms. How calm things used to be! How she envied the ineffable feelings of love which she used to try to picture from her readings." Now he could easily continue: "She was not happy, she never had been. Where did this basic inadequacy in life come from? . . . But if there were, somewhere, a being, strong and handsome, . . . why should she not find him? Oh! How impossible! Nothing was worth looking for. . . ."

The reader, present during the birth of her thoughts, emotions, and images, is completely at one with her because of the presentation. Flaubert uses this free indirect discourse alternating with direct quotations ("But I love him!") to move the reader closer or further or to allow the reporting of what would, in direct discourse, be absurd. Sometimes Flaubert lengthens such passages of free indirect discourse to develop a whole new and uninterrupted tone, the interior monologue, which lends itself to reporting the unimpeded flow of thought. A later generation, removing the logical coherence of the sequence, would develop this into the technique it would term stream of consciousness. Free indirect discourse and the interior monologue, occurring occasionally in earlier English and French literature, had never before been put to the constant use that appears in *Madame Bovary*.[21] Joyce gave it its greatest further extension, in *Ulysses*.

A startling and bold handling of time provided Flaubert a fur-

ther means of remaining impersonal in his presentation while still
controlling his material so as to guide the reaction of the reader.
This device, conveniently, does not risk alienating the reader, who
is for the most part unaware of it, at least as Flaubert handles it.
While Flaubert did not invent the technique, still the extensions he
gave to it were new, and he is the source for most of the later and
extraordinary developments which twentieth-century writing has
produced, especially in Joyce and Faulkner. Flaubert came to realize that for the novelist time is a variable which may be altered at
will. The "external time" of the novel may be made to proceed at
a normal pace, while the internal time of a character races ahead
or slows down, as in Emma's visits to try to borrow money. Or
the internal time may stop, reverse, and then whirl madly back
and forth as when Emma's sanity begins to slip from her on her
return from Rodolphe's chateau after he had refused to help her.
Here the range is from the more normal disjunction of any individual from his surroundings in time as he is bored or excited all
the way to the anguished dislocations Flaubert knew from his
epilepsy.

The external time of the novel, too, Flaubert realized he could
manipulate with equal freedom. Time is crammed and races by at
La Vaubyessard; it creeps the following year at Tostes. Most important, whole segments of it may be wholly displaced and set side
by side for effects of simultaneity never attempted before. The
lowing of the animals and the deputy prefect's speech at the Agricultural Fair, as well as Rodolphe's seduction of Emma, are all
displaced in time so that they occur simultaneously for the ironic
delight of the reader. James Joyce took what was implicit here
and gave it new boldness in *Ulysses*. Then William Faulkner, in
The Sound and the Fury, gave it dimensions unimaginable to
Flaubert but, equally, impossible without his initial impetus.

To undertake his revolution in style was an audacious dream,
and Flaubert knew it. Sometimes he almost cried aloud in impotent fury over his weakness, but at other times, when he had
succeeded, he was beside himself with joy. Something very deep
within him, tremendously voluptuous, overflowed in great gushes,
and he was transfigured, intoxicated. He knew that he would
never really write the prose he imagined; he lacked too many

things. But at least, he hoped, he would have shown the way to a later writer who had more talent than he. Or perhaps one day he would find just the right theme for his capacities.

Two aspects of Madame Bovary were particularly onerous to him. It is true that Emma is Flaubert, but she is, for the most part, that side of him life had taught him to reject. She is, so to speak, all his romantic leanings and errors, with their fatal consequences. Moreover she lives, not even in Rouen, which he detested as a provincial and petty city, but out in the villages of the surrounding countryside. This he had absolutely foresworn. Furthermore, he was writing a critique of a way of life: the book started as an idea, and this idea had to be developed. He was sure it was possible to interest a reader thus with ideas instead of events, but it was enormously difficult and could be saved only by the right style. The whole of the early marriage days between Charles and Emma was a matter of a bourgeois existence and an inactive love; but then this situation recurred during the chaste early relationship between Léon and Emma. They had to be kept interesting through ideas, not through events (of which there were really very few), and new approaches had constantly to be found.

Little by little he fought and won the battle. The early pages all had to be rewritten later, as he learned the techniques of painting, as it were, white on white. Courbet and the painters who followed him were learning to do this, literally, on canvas; Flaubert was making the same conquest with words. But it also remains true that, while both Chateaubriand and Flaubert worked exhaustively over their prose, in Chateaubriand this never shows, and in Flaubert it often does.

Style is, ultimately, a matter of the precise words used, their choice and their arrangement. It is a technical matter, a linguistic one. Full comprehension of Flaubert's style requires observing the specific French words and structures he used, so that any consideration of it in English may fall short of the mark. But conveniently, Flaubert's fundamental concept can be valid for any language: everything must be based in the subject being discussed. The ideas proffered must of course have their source here: this is no more than a rejection of the digressions, usually personal, which had been so popular with the romantics. But Flaubert went much further, holding that even the comparisons and the metaphors must also derive wholly from the subject. They must relate to and come out of the specific person and scene at hand. The truffle image concerning Charles' reminiscences as he rode away is a good one, because this is the way that Charles would have chewed over the taste of the truffles: it suggest him. An image based on recollecting successful whist hands would have been inappropriate because Charles did not know how to play the game. To the objection that the image is not being quoted from Charles' thoughts but is rather in the mind of the author or the reader, Flaubert would have replied that the reader learns about Charles from the image, and its form (in this case, reference to truffles or whist) is a part of that learning process.

In the dismally sad scene outside the convent of her childhood when Emma recalled her dreams of those earlier days and contrasted them with what reality had brought, Flaubert wrote concerning the start of the scene that she came to realize that all these dreams had been real to her and that she was now examining them as one enjoys holding and looking at a handful of broken seashells. The image is good for its suggestion of the beauty of the shells and the strange and melancholy pleasure one can take in their shattered remnants. Flaubert had first thought of it when he was at Trouville. But Emma had never been to the seashore, and this would not have been an image available to her. Its suggestions and reverberations would have taken the reader outside of her: hence it had to be stricken, although no other image occurred to him to replace it. The author must be poetical only to the extent that the material allows it, as in the death scene of Charles, for instance. Flaubert liked to quote the eighteenth-century naturalist and philosopher Buffon, who had affirmed that the relationships present in a beautiful style are perhaps more precious to the reader than even the subject itself.

A further difficulty presented itself. Once the proper phrasing for a sentence or a paragraph had been found, it then had to be linked to the next element by similarly precise transitions. This linking was a doubly difficult matter, because each element had to be true to itself while still permitting the transitions. And a cascading flow of style could be achieved only by such a derivation of each element from its predecessor. Style was not a matter of individual beauties but rather of a continuous, composite whole, often extending over pages at a time. This anatomy or physiology of style was what Flaubert felt was new and essential. And all of this had to be adapted to hundreds of pages of psychological analysis which must be handled in narrations rather than explanations,[22] for explanations introduced the personality of the author as he offered his understandings. Hence even Flaubert's descriptions become in reality animated scenes linked within themselves and to each other by a continuity of style.

To Flaubert continuity of style depended upon precision and exactitude. This, which he had admired in Greek sculpture and architecture, was what gave strength to great art. To speakers of English, accustomed to the comfortable relaxation of English vocabulary and syntax ("I only want ten pounds" for "I want only ten pounds" or the easy blurring of any distinction between "directives" and "instructions"), the notion of precision of language does not seem critical, and the emphasis which speakers and writers of French have long placed upon it seems paradoxical or quixotic if not downright foolish. But a language is a respository of centuries of the culture which has utilized it, and the writer must take advantage of what has been bequeathed to him by generations of his forebears. The availability of imprecision is one of the great heritages of English: how large is a "not inconsiderable amount"? Correspondingly, one of the greatest heritages of French is its remarkable precision; certain turns of phrase in French lose their sharpness of resolution when given the less defined edges of their nearest English equivalent. Flaubert was right in thus understanding what André Gide would painfully rediscover,[23] that the essential genius of French is to tend always toward precision.

La Bruyère, early in the eighteenth century, had insisted that, of all the different expressions which might appear to render a single thought, only one could be right. An author might not be able to find the expression to render a given concept, but it did exist (La Bruyère, too, was a classicist), and nothing but this single correct expression would satisfy a good writer. It might take time to find it, but Flaubert suggested that the writer take his model from hairdressers, all of whom agreed that the more one brushed hair, the more shining it became. Style was the same, and correctness was what gave it brilliance. Flaubert sought to give his book perfection of style. Its Norman coloring (which he detested) would, he hoped, amaze and infuriate all Normans by its telling accuracy. And each speaker in the book has his own style of language; even the peasants, while speaking correct French, talk like peasants, a difficult achievement of which he was very proud.[24]

Flaubert's passionate devotion to the use of words (as well as his doctrine of impersonalism) led Ezra Pound to consider *Madame Bovary* the "culmination of the anterior art of novel writing." James and Proust he found the only authors to have made additional contributions since that time.[25] Walter Pater had meanwhile served to make Flaubert's ideas known in England, using him to exemplify "the latent colour and imagery which language as such carries in it."[26] By drawing on the resources present in the poetic value of language as Flaubert understood them, the English novelists of the end of the century found that, like him, they could present even ugly and sordid aspects of life artistically.[27] In France only Huysmans perhaps followed this lead offered by Flaubert, but James Joyce completely shared his convictions. He had read every line of Flaubert that had been published and knew pages by heart. In his passion for the perfect word and the perfect order of these words he is akin to Flaubert, and both exemplify in their approach to their work the artist as hero and saint.

Flaubert paid similarly heroic attention to the rhythm of the sentences in which he placed these words he sought for so long. He conceived of a poetic prose closely akin to what Baudelaire used in his prose poems. Flaubert did not wish his prose to have the regularity of rhythm of a line of verse, yet it would have its own varying but perceptible internal rhythms. He wished it to be as sonorous as poetry and to have its rich consistency and precision. It was a difficult ideal, in and of itself, and rendered hopelessly so in his own day, he felt, because none of the rules had yet been worked out, whereas the poet had two thousand years of poetic theory to guide him.

The heart of modern literary style lies in the metaphor or

image, the comparison, stated or implied, of one object to another. Not only must every word, then, be right: every object must be so, too. When Flaubert selected the plaster statue of the curate as a symbolic object to fall and break on the trip to Yonville, it was of the right material to break and the proper symbol for the garden he had stood in, which gave its tone to Emma's life at Tostes.[28] The century since Flaubert (and Baudelaire, for poetry) has seen an extension of their concept of imagery; the enormous importance given to imagery probably may be fairly traced back to them, as also the new understandings of the possibilities inherent in it. When Flaubert wrote that nothing indicated a more powerful gift for writing than the construction of an extended metaphor well followed through,[29] he did not yet know Baudelaire, but the poet would have agreed entirely; and the joint impetus they gave to this device has yet to run its full course.

Flaubert thought naturally in images: his letters, often written late at night and when his head ached with fatigue, are always full of them. He wrote to Louise Colet at one point that he was bothered by an excessive feel for metaphor, dominating his other sensitivities. He was, he said, devoured by comparisons as beggars were by lice: he had to spend all his time crushing them; his sentences were crawling with them. And it is entirely possible that as he wrote this extended metaphor (lice—devoured—crushing—crawling) he was but dimly aware that he was employing in his sentence precisely the device he was stating he must learn to curb.

The image as Flaubert understood it is a powerful tool of analysis in itself, and yet it may be abused. It permits a type of open-ended analysis, a device which starts with a direct insight ("I write with too many metaphors") but which ends by extending the insight into a whole range of unlimited perspective ("These metaphors are like lice in that they are omnipresent, disagreeable, and a bother because one must spend one's time removing them and still they are all about"). But the image, as opposed to the analysis, goes further because where analysis gains its power by a precise delimitation, imagery leaves open its suggestions: one's emotions and one's reactions, conscious and subconscious, to the notion of lice. In this case the image is good, quite sufficient, and thoroughly acceptable.

There were times when Flaubert could not resist continuing

them, piling one on top of another, until, as he said, his sentences were crawling with them and some had to be crushed; unfortunately, he was not always able to bring himself to do so. In the great description of Rouen as Emma saw it on her way to her assignations with Léon, he first stated that the city looked as motionless as a painting, but then, describing the painting, he had the islands look like great oblong fish in the river. So the real islands are like painted islands which are like fish; fortunately the river is at least a river. Or in the moonlight scene which Emma and Rodolphe watch on the night before their planned departure, the moon reflected on the water is likened to so many different things so fully carried out that the reader becomes aware of the procedure instead of grasping intuitively what is being suggested: artifice and artificiality have crowded out art.

More successful is Flaubert's typical form, which involves stating a notion analytically and then adding the image to give amplitude and suggestiveness. Of Emma during her feverish efforts to find money to pay off Lheureux, he wrote at one point: "She felt herself lost, rolling at random through indefinable chasms." When Emma found Rodolphe's letter, she fled from the room "as if there had been behind her a terrifying conflagration." (Compare the unimaged statement: "Frightened, she fled from the room.") A moment later, taking his image from the very pseudomedieval readings which had set her off on this disastrous path, he wrote that "her heart beat against her breast as if with a battering ram." Similarly Flaubert insisted that images fit strict canons of accuracy. He agreed when Bouilhet drew his attention to a weak image, "in the mixture of feelings in which he was becoming entangled," because the image of entangling cannot concord with as liquid a notion as "a mixture of feelings."[30] And he urged Louise Colet to abandon a phrase for a tiger, "striped king," on the grounds that it contained two disparate images. Kings are not striped, and so the mind of the reader is carried in two different directions which do not reinforce each other. In every case in *Madame Bovary*, because the image finds its natural place within the character portrayed, the device has allowed Flaubert to remain impassive and impersonal: he appears to have had no part in the statement.

Flaubert built his paragraphs around their imagery frequently, and the more difficult the analysis the more he fell back upon the images to carry the burden. To draw the bare bones of the imagery out of context to display them is to strip away the flesh with which Flaubert had surrounded them so as to conceal their function and operation, and it is, to that extent, improper. One example, however, may not be unduly misleading, although translation adds to the falsification, for to Flaubert as to Baudelaire, the effectiveness of such passages depends quite as much upon their sound to the ear as it does upon what the eye can see and the mind understand and visualize. Flaubert worked ceaselessly to eliminate all inadvertent repetitions of words and sounds, all meaningless clashes the ear could pick up. All this, translation and discussion out of context suppress, but perhaps not fatally.

A powerfully constructed example of texture created by extended metaphor occurs when Léon has just left for Paris, and Emma is discovering her solitude and her melancholy. After an initial paragraph explaining how the next day was funereal for Emma, Flaubert devoted three further, imaged paragraphs to establishing her mood. From this would stem her readiness to be seduced by Rodolphe. The first paragraph stated her regret over allowing Léon to leave without having made him her lover. The second one opened with the statement that this memory of Léon was the center or focus of her ennui. Then, using an image which Emma could have known from any of a number of popular lithographs of the day, he wrote that this recollection "sparkled more strongly than does the traveler's abandoned fire across the snows of the Russian steppes." This image than becomes the basis for a long, developed metaphor. He noted Emma's misery, her efforts to stir up the embers of this dying fire, and her searching about in her memory for what might be used to revive it. She gathered up "everything which could bring some warmth to her sadness." The next paragraph depends for its linkage to this one on the same image and only gradually allows it to sink from consciousness. The paragraph opens, "However, the flames became more peaceful, either because the supply was being exhausted, or because the fuel was heaped too high." Further images gradually lead to the total extinguishing of the fire, "and she remained in a terrible coldness which cut her to the marrow."

The polished final result of all these labors is an oratorical style more closely akin to the age of Louis XIV than to either the Age of Voltaire or even the romantics. It is readily grandiose and makes use of swelling periods. But it is in two ways different and more modern: it easily introduces short, even choppy elements to set off the others or to be set off by them;[31] and it has a richness of texture supplied in general by metaphor to which only authors like Homer, Virgil, and Dante have attained. Flaubert's later works would contract and solidify some of the exuberant fullness of this style, but *Madame Bovary* was, certainly for the rest of the world and probably for France as well, the most read and influential of the works he wrote. Only with Proust well after the turn of the century did the French tradition of the novel find really new openings. Flaubert had succeeded in writing the style he had imagined.

15

The Trial of *Madame Bovary* (1856-57)

Madame Bovary IN THE *Revue de Paris*

I acted like a fool in doing as others do, living in Paris and wanting to publish. So long as I wrote for myself alone, I lived in perfect serenity about my art. Now I am full of doubts and confusion and for the first time I am finding writing distasteful.

> Letter to Louis Bouilhet, June 17, 1856

You will be glad to know that things are going very well for *Madame Bovary*. At any rate I am pleased—so far at least.

> Letter to Maurice Schlésinger of the end of October, 1856

In April, 1856, Flaubert put the finishing touches to the manuscript of *Madame Bovary*.[1] He then had a copy prepared by professionals, which was sent to the printer, while the final manuscript in his own hand he carefully preserved in a special carton made for the purpose. It seemed a part of himself, something he would no more readily part with than he would with his own flesh. The same feeling led him to keep all his drafts and so many of his penned or penciled notes and reflections.

Du Camp had assured Flaubert he was keeping a place in the *Revue* for him, and he was as good as his word. He bought the manuscript at once and paid two thousand francs for it, a good price to an unknown author. Flaubert, much pleased, looked forward to seeing it in serial form shortly and then in book form, along with a revision he might now make of his *Temptation* and perhaps a further work as well. Once he had broken his long silence, the time seemed propitious for a great deal of publishing. He expected his novel to begin appearing in July and to occupy parts of six issues. His only concern was lest Victor Hugo's new volume of poetry, *Les Contemplations*, attract so much of the public's attention as to hinder the sale of *Madame Bovary* when it came out as a book. He could have spared himself the worry: *Madame Bovary* was many long and painful months away from publication.

Du Camp and his fellow editors found much to criticize in *Madame Bovary* and more still which alarmed them. When Flaubert was informed of this, he was furious. Yet it must have seemed presumptuous to Maxime that Gustave should stubbornly reject the wise and knowledgeable critiques the *Revue* so generously offered him. Gustave, for his part, insisted that no one can correct the manuscript of a good author except himself. Chateaubriand would have ruined Voltaire, he felt,[2] and he found that Du Camp was making inept changes in his text. It was an outrage.

The manuscript of *Madame Bovary* was too long; of that there could be no doubt, and the editors of the *Revue de Paris* rightly demanded cuts to lighten the text. A line here or there, even an occasional paragraph, Flaubert grudgingly consented to delete, but he was not happy over it. Was he perhaps sacrificing elements of art in the name of a more facile success? He felt almost soiled at even considering it. Years of his life had gone into the careful elaboration of this text: now a group of men, all of whom he considered markedly his inferiors, were offering advice and insisting that he accept it. He felt discouraged and enraged.

By mid-July the positions had hardened into an ugly disagreement. Du Camp wanted the marriage scene to be cut; his associate wished the Agricultural Fair either eliminated or redone; neither was enthusiastic about the clubfoot operation. When Flaubert received the letter, kindly but patronizing, in which Maxime made his final statements, he was so furious that he wrote "fantastic" across the back of the sheet and crumpled the letter into a little ball.[3]

Flaubert was stubborn, but Du Camp and the rest of the editorial group had little freedom themselves. Readers would not put up with passages that dragged. And then there were the passages which dealt with sex and religion. The government of the Second Empire was dependent upon the support of the conservatives; in

France this group has traditionally feared and disliked a free press. The *Revue de Paris* had already had two warnings over unduly liberal expressions; Du Camp knew that his periodical would be suppressed on the occasion of a third one. What could be better from the point of view of the government than to charge the *Revue* with an offense against morals and religion? Flaubert, on the other hand, knew little of these matters and cared not at all: it was not his periodical, and his principles and prejudices made him insensitive to any but artistic considerations. In point of fact, the *Revue* was suspended for a few days in early 1857 and was ordered out of existence a year later;[4] Du Camp was right to be fearful.

At last, after interminable delays, the initial installment of *Madame Bovary* appeared on October 1, 1856. Flaubert thinking the cause now won, wrote a pleasant letter to one of Du Camp's associates explaining that he had not sought to be disgusting but rather to see whether it was possible, as he believed, to depict ignoble reality artistically. This was why he had had to resist all attempts to persuade him to change: they had really been asking him to write another book.

Minor problems appeared as soon as the work began to come out: a few typographical errors and a foolish matter of wounding sensibilities. Flaubert had had Homais write a pompous and idiotic account of the Agricultural Fair for the *Journal de Rouen*, a real Rouen newspaper. Hearing of this before the appearance of the installment which carried it, Frédéric Baudry, an old friend, reported that his father-in-law, the influential lawyer Sénard, hoped the name might be changed to avoid embarrassment.[5] It seemed a simple enough request, and Baudry suggested calling it, for instance, the *Progressif de Rouen*. Why not? But this was to reckon without Flaubert's intense feeling for the musical and oratorical values of the sounds in a sentence. What would happen, he asked Bouilhet, to the rhythm of his sentences? One or the other of them discovered a happy solution in renaming the paper the *Fanal de Rouen* or *Rouen Beacon*. "Fanal" was close enough in sound to "Journal" to make it acceptable.

At the start of November, Flaubert felt that everything was most auspicious. He had found an attractive apartment at 42,

Boulevard du Temple, near the Place de la République. Early reactions to his novel were all favorable, and he had even been approached by a publisher who wished to bring it out in book form. Bouilhet's affairs, too, were excellent: on November 6 his play, *Madame de Montarcy*, began a highly successful run.[6]

Trouble broke in the middle of the month. Du Camp was readying for the printer the section of the novel describing Emma's ride in the hackney cab with Léon. On the eighteenth he wrote to Gustave: it was no longer possible to treat all of this as a joke, he said. The police would forbid the sale of the issue the moment they saw it. It would be the end of the *Revue*, and this Maxime did not propose to invite. He asked Gustave to stop by the editorial offices so that they could talk over how to handle the cuts.[7]

Flaubert was enraged, but Maxime had no room left for concessions. Even for the preceding issue the *Revue* had required deletions, but Du Camp did agree to publish a note indicating the fact. As he still insisted on deleting the cab ride in the final installment, Flaubert demanded that the *Revue* now state that the author refused to consider the work they were publishing as his. Maxime demurred. Gathering a selection of passages already published in the *Revue* which were more daring than his paragraphs, Flaubert threatened Du Camp with a law suit if he did not publish the disclaimer.[8] By December 12, Maxime had consented; on December 14, a Rouen paper which had been reprinting the installments of the new novel as they appeared announced that it was suspending publication. The following day, December 15, the *Revue* published Flaubert's disclaimer and its own cut text, lacking the ride in the cab.

Flaubert felt curiously indifferent to it all. On the whole people were reacting favorably to his work, and he himself found it worthy of a prize for morality. He had attempted a complex literary wager, and he felt that he had won. Various periodicals of major importance were approaching him; renowned authors were speaking well of him; critical opinion was favorable, and there was even talk of making an *opéra-comique* from his text. And yet the *Revue* seemed frightened and had insisted on deletions. He could not understand their fears. Ironically, his collection of scabrous passages from earlier issues of the *Revue* may have been what came to the attention of the authorities and led them to attack his work.[9] At any rate he and the *Revue* were summoned into court on charges of corrupting public morals.

Madame Bovary IN COURT (1857)

I am afraid I have irritated many people by writing my novel; people don't like frankness; it is immoral to write well.

Letter to Madame Roger des Genettes
of January 16, 1857

The year 1857 is distinguished in the history of French letters by official attacks on the two most important books to be published in France in the century; both were termed offensive to religion and morality. *Madame Bovary* and Baudelaire's *Flowers of Evil* thus leaped to enormous public notice immediately, instead of having to wait out the slower pace normally required for such fame. The process, however, was not easy for either author.

In Flaubert's case threatening word reached him late in December, 1856: the government was considering a suit against him and the *Revue de Paris*.[10] They were anxious days, and he could be grateful that he had acceded to Baudry's request to change the name of the Rouen paper to which Homais sent his article. He now turned to Baudry's father-in-law, Sénard, an old family friend of the Flauberts' and a powerful figure in politics, to defend him.

By New Year's Eve Flaubert was seriously worried that he would lose if he could not have the matter quashed before it came to trial. It had by now become clear that Du Camp's fears had been justified: the government was anxious to crush a liberal periodical on a morals charge. Flaubert turned vigorously to the counterattack, bringing to bear all the weight his family name carried in provincial Rouen: it was essential that the government be made to realize that its position in the whole region would be damaged by attacking the son of the beloved Dr. Flaubert. Moreover, Paris should learn that the family tradition was being carried on into the present by Achille. Letters passed back and forth between Flaubert and his family and friends in Rouen; they hoped the prefect of the department, a powerful official in the French Second Empire, would write a letter to the Minister of the Interior asking that the case be dropped to avoid embarrassing the government in Rouen.

The normally indifferent Flaubert, phlegmatic about such practical matters, now began to display herculean energy as he hurried from office to office in Paris. His enemy was the harder to grapple with in that it was never clear precisely who wished to attack the *Revue* or what government ministry was really involved. Flaubert found that in the face of his efforts overt hostility ceased and the most ingratiating moves were made in his direction: the Minister of Fine Arts went out of his way to speak flatteringly to him in public, and all sorts of important personages, particularly great ladies, were most obliging in the steps they took to bring further pressure. But still in the background lingered the threat of a lawsuit, and it did not seem possible to bring pressure directly to bear to halt it. By the fourth or fifth of January, Flaubert felt sure that the source lay in the Ministry of the Interior: word from the prefect would thus be immediately useful. By the sixth he thought that the Ministry of Justice, too, was involved; but he also knew that the Empress Eugénie was on his side. It was dangerous but exciting.

Two weeks into the new year, Flaubert had succeeded in all his efforts: he had private word that the formal order had been given to drop the case.[11] It had been a close call and he had been badly frightened. What would have been left of his life if he had been condemned? A year in prison in itself would have been hideous; worse would have been the knowledge that every word he wrote thereafter would be watched by the police for the slightest suggestion of obscenity or sacrilege. It would have meant the destruction of his life as he knew it. But fortunately the government machine, stupid as it was, had finally been able to understand and had pulled back. He breathed a sigh of relief and took time at last to notify his friends of what had filled his busy days.

That was January 14; on the next day he learned to his horror that the attack was to be renewed despite all the protection he had found in high places. Obviously there was more to the affair than he had dreamed of, for certainly the backing he had obtained was more than enough to stop a mere ministry from a simple maneuver, easily repeated with a different excuse, to suppress a periodical. Was it perhaps a matter of personal vengeance on those who had presumed to protect him? Was there something else involved? This time the source was too high up in the government for him to be able to locate it. All he knew was that he must now appear in court and run precisely those dreadful risks he had just been describing to his friends and thinking he had escaped.

The case was rapidly called, then delayed, and delayed again. Flaubert used the time in preparing his defense, particularly in searching out passages in the classics of French literature which were stronger in their phrasing than anything in his novel. Du Camp wrote, however, to set matters straight: of course isolated phrases could be found in the classics, but this was not the real issue. Rather the whole tone of the book was involved, its basic brutality, which, to insensitive observers, must appear immorality. This was what Flaubert must consider and the complaint against which his lawyer must defend him.[12]

Flaubert also sought to get famous authors of his day to back him. The poet and statesman Lamartine, author of chaste and ethereal love verses of the preceding generation, offered of his own accord to support him; and numerous men of Flaubert's own generation, realizing that his cause was theirs, too, stepped forward to his assistance. His mood was better, and he even came to joking that after he was imprisoned he would buy a set of chains and a bale of straw so that his portrait could be painted in his cell in proper style.

The trial came on January 29.[13] The imperial prosecutor, Pinard, particularly attacked four scenes: Rodolphe's seduction of Emma, her temporary interest in religion between the two affairs, Léon's seduction, and her death scene. He also pointed to what he called the general lascivious tone, the poetry of adultery, and the profound immorality of the work. He even used what was an ugly word in his period: the book was "realistic." No character in the work, he complained, either condemned Emma or was in fact able to do so. He concluded that art which seeks to live without rules is no longer art.

Sénard made an extremely able defense along lines Flaubert no doubt in part suggested to him. Not content with merely rejecting the accusation, he insisted that the book rested on an eminently moral and religious foundation and constituted an effort to excite the reader to virtuous conduct by inspiring in him a horror for vice. He asked directly whether the reading of Emma's fate would induce any young woman to seek adultery or to flee it. He insisted that, if anything, Flaubert had been too harsh in his punishment of Emma and quoted Lamartine, who found the ending too severe and painful. Also, making effective use of Flaubert's collection of lascivious extracts from the classics of French literature, he noted that the incriminated passages were far less exciting than these.

Essentially Sénard's defense lay in reading the passages preceding and following the ones attacked by the government. In their dreary context of provincial Normandy and ever-declining amours none could sustain the charge that they excited to evil conduct. Sénard's task was won, even before he began to cite Hugo and Balzac or the Great French church writers of earlier days in their analyses of the consequences of sin. The court agreed with him and a week later handed down its verdict. The judges found that the passages offended good taste if taken in isolation; they blamed the book severely because it failed to attain the objective of good literature, which they stated to be adorning and refreshing the spirit by elevating the mind and purifying manners; they objected that the author, in treating of such immoral conduct, had failed to exercise every restraint of language; they drew to his attention that he had gone beyond the limits of literature; but they concluded that his aim had been elevated and that he had not written pornography. They acquitted him, his publisher, and his printer. It was over.

The publishing house of Michel Lévy bought the manuscript and prepared to cash in on the notoriety which the novel had achieved through the efforts of the imperial prosecutor. Praise flowed in to Flaubert from all the major figures in the French literary world, but he found himself disgusted over it all. He had dreamed of success, but not in this way or for this reason, and now he regretted more than ever having published at all.

Everyone sensed that the trial had been an attack not on a book but on a whole domain of literature and on the right to write social novels. How could he ever publish again, Flaubert wondered. Would he do better to return to his original plan and write for himself alone so as to avoid prostituting what he believed in? The trial left him with a lifelong rage against censorship and the feeling that it was both futile and immoral. More than twenty years later, however, he had at least a personal revenge: one of his judges later went out of his mind, and the prosecuting lawyer was identified as the author of scabrous verses.[14]

THE FIRST EDITION

> You have written a good book.
> Letter from Victor Hugo to Flaubert when
> *Madame Bovary* was published

> It is difficult to know where the French novel is going these days. But at least one thing is clear: it is not going far.
> Cuvillier-Fleury reviewing *Madame Bovary* on May 26, 1857

The trial of *Madame Bovary* had whetted the public's desire for the book. Flaubert had prepared an agreement with Michel Lévy on December 24, 1856, selling him the rights for five years at the absurdly low figure of eight hundred francs. Its purchasing power can be judged from the fact that the stenographer who took down the court proceedings for Flaubert received sixty francs a day. As the contract could not have become final until the trial was over, it must only have come into effect some time in February, when it was already apparent that the sales would be very large; Flaubert, to his later intense regret, did not seek a higher figure. About the middle of April copies must have begun to come off the press. The volume was gratefully dedicated to Sénard.[15]

Flaubert sent out a number of inscribed copies. His mother received one from "her old companion." Elisa Schlésinger's was inscribed in memory "of an old and unalterable affection." Gertrude Collier's was "in memory of the beach at Trouville, and of our long afternoons of reading." If Harriet received one, it has not been found. George Sand received one, too, for Flaubert was not a wholly impractical man, and also Michelet, whom he deeply admired. George Sand he did not come to know until many years later, but his friendship with Michelet may well date from this gift and Michelet's kind reply.

There were a number of favorable letters from authors much in the public eye. Champfleury, publicly recognized as the head of the realist school, whom Flaubert knew through Louise Colet's salon, wrote in considerable praise. Victor Hugo sent a kind letter. But on the whole the critical reaction was severe. None of the critics succeeded, according to Flaubert, in pointing to what was really best in his work or in attaching blame to the places which properly merited it; but he found that, with the book now in print, it all seemed very much separated from him. It was just as well. Duranty, editor of a periodical called *Réalisme*, found *Madame Bovary* wholly without interest in an article which could still irritate Flaubert twenty-five years later.[16] Another critic, less polite, termed the novel a dung heap; and a sycophant asked in print how a man could permit himself to be so abject a stylist when Louis-Napoléon, the greatest writer of the French language, sat upon the throne.[17]

The critics were at a loss before so new a work and one for which their only preparation had been the rather poor efforts of the young school of realism.[18] Not even Sainte-Beuve, the reigning critic, knew how to deal with it. Most succumbed to the temptation to tell Flaubert how to do it over again rather better, preferably by turning back to earlier and more comfortable models such as Balzac. Thus it was urged that the novel would have been improved by making Charles more noble so that readers might have wept for him, which is of course exactly to misunderstand the aim and burden of Flaubert's work. Champfleury himself was shocked by certain details which he found offensive to good taste, the ugly infection of the blind man's eye, for instance, or some of the surgical details in the clubfoot operation.

It was Sainte-Beuve, however, who gave or withheld consecration in matters literary under the Second Empire. Flaubert had disliked the critic when he had been unkind to Louise Colet and Bouilhet, and when his role and position seemed some sort of apostasy from the romanticism he had earlier proclaimed. But to Sainte-Beuve, too, the canny fledgling author sent a copy, "With the homage of an unknown writer." He received in reply a long and most flattering letter.[19] Sainte-Beuve complimented him upon his style—at least some one had recognized this quality!—and upon the extraordinary fidelity of the depictions of Normandy. His characters were living people, and Homais was raised to the level of a type. Sainte-Beuve was delighted with the impersonal handling of the irony and the bitterness. The analysis was good but cruel and frightening. He was a bit worried about what happened to matters of ethics in the novel; but at any rate it had been foolish to call the work immoral. He particularly singled out the Agricultural Fair and the moment when Charles and Emma lay in bed dreaming such different dreams of the future.

But there were reservations the famous critic wished to make. He would have liked less detailed descriptions, so that the main points might come out more fully. And above all he would have liked some gentle, pure figure with profound and restrained feelings but drawn with as much veracity and conviction as the other characters. It would have given the reader a moment of respite and would have served as a reminder that there is some good even in the midst of evil and stupidity. He closed by telling Flaubert that he seemed to know everything, and that he was cruel.

The article Sainte-Beuve wrote was a restatement of these points with more elaboration. He added, however, that he sensed in the work a new generation of writers who would bring a new literature. He noted the importance of science, the spirit of observation, maturity, strength, and a tendency to hardness and harshness. He closed with a famous phrase: "Son and brother of distinguished doctors, Monsieur Gustave Flaubert holds the pen as others do the scalpel. Anatomists and physiologists, I find you on every hand!"

Flaubert at once forgave Sainte-Beuve for any errors committed in the past. He wrote the critic of his gratefulness and said he felt repaid for all the pains he had taken with the book, now that he had had these words of encouragement from a critic and author whom he had admired ever since he had read him during schooldays. He proclaimed that in spirit he belonged to the generation of Sainte-Beuve, the generation of 1830 which had made the romantic revolution. He closed by asking permission to call and seek Sainte-Beuve's advice. Such practical discussions were, he said, more valuable than all the esthetic theories in the world. It would be a pleasure and a lesson, he added.

Only one other critical article was really favorable, that by Baudelaire; Flaubert's immense success was made, instead, by the public. Lévy, hurrying a second printing through, wondered if Flaubert would not like to publish at once his *Temptation of Saint Anthony*, which he had been reworking; Flaubert declined. Meanwhile, over his constant denials, readers began to seek for the models he must have copied. He insisted, not quite fairly, that he had copied no one and had sought instead to depict types. But innumerable readers recognized their women friends in Emma, and one gentleman even wrote to thank the author for having avenged him! All the pharmacists in the department, wrote Flaubert, wanted to slap him; and there was a medical officer in Algeria, he later learned, whose wife could have served as a model and whose name was Madame Bovaries.[20] The novel even had the acclaim of the wits and the wags. In Hamburg hack cabs with Venetian blinds, favored by ladies of easy virtue, were for a time known as *bovaries*.[21] And Emma appeared in two of the traditional year-end parodies of notable events.[22]

The hue and cry and even the idiotic praise all made Flaubert less than ever sure that he had done well to publish his novel. So much of what was said about it was so stupid and uninformed. To term his work realism was inept; yet almost no one seemed to suspect that it was more. But the more careful reading public came to have ever more confidence in the favorable reaction with which they had first greeted the book. Far from being another quick success based on a scandal and dying with it, *Madame Bovary* rose steadily in popular esteem.

Writers, too, adopted it, finding in its impersonalism and careful observation the first successful effort to carry out the canons of the new school, realism. Naturalism, Zola would proclaim, arose from it. The scattered formulae of Balzac, he said, found here a clear and concise statement. But all that Zola and naturalism understood of it was the exact reproduction of life, the absence of any subjective, romanticized vision. Composition seemed to them now only a matter of choosing among various real scenes and establishing a harmonious order in their development.[23] It is no wonder that Flaubert, like Chateaubriand before him, was horrified by the works which stemmed from his. The progeny of René were no more unfortunate than those which traced their lineage back to Emma Bovary. This was, however, the penalty to be paid for publishing. Flaubert could no longer caress his dreams of art in private. His book, his thoughts, and even his person were now public property. An age had ended for him and for the novel, and a new one had begun for both.

PART II

Mid-Passage

16

A Noted Author (1857-62)

WHERE NEXT?

I have enough plans for literary ideas to last me the rest of my life . . .

Letter to Louise Colet, March 27, 1853

ALL through the years of writing *Madame Bovary* Flaubert had longed to have done with it in order to turn to other works. At times, it seemed to him that only a study of modern torpor would suffice to let him vent his spleen. He would write a vast contemporary novel passing in review all of the society of his day, a return to the subject matter of Balzac but renewed through his own understanding of form. Alternatively what he frequently termed the fetid subject matter of *Madame Bovary* seemed so disgusting that only escape would do. The "Near-Eastern Tale" which he had worked on in 1846 haunted him over these years, as did the idea for "Anubis," which had been set aside only in order to make way for *Don Juan* and *Madame Bovary*. Another possibility was to take the hallucinations and visions brought on by his epilepsy and turn them into a strange, metaphysical novel filled with apparitions and fantasies, but this must wait till his cure was more certain.

Literature and society both seemed to call for critical works, too. There was the *Dictionary of Accepted Ideas*, which could be made an indirect vehicle for a devastating social critique. Flaubert now envisaged a Preface which would show that the majority is always right, that great men are really inferior to ordinary people, that all originality is dangerous, and that only the leveling of modern, democratic ideas is permissible. The ostensible purpose of the *Dictionary* would then be to put at the disposal of every citizen whatever notions or ideas he might need in present-day society. Flaubert also hoped to write an essay on French poetry, for he felt that France had always misunderstood verse; therefore, prefaces to an edition of Ronsard and to certain of Bouilhet's works would broaden his scope to let him have his say on esthetics.

In fact he had so many ideas that it was almost impossible to imagine being able to choose. Flaubert considered revising *November* but abandoned the task as fruitless. He spent two hours dreaming of a Roman novel and at intervals toyed with the thought of a story set in the eighteenth century. And he continued to have ideas for plays.

In April of 1856, with *Madame Bovary* on its way to Maxime Du Camp for publication in his *Revue de Paris,* Flaubert had to make a choice: two ideas immediately imposed themselves, both of which had come to him during the honeymoon trip to Italy. Ultimately he wrote and published works based on both ideas, though not for nearly two decades. One was the story of Saint Julian, which derived psychologically from his dream about monkeys during that trip; the second was another try at *The Temptation of Saint Anthony.* He hoped to publish both as book-length works in company with *Madame Bovary* in 1857. But only *Madame Bovary* was actually to see print that year.

Flaubert had had passing ideas of writing of the feudal age during the drafting of *Madame Bovary;* now in June, 1856, he turned to it briefly and did preliminary readings for Saint Julian in the Rouen library over the summer. He was intrigued by the details of local color and wrote to Bouilhet of a porcupine pâté he proposed to fit into the work somewhere. He had had Emma and Léon glance briefly at the Saint Julian window in Rouen cathedral, but he deleted this episode from the final version of the novel as irrelevant. Now, too, although he did work at the subject for a few weeks, he soon gave it up for other and more pressing concerns: he would really try to rewrite *Saint Anthony.*

The Second *Temptation of Saint Anthony* (1856)

Saint Anthony weighs on my conscience, and I shan't have any rest until I have worked my way out from under this obsession.

Letter to Louis Bouilhet, June 1, 1856

Flaubert had never wholly abandoned Saint Anthony. While still on the Nile he was thinking of him constantly. On his return, as he meditated on the various subjects for books which had occurred to him during the trip, he was again attracted to the Saint and debated with Bouilhet the wisdom of trying to polish certain passages for separate publication. Du Camp urged that none of them showed Flaubert to good advantage and so he put them aside. Over the winter he remembered with nostalgia how easily he had written these pages; but, pearls though they might be, they lacked a thread and so he feared it was hopeless to try to use them. But as time passed, he accepted less and less the adverse judgment of Bouilhet and Du Camp. Somehow he had not matured his subject sufficiently in the version they had seen and hence the succession of ideas lacked a corresponding succession of events to bear them along. There were all sorts of dramatic elements present, but no drama.

Now, in the summer of 1856, he was at last free of *Madame Bovary*. By the first of June he was back in Croisset and had already started on *Saint Anthony*.[1] Trying to remove the improperly lyrical elements and to strengthen and clarify the structure, he deleted many shorter sections and innumerable turns of phrase which were pleasant enough in themselves but which directed the reader's attention away from the main ideas. It seemed to go well and easily. At the same time he started to draft additional monologues for the Saint. Finally, experience having made him more wary of the censor, he removed a number of passages likely to attract unfavorable attention. The sensual hallucinations which had beleaguered Anthony and which had almost been Flaubert's first idea for the book, he now reduced to a sentence; the visions of Adultery, Fornication, and Uncleanness he deleted entirely. He felt his original concept had been largely sound: it needed only to be made clearer to the reader.

These changes took time, and the weeks slipped by. Moreover, Flaubert found topics requiring further documentation: the heresies, for instance, already discussed in too erudite a fashion in the version of 1849, seemed to need further study, and he read a 1,000-page work on them. By August he was beginning to be bored and bothered by the rewriting; he was coming to realize that the book would tend to be more strange than beautiful. Yet he continued to labor, alternating between hope and despair, and wondering whether his work could ever pass the censor.

As winter came on, it seemed wise to return to the earlier idea of publishing certain scenes separately, and Théophile Gautier's magazine, *L'Artiste*, agreed to take selections to be spread over four issues in December, January, and early February. They appeared just in time for Pinard, the imperial prosecutor, to cite from them to reinforce his charge of obscenity against Flaubert. Publication of the complete work had to be put off, and Flaubert set it aside resolutely. He refused to change his opinion even when Lévy, enchanted with the sale of *Madame Bovary*, suggested risking prosecution anyway to publish while public fervor was still at its height.

Flaubert was, however, no longer in the mood for Anthony. Over the years of writing *Madame Bovary*, he had developed a further idea for his next book: it would be situated in very ancient times so he could describe battles and sieges and all the fabulous world of antiquity, which he had found still alive in Egypt. He wondered about the possibility of something like the Greek and Roman epics. In such splendid surroundings all the details would be luxurious, and the action would naturally take on the grandeur and tragedy *Madame Bovary* lacked. Such a setting could also embody the underlying idea of "Anubis," the story of the woman who thought she was sleeping with a god, which he had abandoned in favor of *Madame Bovary*.

This atmosphere and this fundamental concept he now decided to display in a novel based on the revolt of the mercenaries against ancient Carthage in the second century before Christ. Eventually he called the work *Salammbô*, after the name of its heroine, and within a few days of receiving the favorable verdict on *Madame Bovary*, he began to collect information for it. For the next five years this novel was his principal occupation.

The Need for Tranquility

I know the Paris you dream of, every foot of it; and I tell you that nothing in it is as desirable as a good book beside the fireplace.

Letter to Mademoiselle Leroyer
de Chantepie, March 18, 1857

The author of *Madame Bovary*, and backstage habitué of several theaters, could no longer hope to live as the Hermit of Croisset. Paris was now his home for several months each year, and in fact he enjoyed the city. There was, however, just enough there to ruffle his spirits so that he was often more aware of his irritations than of his pleasures. In the capital friends and acquaintances invaded the sacrosanct privacy that Croisset had always protected. Some were ill and needed visits; others had business affairs with which he felt he could be helpful; Bouilhet kept writing and staging plays for which Flaubert felt his presence and advice indispensable. Sought after by many acquaintances, with an entree to the opera and several theaters, he strove always to go out as little as possible and dreamed of being the same monk in Paris that he so easily was in Croisset.

Relaxation seemed impossible: what would he do, he wondered. Yet he found himself frequently tired to the marrow and morbidly thinking of death. Then his morale would rise again, but not very high nor for very long. Flaubert had never had the simpler social graces, and even now he did not learn to waltz, play cards, or make small talk. Moreover, in the city he could not be at ease financially; his income, quite adequate in Croisset, was insufficient for the obligations Paris imposed upon him, and he found himself having to borrow small sums in order to keep going during the winters. He was infuriated that his friends envied him his income; how could artists be concerned with financial matters?

Successful, admired, and envied, Flaubert was nevertheless unhappy in Paris and took refuge, as always, in his dreams. His numerous government contacts made it easy for him to think of being attached to various official expeditions, and he was seriously disturbed for some little time as he contemplated joining a group going to China: only his mother's need for him kept him from it, he felt. But that did not lessen his misery over missing it. He could dream of owning a house on the Grand Canal, however, and he found the botanical and zoological gardens in Paris moving sites for revery, where one could think of distant places and times long past.

And so Flaubert retreated to Croisset from spring through summer and the early autumn. Here he could rejoice in the wisdom that had kept him a bachelor. Achille's daughter had now reached marriageable age; her wedding, which Flaubert attended, set him to meditating upon his celibacy. Alone in his solitude after the ceremonies, he thought again of the abyss which separated him from his fellows. No doubt the only real happiness in life lay in marriage and in sharing one's life with another; but Flaubert knew that even if he were offered an opportunity to marry he would not accept. To seek it on his own was out of the question.

Living in the country, Flaubert found, had spiritual meaning for him. He was ashamed to discover that, in Paris, he was overcome with longing for green grass and flowers: this was a bourgeois emotion and he was embarrassed by it. Autumn he still loved for its promise of winter. The Seine, its tides swollen at the approach of the September equinox, unfurled real waves against the retaining wall of the garden, and he could look forward to long evenings beside the lamp and fire.

He remained essentially an indoors man, most content to think of nature from the comfort of a warm room. Outside on the river a tug passed now and again, the Seine kept up its murmur, and the tall trees of the garden, now leafless, swayed as the wind whistled through them. Here he could lose himself in the only life he really loved: reading, taking notes, dreaming, and then writing. One idea would lead to another, and he would effortlessly slip down the current of his meditations. That was part of the reason that the next book, *Salammbô*, took even longer than *Madame Bovary* to complete.

At home and far from the hated bourgeois—he once reported that his entire day had been ruined by the sight of one—he lived a quiet, self-centered life, which seemed to his friends to border upon mania. His servant Narcisse happily put up with his eccentricities, and in return Flaubert permitted him conduct not normally tolerated in domestics. On one occasion the man returned home so intoxicated that he could reach his room only with his master's assistance. Once there and stretched out upon his bed, he found himself forced to beg Flaubert to complete his kindness by removing his servant's boots. After a succession of battles with alcohol, however, the poor wretch had to abandon the unequal struggle and give up domestic service.[2]

Flaubert's friends and admirers, aware of his oddities, sought to watch over him. Suzanne Lagier, one of his numerous actress acquaintances, even ventured up to Rouen to assure herself that he was in good hands in Croisset. She found him in an expansive mood: he talked enthusiastically to her of the whirling dervishes of Constantinople and other staples of his fantasies and recollections. She left more alarmed than before. It was even rumored in Paris that he saw no one at all except Narcisse, who was instructed to address him weekly with the information, "Monsieur, today is Sunday." There was also a sea-captain whose vessel occasionally traveled up the Seine past Croisset to Rouen. As he came abreast of Flaubert's house, he dipped his flag thrice in the gesture of homage normally reserved for sovereigns. Flaubert, at first astonished at this recognition from a big three-master, eventually learned of the captain's admiration for *Madame Bovary* and was delighted.[3]

Melancholy moments were the more normal ones. Memories of the past—which he had thought he had not enjoyed living—were apt to crowd in unwanted. At Trouville in 1853 he felt he had put his past behind him and had made his peace with it. Now he knew this was not so. After thirty-five, he wrote, one was separated from one's earlier life as a widower is from his marriage. But this meant only that one could turn back to gaze nostalgically upon it, as upon the events of history. Madame Le Poittevin was still alive, and a few days with her brought back memories of Alfred and all of Gustave's childhood. His youth seemed almost to seep out of the walls of her house and penetrate coldly to the bottom of his heart.

Innumerable small events of daily living stimulated recollections of bygone days and sent his reveries meandering up their melancholy stream. A visit to his old school brought back pains and joys. It seemed to have deteriorated from what he recalled. Even the latrines had been moved. The boys were now as docile as girls in a boarding school, stepping almost mincingly and bowing politely to the faculty. His own truculent youth seemed as distant as Romulus and Remus. Trouville, too, was often in his thoughts. His father's properties there required visits at intervals. Each building, even each shrub, seemed to evoke memories; he became almost drunk with them. There were recollections, too, of his Near Eastern trip to haunt him. Celebrating his birthday in 1857, he recalled that on that day eight years earlier he had been traveling from Memphis to Cairo after sleeping beside the Sphinx and the Pyramids. He could still hear the jackals howling and the wind beating upon his tent.

As Flaubert began work on *Salammbô* in 1857, his health seemed fully recovered. He felt that somewhere around 1855 he had finally put his dread nervous ailment behind him. But neuralgic head pains worried him: he was afraid something was wrong with his spinal column. Bouilhet wisely reassured him that this medical diagnosis was without foundation and that the pains would depart as soon as he abandoned research and returned to his writing.[4] In October, 1858, however, difficulties returned, and he felt as he had in 1844; but this time he knew from experience that it would pass. He was listless and suffered from stomach cramps and pains in his legs and arms. For a month he was miserable with these ailments, but they receded without apparent reason. Periods of depression, too, sometimes set in. His studies for the psychology of his heroine, Salammbô, forced him to inquire into what was known of hysteria in this pre-Freudian age. While there was no coherent explanation of hysterical phenomena, many of them had been observed and described. He recognized the symptoms in himself and, anticipating Freud's discovery, was sure that men were as subject to the malady as women. Thus he was physically ill for two days from rage with himself over disappointment at what seemed his literary inadequacy.

In Paris, Flaubert led a debauched life when he ventured forth from his isolation. In January, 1860, walking the streets of the city one day, he fell to the pavement and injured his face. His mother and niece made him keep to his bed and, for some days, his condition was serious. Bouilhet, who was away, hurried to him as quickly as he could, while from Rouen Achille wrote to doctor friends in Paris for medical advice, for he was afraid that it was a return of what he termed Gustave's epileptiform symptoms— confirmation that he at least suspected the origin of the malady. He lamented the possibility after an apparent cure which had lasted so long. But his brother was turning night into day, and excesses in his work, too, contributed to keeping him in a state of perpetual hyperexcitation: he was doing all he could to bring on a relapse, Achille averred.[5] Fortunately, the symptoms disappeared, but the episode made more humiliating and infuriating a veiled reference to epilepsy in a journalist's attack on *Salammbô* two years later.[6]

Madame Flaubert and Caroline cared for Flaubert while he was bedridden. His mother, though in her sixties, was still vigorous and, except for a brief time in 1858, was almost without illness, as was Caroline. Flaubert continued tutoring his niece in history, and, as she grew into her teens, he invented pet names for her and lavished on her the same warm affection he had given her mother. At sixteen she was his fully formed pupil, and he could speak severely to her of her responsibilities in this situation. She must learn to be serious about her reading and finish a book once she took it up so as to be able to consider it as a whole. She must learn also to carry her ideas through to their conclusions and not be distraught and careless in her thinking as most women were. He told her fondly that he was addressing her as he would a man; this was, he said, the greatest tribute he could pay her.

The New Life: Paris and Friends

Ah! my apartment on the Boulevard du Temple! What
literary feasts it witnessed!

Letter to Madame Roger des Genettes, undated

Important as Croisset was to Flaubert, it could never totally satisfy him. If nothing else, the Rouen bourgeois was even more
unbearable to him than the Parisian. Nadar, the great photographer of the period, recollected meeting a son of one of the better
Rouen families shortly after the publication of *Madame Bovary*.
The young man was startled to find that Parisians liked the new
novel. His tone of superiority was unmistakable as he told the
photographer of his own distaste for it. Then he added that its
author was an unconventional sort of person, not at all acceptable
in Rouen. He attempted to be different and had been loath to join
the National Guard (the ultimate bourgeois symbol of the
period). Then suddenly one day, without confiding in anyone, he
packed his bags and went off on a long trip. The young gentleman explained that, in Rouen, this sort of behavior was frowned
upon.[7]

And so Flaubert would be driven from his retreat at Croisset
back to the Paris for which a part of him always longed. The
great capital was growing fast, expanding in the fifteen years between 1850 and 1865 from less than one million to almost two.
Flaubert's base here was his apartment on the Boulevard du Temple, on the fourth floor and facing south; his study looked out
over the boulevard.[8] His preference was for heavy, ugly furniture,
which he cherished because it was comfortable. This taste tended,
however, to shock his friends, as did his rejection of the contemporary mania for collecting knickknacks, which was as dominant
in Second Empire France as it was across the Channel in Victorian
England. Thick carpets were in every room, as well as heavy
cupboards of carved wood and large divans and armchairs covered
in red leather. A gilded statue of an Indian idol stood on the

mantelpiece overlooking the worktable, which was littered with the heavily rewritten pages of his manuscript.

Flaubert began receiving his friends on Sunday afternoons. These informal receptions delighted him and his guests; as long as he lived, he continued to hold them whenever he was in Paris. The group who came grew larger with the years and included on one Sunday or another a considerable range of the notables of the Second Empire. Writers predominated, of course; but there were painters, sculptors, political thinkers, men of the world, and even a few women, although the tone of the conversation was such that, aside from actresses, women normally did not attend.

Flaubert's Sundays came to be the great break in the boredom of the day for those fortunate enough to be invited. The conversation leaped from topic to topic, from the origins of paganism and the sources of religion to the latest volume of Hugo's poetry, from the Buddha to Goethe. It was a deep satisfaction to be able to think aloud in this warm and friendly atmosphere, recalling pages from the masters, or in imagination reviving lost civilizations. But always, and, as it were, by common agreement, the mysteries of the senses were the ultimate topic toward which everything converged. The unplumbed abysses of bizarre tastes, the monstrous and perverted, the fantasies and caprices and follies of carnal love were the centers around which discussion swirled and which analysis sought to dissect; the Marquis de Sade, a favorite of Flaubert's for twenty years, would be brought into the talk. One of the habitués of Flaubert's Sundays lamented that these conversations would so readily have furnished the materials of a book which could never be written, "The Natural History of Love."

Flaubert was not himself a frequent guest in any other salon, but he made something of an exception for Théophile Gautier.[9] Here, with Bouilhet and Du Camp, he still felt at home. For years he had called himself Gautier's disciple and enjoyed repeating his old friend's phrasings and paradoxes. Gautier, however, used to utter them in the softest of tones, while Flaubert, particularly after dinner, shouted them so loudly that all the windowpanes rattled.

Gautier shared Flaubert's delight in the reiterated joke and in pantomime. After a copious dinner washed down with floods of wine, Flaubert could be induced to arise and do a dance; his favorite he called the Idiot of the Salons. He would demand Gautier's dress coat, put it on, and raise his own collar; then, disarranging his hair and adopting an imbecile expression, he would become the incarnation of brute stupidity, a terrifying caricature as he moved about. Gautier, by now sufficiently excited to wish a role, would remove his coat. Puffing and sweating, his huge buttocks sticking out, he would then perform the Dance of the Creditor. The evening would end in singing.

Close as was Flaubert's relationship to Gautier, his most intimate friend continued to be Louis Bouilhet. They either saw each other constantly or wrote to one another. If anything, Bouilhet was becoming more like Flaubert, joining him now in black pessimism about mankind and finding the company of his fellow man often unbearable. Nothing seemed stupider to him than humanity, and he found his affections, like those of Flaubert and Saint Anthony, going out to the wisdom of cattle and the serenity of the vegetable world.[10]

Flaubert's warm friendship with Maxime Du Camp had suffered during the years of writing *Madame Bovary*, and the experience of publishing his novel in Du Camp's *Revue de Paris* had cooled their relationship further. But the two men continued to have many friends and interests in common, especially their memories. By the end of 1857, or early 1858, much of the old camaraderie had been reestablished. When Maxime left to fight in the War of Italian Independence in 1860, a temporary lapse in his letters was enough to frighten Gustave seriously and to make him realize how much his old companion meant to him. It continued thus for a decade or more.[11]

There were new friends, too. Ernest Feydeau, a nephew of the man who had read *Don Quixote* aloud to Gustave when he was a child, was an archeologist turned novelist; he and Flaubert became fast friends shortly after *Madame Bovary* was published. It was Feydeau who was to carry the banner of realism upon the publication of his somewhat pornographic novel, *Fanny*, in 1858. Its sale was an extraordinary commercial success. Flaubert had read it carefully and had offered close criticisms to Feydeau. *Fanny* marked a turning point in French literature; its main current adopted the brutal portrayals and insensitivity to shock which were to characterize all the later productions of the French schools of realism and naturalism. More readily understood and more easily copied than *Madame Bovary*, it became the norm and obscured the elements of artistic and philosophic idealism which underlay Flaubert's work.

Flaubert was not jealous of *Fanny*'s success but rather shared in its author's delight. Feydeau was in fact of approximately Flaubert's age, but he had considerably less stature as man and as artist. His friends soon noted with irritation that he was copying Flaubert's rages and violence in even more exaggerated form. And as Flaubert neared the end of writing *Salammbô*, he became sadly aware that Feydeau, his "nephew" as he liked to term him, was drifting away, despite all the sentimental bonds linking them. Fundamentally more normal in his perspectives, Feydeau really liked life, accepted it, and willingly joined in its frays. This participation made him a happier man, Flaubert recognized; but it may have had something to do with the slimmer base upon which he erected his more ephemeral fiction.

There were a host of further acquaintances, Dumas *père*, Sainte-Beuve, the historian Michelet, and many others. Jules Duplan, head of a commercial firm, was a devoted and faithful admirer. Constantly he scanned the papers for any mention of Flaubert's name to clip and send to him. Moreover, whenever Flaubert was in Paris, he could always count on Duplan's companionship when he needed relaxation and the warmth of friends. Duplan even helped gather some of Flaubert's materials. Baudelaire, whose poetry Flaubert admired and who returned the admiration in his respect for *Madame Bovary*, was by no means so close as Duplan; but when the poet madly thought he could be admitted to the French Academy, the very temple of respectability, Flaubert was one of those to whom he turned for support, although Flaubert would never consider applying in his own name.

In 1859, needing more information for *Salammbô*, Flaubert presented himself at the apartment of Jules and Edmond de Goncourt.[12] Historians of art, esthetes, novelists, refined sensualists, the brothers had already made their mark in all of these domains, or soon would. They were an extraordinary pair, cultivated to the point of decadence, neurotic, and self-absorbed. Their admiration went to delicacy of sentiment and perception, and hence they were ill equipped to appreciate the bluff and hearty barbarian whom they found Flaubert to be. Nevertheless the friendship among these men, though often strained, lasted through the life of Jules de Goncourt and ended only when Edmond was among those who came to Croisset to bury Flaubert in 1880.

Flaubert, on his first arrival at the brothers' apartment, which was filled with the sort of knickknacks he himself never collected, was like a child wandering about in open-eyed amazement. They found him young, although he was in fact older than either of them, and they remarked on his air of physical strength, his prominent eyes, puffy eyelids, full cheeks, and heavy moustache; his ruddy coloring was heightened by red splotches. They modeled the hero of their novel *Charles Demailly* on him when they published it in 1860. Demailly, they wrote, was powerful and enduring, capable of twenty-seven hours on horseback; but he was a man who seemed to have had something killed inside him in his youth, an illusion perhaps, or a dream; he was ravaged by ennui. The friendship blossomed fast. Gustave gave them a page of the manuscript of *Madame Bovary* and he told them about *November*, which he said sadly was too personal to be published. He endeared himself to them from the start by his obvious and warm admiration for their writing.

Only long years, a decade or more, could, however, bring the brothers fully to accept Flaubert. Their aristocratic natures were constantly ruffled by his provincial noisiness and peasant-like persistence. They recognized his frank openness and loyalty and wanted to like him, but his manias were not theirs. When he declined an invitation to dinner at their apartment because he needed his evenings for work, they found him inexplicable and boorish. The refusal somehow smacked of a pose, and they came to suspect his sincerity because they could not understand it. His mind seemed thick, clouded, heavy, like his corpulent body. He appeared to lack ideas because he could not phrase them with the finesse of the Parisian, bringing them out instead with heavy solemnity. Somehow his whole manner smacked of the village courthouse; his dress was a decade behind the times and he had the exuberance of a large puppy. He was a sort of Homer from Tahiti, violent of gesture and expression but with a bourgeois prudence of action. They wrote that he was a striking example of a man inferior to his books, a careful plodder at best. Yet something of his immense energy seems to have fascinated them, for they continued to see him at frequent intervals in the houses of mutual friends; and they came almost regularly to his Sunday afternoon receptions. To him they were peers with whom he could always talk of literature.

Women

"Woman is the despair of the just man."
Quotation from Proudhon which
Flaubert was fond of repeating

Aspiration toward love was the subject of the three stories Flaubert had been considering while he was still on his Near Eastern trip; *Madame Bovary* had embodied it ironically; *Salammbô* would illustrate it directly. This theme was Flaubert's obsessive literary concern from 1850 until 1862, when he finished his Carthaginian novel, and it had its living counterpart in his own relations with women. Now that he was famous and had his own apartment in the capital, new vistas and dreams and a whole new way of life with women opened before him. He explored many lascivious relationships; he played with warmly flirtatious but more distant friendships; and even austere kinships of the mind and spirit he now came to know and evaluate.

Freedom from Louise Colet had allowed Flaubert to give outlet once again to the lusty desires which had been the base of so much of his sexual life during his student days in Paris before the onset of his epilepsy. Since Bouilhet continued to write plays over these years, he and Flaubert had constant and easy access to the world of Parisian actresses: it richly satisfied each of them and, when they were apart, it formed an important topic in their letters to each other. But Flaubert's understanding of such affairs excluded anything more than refined sensual pleasure. When Bouilhet considered abandoning his mistress of the moment, Flaubert applauded him: a man should never maintain a relationship with one woman long enough for her to begin to intrude upon his spiritual life.[13] Flaubert enjoyed actresses and would, now and then, write to Bouilhet that a visit on the following afternoon would be indiscreet; but constant change was essential.

Flaubert's sexual life was never serious in these years; he always easily returned to his ascetic ways when he retreated to Croisset. Here, when his spirits began to flag after a long session of hard work, he would find himself looking forward avidly to the pleasure of the capital. But he never worked in Paris. Instead he found it refreshing there to plunge into debauchery; even thinking about the city in Croisset could bring new fervor to his writing.[14]

For the most part, all of this was completely normal and, in the Second Empire, was expected of any bachelor. The idea of marriage, however, appeared a hilarious farce to him and to Bouilhet, an attitude which blocked off a whole domain of emotional experience and therefore of maturity. Flaubert's morbid excitement over something monstrous in a hermaphrodite was another matter, that uninhibited ranging of the sexual imagination which led to experiences of the mind and emotions refused to more conventional lives. In him these normally prohibited domains were the vantage points for observing urges and desires which are no less real for being denied and which, transferred to a fictional character such as Salammbô, permit the normally restricted reader to understand them better in himself. To Flaubert, experiencing them was only one more part of living all of life for art. It would not have occurred to him to refrain, any more than it had in the public baths in Egypt.[15]

Women in Flaubert's life had to play all the surrogate roles of sister, daughter, mistress, and wife. Caroline was in most regards a deeply satisfactory daughter; but the other roles were less easy to fill. He denied that any woman could be wife or mistress to him,

COLOSSUS AT ASWAN

Maxime Du Camp was the first European to bring back significant photographs from Egypt, including this one of the now famous statue. The boatmen hired by Flaubert and Du Camp for their trip up the Nile spent days cleaning the sand away from the figure; one of them appears on the left forearm of the Colossus.

TOSTES AS EMMA BOVARY KNEW IT

The small hamlet of Flaubert's novel was a real place, a village where nothing ever broke the even monotony. Emma had to leave it or be stifled by ennui.

REMAINS OF THE SWAN POND ON THE CHATEAU DU HÉRON

This pond, which is now almost filled in, Flaubert visited as an adolescent and later used in *Madame Bovary*. The chateau, La Vaubyessard in the novel, lies to the left. Photograph by author.

FLAUBERT, CARTOON OF 1857

Parodying what many called Flaubert's cruel and relentless analysis of Emma Bovary, the caricature portrays Flaubert as the pitiless surgeon dissecting his heroine's heart.

LOUIS BOUILHET IN THE LAST DECADE OF HIS LIFE

All their friends noted how much Bouilhet and Flaubert resembled each other. Bouilhet's drooping mustache and balding head, his heavy eyes and corpulent body, were all like those of his friend.

FLAUBERT, BY NADAR

The large head, the Gallic chieftain's mustache, and the heavy lower
eyelids suggest Flaubert's truculent gentleness. Nadar was the greatest
photographer of his day in France. Archives photographiques, Paris.

MAXIME DU CAMP, BY NADAR

The portrait simultaneously reveals the successful dandy, the calculating schemer, and the alert sensualist. Archives photographiques, Paris.

SUZANNE LAGIER, BY NADAR

The actress' easy tolerance made her the only woman welcome at Flaubert's Sunday receptions.

and his sister was dead. Towering over all his needs, however, was the longing for someone to be to him the satisfying, fulfilling mother which Madame Flaubert had never been or, paradoxically, had been so fully that now all other women had to be what she still was. But he continued to believe that man is at his best in his aspirations and that the supreme aspiration is love. He spoke in indignation of a popular author of novels which women liked because all the women characters were portrayed favorably. It proved that the author really did not like women, for those who do, he insisted, write books which tell how women have made them suffer.[16]

There comes an age, Flaubert felt, when one becomes frightened: he had reached it. He feared a liaison or any other bond which might threaten his freedom; he both thirsted after happiness and was terrified by the idea. In theory it was all so easy; nothing really kept one from living life in a tolerable way. But everyone, he realized, sought clear-cut feelings, excessive and exclusive ones, whereas only the complex, the gray rather than the black and white, was really practicable. Before the age of romanticism men and women had been more reasonable. Flaubert was still as timid as he had been in adolescence and as capable of keeping a fading bouquet, but he was frightened of marriage. Moreover he knew, as his friend Michelet had written, that even in love possession led to a feeling of despair.

There is a tragic sense in which all of this meant that Flaubert had never really been able to be in love, that he was throughout these years longing for a loss of himself in love which he could never achieve. His friends knew it, despite all his exaggerated protestations about love and its role in his life. Zola, who later knew him well, remarked that women never really respected Flaubert. After a first attraction, they cooled in their excitement over him, sensing what was the fact, that his few liaisons had been burdens to him and that his close attachments were always with men. An evening spent smoking and talking with Bouilhet would always rank above one spent with a woman. He was, Zola was sure, too feminine in his reactions: women joked with him over this and treated him as a comrade or friend, not as a man, a lover, or a husband. Women would never fill more than a sensual or a literary role for him.[17] Moreover, they were essentially this to all his friends, Bouilhet, the Goncourt brothers, Zola, and the others whom he came to know intimately.

Perhaps even those close to Flaubert underestimated the full complexity of his hurt, his anguish, and his desires. Less talk and more real affection would have been more easily accepted. But one does not talk so cynically without pain: Flaubert noted with approbation the Greek jibe that the prostitute and the owner of the public baths are alike in washing the good and the evil in the same basin. He also made the observation that an adolescent loves other women because they resemble the First One (and he capitalized); later a man loves them for their differences.[18]

Despair over fulfilling his aspirations, which were perhaps beyond attainment, lay at the heart of the matter. Love, Flaubert said, had never brought him happiness, but rather upsets, tempests, and anguish. Woman seemed impossible and incomprehensible; for his security he had kept away from her, despite the attraction of the abysses he sensed in her. She seemed always to be seeking the Eternal Spouse. Ascetic or libidinous, she longed for the great love; to cure her pain she needed not an idea but a man, a lover. He knew this sounded cynical, but it was his observation that in woman idealism had always at its base a wild desire for the carnal.

Flaubert's insolent attacks but ill concealed his fears that man of his day was being weakened and feminized by the mother, the wife, the mistress. Woman took from him his virility and his powerful aspiration toward the heights of the imagination and the intelligence. Pure thought she denied and sought to deny to him. Shakespeare alone among authors seemed to have understood her, depicting her as always better or worse than man, hyperenthusiastic, but never reasonable. For man to seek his peace in her was to court disaster.

In addition to Caroline and his mother, a small number of women did impinge upon Flaubert's life. On occasion he would be reminded of Louise Colet. In the summer of 1856 she had transferred her attentions to the realistic novelist perhaps most in the public view, Jules Champfleury.[19] By ill luck a gamekeeper came upon them in the fields. His formal report almost led to the loss of the government pension she depended upon for her living expenses. With a becoming magnanimity Flaubert and Du Camp intervened and succeeded in limiting the penalty to a reduction in its amount. At intervals thereafter she and Gustave met occasionally, but Louise was never able to overcome her erstwhile lover's fear of a resumption; not unnaturally her pride was hurt. Somehow she got wind of a visit which Gautier and another friend paid to Flaubert in Croisset; his letter of invitation noted that he had managed to acquire the complete works of the Marquis de Sade and that volumes of it would be on the night tables of his guests. Louise, hoping to hurt Gustave, spread the news among her friends, as Bouilhet informed him. In 1859 she sent Champfleury to him, but Bouilhet warned that, whatever the aim of the visit, Gustave should be on his guard: there could be no honest motive behind it.[20]

Later that year Louise sought her revenge by publishing the story of her relationship with him in a book entitled *Lui*. It was a terrible, widely ranging attack on him; on Alfred de Musset, with whom she had had an affair while her liaison with Flaubert was continuing; on George Sand, who had been Musset's mistress; on Sainte-Beuve, Mérimée, Alfred de Vigny, and several lesser men with whom she had had relations. Flaubert appears as cold, cruel, and monstrous; his long, slow labors in writing *Madame Bovary* she depicted as the painstaking efforts of a pedant to redo Balzac. She wrote brazenly of the physical frustrations his refusals to be with her had caused. Sainte-Beuve and Flaubert she portrayed in terms intended to destroy their relationship, and she put into Musset's mouth vicious condemnations of George Sand and Flaubert. She also accused Gustave of seeking public glory underneath his protestations of a concern for art alone.

Lui is a vicious book. Flaubert now sought to persuade his friends that he was not annoyed, that it was really very funny and had immensely amused him. But he added maliciously that *Le Figaro*—ever alert to scandal during this period—would be delighted to pay him any sum for the right to publish the letters he had in his files from her. He refused, however, on principle, to reply to anything she published. It was not, he said, her novel but rather the long liaison which irritated him. The book was no more than the latest scratch, coupled of course with all the jibes his friends and acquaintances thought it proper to aim at him. Du Camp, who saw her a year later in Naples, reported that the level to which she had sunk—reciting poetry to make a living—was full retribution for any harm Flaubert might feel she had done him: she was utterly ridiculous. And in 1861, over a new encounter, Bouilhet could comment that she belonged to the race of vampires, of those who never die.[21]

With Elisa Schlésinger it was different. She and Maurice had long since gone to Germany when Maurice wrote in September, 1856, to invite Flaubert to the wedding of their daughter, Marie, whom he had known as a child of four months on the beach at Trouville, when he first met and fell in love with Elisa.

Unfortunately he was too short of money to afford the trip. But he imagined the quantities of alcohol he would have drunk and the dreams of his youth which would have gone through his mind. The day he received the letter he could think of nothing else. On the first of October Elisa herself wrote to press the invitation; he replied, declining but recalling the days at Trouville and dinners at their house in Paris. As he was writing, the first installment of *Madame Bovary* appeared in the *Revue de Paris*.

Next March it was to Maurice that Flaubert wrote, telling him he was forever linked to the best moments of Gustave's youth. Others, he said, found the present passed too rapidly; for his own part it was rather the past which seemed to be devouring him. Two years later Elisa wrote again, and Flaubert replied, recounting what he had been doing since he had last written. Over the winter of 1859 she was again in his mind as he was sorting out his thoughts on women. To a friend he wrote of how he had loved her in his youth, boundlessly, profoundly, and silently, without ever being loved in return. He knew how one dreamed of kidnapping the woman one loved or going with her to Italy or of somehow winning glory and attracting her attention. He also remembered the tortures of the body, the spasms over a momentary glimpse, the sudden paling when she looked at you. Each of us, he wrote, has in his heart a royal chamber. His he had walled up; but he had not destroyed it.[22]

Shortly, in early 1860, Elisa was in Mantes, close to Paris and where Flaubert and Louise had so often met. She began coming here almost yearly, whenever she could. Bouilhet, who also lived here, reported now and again on her presence, always speaking respectfully to her as "Madame Maurice" rather than using the casual tone he and Flaubert allowed themselves for more trivial acquaintances like Ludovica or "Mother Colet." But the long years of strain as Maurice's wife were beginning to take their toll. In March of 1862 Madame Flaubert met Elisa's son briefly and learned from him that she was suffering from a serious nervous affliction. Flaubert wrote at once to Maurice to ask for details. On March 15 she entered a German sanatorium, where she remained for seventeen months. It was some time before Flaubert learned of it. She told her doctor that for years she had been living an impossible marriage and could no longer stand the sorrow and anguish of her family life and the sacrifice of herself. Deeply impressed, he added a note in her dossier on the nobility of her character.

The following December Maurice wrote that she was still ill in the sanatorium. It had been ten months since he had been able to see her. Any emotional strain was beyond her powers: she could not even write to him. Maurice, now a broken and impoverished man, begged Flaubert to send candy so that the grandchildren might have a present on Christmas Day.[23]

The Collier family, on the other hand, almost drifted out of Flaubert's ken. Harriet he seems not even to have heard of during these years. Gertrude he thought of at intervals; he regretted not hearing from her. Once she did write to his mother but then only to ask her help in locating a French maid. At least the contact was not lost.

The actress Beatrice Person, whom Flaubert had come to know before he published *Madame Bovary*, he continued to see. More important in his life, however, was Suzanne Lagier.[24] She belonged to the fringes of a strange development in the Second Empire, the demimonde. It was a kind of social world in the shadows, populated by women who were the official mistresses of one or another of the wealthy men of the period or who, alternatively, through some transgression in their past, were no longer received in the world of society. The women had their own salons and received the most distinguished men of the period. Auguste Sabatier, whom Gautier had nicknamed *la Présidente* and who was a banker's mistress, had such a salon and played an important role in Baudelaire's life. Flaubert sometimes attended her Sunday evening dinners or wrote her occasional salacious letters.

More important to Flaubert from this world was Jeanne Detourbey or, as she preferred to write it, de Tourbey. He met her in the latter part of 1857, when she was a startling beauty of twenty. She excited him enormously, but she seems never to have been more than gently amused at his advances. By 1858 everyone of importance came to her salon, and he was only one of many men writing her that she was driving them mad. She seems never to have gone further than telling Bouilhet to send Flaubert two kisses . . . by mail.[25] But she added excitement and wild dreams to his life while leaving him feeling completely safe.

With most of these women Flaubert had no more than a quick afternoon or evening; with some, such as Jeanne de Tourbey, idle fantasies were all that he could have. But on at least one occasion in the late winter and spring of 1860 Flaubert had a full-fledged affair, wildly vigorous in its activity but not really engaging his spirit. He wrote in detail of his prowess to Bouilhet and received in reply a mock admonition to guard his health. How could he have expended so much virility? But Bouilhet closed more seriously by congratulating his old friend: he would find that his work did not suffer for it. Shortly Flaubert wrote to report he was being more moderate, but he underlined the further statement that he thought it had all been good for his health. In May he was still making secret visits to Paris, but then it seemed all to quiet down and disappear into the past. This had been a complex time for Flaubert: Elisa was in Mantes; Achille's daughter was being married; and he was reflecting on his celibacy. But his decision to continue his life as it was remained unchanged.[26]

With a number of women of his own age or older his relations were entirely spiritual and sentimental. Amélie Bosquet, a Rouen teacher, journalist, and novelist, had given lessons to his niece Caroline. Their relationship began in this fashion late in 1859. She was a year or so older than he and, although their conversations often went on for hours and his letters to her adopted a slightly gallant tone, theirs was a friendship between writers, heady but in no way physical. It lasted some ten years until she wrote a clumsy review of his second *Sentimental Education*.[27] More enduring was his friendship with Madame Roger des Genettes, also a few years older than he, whom he had first come to know through Louise Colet: she read Bouilhet's verses in the Muse's salon. It was a close and deeply meaningful relationship. He taught her to read carefully and to value the life of the mind and of art; she provided a solid warmth of response which he treasured over the decades.[28]

The publication of *Madame Bovary* brought Flaubert another moving friendship with a considerably older lady, Mademoiselle Leroyer de Chantepie, who was born in 1800.[29] She had been very devout but was now tortured by religious doubts. She wrote to Flaubert to congratulate him on *Madame Bovary*. He replied and there began an extraordinary correspondence—they never met—in which she wrote of her anguish and doubt over the dogma, doctrines, and rites of Catholicism, and he urged her to adopt a position above the forms and petty, human additions to religion. She should seek to lose herself in study and in the writing of a long and serious work; but he was counseling her to accept his own solution and not one she could readily make hers. His gentleness with her reiterated complaints over the pain of her doubts comforted the elderly spinster and gave to Flaubert the strange role of director of conscience. A real intimacy developed, and a real tenderness on both sides.

The most meaningful of all Flaubert's relations with older women, that with George Sand, began in 1859 but developed fully only later, when he had finished *Salammbô*. For some time after he came to know her, he was put off by what he feared in her more sentimental literary doctrines. Only with the years did her greatness of personality and warm charm overcome his scruples and lead him to become her devoted admirer.

A relationship with one other woman—no doubt the most important of all—is so shrouded in veils of silence and half-glimpsed fact as to be hard to elucidate. She was Juliet Herbert, an English governess.[30] Her story cannot be fully pieced together yet; but it was surely the most tender and the longest and deepest of his many relations with women. English governesses had followed one another in the Flaubert household to care for little Caroline.

Whoever the governess was in the spring of 1855—and she may have been Juliet Herbert—she much excited Flaubert, as he reported in several licentious letters to Bouilhet. By the following year, 1856, he was working steadily on English with this governess and was having to restrain himself from grabbing her on staircases.[31]

In 1857, however, it seems almost certain that this governess left the service of the Flauberts and was replaced. Bouilhet wrote that it was rather too bad, as she had gotten on well with Madame Flaubert. At any rate it was in this year that Flaubert and Caroline's governess, Juliet Herbert, collaborated in translating Byron's "Prisoner of Chillon" into French. She had definitely come into his life. Shortly, however, Flaubert moved into Paris for his winter season. The following year, in August, she is at least mentioned in excited terms in a letter from Flaubert to Feydeau: he must come to Croisset before the first of September if he wishes to see her, for she leaves for England on her vacation on that date.[32]

Probably by the summer of 1859 Juliet had become Flaubert's mistress. In his letters of this period Bouilhet always asks respectfully to be remembered to "Miss Juliet." But Flaubert was leading so vigorous a sex life that he was presuming beyond his virility; and he was in Croisset, where she would have been the only readily available partner. For the next several years her name flits in and out of Bouilhet's letters, oddly enough only in the middle of the summers. Was Caroline, now fourteen or so, no longer in need of a governess, and did Juliet only come over from England for short intervals to be with Gustave? The documents do not tell, and Flaubert's niece in publishing Flaubert's letters and private papers always suppressed Juliet's name from them, perhaps because she or close members of her family were still alive.

To make it more mysterious, all mention of Juliet seems to disappear for several years after 1862; but when her name recurs in 1865, hers is already a close, profound, and long-enduring relationship with Flaubert. The surest index to what she was like is, no doubt, that Bouilhet calls her by the French term "gracieuse" which includes also the English connotations of "graceful."

The Writer

> . . . for me a book is a special way of living.
>> Comment repeated in a number of Flaubert's
>> letters around 1859

More than five years went into the composition of *Salammbô*. Sometimes writing seemed nearly impossible and Flaubert's work was slowed almost to a halt; at such moments his mood could be terrible. More often, he worked slowly because he loved what he was doing. A word he needed or an idea which flickered across his mind would send him off on hours or days of research, wanderings, and infinite reveries which his monastic way of life rendered easier. In Croisset he allowed nothing to disturb him. He would rise at midday and go to bed around three or four in the morning, falling asleep only about five. He hardly knew the color of the daytime sky.

In Paris, as much as possible it was the same; his only willingly accepted distraction was his own salon, and Sunday evening at Madame Sabatier's circle. While often much of the afternoon would pass idly, by early evening real excitement would mount and he would begin to cover the sheets with writing. For he still needed, as with *Madame Bovary*, to see his thoughts in his own hand on a page before they became real enough to be evaluated. There was at least one occasion when he was so caught up in this work that he did not leave his table for thirty-eight hours at a stretch and at the end was so exhausted he could no longer muster the strength to raise his carafe and pour himself a glass of water.[33] As the novel drew toward its close, he even curtailed his time in Paris so as to hurry its completion.

Writing was still an escape, and writing of antiquity was a particularly effective way to slough off the contamination of the modern world. He looked upon it as others felt about playing the violin: its function was to divert him, and he confessed he sometimes wrote out whole long passages having no real place in his novel and which he would later suppress. A deplorable way to write, he thought, but it was the path he had to follow.

Sometimes excesses of work left Flaubert lethargic and over-come for at least brief periods. The Goncourt brothers, when they came to know him, had grave doubts about his wisdom in this. And perhaps *Salammbô* itself, at best heavy to read, echoes the life of its creator. But in general, as before, work and only work could excite him, and solitude was as intoxicating to him as alcohol. He would laugh happily to himself, walk about his study, and shout aloud the lines he had written, in part to hear their effect, in part from sheer animal good spirits. Night was particu-larly precious for this; when he was at Croisset, he would start the evening session with a long dip in the Seine. Then, all shutters closed, he would settle deliciously into the evening's writing.

While *Salammbô* was of course his principal occupation dur-ing these years, Flaubert occasionally did have to give his atten-tion to *Madame Bovary* again. Late in 1857, Henry Monnier, the novelist, actor, and artist, wanted to dramatize the novel; his own creation, Monsieur Joseph Prudhomme, a character not unlike Homais, fitted him for the task. Flaubert, however, distrusted such shifts from one artistic genre to another; he refused, as he did again the following year with another playwright, although he realized that he might well be losing thirty thousand francs thereby. In point of fact the novel was not dramatized until 1906, when it was put on at Rouen in an adaptation by Busnach, who had collaborated with Emile Zola in staging some of his novels: it was a failure. Several movie versions have appeared, one under the direction of Pierre Renoir with music by Milhaud, but never in a form to satisfy any of the critics. In 1936, Gaston Baty tried to stage it again, but thus far Flaubert's refusal to sanction such a transfer has always proved right.

In 1861, as the long task of writing *Salammbô* was drawing to an end, Lévy decided to put out a new edition of *Madame Bovary;* his original contract with Flaubert was coming to its close and he was anxious to renew it. This gave Flaubert a chance to review his novel and to see in what ways, if any, he would now wish to rewrite it. Wisely, he decided against any but minor changes, realizing the novel was so tightly integrated that it could hardly be tampered with. In fact Bouilhet urged him, at every turn, to leave it completely alone: any change, however minor, was sure to unhinge nearby sentences as well.[34] With a scrupulous weighing of each word, however, Flaubert did discover a few, isolated alterations he wished to make.

Only two criteria seemed to Bouilhet adequate to force a change. One was strict accuracy of metaphor. Of the widow, Charles's first wife, Flaubert had written, querying, "Could she, by her physical contact, efface the image of Emma in Charles's heart?" Now the two men agreed that the phrase must be reworked, for a physical contact could not efface an ideal or unreal image. The only other criterion was the threat of the police. Bouilhet concurred with Flaubert in considering dangerous the statement that Emma was "finding all the platitudes of marriage in this adultery." It implied that in another liaison she might have been happier. They agreed on changing it to the generalized and hence innocuous "in adultery." There were other, minor alterations, but they occupied in all only a few brief weeks at the end of 1861. Essentially, he was writing *Salammbô* during all these years.

17

Salammbô (1862)

An Anti-Bovary

> I'm asking an intelligent man to shut himself away for four
> hours with my book; and I want to give him a sort of orgy
> with historical hashish.
>
> Observation of Flaubert's reported by the
> Goncourt brothers, January 12, 1860

FLAUBERT'S groans and howls over the fetid, bourgeois subject of
Madame Bovary had not been feigned. Much of it had disgusted
him: he complained that he would rather depict crocodiles; the
subject was not in his nature; it was all foreign to him, at best a
useful apprenticeship.

His next book would be one in which he could use his natural
voice, with grandiose turns of phrase, rich and full periods flowing
easily from the pen, and a luxuriant profusion of suggestive metaphors abounding on every page. No reader of it should ever be
able to object that it was only more vulgar realism. *Salammbô* was
in part a sad choice, he pointed out, made in desperation over his
own world, a retreat from it not unlike Saint Anthony's to a
Thebaid, but in time rather than in space.

With Flaubert a new subject tended to begin as a color.[1] *Madame Bovary* had started as a gray tone; *Salammbô* was a deep
violet. Carthage herself, where the action of the novel takes place,
had long attracted him. When he was still only seventeen, he had
written that her ancient civilization seemed something monstrous
and ferocious, filled with horrors and overbearing cynicism.[2]
Quite suddenly after the successful conclusion of the trial of *Madame Bovary*, he selected this civilization as the focus for his
dreams of sumptuous living and dying in the early days of Roman
power. The trial court heard arguments on *Madame Bovary* on

January 29, 1857; on February 7, it acquitted him. Ten days later, on February 17, he had already begun making inquiries about what was known of the ancient Phoenician city, Rome's most dangerous rival in the third century B.C.[3]

Carthage some 240 years before Christ was in the midst of a lull in her long struggle with Rome. Specifically, Flaubert picked the moment when, fearing that they were never going to be paid for their services, her large army of barbarian mercenaries revolted against her. At first, and for long months, he called his new work "Carthage" and thought of it as her story.[4]

The plot and characters must almost have sketched themselves. There would have to be a leader of the barbarians; he would be the hero. That would suggest the woman in the story be Carthaginian for contrast. After a few hesitations, Flaubert selected Salammbô, daughter of the Carthaginian leader, Hamilcar Barca. A second barbarian and a Greek would serve as counselors to his hero. It remained only to integrate the relationship of his hero and heroine into the main events, which were necessarily military. At some point very early in the development of the story line, and perhaps from the start, he must have seen that this ancient and presumably uninhibited setting would allow that realization of complete love, which he had deemed impossible for Emma Bovary and indeed for anyone in the bourgeois world of the Second Empire. He therefore made his heroine almost a priestess of Tanit, the moon goddess, an incarnation of the female principle. Her lover, the barbarian leader Mâtho, became the incarnation of Moloch, the sun god or male principle. When Salammbô gave herself to Mâtho, it was the situation Flaubert had imagined for Anubis. He now had his theme. It remained only to work out the details of the story, a matter he always deemed of secondary importance.

Flaubert settled into a happy flurry of activity. From one friend he sought photographs of Tunis, the modern city which corresponds most nearly to ancient Carthage; from another, factual documentation; from still others, suggestions of what to read concerning life in the days of Hamilcar Barca. No detail was too small, no research too arduous: he even read a quarto volume of four hundred pages on the pyramidal cypress because one stood in the courtyard of a temple at Carthage. He was deeply into that joy of creation which comes—as Camus, too, has noted—during the initial phases of a new work. But, as Camus points out also, there always remains the task of carrying it out, which is a long torture.[5]

By the end of May, Flaubert had read and annotated fifty-three volumes. He was as fully informed as he could be on military matters. He was reasonably sure that he could produce new esthetic effects from the hubbub of this ancient world. But he could not yet really sense what the landscape looked like; and the religious feeling of the Carthaginians, upon which so much of the psychology of his book depended, was still entirely vague for him.

To make it worse, Bouilhet was alarmed over the subject, fearing the police would scrutinize the book carefully when it came out because of *Madame Bovary*.[6] He knew Flaubert had chosen Carthage because he wanted to describe orgies, and this richly sensual Phoenician culture promised to provide the opportunities. Flaubert wrote that the book was to open with the drunken, brawling Feast of the Mercenaries; later there were to be mystical prostitutions by the priestesses, and Moloch was to be appeased by the sacrifice of living children. It was, deliberately, a scabrous subject. As a further worry, the new novel was so similar to *Saint Anthony* that Flaubert feared *Salammbô* might hinder the later publication of his work on the desert saint. And that one he cared about far more.

To breathe life into these precise, accurate data seemed impossible. Bouilhet urged him to cease the unending search for more archeological details, begin writing, and stop worrying. In an ancient subject like this a certain haze was essential; blurred edges were preferable to sharp ones. He should handle it suggestively, not exhaustively. But the counsel fell on deaf ears: by July, Flaubert had read a hundred volumes and was still lost in the emptiness of his subject. His attitude was becoming pathological; he was afraid and he knew it. He could not make his model come clear before his eyes, and without this clarity he was helpless. His art, for which he lived, was becoming anguish. By August he was tired, withered almost, with the fruitless efforts he was making. He determined to read just three more volumes, which he deemed indispensable, and then to begin.

Finally on September 1, 1857, he was, as he put it, resigned. By the end of the month he had fifteen pages and he did not like them. The Feast was beginning to take shape; but when Salammbô finally appeared, she was, he said, so covered with precious stones that no one would be able to make her out under them. In October, shifting his point of view radically, he changed the title of the novel to "Salammbô, A Carthaginian Novel." But was it to be about Salammbô or about Carthage? He would have to choose, for there was not room in one novel for both an adequate portrayal of an exotic civilization and an analysis of love as fulfilled aspiration. His neuralgic pains recurred, and he worried about his health.

In some fashion, Carthage had to come to life for Flaubert. What better means than a trip to Tunisia to see the land for himself? In January of 1858 he decided to leave for North Africa the following April. The winter season in Paris was proving miserable! Most of his time was taken up by importunities of friends. He rejoiced in the thought of returning to the land of the date palm, where he would again ride on a camel and sleep under a tent. He planned a quick trip of only two months, enough, however, to restore him. Madame Flaubert was, as usual, upset; she soon fell ill, perhaps with pleurisy. Bouilhet was convinced her ailment was only chagrin over the forthcoming journey, and Flaubert persisted in his plans.[7]

He left Paris on April 12 for a trip which was to last some eight weeks.[8] He had a beautiful night for his departure. As he sat in the train bound for the Mediterranean, he smoked endlessly; memories of earlier trips flooded back. He was already melancholy anticipating his return to Marseilles. There he had to wait two days for the ship to North Africa. Eighteen years had passed since his meeting with Eulalie Foucaud. His life seemed to keep going back in the same round over and over. After a long search he found the Hôtel de la Darse, where she had lived. The salon had become a store; her room upstairs served now as a barber shop. He went twice to be shaved and noticed the wallpaper had not changed.

Leaving Marseilles, Flaubert crossed first to Algeria. He landed near Constantine and journeyed there at once; thereafter he made several trips into the surrounding countryside. Then he went by ship, via Bône, to Tunis, near which, all were agreed, was the site of ancient Carthage. A number of excursions from Tunis let him see the sites of Utica and the other cities and landscapes he had been vainly trying to picture for himself. At many points he stopped to record the view; he even made sketches of the configuration of the mountains. Finally he went back overland through the plains and mountains to Constantine and the ship back to France.

Although Flaubert had no companions with him on his Tunisian trip, he was proud that he did not feel lonely. He made friends easily: in one place the director of the post office had read *Madame Bovary;* in another he met a doctor who was a friend of friends. Also, his mind was filled with thoughts of Jeanne de Tourbey, with whom he was especially infatuated at the moment; he was writing her love letters, albeit very respectful ones.

He lived most chastely, however, surprising even himself. But at least one woman whom he met, "the spendid Miss Nelly Rosembourg," as he termed her, excited him. In addition, he saw male dancers, quite inferior to those of Egypt, and he had one evening with dancing girls.[9]

Tunisia and Algeria delighted him and seemed wholly familiar. A cool rose garden with a Roman mosaic brought peace to his spirit. The impoverished peasants and their huts, on the other hand, suggested the curse of the Lord. He was constantly reminded of his previous trip through the Eastern Mediterranean. North Africa, he discovered, was a world he already knew! All across the Southern Mediterranean a single culture had always dominated. What he had experienced in Egypt his mercenaries had known two thousand years before him in Tunisia. The trees, the wells, the terrain, the smells were all familiar: the setting of his book began to come to life. The basic religious spirit, too, persisted everywhere: fanatics were the same whether they were Catholics upholding Lent, Moslems observing the Ramadan, or Carthaginians offering sacrifices to Moloch. Many ancient customs persisted. He saw Arab children whose feet had been scorched to toughen them, as Herodotus had described; the natives feared the vampire as in the days of Saint Anthony; and popular humor was

JEANNE DE TOURBEY

The provocative but reserved mistress of a wealthy banker, she long
obsessed Flaubert.

PRINCESS MATHILDE, BY GIRAUD

Patroness of arts and letters and cousin of the Emperor, the Princess opened the world of the imperial court to Flaubert. She readily pardoned his noisy misbehavior at her weekly parties and applauded the best in his writing.

GEORGE SAND, BY NADAR

In her later years Madame Sand was happy to be known as "The Grandmother of Nohant." Flaubert once called her "a great man" and was proud to have her call him her troubadour. For her part she understood how much he needed her indulgence and motherly affection. Archives photographiques, Paris.

MAXIME DU CAMP, CARICATURE BY GIRAUD

Du Camp in the 1860's was still the satiric, urbane dandy chasing success.

FLAUBERT, CARICATURE BY GIRAUD

The heavy eyelids and self-satisfied air exemplify what the Goncourt brothers disliked in their friend. The caricature was almost a calumny, but accurate, they concluded.

TURGENEV, BY NADAR

The amiable Russian, who spent most of his time in Paris, shared with Flaubert a love of literature and a lack of Parisian polish. He was one of two or three people with whom Flaubert could talk easily. Archives photographiques, Paris.

SAINTE-BEUVE, CARICATURE BY GIRAUD

The reigning, official critic, while hostile to *Salammbô*, admired Flaubert's talent and was a friend, though not an intimate one.

THE PAVILION IN THE GARDEN AT CROISSET

This small building served as Louis Bouilhet's workroom during his visits to Flaubert. Today it is all that remains of Flaubert's property, housing a small collection of his personal possessions. Photograph by author.

as course and vulgar as in the days of Plautus. The flowers and the jackals, the people and the look of the sea were now in his eye, ready to be recaptured when he needed them. Many of his notes filtered into his novel; their general tone dominates all of it.

On June 6, 1858, he was back in Paris and hurrying to call on the friends he had not seen for eight weeks. Feydeau, Gautier, Duplan, Du Camp, Sainte-Beuve and others of his men friends he saw in a quick few days, in which he reserved the time to call on Jeanne de Tourbey each evening and to have a night with the actress Beatrix Person. On the ninth he returned to Croisset to sleep for most of three days and to prepare the last of his notes. As a conclusion he wrote an invocation to all the forces of nature which he had been drawing into himself for eight weeks and which he hoped might now be infused into his book. He called unto himself a feeling for plastic form and the spirit of the resurrection of the past. Through the beautiful he must create the living and the true, despite all odds. He closed by begging mercy of the Lord of souls and asked that he might be given strength—and hope. It was midnight when he penned the last word. He had needed the trip, for he had been stifled. At last he could breathe again.

The Writing of *Salammbô*

> I'm afraid my eyes were bigger than my stomach! *Reality* is almost impossible in a subject like this.
>
> Letter to the Goncourt brothers, July 3, 1860

Flaubert happily returned to *Salammbô* once he was reestablished in Croisset in June, 1858. He believed two years would suffice to complete the book. As with *Madame Bovary*, however, he proved far too sanguine, and *Salammbô* was not finished until the spring of 1862.

Slow or rapid in its writing, good or bad, the novel demanded to be written. Not infrequently Flaubert was disturbed over the course it was taking. But, as he phrased it, his struggles would not have been in vain if he could set a few noble imaginations to dreaming. The work would be a failure if the system he was pursuing were false; but one must do what seemed right. And in any case through his writing he was having an orgy with antiquity, as others did through wine. It was, after all, one's aspirations which counted.

Flaubert was right to be very worried. To write the story of the revolt and the endless battles of the Carthaginian mercenaries and then add a symbolic love story involved major hazards. He risked, as he knew, either a false and inflated poetry or banality. His characters seemed only manikins, and so much of his setting was unfamiliar that he had constantly to explain to his readers what was happening. He had acquired a new desk for the writing of *Salammbô*, or perhaps a little earlier when he had first to furnish his apartment on the Boulevard du Temple. More than ink fell on its mahogany top, a friend wrote: she had seen his tears there, too.[10]

These problems were not obvious in June, 1858, as Flaubert returned to writing. Bouilhet joined him almost at once in Croisset, and the two began to rework the structure of the novel. The description of Carthage, which had so worried him, Flaubert removed from the opening pages and put off to a later chapter. As he no longer feared the prudish bourgeois whom he knew would be shocked by the passages, he happily envisaged describing strange and hideous customs and foods. In a moment of excitement, he insisted he was writing of a bordello of little boys. The Goncourt brothers, taking him too seriously, were revolted and nauseated.

Four years later, he neared the end. He was by now surfeited but drove himself day after day to complete it. After a final all-night session he wrote the last line at seven in the morning of April 20, 1862. He could revise it at his leisure, for Victor Hugo's new novel, *Les Misérables*, was attracting the attention of all French readers; when attention had wandered from that work, it would be summer and a poor time to publish.

He could wait.

THE STORY

You are learned, with that great learning of the poet and the philosopher. You have brought a vanished world back to life and you have mingled a poignant drama with that resurrection. Whenever I meet in a writer the two feelings, for the real, which shows life, and for the ideal, which displays the soul, I am moved, I am happy, and I applaud.

Letter to Flaubert from Victor Hugo on reading *Salammbô*

Flaubert begins his novel in the middle of things: "It was in Megara, a suburb of Carthage, in the gardens of Hamilcar." The tone is quiet, impersonal, and external.

The story plunges at once into the Feast of the Mercenaries: it was soon the exotic orgy, full of the strange garments, dishes, and customs that Flaubert had promised himself. Cleverly he introduced the unfamiliar names of things and peoples in contexts which make their general import clear: the reader begins to enjoy his historical hashish.

In the absence of their general, Hamilcar Barca, the mercenaries became drunk, got out of hand, and freed Barca's slaves, among them the Greek, Spendius. The orgy was becoming dangerous when Hamilcar's daughter Salammbô descended from the palace into the garden. Her presence had a calming effect. The hero of the novel, Mâtho, and Narr'Havas, two barbarian chieftains, were particularly intoxicated by her enigmatic, distant beauty. They fought but became separated; when the struggle was over, Salammbô had disappeared. Seeking her, Mâtho ascended the palace steps to the terrace at the top, followed by Spendius, who rightly foresaw that Mâtho would become the leader of the mercenaries. As dawn came, the two men looked out over the city and, in one of the most successful passages in the book, Flaubert describes the city. Gazing toward the open country beyond the gates, Mâtho and Spendius saw Salammbô's carriage disappearing toward the horizon. A white veil trailed behind it, another of numerous such veils in Flaubert's works, most notably Emma's, which Léon kept thinking he saw.

Two days later Mâtho had indeed become the leader of the mercenaries and adopted the wily and unscrupulous Spendius as his counselor. Both Mâtho and Salammbô found themselves in the grip of a paralyzing, melancholy torpor. Shortly, the barbarians, realizing that Carthage had no intention of paying them, laid siege to the helpless city as well as to Utica and Hippo, her nearby allies.

The Carthaginians believed their fate depended upon the *zaïmph*, the veil of the moon goddess, Tanit. Spendius and Mâtho slipped into the city by night to steal it. Once in possession of it, they went to Hamilcar's palace and again ascended the steps to Salammbô's room, "with the strange ease which one experiences in dreams." Henry in the first *Sentimental Education* knew the same feeling, and later heroes and heroines of Flaubert would, too.[11] The sleeping virgin (Flaubert lays especially great emphasis on her virginity in these pages) wakened and cried out. Protected by the Carthaginians' awe of the veil, the two barbarians escaped from the city unharmed.

Narr'Havas, Mâtho's rival for Salammbô, now joined Mâtho because he possessed the zaïmph. The whole area around Carthage then broke into revolt and routed a Carthaginian army in a pitched battle for Utica, which Flaubert describes with speed and clarity. Salammbô, however, fades from the reader's recollection and interest.

The Battle of Utica is not the only event diverting the reader's attention at this point, for Hamilcar Barca now returns from abroad. For the next forty pages Flaubert describes Hamilcar's wealth, character, family, and philosophy before the Carthaginian leader finally makes a sally to attack the barbarians. They are interesting pages, but they interrupt the flow of the narrative. Here the reader meets Hamilcar's little son, Hannibal, whose childish exploits foretell not only his own later greatness but also the childhood of one of Flaubert's last heroes, Saint Julian the Hospitaller, like Hannibal an early prodigy at hunting. There is also a grandiose scene in the epic tradition when Hamilcar meets at night with the elders of Carthage and refuses the command of the army. Only then does Flaubert return to his narrative.

Finally Hamilcar agreed to lead the Carthaginian forces in

order to gain revenge for the misdeeds of the barbarians at their feast in his palace gardens and also for whatever it was—he had heard only rumors—that happened between his daughter and Mâtho in her room the night the barbarian stole the veil.

By a clever strategem Hamilcar was able to lead his army out of Carthage and relieve the siege of Utica. The story now follows the varying fortunes of the two armies, Mâtho's and Hamilcar's, as their forces swept over the Carthaginian countryside; Salammbô disappears, except as a memory in Mâtho's mind. Eventually, for all his cleverness, Hamilcar was penned into a valley ringed by the mercenaries on the surrounding hills.

At one point during the composition of the story Flaubert was going to call it "The Mercenaries." For all these pages this title would have been appropriate. But at last the reader returns to Carthage, to learn that her citizens, despairing of Hamilcar, were switching their allegiance from Tanit to Moloch, from the female principle to the male one of violence. At the same time they were turning against Salammbô because she was Hamilcar's daughter and because she was devoted to the goddess. She now dominates the scene for one of the best chapters of the book.

The high priest of Tanit, Schahabarim, feared that Moloch, and not his goddess, must be dominant; moreover, Salammbô's python, the mystic symbol of her ancestors and of her worship, seemed deathly sick. The eunuch priest, beset by longings and sadistic urges he did not understand, decided to send Salammbô to Mâtho's tent at the mercenaries' camp. Perhaps—Flaubert doubtless had in mind Judith with Holofernes—she would be able to recover the veil from her lover and restore the fortunes of Carthage. In covert language he explained what she must do and arranged to have her conducted to the tent. There she gave herself to the barbarian leader. After he fell asleep, she fled with the zaïmph to her besieged father. At the same moment Narr'Havas deserted Mâtho and joined Hamilcar, who affianced him to his daughter. Thus aided, Hamilcar routed the barbarians.

The story appears to have moved to its climax, and the reader expects to advance rapidly to the end. Unfortunately the historical fact is that much of the mercenary army made good its escape. The reader suspects what lies ahead and joins Hamilcar in lamenting that had he had fresh troops, he could have ended the war in a day. A vast number of pages might have been spared, but Flaubert had more he wished to display of the ferocity of Carthage. Spendius cut the aqueduct upon which the city depended for water. To induce Moloch to send rain, the inhabitants sacrificed their children to him, giving them up to be burned alive: it rained immediately after the sacrifice.

Hamilcar finally trapped one barbarian army in the narrow Pass of the Axe, where he exterminated them. Yet another siege and yet another battle were needed before the mercenaries were destroyed. Tortures, crucifixions, the leprous body of the Carthaginian general Hannon, gore, guts, and decay litter and bespatter the countryside and Flaubert's pages. The end seems almost anticlimactic. Mâtho was forced to run the gantlet from his prison to the square where Salammbô stood with her betrothed Narr'Havas. The moon was rising. She looked down and longed for Mâtho as he died. The sun set; the mob shouted; Narr'Havas put his arm about her waist as she rose to drink to him. But she fell to the ground, dead. "Thus died the daughter of Hamilcar for having touched the veil of Tanit," is the last sentence of the book, printed as a separate paragraph. Flaubert's judgment of some fifteen years later, when he reread the novel for a revised edition, is probably valid: it is too long by a full third.

THE CHARACTERS: SALAMMBÔ AND MÂTHO

> I am going to have a man make love to a woman; and he will think that she is the Moon, while she thinks that the Sun is making love to her.
>
> Comment by Flaubert reported in the *Journal* of the
> Goncourt brothers for November 29, 1860

Salammbô is a virgin, almost a priestess of Tanit: this is Flaubert's constant emphasis.[12] But like the nun Anna Maria of *Don Juan*, she soon found herself longing for something more; she was mysteriously disturbed and sought peace through long hours of prayer. Her nurse told her she needed a husband.

Like other virgins in French literature before her, particularly Atala and Velléda of Chateaubriand, Salammbô then passed through the delicate nuances of the premonitions of love, especially a vague, incomprehensible uneasiness. Indetermination, passing reveries, and a broad but empty vehemence had all been used by Chateaubriand to suggest the exotic woman and make her a fascinating enigma. The Carthaginian virgin experienced the ennui of Emma Bovary, but translated to a new plane because it was not conscious and understood.

Salammbô felt ill-defined but concordant longings for religion as well as for love. In a strange confusion after seeing Mâtho, she sensed an aspiration toward the moon and called in the high priest Schahabarim. For a long time she felt herself mystically related to the moon, her spirits waxing and waning with it; she nearly died during an eclipse. Now she yearned to touch Tanit's veil: the priest refused.

Flaubert patterned Salammbô on the great mystics, including Saint Theresa, who was one of his first models for Saint Anthony. As several of these mystics, Saint Augustine and Pascal among others, no doubt owed something of their visions to epilepsy, Flaubert was right in sensing a kinship with them. In Salammbô he wished to display the premonitory signs and symptoms of hysteria. But in exactly opposite fashion he also felt that ancient woman had no inner complications: Salammbô was to be like a statue. A hysterical statue is a daring contradiction to attempt to realize, and not necessarily possible. Above all Flaubert wished her to be strange and distant as she gave vent to her half-glimpsed aspirations.[13] Unlike Emma Bovary—Flaubert himself points it out—she was not driven by a horde of passions; rather she was a monomaniac, gradually becoming caught up by her *idée fixe*.

When Mâtho appeared in her room with the veil, Salammbô was overwhelmed. Thereafter at night she would hear the steps of the goddess bringing chastisement for her sacrilege—only priests might gaze upon the veil. Looking fixedly for hours at her sacred serpent, she would feel a spiral in her own throat, a second serpent, slowly rising from within to choke her. Together with her despair, however—and in this she was like Anthony in the presence of his temptations—she felt a secret pride, even joy, and regretted that she had not touched the zaïmph, while detesting herself for her desires. For days she would refuse to eat or would burst into inexplicable tears and send for Schahabarim, only to find when he appeared that she had nothing to say. Although she revolted against his domination, she also experienced an unaccountable voluptuousness with this eunuch; Flaubert had felt a similar excitement in Constantinople. Schahabarim recognized the influence of the moon goddess in the misery of the virgin. It is a pity that this delicately nuanced study of incipient love and of the concomitant hysteria resulting from frustration (a generation before Freud analyzed the mechanism) should be buried in these pages, its elements widely separated and the totality apparent only when the dispersed parts are united.

Salammbô's anguished deepened and she came more under the power of Tanit just as Schahabarim was turning to Moloch. She had been the only relief in his arid life, and yet now his own anguish was driving him to torture her by revealing a doctrine steadily more austere as she sought for mystic appeasement; on the other hand, she rejoiced in her own wretchedness before him. Experiencing the same kind of disillusionments Flaubert had felt with Mademoiselle Leroyer de Chantepie and other women, Schahabarim found to his sorrow that, when he sought to explain his religious speculations and doubts to her, her mind soon tired and she could no longer follow him. He would return to the temple feeling even sadder and more abandoned than before. All his concepts had to become physical realities if Salammbô was to understand. She worshiped the sun and the moon, not the principles they incarnated. And, added Flaubert in bitterness over all priests, even Schahabarim did not always keep the distinctions clear.

Sending Salammbô to Mâtho for the veil was Schahabarim's final test of the power of the goddess he was abandoning: the girl's failure would disprove the power of Tanit. But the gods, Flaubert felt, were ironic about such tests. In fact, Schahabarim's doubts had proceeded so far that not even Salammbô's success sufficed to reassure him, for he abandoned Tanit nevertheless.

The descriptions of Salammbô's preparations and her journey to Mâtho's tent are a climax of involved and effective symbolism. The priest's order brought on a hysteria in her that was like the tortured moment when Emma, returning from her fruitless visit to Rodolphe to seek money, decided to take poison. Like Emma, Salammbô was in the grip of a stupor and felt death sweeping over her; circles of fire seemed to float about her. Both women were undergoing Flaubert's epileptic attacks.[14]

Mâtho mingled in Salammbô's mind with the notion of Moloch, much as he had found something of Tanit in her. Her sexual desire for him she converted into a more acceptable longing to regain the veil. Her decision to make the journey brought her immense relief. Upon her return Schahabarim was impotently furious with her, but she faced him with the same indifference she accorded the death of her serpent, whose previous illness had so worried her. She no longer fasted but instead spent her days watching the mercenaries encamped outside Carthage and, so she believed, awaiting her fiancé Narr'Havas.

Salammbô's memory of her night in the tent faded beyond clear recall. She prayed daily for the salvation of Carthage through the death of Mâtho, and she felt confusedly that the hatred with which he persecuted her and her country had something divine about it. The effeminate Narr'Havas disappointed her in his lack of Mâtho's violence. In the last scene, as she stood upon the great platform with the sky above and the sea and mountains about her, she seemed to the Carthaginians the resplendent image of the city itself, its inner genius, and the incarnation of Tanit. Religion and sexuality had become one.

Salammbô is a strange and enticing figure, too frequently lost in the midst of all the other concerns of this novel. But within her are disquieting elements of the naïve dreams of an earlier romanticism and, equally, suggestions of the self-paralyzing decadence which characterized the generation after Flaubert's.

Hers is somehow not the fate of tragedy. She is at once seductive woman and destructive temptress. Essentially passive, except for her trip to Mâtho's tent, she responds with only a tingling of her nerves when passion should lead to action. Her longing is Flaubert's aspiration toward a complete love; yet, far from raising her lover to sublime stature, she tortures, degrades, and eventually destroys him.[15]

Mâtho is her foil and counterpart. Here, too, only the constant diversions from the theme keep the reader from delighting in Flaubert's portrait of this primitive chieftain's love for a woman he confused with the moon goddess. He lay motionless for melancholy hours. He was sure the fury of the goddess was pursuing him: it was as though she had given him a potion. Salammbô's eyes, in memory, seemed to burn into him. When he advanced, she seemed to be moving; when he stopped, she rested. But equally, she was at times so vague it was perhaps all a dream.

At other times Mâtho was overcome with a continual, mad need for action, a male hysteria. Cheeks aflame, eyes bloodshot, and voice hoarse, he walked restlessly to and fro through the camp. To the mercenaries he seemed a man possessed; he inspired a mystic fear. For months after she had cursed him for stealing the veil, Salammbô's voice would ring in his ears, and he would pale as if about to die. He wanted variously to have her love him, to kidnap her, to murder her. He would bring out the zaïmph, feel it, smell its perfume, then plunge his face into it and kiss it while he sobbed.

His frustrated love was coupled with hatred, which he easily transferred to Salammbô's father. In his imagination, killing Hamilcar alternated with wild moments of holding Salammbô in his arms. He sensed the power of Moloch welling up within him; he heard the voice of the god commanding through him. Like Achilles, he was invulnerable and led his troops like a marine god rushing over the flood of battle. Hero and heroine were the divine lovers Flaubert had longed to portray since the distant days in Rhodes. Hamilcar, meanwhile, had become the presiding genius of Carthage; the two demigods confronted one another in a combat of races, Carthaginian against barbarian, which became their personal struggle.

Scenes of Orgy, Love, and Violence

Whatever it may cost, I am going to write this piece of truculent buffoonery.

Letter to Jules Duplan, May 10, 1857

In general the successful scenes in *Salammbô* depict violent, unrestrained energy and the unleashed passions which since adolescence Flaubert had been wont to imagine as characteristic of the ancient world. He felt, however, that he should not describe directly the scene in the tent when Salammbô gave herself to Mâtho: such an approach would have violated his canons of chaste writing. Yet he had to let his reader know Salammbô was experiencing the fulfillment of her aspirations toward love and religion. In *Madame Bovary*, where he had only a physical fulfillment to describe, he had handled the corresponding scene with a quick end of a sentence: "she abandoned herself." Here the situation was more complicated, and he evolved a complex procedure to match his needs.

Salammbô performed a long, careful ritual of ablutions and mystic preparations for her meeting with Mâtho. To music provided by unseen musicians in a scene reminiscent of Flaubert's nights with Kuchiuk-Hânem and other courtesans in Egypt and Tunisia, Salammbô slowly undressed, bathed, and perfumed herself and called her mystic python. He entered and wound himself over her nude body. At first she hesitated, modesty mingling with revulsion at his cold touch. Then, recalling the orders of the high priest, she grasped the serpent by the middle and placed him about her neck like a broken collar whose two ends fell to the ground. Next she rolled his full length about her thighs, under her arms, between her knees. Then taking his head by the jaws she brought his little triangular mouth up to the edge of her own opened lips; half closing her eyes, she bent over backwards under the rays of the moon. He wound his black, circling body more closely about her, and she struggled for breath under his heavy embrace. Like Mâtho, she felt as though she were about to die.

The scene is remarkably sexual and yet remarkably chaste. Moreover, since the python represented the spirit of her ancestors, the genius of Carthage, and something of Tanit, too, Flaubert could—and did—insist in his letters that the snake's embrace was as much religious as physical and both aspects were symbolic only. He termed it an oratorical precaution to attenuate the descriptions in the tent, for here no man was involved. But there is always, he wrote on another occasion, an element of debauchery when an author uses raw colors. On reconsidering, however, he crossed out "raw" and substituted the word he really meant: "true."[16]

When Salammbô suddenly appeared before his tent, Mâtho was struck dumb. Her garments seemed almost a part of her body; they had a special splendor, a quality belonging to her alone, which everything about Elisa had for Flaubert. Mâtho talked almost madly to her, telling her of his obsession with her. He would turn about expecting to find her, and she would not be there. Such a hallucination Flaubert had experienced with Elisa and described in the *Memoirs of a Madman* and *November*. More recently, though, the memory of Jeanne de Tourbey haunted him in this fashion while he rode over the hills and valleys of Tunisia. His love letters to her turned out to have been the first drafts for this page in *Salammbô*[17]

Mâtho, with Salammbô now before him, felt vaguely that perhaps she was the goddess Tanit. Finding she had come only to get the veil, he exploded in rage but burst into tears a moment later and begged her forgiveness. She was hypnotized; the will of the gods, akin to fate in *Madame Bovary*, seemed to engulf her; Moloch commanded. She fell backwards onto the soldier's bed; the chain linking her ankles snapped; and Mâtho's head was on her breast. She cried out, mingling in one utterance all her aspirations: "Moloch, you are burning me!"

Mâtho fell asleep, and Salammbô, rising, observed her broken chain. Memories of Carthage, the suburb of Megara, her house, her room, and all the countryside she had traversed to reach the tent mixed together and whirled through her mind in images at once tumultuous and clear. These were more of the experiences Emma had had on leaving Rodolphe, those Flaubert had not used for Salammbô's earlier scene, when the priest had first ordered her to go to Mâtho.[18]

Mâtho's kisses had seemed to Salammbô more devouring than the flames of a fire or of the sun god. The reader does not yet know how she reacted, however. Now, afterward, Flaubert felt it could be discussed. A Carthaginian who had been nearby and had heard everything entered and cursed her: "I heard you crying out in your ecstasy, like a prostitute, while he described his desire to you." With that the scene closes, by no means as restrained and chaste as in *Madame Bovary*, but still far from lascivious. The reader has ample peace of mind to observe as Flaubert, for the only time in his life, tried to describe fulfilled aspirations.

There are other scenes in *Salammbô* which are more disquieting for their suggestion of a sadistic enjoyment of blood, horror, and torture. In his youthful works Flaubert had tried his hand at many such episodes and had even regretted that the Marquis de Sade had failed to include scenes involving cannibalism or wild animals in any of his works the young man had read.[19] The choice of subject in *Madame Bovary* had excluded all of this, but ancient Carthage did not.

The long, drawn-out death of a mercenary army trapped in the Pass of the Axe provided an opportunity. In preparation Flaubert read widely in medical treatises on starvation and in records of men long at sea on rafts, a subject which had attracted the painter Géricault in his "Raft of the Medusa," the work which had set off the romantic revolution in painting in 1819.

The army pressed blindly through the Pass only to find a gate blocking the exit. Those in front, driven on by those behind, were skewered on nails protruding from it; great pieces of their flesh remained attached. Forty thousand men soon found themselves helpless.

Some paragraphs in the description yield particular pathos, especially those recounting the long, sad hours as the various barbarians recalled their homelands, a scene Joseph Conrad remembered for certain passages in his *Nigger of the Narcissus*. Other moments were there for their brutality, and they did shock Flaubert's readers, as he knew they would. The most barbaric among the mercenaries ate the flesh of those who had died. Gradually the horror the survivors felt gave way before their hunger; all began to eye one another for signs of weakness. Toward the end, famished, they killed without waiting.

The last, exhausted few were trampled to death by Hamilcar's elephants, except for four hundred who were forced to fight each other. Flaubert maintained relative delicacy and poignancy in reporting the reactions of those linked by homosexual affections who were forced to attack each other. Later authors have gone so much further than he in removing restrictions upon what may be written that his prose seems innocuous indeed, and today few are likely to be upset by it. But it is not entirely clear that his novel gained by these elements, however much they may have delighted him. They were to cause him trouble with the critics.

FROM THE EPIC TO THE MODERN HISTORICAL NOVEL

> I have tried to give consistency to a mirage by applying the procedures of the modern novel to antiquity.
>
> Letter to Sainte-Beuve, December 23-24, 1862

Like *Madame Bovary*, *Salammbô* gave new dimensions to French literature, but even more than its predecessor it was overtly based on traditional classical concepts, in this case the epic. While the new novel was by no means so successful as its predecessor, still to later writers its handling proved suggestive and helped form a new genre, the modern historical novel.[20]

The principal classical source of *Salammbô* was the Greek historian Polybius. Other classical authors provided factual data and the atmosphere of an unrepressed barbarian world or else tested techniques and devices. Flaubert reread Virgil now. The precision in the use of words in the *Aeneid* confirmed him in his concepts of style. One critic sensed something of Flaubert's aim when he called *Salammbô* the product of an able classical sculptor.[21] About this time, too, Flaubert noted the idealizing tendency of ancient art, observing that the use of masks in the theater suggested how insistent classical authors were upon remaining close to generalities and types, just as he was.[22]

Nevertheless, perhaps even more than heretofore, Flaubert had little use for those doctrines of restraint and purity which seemed to some of his contemporaries essential to the best works of Greece and Rome. There are scenes in *Salammbô* which would not have occurred in the greatest Greek and Roman classics, but only in the lesser works. These latter, however, particularly appealed to Flaubert, and their uninhibited rejection of all restraints seemed to justify his own excesses.

Critics have often termed *Salammbô* an epic. The novel does owe much to this genre, and the phrase "epic realism," which has been used of it, is at least a step in the right direction. As in the classical epic tradition, Mâtho can be miraculously untouched by arrows, and Hannibal's youth—despite a denial by Flaubert—is obviously miraculous. Hamilcar's standing upon the altar of the god, swearing a solemn oath and predicting a dire future, is in similar vein. Sainte-Beuve even objected that the lascivious serpent was out of harmony with the general epic tone. The locale is the Mediterranean; there is an epic enumeration of the troops. The races and something of the characters have not a novelistic but an epic reality, larger than life and standing in titanic conflict: Salammbô and Mâtho are semi-mythological incarnations of gods, with the supernatural element internal rather than external.

Salammbô is not, for all that, a classical epic. Flaubert was annoyed, perhaps unfairly, that it was considered one, for he had so drastically altered and departed from the epic that he destroyed its possibility within his work. There remains from the classical genre, aside from aspects and details, only the concept of literary beauty. *Salammbô*, for all its various classical elements, is still essentially an innovation, a new genre in its own right.[23]

The most important single inspiration for Flaubert's new ideas came from the romantic historian Jules Michelet, for whom he had felt from childhood that sort of affectionate admiration one has, as he put it, for those artists who seem to satisfy all one's needs and match totally one's own temperament. At school, it had been under the guidance of Michelet's pupil Chéruel that Flaubert's passion for history developed. He had devoured Michelet's

History of Rome, the later volumes of his *History of France*, and other works. Whole pages remained in his memory for their allying of poetry and reality, color and relief, facts and meditations: they were for the boy not so much books, he said, as whole worlds in themselves.

In 1846 Flaubert's enthusiasm for Nero, fed by reading Michelet, had astounded poor Louise Colet, whose temperament hardly coincided here with her lover's. All the barbarians of antiquity seemed in their heady sonorous existence to be of Flaubert's race; as he imagined them in their debaucheries, the soldiers of the legions were the forerunners of the mercenaries of *Salammbô*.[24] The years passed and Flaubert continued to read the new books that flowed from Michelet's pen, admiring not only the erudition but also the immense sympathy which encompassed and understood everything. Through this feeling for the true, Michelet seemed able to embrace men and events and penetrate to their essence. Then he could illuminate a whole epoch with a word. Flaubert hoped to create *Salammbô* with the same combination of painstaking scholarship and imaginative sympathy.

Michelet found a ready response in Flaubert's hallucinatory imagination. The Goncourt brothers noted that their novelist friend was above all a poet, a man of fantasy.[25] The critic, historian, and student of psychology, Hippolyte Taine, visited him as he was finishing *Salammbô* and asked a number of questions about the way his imagination worked. He learned that Flaubert, with eyes closed, found his head filled with pictures. His visual memory included all the details of a photograph, taking in the slightest crack in the floor quite as much as the largest objects in the room. Hence, when he began to write, his problem was never to imagine but rather to clear his mind of the debris his memory furnished. Ideas or objects which stirred his imagination, even an advertising poster, became obsessions dominating his thinking for a day or more at a time. Nature, he noted, could never be a matter of repose for him: rather he absorbed it and felt absorbed by it, remaining almost wholly dulled and stupid as he lay on the sand or the earth.[26] The feeling was as real in the 1860's as it had been on the Nile in 1849.

As he read Michelet, who made history a resurrection of the past, Flaubert's imagination quickened and he could begin the novelist's fundamental task of breathing life into his situations. For him the historical novel must not be a thinly disguised vehicle for nineteenth-century ideas, as it had been all too often for Hugo in *Notre-Dame de Paris* or Chateaubriand in *The Martyrs*. What Flaubert sought instead was the color or beauty of the originals, from which would arise ideas and characters who would be types. *Salammbô*, as historical novel, is in fact directly related to *Madame Bovary*: there is no change in underlying esthetic. In each case a milieu, closely studied, interacts with characters who mold it and are molded by it, Emma by Yonville, Mâtho and Salammbô by Carthage.

Flaubert's first task was to learn as much about Carthage as about Yonville. Unfortunately, as Michelet's *History of Rome* warned him, the vanished city had left almost no records; its very site was a matter of conjecture and dispute. Flaubert's friend Renan, the scholarly historian, provided suggestions and an approach which saw history dominating characters: Salammbô and Mâtho would be the products of their age, as Taine would shortly be demanding. Flaubert wanted the very pores of his book to exude historical truth, and for this he wished to be totally immersed in his subject; in that way he would find the right color naturally and inevitably. Archeology was as necessary to prime his imagination as it had been earlier during the Breton trip of 1847, when his studies of Celtic and other history had set him to dreaming. Therefore, along with classical writings on ancient Mediterranean civilizations, he studied the relevant scholarship of his day. The works of Renan, Maury, and Baudry, whom he knew personally, and dozens of others whom he did not, he mastered over the months and years of preparation.

Flaubert was an unpredictable nuisance to his learned friends, for he knew enough to ask complicated questions and yet not enough to phrase them with the care of a scholar. His frantic letters for information would contain quotations which interested him but no indication of their source. Or he would give title and chapter, but one or the other would be wrong. Yet somehow they all accepted his vagaries and helped him as his work took him from one specialty to another and his documentation grew.[27]

Since he was never going to know exactly what ancient Carthage was like, Flaubert had often to present probabilities or at least avoid absurdities. Errors there are, but they are trivial and do not invalidate the general effect. His method—consciously elaborated—was to use his sources as far as they would go and then to take such further liberties as he needed, striving to remain within the general tone. It was enough that the image of Carthage should approximate the reader's ideals. Flaubert's flair for evocation has stood the test of readings by innumerable North Africans: he did find the tone of eternal Africa and conveyed it in his novel.[28]

Flaubert carefully described and differentiated his barbarians from one another to produce that historical hashish he sought for his reader. The mechanism of each piece of siege machinery he makes understandable. The fabulous gems of Hamilcar's treasure review the splendors of the Bible and Pliny. There is a vicarious delight in perusing the erudition thus displayed; one comes to sense an awesome reality in the strange vision which arises. But the method did not require Flaubert to become the slave of his learning. Thus, although he was privately persuaded that Carthage had no aqueduct in the days of the mercenaries, still, when he needed one for the entry of Mâtho and Spendius into the city, he did not hesitate to fabricate it.

Flaubert's descriptions give a deceptive effect of detailed accuracy, but it is in fact impossible to reconstruct any physical totality from the pages of his book. Rather, there arises, when Flaubert is successful, a particular type of mirage for the reader, the illusion of living a scene, an event, or an emotion. This is the province and the privilege of fiction; when that illusion has at its base careful historical accuracy of detail and tone as Flaubert understood it, then it is the modern historical novel, a new genre in France at least, which to a large extent he created in *Salammbô*.

The real problem was not so much to learn the facts as to give the variegated mercenaries and the Carthaginians the same breath of life the inhabitants of Yonville had. Flaubert was counting on a wealth of detail, much of it technical, to bring them into sharp focus for the reader. Unfortunately since he rejected any concept of restraint, classical or other, after enough pages the repetitions do bore and overly long processions of unfamiliar details finally evoke no more than unfamiliarity. Sainte-Beuve, who was frankly irritated by *Salammbô*, suggested a travel book would have been a better vehicle for Flaubert's erudition, which is so often the enemy of his action in this novel. Many reports of local customs would not have seemed absurd in an account of a journey; but they do here: "In the fourth dilochia of the twelfth syntagma, three phalangists killed each other as they fought over a rat." Also, accuracy may interrupt unity of tone and effect, as in the funeral services for the dead mercenaries of different nations. The ceremonies are alternately grandiose, revolting, or curious, and the reader moves confusedly among archeology, the epic, the elegy, and a clinical report.

The battles and sieges presented a special problem which Flaubert was not able to resolve.[29] And they bulk large in the total novel. He admitted to Sainte-Beuve that he had somewhat forced the events of history in including any siege at all, but as a matter of fact there are really three separate ones. In addition, there are three pitched battles and some twenty pages describing military maneuvers in open country. Flaubert was worried by these repetitions and the proliferation of small details. Bouilhet agreed with Flaubert that he had perhaps been unwise to take a historical event, since he could not radically alter it; but he had, and hence his story was inevitably going to involve recurrent actions and scenes. The *Iliad*, he reminded his friend, suffered from the same handicap but managed to overcome it.[30] Flaubert hoped, however, that his use of detail had removed his work from any resemblance to the *Iliad*. And in any case he had intended to do something other than rewrite Homer. To make matters worse, Flaubert's taste betrayed him. Scenes of battle carnage aroused his imagination by their appeal to his very real sadism. Many—perhaps even most—readers, however, have not shared Flaubert's excitement and have ultimately tired of blood and entrails. For them interest lags and finally disappears from these pages.[31]

There is also the question of the characters. Flaubert's presentation must convince the reader of their validity and hence their credibility. Flaubert once wrote that, if the color of his novel was not unified, if the details jarred, if the customs did not derive from the African culture and the climate and the temperaments of his characters, or if his hero and heroine were not consistent with themselves, then his book lacked harmony and he had failed. This is not, however, quite all that is at stake. The details are sufficiently accurate; little doubt of that, despite contemporary attacks. And the interrelationship of the various elements of the culture seems sound. But Salammbô is disquietingly like Emma Bovary in her ennui, and Mâtho is dangerously like Flaubert in his longing for her. Sainte-Beuve challenged this, and probably rightly. Was the psychology Carthaginian or postromantic? More serious than this, the psychology, good or bad, disappears completely behind the archeology for pages at a time.

The interest of Salammbô for the theory of literature remains great, notwithstanding its real weaknesses as a novel. Flaubert sought to melt together epic grandeur and historical evocation and to develop therefrom characters who would display a valid psychology; he succeeded in part. Mâtho and Salammbô, for all their overtones of nineteenth-century sublimation, could never have existed in the nineteenth century. A new genre had been initiated; there would be time to perfect it later.

RELIGION AND ITS SYMBOLISM

> Now, since every gain has to be paid for by some sort of loss and since every transaction is governed by the desperation of the weaker and by the demands of the stronger, there was no pain too great to be offered to Moloch. Since he delighted in the most horrible tortures and since the Carthaginians were now in his power, he must be appeased.
>
> Salammbô, the decision to sacrifice the children to Moloch

Religion is constantly a theme in Salammbô, in the priest Schahabarim, in Salammbô's religious preoccupations, and in the actions of the barbarians and the Carthaginians. While not infrequently Flaubert made what statements he wished directly and overtly through his characters, often he expressed important concepts through symbols. Madame Bovary had made occasional use of them; Salammbô is constructed around them. There are, for instance, the lions, whose presence, direct or implied, punctuates the book. In the opening pages the mercenaries lie on the ground during their feast "in the peaceful pose of lions as they tear their prey apart." Later they observe with horror the Carthaginian practice of crucifying these animals. Toward the end of the book when the barbarian leaders are themselves crucified, they remember these earlier victims. And at the end, the last soldiers who escape from Hannibal are caught and eaten by lions, who thus provide a recurrent symbol to suggest the temper of the country, the culture, and the men of Carthage.

Around this constant use of symbols Flaubert hoped to link the two subjects of his book, Carthage and the pair of lovers.[32] Salammbô, Tanit, and the veil of the goddess are three images of the same reality and are, in many senses, interchangeable. Thus the reader moves from Salammbô through the veil to the Carthaginians who feared an affront to the goddess or from Mâtho through Moloch to the Carthaginian sacrifice of their children.

Flaubert also used this symbolic structure to aid him in suggesting Salammbô's nature, which he had at the same time to display and yet to keep enigmatic. Very early in the novel, she contained in her own person vaguely religious aspirations and vaguely sensual ones. She longed, like Flaubert, to be absorbed into the night fog, the waves of the fountain, the sap of the trees; she prayed to be allowed to take leave of her body and become only a breath or a ray of light, so as to slip heavenward and be joined to the moon, her mother. In the same way Mâtho's violent nature, his sexuality, and his religion are subsumed under Moloch.

This raises problems. It is quite possible to accept, with Freud, a relationship between religion and sexuality without, for all that, being quite prepared to accept for oneself the level of cruelty and superstition in the Carthaginian versions of this relationship. If the reader refuses this for himself, then the heroism of Salammbô, far being divine, is corrupt for him. Her purity depends wholly upon her ignorance of the meaning of her very real erotic desires and concomitant hysteria; she may then not strike the reader as pure. And similarly religion does not seem adequately subsumed in the children burned alive to appease Moloch. If the reader declines to accept this symbolism, then the linkage between the two subjects of the book, the city and the lovers, is burst asunder and the characters are rejected, not embraced.[33]

In other situations, the reader may not be aware that a religious symbol is involved. Thus Flaubert intended at first to give Salammbô a dance, religious, mystic, and then voluptuous; but considerations of the chastity he wished in literature led him to replace his physical statements by symbolic ones.[34] In *Atala,* when the heroine was about to give herself to her lover, Chateaubriand placed a tempest about the couple; the thunder rumbled, and lightning set fire to the forest. Flaubert, too, had thunder, lightning, and fire in his scene; and in part he was merely following his predecessor. But far more he intended a symbolic effect: thunder was, to the Carthaginians, one more of the manifestations of Moloch. Unfortunately, most readers will need Flaubert's letters to tell them so.

While symbolism carries the main burden of what Flaubert wished to suggest about love and religion, he also made the direct statement that Hamilcar sought the essences behind the symbols. His religion, like Flaubert's, was an attempt to banish from the mind all forms, symbols, and names, the better to grasp the immutable spirit. From this, said Flaubert, he drew a certain peace and serenity born of a disdain for death and for all chance occurrences: stoicism, in a word, as invulnerable to fear as to pity. Hope, Flaubert felt, was always a derogation upon the powers of Providence; and the search for happiness still seemed man's principal source of disquietude.

Religion Flaubert respected, as mankind's most natural and most poetic feeling, a necessity and an instinct. Hamilcar, Salammbô, and Mâtho exemplify this concept. All forms of piety attracted Flaubert, Roman Catholicism above all others. He felt, however, that humanity must abandon the effort to resolve the contradictions apparent on every hand in the universe: how could a limited creature hope to know their resolution? Man's attempts— and here it was the follower of Montaigne and of Voltaire speaking —were all misguided. Neither science nor religion could progress while man insisted on giving such attributes to God that He became like an oriental monarch surrounded by his court or was degraded to the level of a bourgeois.[35]

Flaubert counseled Mademoiselle Leroyer de Chantepie to recognize that priests could not answer her dilemmas, for modern life had already left them behind. Man himself produced his ideas of good and of evil, whether he was a cannibal eating his fellows or a child sucking his barley-sugar candy. Knowledge and art could alone console for the dichotomy of religion and philosophy. And only a love for the facts in themselves and a stoic impassivity could bring peace. Hence Catholicism hated science, Flaubert felt, for science admitted of change. One day, when science turned its methods to the human heart, it would bring light to the agonizing questions the nineteenth century must content itself merely to pose. What Flaubert called "the ardent contemplation of things" could then become the new faith.[36]

For Mâtho and Salammbô to believe they incarnated gods completed their aspirations. For the Carthaginian priests to define the desires of Moloch brought abomination. It was the full fury of Flaubert's wrath against those who would define closely the nature of God that led to the hideous scenes in which the children of Carthage were burned alive in the copper belly of the god. Moloch's spirit roamed the streets creating atrocities because the people of Carthage believed they could thus define him. Definitions of God under the Second Empire were less bloodthirsty; but Flaubert would have held that the error was the same and that history showed the Catholic church could be quite as bloody as anything he depicted of Moloch.

SADISM

> I am indulging in farces which will upset the stomachs of decent people. I am piling horror on horror. Twenty thousand of my good people have just died of hunger; before that they were eating each other; the rest of them will be crushed by elephants or devoured by lions. "Bestiality and murder on every hand."
>
> Letter to the Goncourt brothers of January 2, 1862

In one of the paradoxes he enjoyed, Flaubert suggested he was really kinder to humanity in *Salammbô* than in *Madame Bovary;* he even urged that love of humanity had led him to resurrect one of its lost chapters. The unfortunate fact is that, where the subject of *Madame Bovary* had kept the sadistic aspects of Flaubert's nature on a check rein, he now deliberately chose to liberate them.

The Marquis de Sade offers a convenient center for examination of these aspects of Flaubert's personality. He would have had these traits without Sade, and it is probable that his frequent reading of the Marquis' works is symptom only and in no way cause. But Sainte-Beuve, the Goncourt brothers, and no doubt others thought at once of Sade as the source for this side of his personality. It seemed to many of them a foolish and degrading obsession in Flaubert to be thus preoccupied with cruelty, perversion, and the revolting.[37]

In part his friends were mistaken. Some of what they objected to was the truth and not Flaubert's peculiarities. Hannon's maladies are loathsome, but Flaubert had observed leper colonies in Damascus and knew that such loathsome maladies could afflict mankind.[38] Further, he knew the fascination of the monstrous and what deeply religious questionings could lie behind the effort to understand how the monster, too, was a part of God's creation. He also brought more honesty to the literary discussion of direct sexual desire than was the wont of the Second Empire, which, however much it bragged of its prowess in private, still liked to cover sexuality with a veil of alleged decency in public. In addition, much of what is clearly decadent in Flaubert—and his friends could identify this readily enough—later ages have learned to recognize as being quite as human and interesting as the sort of conventional normality of which the more average man is so cheerfully and so blindly proud. There are thus passages in which Flaubert analyzes rapidly but clearly the unavowed urges of the Carthaginian women who tortured Mâtho to death in the final pages; they longed for him physically and at the same time rejoiced in killing him. Earlier, when Salammbô came to Mâtho, his nostrils opened wide to breathe in the perfume of her body, an indefinable emanation, fresh and cool and yet stupefying. She smelled of honey, pepper, incense, roses, and, as Flaubert put it, of yet another odor. The twentieth century has found no regrettable crossing of forbidden lines in even stronger phrasings.

Yet his friends were right that Flaubert did delight in the revolting, the cruel, and the sadistic, and they were also right in sensing the presence of this fascination in his book. He delighted in accounts of sexual abnormalities of every sort, from hermaphroditism to necrophilia. As early as 1845 he had agreed that cruelty in ideas and principles revolted him, but he found cruelty through sensuality perhaps no more than a need of man, if he wished to exercise the plenitude of his faculties. Later, in Egypt, he had shown a morbid interest in the various forms of torture used by the tax collectors in their rounds, noting that some of the punishments would leave the victim crippled for six months while others left permanent injury. Elsewhere he regretted not being allowed to see prisoners beaten.[39] In *Salammbô* he could describe all these matters.

The heaping up of horrors in his novel is so great that, gradually, the sensitivity of the reader dulls. Beatings are distributed right and left as Flaubert had seen them in Egypt. Homosexuality is indicated in the opening Feast of the Mercenaries and stated directly in the Pass of the Axe. There is a mass prostitution by the priestesses of Tanit, and torture runs through the book: torture of Hamilcar's slaves who have incensed their master; torture of individual captives; torture of two thousand of them simultaneously. Hunger works its ravages in Carthage, in Hamilcar's camp, in the Pass of the Axe. But some of the Carthaginians eat the flesh of the dead mercenaries merely for revenge. Corpses decay and putrify after each battle. Somehow the scale of values shifts, and most of these events seem normal within their context. In part, this is what Flaubert wished.

Even so there remain sensibilities which can be offended. When one of the barbarians kills an enemy, slits his throat, and then sucks the blood out of the open artery till no more will come, it is perhaps not enough that Flaubert notes the other barbarians are horrified. The reader's sympathy for the mercenaries is lessened; since he long before lost any for the Carthaginians, his involvement in the story is sharply and irrevocably reduced.

Perhaps the most revolting single character is Hannon, the Carthaginian general who suffered from leprosy and elephantiasis simultaneously. His breath stank; his eyes burned brightly, but he had no eyebrows left; a mass of scaly skin hung over his forehead;

his enlarged ears stuck out, and huge wrinkles outlined his nostrils. Ulcers covered the formless mass of his body and the overflowing flesh hid even his toenails; from his decaying fingers shapeless greenish matter hung. His lust was all but insatiable and the more attractive captured women were thrown to him. When the barbarians crucified him, his spongy bones and flesh were inadequate to support the body. The details Flaubert gives, relentlessly. But no character in the book seems to mind as much as the reader does. Hence the reader declines, ultimately, to accept either Carthage or the mercenaries as being at one with him.

Unfortunately, an aspect of Flaubert's personality which could not easily be transmuted into art was being unshackled. Any objection to his expressing it he rejected as bourgeois prejudice. All the horrors he depicted are part of humanity, to be sure, and recent wars leave little room for denying their nearly universal validity. But to show them occurring in a barbarous civilization far removed in time is in no sense to invite the reader to discover them within himself. And if the reader cannot do this, then their display is only morbid and, frequently, no more than the sadism of the author. Had Flaubert pursued this line of development further, it seems unlikely that he would be known as more than the author of *Madame Bovary*. In point of fact, however, the writing of *Salammbô* seemed a purge to the malady; and none of his later writing ever showed this vein to such an extent again.

ESTHETICS AND STYLE

> The agonies of the sentence will begin, the torment of assonances, and the tortures of the period. I shall be sweating and twisting about over my metaphors.
>
> Letter to Ernest Feydeau of about August 5, 1857

For intelligent and sensitive readers, Flaubert had incarnated in *Madame Bovary* the best that had come from the rising school of realism. Sainte-Beuve and others waited expectantly for his next production, which would carry the battle forward. They had been disappointed: the years passed, and nothing came from the master. Sainte-Beuve regretfully turned instead to the praise of secondary productions like *Fanny*.[40] And then, when *Salammbô* was finally published, it appeared to be a wild, romantic fantasy, full of exuberant feelings and a lush décor: the leader of the realist school, as he had been baptized against his will, had apparently deserted the battle.

In fact Flaubert was even more scrupulously true to his doctrines in *Salammbô* than he had been in *Madame Bovary*. A rigorous search for the scientifically accurate had been his base; from this he had sought consistently to rise to an ideal which would be true and hence could be portrayed through beauty to incarnate the good. To the basic procedure for *Madame Bovary* he had had to add only something of the understanding and technique of Michelet. Finally, writing was still for him an escape: he proposed to become drunk on ink, since the nectar of the gods could not be had.

The subject of the new novel was different, so the style— which to Flaubert was still a way of perceiving things—had to be different to concord with the new material. He did now concede that some ideas might be impossible to phrase well, and French seemed too often a worn-out language. While the sadism did come from his own personality, its elements were all justified by the subject: only canons of taste could have excluded them, and taste he continued to distrust. It was like the human voice: what it gained in volume it lost in perfection of pitch and in flexibility. It became perverted by being too refined, like women who are too amiable and hence become coquettes.[41]

The rhythm of a sentence was even more important to him than before, and he talked of style at length with Feydeau, Gautier, and the Goncourt brothers. Feydeau agreed, but the others found something ridiculous in taking such pains. It seemed absurd to proclaim style supreme over matter rather than at one with it. And all three agreed that, whatever the importance of rhythm, oftentimes only Flaubert was able to sense it in his own sentences and then only by reading them aloud himself; it all disappeared when others read the page silently.[42] Had Flaubert known how fully his friends disagreed with him, he might have sought to reply that, while most readers do read silently and with no thought of the spoken rhythms, he had never felt that he was writing for most readers and that, for those whose reading he did prize, it still remained important to have a full and sonorous spoken rhythm, albeit sensed only silently.

Occasionally, a new difficulty appears: the search for plasticity and perfection of sound and rhythm may conflict with stating the express and immediate content of a passage. To use the same noun twice in successive sentences is, of course, monotonous, and normally Flaubert used a pronoun to avoid such repetitions. The device will serve even when the pronoun opens a new paragraph: the reader's mind will probably identify an initial "they" as referring to the last topic in the preceding paragraph. But Flaubert now allowed himself to open a new paragraph: "A busy populace from morning to night filled them . . ." The reader must return to the preceding paragraph to find that it refers to the streets.

There are pages of *Salammbô* which are delightful to read aloud. They have plenitude and grandeur, something of the majesty of Milton but seen through a fiery red lens. The lens, however, can become a handicap: in Tunisia under Carthage everything was already blown up to gigantic dimensions, or so Flaubert imagined it. Hence metaphor is displaced by the direct adjective, and the overwhelmed reader gradually loses all feeling for the perspective of the matter. Narration has, in some sense, become as descriptive as description in this extraordinary land seen through this extraordinary lens.

The style marches relentlessly on, crushing everything before it, including, sometimes, the reader. The procedure, for all its massive grandeur, risks becoming mechanical in its onslaught, and French prose was to reflect this mechanical quality for another generation or two, until Marcel Proust introduced a more supple concept of the metaphor and style in general.[43]

Flaubert's style reached fullness and served its purpose best in what were essentially set pieces, the moments of great description which stemmed easily out of the narration and fused back into it insensibly at the end. He insisted, probably correctly, that all of these passages had real narrative reasons for existing, for they helped to move the story forward.

The most effective description in the book, and also perhaps the most useful at the same time, recounts the view which Mâtho and Spendius had out over the city of Carthage when they hurried to the top of the palace in pursuit of Salammbô.[44] It was sunrise. The paragraph was derived from Flaubert's trip to Tunis: it was, transformed to fit his needs, a dawn he himself saw there some two thousand years later than Mâtho. The description, changed to fit the ancient situation, provides the reader with his first understanding of the topography of the city, as the rising sun successively reveals its diverse parts.

The passage* opens dramatically: "But a luminous bar arose toward the East." As in the portrayal of Rouen, Flaubert presented the elements of the city as alive. Forms he allowed to remain somewhat confused, but from the immense jumble there emerges a fairly coherent picture in which outlines are clear and colors slip in easily:

> To the left, far below, the white curves of the canals of Megara were beginning to outline the green of the gardens. The conical roofs of the heptagonal temples, the staircases, terraces, and ramparts, bit by bit, were becoming silhouetted against the pallor of dawn; and all about the Carthaginian peninsula a girdle of white foam vibrated, while the emerald green sea seemed as if frozen in the cool of the morning.

The final image with its heavy "seemed as if frozen" is unduly timid, but the general sense of the advancing dawn impresses itself on the passage, especially through the use of imperfect tenses

---

*"Mais une barre lumineuse s'éleva du côté de l'Orient. A gauche, tout en bas, les canaux de Mégara commençaient à rayer de leurs sinuosités blanches les verdures des jardins. Les toits coniques des temples heptagones, les escaliers, les terrasses, les remparts, peu à peu, se découpaient sur la pâleur de l'aube; et tout autour de la péninsule carthaginoise une ceinture d'écume blanche oscillait tandis que la mer couleur d'émeraude semblait comme figée dans la fraîcheur du matin. A mesure que le ciel rose allait s'élargissant, les hautes maisons inclinées sur les pentes du terrain se haussaient, se tassaient, telles qu'un troupeau de chèvres noires qui descend des montagnes. Les rues désertes s'allongeaient; les palmiers, çà et là sortant des murs, ne bougeaient pas; les citernes remplies avaient l'air de boucliers d'argent perdus dans les cours; le phare du promontoire Hermaeum commençait à pâlir. Tout au haut de l'Acropole, dans le bois de cyprès, les chevaux d'Eschmoûn, sentant venir la lumière, posaient leurs sabots sur le parapet de marbre et hennissaient du côté du soleil" (*TENT*, p. 21).

(there are even more of them in the French). Typically, Flaubert closed this first movement with a note on the atmosphere, the "cool of the morning." The second movement, like the first, opens with the approaching sunrise, but as interest shifts to the city, the imagery is more happily sustained:

> As the pink area of the sky grew larger, the high, inclined houses on the slopes of the terrain grew taller and huddled together, like a flock of black goats coming down from the mountains. The deserted streets spread out; the palms, growing out of the walls here and there, were motionless now; the full cisterns were like silver shields left behind in the courtyards; the lighthouse of the Hermaeum Promontory was beginning to pale.

The silvered flecks of light from the open pools provide accent points in the amorphous mass of the city, as had the shining wet roofs under the rain in the description of Rouen in *Madame Bovary*. More striking, and almost hallucinatory, is the weird reversal of roles attributed to animate and inanimate objects. The lifeless sun, the inert houses, the static streets are all vibrant with life and move, huddle, or stretch out over the city. Conversely, the only elements which suggest life are the motionless palms and the lighthouse beacon, which is beginning to pale. It is an awesome upsetting of all familiarity which builds up about Mâtho at this fateful moment. This strange way of viewing derives from a frequent experience Flaubert had during his Mediterranean trip, when it seemed that landscape was in motion and that light could circulate or be immobile. It bears an intimate relationship to his pantheistic view that nature was alive, and the houses huddling together are like Greek mountain ranges one behind the other which he had described as "pressing together like heads of giants jostling each other in order to see better."[45]

The close of the paragraph is one of those triumphant visions which for Flaubert were the prime attraction of his subject. The air of mystery reached its climax as the living horses strained to welcome their god: "At the very top of the Acropolis, in the cypress wood the horses of Eschmoûn, sensing the oncoming light, put their hooves upon the marble parapet and whinnied in the direction of the sun."

This description Flaubert took directly from notes he made as he watched the sun rise over the site of ancient Carthage. Enough remains from the real sunrise to illumine the imaginary scene two thousand years before, as Flaubert eliminated, condensed, and re-arranged the sequences to reach the ultimate clear and simplified tableau. He found at Tunis the color he had needed for Carthage. The description is imbued with a timeless lyricism drawn from his experience and growing in intensity as did the actual experience, with the dramatic tension and release that accompany watching the slow advance of the rising sun, its quickening pace, and its final bursting over the horizon. But the impact is heightened here by the precise, particularized quality deriving from the archeolog ical elements, whose antiquity reinforces the suggestion of an eter-nal phenomenon. The experience has had validity as long as there have been men to react to it, either in ancient Carthage or among modern readers, though few can ever know except through litera-ture so dramatic a culmination as the response of the horses of Eschmoûn, where the ancient setting and the nineteenth-century lyric experience fused in an ultimate description written beyond time.

Salammbô Is Published

I have read . . . that Colette preferred *Salammbô* to Flau-bert's other novels and I think that I understand the reason. Bourgeois life had changed because all Europe had been affected by two wars and their migrations. Flaubert helped to prepare the ground for modern psychology, he was not a doctor's son for nothing, and it is a measure of his greatness that we respond to different books of his at different times. . . . Perhaps his study of Carthage and the mercenaries (how one can smell the lions!) is nearer to us now with our memories of blitzes and invasions than his greater but nar-rower studies of French provincial life.

Bryher, *The Heart to Artemis, A Writer's Memoirs* (1962)

The spring and much of the summer of 1862 Flaubert devoted to final revisions of *Salammbô*, not completing the work until July 5.

He then sent the manuscript to Maxime Du Camp, who thus had the difficult task of being the first outsider to have to comment on the finished work. He acquitted himself well, giving Flaubert tremendous praise for what he had accomplished but turning before the end of his letter to the objections his conscience would not let him pass over in silence. There were too many battles, too many bellies ripped open, too much hot sun. Moreover, the novel disappeared behind the historical trappings: one interest kept being substituted for another. And he had real difficulties with many of the pronoun references. He wisely urged his friend to have someone read the manuscript aloud to him.[46] Du Camp was a good critic, but he must have known that he came too late. The parts of the manuscript were now too tightly integrated: Flaubert made no further important changes.

The sale of *Salammbô* to the publisher Michel Lévy was a complex and subterranean battle.[47] Flaubert, who hoped for twenty to thirty thousand francs for his novel, had Duplan carry on the negotiations. They were not easy, as Flaubert absolutely refused to let Lévy see the manuscript—this would be tantamount to allowing that he was competent to judge it!—and on the other hand Lévy had most legitimate doubts about the salability of a work on ancient Carthage by the author of *Madame Bovary*. He was worried, too, over the censor's reactions to what so independent an author might have done with this subject. And so very much money was involved! Hoping to increase sales, Lévy raised the question of possible illustrations, only to meet a furious reply by Flaubert: who indeed, he asked, could do a portrait of Hannibal? Or draw the precise design of a Carthaginian chair? If only he could have had illustrations, his task in writing would have been so much easier! He had taken trouble to leave these details vague precisely so that the imagination of the reader might have free play. And now Lévy was proposing to have some idiot destroy the whole illusion by his precision!

Bouilhet joined Duplan in urging more moderation on Flaubert: Gautier was paid only a thousand francs for a novel, and even Academicians received only three. When Flaubert suggested secretly approaching other publishers, his friends pointed out that the highly successful firm of Lévy was probably the only one which could come anywhere near his demands. Slowly he moderated them, from thirty to twenty thousand at first; then he allowed Lévy to read the manuscript; and finally in September they agreed on a price of ten thousand francs and the further guarantee that Lévy could have Flaubert's next modern novel for the same figure.

Flaubert had meanwhile gone to Vichy to relax; he had even hoped to have the money from Lévy to let him make it a more luxurious trip. His mother, who accompanied her son and Caroline, was not well, so that uncle and niece were much together. Flaubert would take a book and Caroline her sketching pad, and they would wander off along the riverbank. He read while she drew, and he would interrupt her when his reading suggested an idea to him or recalled to his mind passages from his favorite authors, which he would then recite to her. Despite his own rejection of the Church, he always accompanied his niece to Mass on Sundays. It was a long and happy month of complete relaxation.[48]

It was just as well, for the reception of *Salammbô* by the critics was not cordial. To begin with, Lévy had had the ingenious idea of letting it be rumored that he had paid thirty thousand for the novel in order to whet the appetite of the reading public. No doubt it did, but it also gave Flaubert's friends serious doubts concerning his artistic integrity. What should one make of his exaggerated claim of being interested only in art when he turned out to be such an adroit businessman, the Goncourt brothers wondered; they began to distrust their friend.[49] Then the book went on sale, and Flaubert worked frantically to get favorable reviews.

A copy went to Sainte-Beuve, about whose reaction Flaubert was deeply worried. He urged all his friends to try to influence the powerful critic. Eventually Sainte-Beuve devoted three successive articles to *Salammbô*. Although he was respectful toward Flaubert, still he had to make many of the objections which critics have been making ever since. More dangerous, he raised openly the question of sadism. Flaubert, seriously frightened, wrote a long letter in reply, answering him point by point but above all complaining of the risks for him which were entailed in such an objection: it might alert the police. When he found that Sainte-Beuve intended to publish this letter, he was even more alarmed and begged him to remove at least this paragraph from the letter. Sainte-Beuve, guessing more rightly than Flaubert, foresaw that the police would not dare to attack the popular author; hence, with only a few deletions he did in fact publish the reply. It is as well, for it helped to set the matter straight.[50]

A number of the critics and criticisms irritated Flaubert. *Madame Bovary* had been called a poor imitation of Balzac; with *Salammbô* it was Chateaubriand's name that seemed on every lip. Flaubert's annoyance was no doubt in part because, after Michelet, Chateaubriand was the greatest modern influence on his work; but he was also right in feeling that he had moved far away from his master. He deliberately left to Chateaubriand all elements of grace and enchantment, preferring for himself color and violence. His was to be the poetry of the reality that Carthage had been; Chateaubriand's was the poetry of a generality. Yet it was Chateaubriand who had opened the way by traveling to Tunis and who had known that he would have later followers. Chateaubriand must have been constantly in Flaubert's mind as he wrote *Salammbô*, just as Balzac had been during the writing of *Madame Bovary*.

Flaubert was right, however: in both novels his concept went beyond that of his predecessors. Unlike Chateaubriand, he was not seeking to offer a conclusion; rather he provided his reader the materials with which to do so. Hence he had to put directly into the text of his book much of the factual information which Chateaubriand had relegated to his footnotes in *The Martyrs*. He lost some of the poetry Chateaubriand had cast as a veil over his material, but he hoped he gained in the truthful presentation of beauty.

Many intimate friends and old acquaintances spoke or wrote enthusiastically about the new novel. Louise Colet arranged through a friend to have Flaubert told of her favorable reactions. He responded with a few pleasant comments about his former mistress. But when he failed to suggest that they meet, Louise was furious and spoke of her total contempt for his character and the terrible repulsion she felt for his premature physical decrepitude.[51] His old friend Ernest Chevalier, now a successful magistrate in Lyon, wrote to wish him praise from all intelligent men and many purchasers among the bourgeois. Reading Gustave's work, he said, had brought back their childhood together and the moments when they had sat together reading the first juvenile works that Flaubert had published in *Le Colibri*.[52] Ludovica wrote affectionately to say her copy had arrived just in time. Knowing that Jeanne de Tourbey had hers already, she was herself almost beginning to be angry; she would read it at once and Flaubert should stop by the next day to hear her reactions at firsthand.[53]

With Sainte-Beuve, Flaubert had done everything he could, but nevertheless his three reviews were not favorable. Flaubert's maneuvers succeeded only in annoying the Goncourt brothers, who felt he was behaving improperly.[54] An occasional critic then and even today has found the novel sound, but in general the reaction, from the very first, had been hostile. The article in December which mentioned his epilepsy was a first thorn in his flesh.[55] A second article in the same newspaper, and the lead one this time, infuriated him by unpleasant descriptions of his physique, his life, and his novel. He was a fat frog trying to blow himself up to the proportions of a bull, a weak and perverted rhetorician, and his book reached such levels of boredom that it managed to become a wholly new phenomenon. Flaubert was beside himself, and the combined efforts of Duplan and Bouilhet barely sufficed to keep him from taking some sort of violent action. His mother, whom officious friends informed of the article, was afraid that her son was about to fight a duel.[56]

Against this background came the most erudite of all the attacks on the book, by a recently arrived German archeologist, Froehner, who was so unwise as to put in doubt Flaubert's scholarship and to correct him with pedantry and superiority. Flaubert was already irritated beyond the point of endurance. When he was informed that in fact Froehner was only a cover for other opposition forces, including Louise Colet, he took up his pen for a terrible reply. For fourteen hours, through most of the night and far into the next day, he worked.[57] Point by point he rebutted Froehner's ill-chosen arguments and with devastating irony destroyed him. When he finished, he felt better. The reply was published shortly.

The Goncourt brothers, to whom Flaubert had read parts of the novel at various times, were seriously worried. Some sections appealed to them, but they missed any over-all effect in these endless details, and the book seemed heartless, a novel of the body, not of the soul, of man. They felt they had a right to hope for more from their friend. Some parts were childish, others ridiculous, and the general effect was mortally boring.[58] The lesser critics stated in public what the Goncourt brothers were confiding to their journal. Flaubert jotted down in his Notebook the bitter jibe that fame consisted in being the occasion of a large number of stupid observations.[59]

Meanwhile *Salammbô* was a huge popular success. By the ninth of December, when the book had been out less than three weeks, four thousand copies had been sold. A second edition was required shortly after the new year began. The novel came out too late for parodying in the year-end reviews of 1862; but it was still talked of enough to appear in those for 1863. *Salammbô* was Flaubert's last great popular success, and he savored his fame.

There was even talk of making *Salammbô* into an opera, a project which had interested Berlioz, who, by exception, had reviewed the novel in one of his articles normally reserved for musical matters. Reyer, too, had thought of it nearly a year before the book appeared, on the basis of advance reports. Once it was published, Flaubert thought of a libretto by Gautier and score by Verdi. Over the months and then the years the project continued to be discussed, but to no avail. Such an opera was not in fact completed for decades and then with a libretto by Du Locle and score by Reyer. In 1890 the opera was at last performed in Brussels and revived in Paris in 1938.

Salammbô had proved, perhaps, not to be a very good novel, but it had provided the occasion for some splendid pages and had opened paths the historical novel could explore for generations. Above all it had to be written: some things a writer must get said or have forever intruding into works where they do not belong. Flaubert's concept of total and uninhibited love, uniting the desires of the flesh and the highest aspirations of the soul, a concept he was sure had existed in antiquity, he had to embody in a novel. He had now done so.

18

Facing the Mid-Forties (1863-69)

The Castle of Hearts

I am *ashamed* of it; it seems to me . . . trivial and petty . . .
it is empty. I have written something mediocre and inferior.
Letter to Amelie Bosquet, October 26, 1863, after
finishing *The Castle of Hearts*

THE umbilical cord had been cut: *Salammbô* belonged to the
public. What would Flaubert do now? A man must live with the
demons that are part of his make-up and strike what compromises
he can with them. Flaubert's love of the theater had started him
on his writing and underlain part of the transformation he had
wrought in the art of writing the novel. The Agricultural Fair in
Madame Bovary reflects this, and countless pages in *Salammbô*
were written—his exchange of letters with Bouilhet makes clear[1]
—in the full consciousness that he was writing scenes as for the
stage. He felt the time had now come to give direct outlet to his
joy in the theater.

As early as 1859, Flaubert had begun to think of writing a
play, and the idea had remained in his mind through all the final
months of drafting *Salammbô*. Bouilhet encouraged him to feel
that he had native talent for the theater.[2] Hence, in the last
months of 1861 he began to think seriously about what he would
write. He was certain that he understood the complex of commercial and personal interests that go into making a play a success,
and he was delighted at the prospect of entering in his own right
this world of the theater where, through Bouilhet, he already
knew so many actresses.[3] Eventually he hit upon the idea of a
féerie or satirical fairy tale woven around a pair of young lovers
who were aided by good fairies and opposed by gnomes allied

with all the bourgeois of the world. The idea was not outstanding; a three-way collaboration among himself, Bouilhet, and a mutual friend made matters worse. The *féerie* rapidly became a monster devouring Flaubert's time as he sought to handle it as he had *Salammbô*, by reading everything in print on the subject before he began to write.[4]

Many painful months went into the drafting of the play. The authors were interrupted by the publishing of *Salammbô* and by the vagaries of the third collaborator, who never seemed to be able to keep his part of the engagement; Bouilhet, too, had other occupations. Long before he had finished the play, Flaubert was heartily sick of it and knew it was a mediocre work. When *The Castle of Hearts* was completed, no director would touch it. Reluctantly Flaubert had to put it aside, but by then eighteen months of intermittent work had been squandered, and 1863 was drawing to a close.

Flaubert's gift was simply not for the theater, however much he learned from it for his novels. *The Castle of Hearts* does contain occasional entertaining lines, sometimes even whole scenes, and the influence of Aristophanes has been seen in certain parts.[5] But this is not so important as the fundamental impossibility of ever staging it. The months that went into writing it and the many, many months which later went into revisions never succeeded in producing a viable work. Like Camus' plays or Baudelaire's translations of Poe, Flaubert's work for the theater—*The Castle of Hearts* was not his last venture—must be understood as the tangential efforts which some creative artists seem to need. Although such ventures are in no direct way related to the mainstream of their artistic development, still these efforts, to which they attached so much importance, cannot be wholly dismissed as errors. Perhaps Flaubert could not have felt the dramatic qualities of the scenes in his novels so fully had he not had, concomitantly, an urge to write directly for the stage. At any rate, as he would have put it, he did what he did because he had to: creation, as he understood it, was not a voluntary choice.

A TIME OF HESITATION

Now that I have no major work in progress, I no longer
know what to do. I dream idly and I flounder about in the
midst of a lot of plans and ideas. But even the least ambitious notion that I half glimpse seems to me either impossible
or inept.

Letter to Madame Jules Sandeau, July 14, 1862

One of the reasons for Flaubert's adopting the project of *The
Castle of Hearts* may have been that, for the moment, the stream
of creativeness which had been carrying him for twelve years
through *Madame Bovary* and *Salammbô* was running lower.
While he was writing his play and for a year thereafter, he was
jotting down in his Notebooks innumerable ideas for further
works.[6] Beneath the apparent fertility, however, lay a much more
real futility. One idea or another would attract him for an hour or
a day or a week, but none seemed so compelling as to demand to
be written.

An old project to write a novel based on his nervous ailment
tempted him now and again; the idea of rewriting *The Temptation of Saint Anthony* attracted him even while he was still finishing *Salammbô*. Or various tales from ancient history seemed natural sequels to the Carthaginian novel. Before *Salammbô* was even
off to the printers, although he was full of dreams for other
works, he was equally full of doubts and fears. Something had
really gone wrong, and writing *The Castle of Hearts* did little to
improve matters.

Three different possibilities kept recurring. The first, which he
was in fact never to write, was the old dream of a novel depicting
the civilizing of the Near East and the barbarizing of the West, to
the detriment of both. Two other ideas, however, also intrigued
him. Eventually both were to become books, *A Sentimental Education* and *Bouvard and Pécuchet*. But, because each raised the
same apparently insuperable obstacle, for long months he began
neither. What was an antiromantic generation to do about roman-

ticism? By 1860 the problem was changing face for Flaubert, and he now easily affirmed that he was an old-line romantic. One does not devour one's childhood; or, if so, it is only to digest the past so as from it to body forth new flesh and blood. In *Madame Bovary* he had castigated romanticism; in *Salammbô* he had, by implication, suggested it could exist only in other ages. But the longings were always with him. As the years went by, he could even say all that was good in him came from this early leaven. And yet romanticism was wrong, fundamentally wrong, he felt. What could a writer do or say about it?[7]

In other words, could he again turn to the modern age? There had been moments during the writing of *Salammbô* when he felt urgent desires to come back in his next book to his own period. Sainte-Beuve, eager to see the realistic school produce a really good work, kept pressing the idea upon him.[8] But then again, whenever he really thought about it, the contemporary world both inspired him with horror and bored him profoundly. Blown about by these contrary winds, he could make for no port. Still, quick flashes of ideas for novels with modern subjects would occur to him, possible story lines or situations that would permit discussing the ways in which, instead of profiting from romanticism, his period was destroying it under the grotesque and the bourgeois.

Salammbô had been out for barely three weeks when, on his forty-first birthday, December 12, 1862, he jotted down in his Notebook that he was about to begin serious work on his big Parisian novel.[9] The second *Sentimental Education* was already in germ. But the task was not to be that easy. Earlier in the year he had become intrigued with the possibilities inherent in his story of two copy clerks, an old idea which went back many years. They would eventually be called Bouvard and Pécuchet. He would explore their minds and through them analyze the society of his age. How could he choose? Gently but firmly Bouilhet urged him to continue to search his mind and heart until he found the subject he really wished to write.[10] And so the months rolled by, taken up but not filled by *The Castle of Hearts*, while Flaubert's fancy proved too vagabond to control and unending ideas burst in unbidden to keep him from the serious business of deciding between *A Sentimental Education* and *Bouvard and Pécuchet*.

The difficulty with the idea of *A Sentimental Education* seemed to lie in putting the ideas together around some sort of story. No main scenes seemed to suggest themselves and—in a phrase he would use when the book was completed—the novel refused to make itself into a pyramid: it had no structure. Hence even under the whiplash of letters from Bouilhet, he continued helplessly to mark time. How could he find amusing events around which he might spin his tale? Bouilhet, questioned, could only send regrets for his inability to think of a plot for his friend.[11] At least, however, the choice was narrowed down to the contemporary period and an effort either to castigate it for having lost all its romanticism or to anatomize how this worked out in practice. The difficulties he was experiencing made him regret not having turned at once to *Saint Anthony* after finishing *Salammbô*, but it was too late now to go back. At last—already into the summer of 1864—he decided definitively to write *A Sentimental Education* and began the readings he felt necessary.

LIFE AT CROISSET

When I observe my solitude and my anguish, I wonder whether I am a fool or a saint.

Letter to Madame Roger des Genettes, Summer, 1864

The Goncourt brothers paid Flaubert a visit in Croisset in the autumn of 1863.[12] They found a severe, somewhat cramped, and very bourgeois tone to the household. Fires were not kept burning as high as they would have wished, and the carpeting had been stinted wherever possible. Even the food was less plentiful than they had imagined, knowing provincial ways and, above all, Flaubert. Only silverware appeared; nothing was of gold. Normans, the brothers recalled, were famous for stinginess.

Flaubert's hospitality, on the other hand, welcomed them from the start, cordial and open. Caroline, now a young lady of seventeen caught between her uncle and her grandmother, they pitied for her shut-in life. She was sent off to bed immediately after seven o'clock, much to her pouting regret. All next day everyone remained indoors, following the preference for immobility which had grown in Flaubert with advancing years. Not even his mother seemed able to drive him outside for so much as a walk in the garden. The brothers noted the lack of horse or canoe.

The day passed upstairs in Flaubert's study, its windows looking out over the Seine and the garden. Heavy oak bookcases, some of which still remain at Croisset today, covered much of the blank wall space. The fireplace had on its mantel a clock of yellow marble which had belonged to Flaubert's father. Balancing it was a bust of Hippocrates. To one side hung the water-color portrait of Harriet Collier; Flaubert told them only that she was a young lady he had known in Paris. It was a poor piece of art, and the girl seemed to them languorous and sickly. Callot's *Temptation of Saint Anthony* hung on another wall, while between the windows toward the river was Pradier's bust of Gustave's sister. A heavy divan-bed covered with cushions and a Turkish coverlet stood to one side, while a gilded idol overlooked the work table covered with green baize. The inkwell was in the form of a toad. On tables and walls were innumerable objects from India, evidencing Flaubert's fascination with that country. The curtains and hangings were gay, Near Eastern in their designs, and, to the fastidious taste of the brothers, somewhat old fashioned. Everywhere there were mementos of Flaubert's trips to the Mediterranean. His taste for the uncivilized Near East seemed a little coarse to his visitors. They found a substratum of the barbarian in this artist's nature.

Visits such as that of the Goncourt brothers were extremely rare in the quiet household beside the Seine. Of lady visitors there were almost none: Flaubert retreated more and more into his anchorite's life at Croisset, content to catch up when he was in Paris. Once again, as during the time of writing *Salammbô*, weeks would go by without his seeing a soul, for Caroline and his mother were not infrequently away in Rouen. His only sure companionship was the band of rats rummaging about noisily in the attic above his head, or, outside, the murmur of the water and the blowing of the wind. The solitude heightened his nervous sensibility.

His mother contributed little to calming Flaubert. She was already seventy when the Goncourt brothers visited Croisset in

1863. They found her still full of vitality and, though aged, still retaining the dignity of a woman who had been very beautiful in her youth. But—though they did not see it—she was as given to nervous upsets as ever, providing the tensions herself when external events failed to supply them. Once she even became so irritated she almost fired poor Julie; Flaubert had to intervene on the old servant's behalf.

Her health was not really bad until August, 1865, when her habitual nervousness brought on an attack of shingles. For several weeks the skin inflammations and neuralgic pains continued almost unabated. Her symptoms tended to disappear—a bad sign—whenever the doctor called, and Flaubert spent several sleepless nights caring for her.[13] With the following year her deafness became much worse, making her far less a companion to her son. In the spring of 1867 she had a first, slight stroke. Flaubert was in Paris, and Bouilhet, in Rouen at the time, wrote a reassuring report. For half a day there had been interference with her speech, a violent headache, and considerable weakness. Bouilhet suggested that it would be unwise for Flaubert to return to Rouen, as she might be alarmed by his arrival. But he also warned his old friend that such an attack was always the prelude to further ones. Flaubert, when he did see her, felt the stroke had been comfortingly mild. But she was now much harder to live with, and he was sad at watching her grow both weaker and more irritable. In late summer he was able to escort her to the great Paris World Exposition, but old age was inexorably taking its toll, and as the writing of *A Sentimental Education* drew to its close in the spring of 1869, Flaubert, who was living in Paris, was receiving regular bulletins on her health from Bouilhet.[14] Her state was alarming and presaged an end which could not be far off.

In 1865 the husband of Achille's daughter committed suicide. Two or three years later the daughter who had been born to them came down with measles soon complicated by pneumonia. The mother was sick herself and unable to be with her child. Shortly the child died, and once again Flaubert wearily took the road which led up to the cemetery, thinking of how many of his loved ones now lay there.[15]

On the other hand, Caroline was growing up fast. In December, 1863, her uncle, in Paris, was informed she wished to be married; she had selected her man; he had made the formal request for her hand. Not all is entirely clear in this matter.[16] Her suitor gave his name as Ernest Commanville; he may even have hinted it was in reality *de* Commanville. He owned a sawmill at Dieppe and imported wood from Scandinavia, which he sold as cordwood for fireplaces or for use in construction; he was reported to be well thought of in commercial circles. He was about thirty and Caroline seventeen, about the age difference normal then—and frequently still—in good society in France. In point of fact, however —and this would have had to come out before the required legal marriage ceremony could be performed—he was illegitimate. To compound it, so were his father and his grandfather before him. But before all this became known, no doubt matters were much too far along for it to be easy to withdraw; Ernest Commanville had a good reputation and had kept his secret carefully.

While Commanville's background was still unknown to Caroline and she was considering marriage, leaning first to one side and then to the other, she wrote her uncle for his advice. He had met Commanville, had had time to size him up, and did not dislike him. He sat down to try to write the letter her father might have written. He urged upon her that the real matter to weigh was her chance of future happiness; he admitted he would be as unsure as she was. The creator of Emma Bovary knew full well—and told his niece—that life required for its nourishment more than poetic ideas and exalted sentiments. But what should you do if the idea of bourgeois existence spelled unrelieved boredom? Madame Flaubert was anxious that Caroline be married, and he agreed that he was, too, so she would not be left alone. Caroline had wept copiously when Flaubert had last seen her. For his own part, the prospect of her going off to set up a new household away from his did not make him feel gay. He even confessed that, of course, he would be jealous of her new husband and would not like him at first. But that did not really matter, he added, for in good time he would forgive him for stealing his niece; he would even cherish him, if he made her happy.

He could not advise her: he could only add up the facts for her. In December, 1863, they appeared clear: Commanville was an honorable man who had asked for her hand in honorable fashion. His background, his character, and his relationships all seemed clear. He was from Rouen: a Parisian might be more entertaining but only if he came from the necessarily suspect bohemian milieu. Coming instead from their own city, he could be known and trusted.

The thought of his niece as the wife of an impoverished bohemian, Flaubert admitted, was unbearable. He would rather see her marry a millionaire grocer than a great man who was poor. If the statement seems crass or unimaginative or suggests even a betrayal of the Parisian milieus he had so loved, Flaubert did not mean it that way. For he knew, both from observing himself for forty years and from knowing most of the outstanding men and women of his age, that such people are not easy to live with, whatever romantic notions young girls might have on the subject. He added at once that such a man would not only be poor: in addition he would have moments of tyranny and brutality. That was why he would not wish such a husband for Caroline. And he knew whereof he spoke. His letter was a confession of his own angular, spiny character and, in part, an explanation of why he himself had never married.

Poor Caro would have to live with her husband in Rouen, and this was of course a major drawback. But Rouen and a decent income were far preferable to Paris and no money. Besides, as the sawmill prospered later, why could they not then come live in Paris?

There was a further difficulty, one too serious to be overlooked. Flaubert warned his niece she could not hope to find a husband of better intelligence and education than herself. If he had known such a man, he would long before this have sought him out and introduced him. Caroline had no choice but to marry a man less gifted than herself, and loving him and being happy with him would not be easy. She should resist all the pressures that would be brought to bear on her to come out with a hasty answer. And throughout she should count on the tender affection of her old uncle.

The marriage was soon agreed upon and took place in April of 1864. Flaubert returned from Paris to spend the last few days

with Caroline. The newly wedded couple set out after the ceremony for the consecrated trip to Italy, traveling across the north
from Genoa and Milan to Venice. Maxime Du Camp, who understood what the separation must be meaning to Gustave and Madame Flaubert, wrote the day before—so that the letter would arrive at its most useful moment—to say he knew they would not
be happy and the house would seem very sad when they returned
in the evening. He would be with them in thought.[17]

The young couple was off, and Flaubert, without ever really
experiencing fatherhood, now knew all the loneliness of a child's
departure. His letters followed them as they went. At Venice, he
hoped they would enjoy traveling by gondola and would rejoice
as he had in the paintings of Veronese and Titian and Tintoretto.
Caro should open her eyes wide while she was there to draw in a
provision for her memory to last the rest of her life. His letters
were constant; and Caro was a good niece to him, writing almost
weekly, so frequently in fact that he could later complain if he
had not heard from her for ten days. But a new and different life
had begun for both.

Flaubert settled back into his bachelor life with his mother to
care for him. His health was not entirely good. The long period
after finishing *Salammbô* and before definitely undertaking *A Sentimental Education* was hard on his nerves. He had boils and skin
troubles and stomach cramps. Du Camp reassured him that what
he needed was a good subject to work on; then he would be all
right. By the autumn of 1863 he was having severe eye troubles,
headaches, acute pains in his knees, and some sort of recurrent
outbreak on his genitals.[18] These problems were particularly irritating to a man who found all physical ailments disgraceful.

A great deal of his time during these years Flaubert spent in
Croisset. Several winters, instead of moving into Paris rather early,
he stayed on to push ahead with his book. Leaving whatever place
he was in continued to bother him, so he contented himself for the
most part with only short excursions: he would go in to Rouen
for the Saint Romain Fair, or he would take quick trips of a few
weeks at most to England or even shorter journeys to visit friends
in the country surrounding Paris. His was in general a sedentary
life despite further dreams of trips to India or China, which he

knew he would never make. On the other hand, in imagination he continued to live in flamboyant past ages among primitive, heroic peoples. He did not need, really, to travel.

The penalty for so much imagination was moodiness, and age did nothing to lessen his periods of terrible depression. Moreover he was becoming more and more irritable. In a single afternoon he managed to call one lady an imbecile and another a turkey, a type of conduct which was hard on his hostesses. Wild rages would take hold of him—Homeric, he called them—and his nerves would explode, leaving him in the grip of a headache for the whole next day.[19] He was better off alone most of the time, but his sensitivities then grew beyond his control. His heart would beat faster almost without cause, and he would break out again in boils and rashes. For him and his friends the only state in which literature could be produced was one of perpetual illness. This had been true of Baudelaire and was constantly so with the Goncourt brothers. Frantic efforts, a permanent anguish, a domestic life which was deliberately narrowed, love completely excluded: this was all necessary to be a writer in the 1860's. Flaubert felt as though he had been flayed.[20]

He was more easily moved now. It seemed almost humiliating how quickly tears could come to his eyes. He had been brought up in a hospital, but he recalled that his father, who had even invented new and terrifying surgical procedures, could not stand the sight of a suffering dog. The melancholy mood which a lovely summer's evening engendered in him made him feel only the more strongly the nothingness of man and led him to wonder whether his way of life could be right: the truly great works of the past had not required such pains. He found himself hating nature for the reflections she evoked in him. Once, as he heard a party of revelers returning from their evening by boat on the Seine under the moonlight, he was forced to close the window: his emotions overflowed as he thought back across the years to Italy and sitting beneath the orange trees of Sorrento with Maxime.

Slowly Flaubert's emotions became more manageable and, particularly at the urging of George Sand, he began to open himself to nature. One January night the moon on the snow was so attractive that he went for a two-hour walk, imagining himself in Russia or Norway and rejoicing as the rising tide in the river made the ice crack: the experience did him good, he wrote to Madame Sand.

His moods were, in general, somber. He could not find that he had wasted his time: but what had he to show for all the years? Only work could console him, as always, but at best writing was a cover for his fundamental sadness. He had known in his youth a period of epic vitality and strength; now as the middle forties came upon him he seemed broken by fatigue, his days passing one after another, all submerged under the black melancholy of his memories. Was this, he wondered, the beginning of the end for him, or only a passing malady? He could not tell.

His childhood seemed to surround him on every hand. Occasional letters exchanged with Ernest Chevalier would bring back the bygone Rouen days. Caro's departure, which emptied his own home, revived the specters of the one in which he had grown up. He recalled Ernest's uncle, *père* Mignot, who used to read aloud to him from Cervantes; he could remember the pictures in the living room. Or Easter would stir up memories of the yearly trip to Les Andelys and the endless pipes he and Ernest used to smoke as they sat there in Richard the Lion-Hearted's castle, Chateau-Gaillard. Contacts with the Le Poittevin family revived the even more poignant memories of Alfred. Flaubert could recall arriving at their old family house, when he would find them all outside walking in the sunshine on the terrace with the aviary off to one side. As he entered, he used to give the laugh of Le Garçon and the easy, happy times would begin again. Alfred seemed constantly in his mind, and now that he knew most of the great men of his age, he measured them against him and always found them wanting. There had never been another affection in his life like that which he had felt for Alfred, he wrote to Alfred's sister Laure, and he could still evoke his face and figure at will and hear or see him as though he were there beside him. He always remembered with respect their dreams and readings and talks. What he had done later had all had its start then, as he sought not to fall below the level Alfred had set for him.

During these years, too, there were visits to the coast, particularly to Trouville. The trips were not easy, and Du Camp sent Flaubert a letter of consolation after one of them. Maxime wrote of being reminded of their return together there at the end of the hiking trip through Brittany: how the memory must have saddened Gustave now! Brittany was, Du Camp wrote, their best moment. Never since had they had an equal to that experience, and they never would: age was upon them now, and they must reconcile themselves to it. The letter reached Flaubert in May, 1863; he had not yet decided to write *A Sentimental Education*, but when he did turn to this novel. Maxime's comment would form its last line.

Flaubert's hatred of the bourgeois continued unabated, and he wrote letters of serious condolence to his niece Caroline for having to live amongst them in Rouen. The city was even worse than it had been in his childhood: now its inhabitants barely supported a single theatrical troupe, whereas two had been fully occupied formerly. He was, for his own part, fascinated by the visit of a troupe of gypsies to the city, especially because of the hatred which these undisciplined souls obviously aroused among his fellow citizens. It was the hatred they felt for the Bedouin, the heretic, the philosopher, the poet, for any man who dared live alone. And underneath this hatred was fear. It exasperated him . . . though he had to confess in the same breath that there were indeed quite a number of things which exasperated him: his native land seemed to have been able to hate every new and good idea that had ever arisen. His present book would state this baldly for their edification.

But not all of Flaubert's hatreds were sound, and in the 1860's he was becoming the victim of his own sense of the grotesque to the point that his judgment was being seriously warped. He cultivated his rages without realizing that they could only degenerate into a lack of self-judgment and self-knowledge.[21] This imbalance had helped to destroy *The Castle of Hearts*; it made him a most difficult guest at social gatherings; his long bachelorhood gave him little training in countering it. His new book would reflect his emotional state by being far less impassive and impartial than *Salammbô* or *Madame Bovary*.

Life in Paris

He is not a Parisian; he even looks a little coarse, like a sort
of peasant brought up in a painter's studio, not at all a man
of the world.

         Taine on his first visit to Flaubert in 1863

In some ways life was better for Flaubert in Paris, and, when on
rare occasions work on *A Sentimental Education* was moving rapidly enough, he spent most of the winter and spring months there.
Neither the writer in him, who loved long hours leaning over his
desk, nor the noisy, overly loud buffoon could ever be at home
there. But being in the capital did enable him to visit the Exposition of 1867 several times and discover a new world, far different
from the one he knew. He found it ugly and unpleasant.

Taine, who came to know him during these years, was struck
with his animal energy. His face and especially his heavy-lidded,
ferocious eyes, suggested it. Flaubert received him for the first
time in a jacket and opennecked shirt. Taine noted the high coloring produced by the numerous capillaries near the surface of the
skin; his hair was almost wholly gone. He bore the marks of his
overwork and the constraints he imposed upon himself, looking
like a cavalry captain a little on in years who had taken to drink.
Great strength and a certain heaviness were the dominant characteristics, excluding all delicacy or finesse, but their lack was compensated by an air of obvious frankness and naturalness. He
seemed to belong to some earlier, primitive age, totally sincere and
without any sophistication. He confided to Taine his hatred for
having to dress formally in order to go out in the evenings,

Taine's summary was that Flaubert represented decadence, a
man and an art dragged from their natural spheres into the world
of erudition and composition. He seemed to have tired his brain
by forcing it too far and too long. This large, muscular man was
as nervous as a woman. He trembled at high-pitched noises, such
as the cutting of a cork, a trait which he had given to Emma

Bovary. His admiration in literature went to authors of the classical decadence, a matter of affinity, Taine commented.[22]

Salammbô opened the imperial court to Flaubert. On January 18, 1863, he received a letter from his friend Camille Doucet, then responsible for the censorship of the theaters, informing him that he was expected at the Princess Mathilde's on the twenty-first and that the Emperor and Empress would be there. Their majesties had expressed a desire to meet the author of the Carthaginian novel so that the Empress could consult him on Salammbô's dress: she proposed to wear one like it at her next costume ball. A flattered Flaubert was delighted to comply. The Goncourt brothers, who attended also, found their friend insufferable in his vanity, but the brothers always did find Flaubert's successes painful.[23]

The Princess had recognized him the moment he entered; he thanked her for the honor of her invitation. Unlike the imperial prosecutor, the Princess had had no difficulty in discovering the excellent and the profoundly moral quality of *Madame Bovary*. On the other hand, she found *Salammbô* markedly inferior, although obviously calculated to win popular success. Over the years she was to grow very fond of her novelist friend, pardoning him his noisy paradoxes and exaggerated rages. She was entertained that she could never draw from him a precise definition of what he meant by the hated word "bourgeois," which (she rightly suspected) meant essentially anything he did not like. She knew he had neither wit nor imagination, although he made up for this in part by his enormous readings. In her private papers she noted that he was the bourgeoisie incarnate, but she added at once: "Heavens, if he could hear me!" She understood and easily forgave his need constantly to astonish and amaze his listener; she found far more important his total sincerity in everything he said and did, however contradictory his positions. She was good and kind to him, and through her he came to know something of the imperial milieu, which he loved to frequent, good bourgeois that he was.

Princess Mathilde had her favorite court painter, Giraud, whose talent was perhaps best shown in the quick caricatures he made of the habitués of her salon. A reproduction of his portrait of Flaubert long hung in Edmond de Goncourt's bedchamber, although it annoyed and irritated him. He was anxious, often, to take it down, but always ended by leaving it up because the resemblance was so striking. The portrait showed the sitter's fundamental lack of aristocracy, which was so important to both Goncourt brothers. The caricature went so far that it became a cruel calumny, they wrote. The bulging forehead looked stupid; the teary lower lid, reddened nose, and drooping mustaches suggested a valet who worked in a soldier's brothel here dressed up for a wedding.[24] It was in truth not a flattering portrait, but then neither were most of Giraud's caricatures, for instance those of Du Camp or Sainte-Beuve.

Flaubert's contacts with the imperial court grew steadily more frequent during the sixties. He often retained the sense of humor to poke fun at his vanity over this, but vanity it was. He was invited to various functions, some formal and public, others more intimate, and he enjoyed himself hugely at both, thinking at intervals of how the good bourgeois of Rouen would feel if they could but hear of his social triumphs. He was amazed at the ostentatious wealth Louis-Napoleon's court displayed. It pleased him, after a while, to be able to take Bouilhet about patronizingly and startle him by the number of people whom he knew. Shortly people began to imagine that he had more influence than in fact he did, and he had to confess with embarrassment that there were many favors he was not able to ask of the court circles. However, as the decade wore on, he found the demands on his time were becoming a menace to his writing.

His was a strangely variegated social world. On a given evening he might dine with some of the men of the imperial family at Jeanne de Tourbey's apartment and shortly thereafter be present at an evening gathering with the Princess Mathilde only to hear himself berated for having spent time with such a demimondaine. The imperial court, from the Emperor down, consisted of clever opportunists; Flaubert and the Goncourt brothers cut odd figures there. Flaubert himself did not seem to know it, but the two Goncourts did.[25]

Louis Bouilhet was puzzled and saddened to see his friend thus move into a world with these shoddy values. Around the middle of the decade he wrote to note that now Flaubert really liked this milieu whereas he himself was moving ever further from it. Bouilhet quite understood that by being in Paris each had more chance to see the other—the consecrated excuse—but he reminded his old friend that what they had known together in Rouen neither could ever find talking to the other on a street corner in Paris. When Flaubert objected violently, Bouilhet pursued his point, urging—and Flaubert marked the margin in red pencil to draw it to his own attention—that nowadays Flaubert's interests and aspirations were far more turned toward the social world than they had been during those fabulous Rouen days when he had told Du Camp off for urging him to come to Paris. This change in their views was why the happy and carefree life they had known a decade earlier could no longer be recaptured. In sum they had lost their independence by agreeing to worship other gods than literature.[26]

This thought would recur in the final pages of *A Sentimental Education*, which suggest symbolically that the best moments in life occur at its threshold only, before dream can be converted into reality and hence wither into disillusionment. Now instead matters like being nominated to the Legion of Honor began to concern Flaubert. At first there was talk of nominating him in 1865; but political considerations interfered, and his hopes had to be set aside until 1866, when he was finally recognized. Such ambition was indeed, as Bouilhet insisted, a far cry from his earlier attitude.[27]

Flaubert's new life reached a sort of culmination the day he was invited to a court ball in June of 1867. He insisted that his presence was really at each instant dedicated to literature and that he would some day use what he observed in a novel. But in fact he was completely ecstatic and found the evening colossal. The Czar of Russia, the King of Italy, the King of Prussia, and other royal personages were present! He could even write to George Sand that the Czar had not pleased him at all. More accurately, though, he wrote to Princess Mathilde that the experience remained in his memory like something from fairyland or a dream. Was he not, he asked her, like Emma Bovary attending her first ball?

Because of his contacts with the court, Flaubert followed political matters more closely during these years. Most of what he saw, however, he found so disgusting that he usually contented himself with condemning it outright and totally. He suspected France perhaps lacked an instinctive genius for politics. But like most Frenchmen in the sixties he seriously overestimated the Emperor and so failed to understand how great a menace Bismarck's Prussia would eventually be. Nevertheless, he had more foresight than most of his acquaintances and friends as the political situation began to deteriorate: at least he understood that France must settle once and for all with the Prussian threat. Moreover, he preferred that it be sooner rather than later, lest Prussia play the role of Macedonia under a new Alexander. As the decade drew toward its close, which would be marked by the Franco-Prussian War, the defeat of France, and the end of the Empire, Flaubert's attention was directed more toward internal affairs, where he perceived how seriously the French were divided amongst themselves, so much so, he felt, that there was no internal danger to the Emperor. He was probably right. Unfortunately, like almost all Frenchmen, he did not dream that Bismarck could crush France at will, and would soon do so.

Throughout these years of his mid-forties Flaubert constantly overspent. His income was not large, some seven thousand francs annually; yet it was enough to keep him from want if only he consented to live sensibly. But this he was loath to do, to the real chagrin of his mother, who feared for what might happen when she would no longer be there to rescue him from the various plights into which he was always getting himself. Each of them, mother and son, wrote to the family lawyer as arbiter, trying to circumvent the other, until finally Madame Flaubert had to take a firm hand with her spendthrift offspring. Thereafter he turned to other sources, particularly to Michel Lévy, seeking an advance on the money which would be owing him for *A Sentimental Education*. After months of delay the publisher finally consented, but Flaubert's pride had been hurt in the meantime. And his debts had continued to rise, too, so that, from loan to loan, he was constantly, like Emma, behind on his payments.[28]

FRIENDS AND ACQUAINTANCES

Nowadays I know almost all the men who are commonly
considered to be the most intelligent of the age.
            Letter to Madame Gustave de Maupassant, January, 1863

As before, most of Flaubert's friends and even acquaintances were
men. Of these the closest was of course Louis Bouilhet. By the
middle of the decade success was beginning to desert him, and
Flaubert joined with the poet-dramatist's other friends in efforts
to get him a government pension, post, or subvention. Obtaining
one turned out be quite difficult, and several painful years went
by before the position of librarian at Rouen became vacant. At
last it was Bouilhet's and, exclaimed Flaubert, he would no longer
have to worry about earning a living. Such security was a sad
contrast with his own ten thousand francs of debts.

This was in the spring of 1867 and all seemed well. But by
early 1868 Flaubert's old friend was seriously ill. He coughed a
great deal and was short of breath; above all he was prey to a
black melancholy. Incidental bits of poetry he still managed to
write, but the energy to start a new play seemed hopelessly beyond him. By the end of 1868 his condition was far graver: he
was suffering from serious hallucinations and inexplicable fears.
He could fall asleep only in the arms of his mistress, where she
could watch over him; otherwise dread of asphyxiation kept sleep
away. Flaubert was deeply alarmed as he hurried to finish *A Sentimental Education*.[29]

Flaubert's rapprochement with Du Camp, successfully begun
earlier, brought the two men warmly together in 1865. In the
following year, as death took some of Maxime's oldest friends, he
turned again to Flaubert, urging that these bereavements were a
warning to them to appreciate what they had. He was writing a
book recounting what his generation had been in its younger days.
At Maxime's request Flaubert went over the manuscript carefully.
Du Camp was grateful, and on his side Flaubert felt it was the best
thing his old friend had written. All men of his age would recog-

nize themselves, he said: and he commented on the odd way such currents would sweep through the air, for his own *Sentimental Education* was an attempt to do the same thing, to explain to a generation which had not lived it what life had been like before 1848.[30]

With the Goncourt brothers, whom Flaubert saw frequently, the situation was, as always, complex. Noting his tendency to exaggerate, the brothers came to suspect his sincerity most of the time. They were horrified at the life he led, calling it that of a galley slave or a Trappist monk. Finally, and perhaps worst in their eyes, they found him vulgar and without taste. His genius, if he had any, was that of an unpolished provincial, they decided, and they disliked him for it. Yet on the other hand there was a winning warmth in the affection he obviously felt for them. And how could one resist the praise he so freely gave their works and which so few other readers accorded them? Hence, despite their distaste for him, the brothers continued to see him regularly, and, when they came to count over the people they knew who, like themselves, lived only for art, they always found he alone fitted their high standards. The friendship endured.[31]

When the Goncourt brothers had visited Flaubert in Croisset for a few days in October of 1863, they found it an exhausting experience. All day long, without pause, Flaubert read *November* aloud to them: they were deeply impressed. Then he overwhelmed them with his various costumes from his Mediterranean trips. After dinner he drew from his papers an incredible collection of documents for their perusal: the confessions of a pederast, a prostitute's love letter, the account of a cripple made worse by treatment—the sort of documents which titillated him or reinforced his certainty that man was a fated creature. The next day was a repetition of the first as Flaubert read to the bewildered brothers the entire series of his travel notes. They were less impressed with these, suspecting that much of the trip had been undertaken to amaze the inhabitants of Rouen on his return; they also regretted that there was not more art in the descriptions. At midnight they begged off hearing any more, although Flaubert spoke of continuing till six. Like many other people, the brothers found him both endearing and exasperating.

Much closer temperamentally to Flaubert was the Russian novelist Turgenev. The Goncourt brothers commented that foreigners shared with provincial Frenchmen a certain lack of ease in Paris and that this was, no doubt, what drew Turgenev to men like Flaubert and Zola.[32] The friendship developed rapidly after they met in 1863. Turgenev sent Flaubert translations of some of his works; Flaubert was delighted with them and replied enthusiastically. Frequently Turgenev would promise a visit to Croisset and then beg off at the last moment. His visits—the first was in 1868—were so delightful, however, that over the years Flaubert kept on inviting him and putting up with his constant failure to appear.

Flaubert first met Turgenev at one of the famous Restaurant Magny dinners which Sainte-Beuve had inaugurated in November, 1862. Flaubert often attended them, enjoying the company of Sainte-Beuve, the Goncourt brothers, Taine, Turgenev, and others there. Only finally in 1868 did he begin to abandon them, disliking the newer members of the circle. Sainte-Beuve was never one of his intimates, but the critic was, like Turgenev, one of the few people who understood literature as he did. They remained warm friends. There were more erudite friendships, too—Michelet, Taine, Renan, Maury, among others—keeping Flaubert posted on the developing science of historiography and the related field of comparative religion.

For the first time now there began to be a certain number of people in Rouen whom Flaubert saw with pleasure. There was, for instance, the aging Dr. Félix Pouchet, today remembered chiefly as one of Pasteur's antagonists. Despite his faulty stand on the question of the origin of micro-organisms—he advocated spontaneous generation—Pouchet was an interesting scientist who, like Flaubert, lived a monastic existence dedicated to his work. Flaubert was devoted to him and was delighted to be able to help his son Georges get various posts. Another Rouennais close to Flaubert was Charles Lapierre, editor of *La Nouvelliste de Rouen*, a local Catholic paper, who knew and admired the novelist and was fond enough of him to play innumerable practical jokes on him. Lapierre was well informed on political matters and could advise his friend, to the extent Flaubert was willing to listen.

Through Lapierre, Flaubert met the public prosecutor Raoul-Duval in the autumn of 1868. A handsome, agreeable, athletic man, he soon became fast friends with Flaubert. As he was an enthusiastic horseback rider, he took to riding out to Croisset to talk of literature, science, economics, history, and other subjects over which his free-ranging mind wandered easily.[33] More important for the years to come was Flaubert's meeting with Edmond Laporte, presumably through Jules Duplan, about 1865. By 1866 Laporte was already being invited to dine at Croisset. Ten years younger than Flaubert, he managed a lace factory near Croisset. He was a willing helper and soon became an indispensable aid in tracking down information. They became very close, exchanged gifts, and soon saw each other constantly.

Wᴏᴍᴇɴ

Men who deeply love Woman cannot love Justice.
From a private note written about 1863
and reprinted in *Notes de voyages*

Flaubert's patterns for his relations with women he had established when he was little more than twenty-five; quite naturally he did not alter them radically now that he was twenty years older. What changes did come, came only with aging still more, and he was barely aware in this decade that a transformation was taking place.

Throughout his forties Flaubert continued—particularly in Paris—to arrange frequent and vigorous assignations; he wrote often to Bouilhet bragging of his prowess. Yet in his precepts he continued to vaunt the advantages of the hermit's life that for the most part he led in Croisset.[34] His two lives came together in their common refusal to allow Woman—or any particular woman—to occupy a real place in his life: he could not find a way to make literature and love coexist. Since choose he must, he chose literature unhesitatingly. Real women were to him hopelessly unsatisfactory; they were, like Emma, always chasing illusions and yet always desirable to man as the ultimate good he might seek. For he knew that, despite all his jibes, he remained profoundly attached to woman and as timid as ever with her.

His outbursts were the index of his pain. Frustrated romantic and inhibited, confused victim of an Oedipus complex, he clung tenaciously to an impossible dream of what a woman could and therefore should be. Love, he demanded, must be a vague feeling of excitement. He insisted that in reality he was still a virgin, since all the women he had ever possessed had been no more than mattresses—his own word—for an ideal woman of his dreams. What he sought, what all men sought, was not a physical ejaculation but a nervous one, an emotion, the trembling that comes over you when you press a woman's hand. And so he asserted that he was in fact virtuous and chaste.[35]

He felt that the low state of the theater and the novel could be traced directly to their practice of making love seem ridiculous. Or was it perhaps somewhat different, he wondered: was this broadside attack on adultery instead highly moral? Perhaps the only way to be cured of—or rather, to be saved from—the passions was first to laugh at them.[36]

Confusion fed upon confusion in Flaubert and in his whole circle, for whom the question of love and of woman was obsessive. Flaubert wondered whether he were in fact of both sexes. Perhaps Du Camp alone of the entire group attained some peace of mind, but only at the price of total cynicism. Of his mistress of many years standing he once wrote to Flaubert that she was a good woman, quiet, not given to bothering him . . . that is to say, she was all that one could ask of her execrable sex.[37] It was not a happy group of men who met on Sundays in Flaubert's apartment on the Boulevard du Temple to talk of love.

Flaubert's relations with women, echoing these conflicts, were strangely ambiguous or contradictory. Ludovica had become too old to play a role of more than nostalgia for him. Suzanne Lagier, now older too, was a warm and lascivious friend to whom all these men could turn in complete and open frankness. Louise Colet remained a distant figure whose escapades interested Flaubert enough that he cut out the reports of them from *Le Figaro*. Jeanne de Tourbey he continued to see with such frequency as to annoy Princess Mathilde.[38]

During this decade Elisa Schlésinger reentered Flaubert's life. Before he completed *Salammbô*, he had already learned from her husband that she was seriously ill. Maurice had continued to write of her pitiful state, but only in August, 1863, did Flaubert learn from Du Camp, who saw her in an asylum near Baden-Baden, that she was suffering from mental alienation and profound melancholy. Later in the month she was able to leave the asylum, and Du Camp could report seeing her on her son's arm. He wrote to Flaubert that she was magnificent, thin, pale, dark, her hair now all white, and her eyes wild. She had aged markedly. It made Maxime think at long, sad length of Flaubert and of all that Gustave told him of Elisa. Her husband Maurice was as assiduous as ever with the ladies. Flaubert considered a trip to Baden-Baden that autumn but was prevented by recurring difficulties with his health.[39]

Elisa, however, improved slowly, and there began to be the real possibility that Gustave could see her again. In the summer of 1865 he managed a visit to Baden-Baden, where they may well have met. In addition and more important, her recovery was so complete that by autumn she was able to return to France, making the first of several long visits to Mantes. Bouilhet was living there and thus easily kept Flaubert informed of the presence of "Madame Maurice," as he and Flaubert always respectfully termed her. Again in the winter and the spring of 1867 Elisa spent many months there, and again Bouilhet wrote of it to Flaubert. They no doubt met on occasion in Paris or Mantes. Although their relationship was in no sense a love affair, old memories must have flooded over Flaubert and colored the way he approached telling Elisa's story in *A Sentimental Education*.[40]

Elisa's age, her white hair, and the inevitable ravages of mental illness were not the only reason why Flaubert did not have a liaison with her: he was, over all these years, deeply enmeshed with Juliet Herbert, probably more moved by her than by any woman since the far-off days when he had first met Louise Colet. But this was the love of a maturer man, continued over the years, an affection imbued with that peace and tranquility he had always longed for. When Juliet left the Flaubert household is not now clear. Perhaps she stayed until Caroline's marriage in April, 1864, after which there would have been no easy way for the child's governess to remain in the household. In the following July, however, she was in Paris with Caroline and was expected shortly in Rouen. Contacts with Juliet, now as before, seem always to have been in the summer or early autumn.

In 1865 Flaubert journeyed to England to be with her.[41] His heart beat faster in the train to Dieppe, and the wait for the boat was anguish. How long the trip across the Channel seemed to take! But Juliet was at the station and took him to her house, where her mother awaited them. They spent the evening there. Over the next days they made trips to Westminster, Kensington, the zoo, and the British Museum and the National Gallery and found time for a leisurely walk down Regent Street. Sunday there was a formal family meal with champagne in honor of the French guest. That evening by moonlight they strolled in Hyde Park. On many others he dined with her.

Together they went down to Hampton Court and spent the night in a hotel. As on so many earlier travel evenings, he took out his Notebook to record the scene. Their lodging was near the bridge; they were on the third floor. Out the window Flaubert saw the meadow cut by hedges* more numerous as they neared the horizon and making a pleasant effect. Closer in, there was a haystack; to the right, the railroad station and, on the riverbank, canoes. Near a door across the way were the carriages of the telegraph bureau. The river, foreshortened in this view, was a pale steel color and the boats looked like flies. Light-colored clouds appeared against a pale-blue satiny sky. He closed his description, as so frequently, with a note of movement: "the moon is rising."

The trip to London was in some sense unexpected: Bouilhet,

---

*"Je vois une prairie coupée par des lignes fréquentes d'arbustes. Elles sont plus nombreuses à l'horizon et font bien—au premier plan une meule de foin—à droite la gare du chemin de fer—à la rive des canots—à la porte en face des voitures du maître de télégraphe—la rivière en raccourci couleur d'acier pâle—des barques dessus comme des mouches—petits nuages clairs. Le ciel est satin bleu pâle. La lune se lève."

for instance, knew nothing of it in advance and could not imagine why Flaubert had left.[42] But it was a good and important time for him, not only because he was with Juliet but also for some of the materials he was able to gather for his *Sentimental Education*. Juliet, who was beside him as he wrote of this to Caroline, sent her former charge an affectionate hug.

In the summer of 1866 Flaubert again spent time in London with Juliet, though on this occasion some of his pleasure was spoiled by the miserable heat which plagued them. Bouilhet, in his role as "Monsignor," this time sent Flaubert two archepiscopal blessings, one for each. Flaubert went to considerable effort to keep his other friends from knowing where he was: there was, for instance, the matter of arranging to be present at a showing of a play by George Sand, who could not be told why it was so complicated for Flaubert.

In August of the following year, 1867, Flaubert again hoped to make his usual visit; unfortunately a bad attack of indigestion prevented the trip at the last minute. There may, also, have been other trips to London, and Juliet may have come to France on occasion; but no evidence of such trips has yet to come to light.

In his forties Flaubert also began a new type of relationship with women, taking a warm pleasure in gentle, courteous, and rather formal flirtations. Amélie Bosquet, whom he had come to know earlier as one of Caroline's teachers, was one of these, and to her he wrote a number of flattering and affectionate letters. Another was Madame Roger des Genettes. She and Flaubert began in 1864 an intimacy, in no sense physical, which was to last the sixteen years till his death. Thinking back many years later, she could remember no discordant moment. Flaubert was often violent, but his heart was always true to itself. She recalled their friendship as a noble and free affection, for despite his gruff air, Flaubert had, she found, a very feminine delicacy; he had at times in her apartment leaned over to caress a flower, which he would refuse to pick.[43]

More important to Flaubert was George Sand, whom he first came really to know during this decade: she had once been the wild feminist, the mistress of Musset and Chopin and Liszt; but she was now the aging and lovely "Grandmother of Nohant," as she liked to think of herself.[44] Of course Flaubert had known of her writings since his own adolescence, and he had rightly sensed in her actions and her portraits her half-masculine qualities. Like Louise Colet, from her eyes up she seemed to him a man.[45] George Sand approved of *Salammbô* and had said so in print. In January of 1863 Flaubert wrote to thank her in a warm and pleasant letter; he asked her for her portrait. But it was, at this time, no more than an acquaintanceship.

In 1866 this warmest of Flaubert's affections really came to fruition. Nearly twenty years his senior, George Sand had like him been through a stormy adjustment to the ambiguous problems of sexuality and, again like him, had now resolved them, although in her case by a total rejection which brought to her the peace Flaubert sought in venal affairs or—on a profounder level—in his relationship with Juliet Herbert.[46]

Sand's very masculinity helped: Flaubert could and did call her "a great man," the phrase he had tried to use of Louise Colet or, more successfully, of his niece Caroline. But in Sand's case, he was right. To this she added charm, the warmth of her motherly affection, and a lifetime of writing. They met often in Paris, they visited each other's homes and exchanged long letters when they were apart. Each occupied in the other's heart a special, indeed a unique, place.

Only the beauty of Sand's spirit could ever have reconciled Flaubert to her novels: their immense and constant personalism, their happily displayed lyricism, and their total absence of any real concern for art must constantly have bruised him. And only her devotion to him could have reconciled Sand to his writing, so cold in its perfection that it hurt her to see him show so little in his writings of the warm and lovable person she cherished.

In February, 1866, Flaubert escorted George Sand to the dinners at the Restaurant Magny; in the spring her new novel was dedicated to him, and she suggested that they take to correcting each other's work, as she and Balzac had been wont to do. In August he was pressing her to visit him in Croisset; late in the month she did come for a few days. He met her in Rouen and showed her the medieval parts of the city. He then took her to Croisset, where she met his mother, whom she found a charming old lady. The house was clean, the service excellent, her host attentive. That evening he read her *Saint Anthony;* she was deeply impressed. The next day, despite the rain, they took the boat to La Bouille and back. Flaubert delighted her; she was sorry to leave the next day. A few weeks later she endeared herself to him still further by seeking to have *The Castle of Hearts* put on in Paris at the Odéon, albeit to no avail.

Almost at once he began to urge her to return for a longer visit, if only to read the play, which she did not yet know. She came back for a week in November, and he did read it to her: though she found many things admirable and others charming, it was too long, too rich, and too full. At two-thirty in the morning they went downstairs for a bite of cold chicken. After more talk and cigarettes, they separated at four o'clock. The days passed quickly. Flaubert was heroic—it was Sand who said so—and walked with her up to Canteleu on the top of the hill overlooking Croisset and the Seine. They visited Rouen museums and attended the Saint Romain Fair. They both worked. He read her the start of *A Sentimental Education,* which seemed very solid to her. And they talked until late each night. She left a week after she arrived.

Flaubert was now completely devoted to Madame Sand; he had never felt quite this combination of emotions about any one: they seemed to understand each other so easily! What he felt was so very personal and private that, fearing she would (as was her wont) use Croisset in a novel, he begged her, if she did, to disguise it so no one else would recognize it: Croisset and her visit must remain for them alone.[47] To be sure, she was too kindly for his taste and too forgiving; she was too taken up with socialism; she valued people too much for their good will and was insufficiently critical of their lack of intelligence. But she had completely captivated him: he was, he proudly signed himself her old troubadour. After her August visit, she had slowly taken to using "tu" with him, much as a mother would with a child; for his part, though, he never departed from the more respectful "vous" to her. She realized his real goodness and could forgive him his real lacks. Each sensed in the other further domains to explore, sensibilities they had but touched upon.

Of course their friendship was at once misunderstood. Flau-

bert happened to write to Amélie Bosquet; she replied at once
with a feline letter telling him she was indeed flattered not to have
been forgotten. Rumor, she said, had doubled the length of
George Sand's visit, and the report was that when she left she had
the ravaged look of a departing mistress. Mademoiselle Bosquet
was as careful to state that she believed none of this as she was to
recount it all.[48]

By the spring of 1868, two years later, despairing of ever getting her recluse friend to visit her in Nohant, Sand again accepted
his invitation to Croisset. They were to travel there from Paris
together. Flaubert, however, found himself forced to leave earlier
than he expected. Some two or three days in advance, he had
returned peaceably in the evening to his Paris apartment and,
around eleven-thirty, was in bed and about to fall asleep, when
suddenly a trombone brayed and a drum roll began: there was a
wedding party across the street. He did not miss a quadrille and
gradually discovered he had been wrong: there were not one but
two drummers.

At six o'clock in the morning the masons arrived for repairs in
Flaubert's own building. At seven, bleary eyed, he rose and went
in search of a hotel room. When he finally found one, he had to
wait three-quarters of an hour before it was ready. Hardly was he
settled before a carpenter began nailing a traveling crate together
in the next room. After a long and fruitless wait for another room,
he left for another hotel. Only a tiny, black hole seemed available.
But even there the shouts of the other guests, the noise of carriages rolling by, and the racket as water pails were dragged across
the courtyard still made sleep out of the question.

By then it was noon or so, and Flaubert returned to his apartment, where he packed his bags. Still unable to sleep there, he
went to Du Camp's apartment and sought sleep in vain from four
to six: still further masons were at work erecting a wall to bound
Maxime's garden. At six he abandoned the effort and went to a
public bath. There his rest was enlived by children's games in the
court and a piano nearby.

At eight he returned to his hotel room, where his servant had
laid his dress clothes out on the bed: he was to go to a ball at the
Tuileries. But as he had eaten nothing, he thought it wise to go to

a cafe first for a snack at least: at the next table a man was suddenly taken ill and vomited all over the floor. At nine, back in his room, he could not face the idea of a formal evening and instead had his servant pack his bag: he would return to Croisset. On the way to the station, his suitcase fell from the roof of the carriage onto his shoulder, giving him marks he still had days later.

George Sand had to travel to Rouen unescorted. This time the visit was shorter—only three days—but its brevity did not matter as the friendship was already warm and close. A few days later she wrote begging him to learn to accept life as it was, fully and warmly. In this she had found happiness herself, and he might, too. In December, when he again refused an invitation to Nohant, she wrote with motherly affection to say that probably he really loved his hermit's life of which he complained so much. But if this were true, he should tell her, so that she would no longer be sad for him. His reply was evasive.

Each was delighted the following New Year's to discover that the other had remembered to write, and as the year progressed, the Goncourt brothers, overhearing George Sand using "tu" to Flaubert, were sure that she must be his mistress. More within the real tone of the friendship, she named one of the rams on her farm "Monsieur Gustave" and sent him a cushion the following autumn. Such a relationship was what George Sand wanted and Gustave Flaubert needed, for it was founded on these far more solid rocks rather than on the shoals of passing fancies, of which each had had more than enough many years before.

A PHILOSOPHY FOR THE FORTIES

Everyone has his bad days, of course! But with enough will power they can become fewer and fewer. You may take my word for it, for I am a past master in melancholy!

Letter to Princess Mathilde, March, 1868

As the forties progress, a man may modify and deepen his essential beliefs, and he may come to understand better their implications and interrelationships; but it is unusual for him so to alter his fundamental concepts as to become unrecognizable compared to his former self. Flaubert, now at that age, settled into his attitudes with a firmness born of long familiarity with them.

Only contemplating the ideal consoled him for the real, and it remained the anchor of all his beliefs. But during this decade he confessed more freely that there were certain beautiful realities at the same time. He was experiencing more fully now the dualism Thomas Mann would attribute to Tonio Kröger, who was as much the artist as the bourgeois and as unable as Flaubert to deny the one or the other. Art was still to Flaubert an escape from life, but he now admitted more readily that it was a sad consolation. He lived, he said, in his ivory tower, which was an excellent way to avoid getting his feet wet, but he added that it was often freezing in his particular tower.

Flaubert appeared to be, and indeed in some sense was, in and of the world of the imperial court. Yet even while this provincial bourgeois rejoiced at seeing himself thus received by an emperor, still the cool, detached observer could recall with cynical disinterest his precepts that to hold any official post made one stupid, to rise in rank was to fall in stature, and all honors dishonored.[49] He watched bemused as houses of prostitution became less common—or were they, he wondered, only better hidden? But a new type of prostitution, that of the minds and souls of men, was growing. Soon perhaps, all the houses where he could buy a mistress for five minutes would be closed, but those where he could have a friend for half an hour were legion. The cafe was replacing the brothel.[50]

Flaubert's hatred of the bourgeois remained undimmed, but perhaps he understood his feeling somewhat more fully. He now knew the word was to him a general term having nothing to do with social or economic status and relating instead to special forms of stupidity. He noted with regret that humanity not infrequently doubled one stupidity with another only to proclaim that the result was respectable: on a similar basis a donkey skin glued onto a chamber pot could be declared a drum.[51]

This stupidity Flaubert found rampant in all levels of humanity, as much a part of the lower classes as of the bourgeoisie. He agreed wholeheartedly with the idea of education for the masses and even accepted the idea that they would one day achieve a kind of morality. But that they could ever be intelligent he flatly denied. The important work of humanity had always been accomplished by a small number of people, perhaps a few hundred in each century, who were the consciousness and the conscience of humanity. To them alone belonged any true elevation of the spirit, which would never be accessible to the masses. When the generality of mankind abandoned its belief in the Immaculate Conception (this dogma, new at the time, was one of his pet hatreds), they would substitute table-tipping or something equally objectionable. They were a collection of animals: one could strive only to make them a bit less evil.

Paradoxically, "the people" was a narrower concept than "the individual," Flaubert discovered, and the masses the opposite of man. A modern Prometheus would have to revolt not against the gods but against the people, whose tyranny was far more dangerous than the older ones because in its demands for conformity it would soon leave no one free. Freedom of the body man now had, but what did it avail if the mind were no longer free? Failure to consider intellectual freedom was the error of the early French socialists like Saint-Simon, Fourrier, or Proudhon, whom Marx had dubbed Utopians.

Underlying all of this, to Flaubert, was the question of religion. He found the Utopian Socialists bathed in religiosity. So was the entire French culture. He saw the source of many of the problems of his age in an exaltation of the notion of grace to the detriment of the notion of justice. Led by the Catholic church, France had abandoned the paths of Voltaire for those of Rousseau, which were based on dubious logic and an appeal to the emotions. Had the Revolution been more concerned with Equity instead of Fraternity, its work would have been more solid and the Revolution of 1848 would not have followed it into the same errors. Flaubert knew to his sorrow that he was a child of Rousseau, but he still sought to be clearheaded enough to regret it: the fog of Rousseau's melancholy, he said, had blinded French to the clear light of justice.

Flaubert particularly deplored the route taken by the Catholic church. Fundamentally antiscientific and renouncing the lucid understanding of a Plato, the church, he felt, had been floundering in confusions concerning alleged distinctions between mind and matter. Spiritualism and materialism were two equally impertinent pretensions of modern man. Upon such false premises and upon the claim that levity and licentiousness were unnatural, Catholicism sought to inhibit in man all that was so very natural to him. These views disgusted Flaubert. The more he studied the Revolution of 1848—or, earlier, the Revolution of 1789—the more profound and disastrous he found the church's influence: Michelet held the same views. Hence, for Flaubert, France's real problem in the 1860's was not the Empire but religion, and he found no temptation or need to join with the opponents of the imperial court.[52]

As Flaubert studied the history of his generation and sought to understand it, he was led to consider the role of the historian. He knew many of the more interesting historians of his own day, and no doubt talked with them and read their books. Relativism was in the air, and he came to formulate his own canon concerning it. Ultimately each historian was free to look at the past as he chose. No longer did Flaubert naïvely seek to come to know "how things had been," as he had at the time of the first *Sentimental Education*. Now, instead, he realized that history was only the reflection of the present upon the past, a particular light which the historian casts backward from his own age upon an earlier one. And so history must constantly be rewritten. Croce, at the end of the century, would not feel otherwise. But, relative though the historian's view must of necessity be, he must still elaborate it, and the historian's view would underlie *A Sentimental Education*.

In opposition to many of his generation, Flaubert felt—as he always had—that abstinence, limitations, or inhibitions were mistakes. Effort was what raised man to the heights. The Great Natures (and he capitalized) had all been prodigal with their resources: "Woe unto those who do not understand exaggeration." One must laugh or weep, love or work, enjoy or suffer, vibrate as much as possible and with all one's faculties. But this his generation had not done. Perhaps this refusal more than anything else marked for Flaubert the bourgeois. Man's worth, he felt, could be measured by the extent to which he was capable of love. One must develop *will power*, and Flaubert underlined the words, to dare to love and so combat the melancholy which was otherwise such a disastrous concomitant of life.

Thus Flaubert made his own peace with his private romanticism. In his youth, he felt, some of his generation had known how to love. Some few, like himself, had at times withdrawn from all contact with women, but by an act of will, not from a lack of vitality. And they had made up for it thereafter; temporary withdrawal had saved them.[53] But there were so few like this; the rest were flabby. This apathy he would anatomize in his second *Sentimental Education*, which would display the listlessness, the emptiness of their existence, their *veulerie*, to use the not-quite-translatable French word for it.

Now that he had come to an easier acceptance of much of romanticism, he had to face the special lyric quality of its literature. He had elaborated an antiromantic esthetic of his own which he could hardly discard now. Could literature be made even more comprehensive than he had earlier imagined so as to include both? Alas, the condition of literature in his day reminded him of Venice: the ancient city of the doges was still beautiful, but it was full of spies and soldiers; indifferent bourgeois came to examine its ruins as it slowly degenerated into an infinite, mournful commonness and its walls tumbled down into the canals. He could hear the frogs leap against the flaking frescoes.[54]

To the immense irritation of the Goncourt brothers, Flaubert still sought bulwarks to guarantee art against the contamination of reality, which nevertheless had to be its foundation. Hence he still held that art must be impersonal depiction.[55] Drawing conclusions belonged to God alone. An objective representation, art must still be created without extraneous impetus, from either government or popular pressures.[56] The artist, he wrote in a sentence to be much quoted by later writers and critics, should imitate what God had done in his creating: act and then remain silent. He had done enough if he had adequately conceived his subject and successfully discovered the manner for expressing it.

Great art must still be impersonal and scientific; but Flaubert now realized there were complications he had underestimated. Archeology, history, and languages were at the fingertips of the writers of his generation, yet the feeling for art was being submerged under this erudition, as earlier the critical spirit had seemed to him to threaten creativity. It was in part a condemnation of his own *Salammbô* and a caveat for himself as he strove to write the history of his generation. As if in prophetic protest against doctrines Zola would enunciate only some years later, he objected that truth could not be discovered by literary fictions. Observation and representation without conclusions were alone safe.

In the 1860's—as opposed to the previous decade—the wide prevalence of statements concerning so-called realism required further definition on Flaubert's part of what he meant by his doctrines. He agreed that one must start with the particular but only in order to generalize and so achieve a logic greater than the random play of event. The truth which mattered, the eternal element, entered only with this generalizing, which was to be achieved by that harmonious exaggeration he had always demanded. Thus a gloved hand was far more interesting than an ungloved one, for the glove generalized the hand. By making it inexpressive, the glove left only the form, anti-natural, perhaps, but retaining movement and hence life.[57]

Flaubert departed most crucially from contemporary realism, he now realized, in his insistence that the artist must interpret, for in so doing he would perforce be idealizing. One attains the ideal only by being real, and one attains the true only by generalizing. The Goncourt brothers snorted, but Flaubert was sincere in asserting to them that pure beauty, which he sought, was to him that which produced in him a state of vague exaltation. He had used a similar phrase about love.[58]

Flaubert still found in classicism his principal roots; he even returned to the study of Greek, but he coupled it with his continued enthusiasm for Michelet. In the course of exposing what seemed to him to be true, the writer must strive for a universal understanding and ability to feel what others, whom he depicted, felt. With enough of this fellow feeling, *sympathie* in French, one could attempt to let justice enter art to make it the equal of the law in majesty and of the sciences in precision.

In reading Turgenev, as with *Don Quixote*, Flaubert found that he lived with the characters, on horseback over dusty roads and eating raw onions with the one or riding over the steppes with the other. It depended on an admixture of a bittersweet perfume, of tenderness and irony, observation and color. One rediscovered one's own emotions, now clearer. But above all it was the good-heartedness which Turgenev's works exuded that delighted and charmed Flaubert. He sensed in them a sort of permanent emotion, a profound, hidden sensitivity, which gained by being contained; they evoked in him a *sympathie* which let him enter into the characters and which even gave a soul to landscapes.

Turgenev succeeded where the cheaply lyric French poet Béranger had failed. Béranger, in Flaubert's view, had been content to report in rhyme whatever had moved him. Flaubert sought instead not perhaps to suppress his emotions—which would be to reject romanticism—but rather to contain them for art.

In the eighteenth century the critic had been a grammarian; in the mid-nineteenth century he was a historian, Flaubert averred. He himself wished the critic to be an artist, to consider the work in and for itself, examining its composition, its style, and the point of view of its author. For this the critic must have a great imagination and an inexhaustible fund of goodness which would generate a kind of ready enthusiasm; finally he must have taste. For these reasons Flaubert came to admire the critic and historian Taine. Taine is principally remembered today for his exposition of the ways in which a creative artist derives from what Taine called his race, his moment, and his milieu. Flaubert was interested, for his own views of cultural history had moved close to Taine's—though perhaps not as clearly phrased—from the time he had elaborated them during the writing of the first *Sentimental Education*. On the other hand, despite his admiration for Taine's *History of English Literature* (1863), he was disturbed that his friend's theories implied a kind of artistic determinism which left no place for individual talent. He himself felt the truth lay somewhere between Taine's causative factors and the earlier notion of a divine gift.

As Taine became interested in artistic creation, he and Flaubert exchanged letters analyzing certain aspects of artistic imagination in relation to pathological hallucinations. Taine's questions led Flaubert to scrutinize the nature of his imagining of scenes and people as he sought to write. He told Taine that what he imagined became for him as real as the objective reality about him. He would begin with a particular scene made up of real objects which he had observed; then his imagination would work with the scene until after a while he could no longer distinguish the additions of his imagination from what had set it all off. But what he imagined —a chair, for instance—was in some sense not limited, however precise it might be. It floated or was suspended: its location in space was not defined. At least in his own case, he reported, artistic imagination could not cover a large area, so that what surrounded the imagined chair hardly existed, in contrast to the real observation, in which the viewer would be at least conscious of the rest of the room. Also, in artistic hallucination a feeling of calmness flooded over him as external reality disappeared and he was fully caught up in his vision.

Creativity had to predominate over observation. Flaubert was intrigued by the case of an English portrait painter who could see his sitter merely by looking at the chair in which he habitually posed. The painter eventually went insane. Flaubert commented that his portraits were probably not good resemblances because, paradoxically, his overly exact memory would have acted like a camera and diminished his powers of idealization, which could alone produce artistic truth.[59]

Idealization, however, must be coupled with rigorous precision. Thus Flaubert pilloried the commonplace seventeenth-century expression *couronner sa flamme*, literally "to crown someone's flame," meaning "to return his love," "to marry," which contains an image no more bold or unusual than the phrase "crown thy good with brotherhood" from "America the Beautiful." He pointed out that only a lack of real feeling for the precise content of the image could allow such expressions: neither a flame nor the good can possibly be crowned. Skill was what distinguished the master, the acquisition of years, without which none of the rest mattered. The writer who had it could take a single subject and write in ten volumes or three pages a narration, a description, an analysis, or a dialogue. If his mastery of style fell short of this standard, Flaubert dismissed him as no more than trivial.[60]

19

A Sentimental Education

Initial Ideas

Everything depends on the original concept.
Observation of Goethe's often repeated by Flaubert

THE novel *A Sentimental Education* was Flaubert's last tribute to Elisa Schlésinger. While it departs from her to discuss most of the major problems of his generation, this love story from his adolescence, which he had first told in his *Memoirs of a Madman*, is the most constant center of attraction of the novel and—Flaubert's hero to the contrary—its most memorable and finest center of interest.[1]

It is entirely fitting that, as Flaubert struggled to find a new subject during the long months after he had completed *The Castle of Hearts*, his first notation concerning *A Sentimental Education* should have been a reference to Elisa: "Journey on the Montereau boat. A schoolboy. Mme Sch[lésinger].—Mr. Sch[lésinger]. Me."[2] The great opening scene of the novel had already begun to take shape.

The story was to be Parisian. In an early sketch Flaubert began to play with the possibilities of a novel on the relationships in the society of his day between the women of good social position and the courtesans or "lorettes," as they were called: each emulated the other in ways which scandalized both. He could deal with a husband, his wife, and her chaste lover; each would know all about the others, and the husband would initiate the lover into the world of the lorettes. There would be a masked ball like those of *la Présidente*, Madame Sabatier, after which the lover would sleep with the lorette. There would also be a major scene in a carriage on the Champs Elysées. In a later scene, the wife, jealous of the lorette, would come to an assignation with her lover; but she would come only two or three times in all, and the effort to make love under these conditions would satisfy neither of them. The lover, in fact, would be surprised that she had come at all. Over the course of the relationship each would love the other when he was not himself loved in return.

There was a final notation in this early sketch, a canceling, as it were, of the earlier idea of the assignation. Only when the lover no longer loved the wife at all would he possess her. But this did not seem quite right either, so Flaubert wrote himself a reminder that either the lover could possess her or she could offer herself at this time. And then, with a sudden realization that this last alternative was the great one which would make the capital closing scene for the affair, Flaubert decided she would offer herself to him but he would decline.

The main threads had been found and the principal roles determined. Most of them would carry unchanged through the completed form of the long novel some five or six years later, and much that was not yet spelled out here could readily be elaborated from these guidelines. The broad psychological situation was established; and the chasteness of the love affair, too, was decided upon.

Flaubert had one further idea, unfortunately. It was to be disastrous for many readers: all three, husband, wife, and lover, were to be cowards—weak, flabby, will-less creatures, none of whom possessed the courage and determination to resolve the situation. Flaubert was thus already posing for himself a problem which would worry him throughout the redaction: how could he interest a reader in such spineless creatures? The wife, luckily, was to be modeled on Elisa; she gradually lost most of her cowardice and took on that aura which had always surrounded Madame Schlésinger in his imagination. But, in unbroken sequence through to the final version, the lover and the husband almost wholly lack features to redeem them. From the first, readers have been struck with this. For some it has not mattered, but many have found their pleasure diminished by such characterizations.

The husband was to chase after other women, yet he was to be in love with his wife as well, to the astonishment of her young lover. He would be the more puzzled in that the husband would naïvely detail his wife's charms to him. On the other hand, the wife was now to be aware of the lover's affair with the lorette. She would refuse him and then be devoured by jealousy when he slept with the lorette. As a matter of fact, she could even have a moment of weakness of which he would be unable to take advantage. At first he would be dazzled by her. Then, as a timid visitor he would be present at intervals in her house, gradually accustoming himself to his desire and assuaging it with prostitutes as Amaury had in Sainte-Beuve's *Volupté*. With time he would become an intimate of the family and even the confidant of the wife; but it would not occur to him that he could sleep with her.

The initial notion of an assignation seemed to Flaubert to be susceptible of enlargement into more subtle avenues: the wife would accept the assignation and the reader would presume that she was going to sleep with her lover. But it would not turn out that way . . . perhaps because the lover would handle the situation badly. There would be external, fortuitous causes, too. And so the critical favorable moment would pass, never to return. The assignation should be in a furnished apartment in the Rue Tronchet, Flaubert added, and its failure would drive the lover into the arms of the lorette, thereby arousing the wife's jealousy.

The husband was to be an art dealer and the editor of an art journal, a sort of businessman-artist, at the start of the novel. He would soon move to producing bronzes and chemical products and then porcelains before finally abandoning art entirely for business. During a brief period Flaubert considered that the wife, on the other hand, following in the steps of Elisa, might end her days out of her mind. Her lover would have abandoned her before this. But Flaubert decided against the hysteria, perhaps because it was too close to reality, perhaps because Elisa did, after all, come out of the asylum and was seeing him again during these years.

Gradually the comparisons and contrasts between the establishment of the wife and that of the lorette became more and more fascinating to Flaubert as they opened up possibilities for a broader social study of his whole generation. These parallels between the honest woman and what in good nineteenth-century fashion he termed "the impure" would, he felt, leave the young man, the lover, as the center of interest. The book would then become, he wrote prophetically, a sort of Sentimental Education, and he capitalized both words.

If these two women were to fill such important roles (and a third would soon be joined to them), than the book could be once again, like *Madame Bovary* and *Salammbô*, a study of eternal woman. It could contain once again the protest of the frustrated Flaubert that, with every woman, there always came limits to what she could understand, boundaries which she could not transcend in order to follow the thought and the spirit of the man she loved. Salammbô had thus disappointed Schahabarim. Now Flaubert noted that a woman could not follow a man when he spoke of art and poetry or even of the feelings. Just when one was about to embrace a woman's soul, one ran into a wall of brass all set about with nails.

The lover's passion, too, interested Flaubert early in his planning. It was to be intermittent, he wrote. And he now began to elaborate an early insight. He imagined again a final scene between the lover and his mistress at a moment when the lover's passion burned low. The wife would come to him and offer herself, but, as Flaubert now envisaged the scene, she would no longer excite him. He would be afraid of finding her distasteful afterwards. The writing, Flaubert noted, must be delicate so that the wife would not be made ridiculous: the former lover must feel pity for her. She would leave. He would watch her get into her cab. "And it was all over." The last sentence, unchanged from the Notebook, marks in the printed text the ending of this scene as it slips timelessly into the past. With it Flaubert bade his final adieu to Elisa, an adieu he had been unsuccessfully bidding ever since the *Memoirs of a Madman* in 1838. But, until now, he had never been able to find an adequate artistic form for it.

A Satire of the Contemporary World

What is particularly serious and strange about your new
work is the "pavement of Paris" in it.

Letter from Bouilhet to Flaubert, 1864

Just as Carthage had been a new area for the author of *Madame
Bovary*, so the big Parisian novel was again opening new ground.[3]
For many years Flaubert had been thinking of a modern novel
which would pass in review all the terrible things of the contemporary world: it would be a kind of revenge for the way his
fellow man had disappointed him. It could be, he had written in
1853, a sort of picaresque novel like *Gil Blas*.[4] In point of fact, *A
Sentimental Education* does retain something of the easy inclusion
of the most diverse matters within the single reach of one novel,
which had characterized the picaresque genre and reached its
satiric high point in France in *Candide*.

A Sentimental Education was to be a naïve depiction of what
Flaubert and his friends had been, so that younger men, who had
not experienced the Revolution of 1848 or known what life had
been before it, might have some understanding of their elders.
For, although he had been little impressed by that Revolution
when it was taking place, he was now certain that it had been a
turning point in French history.

Montaigne had early taught Flaubert that man can never be
more scorned than is his just dessert: and Flaubert delighted in
every spectacle he could find of humanity and its fetishes degraded, disgraced, and condemned. What he called the modern
torpor came, he felt, from man's boundless respect for himself. As
he considered the Socialists who had lost the Revolution of 1848,
it seemed to him that their dream was to seat humanity, mon-
strously obese, in a yellow niche as in the railroad stations, where
it could balance itself from side to side, eyes closed, vacuous, and
beatific, digesting its lunch while awaiting its dinner and relieving
itself into a pot below. He swore he would not die before spitting
out his fury at this idol, and it might well prove to be, he ventured, his sharpest and cleanest blow, perhaps the only truly moral

protest of his age. Of this fury, too, there is much in *A Sentimental Education*.

And so Flaubert set about telling his Parisian story in such a way as to let him dissect the vapid nullity of his age. He would describe the education of all the sentiments or feelings; but it would be other than the first *Sentimental Education*, for there he had had Jules, an alter ego, to phrase his dreams. Here there would be no such character, and Frédéric Moreau (for thus Flaubert named his hero) is only a Flaubert who failed, who never quite saw anything through to its conclusion, one of the flabby-willed creatures whose *veulerie* Flaubert wished to castigate. For him there is no redemption through learning to love beauty and the life of ideas. *A Sentimental Education* is a gray catalog of failure. The lessons of the novel are that illusions alone are beautifull and that life itself, by being lived, will destroy them. This judgment had been Flaubert's as he started into adulthood in the early 1840's. It was still his firmest conviction.

Flaubert's generation contained in point of fact a number of men of iron will, and he knew many of them: Taine, Renan, the Goncourt brothers, Princess Mathilde, and a host of others. He was himself a man of long-sustained determination. But none of this steadfastness, not even in the willowy form of a Jules, was to be allowed to enter the new novel. Whereas *Madame Bovary* and *Salammbô* had shown man's fatal illusions, the new *Sentimental Education* would show only their futile ones. In *Madame Bovary*, society was both the generator of these illusions and their nemesis; in *Salammbô*, man's fate had made him thus. But Frédéric lacks both the dynamic will of Emma and the heroic qualities of Mathô and Salammbô. The *Education* was never intended to be a powerful novel like its two predecessors. It was a deliberate gamble with grayness. But then every book of Flaubert's thus far had been a sort of wager, and the *Education* was not to be his last one.

To shift from a study of provincial customs to an analysis of a sentimental education was to move from the objective and determinable to the subjective and endlessly amorphous.[5] The close analysis of the psychology of love, the central focus of Flaubert's novel, is an old subject in French literature, going back at least to the *Princess de Clèves* in the seventeenth century, if not to

Chrétien de Troyes in the twelfth. Earlier in the nineteenth century Balzac had given it titanic dimensions, while in *Volupté*, which Flaubert had read with passion in school,[6] Sainte-Beuve had lingered over its more delicate nuances. But now, after the mid-century, Flaubert drove out of the subject every vestige of the poetry, the grandeur, and the grace which had embellished it in earlier hands. His would be the novel of universal illusion. Not even his belief in scientism could resist the onslaught. Life was to be reduced to the absurd, to mere chance. The very missing of the assignation would be an accident.[7]

Flaubert insisted that he was being more honest than his predecessors. He saw life as more complex and more varied than Sainte-Beuve had depicted it in *Volupté*. Nor is *A Sentimental Education* truly Balzacian in concept, although, to be sure, Flaubert's lover does come to Paris from the provinces in the footsteps of so many of Balzac's young men. Some of Flaubert's characters would have liked to do what Balzac's had done, but they were quite incapable of such virile determination. All were, instead, victims of that cowardice and *veulerie* which lay at the base of Flaubert's initial concept and which—in contrast to Balzac's visions—he insisted were the reality about him.

Madame Bovary, though in a bourgeois setting, did not have a bourgeois heroine; *Salammbô* was entirely exempt from this taint which Flaubert so abhorred. But *A Sentimental Education* never really departs from it for long. The hero, the various women with important roles, the settings in Paris and in the provinces all have an unrelievedly bourgeois ambiance, despite the origins of some of the characters above or below it. Flaubert had never been able to imagine how such people endured the dreary monotony of their lives. Years before he had written of that atrocious invention, the bourgeois. Why was the wretch on earth in the first place? And what did he do there? How he could possibly pass his days Flaubert considered a grave problem which he could not himself elucidate.[8]

The prominent bourgeois elements in the *Bovary* had bothered him. Now, with no relief anywhere in the *Education*, he was overcome with disgust and boredom as the writing dragged along. Was it not time for him to be allowed a bit of amusement in his life, he wondered? As so often when he was writing of Emma, he vowed he would never again touch a bourgeois subject; he probably believed it.

His basic concept, Flaubert decided, was impossible for, although the psychological state he wished to describe—cowardice and *veulerie*—was entirely new, it tended to disappear inevitably into the crawling mass of the bourgeois background. All sorts of topics which the reader would have enjoyed reading about at length Flaubert had to condense or move into a secondary position in order to establish additional aspects of his milieu. The method, although inevitable, was basically faulty, he feared. The requirement of his age that the artist be scientifically accurate, coupled now with a bourgeois subject, materialistic and positive, made it impossible to evoke that vague exaltation which was the aim of art. But he was too far along to go back.

Really great effects, Flaubert was convinced, could be achieved only with simplicity and with clear-cut passions. But where was there any simplicity in the modern world? As he put it, moral cohabitation with bourgeois characters was turning his stomach and wearing him out. Somehow this must all be made into the unified totality of a work of art. The problem reached one obvious crystallization in the difficulties he found in choosing a title. George Sand, whom he begged to find one for him, was no more able than he, though he read her most of the work at one time or another. Finally the old one of twenty years before, which had crept into his notes early in the planning, was the only name available when time ran out, so it remained. Flaubert was sure that his inability to find an appropriate title meant that his concept of the work was not clear.

Like his earlier novels, *A Sentimental Education* is a story of failure, an account of why ordinary people do not succeed in their lives, for only the artist truly lives. If Flaubert's difficulties with this novel meant that bourgeois failure was an impossible subject, then only an artist could be a valid subject, and the next step would have to be the writing of books about the writing of books. Flaubert continued to reject this idea, for the artist was necessarily atypical and books must deal with the general. Still, what other attractive subject could there be? The final, esthetic solution of *In*

Search of Time Past was already implicit and the *Portrait of the Artist as a Young Man* foreshadowed.

FRÉDÉRIC

I want to write the moral history of the men of my generation; "sentimental" would be more exact.

Letter to Mademoiselle Leroyer de Chantepie,
October 6, 1864

The cast of characters which Flaubert elaborated to carry the burden of his message and his hate is enormous, great enough so that, in fact, on a first reading it is possible to become lost and be unable to distinguish certain of the more important secondary characters one from another. But on a further reading each comes gradually to occupy a particular domain distinct from the others. While all except the heroine make failures of their lives and belong to an inferior sort of human category, each is just enough above the average of his sort to try to become more. Each is irrevocably doomed to his failure, however, in some measure through ineptitude or stupidity but for the most part through cowardice and *veulerie*.

After first intending to give the husband and wife the name of Moreau, Flaubert decided that it fitted his young lover better; he became Frédéric Moreau. The art dealer-husband is Jacques Arnoux; his wife is Marie. Marie had also been the name of the heroine of *November*; the nun in *A Night of Don Juan* had been Anna Maria; and there had been characters with this first name in other works. Hence probably the combination Marie Arnoux was fortuitous only, and Flaubert no longer consciously recollected in his forties that twenty years earlier he had known a prostitute by this name.[9]

There had also to be a lorette: her name became Rosanette, and, since Madame Sabatier, her prototype, was known as *la Présidente*, Rosanette is called *la Maréchale*. As the story evolved, it became wise to add another woman, for Flaubert came to need someone from the upper bourgeoisie, well above the slightly shady

Jacques Arnoux. This is Madame Dambreuse, wife of a powerful and unscrupulous banker. Frédéric will gravitate between Madame Arnoux, with whom his relationship is always chaste; Rosanette, whom he finally musters enough courage to possess; and Madame Dambreuse, who will become his mistress only toward the end of the book, after he has long wanted her because of her position.

While the real structure of the book is around these women, there are a number of men of considerable importance. The would-be lawyer, Deslauriers, plays something of the role of Jules in that he is a close friend of Frédéric's, a character to whom the hero can unburden his thoughts and ambitions. The banker Dambreuse is significant at intervals. A number of others play secondary roles: an actor, a painter, certain figures with political dreams or ambitions, a journalist, a young nobleman. Following each one of them for a time, the reader penetrates into one segment after another of the Parisian panorama. Or, turning to the provinces, there is another woman or, more properly, a girl, Louise Roque, growing into womanhood and in love with Frédéric: he will toy with the notion of marrying her. There is her unscrupulous and scheming father, who wishes young Frédéric for his son-in-law, and a group of wholly minor characters about Frédéric's mother, a lady of fading means and great pretensions.

It is not feasible to summarize so involved a plot as that of *A Sentimental Education*. At the start, the young provincial Frédéric was beginning the study of law, as Flaubert had. On a boat trip returning to his home in Nogent—where Flaubert as a child spent alternate summers—he saw Madame Arnoux and saved her shawl from falling into the river. Here Flaubert repeated for the last time the episode from the beach at Trouville with Elisa. Frédéric fell in love with Madame Arnoux at once, but some notion of the incredible complexity of the plot may be gained from the fact that he fell in love with her not once but four times over during the course of the novel. He started with a small amount of money, learned that his inheritance from his mother would be almost negligible, resolved to conquer his fortune, abandoned hope, and then unexpectedly inherited a considerable sum from an uncle. He was deeply attached to his school companion

Deslauriers but abandoned and even rejected him for long periods of time. He dabbled in painting, considered writing fiction and history, wanted to be a political figure, meandered along the borders of the world of journalism, was flattered to know some of the minor nobility, played the stock market, and through it all sought unavailingly for some kind of reason for living.

He observed the start of the Revolution of 1848 but was far more taken up with his assignation with Madame Arnoux—which she did not keep. This led him to find the courage to ask Rosanette to sleep with him. While France went through this climactic upheaval, Frédéric was enjoying his liaison and left Paris for Fontainebleau with his mistress. It is not only impossible to give a résumé of these events in their proper sequence, it is also entirely unnecessary, for what Frédéric did was always fated to be without importance and specifically what he failed to do does not need to be detailed in its entirety.

As the book draws toward its last pages, each successive event becomes the end of a potential for Frédéric and as such assumes importance in its own right. Arnoux's business dealings became less and less profitable and more and more shady. Finally he was forced to flee the country, but not before Frédéric borrowed money from Madame Dambreuse to try to save him so that his wife would still be there in Paris. When Madame Dambreuse learned of all this, she arranged—through Frédéric's old friend and companion, Deslauriers—to have Monsieur and Madame Arnoux's personal effects sold at auction to cover certain promissory notes she had discovered among her now dead husband's papers. Frédéric thought his other mistress, Rosanette, responsible and abandoned her permanently. Shortly, Madame Dambreuse demanded he escort her to the auction, where she insisted on buying a particular coffer of Madame Arnoux's, to which Frédéric was especially attached. When she refused to stop bidding, he abandoned her, too.

The *coup d'état* which ended the Second Republic and established the Second Empire was breaking out, but this event, too, Frédéric missed: he left Paris for Nogent intending to resume his courtship of young Louise Roque. After all, she was charming and rich. He reached the provincial city to discover Deslauriers had taken advantage of his absence and other liaisons to win Louise for himself. The marriage party was just leaving the church. Frédéric slipped back into the railroad station unobserved and returned to Paris.

The next section, almost the last, begins "He traveled," a single-sentence paragraph which Proust particularly admired. Rapidly the rest of an essentially futile life falls into place. And then two remaining sections, both short, give to the book its end, if not its climax, and suggest whatever ultimate meanings there are to living. In a first and deeply moving scene, Madame Arnoux, now fifteen years older and white haired, suddenly entered Frédéric's apartment to repay money borrowed many years before. When she offered herself to him—with great delicacy and restraint—Frédéric with equal gentleness refused.

In the last scene Frédéric and Deslauriers were together again. They reminisced, exchanged information about mutual friends, and then came to recollect an occasion from their school days when, in fear and trembling, they had picked bouquets of flowers and gone to a brothel. There, terrified, Frédéric had suddenly lost his nerve and fled; since he had the money, Deslauriers had to leave, too. Remembering the details, Frédéric observed, as Du Camp had of their Breton trip: "Perhaps that was the best moment we ever had," and Deslauriers, in the last line of the book, agreed that it probably was.

This ending to *A Sentimental Education*, beginning with the debacle in Frédéric's relationships with various women and leading through the last visit of Madame Arnoux to the judgment of Frédéric and Deslauriers that an uncompleted visit to a brothel was their supreme moment, has delighted some readers, disgusted others, and puzzled still further ones. It has whatever meaning it does have, however, only after the many pages that precede it—the work is longer by a full quarter than *Madame Bovary*—with their complex of events, scenes, and characters.

Frédéric, who thus evaluates his life as the reader watches him for the last time, is a thoroughly mediocre person, not a caricature, to be sure, but so undynamic as to be most risky in a leading role. He does possess a delicacy and a finesse that set him off from the coarser people by whom he is surrounded—a Jacques Arnoux, for whom everything seems permitted, or a scheming Deslauriers, who will defraud his best friend. But compared to the Balzacian heroes who preceded him, Rastignac, Vautrin, and the others, if he is not the first of the unheroic heroes, then at least he represents the last stage before them. And, as Flaubert himself was to confess, inactive heroes are not readily interesting. Even in the first sketches he had noted that Frédéric would never imagine he might possess Madame Arnoux. His appeal and interest do not lie here, but rather in his almost feminine charm, which, wrote Flaubert, always fascinated Deslauriers.

As Emma gave meaning to all the men in her life, here Madame Arnoux gives meaning to Frédéric; his relationship to her in some measure justifies him and gives him his value. His effort and his goal are to enjoy life, although he is not, like Arnoux, a hedonist or an egotist. He needs affection, Rosanette's if he cannot have Madame Arnoux's, and an opportunity to express his own affectionate nature. But a structural problem arises: Emma was the center of *Madame Bovary*, its very active heroine; Madame Arnoux is at best the center of Frédéric's more permanent affections. He often abandons her for long periods of time; for many pages—like Salammbô she disappears completely from the book. She cannot then be what gives the book meaning, however much she may serve to focus Frédéric. Nor is he a satisfactory center, although he resembles Emma in his fantasies. In those qualities, however, which let Emma dominate and give order to her novel, Frédéric differs from her. To be sure, he is a man and she is a woman in a culture forbidding many things to women which it permitted to men; but he used his freedom to disperse his energies, while she concentrated hers. The novel, which must follow him about, becomes centrifugal, too, or at best has so many focuses that unity is denied it.

To complicate matters further, only Frédéric's lack of fixed purpose makes credible his extreme variety of interests. Throughout the book, and, furthermore, in discussions concerning him by Flaubert or by critics, there keeps recurring the fundamental trait which was already present in the early sketches of this inactive hero: he is flabby-willed and a coward. The point is sometimes dodged or even denied in critical estimates of him, for the reader becomes fond of this will-less man; and one does not like to speak evil of friends or even to hear it spoken. Flaubert himself became seriously confused about him, as he had about Emma when he wrote the last portions of his study of her. He once said his novel was written to make people feel at least some pity for these poor men who were so little understood and to prove to women how timid such men were underneath. But timidity is something different from flabbiness and cowardice, and however timid Frédéric is allowed to be, he still has these other, less appealing traits.

The modern reader, whether a willing or an unwilling disciple of Freud, will of course ask whether Frédéric's lack of spine does not derive from his relationship to his mother. Madame Moreau was domineering, and Frédéric was little able to counter her demands and desires. She had long had his career planned for him, she managed his courtship with Louise Roque, and he could never refuse her requests. In fact, she exercised something of the same tyranny-through-gentleness that Madame Flaubert did. But Flaubert—for better as well as for worse—was writing before Freudianism and the coining of the term Oedipus complex to describe this relationship. Its importance for the adult Frédéric, Flaubert understood, if only from his personal life. But it did not occur to him here, any more than it had with Emma, that he could further explain Frédéric's character by relating his childhood in detail.

Flaubert's concern was with late adolescence and full maturity, and here he was within a long tradition. Hamlet's lack of decision seemed to Flaubert what was greatest about the role. Hamlet kept within the penumbra, where problems do not have solutions; Shakespeare was willing to make him less than consistent and hence the all-encompassing figure of modern literature.[10] But after Shakespeare—although Flaubert does not note it—it is not easy to find characters of world literature as fluctuating as Hamlet. Goethe and romanticism had, in fact, emphasized action and had even asserted that solely in doing was there being. Only with certain aspects of romanticism, with René and particularly Sainte-Beuve's Amaury in *Volupté*, does the will-less hero return. But Flaubert goes even further than Sainte-Beuve. Where Amaury imagined a love lasting until death, in *A Sentimental Education* the love, not the lover, dies. And where Amaury tried too little, Frédéric tries not at all. With the turning against romanticism of this whole antiromantic generation, there seemed to be nothing that one might will which did not, even in advance, display its hollowness. Only despair had solid foundations.[11]

To Flaubert, Frédéric epitomized his own generation, which seemed to have wasted its strength. *A Sentimental Education* as a whole participates in this sense of aimlessness, passivity, and drifting. To counter Frédéric there is not even an Homais or a Lheureux, who would here seem almost welcome. Taine, on reading the novel, agreed that it was objectively true, but he added that he did hope one day Flaubert would write of his own belief, which he had justified by his whole life, in an indefatigable and victorious will. Flaubert, however, believed that one did not have will power merely by wishing for it. And he felt it had been lacking in most of the world he knew. That was part of why he hated life.

Frédéric's *veulerie* was in some measure the extension forward in time of the romantic *mal du siècle;* it was to have its heirs as well. In France, Huysmans' novels rapidly moved far beyond Frédéric Moreau; in America, *The Education of Henry Adams* may owe something of its title and its content to Flaubert, for few records of futile will-lessness equal Adams'. A little later T. S. Eliot put in the mouth of J. Alfred Prufrock lines which phrase in English what Frédéric had always felt in French:

> There will be time, there will be time
>
> .   .   .   .
>
> Time for you and time for me,
> And time yet for a hundred indecisions ,
> And for a hundred visions and revisions,
> Before the taking of a toast and tea.

From almost the first pages Frédéric's cowardice shows through. He had been overcome by the apparition, as he termed it, of Madame Arnoux; yet, though he wished to see her again as he left the boat, he lacked the courage and explained to himself that it would do no good. Meeting his old friend Deslauriers shortly, he proclaimed—as Flaubert had in 1840—that like all geniuses he needed a woman to love him.[12] But he renounced in advance any effort to seek her out, for he was of the race of the disinherited and would never know the extent of the genius he might have displayed. He shifted with every wind that blew; and, from the first use of the word "cowardly" in the early sketch to the final proclamation that running from the prostitutes was his best moment, Frédéric was steadily and uninterruptedly a coward. He was immobilized by fear, he rightly accused himself of cowardice over and over again in his relations with Madame Arnoux and with Rosanette, even with Deslauriers. Flaubert, who repeatedly calls him a coward, finally sums him up as "the man of every weakness."

Such a portrait would be unreadable without variety, and here the *veulerie* of the hero does add richness. Leaving Madame Arnoux on one occasion, he was persuaded that finally he had her affections. He sought about him on the street hoping to find at least a beggar to whom he might give alms. None was in sight; and so, within moments, his whim had disappeared. But while it danced before his will, his responses modeled one further shadow in his portrait.

In Frédéric's courtship of Louise Roque in Nogent, the two regrettable traits reinforce each other to make the interest of the portrait. He was in love with her and not merely a philanderer taking advantage of an adolescent girl. But after a short time with her, the inconsequent Frédéric found himself longing to be back in Paris. He invented an excuse, told everyone he would return shortly, and—adds Flaubert—believed it himself. But, like Flaubert with Harriet Collier, he considered marriage for only a moment and then recoiled: the young girl was of course hurt. And Frédéric loses in the reader's eyes when he later denies his affection for her in order to please Madame Dambreuse: how could she think he had loved such an ugly duckling?

Matters are not much better with Rosanette. Frédéric at one point had in fact conquered her: she was his for the taking. At that very moment, however, he had just lost Madame Arnoux, irrevocably as he thought. Overcome by this, he let the occasion slip and impotently watched another man walk off with her. Favorable opportunities with her, however, kept recurring for this fortunate man, but he kept letting them escape him. When at last she did become his mistress, she dominated him entirely, treating him as though he were her property, her thing. Eventually, torn between boredom and desire, he could neither resolve to break away nor determine to remain. Even when happily with her he often felt a wild, bestial longing (the phrase is Flaubert's) for several other women, including Madame Arnoux.

Eventually Madame Dambreuse, too, became his. Spinning madly between them, he took an especial pleasure in the thought that he was being a cad; he felt even more delight when in addition he asked Deslauriers to put Louise off for a while. Soon he was enjoying lying to Madame Dambreuse and to Rosanette for the pleasure of it, sending identical bouquets or letters to each, and telling both the same fabrications. But Madame Dambreuse, too, palled, and he longed to rid of her despite all the money she could mean to him. When he found a suitable excuse in her behavior at the auction of Madame Arnoux's property, he left her.

Frédéric's cowardice and *veulerie* are most apparent in relation to Madame Arnoux. It is not only that he fell in love with her and then got over it so many times or that he was constantly too indecisive and too afraid to carry by storm what he so longed for at intervals. In addition he could believe he had completely forgotten her and then discover he never had. Unlike Sainte-Beuve's Amaury or Flaubert himself, he did not seek relief in prostitutes despite the urgings of his friend Deslauriers. Also, almost without warning he dropped Deslauriers, who needed him, over and over again for the merest will-o'-the-wisp concerning Madame Arnoux. She was of course exacerbating his nerves and enervating him daily, but his certainty that she would never consent to be his mistress kept him silent. He was not even jealous of her husband: the schoolboy hero of *The Memoirs of a Madman* had had more dynamism than this. Yet Frédéric could dream of the happiness of living with her and passing his hands over her long braids or sitting at her knees with his arms about her waist. But he was incapable of such decisive action and hence a permanent anguish stifled him. Like Mâtho, but here in a situation of his own making, he would sit motionless for hours or would burst into tears.

Even positive action in Frédéric degenerated into an inability to will anything and hence an insistence that Madame Arnoux make his decisions for him, of necessity unbeknownst to herself. Debating whether to be a great painter or a great poet, he adopted the former since Jacques Arnoux's dealings in art would then provide a link to her. Later, the most casual of her remarks led him to decide to seek a government post. Neither career, though, did he pursue beyond the first futile steps. And at every turn throughout his love his fear of losing Madame Arnoux by an ill-chosen word or gesture was so much greater than the will he could summon to conquer her that nothing ever could or did come of it—until, of course, in the final meeting, when it was too late.

Frédéric's dreams, unlike those of Emma, the public allows because he is a man. But their impact on the novel readers have never widely accepted. They are willing to be told that Emma had illusions about reality, even if those illusions cut close to ones dear to their hearts. But Frédéric Moreau is far more profoundly unsettling: all of life and reality itself seem now an illusion. From the very first his dreams far outshone the facts. What happiness it would be, he thought to himself on meeting Madame Arnoux, to walk side by side with this extraordinary woman, his arm about her waist, her dress sweeping the yellowed leaves along as he listened to her voice and her radiant eyes observed him. He mused that the boat could stop and they would have but to descend . . . and yet this simple act was no easier to accomplish than stopping the sun. The dream was all he had and all that mattered. But this is precisely the walk he and she took at the very end . . . and he refused her.

Disillusion follows hard upon disillusion in *A Sentimental Education*. Frédéric had barely been reunited with Deslauriers in the opening pages before he learned that their common dream of living together in Paris was shattered: "It was the first of his dreams to collapse." Flaubert also gave to Frédéric the same mad longings he had about himself: he imagined a vast Moorish palace where he would recline upon divans covered with cashmere while Negro pages served him. The dreams were so real that the return to reality crushed him as though he had lost something. Where, then, was reality? And was not the illusion more real than any objective phenomena? Constantly Frédéric found solace and courage only in further illusions. As he was returning to Paris after inheriting from his uncle, his dreams were so vivid that all exterior objects disappeared from his ken while his carriage bore him on through the long hours of the night.

If the only reality is disillusionment, then surely a man of feeling must turn this absurd state of affairs upside down and assert the contrary: illusion is that which is real. Thus the uncompleted visit to the brothel, because it was never carried through to disillusionment, was the best event of the lives of Frédéric and Deslauriers. A paradox, to be sure; but Flaubert was old enough to be willing to risk it. Had he not always asserted that the only meaning life had was ironic?

THE REST OF THE CAST

> To my mind your characters are exact specimens of the average French bourgeoisie of today. All are composites, sometimes crude, sometimes delicate, both good and evil, with intermittent whims, nothing great, strong or determined.
>
> Letter to Flaubert from Taine on reading
> *A Sentimental Education*

"It was like an apparition," was the effect upon Frédéric of his first sight of Madame Arnoux. She was for him all the heroines of the romantic books and, had he been able, he would have added nothing, taken nothing, from her person. The universe was suddenly larger and she was the luminous point toward which everything converged. Over and over through the book Frédéric relived her specialness and was aware of it, as Mâtho had been of Salammbô's. Each word that came from her mouth seemed something new; her comb, her gloves, her rings were special things to him; they had the importance of works of art and appeared almost animated, like people. Indeed, as time passed, all of Paris seemed to exist only for her and the great city with all its voices became an immense orchestra surrounding her.

Henry James called Madame Arnoux the main adornment of *A Sentimental Education*, a book which, aside from her, he did not like. He pointed out that she was Flaubert's one attempt to represent beauty other than sensual. Emma, Salammbô, and even the later women exist only for the senses. Not so Madame

Arnoux, whose character and life give her her beauty. James insists Flaubert made a terrible error, however, in portraying her only through the eyes of so mediocre a person as Frédéric.[13] This opinion, though interesting, is not necessarily valid: Frédéric's very mediocrity leaves him a more transparent observer of this woman who is the center of his life—at least while he is in·love with her. He observes her not so much from his own point of view as from a point of view which she has made him adopt and which is in some sense her own creation. We as readers then see her, too, as she imprinted herself upon him.

Moreover, James to the contrary, Flaubert does not leave the depiction of anyone so crucial as Madame Arnoux entirely to the naïve and malleable Frédéric. Despite his years of protestations about impassivity, impersonalism, impartiality, and objectivity, Flaubert in this new work is constantly and overtly on most of the pages. Thus he enters directly to inform the reader that, as 1847 came on, his heroine was approaching what he called the month of August for women, a moment of both reflection and tenderness. Maturity, which is beginning, colors the glance with a profounder flame, and the strength of the emotions is mingled with experience of life. Nearing the end of moments of emotional overflow, her whole self pours forth in the harmonious richness of her being. As Frédéric lacked most of the qualities necessary to make this judgment for the reader, Flaubert had no hesitation in intervening to pronounce it. And then moving within her—for shifts in point of view abound in *A Sentimental Education* and give it some of its richness—the creator of Emma could add that, sure of not succumbing to her temptation, Madame Arnoux abandoned herself to an emotion which seemed to her a right earned by her sorrow: she entered upon a platonic relationship with him. Emma had exercised her corresponding right by accepting the credit extended by Lheureux; Madame Arnoux was content to rejoice in the presence of her adoring lover.

On the other hand, Frédéric alone sufficed to see a tranquil majesty in all her movements and her tiny hands as made for giving alms or wiping away tears. Her low voice had caressing intonations which mingled with the light touches of the breeze. It was a Frédéric fused with Flaubert who longed to throw himself at her knees but lacked the courage to do so, who felt a sort of religious fear which made him find that her dress, mingling with the darkness of the late afternoon, seemed immense, infinite, impossible to imagine lifting.

The portrait of Marie Arnoux in *A Sentimental Education*, despite what James says, is entirely adequate. She triumphs over even the great Balzacian heroines, very few of whom seek, like her, to be of supreme virtue. And Balzac's Madame de Mortsauf, who does, by aiming at a more ethereal perfection, pays by being less convincing. Alone among the great fictional heroines of Flaubert's century in France, Stendhal's Sanseverina can stand comparison with her. But this is in part, no doubt, because la Sanseverina's role as Italian and as aristocrat makes comparison almost meaningless.

Through Frédéric's eyes we see Marie Arnoux as a calm and serene mother, a sort of Madonna toward whom a religious veneration is in no way inappropriate. Her role as mother to her own children reinforces the image and helps keep her safe. Frédéric not only cannot imagine her nude, he no doubt does not wish to, and he can accept the fact of Arnoux's possessing her with equanimity. Her quiet strength is enough for him, and it guides her steps through the perilous paths Flaubert makes her trace out as her husband's fortunes fall lower and lower. In turn she draws strength from her lover, but only within those bonds which will not put in jeopardy her marriage and her maternity. When, at the end, she offers herself to Frédéric and he refuses her, she can find in this refusal the ultimate triumph of their love.

A Sentimental Education is Flaubert's last tribute to the vision that Elisa Schlésinger had been thirty years before to an adolescent boy on the beach at Trouville. As now, white haired and only precariously out of the asylum, she read that tribute, she must have understood behind the fictions what it all had meant. For she alone knew what was fact as well, and could sense in the fiction what was grateful recognition for what she had been.

Her great foil, Rosanette, is more easily encompassed. Unlike anything in Balzac—for his view of the courtesan is fundamentally romantic—Rosanette is cheap, vulgar, noisy, stupid, and ignorant. She is pure female; hence, after momentarily infatuating and confusing Frédéric (in one of the great passages of the book), she must end by boring him hopelessly. Only the fortuitous event of her pregnancy drags the liaison out; its lingering collapse was inherent from the start. She is a fascinating part of that reduction of romantic dreams to their fundamental hollowness which the book proposes to display on every hand. Rosanette is the destruction of the myth of the courtesan.

Madame Dambreuse, the last of Frédéric's mistresses of importance, is the woman of the successful upper bourgeoisie, essentially frigid, incapable of giving herself as Rosanette can and equally unable to enjoy her wealth and power. Like Rosanette, she reminds the reader of characters in Balzac. But just as Rosanette has had the poetry of the courtesan dried out of her portrait, so Madame Dambreuse—unlike, for instance, the Countess de Beauséant in *Le Père Goriot*—has no heroic proportions and commands neither respect nor pity. She is neither powerful nor appealing nor titanic; she is merely desiccated. All that made Balzac's world so exciting is illusion only and has here withered to dust.

It irritated Flaubert considerably that, as soon as the book was published, readers began to identify the allegedly real people behind the various characters. As with *Madame Bovary*—and, no doubt, with just as little validity—he denied that he had had any models. Yet of course many episodes and many actions of his characters had approximate prototypes in reality. Du Camp was quite certain that he could name them all,[14] and Madame Dambreuse was one of them, for her prototype, Valentine Delessert, had been his mistress, the wife of a man he and Flaubert had first met in Constantinople and whose influence Du Camp had been happy to use. Flaubert, too, turned to Delessert at the time of the trial of *Madame Bovary*. Madame Delessert, long the mistress of Prosper Mérimée, became Du Camp's in September of 1851. When Flaubert wrote concerning Frédéric's seduction of Madame Dambreuse that his hero was surprised at the ease of his victory, he did so because Du Camp had written him a decade or more before that "the thing took place with a charming simplicity which proves a long experience on her part . . ."[15]

Frédéric's liaison with Madame Dambreuse was never an end in itself. She was wealthy and had a social position which he desired. For her part, not unduly aroused either, she undertook to dominate him by sending him flowers, making tapestries for him, giving him a cigar case, an inkstand, and dozens of other small objects, so that all his acts would be surrounded by her presence. He was saved from her only by the fact that Rosanette was equally possessive; and, of course, there lingered in the bottom of his heart some sort of memory of the unobtainable Madame Arnoux.

Madame Dambreuse, sophisticated as Emma never could be, easily played a gamut of roles for Frédéric. Lighthearted or serious, melancholy or reasonable, she was blasé over the passing preoccupations of the day and claimed to be interested instead in a whole series of less transitory feelings. She was wise enough to complain that poets denature truth but clever enough to ask Frédéric to tell her the name of a star. His feelings, however, had none of the ecstasy he felt for Madame Arnoux nor, for that matter, any of the gay, disorderly excitement which Rosanette aroused in him. But Madame Dambreuse seemed inaccessible and out of the ordinary; she proclaimed herself a devout churchgoer. He imagined that she would have delicacies of feeling as rare and desirable as her laces; and he anticipated sudden flashes of modesty in the midst of depravation. So he wished her as his mistress.

Madame Dambreuse has a brittle, surface quality, no doubt because that is the way Flaubert wished her to appear. Perhaps also he was handicapped because this was not a world in which he was at ease and could readily depict. Similarly, Louise Roque, the inexperienced girl from Nogent, is a thin creation. Flaubert's contacts with young ladies in love had never been frequent and had all occurred many years before. No doubt Louise does echo Harriet Collier here and there, but she is at best a shadow figure, present only to provide Frédéric with still one more possibility.

Jacques Arnoux was important for Frédéric because he was Marie Arnoux's husband, but he was also important in and for himself. Unlike Maurice Schlésinger, who was a converted Prussian Jew, Arnoux was from Marseilles and ended his career as a dealer in religious art. Flaubert was at pains to point out there were fundamental resemblances between him and Frédéric which led the latter to feel a certain attachment to him. They shared an obvious common taste in women, a common habit of dreaming beyond reality, a common lack of that persistence which brings the dream to fruition. Halfway between merchant and artist at the start of the book, Arnoux made the gradual decline into shady commercialism which the earliest sketches had planned for him. He was good, kindly, a proper father to his children, and a fond husband who loved his wife. But quite as much as Frédéric he was doomed to failure through inability to face the crushing realities behind his illusions. At times Frédéric hated him for his luck in possessing both his wife and Rosanette. Too late, when Frédéric had possessed Rosanette himself and given her up and when he had refused to possess Madame Arnoux, he understood that his hatred, too, was an illusion. But by then he was ready to pronounce the visit to the brothel his best moment.

The banker Dambreuse and his circle of friends are unique among the characters in *A Sentimental Education:* they knew what they wished and succeeded in getting it. Like Homais, though, they should never have wanted it. Dambreuse was clever, hardworking, and absolutely without honor or even scruples; he would sell himself to anyone who could give him power, which he turned into money. And, unlike Homais, he was never a fool, never made a serious mistake, and died happily in his bed. Not even his wife's infidelities bothered him: he had cut her out of his will in favor of his illegitimate child.

Frédéric's close friend Deslauriers would have liked the power of a Dambreuse, but he was no more than unscrupulous. He lacked the wide vision and colossal boldness of Dambreuse and so was the better suited to his role as Frédéric's confidant. Such dual or doubled heroes offer obvious conveniences. Flaubert had created Jules and Henry in the first *Sentimental Education,* and *Bouvard and Pécuchet,* the other novel he had thought of writing in the 1860's, also revolved about a pair. Frédéric dreamed of love, Deslauriers dreamed of action; he was every bit as ridiculous as Frédéric and equally the victim of universal illusion. Like Frédéric, he, too, looked back to an early moment of illusion as his best because it was never destroyed by the touch of reality.

Although Deslauriers was enough like Frédéric to remain his friend over the long years, still he was four years older. He borrowed a number of elements from Du Camp, for the most part traits Flaubert did not like. Deslauriers wished to make a splash, be an influential person, have three secretaries, and give a big political dinner once a week. He looked back with envy to the days of the Revolution of 1789, when ordinary men like himself could be important. At least at the start of his life, he felt that the future was big with promise; it infuriated him to be held back by Frédéric's indecision. But time and life took their toll, and he, too, ended totally disillusioned.

Leading off into directions which the main characters could not adequately explore are a host of lesser ones. Hussonnet the journalist, who also borrows from Du Camp; Pellerin the artist, who phrases many of Flaubert's theories of esthetics; Delmar the actor; the republican Sénécal; Regimbart, the eternal malcontent; and many others swell the book until this single work seems to have in microcosmic form something of the wealth of diversity and the panoramic scope Balzac wished for his *Human Comedy* in twenty times the number of pages.

Edmond de Goncourt once complained that the characters of *A Sentimental Education* are not really types but caricatures exaggerated beyond what the reader will accept.[16] Out of their mouths, he objects, comes every idiocy of the group they represent; hence the individualizing necessary to a satisfactory type-character does not take place. It is undoubtedly true that, with time, the reader has difficulty in recalling who is who amongst the secondary characters. To this extent—and Edmond de Goncourt uses a secondary character as an example—he is right. Perhaps, however, he pushes too far when he levels this accusation against the major ones. They do, in fact, have their own personalities and stand out in the reader's memory, not only Frédéric and Madame Arnoux but also Rosanette, Deslauriers, Arnoux, even Dambreuse. As for the completely secondary characters, they must, after all, be just that and not intrude their own overly indicated personalities between the reader and those characters upon whom he must concentrate.

And yet, when all this has been said, something of what Edmond de Goncourt asserted still lingers in the reader's mind. In some way the characters of *A Sentimental Education* tend not to have the sharply defined silhouettes of *Madame Bovary*. The reason for writing *A Sentimental Education* was to delineate a type of cowardice and *veulerie* which excludes such definition; characters as clearly drawn as Rodolphe or Lheureux or even Charles have no place here and must give way to the more blurred personalities which Flaubert depicts. The loss for the reader was unavoidable, but nonetheless real. No doubt this dilemma was part of why Flaubert had grave doubts as the story moved along through the years: was the entire plan not perhaps fundamentally a mistake?

AUTOBIOGRAPHY ENTERS

> In writing that scene I must have been troubled by contradictory memories.
>
> Letter of November 19, 1879, to Turgenev,
> who had criticized a passage

For better and for worse, disillusionment is the topic of *A Sentimental Education*, disillusionment with the dreams of romanticism and their liquidation by observation reported through irony. Ennui, which had driven the romantics to seek wilder emotional orgies, here is proclaimed to be the ineluctable character of life itself, and this time there can be no dispelling of it. An occasional vision may seem to promise more, but the attempt to live out such visions shows them to have only further illusions, making the ennui the more bitter. Once again, the visit to the brothel is the only safe happiness because it never put the promise to the test.

A Sentimental Education was the story of Flaubert's own growth through romanticism to disillusionment long before it became Frédéric's. Werther, René, Lara, and even George Sand's Lélia "and others equally mediocre" aroused Frédéric's early enthusiasm as they had Flaubert's. Author and hero are of the same age, and Flaubert enjoyed playing upon the parallels, even in little details such as the moment of Frédéric's inheriting his fortune, which is the only date given exactly, December 12, 1845, Flaubert's own twenty-fourth birthday. The visit to the brothel took place in 1837, approximately when the adolescent Flaubert made his first acquaintance with prostitution. Then Frédéric had Flaubert's miseries as a student in Paris, much like Henry's in the first *Sentimental Education;* he failed, then passed, his law examination; and one of his friends broke in pipes with the same loving care as Flaubert.

Many of Frédéric's attitudes, too, stem from Flaubert. The idea of fatherhood seemed to both grotesque and inadmissible. Frédéric's contempt for agricultural fairs was so great that he refused to attend one, although his absence seriously hurt his political candidacy. He felt Flaubert's generous excitement over bygone ages and had the same literary longing to be the Walter Scott of France or to write medieval dramas. Later he considered writing a comedy or a history of esthetics. When he possessed mistress after mistress but never the one he wanted, he made Flaubert's discovery—shared with Michelet—of the loneliness that can coexist with full physical possession. At the end, when he traveled, he came to know the melancholy of boats, the cold awakenings under tents, the dizzying, dulling effect of landscapes and ruins, and the bitter taste of interrupted friendships. He even attended a performance of a *féerie* and one is almost surprised to find it was not *The Castle of Hearts.*

Frederic and Flaubert differ in what matters, however. While Flaubert was capable of crippling dilatoriness in writing his works and dragged out what another man might have accomplished in a tenth of the time, still his will—at least in relation to literature—was indefatigable. Frédéric's *veulerie* was no more than a possibility latent in Flaubert's nature, which he magnified into a dominant trait for his hero, who was not an artist but a bourgeois.

Many small events in Flaubert's life fitted into *A Sentimental Education.* Calling one day on one of the kept women of the Second Empire, he noticed a man's hat carelessly left on a table and later jotted down in his Notebook that it meant "I am the Master. I am at home here." Frédéric saw such a hat at Rosanette's one afternoon before she became his mistress.[17] Similarly, the splashing fountain which had sounded in the courtyard while

Flaubert and Eulalie Foucaud were making love in the hotel in Marseilles in 1840 now played for Frédéric. It had come back to Flaubert's mind one evening in Damascus; it had overflowed into a basin for Saint Anthony and cooled a courtyard for Salammbô. Now it first added its touch of luxury to Frédéric's dreams of a Moorish palace before resounding in a hotel courtyard in Fontainebleau whither Frédéric and Rosanette fled from the Revolution in Paris to find quiet and seclusion for their love. Now, twenty-eight years after its sound had first lulled Flaubert and his mistress, Frédéric and Rosanette fell asleep to it, too.

In 1846, perhaps remembering a personal occasion with Elisa, Flaubert had written to Louise Colet, that, if ever a youngster should fall in love with her, she should let him steal her handkerchief. How the boy would treasure it, even keeping it with him as he fell asleep![18] Frédéric did manage to obtain a scented handkerchief of Madame Arnoux's and deliciously smelled it in secret; when she dabbed a moist eye with another one, he longed to be in its place. Later, during the platonic phase of their relationship, she freely gave him a pair of her gloves and a week later her handkerchief. The first ride in the Bois de Boulogne with Louise Colet and her child served, too, as the model for Frédéric when he rode with Madame Arnoux, also through the Bois and accompanied by her child, who laid her head on Frédéric's lap. He leaned down and gently kissed her forehead, as Flaubert had.

Louise Roque was created with the help of Flaubert's youth and adolescence. She and Frédéric colored the pictures in a copy of *Don Quixote*, and Frédéric read aloud to her from the great romantic authors, as Flaubert had to Harriet Collier. She also imagined sensual joys in swimming, with the water caressing her whole body.

Quite naturally, many scenes, ideas, even sentences from his previous writings found their way into *A Sentimental Education*. Of course it repeats much from the unpolished *Memoirs of a Madman, November*, and the first *Sentimental Education* of 1845. The entire introductory scene, when Frédéric first discovered Madame Arnoux, derives from these works; and a number of details in other scenes, many relating no doubt to Elisa, recur. That strange veil floating in the wind in *November* and most of the later works is again borne on the breeze here; and the woman's pose with arched back is again a suggestive one for Flaubert, as it had been with Emma and Salammbô. Madame Arnoux adopted it in Frédéric's arms in her final scene with him. A sentence from *November* serves again, slightly recast, to suggest that odd feeling of a moment preceding a separation, when the beloved is already really no longer with one.

The first *Education* was a natural source for the second. From it came perhaps the ideas for an assignation not kept, for Frédéric's near suicide, for the political ambitions of both heroes, for the fact that neither can dance, and for the shawls both husbands present to their wives, as well as for several of the minor characters. One in particular, Mademoiselle Aglaé of the first work, is a rapid sketch for La Vatnaz in the second, a former teacher from the provinces who serves a number of shady purposes in the capital. La Vatnaz, too, had strange golden flecks in the iris of her eyes which Flaubert had already given to other characters, Rodolphe of *Madame Bovary* in particular.

Certain aspects of love which Flaubert had already dissected in the first *Education* could now be explored and expanded. Henry had experienced with Emilie Renaud that terrifying irritation which can come over a man living with a woman who adores him when she has endlessly the same eternally limpid, inept look about her eyes to go along with the same eternal smile. Frédéric faced it with Rosanette. And as Henry had discovered in New York that voluptuousness could not be enough, so Frédéric had to find with Madame Dambreuse that sleeping with her could prove most difficult: an atrophy of his feelings set in.

Resemblances to *Madame Bovary* were legion in the work inevitably, as both dealt with love in the modern world. Frédéric was wont to fix a time by which he would make his declaration to Madame Arnoux, just as Flaubert, Léon, and Charles had. But in *A Sentimental Education* desiccating irony destroys the opportunity: Madame Arnoux left Frédéric to enter a china shop before the appointed moment arrived, and his heroism went for nothing. Similarly, both works describe balls, but the contrasts are more crucial than the similarities. In both Flaubert, who did not dance, gave a strangely obscene account of the movements of the dancers. In the ball at La Vaubyessard, however, Emma thought she was seeing her dreams realized, while in *A Sentimental Education* everything was boring or sordid.

Frédéric, like Emma, was a dreamer, and here the resemblances become very close. Their dreams had a foundation in the conviction that excellence such as theirs merited unusual good fortune. In addition, the sources for both were in their romantic readings. Like her, he was moved by music. And the thought of travel to distant climes sufficed to set either of them to dreaming, a trait which belonged in the first place to their creator. Again, it was Flaubert's belief that led Emma and the others in *Madame Bovary* to fall back upon the concept of fate. Frédéric, too, pleads this excuse, but only when tossing a coin to see what to do: upon a favorable response, he was happy to conclude destiny was pushing him toward Madame Arnoux.

Sometimes the duplications from *Madame Bovary* can be disturbing. An author of great creative powers like Balzac could and did treat the same scene in a number of works without danger. But an author as dependent as Flaubert upon real and precise sources was all too likely to repeat himself when he used the same experience a second time. Emma Bovary had seen her personal property seized for her debts; Rosanette would, too, and Madame Arnoux after her. To be sure, Flaubert strove to vary the details and the structure of the event, but the tone remains too similar not to give the feeling that he was here plagiarizing himself.

More significant are the scenes in the two books where women give themselves. When Emma was seduced by Rodolphe, Flaubert wrote that the shadows of evening were descending and passing through the branches; the setting sun blinded her eyes and silence was everywhere, while something sweet and gentle seemed to be exuded by the very trees. When Madame Dambreuse gave herself to Frédéric, the great trees in the garden, which had been trembling gently in the breeze, ceased moving. Immobile clouds marked the sky with long red bands, and there was, as it were, a universal suspension of everything. Similar evenings and similar silences came back to Frédéric's mind. These two scenes are really the same seduction, though in the first the point of view is the woman's and in the second it is more the man's. It continues to be the same scene as Emma-Frédéric returns home, Emma to a joyous self-adulation as the peer of the heroines she has read of, Frédéric to the comfortable superiority of considering himself now definitively a part of the world of patrician adulteries and high intrigue. The scenes in which Flaubert tried to put into the mouth of a lover something of what he was feeling proved more damaging. Rodolphe's phrases were apt to come forth. When Rosanette in a moment of expansion tried to interest Frédéric, she assured him that their lives were two rivers which must join; Rodolphe had already used the image. And when, more crucially, Frédéric asked Madame Arnoux if she did not feel the aspiration of his soul mounting toward hers and fusing with it, this suggestion, too, was first made by Rodolphe. Frédéric urged the affinities of two souls upon Madame Arnoux, also like Rodolphe, and both men told these women about dreaming of them. These similarities, surely not intentional on Flaubert's part, are disastrous. If he can find no words to phrase the integrity of Frédéric's passion that have not already served for the lechery of Rodolphe, then there can be no distinction between passion and pretense, feeling and fabrication. And a fruitless visit to a brothel will equal a night of love.

Flaubert had varied the forms of attachment in *Madame Bovary* by including not only dominance and subservience but also a preliminary phase of platonic involvement. Frédéric was to know the full attachment of the senses with Rosanette; but throughout the entire *Sentimental Education*, except when he was not in love with Madame Arnoux, he experienced love without satisfaction. This situation, for a Flaubert, was inextricable: of course he must reduplicate. In *Madame Bovary* the material is a brilliant condensation (the Agricultural Fair, the analysis of Léon's frustrated state); in *A Sentimental Education* it is spread over several scenes and many pages. But it is the same material. The fundamental identity is clear if the single page which describes Léon's early feelings for Emma is placed beside the scattered passages deriving from it which concern Frédéric:

Madame Bovary

"What folly," he said to himself. "How could one ever reach her?"

She seemed to him so virtuous and inaccessible that he abandoned even the vaguest of hopes.

But by this very renunciation he placed her in an extraordinary condition. She was separated for him from the carnal qualities from which he could obtain nothing. And in his heart she rose steadily, detaching herself as in a magnificent apotheosis. His was one of those feelings which does not affect daily living and which one cultivates because it is rare and whose loss would be more afflicting than physical possession could be rewarding.*

*Madame Bovary

"—Quelle folie! se disait-il, et comment arriver jusqu'à elle?"

"Elle lui parut donc si vertueuse et inaccessible, que toute espérance, même la plus vague, l'abandonna.

"Mais, par ce renoncement, il la plaçait en des conditions extraordinaires. Elle se dégagea, pour lui, des qualités charnelles dont il n'avait rien à obtenir; et elle alla, dans son coeur, montant toujours et s'en détachant, à la manière magnifique d'une apothéose qui s'envole. C'était un de ces sentiments purs qui n'embarrassent pas l'exercice de la vie, que l'on cultive parce qu'ils sont rares, et dont la perte affligerait plus que la possession n'est réjouissante" (p. 148).

A Sentimental Education

Moreover, he was stopped by a sort of religious fear. Her dress, melting into the shadows, seemed to him immense, infinite, impossible to raise.

By the very force of his dreams he had placed her outside of human conditions.

It was agreed between them that they would not belong to one another.

The charm of her person moved his heart more than his senses. It was an infinite beatitude, such an intoxication that he forgot even the possibility of possessing her.

He would remind himself that opportunities [for seduction] keep recurring, but that it takes only one blunder to end everything.

L'Education sentimentale

"Il était empêché, d'ailleurs, par une sorte de crainte religieuse. Cette robe ... lui paraissait ... insoulevable ... (pp. 285-86).

Par la force de ses rêves, il l'avait posée en dehors des conditions humaines (p. 245).

Il était bien entendu qu'ils ne devaient pas s'appartenir (p. 389).

... le charme de sa personne lui troublait le coeur plus que les sens. C'était une béatitude indéfinie, un tel enivrement, qu'il en oubliait jusqu'à la possibilité d'un bonheur absolu (p. 392).

... se disant qu'on peut ressaisir une occasion et qu'on ne rattrape jamais une sottise" (*ibid.*).

There are other similarities. Monsieur Dambreuse dies and so does a child of Rosanette and Frédéric. The older man's corpse is little described, but the child has purple lips, his skin is pale, his nostrils are pinched and his eye sockets hollowed. The reader has seen this body before: it was Emma's. Over her dying form, the priest, in the ritual of the Mass, recapitulated her life. Frédéric similarly summarized for himself the main events of Dambreuse's tormented existence as he sat looking at his corpse. And a further review of a lifetime is condensed into a paragraph during the sale of Madame Arnoux's personal belongings. The pretext is slightly different each time, but the purpose and the basic technique of a recapitulation at the end of a life are identical.

There is a similarly disquieting recurrence of a strange laugh which had first been that of the devil on the closing page of *The Temptation of Saint Anthony* in the version of 1849; next it had been the laugh, "atrocious, frenzied, despairing," of Emma at the end of her life. Now the soft-voiced Madame Arnoux had it and used it twice, the first time "sharp, despairing, atrocious," the second "sharp and *déchirant*," which may mean either "earsplitting" or "heart rending." It is the same laugh of anguish and agony, but perhaps less appropriate. It may have rung out first when Madame Flaubert realized that her husband was dead and then have recurred—after Flaubert had first described it in *Saint Anthony*—when her son left her for his trip around the Eastern Mediterranean.

Finally, the unpublished *Dictionary of Accepted Ideas*, too, so useful for Homais and Bournisien, again furnished observations to be proffered by characters in the new work. The traditional honeymoon trip to Italy came in for ribbing as did—twice over— the fact that Italy was inferior to its reputation. But here Flaubert was safe: the *Dictionary* was not in print, as were *Madame Bovary* and *Salammbô*, to confound him.

THE GREAT SCENES

> Each scene in the novel is played on the front of the stage;
> but each element takes its turn, and it is not a cold photo-
> graph that the reader has before his eyes but rather a living,
> changing performance, in which each type of person has his
> chance to act along with his group of accomplices or dupes,
> with his own interests, passions, and instincts. The charac-
> ters cross the stage rapidly, but each time they demarcate
> sharply the next step in the path they are pursuing. . . .
>
> George Sand, review of *A Sentimental Education*

All of Flaubert's previous novels had been a succession of scenes
linked by connecting passages: *A Sentimental Education*, too, is
built on this pattern. It opens, in point of fact, with one of the
greatest scenes of them all. From scene to scene the reader moves
along, observing the hero, Frédéric, and through him the other
characters. Although the reader does occasionally have privileged
information about him—for instance the indications from the author that he is a coward—his world is usually observed through
his eyes in a dozen or more major scenes scattered through some
six hundred pages. The reader has no difficulty in knowing where
Frédéric is; each scene is heralded with enough trumpets. And
dialogue is so rare in Flaubert's novels that one does not need to
know the importance he attributed to it in order to react when it
does occur. And thus—or so Flaubert would have it—the reader
slips from scene to scene much as he does at the theater, except
that here no director can misunderstand the signals: the author
alone commands actors and director, stage designer and stage man-
ager, to produce, full bodied from his own brain, the entire production.

Flaubert had announced in August of 1864 that he would
begin his big Parisian novel the next month, after he had made the
trip up the Seine to Montereau in preparation for writing the
opening scene. Actually he could no longer go by boat as the run
had been canceled, so he went by carriage instead.[19] In earlier
years he had made similar trips, especially on the lower reaches of
the Seine between Rouen and the mouth of the river. One occa-

sion in particular, from 1838, still stood out in his memory in 1853 and, presumably, in 1864. He had been going from Rouen to Les Andelys, as he often did, with Alfred Le Poittevin. The two were in one of their periods of unbearable ennui. Not knowing what else to do, they settled at the bar and consumed brandy, rum, and liqueurs, with a rice soup to top them off. There were several Parisian ladies and gentlemen on board, and the wind tore a green veil from the straw hat of one of the ladies. It swirled across the deck and became entangled in Flaubert's legs. A man in the fashionable white trousers of the day came over and picked it up. The opening scene of *A Sentimental Education* had already been found.[20]

The novel begins in Paris along the quays, where the *Ville-de-Montereau* was being readied for the trip up the river to Nogent. With much bustle and noise the ship* got under way, and the banks lined with storehouses, factories, and yards slipped by like the unfolding of two wide ribbons. Among the travelers was Frédéric, but so naturally a part of the scene that the reader barely notices him against the background of the river with its sandy shores. Here and there, logs, which were lashed together, began to undulate as the wake of the *Ville-de-Montereau* struck them—a passage which Proust particularly admired for the way in which Flaubert's eye had become one with the logs and so perfectly reported them that the reader, too, senses their movement.[21]

The ship's wake and the shores under the burning sun were as

---

*"Enfin le navire partit; et les deux berges, peuplées de magasins, de chantiers et d'usines, filèrent comme deux larges rubans que l'on déroule ... (*ES*, pp. 1-2).

"La rivière était bordée par des grèves de sables. On rencontrait des trains de bois qui se mettaient à onduler sous le remous des vagues, ou bien, dans un bateau sans voiles, un homme assis pêchait; puis les brumes errantes se fondirent, le soleil parut, la colline qui suivait à droite le cours de la Seine peu à peu s'abaissa, et il en surgit une autre, plus proche, sur la rive opposée (*ES*, pp. 2-3).

... À chaque détour de la rivière, on retrouvait le même rideau de peupliers pâles. La campagne était toute vide. Il y avait dans le ciel de petits nuages blancs arrêtés, et l'ennui, vaguement répandu, semblait alanguir la marche du bateau et rendre l'aspect des voyageurs plus insignifiants encore" (*ES*, p. 5).

monotonously the same as the endless succession of panoramas. As each turn was rounded, another perspective of low hills, curtaining lines of poplars, and empty countryside appeared. Even the clouds in the sky were motionless and unchanging, and ennui, hanging vaguely over everything, seemed to slow the advance of the boat and make the passengers even more insignificant. In this suffocating atmosphere, the reader drifts along until, like the boat and its passengers, he, too, travels this river of life into a world of monotony, futility, repetition, and ennui.

Frédéric was moving restlessly about the ship when suddenly he came upon Madame Arnoux. The discovery is the familiar one which as adolescent and as young man he had tried so many times to suggest. She wore a broad straw hat with pink ribbons which trembled in the wind as they hung behind her. Her black braids, framing the outer edge of her large eyebrows, came down quite far and seemed to press lovingly against the oval of her face. Her dress, a light-colored muslin with small dots, spread out in full folds. She was embroidering something; her straight nose, her chin, all of her was sharply silhouetted against the blue sky. He watched spellbound, studying each detail, speculating about her life and filled with amazement.

And then it happened; her shawl, long and with bands of purple, began to slip toward the edge of the ship, about to fall. How many times on the high seas or during damp evenings she must have wound it about her waist or covered her feet with it, slept in it perhaps! Frédéric bounded forward just in time to catch it and return it to her. Madame Arnoux thanked him and their eyes met. Her husband, looking for her, called out, and the spell was broken. The story was launched.

There are three scenes in the book depicting formal balls, each designed to advance the plot line but also, especially by their contrast, to display three different levels of society. The first was at the Alhambra, a public dance hall. To be sure of his tone, Flaubert persuaded Jules Duplan to accompany him one evening to observe such a place. The Alhambra was the world of the student and the petty employee who came with a mistress or were out to meet one for the evening. In this easy atmosphere all but Frédéric found themselves girls and disappeared.

Arnoux was present, too, at the Alhambra, carrying on some dubious affair. He escorted Frédéric to the second ball, at Rosanette's where he met the lorette the first time. The atmosphere was as erotic as that of the Alhambra, but not so clearly promiscuous. Watching the quadrilles, he squinted his eyes to see them better and sniffed the warm scent of the women as it circulated like a kiss through the rooms, a cruder handling than the tent scene of *Salammbô*. Rosanette's was the world the student had dreamed of, where love was facile if one had money and where everything concurred to give romance color.

Underneath, as Frédéric rapidly discovered, ran a steady current of sordidness. The oldest and most decrepit man present was Rosanette's protector. As the evening wore on, fatigue and alcohol took their unglamorous toll, letting Frédéric glimpse how little joy touched the lives of these women. Flaubert's is never the sentimental touch of a pitying Victor Hugo; instead, he tears away the coloring romantic authors had lent their fallen heroines. Here tubercular women spat up blood; sweat ran down their faces, spoiling the makeup and showing the pallor beneath. Ugly verity was emphasized by the reddened eyelids of the sleepy guests and the chattering teeth of those who had fevers. Frédéric fell asleep to a dream of having one after another of the women, while a pair of eyes which he could not identify, big and black, watched him. Rosanette rode astride him, driving her spurs into his flanks. The ball had been an orgy such as Balzac had enjoyed portraying. But here there was no enjoyment for author, for participant, or for reader: the horror beneath had been unmasked.

At the Alhambra the women were of the poorer classes. At Rosanette's, they were kept women of a much more expensive sort. Madame Dambreuse, however, belonged to the world of the financial and political leaders of France. In her mansion the veneer of decency was always maintained, but at the cost of a vast ennui. Not even the men could pretend to be enjoying themselves as, with bored nonchalance, they acquitted themselves of the duty of dancing with their unattractive partners. Beneath the surface, however, there was less to distinguish Madame Dambreuse's salon than appeared: her husband's alleged niece, who was present, was in fact his illegitimate daughter. And Madame Dambreuse was furious with the young man who was courting the daughter because he had earlier been her own lover.

The women who filled Madame Dambreuse's boudoir were seated on stools.* Their long skirts billowing out around them seemed like waves from which their torsos emerged, and the low neckline of their dresses easily revealed their breasts. Each held a bunch of violets in her hand. The dull tone of their gloves brought out the whiteness of their arms. Occasionally, when one of them moved suddenly the strap of her dress would threaten to slip off her shoulder. But the decency of the faces tempered the provocations of the clothes; some even had an almost animal placidity. This assembly of half-naked women reminded Frédéric of a harem . . . and of another, cruder gathering which nineteenth-century taste did not allow Flaubert to name.

Like Balzac, Flaubert wished to describe the great parade of carriages and riders along the Champs Elysées. He arranged that Frédéric, imitating Rastignac, should see and envy those who took part in it; and, again like Rastignac, he finally rode in such a carriage, with the striking Rosanette beside him. But his triumph was a downfall: Madame Dambreuse had seen him and had not liked his companion; Madame Arnoux had, too, and Rosanette had even shouted an insult at her. Moreover, friends had forced themselves upon the couple for dinner. Hence Frédéric was now glumly driving toward the restaurant in a line of carriages as monotonous as the flow of the river and the movement of the boat at the start of the novel. But then Frédéric had had illusions; now

---

*"Des femmes le remplissaient, les unes près des autres, sur des sièges sans dossier. Leurs longues jupes, bouffant autour d'elles, semblaient des flots d'où leur taille émergeait, et les seins s'offraient aux regards dans l'échancrure des corsages. Presque toutes portaient un bouquet de violettes à la main. Le ton mat de leurs gants faisait ressortir la blancheur humaine de leurs bras; des effilés, des herbes, leur pendaient sur les épaules, et on croyait quelquefois, à certains frissonnements, que la robe allait tomber. Mais la décence des figures tempérait les provocations du costume; plusieurs même avaient une placidité presque bestiale, et ce rassemblement de femmes deminues faisait songer à un intérieur de harem; il vint à l'esprit du jeune homme une comparaison plus grossière" (*ES*, pp. 228-29).

they were gone. As his carriage neared its destination, it splashed mud on a pedestrian, Frédéric's old friend Deslauriers, whom he had long abandoned.

Sometimes, as with the day at the races, a scene is long and lasts for pages; at other times a page or so suffices, reverberating back to the beginning of the book or anticipating the last moments. When Deslauriers, for his own less-than-honest purposes, told Madame Arnoux that Frédéric was about to marry Louise Roque, she sent him away and turned to the window to look out, just as Frédéric would many years later, when she left him after her last visit. With an uncomprehending eye, she watched a packer across the street nail down the lid of a case; hackneys passed; she went to a chair and sat down. All was silent, like an immense desertion of everything. She wondered aloud at his marrying and suddenly began to tremble all over. Again aloud, she asked herself: "Why this? Am I in love with him?" And then suddenly it burst from her lips: "Yes, I do love him! I do." She found herself exploring something which had endless depth, a profundity greater than could be plumbed. The clock beside her struck, but unlike Emma outside the convent, she had no need to be wakened from nightmarish dreams. She listened instead as the vibration died away and remained seated on the edge of her chair, her eyes fixed, her lips still smiling.

Typical of *A Sentimental Education*, Madame Arnoux discovered she loved Frédéric only when she thought it was too late. When the misunderstanding was cleared up, the mood had changed. Her constant smile Flaubert had already castigated in his first *Sentimental Education*. The fixed, dark eyes staring out into space had haunted him since Trouville and were the eyes Frédéric had seen in his dream after the ball at Rosanette's. They were perhaps also the eyes of Murillo's "Virgin" in Rome.

Madame Arnoux held Frédéric off for many months, but finally there came a time when only consenting to meet with him made any further sense; and so she agreed to an assignation. As Frédéric waited through the long afternoon and listened uncomprehendingly to the distant noises from the outbreak of the Revolution of 1848, the reader shares his almost unbearable tension. He could not know it, but Madame Arnoux was delayed by her child's sudden attack of croup. When Flaubert sent the manuscript to Du Camp for his critique, Maxime also had his mistress read it: she found the wait so unpleasant and so interminable that she begged Flaubert to shorten it![22]

The croup scene gave Flaubert great trouble. He had intended to have a tracheotomy performed on the child; but his attempt to watch one ended in disaster as he could not stand the child's suffering. Rather than risk describing something he had not seen, Flaubert adopted an alternative outcome, the rare case in which the patient coughs up the strangulating membrane and recovers. The account alternates between the anguish of the child and the anguish of the mother, moving back and forth as it had at the Agricultural Fair.

There are similar episodes in Balzac and in the minor novelist Octave Feuillet, in which the illness of a child interrupts an assignation. But nowhere previously had the dread and trivializing hand of coincidence so weighed down upon a scene. Madame Arnoux, after long years of resistance, was about to give herself to her lover; she knew she would, Frédéric knew, and so does the reader. A point had been reached at which her consent was the only acceptable course. Then a totally irrelevant, and hence trivial, cause intervened, as Flaubert had willed it should. And—again as in the early sketches—the psychological moment had forever passed. Frédéric, confused, angered, and despairing, went off to Rosanette, finally finding in his misery the strength to conquer this willing prey. He took her to the apartment prepared for Madame Arnoux; as she was falling asleep after they had made love, she heard him sobbing like a child.

Frédéric and Rosanette soon left Paris for the Forest of Fontainebleau in order to be undisturbed. Over the summer of 1868 Flaubert went there twice himself to prepare for writing the descriptions of the Forest, which are among the greatest in his works.[23] These are some of the few happy moments in the novel, but even here the undertones are ironic, satiric, or tragic. No one is ever pardoned for long in *A Sentimental Education.*

First there was a devastating period of ironic opposition. The beauty and solemn antiquity of the Forest and Palace moved Frédéric deeply but meant nothing to Rosanette. Frédéric at Fontainebleau was Flaubert himself, the seasoned and learned traveler responding vibrantly to the suggestiveness of places long steeped in story. Rosanette was the totally uneducated lorette whose own body had been her sole interest. She walked with her lover through the galleries of the Palace, glad only to use the mirrors to rearrange her coiffure. The memory of Diane de Poitiers excited Frédéric; clearly Rosanette had never heard of her. She failed also to understand and appreciate the special appeal of such empty palaces. As they went out in the Forest, Frédéric recalled ancient legends of the forest saints, but Rosanette was unrelievedly miserable. Frédéric rejoiced in the monstrous, fantastic quality of the trees, but she was again unable to follow. When they fell back upon a surer physical basis, however, they were quite at one, and Rosanette seemed almost a part of this Forest to her lover.

It was probably only in 1870 or later that Flaubert jotted down an irritated observation which aptly summarized Rosanette at Fontainebleau: "That something or other which is so limited and so exasperating and which makes up the very basis of the female personality."[24] Frédéric now discovered this limitation in Rosanette as she trivialized and personalized each moment while he was losing himself in the impersonal melancholy of history. Flaubert, taking over as completely as he had in the description of Yonville, told the reader baldly what lay before the two visitors. The ten windows* of the arcade were wide open, he wrote; the sunlight made the pictures shine, and the blue sky beyond continued the ultramarine of the painting within. From deep in the woods, whose misty tops filled the horizon, there seemed to come echoes of hunting cries and calls on ivory horns and of the incredible ballets in which princesses and noble lords dressed as nymphs and woodfolk

*"Les dix fenêtres en arcades étaient grandes ouvertes; le soleil faisait briller les peintures, le ciel bleu continuait indéfiniment l'outremer des cintres; et, du fond des bois, dont les cimes vaporeuses emplissaient l'horizon, il semblait venir un écho des halalis poussés dans les trompes d'ivoire, et des ballets mythologiques, assemblant sous le feuillage des princesses et des seigneurs travestis en nymphes et en sylvains, époque de science ingénue, de passions violentes et d'art somptueux, quand l'idéal était d'emporter le monde dans un rêve des Hespérides, et que les maîtresses des rois se confondaient avec les astres" (ES, pp. 460-61).

assembled beneath the trees. They belonged to an age of ingenuous knowledge, violent passions, and sumptuous art, when man's ideal was to carry the world off into a dream of the Hesperides, and the king's mistresses seemed to fuse with the stars. Poor Frédéric, to whom all this is addressed, could tell from the total silence of Rosanette that it meant nothing to her, and he was not the dupe of her undeveloped remark that "it brought back memories." Somehow, though, she seemed even prettier for her effort at seriousness, and Frédéric found himself excusing her easily.

Again and again the same mechanism recurs. Flaubert, in his own name, recounts a situation or describes a particular type of nostalgic charm. Frédéric responds. And Rosanette fails him. She primps, claims knowledge she does not have, yawns, recoils . . . works every change on failing to be moved.

Gradually nature itself became what charmed them, and Rosanette, artificial though she was, was not incapable of reacting to it: a second phase began. She and her lover rode about the Forest in an old carriage. Images of disuse and death surrounded them on every side: the ditches* beside the road were full of brush; here and there an old, unused forest road appeared, its path filled with grass. A cross would extend its arms at intersections; elsewhere aged posts were tipped at the odd angle of dead trees; moss filled the worn wagon tracks. Rosanette and Frédéric felt alone, far from the world, together. As they breathed in the wind, they sensed within themselves the pride of a freer life with a superabundance of strength and a nameless joy.

Rosanette did not respond as much as Frédéric in the Forest;

---

*"Les fossés pleins de broussailles filaient sous leurs yeux, avec un mouvement doux et continu. ... quelquefois, un chemin, qui ne servait plus, se présentait devant eux, en ligne droite; et des herbes s'y dressaient ça et là, mollement. Au centre des carrefours, une croix étendait ses quatre bras; ailleurs, des poteaux se penchaient comme des arbres morts. ... plus loin, de la mousse avait poussé au bord des ornières profondes.

"Ils se croyaient loin des autres, bien seuls. ...

"Debout, l'un près de l'autre, sur quelque éminence du terrain, ils sentaient, tout en humant le vent, leur entrer dans l'âme comme l'orgueil d'une vie plus libre, avec une surabondance de forces, une joie sans cause" (*ES*, pp. 465-66).

but bit by bit she began to react in her own way. When she did and chattered happily along, he watched* alternately the black beads of her hood and the juniper berries, the folds of her veil and the volutes of the clouds. When he bent near to her, the freshness of her skin mingled with perfume of the woods. Reliving the romantic images of familiar Lamartine poems, they observed the sky coming down to the jagged tops of the trees, in the distance the bell tower of a church, a river to the left seeming motionless along its winding curves. Frédéric was sure for the rest of his days he would be happy with that intimate happiness inherent in the life and the body of this woman. He seemed to discover a whole new beauty in her which was either the reflection of the things about her or something their secret powers brought out in her.

They paid no attention to the occasional roll of a drum from the neighboring village. There might be a revolution in Paris, but what was happening to them was more important. And so Rosanette was led to talk of her youth and what it had been like to be a child of impoverished parents. She told Frédéric of the loss of her virginity: the story was Suzanne Lagier's.[25] This whole section—as all principal ones—Flaubert recounted in direct discourse, but no other passage in the book has such a preponderance of it for so many pages. Flaubert calls her "the poor *Maréchale*," bringing in once again that revelatory adjective.

There are a number of great paragraphs of description of the Forest of Fontainebleau, but one is particularly well structured.

*"Le bras sous la taille, il l'écoutait parler pendant que les oiseaux gazouillaient, observait presque du même coup d'oeil les raisins noirs de sa capote et les baies des genévriers, les draperies de son voile, les volutes des nuages; et, quand il se penchait vers elle, la fraîcheur de sa peau se mêlait au grand parfum des bois. ...

"Le ciel, d'un bleu tendre, arrondi comme un dôme, s'appuyait à l'horizon sur la dentelure des bois. En face, au bout de la prairie, il y avait un clocher dans un village; et, plus loin, à gauche, le toit d'une maison faisait une tache rouge sur la rivière, qui semblait immobile dans toute la longueur de sa sinuosité. ...

"Il ne doutait pas qu'il ne fût heureux pour jusqu'à la fin de ses jours, tant son bonheur lui paraissait naturel, inhérent à sa vie et à la personne de cette femme. ... Il lui découvrait enfin une beauté toute nouvelle, qui n'était peut-être que le reflet des choses ambiantes, à moins que leur virtualités secrètes ne l'eussent fait s'épanouir" (*ES*, pp. 469-70).

The first part is organized around the sunlight which penetrates into the forest in varying ways. The opening sentence establishes the broad divisions of the scene and a second picks out details; in both, light is the agent:

> The light, in certain places illuminating the edge of the wood, left the backgrounds in shadow; or else, attenuated in the foregrounds by a sort of dusk, it spread purple vapors, a white clarity, over the more distant areas. In the middle of the day, the sun, falling vertically on the wide green areas, would splatter them, suspend silvery drops on the tips of the branches, stripe the grass with strings of emeralds, cast spots of gold on the layer of dead leaves; [Thus far the light and the sun have introduced dynamic movement. Now, in a dramatic shift, the onlooker becomes central, with his power of image making.] when you tipped back your head, you could see the sky between the tops of the trees. Some of them, very tall, looked like patriarchs and emperors, or, touching each other at their outer edges, formed sorts of triumphal arches with their long trunks; others, growing on a slant, seemed like columns about to fall.*

All at once the Fontainebleau episode was over. Frédéric read that Deslauriers was wounded, announced his immediate departure, and was shocked at the egoism of Rosanette, who noticed only that she was to be left; he departed madly for Paris, where his presence turned out to be wholly unnecessary. It had all been for nothing: the trip, the revelation of Rosanette's limitations, their momentary closeness, and his abandoning her for his friend. Such futility prefigured the end.

Madame Arnoux's visit to Frédéric is the next-to-the-last epi-

---

*"La lumière, à de certaines places éclairant la lisière du bois, laissait les fonds dans l'ombre; ou bien, atténuée sur les premiers plans par une sorte de crépuscule, elle étalait dans les lointains des vapeurs violettes, une clarté blanche. Au milieu du jour, le soleil, tombant d'aplomb sur les larges verdures, les éclaboussait, suspendait des gouttes argentines à la pointe des branches, rayait le gazon de traînées d'émeraudes, jetait des taches d'or sur les couches de feuilles mortes; en se renversant la tête, on apercevait le ciel, entre les cimes des arbres. Quelques-uns, d'une altitude démesurée, avaient des airs de patriarches et d'empereurs, ou, se touchant par le bout, formaient avec leurs longs fûts comme des arcs de triomphe; d'autres, poussés dès le bas obliquement, semblaient des colonnes près de tomber" (*ES*, pp. 465-66).

sode of the book. Edmond de Goncourt wrote to Flaubert that he knew no scene in any work which touched him more or was sadder or more tender; it depended upon no tricks for its effectiveness.[26] Frédéric's mind had been unoccupied and his heart inert for many years; and then, as suddenly as on her first appearance, there she was before him. Quite early in the visit he ceased being honest with her: she saw a portrait of *la Maréchale*, thought she recognized her, and questioned Frédéric, who emphatically denied knowing the sitter. They talked of their past and the love they had had for one another. Then Flaubert made a most unusual slip (although there are two or three others in this work). When Frédéric asked Madame Arnoux how she first discovered his love for her, she referred to an occasion on which he had kissed her wrist. Such an occasion did occur in the book, but it was in the middle of a somewhat unpleasant tangle, and it was Rosanette's wrist, not Madame Arnoux's, that Frédéric kissed.

After going out for a walk, they returned to the apartment and Madame Arnoux removed her hat: her hair was white. It gave Frédéric the same shock Flaubert must have had when he first saw Elisa after her stay in the asylum. To allow himself a moment to recover, he sat at her knees and spoke to her once again of what she had meant to him and the special quality she had seemed to have. The music of his own words intoxicated him as much as Madame Arnoux. She leaned toward him, her breath was on his forehead, and he could sense her body beneath her clothes. Their hands met, and the tip of her shoe appeared outside the hem of her dress. He told her, almost fainting, "The sight of your foot upsets me." She stood and told him how grateful she was, at her age. A moment later he held her in his arms, she leaned back in that arched pose, eyes closed and lips parted. But when Frédéric did not take her, she pushed him away and told him, under pressing, that she had intended to make him happy. For a sudden moment Frédéric felt wild desire; but it was countered by a sudden revulsion. To have Madame Arnoux would be a sort of incest.

Had Frédéric stopped with this quasi-filial, quasi-religious feeling, the picture would have retained at least that purity of an inhibited sort which had always characterized his relationship to her. But there was more. Twenty years before, Du Camp had noted to Flaubert that no man ever fails, after having a woman, even one who has long resisted him, to feel a terrible fear: how is he going to get rid of her? When Rodolphe had debated seducing Emma, he had had the same worry. Now Frédéric felt it: there would be disgust for her afterwards. And what a nuisance she would become. So he turned and rolled a cigarette. In a moment she kissed his forehead, cut off a long lock of hair for him, and left. He watched her get into her cab, as she had watched the cab on the afternoon she discovered she loved him.

"And that was all" are the last words of the episode. The romantic clichés of constancy over the years, the joy of finally fulfilled desires, the notion that love will never cease or alter, these, too, were now labeled illusions and crushed by white hair, age, and vanished appeal.

While critics have always differed about *A Sentimental Education* as a whole and about many of its scenes, no single episode has aroused so much irritation and admiration as the last in the book, when Frédéric and Deslauriers, after many years, came together again. It happened "by the fatality of their natures," Flaubert wrote. Such a reunion formed a relatively easy excuse to recount what had occurred to each of his characters—although the reader may reasonably object that the device is too obvious. Frédéric had managed to dissipate two-thirds of his fortune and was now reduced to some nine thousand francs yearly, or only a bit more than Flaubert himself had. Rosanette, still following the model of Suzanne Lagier, was now very fat, enormous even; and the two men regretted her formerly slim waist. Like Suzanne, too, she had a small son.

The real interest of the scene, aside from providing a mechanical means to end the novel, lies in the recalling of the visit to the brothel, which had been hinted at several times at the start of the work. To agree, as the two men did in the last lines, that this unfruitful visit ending in an undignified flight was their best moment constituted the parting slap which Flaubert wished to administer to his generation.

What does this judgment say? That an event which was not

consummated was superior to any that were, that illusion is always superior to reality, that dreams are always shattered unless preserved totally from the consuming breath of actuality. The reader moves from puzzlement to rage or to acquiescence, depending upon his own view of ultimate meanings in life. But for Flaubert this verdict had been clear and indisputable ever since he had begun to formulate his pessimistic view of life in the late 1830's. When he reconstituted his philosophy after the onset of the epileptic crises, it was on the basis of a determined stance outside of life, which he would observe only from a distance. And, specifically in relation to sexuality—which forms the core of this episode —he would remain untouched. When, in Egypt, he had walked up and down the prostitutes' quarter refusing their advances in order to enjoy more fully, or had risen from Kuchiuk-Hânem's couch to step into the street and contemplate the night, he had been preparing the ending of *A Sentimental Education*. Nonparticipation alone permitted the full savoring of life, the retention of the innocence of the ideal and the illusion. For the first time Flaubert was stepping from his own preserves as artist to tell his fellow men what course lay open to those who were not: they could at least understand that illusions must be preserved if they could not be enshrined in art. One could stand on the threshold of the brothel, even if it were denied one to write of such restraint.

Jules, in the first *Sentimental Education*, retained the feeling that his own time of youthful illusions had been the poetic period of his life, par excellence, a sort of golden age for his emotions. But Jules is more Flaubert than is Frédéric and the illusions of the second *Sentimental Education* relate not to idea and ideal but to event. Moreover, when Du Camp first used the last phrase in his letter to Flaubert, he was speaking of the trip through Brittany, an event whose only unreality was that it was memory. At least for Flaubert and his friends, the period of dreams had been a noble one and the best moments had been actualized. It had not been so for all the Flauberts who failed, all the Frédérics of his generation, marked by *veulerie* and cowardice.

A Sentimental Education, like Joyce's *Ulysses* later, comes full cycle and ends the reader where he started, the wiser only for understanding now what the veiled references at the start signified. Such a cycle, however, with a full return to the beginning, can come only in a work of art; but not even Frédéric, privileged being that he is as a character in a novel, can relive the brothel episode. The final message, like the entire book, proves devastating, and his generation and all those that have come since have included many readers who have declined to accept it.

THE REVOLUTION OF 1848

As I study this period, I'm discovering a host of things from then that explain present-day matters.

Letter to Jules Duplan, January 24, 1868

From the very start, Flaubert's *Education* was to be far more than *Sentimental:* that was part of why he found this title inadequate. The book dealt with the art and the finance of his period, its upper social levels and the demimonde, its commerce and its industry, quite as much as with its love life. But for him the principal event of his generation had been the Revolution of 1848 and, almost from the outset, it was to occupy a central position in the novel.

"With Louis-Philippe's abdication something disappeared which will never return," Flaubert had written to Bouilhet from the Near East in 1850.[27] Hence like *Salammbô, A Sentimental Education* has two main focuses, the personal lives of its principal characters and the major political events which put an end to a whole world Flaubert had known. Fiction and history fuse throughout the long episode of the Revolution—nearly seventy-five pages—which opens Part Three. It was a *tour de force* which caused Flaubert much anguish as he struggled to insert his characters and their necessary actions into the fixed data of the events which actually transpired. The background threatened constantly to overwhelm them, as it had so dangerously in *Salammbô*. This was, he fully realized, the grave risk of the historical novel as he conceived it; and the difficulty was compounded in his situation, since his characters, this time, were so much less interesting than the real people whose deeds he had to mention. Moreover, there was the delicate problem of what to choose among the vast body of data available to him.

Despite all his difficulties and the dangers he foresaw, Flaubert was on the whole successful. His novel has remarkable historical accuracy and one does follow the progress of the Revolution. On the other hand the reader is not forced to keep track of history in order to follow the lives of the protagonists. Perhaps the only failure of technique is that the modern reader—for whom these events are long past—has real need for the copious explanatory footnotes which accompany most editions today.

This section of the novel is a chronicle of 1848. Flaubert had long been convinced that he had great gifts for political intrigue; *A Sentimental Education* was to be his occasion to demonstrate his political insight. Unfortunately, as with *Madame Bovary*, the demonstration had to be in reverse, shown only ironically through the catastrophic errors of all involved. Deslauriers incarnates the revolutionary for personal gain; Sénécal's ferocious desire for power and for justice is coupled with a fanatic desire for order which leads to his becoming a police agent; their friend Dussardier is the idealist seeking to protect and elevate the weak and the downtrodden. And it is in the ironic nature of Flaubert's view of the world that Dussardier should finally be shot by Sénécal.

Some of the events of 1848-52 Flaubert had witnessed personally. He and Du Camp had attended one of the Reform Banquets which preceded the outbreak of the Revolution.[28] Flaubert and Bouilhet had gone into Paris on the following February 23 to study the actual fighting. They considerably misunderstood what was happening: although they did notice the firing, they went off with Du Camp to listen to Bouilhet recite some of his poetry. Frédéric's conduct stemmed from that of Flaubert and his friends. And when, on the twenty-fourth, Frédéric walked about Paris and witnessed various events, he was retracing the steps Flaubert and Du Camp took and which Du Camp had in part related already in a volume of his. Flaubert may even have used Du Camp's notes;

he certainly took none himself.[29] Again, by pleasant good luck, he was in the capital at the time of Louis-Napoléon's *coup d'état,* which Frédéric missed in order to go to Nogent, where he hoped to marry Louise.

A Sentimental Education involves a great deal more than the mere external events of the Revolution of 1848, for Flaubert proposed to treat of the major attitudes and theories of the Utopian Socialists. He even put off beginning his novel for some months while he read their publications. Finally a worried Bouilhet became almost sharp in his admonitions to start writing.[30] Flaubert did at last, but he returned once more for long months in 1866-67, reading widely and asking older friends like Sainte-Beuve and George Sand for further suggestions.

In the novel, as the long pent-up rage of the mob burst loose, Frédéric moved from one part of the city to another to watch the rioting. At first all seemed to be play acting. But as the fighting grew more bloody, even the peaceful Frédéric "felt his Gallic blood surging" under the magnetism of the excited crowds. He trembled all over and was seized with an immense love, a sort of supreme and universal tenderness, as if the heart of all humanity were beating within his breast. These high hopes, which so many of his generation entertained, were what had made the outcome of the Revolution so bitter a farce to a Flaubert, a Baudelaire, a Hugo, a Leconte de Lisle, and countless thousands of others.

The Socialists were the particular bête noire of Flaubert. Already in the Levant he had declared them monstrous in their stupidity.[31] Now as he read and reread them in the 1860's, he was appalled. They all shared a common hatred for liberty, for the Revolution of 1789, for any sort of sound philosophy. Essentially medieval in outlook, they turned toward the past, not the future as they claimed. Their debt to religion was crippling; they had pillaged de Maistre and Lamennais. What despots they were! Flaubert's righteous indignation grew as he read. All of them, he came to state, based their belief ultimately on biblical revelation and sought to have man expiate some sort of original sin.

Deslauriers expressed much of Flaubert's thinking, attacking Saint-Simon and the other Socialists as a band of jokers who wished to redo Catholicism under a new guise. Sénécal illustrated the nature of the problem. Defending the position of the Revolution, he demanded the application of the principles of the Gospels, to which he added garbled elements from Rousseau and the nineteenth-century thinkers. He envisaged a virtuous democracy which would be a cross between a small farm and a factory, "a sort of American Sparta in which the individual would exist only for society."

As the Revolution faded into dissension and chaos, Deslauriers was again charged with expressing Flaubert's views. He complained that the hopelessly inept masses, prostrating themselves before one god after another, could always be bought by anyone who promised to feed them. Frédéric, too, castigated the revolutionaries as petty bourgeois and fools who had defrauded the workers of almost everything. Progress could be accomplished only by an aristocracy, perhaps only by a single powerful man.

The reactionaries, however, fared no better. Flaubert pointed out that they lacked the indispensable man to guide them to true conservatism; Thiers, their nominal leader, was as inept as the Socialists. The party was doubly damned: since salvation lay only through them, their failures made them criminal. Still worse, when they regained power, their cruelties and brutalities equaled those of the Socialists. The common sense of the nation seemed upset and, added Flaubert, there were men who remained idiots forever after. The divine right of kings and the sovereignty of the people were two equally absurd notions. For too long metaphysics had reigned in political thought, and all of society was rotted. It was time to treat political theory scientifically, as it was for esthetic theory. Otherwise chaos would always reign, changing only in the particular forms of idiocy worshiped at the moment. Thus patriots, Socialists, and reactionaries among Flaubert's readers could each find his own dish and put the book down with distaste or with fury at its author. Only time could heal these perspectives, and there has not yet been that much time.

ESTHETICS AND STYLE

Unity arises in art as a result of the transformation the artist imposes on reality. This correcting, which the artist accomplishes by his use of language and his redistribution of the elements drawn from reality, is called style and gives both its unity and its limits to this new universe.

Albert Camus, *The Rebel*

Camus has observed that the French novel has always sought to unite the fatalism of man's conditioned destiny with the notion of art, which is man's supreme manifestation of his liberty. It has been a sort of ideal terrain upon which the forces of destiny could struggle with the power of man's free will, giving him an opportunity for revenge and a chance to surmount his difficult fate by imposing a form upon it. It remains to determine to what extent Flaubert succeeded in imposing a form upon his material in *A Sentimental Education*.[32]

Nature is beautiful only to those who know how to look at her, proof to Flaubert that everything is subjective.[33] But equally he felt his novel was written in terms of certain scientific exigencies over which he had no control. In fact, any novel must be scientific, that is, it must remain within the limits of general probabilities. In addition, his particular novel was attempting to combine the epic and the satiric in an historical framework. It was to be a kind of "epic of mediocrity," as Gide later termed it, a satire of his generation. It was also to record, still within the novel form, the moral, political, and emotional history of his generation. Lastly, *A Sentimental Education* was to have the essential quality of all art for Flaubert: it must produce a vague exaltation in the reader through his participating in the lives of the characters.

It cannot be seriously maintained that *A Sentimental Education* is the entirely successful resolution of the wager involved in seeking to unite all these themes and subjects. Rigorous scientific demands, a bourgeois subject, fixed historical data, mediocre personalities, and an effort to produce in the reader a vague exaltation: no wonder Flaubert staggered under the burden, which a lesser man would not have undertaken. As he neared the end, even he declared that the attempt had been foredoomed.

Flaubert used to say of his novel that the trouble was it did not form a pyramid. This was apparent even in the initial planning, which is one reason why he put off starting for so very long. Many years after it was completed, he still affirmed that the *Education* lacked that falseness of perspective which is essential to art. It offered no progression of effect, and hence the reader had the same impression at the end that he had at the beginning. Somehow Flaubert had been so preoccupied with adhering to reality that he had failed to choose adequately within what it offered him. No one, he felt, had pushed probity further than he had; but since art and reality were separate domains, he had failed.[34]

Flaubert also feared, even when far along in the writing, that his book suffered for lack of a main scene. To him it seemed to have no set pieces, not even any metaphors, because any embroidering that he might have done would have rent the basic fabric. He was worried but he need not have been. The work abounds in major scenes, the initial one on the boat, the dinners and balls, various episodes in the Revolution of 1848, the whole stay of Frédéric and Rosanette in the Forest of Fontainebleau, and countless others. And of course it closes with the great scenes of the final visit of Madame Arnoux and the conversation between Frédéric and Deslauriers.

Flaubert intended *A Sentimental Education* to be impersonal, impartial, impassive, and objective. In fact, however, he was constantly and obviously present in his novel. Taine wrote him that he kept discovering the author's private feelings everywhere; he doubted, though, that readers who did not know him could do so.[35] Maupassant, writing a little later and hence with more experience of what readers did discover, could be more perceptive. Speaking of Flaubert's manifest exasperation over human stupidity, he conceded that Flaubert's works did have a bitter savor which came from his constant discovery of mediocrity, banality, and stupidity everywhere. Flaubert, Maupassant pointed out, noted it in *A Sentimental Education* in almost every paragraph, by a word, by the slanting of a phrase, or by the general tone. Hence,

Maupassant felt, the distaste which a number of readers experienced in reading the work.[36]

Speaking of Thiers, whom he hated, Flaubert once asked how he could legitimately express his adverse opinion without appearing to be an imbecile later on. He decided, as before, that the best procedure was to content himself with depiction: dissection was a vengeance. And yet he promised his friends he would give the political leader his due, and he did by having one character declare Thiers's writing as beautiful as his thoughts were profound. Since probably not even Thiers thought his prose remarkable, the intent was clear. George Sand was worried and begged him to be generous. He promised to show her the manuscript and remove anything ill tempered or nasty; he did read it to her, but to no avail. She would have had to ask for a complete rewriting, and then it would have been another book.

Many of the devices Flaubert employed to express his own opinions he had elaborated earlier for *Madame Bovary*. The "poor" little face of Madame Arnoux's sick child joins the "poor" *Maréchale* in revealing Flaubert's sympathy, as had the "poor" hands of the dying Emma. Deslauriers not unreasonably phrased Flaubert's views on political theory; the artist Pellerin felt his nostalgia for bygone ages. Madame Arnoux observed correctly that her husband had been the only honest man at a dinner party. But in *A Sentimental Educaton*—as opposed to his earlier novels— Flaubert seems for the first time curiously unaware that such statements must be made by characters whom the reader can trust. When Pellerin expresses Flaubert's own doctrines on esthetics, the reader becomes uneasy. Is this bumbling charlatan to be believed when he asserts that so-called realism is silly and when he insists upon grandeur and impersonal exaltation as the aims of art? Or that these must be based upon ideas, of which he has almost none? He speaks for Flaubert and not for himself, but this the reader cannot know.

Ironic juxtaposition had been immensely effective in *Madame Bovary*, as in the Agricultural Fair. Here, too, Flaubert used the device as a means to avoid having to intervene himself; he could limit his role to arranging the sequences. When a desperate Frédéric returned from Fontainebleau to Paris during the Revolution, he hurried down to the Seine; at a window an old man was weeping over what had happened. The river, however, flowed as peacefully as before, the sky was clear and blue, and in the Tuileries Gardens the birds were singing.

More complex and richer in ambiguity are the oppositions between Frédéric and Rosanette at Fontainebleau. Royal residences, Flaubert explained, have a particular melancholy about them when, in their old age, their emptiness suggests the flight of time and the impermanence of man. This direct intervention by the author described the setting and, presumably, a reaction of Frédéric's. Now, using ironic juxtaposition, Flaubert had only to add that Rosanette was overcome with huge yawns.

At times, apparently unaware that he was intervening, Flaubert would state that "Madame Arnoux did not see that . . ." or "Frédéric told everyone, and believed himself, that . . ." Such devices can add richness when it is not entirely clear whether it is Flaubert or a character who is making the observation. During the visits Frédéric and Rosanette made to their child at the wet nurse's, "the two women would chatter on for hours, uttering unbearable stupidities."

Aphorisms and general observations, a long tradition in French literature, had already had their place in *Madame Bovary*. Although they were less common in *Salammbô*, they are constant here: "There are men whose only mission in life is to serve as intermediaries for others; one crosses them like a bridge and goes on." There can be no doubt who makes the assertions, and a large proportion of them are contemptuous. Hence, perhaps without being consciously aware of it, the reader elaborates an unpleasant picture of Flaubert: "Certain men delight in making their friends do disagreeable tasks." Or there are fuller statements, for instance the disillusioned and cynical assertion that "women's hearts are like those pieces of furniture with secret drawers; with vast effort and many broken nails, one gets them open to find only a dried flower, bits of dust, or nothing at all!" Maupassant was right: the reader does learn Flaubert's bitter view of humanity. And he will not necessarily concur or even—if he senses himself attacked—be willing to allow it.

Such aphorisms proved insufficient to carry the burden of

Flaubert's scorn for his fellow man. For conservatives who were shocked by the audacity of certain Socialist theories in 1848, he observed that these ideas had all the novelty of Mother Goose and had been amply debated for forty years. He went on to affirm that they frightened the bourgeois as much as a rain of meteors would have; and he capped his insults with the observation that these ideas aroused indignation by virtue of the law that any idea, merely because it is one, always provokes hatred in such people. Later, he went on, such concepts would draw praise in proportion to the amount of this execration. He also stated that the corollary of this law was that any idea, however mediocre, is always superior to its detractors.

Flaubert did not leave the liberals in peace, either. He informed them that in 1848 France no longer felt a master over her and so began to whimper with fright like a blindman who cannot find his stick or a muling child who has lost his nurse. Now all groups had grounds for complaint, precisely as he wished, to match his all-encompassing hatreds. He continued to maintain his familiar esthetic canons as before, but he was now confusing an impartiality in which no one is blamed with one which deals out blows to all sides equally.

Flaubert's intrusions of this sort have succeeded in annoying a very considerable number of readers, and their antipathy may exceed their pleasure; nevertheless the novel can charm and always has delighted many others, for Flaubert made advances in style here which are not to be found in his earlier works. Thus, a strange, ambiguous form of intervention becomes prominent now. The technique sets the page apart not only from the reader but, oddly enough, from the author as well, for Flaubert offers suggestions which were "perhaps" the true explanation or situation: Frédéric's writing of others is "perhaps the only way not to suffer." Sénécal, taking leave of Frédéric after a long talk, made a confession which—Flaubert adds in parentheses—"was the aim of his visit perhaps." Reader joins author in speculation about what these creations of his were doing. No one, apparently, really knows, and the rich ambiguity of life is respected. The contemporary novelist, Alain Robbe-Grillet, has objected to earlier fiction on the ground that meaning in the world can never be more than partial, provisional, or even contradictory. How then, he asks, can the work of art claim to illustrate any a priori meaning whatsoever? If reality has a meaning, he insists, the contemporary artist does not know it.[37] Flaubert's "perhaps" leaves his position safe.

Another device which has a strange effect upon the reader appears in descriptions where Flaubert wished one to sense the look of certain places: Fontainebleau, the site of the porcelain factory, the countryside about Nogent, and others. Unlike Yonville, these sites are real; and unlike Carthage, they were still in existence and familiar to many of his readers. Moreover, Flaubert had visited them and seen for himself what was there. He seems to have become intrigued with the possibility of suggesting the physical presence of the reader at the site. Hence, everything which is permanent, there at the time of the novel and still there at the time of the writing, he described in the present tense, reserving past tenses for what was only temporarily present or occurred only at the specific moment his characters were there. When Frédéric went out to see Madame Arnoux at her husband's factory outside Paris, all these tenses came into play:

> A great flat boat was going downstream with the current . . . a woman passed . . . He found himself on an island, where one sees on the right ruins of an abbey. A mill was turning, damming up the entire width of the other branch of the Oise River, which the factory overhangs. The size of this building greatly astonished Frédéric.*

Free indirect discourse, already common in *Madame Bovary*, appears in even more nuanced situations, as when Frédéric, upon his return from the Dambreuse ball, summed up his evening while he prepared for sleep. Using free indirect discourse, including even a parenthetical thought, Flaubert phrased Frédéric's musing: "First of all, his evening dress (he had observed himself in the

---

*"Un grand bateau plat descendait au fil de l'eau ... une femme passa. ... il se trouva dans une île, où l'on voit sur la droite les ruines d'une abbaye. Un moulin tournait, barrant dans toute sa largeur le second bras de l'Oise, que surplombe la manufacture. L'importance de cette construction étonna grandement Frédéric" (*ES*, p. 275).

mirror several times), from the cut of his coat to the bow of his slipper, left nothing to be desired." From this Flaubert slipped easily to direct questions and then back again to indirect, before finally becoming the traditional omniscient author stating what happened next. He is reporting Frédéric's speculations on Madame Dambreuse: "It would be tremendous to have a mistress like her! Why not, after all? He was surely as good as the next man! Perhaps she was not so difficult to get! Next Martinon came to mind; and, as he fell asleep, he was smiling in pity over the poor man."*

As with his earlier novels, Flaubert gave constant, scrupulous attention to the details. The adjective "monotonous" recurs with just enough frequency and in sufficiently startling places to set the tone: the grass as Frédéric approaches the Arnoux factory is of a monotonous green; the men's ties at an evening party have a monotonous whiteness. Images foreshadow the synesthesia so popular with a later generation: "the silence, which was profound and absolute, a black silence." Occasionally, however, in *A Sentimental Education* the care and attention can become obvious and preciosity enters, an ill-assorted partner for the almost frozen majesty of so much of Flaubert's writing. There is a kind of self-conscious pirouette to a sentence describing Madame Dambreuse: "She wore a mauve gown trimmed with lace, the ringlets of her coiffure more abundant than usual, and not a single jewel."†

Concision is effective in such sentences; it can become a defect. In a formidable sentence Flaubert described three sorts of women

---

*"Frédéric, en se couchant, résuma la soirée. D'abord, sa toilette (il s'était observé dans les glaces plusieurs fois), depuis la coupe de l'habit jusqu'au noeud des escarpins, ne laissait rien à reprendre; il avait parlé à des hommes considérables, avait vu de près des femmes riches, M. Dambreuse s'était montré excellent et Mme Dambreuse presque engageante. Il pesa un à un ses moindres mots, ses regards, mille choses inanalysables et cependant expressives. Ce serait crânement beau d'avoir une pareille maîtresse! Pourquoi non, après tout? Il en valait bien un autre! Peut-être qu'elle n'était pas si difficile? Martinon ensuite revint à sa mémoire; et, en s'endormant, il souriait de pitié sur ce brave garçon" (*ES*, pp. 232-33).

†"Elle avait une robe mauve garnie de dentelles, les boucles de sa coiffure plus abondantes qu'à l'ordinaire, et pas un seul bijou" (*ES*, p. 224).

present at the Alhambra seeking three sorts of men and wearing gowns of three different colors: "Lorettes, shopgirls, and prostitutes had come there, hoping to find a man of wealth, a lover, a gold piece, or simply for the pleasure of dancing; and their gowns with tunics of water green, cerise-blue, or purple, passed and moved about among the ebony trees and the lilacs."* There is, of course, a certain pleasure in piecing it all together—it does work out—but the novel has been interrupted while the author performed a *tour de force*. And surely he cannot be thought of as absent from the page.

Transitions from one paragraph to the next continued to demand Flaubert's attention. The sentence stating that France wept in terror at no longer feeling a master is the final one in its paragraph. The next paragraph, switching subject completely, does so by an ingenious recall: "Of all Frenchmen, the one who trembled most was Monsieur Dambreuse." On occasion, however, a kind of stiff self-consciousness makes the reader aware of the technique, and what should be an imperceptible transition becomes an interruption. For really no inherent reason one paragraph ends with the statement that Frédéric became as punctual as Regimbart. The remark serves only to validate the opening sentence of the following paragraph: "Every day Regimbart . . ." But the reader's mind was too far from Regimbart when he entered as a point of reference for the device to be anything but distracting. So many transitions are so well motivated that it is a surprise to meet fortuitous ones, like the occasion on which Frédéric, walking aimlessly, looks up to see the sign in front of Arnoux's and so enters to pursue the acquaintance begun on the boat. Life, Flaubert would have responded, is like that, equally fortuitous, ephemeral, and trivial.

Flaubert's views on form occasionally raised serious difficulties. Less and less did they include observance of the simple requirements of grammatical structure or elementary composition: the

---

*"Des lorettes, des grisettes et des filles étaient venues là, espérant trouver un protecteur, un amoureux, une pièce d'or, ou simplement pour le plaisir de la danse; et leurs robes à tunique vert d'eau, bleu cerise, ou violette, passaient, s'agitaient entre les ébéniers et les lilas" (*ES*, p. 101).

demands of harmonious sound or flow could at any time supersede more pedantic rules for correct French.[38] Du Camp, who was certainly being pedantic, found some 251 allegedly incorrect phrasings in the manuscript of *A Sentimental Education* when Flaubert submitted it to him.[39] While many of these are no more than trivia, still readers will join him in his objection—which Flaubert declined to recognize—to the statement that one o'clock struck slowly. And, as Du Camp's mistress pointed out, there are innumerable pronoun references in the novel which—though actually correct—are so confusing that one has to read the passages several times to understand them.[40]

Flaubert's interest and concern for style were elsewhere, in his concept of it as a special way of perceiving. The problem was as fundamental a matter as how one looked at simple physical objects, for that seeing would then condition the mode of description, making demands which far transcended mere antecedents for pronouns. After *la Maréchale* had described to Frédéric how her mother had arranged the sale of Rosanette's virginity, Flaubert let the unperturbed indifference of nature make the ironic comment he needed; but to do so he had to see all nature about them actively pursuing its own course. The leaves* rustled; in a clump of grasses, a large foxglove swayed; the light flowed like a wave over the turf; and the silence was cut at rapid intervals by the grazing of a cow which had moved out of sight.

Light Flaubert frequently called upon to move or play about his characters in this fashion. The porcelain globes† of a lamp poured out a light which undulated like white *moiré* satin against the walls. Or a lamp cast a luminous circle‡ on the ceiling, whiten-

---

*"Les feuilles autour d'eux susurraient; dans un fouillis d'herbes, une grande digitale se balançait, la lumière coulait comme une onde sur le gazon; et le silence était coupé à intervalles rapides par le broutement de la vache qu'on ne voyait plus" (*ES*, p. 472).

†"... les globes de porcelaine versaient une lumière qui ondulait comme des moires de satin blanc sur les murailles" (*ES*, p. 224).

‡"Un cercle lumineux, au-dessus de la carcel, blanchissait le plafond, tandis que, dans les coins, l'ombre s'étendait comme des gazes noires superposées ..." (*ES*, p. 239).

ing it, while in the corners shadows spread like black veils super-imposed one upon another. A white light* falling on Rosanette from the candelabra infused her skin with mother-of-pearl tones, put pink on her eyelids, and made her eyeballs shine. Light was to Flaubert the agent creating what it falls upon, as it had been in Greece.

Perhaps the greatest single example is the description† of the afternoon sunlight as Rosanette and Frédéric returned from the races in their carriage and drove down the Champs Elysées. They looked out on the rising vapor, through which the sunlight shone. "Passing under the Arc de Triomphe, it spread out a reddish glow at a man's height, which made the wheel hubs, the door handles, the ends of the shafts, and the rings on the seats sparkle." Now, changing to a new subject—but the reader realizes this only slowly—Flaubert described the individual trees and people as forming great wholes. "And, on both sides of the broad avenue, like a river in which the manes, the clothes, and the heads of people were undulating, the trees, shining from the rain, rose like two green walls." The description closes on a return to the sky and its feel and color, essentially a return to light: "The blue of the sky, above, reappearing here and there, had the softnesses of satin."

The effect of this light is hallucinatory, and hallucinations in *A Sentimental Education* run the gamut from such odd modes of perception to nightmares, as when Frédéric fell asleep after the ball at Rosanette's, through hypnagogic dreams as characters doze, to artistic and finally quasi-epileptic hallucinations. Sometimes no more than a character's effort at recall was involved. Frédéric, in the carriage on the way to Nogent, remembered his first meeting with Madame Arnoux so vividly that he became aware of objects

---

*"... cette lumière blanche pénétrait sa peau de tons nacrés, mettait du rose à ses paupières, faisait briller les globes de ses yeux ..." (*ES*, p. 304).

†"Passant sous l'Arc de Triomphe, il allongeait à hauteur d'homme une lumière roussâtre, qui faisait étinceler les moyeux des roues, les poignées des portières, le bout des timons, les anneaux des sellettes; et, sur les deux côtés de la grande avenue, pareille à un fleuve où ondulaient des crinières, des vêtements, des têtes humaines, les arbres tout reluisants de pluie se dressaient, comme deux murailles vertes. Le bleu du ciel, au-dessus, reparaissant à de certaines places, avait des douceurs de satin" (*ES*, p. 299).

he had not consciously noticed when he was with her. At other times, it was still only his lively imagination at work: calling on Madame Arnoux, he saw the alcove containing her bed and came to imagine her head on the pillow so clearly that he had trouble in not seizing the real woman before him.

In Frédéric hallucination could become almost a deliberate creation. Resting beside Arnoux while sharing his guard duty, he noticed that his companion had fallen asleep with his gun so placed that if it were accidentally discharged, it would kill him . . . and free his wife. Like Saint Anthony meditating upon evil, Frédéric found he really wanted to commit the murder and became frightened: "In the madness of his dream, the rest of the world began to disappear and he was conscious of himself only through an intolerable tightness around his chest."*

The dream about Arnoux was deliberately produced; or at least Frédéric was consciously collaborating in its production. Sometimes the hallucination passed beyond voluntary control. When he considered the idea that he was the father of Rosanette's child, he found it grotesque; but as his thoughts wandered on, it occurred to him that the mother might have been Madame Arnoux. "And his dream became so gripping that he had a sort of hallucination"† and imagined the little child before him on the rug.

Madame Arnoux several times triggered these experiences in Frédéric, as Elisa had with Flaubert in the early days, when he would imagine she was behind him. After Frédéric's inheritance allowed him to return to Paris and thus see her again, "with the clarity of a hallucination, he saw himself beside her . . . At the door his tilbury—no, a coupé rather—would be standing."‡ He could hear the noises made by the horse. He would receive her

---

*"... dans la fureur de sa rêverie, le reste du monde s'effaçait; et il n'avait conscience de lui-même que par un intolérable serrement à la poitrine" (*ES*, p. 453).

†"Et sa rêverie devint tellement profonde, qu'il eut une sorte d'hallucination" (*ES*, p. 516).

‡"Avec la netteté d'une hallucination, il s'aperçut auprès d'elle. ... à la porte stationnerait son tilbury, non, un coupé plutôt: un coupé noir, avec un domestique en livrée brune; il entendait piaffer son cheval et le bruit de la gourmette se confondant avec le murmure de leurs baisers" (*ES*, p. 140).

and her husband in his house, which he furnished in his imagination. This life would last indefinitely, he felt, just as Charles Bovary had about his dreams for little Berthe. The stream of consciousness was being foreshadowed when Frédéric imagined a tilbury and then corrected himself; sounds, too, made the dream richer, though it lacked odors or tastes. It ended by approaching the epileptic seizures Flaubert knew: "These images were appearing so tumultuously that he felt his head beginning to turn."

The image of "moving with the extraordinary ease one feels in a dream" recurs, too, on one of several walks during which Frédéric slipped into a dream state. After an unfruitful visit to Madame Arnoux, he moved at random, seeing nothing, striking his foot against stones, and losing his way. He was brought back to himself only by a sound, as was Emma Bovary outside the convent, in this case the noise of the worker's shoes as they left the factory. Earlier, after his first dinner at the Arnoux home, he walked the streets of Paris, equally unconscious of where he was, of space itself, in fact. He went on aimlessly, lost, drawn forward by an invisible force. This time he was revived by feeling the damp air about him: he had returned to consciousness along the quays of the Seine.

Other characters, too, lost their sense of time while walking; but it was reserved to Frédéric to have the onset of an epileptic attack. Seeking desperately for a friend once, he was trying with all his forces to recall the cafes the man used to frequent: "all the names . . . spurted forth from his memory at the same instant, like the thousand elements of a piece of fireworks." Flaubert and Emma Bovary had both experienced this before Frédéric: it was the greatest anguish any of them knew.

THE NOVEL APPEARS

You must be tremendously glad the writing is done, and I
share your joy.

Letter from Louis Bouilhet to
Flaubert, May 22, 1869

As spring moved toward summer in 1869, the huge manuscript of
A Sentimental Education drew to its close. Once the fundamental
planning had been established, the writing had presented fewer
problems than *Madame Bovary* or *Salammbô*; no Agricultural Fair
or ancient battles with long-forgotten siege weapons challenged
Flaubert. Instead he had faced the daily grind of trying to write
interestingly about boredom, of breathing enough life into lifeless
characters to make them interest a reader. He was understandably
overjoyed to have his task at an end.

Princess Mathilde, who expressed an interest, found herself
trapped with her entourage for five long afternoons while an
elated Flaubert read every line of it aloud. Such occasions were
solemn ones to him. Zola remembered how he used to read in a
sonorous voice, bringing out the rhythms and uttering the sentences as though they were part of a recitative, so as to display the
musical value of the words, but without adding emphases. It was a
sort of lyric declamation, and he had an elaborate theory about it.
In major passages, as he approached the final effect, he would raise
his voice till it thundered and the ceiling trembled. When Flaubert read to Princess Mathilde, she noticed that the slightest noise,
a pencil on a piece of paper or the rustle of a dress, would bring
signs of impatience from him; but he was as happy as a child over
her praise.[41] To Caro he confided he thought he had read remarkably well.

It was time for Du Camp to see it. He read the manuscript and
found the 251 errors; but he also wrote his friend a letter of
explanation, telling Gustave that he had indeed accomplished a
tour de force in writing such a book on a subject which was not a
subject, without any real plot or actions for his characters to per-

form. He pronounced the work interesting and some of the scenes very good, particularly the final visit of Madame Arnoux to Frédéric. And naming the real people behind the characters, he congratulated him on his renderings of Schlésinger and *la Présidente*. Then he began to suggest cuts and complained of the innumerable elliptical constructions meaningful only to Parisians of his day and, even among them, perhaps only to writers and journalists. The title, too, was misleading: it should be "The Story of a Ninny" or "Mediocre People."

Flaubert screamed in pain and wrote a protesting reply; several further letters were exchanged. Du Camp maintained his original points and went further to insist that Flaubert was using a form of the spoken language even when writing in his own name. The book was becoming a literal representation of what people actually said: why bother, then, to write?[42] Eventually furious and alternating between a longing to reject the corrections entirely or accept them all in exasperation, Flaubert made up his mind to cull what seemed inescapable from them. It is probably not without significance that this was the last time he submitted a manuscript to his friend.[43] He then reread it himself one final time, "to remove the grammatical errors," but without any feeling that these corrections would help him in the eyes of the critics.

In August proof began to arrive. By September the canny Michel Lévy had begun to place brief references to the new novel in the newspapers, and on November 16, the day before publication, extracts appeared in several papers. But within a week of publication, it was clear that *A Sentimental Education* was not going to be a success. Most of the people to whom Flaubert sent complimentary copies failed even to acknowledge receipt. While the imperial court liked it, the critics objected violently. Its form bewildered almost all of them: it seemed to lack all composition, to be a series of sketches and not a picture. It was called a set of memoirs, detached episodes, a chronicle, notes, anything but a novel. Its characters met one another but never seemed to join; even George Sand found them too passive. They moved through events which lacked any cause and had no effect. Those who read carefully realized that they were not dealing with an impassive author and an impartial work. Flaubert's massive contempt for the human race exasperated a number of critics, who protested in the name of humanity against what seemed an insult. Even Taine wondered, along with Sand, why there could be no redeeming side, why the perfectly real people who did accomplish things played no part in this book.

As he reported to Madame Sand in a lengthy letter, Flaubert himself was called every sort of name in one article or another; even his friends avoided discussing the book when they met him. Although the sales were sufficiently good to satisfy Lévy, they could not compensate Flaubert. As he put it, he had received few laurels and was as yet unwounded by any rose petals. The professional patriots and the conservatives understood his attacks on them and responded violently. Others compared him to the Marquis de Sade, especially for the brothel episode. He proclaimed he was unmoved, but he did ask George Sand to write an article in his defense. Perhaps the cruelest blow was Maxime Du Camp's expression of sympathy. Flaubert came to feel there were personal hatreds against him in the attacks. Certainly this was true of Amélie Bosquet, whom he had helped many times. She wrote a hostile review in the belief that she was the model for one of the minor characters whom he had treated rather badly.

During the first few months, Flaubert could reasonably expect that matters would turn out as they had with *Madame Bovary* and that in a short time the morality of the new work would be accepted. Hugo wrote to congratulate him for displaying the penetrating eye of a Balzac, but with style in addition. An occasional reviewer did see some of what he had intended. His old friends Banville and Mademoiselle Leroyer de Chantepie published favorable judgments. But by January of 1870 it was apparent that the general tenor of all the articles would long continue unfavorable. George Sand wrote to comfort Flaubert, assuring him that these reviews in no way affected his book, which was good. It had simply not appeared at the right moment because it stated the disarray of France so clearly it wounded live sensibilities. In the course of time, when readers would no longer have to recognize themselves so totally in the novel, its day would come.[44]

Time did pass and popular success was still refused to the novel; it does not today have the wide appeal of *Madame Bovary*.

Flaubert came slowly to what is perhaps a sounder view. Nearly a decade later he was talking with a younger author who particularly admired it: Flaubert thanked him almost effusively. To explain why the public did not share this view, he reverted to an image he had used at the very first, in 1863. Joining his hands together by their upraised tips he said: "The book is not constructed like this. The public wants works which praise its illusions, whereas *A Sentimental Education*—," and he let his hands fall back as though all his dreams were collapsing beyond hope. Then he fell silent. His work had not been understood.[45]

Theophile Gautier's son, writing privately to his father, used a phrase whose prophetic value he could not suspect. The book was, he complained, "a slice of life" about a simpleton who resembled Wilhelm Meister a bit but lacked his poetry.[46] Yet in fact this element of which Gautier's son complained, the notion of portraying "a slice of life," was what the next generation of authors was going to undertake. Much of Huysmans, as well as of his lesser companions, is a direct outgrowth of this attempt; and French naturalism would not have taken the turn it did without *A Sentimental Education*. Then, in the final decade of the century, the doctrine of the slice-of-life started a renovation in the theater which gave impetus to a whole generation of playwrights, directors, and actors.

Yet young Gautier's critique is not without foundation: all these works deliberately display life without poetry. One's reaction to them depends entirely upon whether, in advance, one has decided that life does lack all poetry. No reader who believes this will have trouble with *A Sentimental Education;* and no reader who denies it will ever be convinced by Flaubert's novel. Hence it is quite likely that *A Sentimental Education* will continue to be the delight of some, while to others it can never contain more than magnificent paragraphs lost in a book whose philosophy they reject along with—and perhaps too hastily—the entire novel.

PART III

Tribulation

20

The Old Order Passes (1869-72)

DEATHS

I have no one left to talk to.

Letter to Madame Roger des Genettes,
June 23, 1870

As the writing of *A Sentimental Education* drew to a close in the spring of 1869, Louis Bouilhet's health was giving serious concern; he was himself convinced that his end was near.[1] Most of those who knew him well, however, recognized no more than his obvious hypochondria and tended to discount his statements. To make his mental state worse, in June he was encountering difficulties in his efforts to get his current play accepted. When he learned from Flaubert that it could not be put on for months, his spirit broke. He wrote that he was too old to send a challenge to the directors of the theater but that he could no longer accept the old stories of literary fraternity: it was rather dog-eat-dog, and he felt himself a sick man, unable to avenge himself. He hoped a later justice would avenge him; this thought alone kept him from tears.[2]

Flaubert was able to adjust matters, but Bouilhet remained in such a nervous state that taking the cure at Vichy seemed necessary. He left toward the end of June, overcome with melancholy and worrying all his friends by his apparent determination to be sick, so odd in a man who had formerly been so gay. He lived in constant terror, though for this he knew no cause. Flaubert was sympathetic but also personally inconvenienced, as he was awaiting Bouilhet's recovery to go over *A Sentimental Education* for the last time with him before sending it to the printer. Bouilhet's ill health was upsetting Flaubert's vacation plans, but he sought to be patient.

From Vichy, Bouilhet was soon sent back to Rouen. Here he at last consented to see Achille Flaubert, whom he had been afraid to consult for fear of learning the truth. He was declared beyond hope: it was albuminuria, the abnormal presence of albumin in the kidneys, a disease still desperately serious today and from which one inevitably died in Second Empire France. At first Bouilhet seemed to rally; Flaubert visited him almost daily and was delighted to see his appetite excellent and the swelling in his legs diminishing. On Saturday, July 17, Flaubert saw him in Rouen before leaving for Paris. Bouilhet had received a visit from his sisters; their brutally insistent efforts to save his soul had scandalized even a canon from the cathedral. Flaubert set off in good cheer. On arriving in Paris, he called on the Goncourt brothers, where he even joked about his own good spirits, which derived, he said, from those lost by all his sick friends. The brothers, often unwell themselves, found the remark in bad taste.[3]

While Flaubert was thus away in Paris, Bouilhet became delirious around five on Sunday afternoon and began to compose aloud the scenario of a medieval drama on the Inquisition, as he and Flaubert had been doing for twenty years. He was tremendously excited and kept calling Gustave. Then a fit of trembling seized him and twice he muttered adieu, while seeking to bury his head on his mistress's breast. A moment or two later, very gently, he died.

It was not until Tuesday, at nine o'clock in the morning, that the telegram reached Flaubert. He was alone. He packed his suitcase, sent word to Du Camp, stopped by Duplan's office to tell him, and then sought to pass the time by walking the streets until his train at one o'clock. He noticed that the day was very hot, especially on the streets and in the railroad station.

The trip to Rouen was excruciating, as he shared a compartment with a prostitute who was laughing, singing, and smoking cigarettes. She stretched her legs out on the long bench. Passing Mantes, where Bouilhet had spent so many years and from which he had reported on Elisa's movements, was particularly difficult. The girl, seeing his pallor, offered him her Eau de Cologne; it revived his spirits somewhat. He was dreadfully thirsty, more so, he later wrote Maxime, than they had been in the desert.

Flaubert was one of two chief mourners; at least two thousand people followed the coffin. He was bitterly aware of the grotesque aspects of the funeral procession. Fortunately for him hallucination took over: Bouilhet first seemed to be inside him commenting to him on what he saw, then walking beside him as if someone else were about to be buried. The heat was atrocious; Flaubert was dripping with perspiration as they climbed the hill to the cemetery. The plot selected was close to that of Flaubert's father. As the bier was placed over the grave and the speeches were about to begin, Gustave collapsed. His brother led him away.

Flaubert had known Louis Bouilhet for thirty-seven years. His counselor, his guide, his compass, he said, were gone. Bouilhet had been his literary conscience and his judgment. What further need was there to write? He had always really written for him. He knew he would continue, from habit, but the delight had gone. He termed Bouilhet his midwife, the one who saw better into his own thoughts than he could himself. The loss was irreparable.

A group of Bouilhet's friends felt that a small monument to him would be appropriate, and Flaubert was named head of the committee to receive funds and carry out the project. Juliet Herbert sent twenty francs. Flaubert was also one of three executors of the estate, which consisted largely of unpublished literary works. Throughout the last days of his illness, Bouilhet had had his long-time mistress beside him constantly. Fearing that the end was near, he had wished to marry her. She had refused, for he would then have known how sick she believed him to be. Flaubert was determined that she and their son should get as much as possible from the estate, and he set to work to stage *Aïssé*, the play Bouilhet had been hoping to have accepted.

Finding a producer was not to be easy. *Aïssé* had not pleased directors and needed radical revision. Flaubert spent much time attempting to carry out their suggestions, but to no avail. The play was not, in fact, put on until some two years later. In addition there were unpublished poems from which he hoped to get money for Bouilhet's heirs. Michel Lévy, whom he approached, explained that books of verse did not make money. At best he would agree to put out the volume at no cost to Flaubert; but there would be no royalties. No better terms could be found, and Flaubert sadly accepted.

Bouilhet was but the first. Sainte-Beuve, long ill, died on October 13, 1869. Flaubert, who had stopped by often for news of the patient, called some five minutes after he died. The small band of those with whom Flaubert could converse was disappearing. Sainte-Beuve had not been an intimate friend, but he had loved literature, and there were few left who did. He was one of those Flaubert felt would have appreciated the style of *A Sentimental Education*. Bouilhet had died too soon to hear the last two chapters, which mattered so much to Flaubert; now Sainte-Beuve was dead without having read a line of the novel. The feeling of solitude began to close in. The winter passed without further losses for Flaubert, but Jules Duplan died on March 1, 1870. Flaubert locked his doors and refused to receive anyone. After Bouilhet, Duplan had been his most intimate friend.

On June 20, 1870, Jules de Goncourt died. The Goncourt brothers had judged Flaubert more harshly than he knew, but they shared his convictions about art. In later years Edmond would judge Flaubert severely, insisting that his talent was no more than second rate and markedly inferior to his own. But Jules's death brought Edmond, who had rarely been parted from his brother, closer to Flaubert. Edmond wept openly at the funeral, as did Gautier and Flaubert. Of the seven founders of the dinners at the Restaurant Magny, only three now remained. Flaubert's head seemed full of burials; he was like an ancient cemetery, overflowing with tombs. And his life was now completely solitary.

THE LIVING

> Almost all the people I know are unbearably dull and ignorant. I alternate between the boorish and the futile.
>
> Letter to his niece Caroline,
> July 14-15, 1870

Only Goncourt, Turgenev, and George Sand remained of those who understood the world as Flaubert did. Except for George Sand and Juliet Herbert, he had no close women friends.

Turgenev he saw in Paris at intervals; though the Russian kept promising to visit Croisset, he seldom did. From time to time Flaubert did see a few other friends, Renan and the scholar Maury among them; but no one was left who could fill the gaps caused by death.

Emile Zola Flaubert came to know in 1869. He was twenty years younger and had to make his living from his pen; hence he was constantly forced to have preoccupations other than art. He could never be an intimate friend. Moreover, his temperament was quite different from the happily ferocious Flaubert. Zola found the older man full of paradoxes, an impenitent romantic who overwhelmed him for hours with a deluge of stupefying theories. Only later did he change his first verdict that Flaubert the man was far inferior to the author, as he came to realize Flaubert's grandiose qualities, the epic ones, he called them. But he never ceased to wish that Flaubert might also have a lighter touch and surer hand in social intercourse. Zola pointed out that the descriptions of Madame Dambreuse's salon, which Flaubert suggested looked like a harem or a brothel, were not written by a man at home in such milieus. To be sure, Zola freely confessed that *Madame Bovary* was one of the two or three works which had really formed him as writer; he looked to Flaubert as a master. But it was not a look of full acceptance, and Zola never placed art at the summit of his goals.[4]

There were still Madame Flaubert and Caroline. His mother's physical state gave no alarm, but she was very weak and, most of the time, very deaf. Early in 1870 she became afraid she had breast cancer but kept her fears to herself and tried, unsuccessfully, to show nothing of her worry. Conversation with her was almost impossible and good days were rare. Caroline, unfortunately, was often away and was in Scandinavia at the time of Bouilhet's death. Her uncle missed her particularly, although he had been delighted that she could get away for the trip and admitted he had envied her. He urged her to follow his own practice of taking copious notes. But as August advanced and he realized more fully the gap Bouilhet had left in his life, he wrote to her of how tremendously he was missing her: the image of his dead friend obsessed him. When further deaths left him even more alone, he wrote repeatedly of his longing for her. If only he could be near her, even for a few hours, just to see her! How he regretted her being too far away for quick visits! Some of the letters suggest *père* Goriot's overwhelming affection for his daughters, and the resemblance is ominous.

Neither did the state of France encourage Flaubert: she seemed as stupid as ever. He pitied Caro, surrounded as she was by bourgeois: she would not find them dazzlingly poetic. The number of imbeciles, in point of fact, appeared to be rising, and most of the people he knew were intolerable. Perhaps he was becoming old: everything bothered him. Each evening he would take a turn in the garden and go over his memories, for there was no one with whom to talk. It had been a year of malediction, he felt, and he was unable to summon fresh enthusiasm to counter it.

George Sand, seeking to comfort Flaubert, urged him to hunt out new affections. He replied that he would be delighted . . . were it possible. All his old friends were married and had their own quiet, bourgeois occupations, business or hunting or whist. Not a one was capable of spending an afternoon with him to read a poet. As for a mistress, Croisset did not furnish the commodity, and in any case he had never been able to mingle Venus with Apollo. There was no solution.

Flaubert's intellectual entourage no longer existed. But how could one be interested in anything other than style? There was not a single house in Paris in which literature was a normal topic. When it did come up in conversation, it was always in terms of success, utility, morality, or some other extraneous matter. And Sand and Turgenev, the two remaining people with whom he could talk openly, lived so far away from him! There seemed no escape from his melancholy.

For the first time the truculent Flaubert began to show a softer disposition. Tears came more easily to his eyes, sometimes even because of his difficulties in writing. In a series of notes which he made around this time, he reexamined some of his fundamental beliefs. Noting that all his close friends had "left him for a woman," he asked himself whether it were not his conduct that was monstrous rather than theirs. At fifty he still had the same devotions they all had had at eighteen. As he considered the sex life his bachelorhood left open to him, he recognized that the social code approved of him and damned the woman. But he asked himself what advantage a man derived from one further adultery, when the slightest love affair could cost any woman her position, her fortune, or even her life. He concluded that it was up to the ladies to make the advances. He also observed that, at fifty, intelligent men did—and with serious intent—those things which would have made them roar with laughter at twenty-five. And a final consolation: he could honesty say the humility of the philosopher was greater than that of the devout person. Could he achieve it for himself?[5]

Against this background minor worries about money seemed an annoying and improper distraction. As soon as *A Sentimental Education* was completed, Flaubert asked George Sand to approach Lévy about the contract for it to see what could be done to improve it. She came away from the publisher with the feeling that he was prepared to pay ten thousand francs per volume, more if it sold well. This was just as well, for Flaubert was, as always, short of money. When Lévy gave him a first six thousand francs over the summer, however, Flaubert's finances seemed sound again, and he assured George Sand that he would always have his independence and his liberty because he would always prefer to give up whatever he must in order to preserve them and it was no longer a source of anguish to him not to live in a Moorish palace. When *A Sentimental Education* had been out a few months and he again needed money, the market for the novel no longer looked so hopeful. Lévy had dropped his figure to eight thousand per volume, and his only concession was an offer to advance three or four thousand against Flaubert's next work, to be bought at the same figure. Fortunately Flaubert, never very careful about these matters, discovered quite suddenly that he had some three thousand francs on deposit with his nephew; hence he did not need to take up either Lévy's or George Sand's kind offer to lend him money. But presumably his worries lay behind a note he made for himself a few months later on the impossibility of paying for literary property.[6]

Financial worries were part of Flaubert's decision to abandon the apartment he had occupied and loved for a dozen years: the rent was too high and its location on the Boulevard du Temple involved him in expensive cab fares. Moreover, it was far from where Caro and her husband were settled. In the spring of 1869, he felt that the time had come, but until Du Camp and another friend found him a new place, he put off making any positive move. The moment he saw the place they proposed, he knew he wanted it. It was at 4, Rue Murillo, in a new building located on land which until about 1848 had formed part of the Parc Monceau. By the first week of June he had already signed the lease and was choosing material for draperies. His mother was planning a trip to Paris to see the new apartment.

The change from the Boulevard du Temple to the Rue Murillo was what all moves had always been for Flaubert, pain and anguish. As his beloved furniture, the divan and the leather chair particularly, left the old apartment, all his memories flooded over him again. This was only natural: twenty years later, in 1888, Edmond de Goncourt paused in front of the building for a moment of sad recollection. He remembered the noisy Sunday afternoons with their battles of words and violent language and the witty and bold Suzanne Lagier. The stucco was falling off the walls in 1888; the drawn shades showed the apartments to be unoccupied; and over the empty ground floor a sign proclaimed: *Cabaret de la Folie.*[7]

Flaubert himself knew that only a return to writing could save him from his melancholy. He had admitted to George Sand his need always to be working. Would he ever find the right subject? By now he had really begun to imagine what a novel should be: but there were two or three other works he had to write first.

With the completion of *A Sentimental Education,* Flaubert was again free and did, in fact, turn to several major projects; but he also allowed himself to be tempted into time-consuming by-ways. There was the matter of rewriting Bouilhet's *Aïssé,* which was a *féerie.* The play reminded him of his own *Castle of Hearts,* which he got out again. It seemed more promising than he had remembered and, after showing it to a theater director, he spent six weeks improving the manuscript. Nevertheless, it was refused again.

At Christmas, Flaubert took the manuscript with him on a

long-promised visit to George Sand in Nohant, where he read it aloud to her. He enjoyed the reading—as he did his entire visit—and his audience enjoyed hearing it. But Sand knew the play could not be successfully staged and noted the fact in her private journal. Flaubert's compensation was his chance to laugh and be gay in the warm surroundings of Nohant. When the others took to dancing, Flaubert—as he used to do years before with Gautier—dressed in women's garb and did a Spanish dance with one of the other men guests. In George Sand's mad house no one would have found anything anomalous, and Madame Sand contented herself with noting that it was grotesque.[8] Another theater asked to see the manuscript of the ill-fated play in February of 1870 but took only a week to refuse it. Again it returned to Flaubert's files.

Now he resolved once and for all to write only for his own personal pleasure. An author must always go on writing, he told a young man who asked his advice about a literary career. Posterity alone decided who had been great, and Voltaire never suspected that *Candide* would be considered his masterpiece. So, discouraged though he was, he continued to jot down ideas for further novels. "Under Napoleon III," which was to show the Democratic Hero and the degradation of Man by Woman (the capitals are his), would probably have picked up where *A Sentimental Education* left off and have allowed Flaubert to express still further his contempt for his generation. It is hard to believe that additional works expressing this view would have been major additions to what he had alreadywritten, so perhaps it is not serious that he did nothing more than make notes for this work. Significantly, one of the characters was to be like Harriet Collier, while in another sketch one woman was to have something of Gertrude.[9]

One thing after another interrupted Flaubert's work during the spring of 1870, and he became more and more irritable. For the first time in perhaps thirty years, suicide again seriously attracted him. It did seem to him that a belief in the afterlife was no more than vanity on the part of man, or a play on words; for only the continuation of the self mattered and that, at any rate, appeared unlikely. Hence on April 4—five weeks after Duplan's death—he noted that the thought of suicide was among the most consoling of all for man. Since nothing further could affect you once you were dead, at each new grief in this life one could say, "Yes—but whenever I wish, it will no longer be." And so life passed—slowly.[10] His pessimism and his resignation were, as he well realized, the view he had already come to in his late teens. The ending of *A Sentimental Education* was perhaps right after all, even in his own case.

Louis Bouilhet had left a number of unpublished poems. The edition Flaubert was putting together for publication gave him the opportunity to write a Preface in which he could express directly his and Bouilhet's ideas on esthetics and style. He enjoyed doing it: it was the only poetics he ever published. He worked hard, especially during the spring of 1870, and finished it in June. He had reread all of Bouilhet's poetry and was deeply moved as he relived various moments they had shared. Some of the memories went back to the time when the two of them, as mere children, had sat together on the same school benches. At Croisset, where he worked on the Preface, Bouilhet's ghost seemed everywhere—behind every bush in the garden, on his divan, in his dressing gowns, which Bouilhet used to wear.

Despite these numerous and varied projects, the period after *A Sentimental Education* was not like that which followed *Salammbô*. He now realized in the difficult months after finishing the Carthaginian novel that he should have turned at once to *The Temptation of Saint Anthony* before becoming entangled in other projects, for the desert Saint remained what he had always been, an obsession he must some day work out of his system.[11] Now, as soon as the manuscript of *A Sentimental Education* went off to Du Camp, he turned to Saint Anthony and began rereading his notes. By June 9 he had begun; by the nineteenth he realized he must redo the entire fabric. As the month ended he was deep into new readings, including Renan's *Saint-Paul*, which had just come out. *The Temptation* was well launched and *A Sentimental Education* for the most part behind him, when Bouilhet's death intervened.

For a long time Flaubert could not return to *Saint Anthony*, although he knew it was what he needed to regain his composure. Then, when he was again free, he allowed himself to be distracted once again by *The Castle of Hearts*. Perhaps it is as well that no director would accept the play, for this forced Flaubert back to Anthony early in 1870. His work was largely documentation. Delays over his Preface to Bouilhet's poems further held up his work, but in April he was back at it and eager to be through with his readings.

Little of the earlier versions of *The Temptation* could be salvaged; Flaubert was all the more eager to be left alone to work at it. As June wore into July, he was searching for a new link to bind together the various hallucinations of the Saint. He missed Bouilhet, someone for whom to be writing each week, yet he needed the writing to take his mind off his dead friends. By July 9 he was sure that he was ready to start.

Work on *The Temptation* and revisions of Bouilhet's play Flaubert expected to keep him busy for some time to come. In August he would perhaps go in to Paris briefly, but he would soon return to Croisset. Around the end of the month he would take a vacation in Dieppe with Caro; he would go to Paris only in October to watch over the rehearsal of *Aïssé*. He may have intended also to make a secret trip to see Juliet Herbert.

In all of these plans Flaubert was, like most Frenchmen that summer, considering only his private interests. International politics figured not at all. In point of fact he had been convinced that politics as a subject for thought was probably dead, a futile discipline like theology. In the eighteenth century such issues had occupied thoughtful men, but, since 1815, the state had taken over and all further discussions of statecraft had been concerned only with external forms. French doctrines and parties, Orleanist, Republican, Imperial, were meaningless since they had all proved capable of including the most contradictory notions. The various flags had been so soiled that it was better to have none at all. And the Empire was proving universal suffrage to be just as stupid as all other schemes. The problem with politics, as with esthetics, was to establish a scientific underpinning. Until this foundation had been developed, politics had no interest for him.

Flaubert was surely justified in finding the politics of the Second Empire an unsavory topic. But, as he and all his fellow citizens were about to discover, these matters could not be ignored. The Franco-Prussian War would soon break out, changing the lives of every living Frenchman from thence forward. France declared war on Prussia July 19, 1870.

THE FRANCO-PRUSSIAN WAR (1870-71)

What hurts me so very much is, first, the eternal ferocity of mankind, and, second, the conviction that we are entering upon a hideous world, from which the Latin races will be excluded. All elegance, even material, is over for a long time. A mandarin like myself has no place any longer in such a world.

Letter to his niece Caroline,
October 28, 1870

When war broke out, Flaubert's initial reaction was disgust with his countrymen for their stupid enthusiasm. He was afraid that mankind had regressed to wars between races, to war for the pleasure of making war. His affairs seemed little upset and he continued them as before, hoping to lose himself in his writing; he had also to attend to the irritating matter of getting his nephew to pay certain bills with the money he had on deposit with him. When Ernest asked to see the bills, Flaubert consented, although he did not understand. Ernest left his wife a note about the matter, observing that one should never pay bills until one had to, but Flaubert did not see the note. In a further exchange of letters, however, he did learn that the young ménage had financial problems; he added these personal worries to the broader ones about his country. Fortunately *Saint Anthony* was moving along nicely.

After a few minor French victories it became clear that the French armies were no match for their Prussian opponents. Flaubert was deeply troubled. There seemed no way to avoid condemning everything before him. The French, so proud of their civilization, were behaving like barbarians, too, and looked forward to the fight. Before a hundred years were out, he was sure, there would be battles involving millions of men. Prussia would be terribly beaten now, of course, and perhaps such bloodlettings were necessary. But if so, humanity was far from the ideal humanists had of it.

France was paying for her foolishness and her materialism, Flaubert felt. Giving the vote to the masses had led infallibly to nonsense: if she had been governed by people like himself and his friends, none of this would have happened. Too, she had become soft and dependent upon her material wealth: now she was being forced back to real values. But the Prussians, he soon decided, were even worse. If it were not for his aged mother, he would have volunteered for the army. Instead he served as a male nurse in his brother's hospital.

The Empire, Flaubert foresaw, could last only days; but still he felt it the duty of Frenchmen to defend the regime. It was not a pleasant prospect, for he was quite sure that revolution would follow upon a peace treaty; social upset and poverty were facing all of them. Meanwhile even the domestic scene was full of idiocy: a demented Rouen husband became convinced that the Prussians were raping his wife. In fact no Prussians were yet near Rouen, but he compensated for their absence by mistaking his wife for one of them and trying to strangle her.

By the end of August, France's situation was hopeless. Flaubert's mood shifted: he turned more optimistic and began to feel bellicose himself. His mother gradually resigned herself to the idea that, if Paris were besieged, he would take his gun and leave; he was almost gay at the thought that he would no longer have to stay on at Croisset, where relatives were now flocking from more easterly provinces. One of them wakened him each morning by going out into the garden and spitting so noisily that sleep was impossible; alternatively his mother's arguing roused him. His impotent fury took itself out in headaches and serious stomach cramps. He felt he was losing his mind and feared that he had cancer; he vomited frequently. Rage, shame, and chagrin kept tears near the surface.

Mistaking his wishes for reality, Flaubert seized upon every favorable rumor. Stories of brilliant military successes were common in Rouen, and these he avidly accepted and passed on to all who would listen. But in fact the disastrous Battle of Sedan was being lost on September 1, 1871, while he was assuring his friends of French victories.

Rouen had now to plan for its defense, the more earnestly as the military authorities seemed to have no plans. When a blockade shut down the factories, poverty in the city became dire. A few days later Flaubert was made a lieutenant and began to drill his company, going himself into Rouen to "take lessons in military art." He found a confusing spectacle there as a dozen different opinions clamored for acceptance. Report had it that the Prussians were about to destroy Paris; but rumors were also widespread of secret chemical discoveries which would give victory to France. Each time he returned home, he found a houseful of people weeping and moaning. In his letters he took to cursing at the entire female sex, even when writing to women.

Meantime the Republic had been almost surreptitiously declared in Paris. Flaubert wondered how anyone could still believe in such phantoms at a moment when the most radical positivism was beating them against the wall. He would fight for the Republic—one should, of course—but he did not believe in it. Meanwhile he and Dumas strove valiantly to defend the reputation of Princess Mathilde, who had been accused of trying to slip out of the country with millions in gold from the national treasure. Oceans of sorrow seemed to be sweeping over him: they all deserved what was befalling them, for they had so long refused to deal with the truth honestly. His self-esteem as a Frenchman was destroyed.

On September 15 the Prussians reached Paris. Caroline was on her way to England and hence safe; but the provinces would be ravaged so long as Paris held out. Rouen had decided to capitulate at once, but the surrounding countryside was determined to defend itself. Flaubert found himself able to return to writing. He also drilled his men regularly and longed for direct combat, joining with his friends in the resolve to go to the aid of Paris if the city were besieged. Perhaps, after all, the tremendous revolt against authority which was going on in France might result in making more of a place for the individual. The most hopeful rumors continued to circulate, keeping his spirits up. To his old friend Feydeau, who was literally dying of hunger, he cheerfully sent money. The poor around Rouen on the other hand, he was determined to shoot when he made his rounds with his militia.

France, Flaubert regretted to observe, was learning to be vicious; it would destroy her. For the rest of their days all Frenchmen then living would be condemned to think about the Prussians, since the society arising from the war would necessarily be republican and militaristic. All gentility—in Montaigne's phrase— would have disappeared. He considered himself finished.

France now underwent a succession of dreadful defeats. Flaubert told his men he would shoot the first of them to retreat; he invited them to deal with him in the same way. This promise of action served to revive his flagging spirits, and he wrote happily to Caro that Juliet's letters suggested his niece was accustoming herself to London. He urged her to visit the places where he had gone with Juliet: the British Museum, the National Gallery, Kensington and Kew, the banks of the Thames, or Greenwich. Later he regretted that Juliet was unable to stay in London with her, but Mrs. Herbert's family could help to console her.[12]

Gradually the inescapable facts asserted themselves. France was being defeated. No provincial army was being formed; Normandy would not fight; and the Republic was even less able to defend itself than the Empire had been. Flaubert's anguish was acute. While others were more to be pitied for their harder lot, still he insisted that none suffered more than he, because he had always cultivated his sensibility. In disgust over the lack of discipline among his men, he resigned his commission, as did his captain and his subordinate. He longed to be able to leave France and go somewhere where there was no sound of drums, no need to vote or fight or live with the eternal ferocity which had been let loose.

He assured Caro he was trying to be courageous and reasonable. But what did he have left? All his friends were gone. The only affections in his life, hers and Juliet's, he was deprived of. The circumstances of his home life were intolerable, but he could not honorably leave. The future would be worse. The Paris they had all known would never exist again. And yet in the midst of it, he loved Paris and France, perhaps more than ever before.

In November the Prussians were nearing Rouen and would

soon be at Croisset. He and his mother would move out rather than share it with them. How could this nation of scholars commit such abominations as he had read of, even worse than those of the Huns because the Prussians were systematic, cold, and deliberately calculating; neither passion nor hunger excused their conduct. He was about to leave for Brussels with Dumas *fils* when a minor event held him briefly at Croisset; and then it was too late.

The Prussians entered Rouen in early December; ten men, three officers, and six horses were quartered at Croisset. To Flaubert's surprise all behaved correctly. If only Caroline could return to Rouen! The burden of his mother was maddening. His free time went to running errands for the Prussians, who had to have hay and straw for their mounts. And there was the constant shame of hearing their boots and sabers on the pavement and of having their horses whinny in your face. For three long weeks Rouen was cut off from all news; Flaubert's spirits sank to their lowest yet. As he looked back, the past all seemed to have been a paradise. The presence of the Prussians had polluted Croisset for him; he would never set foot there again. The future—it had been Emma's experience—was a great black hole: merely to think of it made him dizzy. His only hope lay in death, for life now held only chagrin and abjection. He wondered if he would ever see his niece again. In almost every letter he urged her to return at once from London: surely the alleged dangers were exaggerated! And he pressed her husband in similar fashion. He felt the end of the world had arrived.

On January 27 after a heroic defense, Paris capitulated, thus opening the way to the end of hostilities. Two days later the Prussians left Croisset, but Flaubert remained inconsolable and refused to wear his Cross of the Legion of Honor. Paris should have let herself be burned to the ground. He would ask Turgenev how to become a Russian. If Croisset belonged to him, he would have it demolished.

In mid-February, however, Caroline returned from London, and he found his horizon brightening. He even sought to begin work again, only to find he was not yet ready. His niece knew how gradually to restore his calm and to accustom him to accepting the picture of a world which would take Prussia as its model.

In March, Flaubert was finally again in touch with Du Camp, only to learn of the anguish he had passed through. In January his mistress, Adèle Husson, whom Flaubert always addressed by pet names such as "Dear Twin," had gone insane. She suffered from a suicidal mania and had constantly to be watched. Nothing could be done for her; Du Camp was crushed.[13]

To help restore himself, Flaubert now left on the trip to Brussels he had earlier contemplated. In Belgium he visited Princess Mathilde for four good days; to Flaubert she would always be Her Highness. Here he heard of the heart-rending love letters Adèle was writing to Maxime as she was about to be put into an asylum for her own protection. Problems at the frontier now made it difficult to return to Rouen via the direct route as he had planned. He returned instead via London so as to have the comfort of seeing Juliet again.[14] He reached there in late March but was soon eager to return and start work again. He was recovering.

At last on April 1, he consented to return to Croisset, where he hoped to pick up *Saint Anthony* once more and forget a France he could not accept: the Commune, the insurrectionary Paris government which took over for some two months, seemed quite as bad as Napoleon III or the Prussians had been. He felt odd at being settled in his own home again, but to his surprise he was quite comfortable and even happy there: his room and study were neat and clean. Life picked up again as though the Prussians had never been there. He rather hoped to have the chapter on the heresies written by the end of the month.

Flaubert found a sort of gentleness in quietly recollecting the past. The first Sunday he passed thinking of bygone days when Bouilhet would appear with his notebook of poetry under his arm, or when relatives now dead would walk about the house, or, above all, when Caroline as a young girl would run around the garden in her little white apron. He knew he was becoming a sentimental old man, taking his pleasure in living in the past. But adjustment was easier that way. He learned a few days later of the death of Maurice Schlésinger, which had occurred the previous February.

LIFE GONE AWRY (1871-72)

> The odor of the corpses disgusts me less than the miasmas of egoism being exhaled from every mouth. With a very few exceptions, everybody seems to me to be ready for a strait-jacket.
>
> Letter to George Sand, June 11, 1871

After the Prussian invasion, Flaubert at first felt nothing could startle or hurt him again; but a trip into Paris when the insurrection was over awakened his revulsion once more. The Parisians seemed pathological. They had always refused to take anything seriously, preferring *la Blague,* that art he had never mastered. Hence they could only respond with stupidity and cowardice to the unpleasant reality before them. Each half of the Parisian population was eager to strangle the other and made no secret of it. Everyone admired the Prussians and tried to imitate them, just as he had foreseen. He tired of hearing about ignoble workers, inept bourgeois, stupid peasants, and hideous clergymen. Antiquity and Saint Anthony were a relief. It was as useful to turn phrases as napkin rings. And one became slowly accustomed to doing without Paris. He comforted himself with the thought that the Age of Pericles had been atrocious but had still witnessed the production of great works; his own was no worse.

The continued presence of the Prussians was an infuriating reminder of the war; they did not leave until late July, 1871. Meanwhile Flaubert lived alone with his mother, who could no longer walk. The only variation from the absolute and monotonous uniformity of his days was the occasional passing of a Prussian patrol. He sought unavailingly to bury himself in his work and so forget his rage with his compatriots for being distracted from their hatred of Prussia by their hatred for the Commune. As the summer passed, he came to realize his rage was foolish, for attempting revenge against Prussia would only invite a new invasion and new catastrophes. He felt the crushing hatred of the entire Prussian people. Matters were different now from the days of Napoleon, whose armies had certainly committed horrors in Germany: the Napoleonic armies had been composed of the dregs of the French nation, whereas in Prussia the entire people was involved.

Flaubert's hatred of his compatriots, which had spread across so many pages of *A Sentimental Education,* grew as he watched the sorry spectacle of the early days of recovery from the war. He was disgusted and would have enjoyed being able to drown them all in a latrine; he wondered if France had been sufficiently punished. It bothered George Sand, who loved him despite his truculence, that at his age, when some mellowing might reasonably have been expected, he should remain so violent. She tried to tell him with gentle firmness that he could not hope to live solely for his family and a small group of friends. Surely the cataclysm they had just endured showed this. Man could not isolate himself or deny his bond with his fellow man. There was no good to be found in contempt and malediction, as one belonged to the human race and man's life consisted in loving. When Flaubert railed at "the people," he was cursing himself. Time spent in irritation over the stupidity of others was wasted.[15] Her advice was not far different from what Maxime Du Camp had written twenty-five years before; nor was it any more visibly effective now than his had been.

The more Flaubert considered his country, the more he felt it essential to live apart, at the top of an ivory tower. The Third Republic lacked any kind of elevation and hence might perhaps prove more solid; but this was the first time that mankind had been so cynical as to try to govern without principles.

So long as universal suffrage remained the basis of government, Flaubert felt France was beyond hope. Sheer weight of number prevailed over intelligence, education, background, or money, any one of which was more important. A Flaubert was worth as much as twenty other voters from Croisset. The masses, eternally minor, must have freedom but not power, for the vaguer an idea was, the more popular enthusiasm it would arouse.[16] Only a government of mandarins could save them. Flaubert never stated clearly how they were to be named; but they would clearly agree with him. He was a firm believer in the hierarchy, even, said Zola, respectful and gullible before it; a princess or a minister was, in his eyes, something other than the common run of mankind. He bowed and accepted, to the amusement of his younger friends.[17]

Part of Flaubert's bitterness was doubtless a reflection of his extremely unpleasant home life. His mother was helplessly weak and a sad spectacle of physical decay. In July, 1871, as she prepared to receive a visit from Caroline, she managed a short letter to her, telling how she longed and needed to see her again; she had undertaken a new diet of fortifying foods to be at her very best for the visit. For this she needed a small meat press of the kind which, years before, she had used in bringing up her granddaughter and which had been so successful in raising Caroline to become a strong and beautiful woman. Could Caroline bring one with her when she came? How Madame Flaubert yearned for a little strength to stand up on her own legs! If her granddaughter would have anything to do with her when she saw her, Madame Flaubert would be happy. And she urged her again not to forget the meat press. Caroline saved the letter.[18]

Most of the time Madame Flaubert could not be left alone. Her son would have liked to go to Nohant to visit George Sand, but it was not possible. Caroline and he took turns being away, and he had just used up his turn when George Sand invited him. When he did take his rightful turn later, he had hardly departed before Madame Flaubert was peremptorily demanding his return. He wrote to his niece in a fury to insist that at his age he really had a right, once a year, to go off and do as he pleased. Caroline was to report his displeasure to her and indeed to scold her severely. But she was then to give her a warm hug and make up to her. Upon his return and Caroline's departure it was Elisa Schlésinger's request to come see her in Paris which he had to decline: he had just been away.

When Flaubert had learned of the death of Maurice Schlésinger in April, 1871, he had written to Elisa, and she had replied. His second letter, calling her "Old friend, always dear, yes, always," spoke of the hope he had entertained that she would now come live in France; he might then have spent his last years not far from her. In September of 1871, however, she at least visited France.

Unable to go to Paris to be with her, Flaubert wrote again, urging his invitation upon her. Why should she not stop by, if—as she said—she had to go to Trouville? He explained his inability to leave his mother alone and then, calling her "Dear old Friend, Eternal Tenderness," he explained this was why he could not go to Trouville, where, as he reminded her, he had met her: for him, its beach would always bear the imprint of her footsteps. The ghost of the adolescent boy he had been was writing to the ghost of the woman she had been. They had, he added, so many things to say to each other, of a sort that were said badly on paper. The years had wrought their changes, as he knew. And Elisa must not misunderstand. After all, it was Flaubert who had created the last interview between Frédéric and Madame Arnoux. And so he assured her his mother would be delighted to receive her, and he urged her to come for the night or at least for dinner. In early November she did.

By January of 1872 the situation at Croisset was becoming—it is Flaubert's own word—intolerable. Neither he nor Caroline could imagine what to do with poor, aged Madame Flaubert. Achille's wife suggested installing a nun to help take some of the burden; but Flaubert smelled a project to allow his sister-in-law to pry into his affairs. He refused violently. There was nothing to do but face a life in which he and his niece would take turns relieving each other of the burden of this unsociable, impossible woman. What a falling off it was! It hurt him to feel impiety rising within him.[19]

Five months later the end came. On April 5, 1872, Madame Flaubert's death agony began; it lasted thirty-three hours. Afterwards, a broken Flaubert could do no more than pen one or two-line notes to those who must be informed. To no one, apparently, could he write the sort of full description he had of earlier deaths.

The first ten days were dreadful. Since Gustave had his own fortune, Madame Flaubert had willed Croisset to her granddaughter but with the proviso that her son was always to have his apartment there. He was not sure, however, that he could stand the solitude. On the other hand, nothing drew him to Paris. Gautier was his only remaining friend from the old days; and Theo was a dying man. It was not easy to remake a whole life at fifty. But after ten days he once again noticed the birds singing in the trees and the leaves coming out as spring advanced. If only he could write: it would be his salvation.

He now discovered what he had always known, that his mother was, of all human beings, the one he loved the most. The woman he had railed at for conceiving him in lust, whom he had assured would never have a rival, whose absence most hurt him in the Near East, whom he always complained of but could never live without, had now left him forever. He suffered as though a part of his entrails had been torn from him. During the inventory and the division of her property, he felt as if they were despoiling her.

Then peace descended. Three weeks after her death, he rediscovered calm and tranquility. Once again the Prussian invasion seemed the worst moment of his life; he could again pick up his writing. Everything passed, because one tired of it. Croisset was so peaceful and lovely. An infinite gentleness arose from the silence; the memory of his mother floated near like a vapor which enveloped him. His niece's health began to concern him; he asked her to take especial care of herself. Nostalgia for the past was anguish enough, without adding worry for the future.

He was secretly but profoundly ill, he felt. At last, in 1876, it was as though the fog were dissipated and once again he could be himself.[20] Meanwhile, just as he had kept some of his sister Caroline's clothes twenty-five years before, so now he kept some of his mother's as relics to be visited upon occasion. Charles Bovary had felt the same way about Emma's clothes; and Félicité in *A Simple Heart* would have this veneration for her mistress's wardrobe.

In July, 1872, some three months after his mother's death, Caro wished to go to Luchon, where the waters were felt to be good for her. As Ernest was unable to accompany her, her uncle went along. He had already had to accompany his mother to Vichy several times and knew that he hated the total monotony of watering places. The meals at the general table, the bells summoning the guests, and the animal-like existence which brought all down to a common level were the modern dream of equality and democracy; he loathed it.[21] But his spirits revived when he made an excursion with his niece as far as the Spanish border and was suddenly transported beyond all this world he hated.

Over the long months since the restoration of peace Flaubert had not forgotten Louis Bouilhet or his heirs. By June, 1871, he was already engaged in persuading the Odeon Theater to put on *Aïssé*. It took months to convince them, but at last, as the winter began, the director agreed; Flaubert wrote to Lagier about the possibility of a role in the play. In December he was struggling to assure favorable reviews. The first night, January 6, was excellent, he felt. But he was furious that he had had to get properties himself and handle much of the business of staging that evening. Despite his efforts the press reviews were wretched and the actors played to nearly empty houses. Almost at once the play had to be withdrawn; with it went the final hope of any money for Bouilhet's mistress and son.

Aïssé was timed to open just after the publication of the volume of Bouilhet's last poems. Flaubert lovingly reworked his Preface and all through December seemed to be living with his friend. The volume, however, excited little comment. Silence seemed to be descending inexorably about the memory of the dead poet and playwright.

Flaubert headed the commission to prepare some sort of monument to the poet; it would be presented to the City of Rouen. At last in August of 1871 the money had been collected, and Flaubert formally offered a fountain to the municipal council: it would be decorated with a bust of Bouilhet. At first the idea occasioned little discussion and was accepted in principle. But then, to the stupefaction of Flaubert and his committee, the fountain was refused in December, just as the volume of poems was coming out so unsuccessfully and as *Aïssé* was about to open and close. The city fathers—for once right in such a judgment—questioned whether Bouilhet's worth were sufficient to warrant such public homage. But to raise this question was of necessity to put Flaubert into a fury. He eventually replied with a lengthy letter which he heartily enjoyed composing. He even used as an argument against the municipal council a meeting of the Rouen Academy at which the eulogy of Bouilhet had been pronounced, for through devious means Flaubert had written it in part himself.[22]

He also attacked the councilmen directly: they lacked, he wrote, even the protective instinct of an animal in defending its most precious possessions, in their case money. Their ultimate in-

tellectual effort, he proclaimed, was to tremble before what they
imagined the future would bring. "Conservatives who conserve
nothing," he closed, "to be respected by those below you, respect
what is above you. Before sending the populace into the schools,
go there yourselves. Enlightened classes, enlighten yourselves."
Flaubert sent the letter to the Paris newspaper, *Le Temps*. He
probably was not unduly confused about the extent to which his
intervention helped the cause of Bouilhet's monument: his letters
may even have delayed it. For three days or so the quarrel occasioned quite some comment, then subsided into the forgetfulness
common to any large city. There the matter rested while Flaubert
fumed.

His mood was ferocious. He wondered about doing something
with *The Castle of Hearts,* which Bouilhet had worked on, and at
Lévy's suggestion he sought to revive an earlier play of Bouilhet's
which had been fairly successful in its first run. But then began a
fight to the death with the publisher.[23] Somehow he and Flaubert
had failed to understand each other. Lévy expected Flaubert to
pay for the printing costs of Bouilhet's volume of poems, but
Flaubert thought Lévy was advancing them. Flaubert was so
angry he became physically ill. Some two months later the printer,
also furious, insisted Flaubert remove from his shop the copies of
the volume which were still there obstructing his working space.
Unfortunately Bouilhet's son declined to side with Flaubert when
Lévy, as a compromise, offered to advance the needed money for
a year. Sainte-Beuve's former secretary and George Sand intervened, trying to restore amicable relations between editor and author, but the dispute had passed beyond repair. Flaubert's contract
with Lévy ran out in 1873; he determined to do no further publishing until that time and then to change publishers. *The Temptation of Saint Anthony* he had actually completed, but now he set
it aside.

The death of his mother had brought a solitude more absolute
than anything Flaubert had yet known, as he realized when Caroline returned to her husband after the funeral. Mealtimes were the
worst, alone with himself at the empty table. He had to adapt
himself to this life, however, for, after brief thoughts of travel or
living elsewhere, he realized he did not have the means. And so,

sensing the years catching up with him, he found the past invading him even more than before. He was rolling back through his memories and losing himself in them, with all the tenderness and the impotent angers of an old man. Perhaps, after all, the future for him was contained in a ream of white paper to be covered with black ink in order not to go mad with boredom.

Flaubert continued to have few friends. Du Camp almost disappeared from his ken for many years following the Franco-Prussian War; after the exchange of one or two letters the two men appear to have remained without contact until 1877, and Du Camp seems hardly to have crossed Flaubert's mind. Turgenev he kept hoping to see in Croisset; but although the Russian promised to come, the months stretched out into years and he remained away. They saw each other frequently in Paris, however, and in February of 1872 Flaubert finally met Turgenev's mistress, the opera singer Madame Viardot. Twenty-seven years earlier he had seen her name carved on a pillar in the castle at Chillon; just before he had left for his trip to the Near East, he had heard her sing and found in the beauty of her voice some appeasement for his anguish at leaving his mother. Now at last he was meeting her; he found her odd. He saw something of Victor Hugo, whom he had met in 1843 in Pradier's studio and with whom he had corresponded during the poet's exile under the Second Empire. Hugo was unassuming and charming, which surprised and delighted Flaubert. From time to time he was invited to Hugo's house for dinner. He saw much of Edmond de Goncourt and, in Croisset, he continued occasionally to see Edmond Laporte, who would later occupy the most important place among all his friends; but at this time he still had to explain to Caroline who Laporte was.

In these years after the war Flaubert really came to know young Guy de Maupassant, whose mother had been Laure Le Poittevin. Maupassant would have been welcome in any case as a friend of Bouilhet's—whom he knew for some two years before meeting Flaubert—but as Alfred's nephew he was especially dear. The two became so close it was rumored, quite without foundation, that Maupassant was Flaubert's son. Listening to Flaubert talk, he could recapture what his uncle must have been. He was profoundly moved, for his mother had brought him up to venerate Alfred, and he loved his memory as though he had known him or been his son. He came almost to feel he had been present, too, at the literary discussions between Flaubert and Bouilhet: he seemed to belong far more to that generation than to his own, which bored him profoundly. For Flaubert, Maupassant was a return to his youth, particularly as he shared vicariously in the younger man's lusty exploits in Paris brothels.[24]

After the death of his mother Flaubert needed his friendships with women more than before, although he told Zola they could never touch him for long. Zola felt they knew this and hence treated him more as a comrade than as a potential lover. Maupassant, who knew him more intimately than did Zola, sensed how much of the paternal there was in his relationships to women. He tended to treat them like grown-up children, incapable of understanding elevated matters but to whom one could tell all the little intimate sorrows that endlessly cut across one's life. At a distance he judged them severely; but when he was with them he responded to their consoling charm, delighted in their delicacies and sweetness, and sympathized with their illusions. Their eternal preoccupation with love exasperated him, but the sort of passionate atmosphere he found all about them fascinated him and, despite himself, he was drawn to them.[25]

Toward George Sand he continued to feel abiding affection. He respected and loved her and longed to have her visit him at Croisset. Misunderstanding certain aspects of what he wrote about Madame Flaubert's will, she thought he needed money and wrote at once to offer it. He declined with thanks but assured her that if he had needed anything she was the person to whom he would have turned. Now, with his mother dead, he pressed his invitation to come to Croisset: he would so like to have her in his house again. She would sleep near him, in his mother's room.

Princess Mathilde returned rapidly to France after the war. To Flaubert so quick a return constituted an unseemly acceptance of the overthrow of the imperial family, so that something of the admiration he had felt for her was diminished. But, just because she had fallen from her high post, he continued his warm affection and respect.

Louise Colet, after many years of silence, suddenly turned on Flaubert when he published Bouilhet's posthumous verses, claiming he was seeking to publicize himself. He and George Sand, whom she had villified previously, exchanged sympathetic letters, as he also did with Sainte-Beuve's former secretary, who had similarly excited her anger. All agreed she was out of her mind.[26]

When his mother died, Elisa Schlésinger wrote to offer condolence. Flaubert, too overcome to reply, let time slip by until she wrote again asking if he had forgotten her. He replied, pleading his crushing burden of fatigue. In fact he had been writing to all and sundry; but Elisa could not know that. It was already late May: could she not remain in Paris until June 20, when he would be there? And he called her his "always beloved" in closing the letter. He did go to be present at the marriage of her son. To be thus physically with Elisa, but a white-haired, broken Elisa marrying her grown son, was no doubt serenity to the man who had given his love for Elisa its final outlet in *A Sentimental Education*. Now only the tenderness remained; and to that, presumably, these days he gave full expression.

During the time immediately after the war Flaubert turned to three lovely women, Mesdames Brainne, Lapierre, and Pasca. Madame Lapierre was the wife of a Rouen newspaper publisher, an old and good friend of Flaubert's. Her sister-in-law, Madame Brainne, was a widow. Madame Pasca, an actress who had played leading roles in plays of Dumas *fils*, was a close friend of the first two ladies. Flaubert liked to call them his Three Angels, a term he seems first to have used in May of 1871. All three, sensing how safe they were with the aging but confirmed bachelor, enjoyed a delightfully flirtatious relationship with him. They collaborated on a letter one day, sending him their most affectionate embraces and threatening to call upon him in the very near future, coming together however.[27]

Flaubert was perhaps fondest of Madame Brainne. Her husband had died in 1864, and she enjoyed the boisterous flirting which he carried on with her, perhaps not exclusively in his letters. In them at any rate he would insist that the memory of her *persecuted* him—and he underlined—and that he was more serious than she imagined. Eventually first names began to be used. Flaubert kept prudently to explanations of why he was too old for that sort of thing; she seems to have stayed within comfortable expressions of the hope she meant something to him.

Many of Flaubert's letters to Madame Brainne carried equally warm greetings to the other two Angels, but Madame Pasca seems perhaps to have occupied a lesser place. Edmond de Goncourt thought, many years later, however, that he remembered Flaubert's commenting intimately on her charms.[28] All three women flattered their famous and lonely friend, and, because one or another of them was almost always in Rouen, they did much to alleviate his loneliness.

Flaubert had constant difficulties with money during these years. Although he had a modest but assured income, he was often seriously short of ready cash. Keeping accounts exasperated him, and he was rather proud of having no head for figures at all. Of course the death of his mother made him considerably wealthier than he had been; but this only encouraged him the more to live off his capital. His practices surprised and alarmed his nephew, who managed some of his financial affairs for him. The arrangement, however, allowed Flaubert to think still less about money matters and to protest even more loudly about his incapacity for them. Hence he continued it.

Perhaps his own difficulties explain why Flaubert was not unduly alarmed that Ernest and Caroline continued to have problems themselves. Just before the war broke out, he had been worried for Caro. As soon as peace returned, in April of 1871, he was again alarmed for her. By December their financial situation was serious and he intervened both with Raoul-Duval, a power in the local provincial scene, and with Princess Mathilde. He refused the Princess' suggestion that she might get a mortgage on her residence, Saint-Gratien; but he willingly accepted her proposal to act as intermediary with the Rothschilds. Fortunately all blew over in due course.

Flaubert's mental state did not markedly improve after the war. The long months of shame, rage, and chagrin had molded him. He could and did seek for some sort of insensitivity to public and private misfortune, but events kept interfering and he was no longer able to insulate himself enough not to be upset. He was invited to Vendôme to take part in the ceremonies inaugurating a statue of Ronsard. Dining the night before with Edmond de Goncourt, he was already in a hyperexcited state, insisting on a private dining room so as to be able to remove his coat and shoes and making violent statements about politics, literature, and the wretched life he was leading. Then he learned the minor littérateur Paul de Saint-Victor was to be at the ceremonies. Saint-Victor had not acknowledged receipt of his complimentary copy of *A Sentimental Education,* and his political activities had further annoyed Flaubert. He was already unhappy about having to put up with large crowds: when he learned he would have to make the trip to Vendôme in the company of this man, he abandoned the whole idea, turning back instead to Croisset. His misanthropy was beyond his control, and only alone could he reach some sort of peace. Edmond de Goncourt, hearing all of this, sympathized and agreed that all the people of his day with some artistic sensitivities were equally thin skinned, sick, and either unbalanced or near to it.[29]

Flaubert was deeply pessimistic, noting that humanity always persecutes its great men.[30] Even when he was feeling physically more fit, as he was at intervals, his disgust and despair were constant. Only writing could help him, and he was often too distraught even for that. The quarrel with Lévy and then his mother's death had taken a great deal out of him. His irascibility was becoming so great he was himself embarrassed and alarmed. The doctors could suggest only that he smoke less, a counsel he followed half-heartedly and with little hope of benefit.

Nature, in these months, began to offer him more serenity. He could not lie down on the grass and relax—he felt as though he were already in the grave with lettuce growing up from him—but he did go for a walk from time to time. Once he came upon a cow with a newborn calf lying beside her. The sun shone on the dried autumn leaves. He was so moved by the sight that he leaned over and kissed the calf's head. Looking out one night at the Seine as he was writing to Caro, he saw the brilliant moon through the tulip tree by his window. The passing boats made black shadows on the river; the trees were mirrored in the water, and the noise of a pair of oars cut the silence regularly. The gentleness of the scene he first called "infinite" before settling for the more modest "without equal." Its beauty had moved him to a care in description he usually reserved for his novels.[31]

As Flaubert sought, usually unsuccessfully, to turn his attention to literature and there find peace again, his long trend toward classicism, which had begun with Rachel, continued. Writing which did not concern itself primarily with esthetics seemed to him immoral, for esthetics he now proclaimed a higher Justice (the capital is his). Romantic sentimentality had obscured the intimate relationship between esthetics and ethics, but it must be uncovered anew. To Zola he declared that everything had already been said and therefore the task of the artist was to try to say it better.

Romantic he remained, in temperament and taste; it gave him his creative power.[32] The lyric response was the fundamental one, and he now easily termed himself "an old fossil of romanticism." The conflict no longer bothered him, because he had learned to master it by perfection of form. If some of his hatreds had pierced the surface in *A Sentimental Education*, he had been unaware of their intrusion; he felt secure for the future. But, in fact, hypersensitive, melancholy, alone, and misanthropic, he lived on the edge of the abyss. In 1871 he had considered suicide. In 1872, reworking his *Temptation of Saint Anthony*, he turned back to an earlier source of peace and security, which had not often been in the forefront of his mind over the intervening twenty-five years, the belief in pantheism which had so excited and comforted him in the 1840's. Now he wrote in his Notebook: "The ultimate refuge, the supreme consolation, is to know that one belongs to the Cosmos, that one is a part of Order."[33] This would be Saint Anthony's consolation, too.

21

The Temptation of Saint Anthony (1874)

THE OBSESSION OF A LIFETIME

This is the work of my whole life; the first idea came to me
in 1845 in Genoa, looking at a Breughel painting, and since
that day I have never stopped thinking of it and doing reading for it.

Letter to Mademoiselle Leroyer de Chantepie, June 2, 1872

WRITING *Saint Anthony* was the work of Flaubert's whole life
because he viewed his profession as a kind of priesthood and was
fond of pointing out the resemblances between his life and that of
a monk.[1] Furthermore, the subject, temptation, he could consider
universal. The original form of the story he had already enlarged
in the late 1840's to include temptation not only by the Seven Capital Sins but by almost anything desired or desirable. The first version had emphasized the romantic longings of the younger Flaubert.
As he grew older, other preoccupations had supervened; hence the
Anthony to whom he returned after he finished *A Sentimental
Education* was a hermit of quite different cast.

There is a sense in which most of Flaubert's works deal with
illusion. *Madame Bovary* dissected the shoddy ones induced in
young women by reading the poorer works of romanticism.
While *Salammbô* displayed a wonderful age in which men and
women were able to incarnate the sun and the moon in a colossal
love which shook their universe, Frédéric Moreau, condemned to
live in our latter-day world, had to learn that illusion is the only
reality and that therefore his best moment had been an unrealized
one. *The Temptation of Saint Anthony*, following immediately
upon the *Education*, had the same message, as *Salammbô* had been
a return to the problems of *Madame Bovary*. Saint Anthony,

however, could offer its message directly, for its framework allowed the overt discussion of philosophical ideas in a way rarely possible in the previous work.

Preparations for *Saint Anthony* went slowly in 1869 and early 1870, as there were many demands on Flaubert's time. Then the Franco-Prussian War interrupted him, and all the papers relating to the Saint were buried in the garden at Croisset. In April of 1871, however, tired and broken, he returned to his home to try to pick up the pieces of his life. His niece encouraged him to go back to his beloved Saint, and he did so before April was over.[2] For the next fourteen months, until June 20, 1872, *The Temptation* was his principal occupation and his principal solace.

The new version—the only one published in Flaubert's lifetime—was tightly organized. Anthony experienced the traditional temptations by the Seven Capital Sins but then underwent temptation by Knowledge and learned Flaubert's new position that all religions resembled each other, all were partial truths, and none was absolute. Tempted then by the Devil himself, he discovered all was illusion, perhaps even illusion itself. In a last lyric section he observed life being born out of matter and longed to return into matter himself.

The Temptation of 1874 opens in a strange atmosphere. To establish it, Flaubert borrowed part of the description of the weird illumination he had seen and closely described in Greece two decades before. He used the pearly light and clouds rising like a mane to the zenith and especially the hard, bronze-like look of everything, with a sort of gold dust floating in the air and mingling with the vibration of the light.[3] The Saint was alone before his cabin considering his ennui and reviewing his past life. This initial monologue traced most of the desires which motivated the later pages and displayed Anthony's tense state. Salammbô and Anubis returned covertly as the Saint described the women who came to him because they needed suprahuman voluptuousness and had seen gods calling to them in their dreams.

Anthony passed easily to imagining other lives he might have lived, each desirable because it would have given outlet to one or another of the Capital Sins; in particular he suffered from pride in knowledge. Excited by the succession of his thoughts, he fell into a trance, experiencing in some detail one of Flaubert's epileptic seizures and setting the framework for the hallucinations which overcame him thereafter.

In a series of visions Anthony again imagined satisfying each of his sinful desires, but this time in stronger fashion. In a foretaste of one of the main themes of *Saint Julian*, Anthony gave the first of numerous indications that he felt a blood-lust, as Julian would. He imagined that violence might bring relief from his tensions and saw himself in the gory sack of Alexandria, where he walked ankle deep in blood he had shed.

Episodes crowded in rapidly. The Saint saw interior court-yards like the one which had attracted Flaubert's attention in his Damascus hotel. Nebuchadnezzar and the Queen of Sheba re-appeared from the earlier version, now sharpened by Flaubert's se-vere pruning. She offered the Saint satisfaction of his desire through her magic. Then she promised that her fantasy would soothe his ennui, her body his lusts, her wealth his every whim. She was the refinement of an advanced civilization, no longer a mere erotic symbol. Taine was delighted with her.[4]

Anthony's former disciple Hilarion appeared next. Flaubert distinguished three types or levels of fantasy and the fantastic. That of the ancients depended upon sorcery or talismans. A higher level, primed by poetic imagination or desire, involved thought, the dream, the internal being. But the highest level, that of knowledge, was alone creative.[5] Anthony readily imagined sor-cery, the first level, and mentioned it in his opening monologue; the Queen of Sheba had offered it to him. Fantasy based on desire and imagination had entered when he imagined the women offer-ing themselves to him. He had heard their voices and saw their torsos in a swaying palm trunk. The third stage, knowledge creat-ing fantasy, had had to await the arrival of Hilarion. He embodied much of the roles of Logic and Knowledge in the earlier versions and now destroyed the Saint's confidence in his religion by tempt-ing his pride and confusing him with arguments. When Hilarion suggested observing areas outside of dogma, where belief was not fettered, Anthony gladly accepted. The Procession of the Heresies followed, radically rewritten and shortened. The sequence ended with Apollonius of Tyana offering to explain the cosmos to Anthony. Upon his refusal, Apollonius left.

Taine objected that Flaubert was unfair to the heretical Christian sects here, for he had used their worst enemy as his source. But he did allow that this was perhaps the sort of belief Anthony would have had.[6] And the strangeness adds to the effectiveness of the passage. Priscilla's description of her first meeting with the prophet Montanus was drawn from Flaubert's illness. She heard extraordinary things from Montanus' lips and was transported. Flowers as broad as the sun whirled before her eyes, and a golden harp vibrated in space. Then she fainted. Saint Anthony was having a hallucination of a woman having a hallucination, and both were described in terms of Flaubert's own seizures!

In a moment of clarity between visions, Anthony meditated on the enigma that these people, too, wished to direct themselves toward God. By what right could he curse them? Perhaps he would have learned more had they not disappeared so soon—and thus he induced the next hallucination in himself.

Anthony now shared one of Flaubert's waking visions. Long before, while visiting Arles, he had imagined the arena filled with the knights and senators, courtesans and soldiers, who used to be there shouting and screaming under the hot sun. Anthony now saw this, too. And he heard mention of Saint Polycarp, who was to become one of Flaubert's favorites.

Anthony was fascinated by what he heard and longed to know of other religions. Aided by Hilarion's comments, he observed the Procession of the Gods. He passed from raucous laughter to sympathy and then to the realization that they had as much truth as he. There was no need now for Death's whip to urge them on their way. Anthony watched; they entered and disappeared. At no point did he return to consciousness.

Hilarion urged respect upon Anthony and informed him at one point that he had just witnessed the beliefs of several hundred million people. When the Saint saw Isis faint, he leaped forward to sustain her; Hilarion reminded him she was the goddess of his forebears and he had worn her amulet in his cradle. She disappeared; he was overcome with embarrassment and then tears.

Unable to hate the pagan gods, he pitied them instead. Hilarion pointed out that they all phrased man's aspirations. And so many of them paralleled Christian beliefs or practices, especially the Hindu gods and the Buddha, who had a new importance now in this discussion of reality and illusion. Through most of the month of June, 1871, Flaubert studied the religion of India with Renan's help.

The Greek gods, too, Flaubert profoundly modified. Whereas his lyric interventions had marred the earlier versions, he here remained impassive for the most part. The passage opens with all the gods together on Mount Olympus in a vast tableau. Hilarion speaks of their serene harmony. In general the gods say and do only what Anthony might have imagined. Flaubert's earlier mockery is absent, and only joy or pity remains. Hilarion explains to the Saint that the Greek gods attended every aspect of daily living, giving it a divine quality and guiding mortals toward freedom and beauty. The religion they established had passed, but their values carried forward into later ones. Anthony, sighing, recited the Credo.

For all his resolution not to intrude, Flaubert's wrath against his contemporaries was too great to be contained. In a new speech Jupiter expressed his contempt for men, but it was particularly Frenchmen in 1872 whom he described. He castigated their meanness: they had the hearts of slaves, forgot injury, abjured their ancestors, and failed to keep their oaths. Everywhere the stupidity of the masses triumphed and with it the mediocrity of the individual and the hideousness of races. Fortunately, Jupiter did conclude somewhat as he had before, that his spirit would survive wherever there remained one head retaining respect for thought, hating disorder, and conceiving of law.

Minerva's speech was wholly changed to become a description of the Panathenaic Procession of the Parthenon. Neptune regretted the disappearance of gaiety from the sea. Mars, however, again broke the illusion to castigate a world in which numbers, machines, and ruses had become dominant. Flaubert's own interests showed in a reference to Moloch, devourer of children—it had been men only, before *Salammbô*—and in praise of the heroes of the Battle of Thermopylae, a story which would tempt him during his last years. A new and moving description of Venus suggests the Botticelli painting which Flaubert had seen in Florence but had not used earlier; her condensed speech, however, lacks the lyric force of its predecessors.

The Roman domestic gods had hardly been mentioned in 1849 and 1856. Now they acquired considerable importance since Flaubert wished to emphasize how much a religion was a way of life and an embodiment of a culture, as Renan thought. It delighted Flaubert to lead his Roman through all the rounds of his daily living with a little god to preside over each occasion.

Jehovah's speech, too, Flaubert condensed, deleting all reference to his being displaced by Christ, Mary, the apostles, or the saints. When the last of the Greek gods left, there was total silence: it was the end.

Hilarion's turn had come at last, and he named himself: Knowledge, the third form of Flaubert's fantasy, the creative one. His kingdom, he affirmed, was as broad as the universe and his desire limitless. His path was always forward, freeing the mind and weighing worlds, with neither hatred nor fear, pity nor love, and without God. Flaubert wished the reader to accept what Hilarion stated; his tone was peremptory. But it is not easy entirely to accept what this strange being says—he has, after all, apparently been responsible for so many illusions and is himself the product of Anthony's diseased mind. The reader cannot be entirely happy with him as guide, any more than he was with Pellerin in *A Sentimental Education*.

This issue becomes even more serious. In Flaubert's world of 1874, knowledge was no more a safeguard than religion. When Hilarion offered to show Anthony the Devil, the Saint agreed. And now the reader is asked to take the Devil as a reliable witness on the nature of man and the cosmos; but he is less than satisfactory in this role, and the reader requires some pages before he adjusts. As he had in several of Flaubert's youthful tales, here again the Devil took Anthony high into the air to survey the universe. When his guide answered his questions, the voice seemed to be only an echo of Anthony's own thinking or a response of his memory. In the ensuing dialogue, he and the Devil linked together the earlier arguments on reality and illusion. Dazzled by the infinite extent of space, Anthony realized his finite mind could not encompass it and that, since matter is a part of God, He cannot be an individual or be moved by prayer. The petty requirements of man's limited intellect do not make the laws of the universe. Even good and evil concern man alone, not God. Anthony lamented that this was like a death more profound than death itself.

Now ready for vaster concepts, Anthony learned form itself might be an error of his senses and substance a creation of his own imagination. Or perhaps the world was a perpetual flux and appearance the only reality. But was Anthony even sure, absolutely sure, that he was alive, the Devil asked. Was there perhaps nothing at all? The Saint had to confess that truth lay beyond the power of humans to attain. Illusion was the only reality, if it in fact existed. He now knew Flaubert's melancholy truth.

After a moment of consciousness, Anthony fell into hallucination once again. Two women now confronted him, personifying the two greatest illusions of life, Voluptuousness and Death. Both had had dialogues in the earlier versions, but Death was now no longer the romantic concept of the Infinite and the Perfect. Rather, under the influence of Schopenhauer, she had become nothingness, "an illusion at times masking the continuity of life." The two women who incarnated these symbols offered Anthony most of the types of fantasy he had noted in his second category, poetic imagination and desire. They appealed not at all to magic and sorcery, but rather to his dreams, desires, and thoughts. Death called herself consolation, rest, forgetfulness, eternal serenity; Voluptuousness offered him sleep, joy, life, inexhaustible happiness. But he rejected both and felt himself eternal.

Anthony speculated about the nature of the universe. If substance is really unique, then why are forms so varied? He longed to see the primordial figures that underlay all life and linked thought and matter, constituting being. The question was enough for his brain to produce the hallucination—from earlier versions—of the Sphinx and the Chimera, the Unknown and Fantasy. Their skepticism was consoling because it dissolved thought and took away the source of anguish. The desire to know God, the Sphinx told the Chimera, was fruitless, and all those who sought this knowledge she had devoured.

When the Sphinx and the Chimera left, the Procession of the Fabulous Monsters entered in an inextricable confusion, as animal and plant, and then plant and mineral, merged. Throughout February of 1872 Flaubert read widely in medieval sources to find appropriate animals, and Maurice Sand sent him sketches of imaginary monsters. But almost without exception the entire procession is composed of careful condensations of what Flaubert had written in 1849, with a few corrections from 1856. And it is no more possible to take this seriously now than it had been for Du Camp and Bouilhet in 1849: "The Tragelaphus, half deer and half bull; the Myrmecoleo, lion in his forepart, ant in his hindpart, and whose genitals face backwards; the python Aksar, of sixty cubits in length, who terrified Moses . . . ," and so forth.

The passage becomes gripping only in the last page or so of the book as monstrous beings begin to fly about. Here, borrowing directly from effective material in the version of 1849, Flaubert depicted first those beings which were combinations of real ones, owls with serpent tails, and the like, crowding about Anthony. This time, however, he also essayed the sort of horrors which Breughel had imagined, animal shapes degenerating into vegetable, and mineral forms which were disquietingly alive. Delirious, Anthony observed the microscopically small and saw life itself being born from matter. The vision produced the final lyric passage which, though taken from earlier versions, now attains its force from being the last words of Anthony in the book, his cry of delight and excitement,* and his yearning to be an animal, to bark or swim or bellow, to have wings or a trunk. He longed to be in everything, emanate with the perfumes, flow like water, vibrate like sound, and ultimately to penetrate each atom, descend to the base of matter, be matter itself.

*"O bonheur! bonheur! j'ai vu naître la vie, j'ai vu le mouvement commencer. Le sang de mes veines bat si fort qu'il va les rompre. J'ai envie de voler, de nager, d'aboyer, de beugler, de hurler. Je voudrais avoir des ailes, une carapace, une écorce, souffler de la fumée, porter une trompe, tordre mon corps, me diviser partout, être en tout, m'émaner avec les odeurs, me développer comme les plantes, couler comme l'eau, vibrer comme le son, briller comme la lumière, me blottir sur toutes les formes, pénétrer chaque atome, descendre jusqu'au fond de la matière,—être la matière!" (*TENT*, pp. 200-201).

Against this background, the closing vision had to be different. The Devil had been nowhere present in this scene; he could not end the book with his hideous laugh. Rather the sun rose, the bank of clouds opened as it had that day in Greece, and in the midst of the blue sky there appeared the disk of the sun with the radiant face of Jesus Christ in its center. Anthony made the sign of the cross and set himself to pray.

The work remained Flaubert's favorite until the end of his life. It was dedicated to the memory of Alfred Le Poittevin, although —such is the irony of publishing—the name was misspelled and no one caught the error until after the first printing.

Saint Anthony was an effort to create a precise ethical mood and to raise—in terms of an unbalanced temperament—specific fundamental questions. What was real in all this mad rush of apparent sensations and perceptions? Anthony's cabin, the stones before him, and the sand had no more reality than his dreams. "Like a brute beast, he believes in the reality of things," jeered Apollonius, as he left to rise far beyond the realm of forms, beyond the earth and the skies, to where the Ideas and the Incarnate Word reside. There they would grasp in all its infinity the Eternal, the Absolute, Being itself. Apollo, too, aspired to leap up beyond forms into the Idea. This, the interrelationships among Reality, Form, and the Idea, was Anthony's principal query.

Hilarion, Anthony's new guide, differed from the earlier ones, Logic and Science, for this reason. He did not concern himself with the goodness of nature, the ultimate foundations of good and evil, or the like, and he had no aggressive hatred for religion. For the most part he was content to raise questions; he did not imply they had answers. It was enough if they destroyed the placid, narrowing certainties within which Anthony moved. If he could persuade the Saint to rise above his dogmatism to a level of detachment and impartial enquiry and evade entirely the unanswerable question of faith itself, he would be satisfied.

Flaubert wrote in one of his Notebooks near this time that there should be some kind of midterm between archeology and modernity, between the past and the merely ephemeral. Could one not find a ground between a deliberate search for the archaic and an equally deliberate pursuit of realism so as to achieve a result embodying neither what was dead nor what should never have been born?[7] *The Temptation* was such an attempt. One aspect was Flaubert's quiet, historical presentation. In the first version and in the second as well, he had sought drama around the Saint's struggles against his temptations. Here, instead, the reader observes his actions, sympathetically, to be sure, but without participating in them. It is enough to have seen how things were; dispassionate understanding is the goal.

Flaubert was acquainted with many of the leading authorities on the various aspects of his subject. Renan he knew well, and Baudry and Maury were childhood friends. Once again, as with *Salammbô*, his lack of training as a scholar drove his friends to wrathful explosions against his careless inaccuracies. But his persistence and their tolerance produced a work which met with a few erudite objections when it did appear—no mean feat for an amateur in a highly specialized field.[8]

Edmond de Goncourt was troubled by *Saint Anthony*, nevertheless. The final version Flaubert cut until it was only one-fifth as long as the first and one-third as long as *A Sentimental Education*. Even so, its mass of archeological detail is not readily meaningful or exciting. Goncourt felt it was as though Flaubert had dumped his notes, pell-mell, onto the page. He had chosen a brilliantly colored period like Salammbô's again and tried to dazzle his reader, but the result was neither intelligent nor original. At best it was laborious ingenuity.[9] The objection was well taken. When Anthony looked out over Alexandria's two ports, Flaubert paused to name them in a parenthesis.* He then characterized the ports as round, like two circuses, and separated by a jetty joining the city to the island surrounded by cliffs, on which the lighthouse stood. It, in turn, was four sided, five hundred cubits high, of ten stories, and with a mass of black coals smoking on its summit. Flaubert's belief that excess was always good, a proof of idealism and evi-

---

*"Il embrasse, d'un seul coup d'oeil, les deux ports (le Grand-Port et l'Eunoste), ronds tous les deux comme deux cirques, et que sépare un môle joignant Alexandrie à l'îlôt escarpé sur lequel s'élève la tour du Phare, quadrangulaire, haute de cinq cents coudées et à neuf étages, avec un amas de charbons noirs fumant à son sommet" (*TENT*, p. 21).

dence of a willingness to go beyond need, can sometimes eventuate in absurdity.[10]

In more fruitful fashion, the historian's detachment as opposed to the romantic's personal involvement allowed Flaubert the calm acceptance of all religions. One neither accepts nor rejects; one admires. He had abandoned Chateaubriand and, under the tutelage of Renan, developed instead the implications of the insight he had had as far back as Brittany concerning the basis of religion. He had restated his concept in the 1850's to Louise Colet: religion was a philosophy which had achieved the form of art. Its generating force, the religious feeling, essentially superstition, was the same throughout all humanity, corresponding to the same needs and dying or being replaced for the same reasons everywhere.[11] Freud, who thought highly of *The Temptation*, would not have disagreed.

Many scenes do recur from the earlier versions, but even they are usually changed. The Heresies appeared only so that Anthony might come to know them. They did not so much tempt him as expose their beliefs for his consideration. Hilarion told him to listen to all arguments and disdain none. When he became sufficiently confused about the nature of miracles and the contradictions in the Bible, he found himself freer; his thought now struggled consciously to escape from the prison it had been inhabiting.

To Flaubert, the child and the barbarian or the primitive do not distinguish between the real and the fantastic;[12] hence Anthony, experiencing a psychological and neurological phenomenon, hallucination, had little difficulty understanding its implication that reality was ultimately illusory. Taine anticipated Freud in admiring Flaubert's handling of the literary problem of the hallucinations. On the one hand, as Taine wrote to him, he had had to describe a real hallucination as an ascetic of 330 A.D. would have lived it with all the incoherence and illogical leaps of the imagination, the jumble of phenomena, and the suggestions of impaired intelligence and mental illness that go along with such a psyche. But on the other hand, he had also succeeded in depicting a vast metaphysical orgy as the various systems clashed against one another.[13]

The transitions from idle musing to hypnagogic dream to epileptic seizure are detailed and insidious. The Saint's ennui was the generating factor in the opening pages, as he imagined previous days when he did not feel so much anguish. His chagrin became so great he burst into sobs as Mâtho and Frédéric had; the nervous tension was beyond control. He had a visual hallucination in which the arms of the Cross seemed to bend into the shape of the Devil's horns; he heard voices; he saw the things he coveted. A tumultuous horde of hallucinatory visions irrupted into his brain; it was an epileptic seizure.

This was the fullest account Flaubert ever wrote for publication of what went on during his attacks, although of course no reader could divine what it was. Weird objects began to pass before Anthony's eyes, a water puddle, a prostitute, the corner of a temple, a soldier, a chariot with two rearing white horses. Emma had seen such visions crowding suddenly in upon her; Salammbô, in Mâtho's tent, had thus recalled her home and her ride to the camp; Frédéric had had the names of cafés flood into his mind, and parts of the bodies of the women at Rosanette's ball had floated madly before his eyes as he went to sleep.

Anthony found the images arriving suddenly, in jerks, standing out against the night like scarlet paintings on ebony. Emma and Frédéric had both had this experience of the memory discharge being sudden and instantaneous, like the thousand elements of an exploding piece of fireworks. Then the movements sped up and the objects passed before Anthony's eyes in dizzying fashion. But sometimes they would stop, grow paler by degrees, and melt; or else they would fly away and immediately others would take their places. Emma had seen globules of fire burst in the air like fulminating caps and turn round and round before moving off to melt upon the snow. Salammbô's confused memories of her night in the tent dashed about as in a whirlpool in images which were tumultuous and yet clear; Frédéric's memories, too, arrived in mad, disjointed fashion, so much so that his head began to grow dizzy with them.

Anthony closed his eyes, but the hallucinations only multiplied, surrounded him, besieged him, as Emma found the balls of fire multiplying, approaching, and finally penetrating her body.

Anthony, like Emma and Frédéric, was terrified; he could feel nothing beyond a burning contraction in his stomach. Emma and Salammbô had been in a stupor; Frédéric was conscious of his existence only because of an intolerable pressure on his chest. For Anthony there was also a din within his head; Emma felt her arteries beating as though deafening music were filling the country-side; Salammbô had suffered from a pounding in her temples.

Perhaps alone of Flaubert's heroes, Anthony now perceived an enormous silence separating him from the world; he sought to speak but found it impossible. He was like the earlier heroes and heroines, however, in feeling the general bond of his being dissolving; unable to hold out any longer, he fell upon his mat.

Then began the succession of visions which filled the Saint's night. At first, as each ended, he recognized it as vision only; but his periods of hallucination grew longer until he eventually remained unaware of external reality for fifty pages. The conversations with Hilarion when he first appeared and the Procession of the Heresies occupied all this time. After it, Anthony dreamed of fire and awakened to discover his beard had been singed by embers from his hearth. Only brief moments of consciousness interrupted the Procession of the Gods and the long, confusing conversation with the Devil. On recovering, however, Anthony remembered everything and considered suicide. The ending of the book was almost unbroken hallucination.

The Temptation of Saint Anthony meant so much to Flaubert and occupied so much of his life that one wishes it were great. While this outline can be legitimately drawn from it and is presumably the basic structure he meant his reader to sense, still long arid stretches of *Saint Anthony* are only mildly curious in an antiquarian sort of way. Some of it is inescapably dull and unconvincing or uninteresting. Furthermore, the psychological framework of the Saint as epileptic is clear only when one knows what Flaubert's symptoms were. The epileptic experiences of an Emma Bovary or a Salammbô or even a Frédéric, all less complete and occupying only a page or so, are far more comprehensible to the reader, who understands behind the event the psychological anguish of the experience even if not its physiology. For Anthony, who falls into a trance before fifteen pages are done and who never fully comes out of it, the reader feels curiosity, but little true pity. And, like Anthony, for the most part he merely observes. Uninvolved in the action, his concern never rises far above a quiet indifference, as Flaubert strives his best to display his ultimate wisdom.

Perhaps Flaubert sensed something of this. At any rate, he set the manuscript aside for several years, as he had long been saying he would. His fight with Michel Lévy left him with no urgent desire to publish until that contract ran out; nor did his contempt for his countrymen invite him once again to offer them a book of his. And so he put *Saint Anthony* away and went to Paris to be with Elisa, saying only that he would perhaps publish it along with the other volume on which he was working, *Bouvard and Pécuchet.*

22

Bouvard and Pécuchet

THE OTHER LIFELONG OBSESSION

An old idea that went back to his youth.

Emile Zola on Flaubert

THE basic framework of *Bouvard and Pécuchet* is the story of two copy clerks who retire to the country when one of them comes into an inheritance. During this retirement they investigate most of the fields of human endeavor and find all of them fruitless at best, harmful all too frequently, and always stupid. At the end they return to copying. Like *The Temptation*, the new work had its roots in Flaubert's youth. Its earliest form was his first published work, which had appeared in *Le Colibri* in 1837, already a satiric account of the limitations of the copy clerk. Flaubert was still at work on this last incarnation of his clerks when he died in 1880.[1]

Over the course of nearly a lifetime the idea for the book evolved, changed direction, and took on new dimensions. It crystallized in its final form only during the actual writing, which began in 1874, or nearly thirty years after its genesis. Rather early in this development came the idea for collecting foolish ideas and foolish statements, the latter usually referred to by the French word Flaubert always used for it, his *Sottisier*, the former being his *Dictionary of Accepted Ideas*. These he had been pillaging for his novels ever since he had created Homais, who is in part a precursor of Bouvard and Pécuchet, an incarnation of bourgeois stupidity.

Until late in the 1860's Flaubert was wont to refer to his project as the "History of Two Woodlice," a title which adequately expressed his contempt for his proposed heroes. But his ideas remained to a considerable extent vague and formless. In fact they seemed to defy formulation, which is one of the reasons why he set the notion aside in 1863 and preferred to try *A Sentimental Education*. Yet before abandoning the project, he had at least established the framework: a meeting of the two men, their experiences in the country, and their return to copying. Moreover, a great many of the topics they would explore were taking shape in his notes. A number of actual sentences, crucial and often satiric, he had already found; and he was searching for what they would copy and what its import would be.

For the basic structure there can be little doubt that Flaubert was indebted to a short story he had read. When Alphonse Daudet showed the original to Edmond de Goncourt some eight years after Flaubert's death, Goncourt felt the resemblance amounted to plagiarism.[2] That word is perhaps a little strong, but the relationship is uncomfortably close. The original work, however, has never been read since it was last reprinted in 1858; and *Bouvard and Pécuchet* is as alive as when it was first published.

What would these two copy clerks have copied, which would have formed the second volume? Flaubert died before completing it, and he had slowly changed his mind over the years. Initially they were going to copy anything and everything: their material, however, was going to include the *Sottisier*. In fact, it really generated the need for clerks to copy it, so there could be a reason for printing it. Jules Duplan was almost Flaubert's collaborator here in locating and transcribing materials. Even after *A Sentimental Education* displaced *Bouvard and Pécuchet* late in 1863, Flaubert continued to gather materials for the *Sottisier* and to encourage Duplan to do so, too.

As the years passed, Flaubert began slowly to change his concept and to glimpse another and far more interesting one. A transition stage is evidenced by a plan to have them discover an "album." A popular pastime with the ladies at this time consisted of keeping a bound volume in which they asked their friends and famous acquaintances to jot down thoughts or verses. Louise Colet had had one; so had Madame Arnoux. Such an album Bouvard and Pécuchet would undertake to copy: their text was already, then, beginning to be structured.

The next step was natural and may have arisen from the effort to include the *Dictionary of Accepted Ideas* among those items the two clerks would copy. Flaubert decided to give them far more critical intelligence than they had had heretofore: they would compile the *Dictionary* themselves. It would be, he now decided, a terrifying critical encyclopedia, ironical and farcical. Idiotic quotations from all of mankind would find their place here, cited with apparent solemnity but delivering in reality a whiplash in the face of that very humanity.

A concurrent problem was finding a way to involve his pair in their various investigations. How could they be led to explore field after field? The difficulty was akin to what he had faced with Anthony. In fact the grouping of materials is by subject matter and related to the intellectual relationships of one discipline to another. But to the reader (or so Flaubert hoped), the transitions all relate to natural, not to say inevitable, decisions taken by the two men. This was the solution Flaubert discovered in 1872 when he returned to work on the book. The buying of the country place, a farm, would lead naturally to the study of agriculture. Their failures in this domain would lead them to chemistry to understand better what they were doing. Later they would be out of doors in the evening and would observe the stars: a natural curiosity would lead them to study astronomy. It also occurred to Flaubert now that it would be well to have them hated by everyone because they were different. Bouvard and Pécuchet had taken their first long step toward becoming the incarnations of their creator.

A new attack on the over-all plan brought further perfecting. Astronomy could readily be grouped, Flaubert perceived, with geology and zoology: the transitions should be easy to invent. New domains, too, began to be added, esthetics and poetics, and phrenology. Moreover, a convenient inheritance could be used to motivate the move to the country at the right moment. Such random events were of the stuff of life, like the croup of Madame Arnoux's child. Above all the two clerks were to become more like Flaubert: he would emphasize their ennobling effects upon each other. He noted that the friendship between two men was the finest thing on earth: by the very fact of their friendship, the clerks would develop a deeper ethical sense and wish to have more ideas. Flaubert and Chevalier, Flaubert and Le Poittevin, Flaubert and Du Camp, Flaubert and Bouilhet were thus insensibly displacing the two woodlice. The unresolved question was whether this sympathetic understanding would sufficiently displace Flaubert's earlier hatred and comtempt.

What the ending of the book might be, what its summary and its conclusion should contain also needed elaboration; and they too, would have to reflect the shift in Flaubert's point of view toward his protagonists. It now occurred to him that, as the labors of the two clerks to understand new subjects drew to its close, the prefect could write a letter to the local doctor: should Bouvard and Pécuchet be put into an asylum as dangerous madmen? The doctor was to reply that this was not necessary as they were not dangerous, but merely inoffensive fools. But those fools had now become Flaubert, too, and so he added that this letter from the doctor would résumé and judge the book and the two clerks would obediently copy it. It was the transposition onto the modern plane, bitter, ironic, and almost unbearable, of the ending of *Don Quixote*, when the knight himself abjured everything he had lived for. So written, the book could aspire to a place beside its predecessor.

The remaining discoveries merely expanded the list of subjects or attended to mechanical problems. Since each new experience had to end in failure for the two men, Flaubert feared the reader might come to understand the underlying method and hence anticipate the failure before it occurred. He was right to be alarmed: when the reader is no more than a quarter of the way through, he is fully aware of the method and may refuse to accept the structure. But when Flaubert came, quite late in the writing, to see that, as with *Salammbô* and to some extent *A Sentimental Education*, his basic plan was flawed, he was too far into it to pull back. It had to stand or fall as it was.

If Bouvard and Pécuchet were to investigate every field of human endeavor, then their creator would have to, also; and that would mean months and indeed years of study before he could undertake the book. What remained of 1872, all of 1873, and much of 1874 went into the task, although with interruptions.

Chemistry, medicine, agriculture, religion, philosophy: on and on and on he went. Slowly, from the very fact of the readings, the book began to take precise shape in a succession of draft plans.[3]

Roughly, each chapter would deal with one discipline: all the sciences, histories of every sort, literature, love, or education.[4] Within these tight frames Flaubert had to be adequately comprehensive while still inventing sequences the reader would find plausible. By the summer of 1874 all the various topics he wished or had to discuss had found their appropriate niche; on August 1 he set to work, almost exactly two years since he had begun his readings in August of 1872.

From the start Flaubert knew the new work was a terrifying undertaking; but it could also be a kind of total, all-embracing statement of the wisdom of a lifetime. Since every topic must appear, every idea Flaubert had could be displayed. The prospect excited as much as it frightened him. Besides, as always, work was a way not to suffer from the world about him, not to be submerged in memories of a world now dead.

When finally he could no longer put off writing, he felt he was embarking upon a long voyage into unknown regions from which he would not return. He was right; but that was still six years away. A year and a half later personal and other difficulties forced him to put the manuscript aside: it was the late spring of 1875. When he could at last summon the strength to return to it, two years had passed, and it was March of 1877. Work then proceeded uninterruptedly and—for Flaubert—relatively fast. When death put an end to his labors in May of 1880, he had nearly finished the final chapter; he expected a few months to suffice for arranging the second volume. He had almost completed the journey.

A LAST TESTAMENT

Since I intend to express a few fundamental verities in this
book, I hope in this way I will get them out of my system
and then be able to be more Olympian, a quality which I
lack absolutely at the moment.

Letter to George Sand, December 12, 1872

Bouvard and Pécuchet was always intended as satire, from the
early caricature of the copy clerk in 1837 through the collection
of mankind's idiotic ideas and statements gathered over thirty
years and on to the final plan for reviewing all ideas, knowledge,
and endeavors. But what precisely was to be satirized? Was everything that mankind did wrong? Was some of it right? If so, were
Bouvard and Pécuchet ever to be right? And could Flaubert succeed in maintaining one position in regard to all these issues, particularly when the book, like all of his, would be written over
many years and, in this case, had been thought of over decades?

For some of these matters Flaubert had clear answers, for some
his answers were hazy or contradictory, for others he had no answers at all. His shifting stances were a matter of temperament:
he was in part a satirist and found that his society, like all societies,
offered matter for his correction. But more than this, his often ill-
considered violence, his enormous rages, and his cult of exaggeration found common outlet in vitriolic explosions whose only purpose and justification were to give relief to their author. They had
no external basis in the society about him: they were not satire.
When he condemned people or customs to erasure from the face of
the earth or when he wished to drown all his contemporaries in a
huge latrine, he was expressing his own private concerns and difficulties; he was in no sense making an objective, satiric statement.
Those who knew and loved him understood and forgave him his
outbursts in their company. But when he proposed these excoria-
tions in a carefully written book, they were still no more than the
unconsidered responses of an organism long unable to stand the
pains of living. And this, for the reading public, cannot make a
book.

Unfortunately neither Flaubert's habit of violent concern nor his wide reading necessarily made for sound thinking. They could at best improve the quality of his thought, and in many cases Flaubert's friends had long found him deficient here. While they continued to love him for his other qualities, his exaggerations and intemperance did not support his conviction that, if France were governed by mandarins, he would be selected as one of them.

Madame Bovary had been great because the lyric tendencies of Flaubert's nature (which were as great in his loving as in his hating) were in check. *Salammbô* had not encouraged his readers to value highly his taste when left unbridled. And *A Sentimental Education*, however great in the minds of many readers, still left others with the gravest doubts about his capacities for analyzing and dissecting a society. There were consternation and alarm amongst his friends as word spread about his new project, for in it Flaubert the philosopher was to have his day.

The new book has been seen as *An Intellectual Education*, a counterpart to the earlier sentimental one. The sights are lowered and only the flat, the vulgar, and the ridiculous are the targets; the area, though equally broad, is on a lesser plane. Illusion will of course be the final insight, but here the protagonists will have only the illusions of the mind, which are no more than folly, where Emma, Salammbô and Mâtho, Frédéric and Madame Arnoux, even Anthony, had in some sense been ennobled by their illusions. They were the better for having had them, but no one is the better for having been a fool, above all when it happens not once but a hundred times over and always in the same way.

Bouvard and Pécuchet are as full of foolish illusions as Frédéric Moreau. As they began to contemplate having a country place, they pictured themselves in shirtsleeves pruning their roses and turning over the ground. They imagined waking to the song of the lark and rising to follow the plow. They would pick apples and watch the butter being churned or care for their beehives and listen with delight to the lowing of the cattle. They would live off the products of their own land and could do as they pleased: they would let their beards grow! The reader does not have to be a country dweller to know this will not be the reality; he begins to sneer in contempt.

Illusion is everywhere in the book: it must be, or the point is not proved. All knowledge is illusion, all human affection is illusion; reality itself (Anthony's ultimate discovery) is illusion. The reason for Flaubert's turning to *Bouvard and Pécuchet* in 1872 and not in some other year—or ever—is what it always is for any author at any time, the particular conjunction of events in his life at this moment. Only human idiocy and human illusions were then a sufficiently insistent concern to demand outlet. He saw it as a book in which he would exhale his wrath with his contemporaries for their sins. Like the ancient Hebrew prophets whom he enjoyed reading, he would let loose upon them what had been stifling him in his rage, he would vomit forth his disgust even if it shattered his own chest. The flow of his bile would be broad, copious, and bitter, he vowed; he hoped only to be able to live long enough to complete it, for it was to be his last testament, his ultimate statement and bequest to his fellow man.[5]

THE OPENING CHAPTERS

> It may turn out to be funny.
> Letter to Madame Roger des Genettes,
> September, 1873

An objective evaluation of *Bouvard and Pécuchet* is probably impossible, and every reader who has ever judged it has in the process judged himself. Moreover, although Flaubert is dead, his *Sottisier* has never been closed and, as the reader opens his mouth to offer a critique, he knows that he will be contributing new items to the collection. For, while *A Sentimental Education* has divided critical opinion in orderly and mannerly fashion, *Bouvard and Pécuchet* has divided it violently. If the world merits drowning in Flaubert's vomit (or the reader's), then one approaches this book tolerantly, forgives partial and incomplete demonstrations, and finds the exaggerations no more than artistic license: after all, Emma's death was not handled by understatement and, with the exception of Lamartine, no one has objected to that. If on the other hand the world must ultimately be understood and hence forgiven, then the reader will not allow the partial proof and must object that the argument has not been sustained and that the conclusion does not follow. Where some readers find perceptive insight and brilliant rapier play, others see prejudice, immaturity, and the clumsy maneuvering of an ungifted buffoon.

Fortunately all readers agree on the opening: it is one of Flaubert's best and raises high the hopes of each new reader, whatever his preconceptions about man and his world. *Salammbô* had opened with exotic, epic overtones: "It was in Megara, a suburb of Carthage, in the gardens of Hamilcar." In ironic contrast, *Bouvard and Pécuchet* begins instead: "Since the temperature was 91 degrees, the Boulevard Bourdon was absolutely deserted."* The tone of the bourgeois work is already established.

It is an extraordinary opening.† The stage is empty, as opposed to *Salammbô*, or *Madame Bovary* or *The Temptation* or *A Sentimental Education*. Here no one, absolutely no one, is present. Nor is the date given in this motionless, timeless world. It will not appear for fourteen pages. When it does, it is approximately 1838, only two years earlier than the opening of *A Sentimental Education;* but this work will deal with characters a whole generation older. When, eventually, the two protagonists enter, they alone then occupy the stage for most of the book, a simplification reminiscent of early Greek drama.

The Boulevard Bourdon is not far from where Flaubert had lived for so long on the Boulevard du Temple. The second paragraph locates the scene as near the Canal Saint Martin, much of

---

*"Comme il faisait une chaleur de 33 degrés, le boulevard Bourdon se trouvait absolument désert" (*BP*, p. 1).

†"Plus bas, le canal Saint-Martin, fermé par les deux écluses, étalait en ligne droite son eau couleur d'encre. Il y avait au milieu un bateau plein de bois, et sur la berge deux rangs de barriques.

"Au delà du canal, entre les maisons que séparent des chantiers, le grand ciel pur se découpait en placques d'outremer, et, sous la réverbération du soleil, les façades blanches, les toits d'ardoises, les quais de granit éblouissaient. Une rumeur confuse montait au loin dans l'atmosphère tiède; et tout semblait engourdi par le désoeuvrement du dimanche et la tristesse des jours d'été.

"Deux hommes parurent" (*BP*, p. 1).

which was covered over in 1860 when Haussman remade the face of Paris. The canal was motionless, ink colored, and dull to look upon. Beyond it the white façades under the vibrant sun dazzled the eye, and a confused noise arose through the hot, sleepy, idle atmosphere; the melancholy of a summer's day spread everywhere. The monotonous, sodden fixity of it all numbs the reader by its torpor: the bustle in the opening scene of *A Sentimental Education* would have been out of place, the sort of note one must be induced to forget, for in this novel nothing ever occurs.

The fourth paragraph of the book consists of three words: "Two men appeared." At once and steadily throughout the book Flaubert sought to differentiate them. And in fact the words are there on the page to do so—providing the reader were ever to become convinced that the protagonists are living human beings and not merely clotheshorses upon which Flaubert hung ideas. They are different; but the reader does not remember it and always refers to them in his mind as a pair. He learns as they approach a single bench that their clothes are different, their figures opposite, their faces dissimilar. What he remembers is that "when they reached the middle of the boulevard, they sat down, at the same moment, on the same bench."* The last clause, typical in its being broken into three parts, is such effective Flaubertian prose that it drowns any effort to keep them apart. Each takes off his hat, each finds the other's name written on the hatband of his neighbor, each speaks to the other of it, each discovers the other is a copy clerk, and each is delighted by the other.

Their initial conversation is one of the most successful scenes in the book. Their opinions, freely given and warmly received, come for the most part from the *Dictionary of Accepted Ideas*: they have a long road to travel before they will be able to put its items together for themselves. How nice it would be to be in the country! But the suburbs were unbearable because of the noise

---

*"L'un venait de la Bastille, l'autre du Jardin des Plantes. Le plus grand, vêtu de toile, marchait le chapeau en arrière, le gilet déboutonné et sa cravate à la main. Le plus petit, dont le corps disparaissait dans une redingote marron, baissait la tête sous une casquette à visière pointue.

"Quand ils furent arrivés au milieu du boulevard, ils s'assirent, à la même minute, sur le même banc" (*BP*, pp. 1-2).

from the bars. Still, they were tired of life in the capital. But one was even hotter on the street than in one's apartment. Women, they agreed, were frivolous, sharp tongued, stubborn. On the other hand they were often better than men, though sometimes they were worse. It was better to live without them. The two condemned the tobacco monopoly and the operations of the government offices charged with the upkeep of the roads; business and the theater, the navy, and the entire human race came within their survey and were included in their contempt.

In the teeth of this idiotic exchange Flaubert asks the reader to accept the notion that each discovered a part of himself in the other and felt that sort of expansion and tenderness which young love inspires when it is new. The pair continued for hours, and it was all the same: the reader's contempt mounts. Medicine was a glorious conquest, but how much one had to know! If only there were time! Earning a living took so many hours! At last, when Bouvard persuaded Pécuchet to walk back with him to his door, Pécuchet, agreeing, insisted that Bouvard had cast a spell over him. The spell has not included the reader, and the satire is complete, effective, and devastating. The two copy clerks are idiots and hugely entertaining.

The bond was established between Bouvard and Pécuchet. Each found the other of his own age, each was surprised, having thought the other much older; the ways of the Lord in bringing them together were inscrutable but wondrous. Their meeting, they agreed, had the importance of an adventure. The point of view, internal to Bouvard and Pécuchet and to the event, is valid; rejected by the reader, it establishes the irony.

Each of the two men had one close friend and introduced the other to him, and each found the other's friend inadequate. The union of Bouvard and Pécuchet was so solid that each agreed with the other's verdict. They took to dining together and to making excursions in their free time. At the Louvre they tried to be enthusiastic over Raphael; in the library they wanted to know the number of volumes. Bit by bit and not always foolishly, their horizons widened and they had more ideas. Wherefore, wrote Flaubert, they had more suffering. A stage coach made them long to travel; the flower market made them sigh for the country.

They were becoming like their creator, having even to give up walks in the country because the days following were so sad.

Bouvard's inheritance changed everything. Pécuchet took it for granted his friend would share it with him; and Bouvard did, too, in contrast to Frédéric's annoyance that Madame Dambreuse automatically assumed he would still want to marry her after her loss of fortune. With much searching, they found a place to live in Normandy, near Caen.

Pécuchet accompanied the baggage in a journey chaotically reminiscent of *Don Quixote*. The inns were wretched, it was cold, and rain was falling; then an axle broke, shattering the china. After nine days the wagon reached the neighborhood of the house; turning into country lanes, it came to a final halt in a plowed field. Darkness had fallen long before, and Pécuchet was hopelessly lost. Struggling to find some human habitation, he stumbled upon Bouvard . . . but then could not find his way back to the wagon. Bouvard, for his part, had got into the wrong coach in Paris, had fallen promptly asleep, and wakened only to find himself in Rouen. He had set out the next morning and arrived just in time to meet Pécuchet. Flaubert's account was like Emma Bovary's move from Tostes to Yonville, but this time it rode on unbridled exaggeration and reached the proportions of Cervantes's epic farce which had enchanted the boy Gustave.

After a warm dinner and a quick visit to the garden, the two men fell asleep for their first night in their own home. In the morning they discovered that everything was in dreadful condition and the land almost beyond hope of saving. But soon Bouvard, the lecherous one of the two, planted tomatoes, at that date still thought to be aphrodisiacs; Pécuchet, his feet more solidly on the earth, began a compost pile, gathering manure from the road to enrich it.

The comedy is obvious, the satire evident and entertaining. Bouvard and Pécuchet visited a neighboring farm, where everything prospered. Later, when the owner is satirized as a fool, the reader understands that even in Flaubert's world almost anyone can run a farm: only the consummate and total folly of this pair prevented them from succeeding. The world is solid enough and adequate: the fault lies with the two clerks. And they are very funny.

Springtime, the salvation and temptation of many an amateur gardener, makes a certain number of plants come up inevitably for them. Supposing therefore that they have especial gifts, the two decide to farm their own lands. The pattern, to be followed throughout the book, now begins to be set out. For silly reasons they undertake an enterprise; then they turn to their books and read about it, spending money like the fools they are. Soon they discover on the one hand that it is not that easy after all and that, more confusing to them than to the reader, their books are in conflict. The reader who is a gardener or a farmer will respond that there are good books on these subjects and bad books, and that only a fool believes that something is so because he has read it in a book. But the issue seemed a serious one to Flaubert, and he raised it anew with each topic they investigated.

Soon, of course, Bouvard and Pécuchet were driving their farmer out of his mind. The comic elements surrounding the city man who goes to the country to tell countryfolk how to live are quite familiar, and the reader, of course, chuckles as Flaubert has his pair make all the inevitable, ludicrous errors. The details may be a bit complex for the city dweller to follow, but he easily understands the general situation and is happily occupied in laughing. When Pécuchet abandoned farming for gardening, the reader expects him to ruin everything he touches and laughs gleefully as it works out that way. But the pages turn more and more slowly for the reader as the procedure becomes more and more predictable. Forty pages into the book the whole system is so obvious that there is some question about the wisdom of reading further.

As the farm-and-garden episode is drawing to a close, the two fools draw a foolish conclusion: each situation in a garden or farm is uniquely individual and dependent upon a unique combination of factors. Hence there can be no rules, and the effort is foredoomed. Many readers, however, have succeeded in raising lettuce or radishes, pansies or daffodils, and know that the feat can be accomplished. That Bouvard and Pécuchet were unable to do so is their ill luck and may make them uninteresting; but it never occurs to the reader to suppose they have discovered a law of the universe. In the first place, of course, they are wrong, as the rows of lettuce and radishes or the beds of pansies and daffodils exultantly proclaim to any gardener and his friends. In the second place, if it were true, Bouvard and Pécuchet knew so little and were so inherently naïve and stupid that their experiences validate no conclusions whatsoever, except concerning naïve fools. The reader may notice with alarm that he has completed only part of the second out of ten chapters.

The Method Collapses

> Since the two heroes are limited and stupid . . . , their disillusionment and misadventures are necessarily flat; the reader comes to expect them and does not find them interesting. It is like watching two snails climb Mont Blanc: the first time they fall, you smile; the tenth time it is unbearable. Such a subject could hardly be carried out to a hundred pages at the most.
>
> Letter from Taine to Turgenev on reading the first chapters of *Bouvard and Pécuchet*

Once the reader has become aware that a system is at work, he understands that Flaubert is no longer attempting to portray honestly. The reader then balks, just as Flaubert himself had all through his youth, when he used to complain that authors like Chateaubriand falsified their writing by their preconceptions. Chateaubriand's stemmed from his Christianity and Flaubert's from his pessimism, but both were preconceptions and either was ruinous to a work if the reader did not share it.

The two clerks now began an unbroken succession of errors. Having landscaped their garden in hideous fashion, they felt the need to show it off by giving a formal dinner, a clever transition to introduce a number of characters who people the background of the story. The dinner was of course a catastrophe. In the next episode, the two undertook to make their own preserves: everything spoiled or exploded. The reader, however, knows that many rather simple-minded kitchen maids have long since mastered serving a dinner or preserving foods. If Bouvard and Pécuchet—or Flaubert—were unable to, that is another matter, but not an important one. The two turned to the study of chemistry; at once they were confused. They discovered that simple bodies are perhaps compound and that the differences between acids and bases are not as clear as Flaubert would have wished. Even the unscientifically minded reader has by now lost confidence in his guides and takes it for granted that there is an explanation for the alleged hurdles, even though it may lie beyond the reader's competence. Bouvard and Pécuchet canvassed the other major branches of science and failed at all of them and were again irritated when their authorities did not agree.

As Flaubert thus summarily dismisses one area of learning after another, the reader would undoubtedly put the volume down, were there not other aspects to hold his attention. Even in these rather arid chapters, written before Flaubert himself set the manuscript aside in 1875, these others are present, albeit infrequent and never loud. They are why the reader continues the book.

There is an occasional deepening of the tone as Bouvard and Pécuchet learn more and hence begin to ask more searching questions concerning the aim of the universe. Bouvard even suggests that perhaps there is none; Pécuchet for the moment must content himself with muttered demurrers. The reader, rightly, hopes for more in this vein as the two clerks develop; and he reads on.

There is also a frequent comic note in these pages. Flaubert's sense of humor was never delicate, but where laying about with a heavy club was appropriate his blows were as stout as the next man's. His pair was amazed that fish should have fins and birds wings, and geology pleased the priest by confirming the Deluge. A terrified Bouvard dashed off looking like a winged turtle. If this is not wit, at least one may chuckle. And such moments help to carry the reader over pages where Flaubert explains the relative merits of the Plutonian or Neptunian theories on the origin of the world or objects to fancied difficulties in geologic nomenclature.

When the reader, however, is about to give the clerks up as too uninteresting for further pursuit, Flaubert recounts Pécuchet's sudden awareness of the universe all about him as, for the first time, he looked closely at it and experienced that pantheistic peace which Flaubert had known in his younger days before he had come to hate nature. A border* of moss marked the edge of the hollowed road; it was shaded by ash trees, whose summits swayed gently; scented flowers and shrubs perfumed the heavy air. Pécuchet, his intelligence dulled, meditated idly on the countless existences about him, the buzzing insects, the springs hidden beneath the grasses, all of nature. No longer seeking to pry out her mysteries, he was instead satisfied to be enchanted by her strength and lost in her grandeur. The prose is a return to the Flaubert of the great novels as the concept rejoins *Saint Anthony*.

THE READER RESIGNS HIMSELF

> People don't like literature.
>> Bouvard and Pécuchet's summary of their investigations
>> into literary criticism

Bouvard and Pécuchet is not a novel, and it is unfortunate that the reader keeps hoping that it will be, for it was never Flaubert's intention that it should be read as one. It is not supposed to entertain but rather to improve the reader. Eventually he resigns himself, understanding that there will be enough worth in it and enough humorous episodes so that he had better not put the book down, tempted though he may be in the arid stretches.

The fourth chapter treats of history, the fifth of literature. Flaubert, who had written so casually in the 1840's that before

---

*"Une lisière de mousse bordait un chemin creux, ombragé par des frênes, dont les cimes légères tremblaient; des angéliques, des menthes, des lavandes exhalaient des senteurs chaudes, épicées; l'atmosphère était lourde; et Pécuchet, dans une sorte d'abrutissement, rêvait aux existences innombrables éparses autour de lui, aux insectes qui bourdonnaient, aux sources cachées sous le gazon, à la sève des plantes, aux oiseaux dans leurs nids, au vent, aux nuages, à toute la nature, sans chercher à découvrir ses mystères, séduit par sa force, perdu dans sa grandeur" (*BP*, p. 119).

undertaking a historical novel the author must know all the facts, now demonstrates that, since this is impossible, historical fiction cannot be written. But the reader discounts the statement: after all, Flaubert had written *Salammbô* and, in the interim period while he was not working at *Bouvard and Pécuchet*, he wrote two more pieces of historical fiction. Manifestly he himself had some sort of resolution of the problem, even if he was not telling it in these pages. The paradox is, however, ingenious; and the reader has ceased to take Flaubert seriously and hence to argue with him.

Many other passages are entertaining. Topics fly by, which makes each one easier to read. Transitions are more cavalierly treated: seeing an old soup bowl is now enough to change the interest of the pair to old pottery. The earlier uniformity of their stupidity is now relieved by dialogue and dispute as Bouvard and Pécuchet take opposite sides. Their chaotic doubt becomes amusing: finally they have not a single solid idea left.

Alternatively, the two clerks sometimes express interesting insights. When Flaubert suggests how different our view of Julius Caesar would be if we read, not his *Commentaries on the Gallic War*, but those of his opponent Vercingetorix, the reader may pause for a moment's thought: a familiar point has been well put. When Bouvard and Pécuchet turn to literature, a commentary on Walter Scott phrases the enchantment that the romantics always found in him, and a rejoinder defines the revolt of Flaubert's generation: Scott's effects are artificial and repetitious; there are too many dialogues; and his prudery is unbearable.

Bouvard liked the novels of George Sand. Pécuchet read them and was delighted that each presented a thesis, but Bouvard condemned the practice. Then, after a brief interest in the theater, the two turned to Balzac. Their initial pleasure soured as he came to seem exaggerated and fantastic. But it is disturbing to the conventional reader that novels which it would fill much of an entire lifetime to read, Bouvard and Pécuchet crowd into no more than a few months. Verisimilitude, that ideal truth of art which Flaubert earlier sought with so much care, he here abandoned entirely in order to make room for developing directly the truth with which he was so passionately concerned and which somehow neither *A Sentimental Education* nor *The Temptation of Saint Anthony* seemed to him to have phrased adequately: all of life is an illusion, no part of it will withstand examination. He now insisted on being allowed to state this directly and fully, unhindered by any of the normal restrictions of the novel.

There is one privileged exception to this universal illusion. It is never discussed at length by Bouvard or Pécuchet, but it is not argued away, either. It arose, for instance, when the two clerks read Hugo's *Hernani* aloud, as Flaubert had so many years before to Harriet Collier: they were as deeply moved as he had been. Then Flaubert added in his own name that art has power to move even mediocre people like them. Art, then, is not illusion and withstands the onslaught of universal doubt as, a generation later in Proust, it will withstand the erosion of time.

Grammar, style, and esthetics Bouvard and Pécuchet rapidly swallowed and rejected: all are nonsense and illusion. Often the contradictions Flaubert displayed he put most amusingly; often Bouvard and Pécuchet amaze by their erudition. They are not characters with the normal prerogatives and limitations of such beings: they are Flaubert and his readings, Flaubert and his hates. Unbound by time or space, intelligence or wealth, in their short span of freedom they live and above all read most of what Flaubert had been able to encompass. And they exemplify or excoriate what he hated and the folly and downright silliness he thought he saw about him. *Bouvard and Pécuchet* is not an encyclopedia, despite Flaubert's claims, for that would imply some criterion of objectivity. It is instead akin to the final pages of *Madame Bovary*, which pillory Homais and Bournisien, the bourgeoisie and the Church, those perennial hates of Flaubert's. And *Bouvard and Pécuchet* is as good or as bad as those pages, but this time there are four hundred of them.

The book also returns to a number of Flaubert's earlier topics, the Revolution of 1848 among others. Although he had had no new ideas concerning it, he decided to treat it again here. The Socialists were still vile tyrants, the Conservatives equally dreadful, the masses unimaginable, and universal suffrage hideous. The only marked change in Flaubert was, perhaps, that his disgust with the Conservatives had been nourished by watching their mismanagement of the new Third Republic. This was not enough, however, to justify a return to the old material; but his consuming hatreds had burned away his critical sense. The reader familiar with *A Sentimental Education* moves here with leaden feet.

The seventh chapter deals with love and restores confidence in Flaubert: it is very funny. Pécuchet, a virgin, fell in love with their serving girl. He did her work for her, even getting up early to clean Bouvard's shoes. His reward was a painful bout with venereal disease. Meanwhile Bouvard, rather beyond such things in years, courted a widow who coquettishly accepted his advances in the hope of getting some of his land from him. He discovered this the day Pécuchet found he could no longer walk without discomfort: the conversation between the two is in the long tradition of such broad farce. There is a good deal more to love than this, as the creator of Emma, Salammbô, and Madame Arnoux had once known; but this satire is at least entertaining. Also—and it is a great relief—the chapter does contain some action. Bouilhet, dramatist that he was, might have barred Flaubert from writing so many of the preceding pages, which are blurred into dullness for lack of any relieving action.

Chapter Eight is rather hard on the reader: it treats of nonsensical, cultish beliefs. It starts humorously enough with gymnastics. But then Bouvard heard of table-tipping, a popular pastime in France around the middle of the century. This sets off a review of such beliefs. And there are so many of them: hypnosis, spiritualism, magic, the divining rod, before at long last the clerks turned their attention to philosophy. Moreover, Flaubert's position becomes almost impossible to determine, for over and over these cults produced the desired effects: the reader is asked to believe that the silliest forms of divination prove successful here far beyond the play of normal coincidence. Who is deceiving whom about what? Bouvard and Pécuchet believed all this nonsense. But they also believed that great literature exists and can move even mediocre people. Flaubert believed in literature; did he believe in table-tipping? If his demonstration that the accepted verities are illusory has any validity and meaning, then conversely the demonstration that accepted illusions are truthful has the same validity . . . or lack of it.

The two clerks turned next to philosophy. They were proud

of themselves and contemptuous of their earlier studies. But—and one foresees it—here, too, they found only confusion and disagreement. Their conclusion was that philosophy consists of explaining what one understands almost not at all, by means of words which one understands absolutely not at all. Voltaire was more concise when he divided metaphysics into what everyone has always known and what no one will ever know.

Rather suddenly and not entirely satisfactorily, *Bouvard and Pécuchet* turns serious. Bouvard, like Anthony and Flaubert himself, came to doubt even the existence of matter and held that the certainty that nothing exists (however sad that may be) is at any rate something certain; few people, he added, are capable of such austerity. But this transcendental attitude made them proud of themselves; it led also to their sad decision to commit suicide. Lest we take them seriously for too long, however, Flaubert intervened to have them desist. Their reason: they had not yet written their wills.

As contempt displaces respect, the reader returns to firmer ground, only to be baffled again as the two, almost by chance, attended the midnight services on Christmas Eve in their local church. The nave, the lights, the crowd of the faithful, the priest, and the service all combined with the warm atmosphere to bring them a strange feeling of peace, perhaps the only one they ever knew. It was Flaubert in the Breton churches watching the peasant or sailor kneel and find solace. In spite of themselves they were touched. They joined in the singing, moved as though by a new dawn.

A confused reader moves into Chapter Nine, not quite sure who is to be considered idiotic: the two clerks, Flaubert, or himself. But at any rate Bouvard and Pécuchet have had a religious experience. Flaubert himself was acutely aware this would be a difficult chapter to write, for it was to treat of orthodox religion, and he wished to give both the religious and the philosophical point of view with equal force. It is not entirely clear why he considered this wise.

If the reader were, like his clerks, the victim of illusion, then Flaubert may have thought the reader would assume the mandarin author had the truth. In that case the reader would learn that religion and philosophy are equipoised. But literature is not life and can never have more validity than the insights, conscious and unconscious, of its creator, which it imposes by esthetic and not by magisterial means. Flaubert's insight would appear to be, once again, that there are no insights and all is illusion. Moreover, all illusions, including religion and philosophy, are equally valid and equally foolish. If this be his point, what then did Bouvard and Pécuchet experience on Christmas Eve? The literary problems which would later be called point of view are so badly resolved here that the reader moves forward hopelessly confused. Are the clerks wise or foolish in Flaubert's mind? And whichever he thinks, is he wise or foolish? The reader may not be convinced that this confusion is worth his time, even after the experience of the contemporary novel based on confusion.

The chapter seems to lack coherence. As with literature, Bouvard and Pécuchet constantly brushed against what seemed to be firm truths like the earlier assumption that *Hernani* is good, but this did not shake the invincible conviction of Flaubert that all was illusion. Many beautiful things are said of the Gospels and of Christ, who displays heaven and seems to require nothing theological of the believer, nothing in fact except a pure heart. The two men came to understand that only this purity and simplicity were required of them if they would find peace. Without trouble, they o'erleaped the hurdles miracles might otherwise be to a rationalist and seem well on the way to some sort of solid discovery.

A gnawing doubt may assail the reader: how can these two possibly be right about anything? Fortunately they will not long even appear to be so. They became the protégés of the nearby count, of course a devout man and of course an idiot. Then they exaggerated their virtues and turned to the buying of shoddy religious art from a broker like Jacques Arnoux at the end of his life. Soon they were overwhelmed by the commercialism of modern religion. Not even their first communion seemed to them as meaningful as they had hoped. Apparently, then, the dream is always superior to the reality, and Flaubert's last book says only what he had already said in *A Sentimental Education* and *The Temptation of Saint Anthony.* But in those works he had spoken clearly. Here, the reader may say it, if that is his pleasure; but Flaubert does not say it unequivocally, and the reader need not read the book to make his own private assertion. He remains confused.

An effort by Pécuchet to find the truth by quizzing the abbé Jeufroy is ridiculous and futile. The reader, conscious of the mechanism, supposes in advance that it will be so. And Pécuchet adopted what the informed reader knows is Flaubert's own view, that all religions have much that is useful, good, and venerable. But the reader who is not informed of Flaubert's private view cannot divine that this is supposed to be any more true than the midnight service on Christmas Eve, devoted to one and only one religion. While one does recognize the arguments already offered in *Saint Anthony,* such repetition is in itself dubious and a poor substitute for a reliable point of view.

The chapter seems about to close on Pécuchet's assertion that he would become a Buddhist, when he and Bouvard returned home to discover their servant on his knees in ecstasy, praying. Bouvard called the servant a fool; but Pécuchet reminded him that this simple man was perhaps perceiving things they would give anything to see if they but knew how. The object of devotion was not so important as the devotion itself, for the essential thing was to be able to believe. And very quietly Flaubert closed the chapter: "Such were Pécuchet's objections to the remark of Bouvard." The episode and final comment seem honest enough and sufficiently reliable. But then what do the many, preceding pages signify?

The final chapter, the tenth, on education, helps but little. It is not a very good chapter, as the two clerks undertake to bring up a young boy and girl; and it becomes unbearably repetitious of earlier moments, despite a number of broadly comic moments, such as a very funny description of two peacocks making love. Gradually everything collapsed about Bouvard and Pécuchet, who were deprived of the children, hated by their neighbors, and suspected of dangerous madness by the authorities; they withdrew from all their pretensions and turned to copying as the chapter closes and the first volume ends.

The Second Volume

> . . . the second volume, already three-quarters done . . .
> Letter to Georges Charpentier, May, 1879

Flaubert did not live to finish putting the second volume in order and preparing it for the printer, but over and over he reiterated that the manuscript was nearly complete and would require only a few more months, four to eight at the most.[6] Hence, of course, the work must have been nearly ready in his papers. And it was. But what he intended is so incredible a misjudgment of what the reading public would accept, even from a mandarin, that critics have long refused to recognize the obvious fact: Bouvard and Pécuchet, after some random copying of whatever fell into their hands, were to copy Flaubert's *Sottisier*, page after stupid page of the silly errors people make when they become infatuated with the flow of their own words and allow sense to slip from their grasp. "May the Provisional Government last forever!" is an adequate sample. As a single example, this may amuse; reduplicated for hundreds of pages such stupidity is not readable. But the documents for Volume Two all exist still in Rouen: Flaubert and Duplan had been gathering them for years. Moreover Flaubert had endlessly made use of friends' time to copy material for him because it left him free to hunt for further idiocies: he had only to mark the margin. Not all of this foolishness now in Rouen could possibly have gone into one volume, but even supposing the best were selected, the work would have remained unreadable. It is as well that death put an end to matters before a publisher had to refuse the volume.

After random notes copied without regard to content, the two clerks were to pass to résumés of works already read, a device Flaubert had already used far too much in the text itself. It served well enough to bring out the errors which intrigued him, but it makes very dull reading. Next the copyists were to have a crisis and feel the need to classify what they were copying, a sort of recapitulation of what their author had done with the material.

They would then choose, as Flaubert had before them, idiotic passages of purple prose; or they would compare records of ugly crimes committed by proletarians with crimes committed by kings, or contrast the benefits of religion to its crimes. Then they were to put together the *Dictionary of Accepted Ideas*. They were also to take to adding footnotes of their own to what they copied. Perhaps they would even have copied a few short stories to leaven the loaf, the *Night of Don Juan* among them. And, of course, they could readily have pillaged their own remarks in *Bouvard and Pécuchet*, not to mention all of Flaubert's earlier works, for he had often used the *Dictionary of Accepted Ideas* and had made a few silly mistakes himself, as he well knew.

It would have been a game of a ghastly, grisly sort. Flaubert would have enjoyed it, and so would some of his friends. But it is doubtful that many readers would have, for long. Numerous pages here and there would have appealed even to readers less totally contemptuous than he; and some readers have always been found who share Flaubert's nausea. But for the most part, his testament is more acceptable if this is not its phrasing.

THE CHARACTERS

> One day we were talking about names, and I said I had found a wonderful one, Bouvard, for the novel I was working on. Flaubert's face took on a strange expression. He drew me aside and, overcome with emotion, begged me to leave this name of Bouvard to him. I laughed and assured him he was welcome to it. But he remained serious and very much touched; and he kept repeating that he would not have continued with his book if I had kept the name. For him the whole work was incarnated in those two names, Bouvard and Pécuchet. Without them he could no longer imagine it.
>
> Emile Zola in *The Naturalistic Novelists*

The sound of the name Bouvard recalls Bovary, as the Touache family from the former novel recalls the Tuvache of the latter and as the various Maries and Marias re-echo through Flaubert's novels. But there is a change here in the characters, for they are now more abstract. Bouvard and Pécuchet do not live as did Emma or Frédéric; they exist in order that beings who can think and speak (and so be written about) may move through positions calculated to bring out certain responses in them and thereby prove a thesis. Without the thesis, they would not live, whereas Emma lived and wept in twenty villages, as Flaubert had observed. Toward the end of the book, but even there only at intervals, the pair does occasionally move the reader to that spontaneous sympathy which full-fledged characters so easily evoke; but for the most part they are only puppets mechanically pushed from disaster to disaster by the playmaster who created them for this and for this alone. In contrast with *Candide*, a vacuum seems to surround Flaubert's protagonists.

The last version of *Saint Anthony* had already begun the trend away from individuals and toward types as the starting point for the creation of a character. Anthony was to be the desert hermit of the fourth century, a type, not an individual. And he never acquired the individuality of an Emma, a Charles, or a Mâtho. Bouvard and Pécuchet pushed further. Their interchangeability suggests the nature of the difficulty, in contrast to Flaubert's differentiation of Henry and Jules or Frédéric and Deslauriers. Flaubert had been wont to hold that the novelist must start with the individual and move to the type. He had begun with real people and moved to characters: Elisa to Madame Arnoux, Maurice to Jacques Arnoux, or Louise Colet, Ludovica, and others to Emma Bovary. Then the fictional character, individualized in his own right, could be raised to the level of a type, Emma as modern woman, Frédéric as modern man. In *Anthony* somewhat, and throughout *Bouvard and Pécuchet*, the type is the starting point and never does become individualized.

The substitution of types for individuals as characters offers the reader the contemplation not of humans but of abstractions or categories. Of course, then, any event subsumed in that category may occur to the protagonist. And this had been the case with *Saint Anthony*. He was to have a difficult night, and it would go on as long as the author cared to prolong it. Flaubert might take pains—he did in fact—to establish some sort of psychological motivation for each new episode in *Bouvard and Pécuchet*. But there was no inherent necessity in any of them: any one could have been dropped at will, or more might be added. It would make no esthetic difference. Emma, on the other hand, without a platonic phase with Leon, would have been a different woman and would have had a fate at least somewhat different, for she is a true character and hence is, like a living person, in some measure the sum of the experiences she has had. It is a necessary function of Bouvard and Pécuchet that they not be formed by what occurs to them and not be the sum of their experiences in any sense. Further chapters could easily be added—the two men do not explore games, for instance—and each reader will have his own choice of chapters which might have been left out; but in neither case would the artistic unity of the book be affected.

The same dehumanizing, but carried still further, affects the secondary characters in *Bouvard and Pécuchet*. They must not infringe upon the drawing power of the two clerks, who are constantly to absorb our principal attention; hence the secondary characters have almost no individual existence of their own. We have met them all before, and they could all be exchanged for their peers with no change whatsoever. They have roles rather than personalities: the individuality of the girl who gives Pécuchet his venereal disease is not significant.

This abstract quality in the two clerks does not easily accommodate that affection Flaubert always came ultimately to feel for his characters and the ensuing desire he had to endow them with his own habits, manias, and philosophy. He was truculently an individual and his traits, always strongly marked, blend ill with these figurines. In his earlier novels only his intimates would have known the secret pleasure he was taking in having a character live and act as he had. Men do court women by lamplight; hence only those who knew the circumstances surrounding Flaubert's first night with Louise Colet could recognize its recurrence in *A Sentimental Education* or identify it again when Bouvard courted Madame Bordin. Similarly, few readers could identify Flaubert's own first sketch for *A Sentimental Education* in the words phrasing the plot of a novel Bouvard and Pécuchet considered writing about "a woman, her husband, and her lover." This much is harmless. The clerks' capacity for suffering, however, which grows with each succeeding acquisition of knowledge, is understandable in Flaubert but strange in two such insensitive beings as these. Each found the other's manias exasperating. Pécuchet could be bothered by the song of a rooster; the scent of roses nauseated him. Like his creator, he hated the countryside.

Flaubert also consciously gave his clerks many of his cherished insights and beliefs.[7] They acquired his own driving passion for truth in itself. A character who had this need would pursue it (or tragically fail to do so). But these are only marionettes: when the need had been stated, it was enough, and they could then be diverted to other concerns. Bouvard and Pécuchet, even when incarnating Flaubert, did not long endure under the burden. Momentarily they might yearn for horses and carriages, great wines and beautiful, complaisant women, or philosophic knowledge. But these are no Frédéric Moreau, and we have not come to know them to learn the consequences of harboring these illusions. The fantasies enter, pirouette a moment, and leave the stage at once, another set of illusions just like all the rest. Nor can more lasting insights, sensitivities, or convictions properly move us in such people. Flaubert had forgotten his own precept that literature is neither science nor religion nor philosophy: it cannot prove anything.[8] Only by its characters may it convince. But the breath of life is not in this work: in its place mannekins act out Flaubert's all-encompassing contempts.

Some novels are at the very center of a man's life: *Madame Bovary* was such a work. Others represent their author's outer limit, that place where his reach ends or his view is about to be extinguished: *Bouvard and Pécuchet* was this sort of work, proclaiming that Flaubert could extend his grasp no further, could identify no landmarks beyond, for all was slippery, unsure, and unknowable. The reader's problem is to measure his grasp against that of Flaubert, his eye against his; and this is not necessarily a wise wager for Flaubert to have set. It takes a Marcel Proust to match himself, nothing daunted, against a Flaubert as novelist. But as thinkers, may not many men enter the lists against him? Flaubert, a self-proclaimed mandarin, had no doubts concerning his powers; one remembers Socrates did.

Flaubert had hoped, in early manhood, that art and science would one day meet at the summit. Of art he always felt sure, and his faith in science had been, like that of his age, boundless. But as the years had gone by, somehow his high hopes had not been fulfilled: the truth had not been attained, and neither science nor its larger context, knowledge, seemed to have brought happiness. Montaigne could have told him all of this, had Flaubert but listened. But now Renan and many of the other leading thinkers of the generation were themselves coming to skepticism as the only safe position. Flaubert joined them; however, with him, skepticism had to become total. Hence his denial of reality and his imperious need to proclaim this in a work whose realistic trappings were slight and whose import was allegorical: knowledge is unsure, art is elusive, and they will never meet at the summit of that pyramid. Humanity had been judged and condemned to futility. Flaubert, who used to withhold judgment, saw no reason to withhold the verdict that nothing could be judged, for nothing existed.

A Sentimental Education had proclaimed the dream always superior to action. *The Temptation* had passed all religion, knowledge, and even existence in review and found them all transitory illusions. *Bouvard and Pécuchet* repeated the indictment. But is the demonstration convincing? In *Candide*, Voltaire made fun of error, but not of reason: the falsity of Pangloss' foolishness may be known. In *Bouvard and Pécuchet*, nothing may be known, not even the falsity of error. But because Bouvard and Pécuchet are too limited to be able to cultivate their gardens, must one assume that Candide could not cultivate his?[9]

Flaubert would have held his clerks' sin was that they drew conclusions. No one should, ever: not even God does. But the clerks conclude stupidly, and hence irrelevantly for the reader, who declines to assume he is that stupid. If they cannot find answers, other characters even in this book do, their neighboring nobleman-farmer, for instance. Later they considered presenting themselves for election to the post of deputy: Flaubert's notes show he thought they would make good deputies because they had read widely. Then, apparently, people who would make good deputies do exist. The failure of Bouvard and Pécuchet to win election was to demonstrate the stupidity of the masses. Now the reader, aghast, wonders how Flaubert ever thought these idiots, incapable usually of the most elementary successes, could possibly manage the affairs of others: as mandarins, they are even less adequate than their creator.

Bouvard and Pécuchet do not become reliable witnesses for the reader. It was a problem Flaubert had long been carelessly ignoring. They quite often interlard their idiocy with Flaubert's cherished doctrines, but the reader declines to accept them on their own authority. He is forced into an unwelcome choice: he must reject either the world or his guide. Readers have been found painfully skewered on each horn of the dilemma.

The Comic

The sense of the comic is Virtue's only consolation!
Letter to George Sand, April 8, 1874

Flaubert envisaged *Bouvard and Pécuchet* as based upon the comic view of life, which he had long held to be the highest. By making the entire work comic, he would make it all palatable. And, had he been successful, perhaps it would have passed muster. After all, one does not ask of *A Midsummer Night's Dream* whether Bottom the Weaver could logically be believed to have the head of an ass. If the comic view had adequately buttressed *Bouvard and Pécuchet*, it might perhaps have suppressed corresponding questions about his two heroes.

The present form of the work is not what Flaubert would have published, and it has been urged that he would have considerably reworked the manuscript, if he had lived to see it through to the printed form. This is most doubtful. Once his other works had reached this stage—a clear copy in his own hand—minor deletions and a few clarifications were the only changes he normally made; his books were always too tightly constructed and linked paragraph by paragraph for more to be possible. Hence the manuscript may be considered to contain the essential of the comic view he would have published.[10]

Flaubert knew he might drown in his attempt; but he was more attracted by the notion that, if he succeeded, the earth would not be big enough to bear him. In the chapter on the sciences, he sought, and believed he had obtained, the comedy of ideas, for he found all exceptions irresistibly comic disproofs of the possibility of science rather than indications of domains requiring further investigation. The reader is thus forced to the conclusion that Flaubert's ideas of science, especially the meaning of classification and the use of hypotheses, were learned but inept. Too much of the book is based upon this, and the only comic element is his arrogant fury at the efforts of his scientific friends to explain matters to him.

Flaubert's sense of the comic had never been more than jejune. Le Garçon had been an adequate—or pardonable—creation of adolescents; but to continue to rejoice in him on into manhood betrayed a failure to develop that more delicate sense of the comic which marks maturity. This lack had ruined his *Castle of Hearts* and damaged other works as well. When it failed him in *Bouvard and Pécuchet*, whole scenes fell to pieces. And he constantly counted upon it. Maupassant, who enjoyed Flaubert's sense of the comic, found the work imbued with a special, sinister comedy, as all those beliefs paraded through the brains of these idiots who personify humanity.[11] Like most judgments of *Bouvard and Pécuchet*, it reveals as much about the critic as it does about the novel.

There are, to be sure, many funny pages. Pécuchet trying unavailingly to find the Big Dipper or both men delighting to learn that the seat of taste is the tongue and the sensation of hunger arises in the stomach are securely comic in ways Flaubert no doubt borrowed consciously from Molière. Tradition helps, too, when Pécuchet planted a dunce's cap—in France they have long ears—on his pupil for his stupidity and trapped himself, as the boy began to bray so loud and long the cap had to be removed.

Whole scenes may indulge in a sort of raucous comedy out of Molière or Cervantes. Bouvard, attracted anew to the widowed Madame Bordin as he watched her hang her laundry, sat beside her lustfully admiring the rise and fall of her bosom as she caught her breath. Leaning his head against her knee, he took her hands. The wind blew the freshly hung sheets aside and displayed two peacocks making love: Madame Bordin, much affected, was about to consent to marry Bouvard. Suddenly she discovered to her consternation that the clerks' young charge had been watching their attentiveness to the peacocks and Bouvard's caresses. At this moment the farm horse broke loose from his tether and galloped about the barnyard. The laundry line snapped, the horse entangled himself in it, and the laundry was dragged through the mire. Everyone rushed about in a madcap scene recalling Cervantes and foreshadowing Snopes' mules in Faulkner. The horse was beaten, and Madame Bordin was furious over the recollection of her compromised position. Flaubert had returned to *Don Quixote*, the book which, as a child, had sent him off in pursuit of literature. But there are not enough of these scenes for the work to depend upon them for its support.

PORTRAIT OF THE ARTIST AS AN OLD MAN

> The difficulty in a subject like this is to keep varying the phrasing. If I succeed, it will be—and I am speaking seriously—the peak of Art.
>
> Letter to his niece Caroline,
> October 15, 1874

Bouvard and Pécuchet will never be everyone's dish; yet it contains moments which many will always relish. In addition to the comic episodes, on a number of occasions Flaubert fell back upon redoing scenes or motifs which had already proved their worth in his earlier writing. Molière's repeated use of his own young lovers or Balzac's reuse of his courtesans are similar: every older writer tends naturally to borrow from himself. When Bouvard was still hopeful of winning Madame Bordin, the pair went for a walk in the woods. The sun,* which had been hidden, reappeared and set the leaves to shining; it cast luminous spots here and there in the tangled thickets. Three sparrows were uttering their little cries and hopping about on the fallen trunk of an old linden tree. A thorn bush in bloom spread out its pink blossoms, and the heavy lilacs bent toward the ground. The reader, recalling *Madame Bovary*, is on familiar ground of which he is fond.

The standard devices of any experienced professional writer help to sustain Flaubert when he starts to falter. It helps even a less-than-great passage when its author has had the long and varied practice which only age can give. When Bouvard fainted on learning of his inheritance, short, staccato clauses phrased the bustle about the prone body. The close observation of the way light flowed out from lamps dramatized dull occurrences. The mazes of long and involved sentences Flaubert threaded with sure tread. The interplay among the free indirect discourse and the classical indirect and direct discourses allowed nuances of reporting in even tedious matters.

Defects present in earlier works also recur here, and some are more marked. Pronoun references are sometimes unclear; and even the pronouns themselves are omitted in an unfortunate sort of telegraphic style occasionally. The easy sequence of events unhindered by the author's presence wavers at intervals, and a stable point of view becomes blurred. Pedantry, which Flaubert had skirted in *Salammbô* and *Saint Anthony*, here harms many pages as he gives his readers lessons including long quotations and even page references.

As the planning of the book drew to its close and the writing began in 1874, Flaubert had grave doubts: was the basic concept of the book false? Turgenev, like Taine, assured him that he must work quickly and lightly. As the months and then the years passed, he continued to feel that he could not, for that would be to turn the work into a fantasy. Which was only to say that his

---

*"Le soleil avait reparu, faisait luire les feuilles, jetait des taches lumineuses dans les fourrés, ça et là. Trois moineaux avec de petits cris sautillaient sur le tronc d'un vieux tilleul abattu. Une épine en fleurs étalait sa gerbe rose, les lilas alourdis se penchaient" (*BP*, p. 175).

touch never had been light and could not now become so. He feared that anything less than a massive, overwhelming blow would fail of its effect. By moving slowly and by going into details, he would end by seeming to believe in his story and so would make his reader take it seriously, even be frightened by it. Moreover, he said erroneously, he was incapable of doing a short work.

Perhaps no one has ever phrased better what was wrong with his book than Flaubert himself when he said he knew his two heroes were not interesting. But they had to be the way there were, he added. His work was like a filing cabinet with drawers, which was bad enough; but in addition there were too many drawers. The defect was inherent in the subject, he insisted: he had sought to mask it, not to suppress it, for the work itself would have gone in the attempt.

With *Madame Bovary*, Flaubert had broken ground for a new type of novel. *Salammbô*, *A Sentimental Education*, and *The Temptation* had been similar new attempts; and any further works of his must necessarily also be new in form, for form and content were one. If *Salammbô* launched a new historical novel and *Saint Anthony* perhaps a new dramatic one, *Bouvard and Pécuchet* was to launch still another. What he had done, he knew had no name in any language; and he could not keep his reader from picking up his work and calling it a novel. But could it not at least be called a philosophical novel? It was to be his testament, he repeated, the sum of his experiences and his judgment on man and his works. It did not succeed; indeed to many readers it has seemed unreadable, or nearly so. But in attempting to give form to the philosophical novel, it was useful, illuminating, and to Flaubert necessary.

He had anatomized—at the philosophical, not the psychological, level—how two copy clerks investigated human folly, withdrew to record it, and found themselves, despite their intent, forced to give it order and to align their observations so that they would become meaningful. They had become creators in their own right, artists in fact; and Flaubert hoped in Volume Two to complete showing why. While this was the end of their road and not the beginning, James Joyce was inherent here. Ezra Pound reported that Joyce knew Flaubert's works intimately. In his *Portrait*, said Pound, Joyce did not surpass *A Sentimental Education*. But almost alone of later writers, he fully understood the important newness of *Bouvard and Pécuchet*, and, in *Ulysses*, for the first time was able to go beyond it.[12]

Flaubert's spiny and difficult *Bouvard and Pécuchet* is not a success. But it stands gigantic as a forthright effort to declare that the novelist may depart from holding up the mirror to nature and seek instead to produce a purer art, as philosophy displaces psychology and the ultimate problems of man's destiny stand forth unclouded by the petty individualness of mere characters. If it failed, it was a worthwhile try.

was too complex for an inexperienced playwright to handle quickly and easily. Then bit by bit the audience, however sympathetic to the author, came to realize the situations were all stereotypes and the characters all puppets. Flaubert's disdain was too great for the audience to accept and his attack on democracy too obvious to be convincing.

As the audience became aware that the play was impossible and not even the prose they admired in the novelist was going to appear on stage, a feeling of pity and compassion for Flaubert spread through the hall. For a long time the respect they all felt for him kept them within bounds; but then they began to whisper to each other. It seemed impossible to those who did not know Flaubert that his comic sense could be so crass and so heavy. Sympathy gave way to bewilderment and then to annoyance. The play was an obvious failure.

When it was all over, there was consternation backstage. The actors and actresses disappeared: no one wished to be with the author. Even the stagehands were avoiding him. Edmond de Goncourt found him trying to say he did not care. But forty years of dreaming of theatrical success lay behind this evening. He sought to console himself with another heroic meal after the performance was over: this time, two dozen oysters, three slices of roast beef, a truffle salad, coffee, and liqueurs.

The critics the next morning tried to be nice, to explain it all away. But the facts were there: it was an unbearably bad play. Flaubert was too far out of the world of politics, which he despised, to offer more than obvious caricatures. He wrote to George Sand, seeking to be brave and honest about the failure. Yet how could the audience have laughed when his poet said, in 1874, that he still loved the romantics of 1830? Flaubert found this mockery unpredictable and somehow immoral of the spectators. But in a play containing only contemptible people, of course the audience thought the poet as stupid as the rest. The fault lay with Flaubert, who mistook his own phobias and hatreds for widely shared emotions easily adapted to the theater.

After the fourth performance there was nothing for it but to withdraw the play. Flaubert received his customary guests the following Sunday, trying to act as usual, but his disappointment was apparent. When he returned to Rouen, his friends and acquaintances there spoke to him with lowered voices when they were forced to mention the play at all. It was his last venture into the theater, the end of another dream.

A NEW PUBLISHER

Lévy has hurt me very deeply in a very sensitive spot, the memory of my poor Bouilhet. Our disagreement cannot be healed over.

Letter to George Sand, December 12, 1872

Remaining in a constant rage against the publisher, Flaubert had refused to let Lévy have *The Temptation of Saint Anthony* and even enjoyed torturing him by allowing vague rumors to circulate that he was about to give the manuscript to another editor.[4] He wished never to see him again; pardon was out of the question. Months passed and he seemed calmer: at least the thought of Lévy no longer set his heart to pounding. Then the publisher was awarded the Legion of Honor: it was too much for Flaubert, who abandoned wearing his own decoration until 1875 when Lévy died.[5]

Meanwhile, in 1871 the young Georges Charpentier had succeeded his father as head of the extremely successful publishing house which bore their name. Inheriting an excellent list of earlier authors, he was determined to add to it the best writers of his own day and in particular Flaubert. His salon was a major literary meeting place; his taste was excellent; and his wife, whose portrait Renoir was to do twice in this decade, presided easily over the salon for him. Earlier, in September of 1872, Flaubert had learned that Charpentier wished to buy Lévy's rights to his works, but for the moment Flaubert refused to consider anything concerning publishing.

By the early spring of 1873 Lévy's rights to *Madame Bovary* and *Salammbô* had expired and Flaubert was free to resell them; but he preferred to do without the money rather than again incur the commercial horrors he had experienced, he felt, with Lévy. Charpentier, however, was tireless. In June he called and persuaded Flaubert in principle to accept him as publisher. The two talked of how the novels would be printed and agreed, for the *Bovary*, on including an Appendix to contain the formal charge against the novel, the speech by Pinard, Sénard's reply, and the text of the court's decision. There would be no commentary; now that nearly twenty years had vindicated Flaubert, merely to print what Pinard had said was revenge enough. In August everything was settled to the entire satisfaction of both. Flaubert was very fortunate, for he had acquired a sympathetic and understanding friend who stood by him over the years.

Charpentier in due course even asked Flaubert to serve as godfather to one of his children. Flaubert was secretly both embarrassed and pleased. It concorded, he admitted, with the ecclesiastical impression he enjoyed creating by his garb and his hermit's life. And the request was a deliberate tribute to the author of *Saint Anthony*. Protesting his shame vigorously, he announced widely to his friends that they would shortly see him "at the foot of the altar" for the event.[6]

Quite naturally Charpentier had wanted to publish *Saint Anthony*. In December of 1873, as rehearsals for *The Candidate* were about to begin, Flaubert gave in and grudgingly allowed publication of both the new play and *The Temptation*. He hoped, however, to be compensated by making a great deal of money from *Saint Anthony*, for there was not only a French sale but also a Russian translation, thanks to Turgenev, for which he would be paid an additional three thousand francs. Flaubert felt strangely sad on letting the manuscript out of his hands. By the time he had corrected the final sheet of proof, he was even more regretful, for the Russian censors had refused permission to put it on sale there.

On March 11, 1874, *The Candidate* began its ill-fated run; on April 1, *The Temptation of Saint Anthony* appeared. Despite the failure of the play, *The Temptation* sold well at the start; by April 8 the first press run of 2000 copies had been sold out. Publisher and author were hopeful, although there had been attacks by a number of critics.

Théodore de Banville, poet and admirer of Flaubert, wrote his old friend an ecstatic letter on receipt of the volume. Madame Brainne told him that it was a marvel and that he had lost by not coming to see her at once: one could not really tell how far admiration might have led her. And a Protestant professor of theology at Strasbourg wrote in praise; years later, when Caroline Commanville's first husband had died, she would marry the professor's brother-in-law.[7]

Aside from these, almost all the critical appraisals were unfavorable. Even his copyists had been staggered by the work, and hardly any of his readers was able to make sense out of it. It was too uniquely based upon what amazed and delighted Flaubert to have a wider appeal. While the book continued to sell well and so pleased Charpentier, few rallied to public defense of its author. He was, in fact, startled by what seemed to him again the personal character of the attacks. He resolved to put the whole matter out of his mind.

As time went by, Flaubert felt the hurt more rather than less. His play and *Saint Anthony*, both dreams from his childhood, had failed. Not even the elite had liked them. Edmond de Goncourt had most unkind reservations about *The Temptation*; Taine had doubts; Zola found it an attack on humanity.[8] The book was to be rediscovered and enjoyed only by the next generation. Huysmans delighted in it; Anatole France would write *Thaïs* in part under its influence; and Joyce would prefer it to all Flaubert's other works except *Saint Julian*, the tale he was shortly to write.[9] But for the moment, the work was a failure among those whose judgment he valued, except for Turgenev.

Flaubert returned, saddened, to *Bouvard and Pécuchet*. The preceding year he had made a number of excursions in the Paris region trying to find a site for the country residence of his two clerks: nothing had quite satisfied him. As the summer of 1874 came on, he made a long trip into Normandy and finally found what he needed, between Caen and Falaise, a stupid site in a beautiful countryside, as he described it. He and Laporte went together, reviving something of Flaubert's young manhood and the trip with Du Camp. They bounced over country roads, ate in little inns, and slept wherever they could find beds. Flaubert initiated his companion into the great Norman drink, Calvados, a sort of cider brandy. The trip was a time of solid good spirits.

The long stint of readings and preparation for the new work was drawing to a close; Laporte was endlessly helpful in copying materials; he and Guy de Maupassant hunted out further stupidities which could be used. And all Flaubert's specialist friends were being pressed into service for technical data. At last, taking his courage in hand, he sat down at his desk to write on the morning of August 1, 1874. By four o'clock, after an afternoon of torture, he had found the first sentence and sent it off to Caro, as he had promised he would. But five days later he had to send her a revised version (the one which remained thereafter), for not even a full day's work had sufficed to perfect the opening of *Bouvard and Pécuchet*. His last long work was under way.

A WRITER AND HIS FRIENDS

If we were to hunt about a bit, couldn't we perhaps put together a little group of *émigrés*, which would be pleasant? For we are all of us *émigrés*, left over from another age.

Letter to Madame Roger des Genettes,
September, 1873

Croisset in the 1870's was as serenely Flaubert's home as it had been before the Prussians had, as he thought, forever ruined it for him. Maupassant remembered how he enjoyed being able to look up from his work as the great ships passed, their masts appearing almost to touch his walls.[10] As they moved down river, they seemed to carry his dreams with them out onto the far oceans. Often he would get up from his worktable to stand in the windows, filling the frame with his heavy head and chest, which reminded one of ancient Gallic chieftains. To his left he could see the thin spires of Rouen's churches against the sky, answering the high profiles of the factory chimneys and their plumes of smoke on the far bank. Beginning directly across from him, pastures filled with red or white cows extended all the way to the forest on his right. From one side to the other stretched the calm, broad river, its islands covered with trees. It disappeared into the distant curve of the great valley it had hallowed out.

The view was a proud and tranquil one, and he loved it. Observing this panorama was as near to nature as he allowed himself to come these days, for he had long since abjured any direct contact with her. The active swimmer, the avid canoer, the toughened horseman of his youth were all behind him now. At most, when guests were there, he would walk up and down the path among the lindens as he had two decades before with his young niece during the years of writing *Madame Bovary*.

His costume was the delight and amazement of those peaceful bourgeois who came to know of it. A loosely cut pair of trousers was held up by a silk cord about his waist; over them he wore an ample, flowing dressing gown whose bottom edge swept the ground. In winter it was made of a heavy brown cloth; in summer he changed to a lighter, white material with colored designs. On his head he placed a small silk skullcap, which made him look like a priest, and his long, slightly curly hair would dangle down over his shoulders. His ruddy face was cut across by his thick, drooping mustache, white now. The heavy, dark eyebrows emphasized his eyes as they scanned the page searching for unwanted assonances. At intervals he would toss the quill pen in his hand onto a flat Oriental pewter plate, raise his sheet to eye level, lean upon one elbow in his high-backed oaken chair and begin to declaim his paragraph. This was still the final test.

It was much the same in Paris, where as before he received his friends each Sunday from one to seven in his bachelor apartment. When the bell announced his first guest, he would throw a red silk cloth over the manuscript sheets on his worktable and go open the door himself. The most interesting writers of the day would appear: Turgenev and Taine; Daudet and Zola with the other members of the naturalist group, Huysmans, Hennique, Céard; and others, the erudite Baudry, the journalist Catulle Mendès, the poet Hérédia; and, usually the last to arrive, Edmond de Goncourt. The little salon would be full and guests would spill over into the dining room. With broad gestures which made him seem about to take flight, Flaubert would go from one to another, his

long robe flying behind him in his brusque movements, full of
enthusiasm or indignation, his resounding eloquence bursting
forth. He delighted his guests by his furies, charmed them by his
goodness, and amazed all by his prodigious erudition; to some of
the younger men he seemed to possess impossible stores of learning and to be capable of leaps of the mind unknown to them.
Then as the afternoon drew to a close, one after another would
leave, till Zola remained alone at the very end. When he, too, had
left, Flaubert would lie down to rest for an hour before changing
into formal clothes to go to Princess Mathilde, who nowadays
received each Sunday evening.

Those who, like Maupassant, loved Flaubert found him gay
and good, Rabelaisian in his laughter and still enjoying jokes carried out over the years. He laughed often with a happy, open
abandon which seemed more natural and normal to him than his
frequent exasperation with humanity. But there were many people
who knew him well and who did not find him an easy person to
be with. Zola found discussions with him almost impossible, for
Flaubert could not tolerate disagreement. When he met opposition, he proceeded by violent affirmations and rapidly lost his temper. But still it was Zola who accompanied him to his apartment
after dinners which they attended together. Otherwise Maupassant usually went with him, for he dreaded an attack of epilepsy
at such moments.[11]

Flaubert was that ill-assorted combination, the aging bachelor.
He enjoyed being with people, really liked them . . . and could
not stand the conversations they imposed on him, just as he liked
to dream of sumptuous elegance but in fact preferred to live very
simply. Many of his acquaintances, Huysmans and Anatole France
among them, found him painfully lacking in intelligence, even
quite stupid on occasion. But there were many others, and perhaps
greater ones, who did enjoy his company and who appeared regularly at his Sunday afternoons or who were proud to be invited to
Croisset. Turgenev and Goncourt were, however, the only remaining people with whom he could talk and be understood.
Feydeau, his "nephew" of the preceding decade, was now estranged from him and was publishing works, like his earlier
Fanny, whose only interest was their pornography; it saddened

Flaubert. His death in November of 1873, while not the loss of an intimate, marked at least the passing of another man of whom he had been fond. Victor Hugo, now returned from his self-imposed exile during the Second Empire, he saw frequently, particularly when he could have him alone without his customary cortege of political personalities. He also tried to be helpful himself to those of his friends who needed him, backing the candidacy of Berthelot to the Academy of Sciences and using his influence wherever it could help. For his own benefit, however, he refused all such moves and repeatedly declined the suggestions of friends that he present himself for the French Academy.

Edmond de Goncourt was a special case among those close to Flaubert. They saw each other almost weekly when Flaubert was in Paris; and yet Goncourt confided to his diary at frequent intervals his continued distaste for his friend's coarseness, heaviness, and lack of tact. Goncourt found him so high strung that he upset any group he was with; he was full of petty vanities, hopelessly provincial, and painfully ordinary. He was even the victim of his own exaggerations in talking. And yet Goncourt continued to frequent his Sunday afternoons.[12]

Flaubert's friendship with Guy de Maupassant grew very close beginning in the latter part of 1872. He found the younger man witty, well read, and charming. Moreover, he was Alfred's nephew. His way of lowering his head as he recited poetry was so much like his uncle's that watching him almost frightened Flaubert, as though he were seeing a ghost. The younger man became his disciple, and Flaubert encouraged him to pursue his efforts to write verse, although he did confess he suspected Guy of being lazy. He also undertook to find him literary posts so that he might gain experience and perhaps a little money.

They shared a common delight in obscenity, too. Maupassant composed a play which led Flaubert to address him as "Lubricious Author, Obscene Young Man." It involved a newlywed couple, who, by a disastrous mistake, spent the night in a brothel they thought was a hotel. Its tone may be judged from the opening scene, in which a young theology student is washing contraceptives. In April, 1875, there was a private performance which excited Flaubert and to which he invited Turgenev.[13] By the following winter young Maupassant became a regular guest at Flaubert's Sundays. He responded with a most flattering article on his friend and mentor.

During these years Flaubert's friendship with the industrialist Edmond Laporte ripened. As they both lived on the river, they corresponded by sending letters back and forth via the riverboat. In September of 1872 Laporte gave his friend a greyhound. Flaubert, who was with Juliet Herbert in Paris at the time, asked that the dog be named Julio "for a number of mystic reasons." And Juliet is probably not the only reason for the name: it embodied more of those sounds which recur obsessively in Flaubert's names. There had already been Djalioh and Djali and Jules; there would soon be Julian. There were other presents, and the two men went off together to locate a site in Normandy for Flaubert's two clerks. Visits became constant in 1874, when Flaubert finally began the writing of *Bouvard and Pécuchet*.

WOMEN

> That was a lovely letter you wrote me. I've reread it three times, as though I were still a young man.
> Why can't I be any younger? Why not? Why did I meet you too late! My heart is as young as ever, but my sensitivities have been rubbed raw in some areas and blunted in others like an old knife that has been sharpened too many times; it has nicks already and more keep being made.
>
> Letter to Madame Brainne, March 31, 1872

In this last decade of his life, as he made his peace with being in his fifties, Flaubert softened toward women. His friends knew it and were not fooled by the harsh and sweeping generalities he still uttered when irritated. Once when he was trying to explain what a lecherous, unprincipled Lothario he was, Daudet interrupted to tell him with finality that he was perhaps a cynic with men, but that he was a sentimentalist with women. Flaubert laughed and had to confess it was so: he had even caught himself calling his prostitutes his "little angels."[14] Now, when it was too late, he knew that all tenderness was lacking from his life; he minded it. But marriage was out of the question, as he explained when George Sand again urged it on him. He had lived a solitary life too long and was too accustomed to having his own way; he was too old and too poor. And then, he added, there was at the bottom of his being an ecclesiastical element which others little suspected. One thinks of the various curés in Balzac, aging, self-centered, and totally egotistical in their lives.

A number of women Flaubert saw somewhat casually. He dined with Adèle Husson, Du Camp's old mistress, who had now recovered her sanity. Sarah Bernhardt wished to make a bust of him, finding his head full of character; Flaubert refused on two separate occasions, but was flattered. Mademoiselle Leroyer de Chantepie wrote once again; and Flaubert noticed some verses by Louise Colet, some of which he was surprised to find good.

Now that age had set its grip upon him, Flaubert felt most comfortable with the women he had known many years. Suzanne Lagier reappeared at his Sunday afternoons, her language as free as ever and her tales of her past lovers exciting even to the hardened group around Flaubert.[15] He attended Princess Mathilde's receptions and she visited him in Croisset where, although he did not have accommodations suited to royalty, at least he could show her the nearby ruins of Jumièges. He was also a not infrequent visitor at her country estate, Saint-Gratien, at Enghien, ten miles outside of Paris.

George Sand had been something of a mother to him for half-a-dozen years before Madame Flaubert's death; after it she played the role even more. Sensing what confused emotions must be engulfing him when his mother died, she wrote to him about the end of his long, cruel period of worry and the searing pain one felt after the struggle was over, a bitter way to earn relief. And so she wrote that she opened to him her maternal heart, which would, she knew, replace nothing, but which suffered with and for him.[16]

Madame Sand's task was not alone to offer consolation. Again and again she wrote that she was displeased with his unsociability and his dissatisfaction with life. His trouble, she told him, was that he imagined happiness to be possible and hence, when he faced its absence in his own life, he was angered and amazed instead of accepting unhappiness as man's chronic state. She blamed him for fleeing from his friends and refusing their love and affection. On receiving her letter, he wrote to Princess Mathilde that Madame Sand's perpetual preaching bothered him: he would reply with insults about democracy, in which she believed heartily. It would, he said, make him feel better.

Madame Sand continued to write, asking if he were incapable of forgiving and forgetting. It was almost as though he were vain and self-centered, she wrote, whereas she knew he was good and kind. Life, she assured him, was ill arranged, painful, and irritating for everybody, but he should stop ignoring all its immense compensations. To forget them was to be ungrateful.

In April of 1873 Flaubert overcame all his hesitations and accepted George Sand's invitation to visit her at Nohant again for a week.[17] His behavior was odd: as before, he dressed as a woman and danced. He looked very old and tired and could not easily stand the noise of so many people about him. Madame Sand feared he lived too cerebrally: his body showed the strain. In words she could not know echoed those of Du Camp thirty years before, she added in her diary that one lives more through character than through intelligence and greatness. She was exhausted by his visit. She loved him dearly, and he was an excellent man, but so exuberant that he overwhelmed them all. Turgenev, whom they knew far less and loved far less, they missed far more, for he had a simple, easy grace and was charmingly kind. Her sadness over all this pierces through. Flaubert, wholly unaware of it, wrote her naïvely of missing everyone and everything about Nohant: how good they had all been, how warm and witty! Why could he not always live nearby? How badly life was arranged! A few days later, on May 1, 1873, at Pauline Viardot's house he saw her for the last time. A year later to the day he was again there and rejoiced again at hearing Madame Viardot sing, but he remembered and missed his old friend, as he wrote her.

Of course they continued to exchange letters. George Sand struggled in vain to tell Flaubert those simple truths of living for life itself and for people, which it had cost her dear to acquire and which she longed to give to him. He loved literature too much, she finally found the courage to tell him: his devotion would kill him, but he would not in turn succeed in killing human stupidity. What hatred he felt for it! Wisdom was a goal even higher than art, which was never more than the expression of it. Moreover, wisdom included the beautiful, as well as the true and the good, and enthusiasm, too. It could teach him to look beyond himself to something more elevated, which he could assimilate through contemplation and admiration. But, she added sadly, she knew she would not succeed in changing him or even in making him understand how she envisaged and sought to grasp at happiness, which to her lay in the acceptance of life however it might present itself. She suggested there was someone else who might be able to help him, Victor Hugo.[18] In this she was perhaps wrong: she had not herself been taught the lesson by being told it.

George Sand's son, Maurice, seemed often to Flaubert to be the man he most envied.[19] In part, no doubt, this was because he really was Madame Sand's son and not an adoptive one like himself. But it was also because his life appeared so good to Flaubert, so regular and normal and sound. Maurice seemed to incarnate the full measure of human happiness. Slowly now Flaubert was coming to realize he had been wrong over all these years in the way he had ordered his life: if only he had married and so been able, like Maurice, to have two little daughters! But then, man is not free and he had only followed out his destiny, which had slowly pushed him along until now he found himself in the center of a vast void, while awaiting the moment to enter the eternal one.[20]

It was perhaps predominantly Maurice's children that made his life seem so good. Flaubert was sure he himself had been born with every sort of tenderness in his heart. But he had been a coward in his youth, he knew: he had been afraid of life. Now he was having to pay. He had gone along from day to day pursuing literature as his only goal and looking neither to the right nor the left. Without his quite realizing it, everything he cared about had disappeared, and now he was absolutely alone. He saw what he had missed when a son was born to one of his servants. The man's ecstasy he would earlier have found ridiculous, he admitted: now, he envied him.

Flaubert's own childhood, in some ways so far behind him, was also very close through the presence of another servant, Julie, who had brought him up from childhood and had always been there as part of his life. In 1873, already an old woman, her sight had begun to fail because of a cataract; but the idea of an operation and the hospital so frightened the aged peasant woman that she put off surgery. By midsummer of 1874, she was nearly blind, and could postpone it no longer. Visiting her in the Hôtel-Dieu recalled so many earlier moments to Flaubert, and seeing the elderly woman lying there reminded him of his mother's death. It was all he could do to hold back the sobs. Coming home alone from the hospital was particularly solitary. He had just returned from the expedition into Normandy with Laporte to locate Bouvard and Pécuchet: that, too, had been full of memories. At last Julie could be brought back to Croisset, where she was enchanted to find herself among familiar things which she could again see. Flaubert confided to his niece how much Julie revived memories of his mother and his youth for him.

Caroline remained very close to him. He continued to counsel her, as he had for twenty years, on her readings. What an ideal existence it would be, he wrote, if only they could live together at Croisset! But then he went back over his letter and added "for me," recognizing that the young must live with the young. His affection for her was, as he sometimes realized, by no means always wise. Caroline spent six weeks with him in the summer of 1873; his loneliness afterward was, he confessed, like that of a mother or perhaps of an old nurse. When she did not write to him at once, he wrote that "her nurse would have her milk turned." And he complained whenever he found her letters or visits too infrequent.[21]

Of affections toward women his own age, Flaubert had few. But there were his Three Angels, particularly Madame Brainne. To her his letters—and no doubt something of his conduct—became very bold during these years. First names replaced the more distant formality, but *tu* never displaced *vous* for either of them. To her he recounted in somewhat complacent detail the delight he would take in placing kisses everywhere upon her or his thoughts of her bosom and how he would love to devour it. He would even enjoy being the covering over her four-poster bed or the tub she bathed in. And of course he protested the rigorous limits she placed upon his actions. They were both enjoying a harmless game.

For Juliet Herbert, on the contrary, he felt a serious and complex affection, which can be somewhat divined through the haze of partial knowledge.[22] In 1872 she was in Paris. Flaubert wrote to Madame Brainne that he was to be in the capital doing research; to others he wrote only that he would be away from Croisset. They had two weeks together before she left him to return via Caroline's house to England. Afterward he went briefly to Princess Mathilde's, but found himself so sad he invented an excuse to get away sooner than he had expected and return to his customary solitude. There the long past weighed down upon him despite his efforts to forget it in his work. As the bad weather grew steadily worse outside, he hoped that Juliet's Channel crossing might not be too bad or that she had put it off awaiting better weather.

Some ten days later, on October 5, Flaubert had digested his sadness and went out of doors in the afternoon to walk his new dog Julio. He watched the sunlight falling upon the yellowing leaves and meditated upon the books he still wanted to write. Memories, too, crowded in, for there were no more dreams of the future left to him: the bygone days began to shimmer gently in a luminous vapor. Against it, he wrote to Madame Roger des Genettes, a few beloved faces stood out, cherished phantoms stretching out their arms to him. It was, he wrote her, a dangerous dream and must be pushed aside, however delectable it was.

Madame Roger des Genettes could be forgiven if she assumed that hers was the face he saw against the mist. But he wrote the same day to Caro to assure her that she had been wrong in supposing that while he was with Juliet he had not missed her. And, describing the same afternoon walk, he told her how much he missed having her with him then, too. He diagnosed his current excellent humor as coming from the progress he was making with *Bouvard and Pécuchet*. During the same evening he also found time to write a fond letter to Madame Brainne, closing with affectionate kisses for her.

A letter to Elisa gave the fullest account of what was in Flaubert's heart. He opened by calling her his Old Friend, his Old

Affection, and he confessed he could not see her handwriting without being moved. He longed to see her and hoped she would come to Croisset, where he would have her sleep in his mother's room. He then described the same walk in the same terms, but this time he added that the face which stood out resplendently from all the others was hers. And he closed: "Yes, yours. Oh poor Trouville!"

All the letters were honest; all said what he meant. They were never intended to be read, one after another, by the same reader. For that, they would have had to be written very differently, which could, of course, have been done. As it was, each of the women who received one read it her own way and knew, as well as one ever knows with any letter, what was in the heart of the writer. For Flaubert loved them all, but differently. Madame Roger des Genettes was Louis Bouilhet, the salon of The Muse, a long literary correspondence, a beloved friend. Madame Brainne was one of the few women he knew who would not laugh if he used terms of strong affection; and aging bachelors need to believe they can still attract women. Caro was his adored niece, the daughter he did not have, the only living memory of his sister. And Elisa had wakened him to love almost forty years before and been that particularly gentle incarnation, a boy's first affection, which he had treasured and made the focus of his wandering amorous fancies until more concrete centers could be found. She was Trouville and his adolescence. If he also wrote the paragraph to Juliet, it, too, was honest and meant to her the abiding presence of his affection.

Flaubert may have written to Elisa after this evocation of Trouville; but if he did, the letter has not come to light. In 1875 she entered an asylum at Illenau briefly. Again in 1881 she had to return to it. Du Camp saw her there; she had many lucid moments but was never able to be out for long. She died in 1888.

How many contacts there may have been between Flaubert and Juliet Herbert is not entirely clear, and each reader must guess for himself what they meant to him and to her. In August of 1874 Flaubert was again preparing to leave Croisset to see her in Paris. They had nearly three weeks together, and he wrote to Laporte (for men are rarely able to remain wholly silent about their exploits) that he had been gigantic in his prowess.[23] To Princess

Mathilde he stated, in opposite fashion, that he had been in the capital only forty-eight hours. It may be no more than coincidence, but Juliet next reappears, in the documents now available, only two years later and again it is August. Flaubert was forwarding a letter to Caro from her. She was to be traveling.

MELANCHOLY YEARS

> I still have the grippe, and it has produced a general fatigue accompanied by a violent (or rather a profound) melancholy. While I sit here spitting and coughing by my fireside, I have been mulling over my youth and thinking of all my dead ones. I have been rolling in Blackness . . . Never have I felt so abandoned, so empty, so bruised.
>
> Letter to George Sand, February 28, 1874

When Flaubert returned to Croisset from his visit with Juliet Herbert in 1872, he could honestly and sadly report to his niece that his only distraction was his new dog. His retreat there was intended to shut out a world he hated but which impinged upon him nevertheless. In October of 1872 Gautier's death pierced his defenses. Although long foreseen, the loss of Théo crushed him. Unfortunately the telegram announcing the funeral was mailed to him, so he learned of it only as the ceremony was actually taking place. He had already arranged a meeting in Rouen concerning Bouilhet's monument; fearing that remaining away would seem a pose, he kept the appointment. After the usual frustrating session, he went on to the Hôtel-Dieu, where Achille's wife talked to him lengthily of the heat. Then he had to cross the entire city to call upon Madame Lapierre and Madame Brainne, whom he was to escort to the Saint Romain Fair. Never in all the times that he had looked upon his fellow citizens of Rouen had they inspired such disgust in him: he longed alternatively to weep and to vomit. His mind kept returning to Gautier and Théo's lifelong love of beauty. The hideousness of the world had killed him.

Flaubert's two Angels understood his feelings and walked

quietly with him to the cemetery. They remained outside the grill so that he could be alone with his grief as he stood in silence by the tombs of Caroline, his father, and his mother. They kept their old friend with them until it was time for him to go home to bed. His dog overwhelmed him on his arrival. As he reflected on Gautier, the modern world seemed to have no place left for people whose real love was art. Théo had been his oldest living, intimate friend. He had respected him as a master and loved him as a brother. He did not pity but rather envied him.

More than ever now, since there was no one left, Flaubert fled the world about him. To George Sand he asserted he did not believe happiness possible; but tranquility at least should be a dream one could achieve. He had urged this upon Louise Colet in 1846. Hence, he wrote, he fled society: contact with his fellows revolted his sense of justice. In solitude at any rate no one could annoy him. It appeared to be his natural way and hence the right one for him.

As autumn moved into winter in 1872, Flaubert began to feel as though he had an incurable malady bringing on invincible melancholy. In addition to the loss of all his beloved ones, there was also the political scene: it was more than he could bear. When he had seen his country go down before the Prussian armies, he had discovered patriotism; now the state of France made him desperately sad. The ruling classes had lost all sense of how to govern. It was like reliving the end of the Roman Empire and watching barbarism inevitably conquer. He had always sought to live in an ivory tower, but now the tower was surrounded by a rising sea of filth. His wrath mounted, and he turned on anyone he met. *Bouvard and Pécuchet*, the receptacle for much of this wrath, suffered for it.

Flaubert's political attitude was all too defensible. He correctly realized the Conservatives, with whom alone he felt a kinship, were playing into the hands of the opposition by their stupidity and blindness. The early history of the Republic was to prove him correct, as a form of government no majority wanted gradually entrenched itself and became the dismal political structure of France for the next seventy years. The country was to witness the decline and eventual disappearance of the old conservative groups, which helped make possible the uncontrollable regimes that followed. Their succession of scandals would not have shocked him: he had foreseen them and was consoled only by the thought that he would not live to experience them.

The months dragged by, and Flaubert's melancholy gave him no more than momentary respites. He was so irritable he had to decline George Sand's reiterated invitations to visit her that winter: it would be cruel, he feared, to inflict his company upon those he loved. A long bout with grippe after the New Year heightened his misanthropy until he could seriously report to Edmond de Goncourt that indignation alone sustained him. The sixth of April was the first anniversary of the death of his mother; in May he moved back out to Croisset, so full of her memories. His first action was to visit her room.

As he reflected upon his unhappy generation, he came to wonder whether it perhaps lacked the capacity for enjoyment. Their elders, the great romantic generation, had had such high spirits! With more clairvoyance he might have asked instead whether he himself did not perhaps lack the perseverance to enjoy, the will power to do what had to be done, in anything except literature. However much Flaubert must have known George Sand was right that he must take a saner view of mankind, it was easier—it had always been easier—to claim that his state was natural and inevitable and the destiny to which he was fated. He had been telling this to his intimates ever since Louise Colet and Maxime Du Camp had made similar objections three decades before. When he was not writing, he was, like many of his generation, in part Frédéric Moreau.

Through it all he worked. Notes for *Bouvard and Pécuchet* and, with the return of warm weather in 1873, work on *The Weaker Sex* and then *The Candidate* filled the hours and let him escape living. In the eleven months from September to August, he read some two hundred books. Work was his only safety, and he clung to it, refusing even to pause long enough to admire a beautiful autumn day. He stepped out to enjoy the air, took a turn on the terrace, and returned to his study.

By the winter of 1873, Flaubert's physical state was beginning to cause everyone alarm, including finally himself. As he came to the end of writing *The Candidate*, the floor was beginning to rock under his feet, and he felt a constant oppression. It was a condition he had known when he was younger: it was time to stop. In the following February, there was the failure of *The Candidate*, and in April the poor reception accorded *The Temptation of Saint Anthony*. By then his doctor was calling him an hysterical old woman and he was having to agree. He was tired to the point of exhaustion, driven beyond the ability to fight back, reduced almost to impotent whining. The state of his health was indeed becoming dangerous.

SWISS INTERLUDE (1874)

I have just finished a two-hour walk, sweating like a horse, puffing like a seal, groaning like a donkey, and stopping every twenty paces. But I am following "my doctor's orders"! I am getting exercise and I am resting.

Letter to Caroline, July 1, 1874

Flaubert was sufficiently sick for his doctor to have to intervene. He must get away and cease this impossible existence. He was allowed the two weeks in Normandy with Laporte before taking off for Switzerland, where he was to have three weeks of complete rest and relaxation at Kaltbad-Righi. He rather looked forward to the excursion and was curious to see whether his morale would be better upon his return: it could hardly be worse.

Flaubert was right in sensing that his morale was the fundamental issue. But how could he feel otherwise? The universal stupidity seemed so all-encompassing he suggested the period was like the time of Noah: decent people should set about constructing themselves an Ark at once, for they were threatened with an inundation of cretinism. He even burst out during a dinner at Princess Mathilde's, insulting a guest who had dared to differ from his tastes in literature. As Flaubert put it, the poor man would not soon again belch forth such idiocy. He also admitted his violence had cast something of a pall over the other diners.

Flaubert's arrival in Switzerland was not auspicious. The countryside was, to be sure, beautiful, and he was reasonably comfortable; but he was exhausted and ten hours of sleep at night seemed only to call for three more during the afternoon. His mind was empty, his body worn out; he was content to gorge on the food and smoke endless pipes. But within the first few hours his fellow guests at the hotel had aroused his loathing. Naturally—the word is his—he refused to eat at the common table and insisted on being privately served. Many of the others were Germans: it was unlikely, he wrote, that he could open his mouth throughout his whole stay. He would try instead to work at a few ideas for books.

The other guests spent most of their time eating or drinking. A day or so of watching them made him long to go out and embrace a calf in a pasture. The men were dreadful, but their wives were worse, simply hideous and wearing dresses which added to the disagreeable effect of their anatomies. When Caroline urged him to begin a flirtation with one of them, he was forced to confess it was beyond his powers. He listened to one torturing a Chopin waltz in a fashion calculated to put all the cows in Switzerland to flight. The ladies pushed the love of the instrument to the point of delirium. The gentlemen's vice was the telescope on the hotel terrace. One or another of them was always before it uttering exclamations, his hat pushed back and his bottom sticking out.

Not even in Switzerland could nature appeal to Flaubert. In fact the distaste he had anticipated proved far less than the reality. He would happily have given all the glaciers in the world for a library, a theater, or a museum. Nature bored him: he longed only to say quietly to her that he knew she was beautiful and he had come out of her. In a few more instants he would return into her, but for the moment, could she not leave him alone? He wished for other distractions: if only he could leave for Venice! Yet he must restrain himself and complete his rest period. Although each day he exercised for two or three hours, still he was losing his appetite; a prolonged stay would make him a hopeless hypochondriac. His face, however, was less flushed and his breath less short, as his doctor had hoped. But two weeks of this regimen drove him nearly out of his mind. As he well realized, the trouble was that, having nothing to do, he was forced all day to think of himself; hence his boredom and melancholy. At last, on July 19, he left for Paris by slow stages. Laporte met him en route.

THE MOOD DARKENS

My mood would make ebony look pink.

Letter to Madame Roger des Genettes,
November 4, 1874

Flaubert was still a tired and sick man: his stay in Switzerland had done him only a very little good. The world seemed impossible, and the only wise course was to disappear as soon as possible. A few days after his return, on August 1, 1874, he began to write *Bouvard and Pécuchet,* hoping in vain that this would bring relief He wrote Caro he was afraid he was becoming like his mother in her later years; his niece must have thought inwardly he was right. His health, however, was a little better, and he enjoyed two or three vigorous weeks in Paris with Juliet. He returned somewhat ill; but convalescence came rapidly and with it a moment of real happiness and well-being.

Flaubert settled into the quiet monotony of writing his novel. His only companions were his memories, and though they overwhelmed him, still they were better than looking at the contemporary scene. Yet each passing year had made him less able to stand the solitude which had grown up about him, for each increased his melancholy. Only Victor Hugo, Goncourt, and Turgenev, of all his circle of acquaintances, seemed to belong to his world any more. He found himself more and more often thinking back to the past and recalling his dead friends and family.

His health, which had been momentarily better, relapsed again and he began to suffer stomach cramps, intestinal discomfort, and extreme nervousness. The machine was giving out. By the start of 1875, he was convinced he had been a very sick man for months; the others about him seemed the same. He wondered if it were the sickness of France herself, which was contagious. He sought for a spirit of resignation, but could not find it.

In February, 1875, Flaubert came down with grippe. It lasted some time and left him even more aware of how unbearable he was to all those about him. To calm him and relieve what Flaubert called his rheumatism, his doctor prescribed potassium bromide. The medication produced a strong skin reaction, making him look like a leper. Daudet, who knew something of how much and how often he was taking the drug, believed that its sedative effect upon him was very strong and was perhaps even related to his slowness with words, at least in his later years when Daudet knew him.[24]

Late March found Flaubert still depressed and suspecting that he must have some hidden illness. As April began, he no longer believed in his book. The prospect of the difficulties it presented crushed him in advance, and he could work only by exercising his will power to the limit: his work was drudgery, a task.

FLAUBERT'S FINANCES

> Surely you don't imagine that I am going to *check on the servants' household expenses!* Suicide would be sweet compared to such a prospect; I would rather groan and be resigned.
>
> Letter to Caroline, November 9, 1872

Flaubert had long been a spendthrift. As a student in Paris he had exceeded his allowance regularly; in his trip through the Near East he had had to make heavy demands upon his mother; during the last decade of her life he had given her cause for serious alarm on this score. Now she was no longer there to keep a restraining hand upon him.

In the early 1870's Flaubert knew he was still spending too much. Poor Caro felt she must undertake the watchdog role her grandmother had had; she wrote a letter of much-needed advice. Her uncle was wrathful: she must have known it would sadden him to be reminded of his poverty! His life was abominably arid, lacking in all pleasures and distractions, and without any outlet for his affections. He was not going to push asceticism any further. He suggested they never mention the subject again.

Although Flaubert had silenced his niece, the subject intruded itself upon him from other quarters throughout 1872. In 1873, however, a new prospect opened: with the lapsing of his contracts with Lévy, he was free to sell the rights to his books. Lemerre offered one thousand francs for *Madame Bovary*, which he gleefully accepted in order to purchase plaster casts of two bas-reliefs from the Parthenon metopes and some household linen. His works had finally brought in something that could be used for his mother's house.

Another aspect was less pleasant. For many years Flaubert had always left a considerable amount of his uninvested funds with his nephew, who was after all a businessman and knew about such things. Ernest was to send him the interest at intervals or, as occasion demanded, to pay certain bills for him or send him money. In August of 1873 the arrangement began not to work very well: Flaubert had increasing difficulty in getting necessary cash from his nephew, and he was surprised to receive from one of his furnishers a notification of an overdue bill which he thought Ernest had paid a year before, when it was first submitted. Ernest sent his uncle the thousand francs he wanted at once.

The winter of 1873 saw the Commanvilles very busy with their sawmill. Ernest had to make several trips, particularly to Scandinavia, and, although his health was beginning to give cause for alarm, he had to keep hard at work. Flaubert offered the affectionate advice that health was more important than anything else: he should let business go for a while and rest.

In the autumn of 1874 there was still no improvement in Ernest's health or finances. In September bills were still coming to Flaubert unpaid, and he had to underline his request that Ernest take care of them at once. There was also the puzzling fact that the young ménage was attempting to sell a villa of theirs. By October Flaubert began really to insist that Ernest give him some sort of accounting of where he stood. His nephew was to send five hundred francs at once and another five hundred shortly: he was also to pay the quarterly rent. And they would have to settle upon some regular method for payments: otherwise, Flaubert wrote in horror, one day he would wake up and find himself penniless. Meanwhile, a German translation of *Salammbô* was to come out and that would tide him over. He also set about serious efforts to sell a large farm of his at Deauville.

As 1875 opened, Flaubert was worried by having no news from his niece.[25] The price of lumber dropped disastrously during this period; it is possible that he was already aware of impending trouble. For some months he avoided writing to friends until finally he was forced to apologize and blame his silence on his depression, which would have led him to write only unpleasant things. He was haunted with melancholy thoughts of the past. Whenever he took the Paris-Rouen train, seeing Mantes reminded him of Bouilhet, who had lived there so long, and, no doubt, Louise Colet as well. Alfred Le Poittevin kept coming to mind; in Paris, daily reminders of the dead Duplan were about him. To George Sand he wrote in late March that, like all old men, he was lost in memories of his childhood. He expected nothing more from life. He seemed to be traversing an endless solitude, going he knew not whither. And he was himself at one and the same time the solitude and the traveler . . . and the camel.[26]

COMMANVILLE RUINED (1875)

We have been living in this infernal anguish for almost four months now. Even if everything turns out as well as it can, we will hardly have enough to live on (for the moment at least); and I'm very much afraid that sooner or later I'll have to give up Croisset. That would be the final blow to me. You can't start life over at my age.

Letter to Madame Brainne, July 18, 1875

Over the course of April and May, 1875, Flaubert was brought face to face with what had been earlier presumably no more than an ugly suspicion: his beloved niece was facing financial collapse. Caroline and Ernest explained their desperate straits; he offered his own fortune at once. What moneys of his Ernest was supposed to have were in large measure gone already; but Flaubert could make more vigorous efforts to sell his Deauville property, convert his capital into an annuity, and still manage to live, albeit less well. He would at once abandon his apartment on the Rue Murillo and move to cheaper quarters near his niece. To George Sand he explained that it would mean more room and an end to his solitude.

On May 10, Flaubert returned to Croisset a broken man. His servant and the dog met him on the doorstep. He put away his things and tried to sleep, but a headache prevented it. After a walk and a bite to eat, he tried again to sleep, but Julio, who had been at Edmond Laporte's with other dogs, moaned piteously. It so concorded with his own mood that he minded it not at all. In the morning he arose and set about his dismal tasks, giving notice to his Paris landlord, writing a few other letters, seeing his doctor. The garden was charming and the house clean: Caro could come visit him when she wished. The river was unrippled and there was total silence about him. He had not yet had the courage to go into his mother's room. He wrote Caro that if only he could see Ernest again confident about the future and earning some money, and if the sale of Deauville brought him enough to protect himself and Caroline, and if *Bouvard and Pécuchet* would move along nicely, then he would not complain of life. George Sand was right: he had no idea that life was not always perfectly arranged for other people and so demanded enormously for himself.

How drastic Commanville's situation may have been is hard to estimate, but his deficit probably approached two million francs, a huge amount when one thousand was a good figure for reprinting *Madame Bovary*. To complicate matters, Flaubert was a man of extraordinary naïveté. While he was an extremely penetrating observer of characters he himself created, he was quite unable to see life about him with any lucidity. His own complete integrity, his faith in his family and friends, and the generosity of his nature all left him at the mercy of unscrupulous people.[27] Ernest Commanville, and perhaps his adored Caro, were unscrupulous and hard pressed.

The summer was frighteningly bad. Later Flaubert was to say that it had driven him almost insane.[28] As the truth of the situation began to become clearer to him, he was overwhelmed by it as though he were sick. He abandoned all hope; even *Bouvard and Pécuchet* had to be put aside. He could write no more; he was empty. The present was unbearable, the future terrifying.

By July Flaubert had come to suspect that his niece and nephew were not telling him everything. He was not sure whether it was better not to know and so to imagine things, or to know and be unable to bear the situation. He kept asking when his anguish and uncertainty would end, and his days began to center around the arrival of the mailman. But the letters, when there were any, could only make it clearer that worse disasters were ahead, as Caroline began to warn him he must prepare himself for having to give up Croisset and everything he owned. It seemed unfair and impossible to him: he had already given up almost everything long ago in order to lead an austere and laborious existence. They could not now wish to take from him what little he had clung to. The idea of leaving Croisset he could not accept. Perhaps even worse was the thought that Caro would now be vulnerable. He was crushed, and said so.

Flaubert never knew more than parts of his nephew's financial problems. The difficulties lay in several areas once Ernest's credit was destroyed and he found himself unable to meet his bills. On the one hand, several members of the family and also certain close friends had, like Flaubert, happily entrusted their funds to him. As Flaubert began to understand that all of these funds might be lost, too, his worry grew. But beyond these, there were the normal commercial debts for which Ernest had signed notes, particularly with his Swedish suppliers of wood. Flaubert's anxiety about what they would do knew no bounds, for they could force bankruptcy and hence bring dishonor to his niece and nephew. He had never imagined anguish like this, having always—though he did not know it—led a sheltered existence. The waiting was the most unbearable. Caro had assured him that she would telegraph if the news were good, and he found his days now passed in watching for the arrival of the telegraph boy. He did not come. Flaubert again wondered if news were being kept from him. He was, he wrote, too old to stand such cruel blows, which may have been part of why Caroline hesitated to tell him more.

Commercial papers accidentally passed through his hands at times, but he knew little of the business world and absolutely nothing of Ernest's affairs; hence the bills and notes meant little to him. Banking firms in Rouen, too, were involved, and Flaubert had indirect and optimistic word about their attitude. One of the partners was named Pécuchet. For a moment in mid-July Flaubert hoped for an early end of the affair and a visit from his niece to comfort him, but the hope was short lived. Headaches, tears near the surface, and a persistent dull feeling were his constant companions.

One day a long-continued rain came to an end, the sun shone, and the white sails began to pass on the river again: it broke his heart to think he must leave all this. At last he began also to glimpse the fact that any arrangement Ernest could make would still mean the loss of all his nephew's capital. What could Ernest then use to earn a living? It was frightening. But most terrifying of all to the bourgeois Flaubert was the fear of Ernest's bankruptcy. He had supposed up to then that death was the worst of evils; he now knew that to watch impotently while those you loved were humiliated was far worse.

Everything of Flaubert's that Ernest had had was lost: would his nephew at least be able to pay him the interest? It seemed doubtful. Flaubert asked Turgenev to write to George Sand for him: he lacked the strength and courage himself and could only wonder how long it would take him to die, for his old age was going to be lamentable. Turgenev did write her, adding his private fear that their old friend was even more wounded than he realized. All that was left was sort of tenacity which had no energy infusing it and a self-concern which had no part of vanity. He was defenseless against misfortune and unhappiness. A few days later Flaubert himself wrote Madame Sand that all he wished now was to be able to die very quickly.[29]

July was difficult, and Flaubert could only hope Ernest would be able somehow to ride out the month, as it was clear his Swedish creditors would not agree to help before then. Ernest did make it. By mid-August, Flaubert thought he knew his nephew's net liabilities at that time amounted to another million and a half francs. It hardly looked as though any of them would have enough to live on, even if they did survive the next few weeks. His niece was trying to find ways to use her fortune to help; but because of legal protections surrounding her dowry she could not bind herself to pay her husband's debts. All that could be hoped was that the bank would accept her signature on a note, providing it were also cosigned by someone of excellent financial standing. For the moment the problem was to find fifty thousand francs quickly in this fashion, with a promise of repayment at the rate of five thousand a year. Edmond Laporte stepped in at once: his signature was good for half of it. Caroline added a postscript to a letter of her uncle's to thank him for helping to save her.

Raoul-Duval was cosigner for the rest, and he also began independent moves to help his friend. Having spent much of his life in politics, he knew that the government could be persuaded to help a famous author. Allying himself with another old friend of Flaubert's, Senator Bardoux, he began arranging for a government pension. When Flaubert learned of it, however, although he was grateful and proud, he felt he must refuse; he hoped his friends would understand. But he did ask whether they could perhaps find him a sinecure in Paris, an honorific post in some library, for instance, which might give him three or four thousand a year and an apartment, as at the Mazarine Library.

This was in August. As the month drew to a close, it seemed more possible to avoid bankruptcy. The family honor was saved, but very little more. Flaubert had found a purchaser who would pay a good price for his farm at Deauville. Now Caroline revealed a little more of the disaster. It would take the entire amount realized from the sale to buy up a pressing note of Ernest's. If Flaubert declined, Ernest would be forced into bankruptcy at once. Her uncle agreed, although it was a further two hundred thousand francs and his last piece of property. He was worn out and wrote again to Bardoux to urge his need for a sinecure.

At least as early as July, Flaubert had begun to think of taking himself off to Brittany to visit his younger friend, Georges Pouchet, who was working at a marine laboratory at Concarneau. Two months there might restore him to better health and some peace of mind. Ernest worked out the itinerary, and Flaubert made it in two days of difficult travel, arriving exhausted and hungry at Concarneau on September 16. He had a pleasant room overlooking the port.

At first his thoughts were only of the past and Ernest's affairs. They were supposed now to go through smoothly to a liquidation; but until everything was complete, he could have no peace. Further waiting seemed more than he could bear. His hand trembled so much that he could hardly hold a pen, and sobs seemed always close to the surface. To make matters worse, the return to Brittany reminded him of his previous trip there, and the port of Concarneau was much like Trouville in its early days. The past submerged him everywhere. He walked about, went swimming, and watched the fish in Pouchet's aquarium. But over it all hung the pall of Ernest's debts, for he was coming to realize more and more clearly that not only had he lost his fortune but also they had undertaken to repay obligations they could not meet. At night his dreams were funereal: Croisset filled them, or dead friends.

After he had been at Concarneau about a week, Flaubert found himself thinking of a short story he wanted to try writing in lieu of *Bouvard and Pécuchet,* now indefinitely postponed. It would be *The Legend of Saint Julian the Hospitaller,* a project which perhaps went back to 1846 and on which he had worked briefly in 1856. Writing it would be a sort of daily task, something to occupy his mind. But as the days dragged by and there was no word on the liquidation, his anguish grew. What could have gone wrong, he asked urgently of Caro?

On the last day of September, Flaubert's wait was over and his property went to cover Ernest's note. A whole lifetime dedicated to learning to live in a particular way, of sacrificing everything else to his writing, he had had to give up in the space of some five months. He had now to admit that he had been wrong: all his efforts to protect himself had been insufficient. But at least nothing more could be demanded of him, he comforted himself.

In fact Flaubert knew there was more: he might lose Croisset and he might have to seek a job. Both prospects were beyond him, he feared. He felt old, decrepit, unable even to undertake the brief

Saint Julian, unimportant though he considered it. Later, if he felt better, he would return to *Bouvard and Pécuchet;* but for the nonce serious work was beyond him. He asked Ernest to advise him whether to approach Bardoux again about a job: he hated the thought, since any paid occupation was in his eyes a falling off. But if it had to be, he was willing to make the request.

As time passed and the days of anguish slipped slowly behind him, Flaubert began to find solace. Nature, which had offered him the peace of pantheism in his youth but which had so long seemed hostile, again brought relief. For two long hours one afternoon he went boating: the sea was calm, the temperature warm, the sun splendid; he was able to forget himself. Landing on a little island, he lay on his stomach on the grass and idly watched the circling gulls and the waves bounding onto the rocks. The sardine boats were returning; the crescent moon appeared and whitened one whole side of the horizon. He felt a tranquility he had not known for months, perhaps for years.

George Sand now wrote to Flaubert. She knew what Croisset meant to him and offered to buy it from his niece, if she had the money, so as to let him live out his days there. He replied quickly, assuring her that the danger of losing it was less imminent; but it had brought him a comforting gesture from an old friend. Meanwhile, however, assuming that he could keep Croisset, he still had to find a minimum of six to seven thousand francs a year in order to live.

With each passing day Flaubert spent longer outdoors, until he was taking four-hour walks and feeling much better. He was also returning to hard, daily work at his short story. He was again spending hours in his search for perfection: in one case, a whole afternoon went to polishing ten lines. It was not easy, and there were many hours of complete prostration when he felt he was too old to remake his life; but more and more he began to face his new world, not pleased with it, perhaps, but no longer overwhelmed.

THE CONQUEST OF WISDOM

I am becoming more calm. The worst part is I feel mortally
wounded.

Letter to Madame Roger des Genettes,
October 3, 1875

If wisdom consists in part in an honest and adequate observation
of life and in a willing acceptance of what one thereby learns,
Flaubert had never been very wise. In *Madame Bovary*, a delicately balanced combination of forces had let him see in Emma as
much of the tragic as of the contemptible. But beginning with
The Castle of Hearts and extending in all-but-unbroken sequence
thereafter, Flaubert's works had reflected and defined his rejection
of life. He had lived outside of—or at most beside—it, a luxury he
consciously allowed himself and which was made possible for him
by his wealth, his ego, his mother and niece, his admiring friends,
and the very bitterness of his spirit. His was, he felt, the soul of a
mandarin, superior to all but two or three chosen friends, Le Poittevin, Bouilhet, or Turgenev.

Now all Flaubert's defenses had been swept away in the engulfing tide of Commanville's ruin. His own wealth was gone, as
were his friends! In his own hour of need, he discovered one
could have needs. His impoverishment, as much of the spirit as of
the purse, opened his eyes for the first time to the real existence of
human frailties, not contemptible but natural, part of man's estate
and meriting compassion, not disdain and reproval. Where his
contempt had separated him from all mankind, now his suffering
made him one with it—or at least with that part of it whose
suffering he could imagine and hence share. Moreover, for the
first time he was hurt in his affections. Commanville he had accepted for his niece because she would thus have financial security
even if not a husband akin to her in spirit. Now she had neither,
and he had only his affection left to offer her: it was not enough.
He was ready now, with a new wisdom, for a new kind of life
and a new kind of literature; he needed only enough tranquility to
write it. It was his good fortune to be granted it, at least briefly.

To be sure, as 1875, his year of disaster, drew toward a close, he prayed daily to be allowed a prompt and easy death. In more sardonic mood, he enjoyed repeating Littré's dictum: man is a highly unstable chemical compound and the earth a very inferior planet. But in reality for the most part his morale was higher and his outlook more hopeful than they had been in the gray-black days behind him.

In his new apartment at 240, Rue du Faubourg-Saint-Honoré, he was on the corner of the Avenue Hoche, about halfway between the Arc de Triomphe and his former place beside the Parc Monceau. Daudet, who dedicated his new novel, *Jack*, to him, was particularly assiduous at Flaubert's Sunday receptions. Zola, Edmond de Goncourt, and, above all, Turgenev, were almost always there. His life was again much as it had always been. He dined weekly with Princess Mathilde, was interested in the doings of other old friends, and even found the energy to call again upon Victor Hugo. Younger men also sought him out: Mallarmé sent an autographed copy of his *Afternoon of a Faun* inscribed "To the Master."[30] But the new poetry of Verlaine, Rimbaud, and Mallarmé he could not enjoy.

Flaubert's financial affairs became more bearable as the months went by. For one thing, Ernest, an inventive man, albeit unscrupulous, constantly had new ideas for saving the situation. For many months Flaubert's hopes kept rising with each new project. One may buy some happiness briefly that way, and until midsummer of 1876 Flaubert did. While he still did not relish a world in which money preempted so much of his attention, still, it was bearable, and he could not only look back enviously to the Greeks, whom he imagined to have lived without such worries, but also forward to a time, in the indefinite future, when his own affairs would be better.

Health was another matter. The long months of strain had taken their toll from all of them. Over the autumn Caroline had been plagued with almost incessant migraines. By midwinter she was seriously ill, and his nephew was troubled by a bad cough. He himself suffered an attack of shingles in the spring. On March 8, 1876, Louise Colet died. He had not seen her for many years, but as he had written of Charles Bovary's first wife, after all, she had loved him. No doubt it had been in her own way, and their liaison had not all been happy, but a somewhat chastened Flaubert now knew that life rarely is so. Hence, when he had thought of her at all in the year or so before her death, he had tended to be more gentle than theretofore. At intervals, details in his relationship with Madame Roger des Genettes or Leconte de Lisle, both of whom he had first met in Louise's salon, had set him to reminiscing. Her little apartment came into his mind now, and he went slowly back up the course of all his memories of her. He spent the afternoon thus, but then resolutely put her out of his mind. But then, barely at the beginning of his life, the Charpentier baby who had been his god-child died of meningitis after an agony which lasted eighty hours. The child's death tore at his heart. He had had his fill of burials: now he wanted only his own.[31]

Flaubert was becoming more stoic, but there was one death which broke his control completely, although he must have known it was coming: the loss of George Sand in June of 1876.[32] He felt as though he were burying his mother a second time. He hurried to Nohant, where he learned the pressures of public opinion were requiring a religious funeral. This betrayal of her beliefs hurt him; he regretted being unable to kill the reporter from *Le Figaro* for his unfeeling attitude.

Alexander Dumas, Renan, and others of Flaubert's old friends were there. George Sand's son Maurice was overcome. Flaubert himself broke down when the casket passed before him and also while he was embracing Maurice's child Aurore: her eyes resembled her grandmother's so much that it was like a resurrection. As the good countryfolk gathered in the soft rain and the mud, fingering their beads while they prayed, it seemed to be a chapter from one of her novels.

Flaubert returned to Croisset, where his servant met him and at once drew him a huge mug of cider, which—to the man's consternation—he emptied. At dinner he enjoyed observing the familiar silver soup tureen and his old sugar bowl. The silence all about him seemed somehow tender and beneficient. He looked at some of Caroline's paintings on the walls and the small chair she had used as a child. His mind turned to his dead mother, but now in a spirit of peace and gentleness. Never had a return to Croisset been less painful.

As the days went by, the doves cooed, the boats slipped noiselessly by on the river, and his writing moved forward easily. He was strangely relaxed, enjoying the green countryside and the silence and swimming vigorously each day. He was convinced—perhaps more than the years since have justified—that George Sand's high place in literature was secure and that over the ages other hearts would beat in sympathy with hers as readers came to know her through her books. He wrote to Maurice of how very feminine "this great man" had been and of her immense tenderness. Maurice could console himself that he had been a joy to her: she had often spoken of him as a blessing. Flaubert's own return to writing the previous autumn, he added, had been her work; she had found the way to bring him back to respect for himself.

George Sand had watched over him with motherly care, helping by her offer to buy Croisset but supporting him far more through her endlessly repeated counsel to come to terms with life itself. Where he made his readers desolate, she sought to console them, she pointed out. He kept apart from life and from his characters, whom he watched as they moved about. While she agreed (not wholly correctly) that he made no overt judgment of them, still, she insisted, readers could divine his opinions and were saddened by them. There was more than literature involved: his real difficulty was that he lacked a firm and broad view of life. Art, she kept reiterating, is more than depiction. True painting, she affirmed, is full of the soul of the man who holds the brush. Criticism and satire could show only one face of life.[33.]

For nearly a decade George Sand had been urging her philosophy on her friend, never annoyed that it always fell on deaf ears. But now that real catastrophe had struck and involved others in addition to himself, Flaubert was at last able to hear what she had always been saying. *Saint Julian* he wrote in a new spirit. Upon its completion he turned at once to a second story, putting off his satiric *Bouvard and Pécuchet*. The new tale was to be called *A Simple Heart*, and it was written in part for her. Many years earlier, he had returned to the contemporary world in *A Senti-*

mental Education in part to answer the desires of Sainte-Beuve, who had died just before the novel was completed. So it was again with this story, which George Sand never saw. She would have been pleased to see that she had succeeded.

June and July of 1876 brought more of what was by now a familiar financial picture. Ernest was not doing brilliantly, but he was earning enough for the bare support of his wife and uncle. The young couple even felt well enough off to make a trip to spas in the south of France during July and August, although Flaubert was himself so penniless during this time that he was unable to entertain Princess Mathilde for luncheon at Croisset.[31]

Flaubert's aging servant Julie was again unwell. The operation on her eye had not been more than a palliative, and now in this summer of 1876 she was ill in Rouen and miserable. He was not sure what to do, for his servants had no warm welcome for her, as her care would fall upon them. Achille, who had treated her, warned his brother that she had a chronic inflammation of the eye and would require someone to look after her. A month later, however, in July, Flaubert brought her out to Croisset. She seemed very thin and weak but, though almost completely blind, she was delighted to be back there "because of the country air." One or another of the servants had to walk with her daily, but it made Flaubert happy to see her regaining strength with each day.

Flaubert was ready once more to survey his life and contemplate the future. It was as though he had been sick ever since the death of his mother four years before. Attending the funeral of Madame Sand had in some way been traumatic: he was at peace with himself for perhaps the first time in his adult life. He felt younger and, like Pécuchet, dared to give up his flannel underwear with no ill effects. He now had the strength to resume the life at Croisset he had thought he was abandoning forever the preceding September when, half-dead with discouragement, he had left for Brittany. Life was not ideal, but it was tolerable. And he had learned how to tolerate it. Dumas, he learned, had called him an idealist. He was happy to agree.

His days were full. He swam, once even struggling manfully against the tide until he almost threw his hip out of joint. And he worked far into the night, for writing was again his outlet, and the dawn frequently had risen before he went to bed. He would never learn to be economical, he wrote to his niece; but at least relatively he looked forward to a long period of peace. More than that, he said, one should not ask of the gods.[35]

In September, Gertrude Collier Tennant paid him a visit: all the intervening years seemed to disappear, and she and he were back in their youth. He blessed her for her thought in coming to see him. After her departure he wrote urging her to return and telling her he always thought of her as his youth. It would be cruel not to continue, now that they had renewed the contact. She should come to Paris for the winter with her two daughters. As for her surprise that he should have written a story with so warm a title as *A Simple Heart*, he insisted she, of all people, had no right to suppose him incapable of affection. For some months they exchanged letters: it did him good.

From his new-found tranquility Flaubert had to find the strength to envisage a future where money problems would be his for several years. At times matters would look more hopeful. In October he was sure things were taking a turn for the better; but all through the autumn and early winter he was seriously short of money and having constantly to write and then write again to Caroline and Ernest to send him cash, although he had reduced his expenses as much as he knew how. It was humiliating, but he had no choice.[36]

Croisset was a source of peace. Settled quietly there, he felt no need for outside distractions. His servants sufficed for all his needs. His memories were there: he could, when he wished, go quietly to his mother's room for meditation. He kept a hat of hers and the fan which she had used when she came to meet him at Italy. He liked to see and touch them from time to time. The passage of time enhanced rather than effaced his relics for him.

Croisset gave him easy access to the open countryside, which he now needed. Long walks back from Rouen and frequent moments out of doors were rebuilding his shattered health, and he began once again to feel sturdy and to rejoice in returning vigor. He took to noticing with all his former keenness the smell of the fog or the precise look of the leaves. He even wished he could be a calf and eat the grass, again a desire for communion with nature. One evening, although he had already had one walk, the moonlight was so beautiful he could not resist its enchantment and, leaving his work table, he returned to the garden. Croisset also brought him close to old Julie, who would come in to talk with him after dinner while his fire was being attended to. They would reminisce about events and people of long ago whom he and she alone remembered. The imagery of her peasant language added piquancy to her phrasing.

As Christmas approached in 1876, Flaubert's anguish and doubts crystallized in a new awareness of the meaning religious belief could give to them: he decided to attend Midnight Mass on Christmas Eve. He worked for ten uninterrupted hours that day. As twelve o'clock drew near, he stopped, paused long enough to write of his decision to Turgenev and Madame Roger des Genettes, and then changed and set out for the mile walk to the nearby orphanage run by nuns. He knew he was being romantic and admitted it freely to Caroline in a letter on Christmas Day. The service had moved him.

Christmas and New Year's were now times for recollection rather than anticipation. On Christmas Day, replying to a letter of Gertrude Collier Tennant's, Flaubert thanked her for remembering Trouville as it was and for hating the modern city. The best of his youth, he wrote her, had been spent there. But all the waves that had rolled over it since had not effaced his memories. He wondered if the long lapse of years embellished things. Was it all as beautiful and good as he thought he remembered it, with her, her sisters, and Caroline? What a gulf between then and now! She would understand.

The thirty-first of December that year seemed a good moment to write his niece what New Year's Day had been like when he and her mother had been children. And so he traced the picture of a then young Julie taking the two children by the hand to make the rounds in the chill January weather to visit all the family friends. Instead, this year, he would spend the day working on a third short story. It was pleasant, a few days later, to receive a letter from Emile Zola telling him how much all his friends in Paris missed him.

Serenity was not easy to achieve or to maintain. There were

moments when the amiable falsehoods upon which in part he built his life appeared in their true light. His Three Angels were very dear to him, but he could not always conceal from himself that, although they were fond enough of him as person, still his ideas frequently shocked them and they no doubt often deemed him of not quite sound mind. Long before, he had recorded in one of his Notebooks the sorrow the artist feels when a woman of whom he is fond does not share his admirations and he cannot move her.[37] The uncomprehension of his Three Angels was not easy to accept and could pierce his defenses to make him unhappy.

Money was the eternal worry, and in January of 1877 there was another crisis. To his dismay Flaubert discovered, quite by accident, that the caretaker in the cemetery had not been paid for years. In a deep and very intimate part of himself, Flaubert cringed. Nor did he have enough to meet the bill. He had to implore his niece and nephew to do so.[38] At this time, too, Laporte came into financial difficulties. He smilingly put a good face on it and said he was grateful because it brought him and his friend together in another way! Despite his own problems, Laporte continued to try to help Flaubert and Ernest, although some of Laporte's actions did not meet with the full approval of Ernest and Caroline.

The situation was becoming alarming.[39] On January 12, 1877, Flaubert had only half a franc left! Four days later he received one hundred francs from Ernest, but he had been under harsher privation than he had known since his student days in the Latin Quarter. He had not even been able to send his maid to Rouen for lack of passage money for her. He wrote in violent protest.

Under pressing Ernest confessed that his financial affairs were worse than he had earlier admitted: his Dieppe sawmill was so heavily mortgaged that he could no longer carry on. And these mortgages were prior claims upon it, which must be repaid before Flaubert's mortgage could be considered. For this worthless piece of paper all the 200,000 francs from his Deauville farm had gone. Sale of the factory, a hope with which Ernest and Caro had long deluded him, would bring him nothing. He turned in every direction to try to raise more money for Ernest, but his resources were, by now, minute compared to the catastrophe before his nephew. There seemed no way out.

Then, inexplicably, affairs looked up and there was money again. Flaubert was reassured and celebrated by ordering a new dressing gown and slippers. He permitted himself to scold his nephew for delays in sending him cash and announced that, upon his arrival in Paris for the final stages of publishing his *Three Tales*, he demanded good wines, fine liqueurs, pleasant company, pocket money, joyous faces, and witty conversation. He prepared himself to enjoy them.

THE ESTHETIC DEEPENS

The whole problem lies right there: to be a poet without being a fool.

Letter to George Sand, June 3, 1874

He was too old to change. This was Flaubert's repeated cry to his niece over all these months. Hence the Flaubert who wrote the *Three Tales* brought a familiar fifty years of living to the task. Although the suffering of others had become more meaningful, their stupidity had not and, as before, his contempt was matched only by the violence with which he phrased it: the fleas on his dog Julio seemed to him quite as important as three-quarters of the human race. What could there be in common between him (or any intelligent man) and them? "Bourgeois" he continued to call them; and their stupidity was almost a personal enemy for him. It was the counterpart of his violent enthusiasm and admiration for what he found superior. To other friends who shared his pessimism and disgust he could affirm that his whole life now had become a moral crusade to show to his fellow man the extent of the danger. The chief moral problem before society was to keep this universal stupidity within bounds. Although it could not be crushed out of existence, at least his efforts to analyze it were steps in the right direction: an illness diagnosed was already half cured.[40]

While it was harder to cling to his principles in near poverty and distress, Flaubert had abandoned none of them. He sought to live a life as quiet and ordinary on the outside as it was violent and original within, where the artist dwelt in an inviolate sanctuary hidden from profane eyes. Success he continued to scorn and he labored for eternity, but nowadays Olympic detachment seemed impossible to achieve. Classical serenity and perfection he still revered, but he happily acknowledged his romanticism, too, remembering with truculent pride younger days when he had insulted the insipid neoclassical poet Casimir Delavigne or noisily insisted Béranger was not the greatest poet of all time. Literary criticism he felt misunderstood by his contemporaries. Now they had all adopted Taine's doctrines, which obscured the work of art behind the scientifically understood factors deemed to have produced it. They supposed that the critic had adequately discussed a work of art when he had explained its surroundings.

Placing himself where the critic must, on the terrain chosen by the artist, Flaubert could admire or evaluate with equal ease Chateaubriand, Hugo, Balzac, or Zola. Naturalism was fighting for the right to exist during these years and, while he disliked much about it, he joined in the efforts to sustain it. Zola was perhaps wrong in trying so hard to found a school and be true to foolish principles; the notion of naturalism was as silly as that of realism, which had preceded it. But *L'Assommoir* had grandeur of movement and undeniable truth. It was, no doubt, too much of one tone, but it was a powerful work. He sought to bring his friends to agree with him.

Chateaubriand was another matter, and Flaubert took an unalloyed pleasure in repeating aloud from memory his favorite passages from *René* or *Atala*. François Coppée remembered the way he would recite, bringing out the rhythm of the sentence and the majestic sonorities. When he had finished, he would pause, silent and exhausted. Then, unable to repress himself any longer, he would seize his listener by the arm, look into his eyes, and seek his assent that it was stupendous.[41]

Balzac was more complex. During these years his *Correspondence* was first published: Flaubert read it with mixed feelings. The artist in Balzac did not come off well, he felt: so much preoccupa-

GUY DE MAUPASSANT, BY NADAR

Son of Flaubert's childhood companion, Laure Le Poittevin, and a fellow writer, Maupassant became Flaubert's devoted disciple and loving, watchful friend in the last years of his mentor's life. Archives photographiques, Paris.

VICTOR HUGO, BY BONNAT

Long an idol of Flaubert's youth and in the 1870's the patriarch of
French letters and a powerful figure in the Senate, Victor Hugo was a
wise guide and staunch friend in the last decade of Flaubert's life. Archives photographiques, Paris.

MADAME PASCA, BY NADAR

A talented actress and attractive woman, Madame Pasca was one of
Flaubert's "Three Angels," the close friends who comforted and flattered the aging novelist in his difficult last years. Archives photographiques, Paris.

MADAME BRAINNE

The closest to Flaubert of his "Three Angels," Madame Brainne was a safe friend with whom to carry on a warm flirtation.

MADAME LAPIERRE

Although perhaps less dear to Flaubert than his other two Angels, Madame Lapierre, the third Angel, lived in Rouen and was a warm and steadfast friend when Flaubert was in Croisset.

FLAUBERT'S NIECE CAROLINE

Flaubert helped to bring up Caroline after the death in childbirth of her mother, Flaubert's adored sister. Caroline was his pupil, his constant concern, and later the source of his greatest anguish when the financial ruin of her husband entailed Flaubert's as well. Her almost masculine face, its eyes recalling her uncle's, reveals the determined and self-centered woman she was.

MADAME FLAUBERT IN ADVANCED YEARS

Throughout Flaubert's life his mother was his dearest companion and only permanent attachment. Her death in 1872 was a loss from which he never fully recovered.

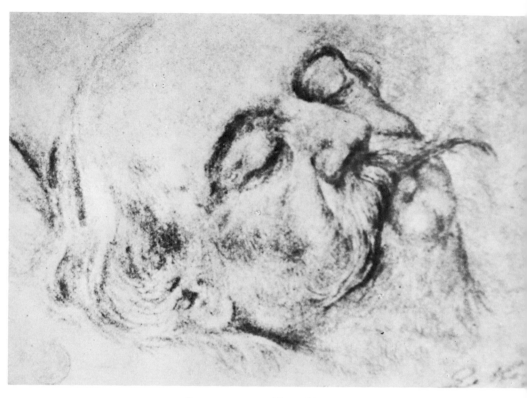

SKETCH OF THE DEAD FLAUBERT

Both the turmoil he experienced and the ultimate peace for which he so longed mark the features.

tion with himself, his debts, his furniture, and his printing endeavors seemed to exclude all consideration of art, of religion, of humanity, or of learning. He seemed famished for glory and uninterested in the beautiful. He was concerned for Catholicism and for politics; he longed to be a deputy or become a member of the Academy. His ignorance was appalling. His highest literary admiration was for Walter Scott, whom even *Bouvard and Pécuchet* would shortly scorn.

This was all familiar ground. But a man, even of fifty years and more, does not necessarily go unmarked through the anguish which Flaubert had experienced: unbeknownst to himself he had learned from it. And so his evaluation of Balzac contained insight which he could not have possessed when he was younger. The earlier man's letters were, he wrote, an edifying document to read. What a life he had lived, and what suffering he had known! What an example he offered by the way he had met the tortures life inflicted on him! One ended by loving him despite his flaws: he was a good man. When Caro wrote that he must have been like her uncle, Flaubert replied with deep satisfaction that Théophile Gautier had often said listening to him was like hearing Balzac again, and that the two would have cherished each other. When George Sand had written to Flaubert that he saddened his readers where she sought to console them, he had replied that he depicted what he saw, and he could not have different eyes. In this he was wrong; his eyes had already opened to much they had never seen before; but this he did not yet know.

Madame Sand also asked him to let his beliefs illuminate his writing; failing this, he appeared not to have any principles.[42] In despair he replied that in fact he was being suffocated by his principles and rages and indignations . . . which was not precisely what she had meant. These, however, he insisted he must not show.

Flaubert's hatreds had become what all hatreds long continued must become, devastating blind spots and weaknesses against which he no longer even knew he needed defenses. His inner ragings and his perceptions of external phenomena had so fused that he no longer distinguished between them: he had become the prisoner, not the master, of his hates. When George Sand accused

him of writing only criticism or satire, he replied that he had
never intended to do either, that he had always sought to go to
the core of whatever he was dissecting and to express its greatest
generalities, avoiding the accidental and the dramatic, the monster
or the hero. His theories had not changed for thirty years; but his
practice had.

Flaubert's preoccupation was, if possible, even more with
beauty than before. His efforts to think clearly and well he now
made almost exclusively in order to write well. He regretted, with
George Sand, that his views on life were not more inclusive: it
would mean better writing. But this the artist did not have for the
wanting of it. On the other hand, simple integrity and hard work
sufficed to attain to an accurate depiction, and the true was, as
always, the basis upon which one started.[43]

Only the pursuit of beauty mattered. This was what so separated him from his fellow writers: passages in the great authors
which left him ravaged with horror or admiration left them quite
unmoved. Edmond de Goncourt was happy, Flaubert said, when
he had overheard a phrase which he could use in a book, because
it was real; for his own part, he was happy when he had written a
page without a repetition or an assonance. He was chagrined that
his friends so misunderstood him. Zola saw only that he seemed
terrified at having to imagine something instead of finding it in
reality.[44] Maupassant, more sympathetic and more perceptive, understood and contented himself with admiring the excellent memory Flaubert could draw upon in his research. He knew an incalculable number of facts and could remember the book, chapter,
and page, even the paragraph, in which he had read a detail years
before and go to it unerringly upon his shelves.[45]

With the writing of the *Three Tales*, Flaubert found himself
discovering unexpected possibilities and new excellences in French
prose: it required only the persistence to polish it sufficiently. He
could still remember the day in Athens when he had stood at the
entrance to the Acropolis overcome with the violence of his admiration as he studied the wall of the Propylaea, a bare wall but of
such perfect masonry that not a joint appeared. Could not a book,
independent of what it said, have the same effect? In the precision
with which its parts were assembled, the rarity of its elements, the

polish of its surface, the harmony of its totality, could it not have an intrinsic virtue, a sort of divine force, something eternal akin to a principle? As he sought to grapple with the newly formed thought, he knew that it was indeed very old and he added that he was speaking in Platonic terms.

There was, Flaubert was mystically sure, a necessary relationship between the precise word one needed to express a concept—and it was here that he used his famous "le mot juste"—and the most musical word for it. Why, he asked—though surely echoing an experience granted to few—does one always produce a line of verse in compressing a thought to its limit? The Law of Numbers, he was willing to affirm, governed feelings and images. What was to the casual observer only external form was in reality internal, integral, the essence of what others mistakenly called the content. His search, then, for what seemed external beauty was in fact a method for penetrating to the heart of his matter. An unwanted assonance or a repetition was an easy index of error. When one finally had the right word, everything dropped into its harmonious place. For, he told Maupassant, there existed only one way to express something, one noun to state it, one adjective to qualify it, one verb to animate it.[46] This mysterious harmony he never ceased seeking through all the fluid, evanescent elements of French prose, for his anguish but also for his surest joy.

Such clear-cut statements of mystically sensed relationships were the result of having lived with these intuitions so very long; they did not, however, reflect Flaubert's new emphasis arising from the years of despair and catastrophe he had just been living. These revolved about the remaining element of the Platonic triad, the good. For the first time, perhaps, he faced directly the issue of morality in his books, no longer contenting himself with insisting that it was enough to have paid attention to truth and beauty. Under the ceaseless prodding of George Sand, he had burst out in a letter to her that if the reader did not draw from a book the ethical conclusions which must be in it, then either the reader was a fool or the book was false. If the depiction were true (he did not say real), then it was good. Obscene works were immoral precisely because they lacked this truth: life was not like that.

George Sand had won. She could not be sure of it, and Flau-

bert did not know it. But the victory came as he struggled to
write *A Simple Heart*, which would enshrine all that she had so
long wanted and waited for. He could make no use of her metaphysics or of doctrines dear to her concerning progress, fraternity, or democracy. He had written her that he sought, without
being able to find it, for that idea upon which everything else
would depend. In fact he had found it. In *Saint Julian*, which he
was finishing, it had been implicit; in *A Simple Heart* it would be
exemplified; in *Hérodias* it would be explicit, for by then he
would know it consciously. He had been mistaken when he had
written that his temperament was beyond change and hence his
esthetic, too. As rage had come to dominate him in the 1860's and
early 1870's, his esthetic had been deflected; now wisdom, painfully acquired, was setting it right again.

One of the most moving works of the decade was Renan's
Prayer on the Acropolis, published in 1876. Flaubert wrote to
thank him for writing it. Its periods unfolded, he wrote, like the
Panathenaic Procession on the Parthenon. To Caro he called it a
summa of intellectual man of the nineteenth century. The *Prayer*
was an invocation to Minerva, incarnation of simple and true
beauty, whose cult meant reason and wisdom, and whose precepts
were an eternal lesson of conscience and sincerity. She conferred
her initiation upon the Athenian at his birth with a smile. But as a
northerner, Renan confessed, he had been able to acquire her wisdom only by reflection and long effort. And he could never forget
his youth in a distant land worshiping in other temples dedicated
to lesser divinities, for he was charmed by the barbarian magic of
Christianity. Moreover, all nobility had disappeared from the
world of his day. A leaden pall of stupidity lay over the world
and stifled mankind. The Apostle Paul had made it a crime to love
Minerva, goddess of order, image of stability.

Minerva had been the source of every virtue, the wellspring
from which the Athenian drew his wit and hence his true faith, his
eternal gaiety, the divine childhood that informed his heart. The
world would be saved by her alone; and in a burst of faith Renan
swore to be true to her, to resist his skepticism, his restless doubt,
his vagabond fantasy. For when the true has been found, why
question, why struggle, why resist?

But could one follow Minerva today? The modern world saw good shading imperceptibly into evil and found nothing absolutely lovable or hateful. In this suspension and refusal to conclude, lay its wisdom. All past truth had perished; all present ones must, also. Renan knew this was the prompting of his weakness, but such evil was in him and could not be denied. A literature or a way of life based upon Minerva, wholly sane and wholly sound, could now arouse only ennui. Renan repeated the word, admitting the goddess would smile at his naïveté. But if his world was corrupt, must he not admit it? And the world, alas, was bigger than she had known. Had she, too, seen it all, not even her forehead would have that Olympian calm; and her head, enlarged, would have had to include conflicting notions of beauty.

And so his conclusion was foreordained. A vast river of forgetfulness sweeps us forward into the nameless abyss which is the only god. The tears of all the peoples are true tears; the dreams of every sage include parcels of truth. And life is only symbol and dream. The gods each pass, and no outmoded faith must be a chain: it is enough that we swathe them reverently in the purple shroud reserved for the sleep of dead gods.

There, too, Flaubert, too, had sought with reverence to lay them, in *The Temptation of Saint Anthony*. But now, as with new wisdom he took up a new book, he had a new faith which, he would suggest, was beyond time.

24

Three Tales (1877)

Saint Julian The Hospitaller

I had a dream about three weeks ago . . .

Flaubert's *Notes* on his trip to
Italy in 1845

THE temptation to take advantage of the insights into Flaubert which psychoanalytic techniques offer is probably as great as most of those suffered by Anthony; but when the subject in question is a long-dead author it is probably wise to invoke all the assistance which the desert saint called upon so eloquently. Flaubert's responses to stimuli cannot be tested; the private significance of his symbols can never be more than dimly glimpsed. And yet this discipline sends probes into areas where the creation of literature takes place. Perhaps, then, if one recognizes the dangers and hence the limitations, it may be possible—without having succumbed to the devil—to have recourse to some of the approaches of psychoanalysis to understand the sudden change and burst of creativity in Flaubert from the autumn of 1875 until the spring of 1877. For during this time his state was precisely one of those that this discipline proposes to elucidate and which it may even seek to induce.

When Flaubert left Croisset to be with Georges Pouchet at Concarneau in September of 1875, he was a broken man whose existence lay shattered about him. The present was unbearable; the future promised to be worse. Only the past, which he had railed at when it was present, seemed to offer consolation, and unbidden it rose about him, soliciting his attention and offering its comfort. When he was ready to write again, it was not his current hates and disgusts that demanded outlet: *Bouvard and Pécuchet* had sat untouched for months. He knew he had not the strength for a work of its compass. And, perhaps, beneath the conscious level he sensed other stirrings. These grapplings it is tempting to scrutinize so as to understand the better the sense in which past was present in the often unwanted memories in his subconscious. Precision of analysis is impossible, and detailed interpretations are doomed to error in advance, but certain broad lines may be sketched.

Upon his return to writing, Flaubert specifically selected the story of Saint Julian as his subject. The medieval legend as Flaubert reworked it bears a close and obvious relation to a dream of his. But the dream precedes the writing of the story by thirty years! The problem is to link the two, however broadly.

The dream is the most suggestive starting point. One afternoon during the trip which Flaubert made with his family to the Mediterranean and Italy in 1845, he was in a garden on the Riviera admiring the roses and observing a small monkey.[1] Either the actual seeing of the monkey or, later, the task of writing up the event in his notes, led him to speculate on monkeys in general and to note that, when he observed one, he was never quite sure whether he was looking at the monkey or the monkey was looking at him. He added that monkeys are our ancestors, a concept which was already in the air in these pre-Darwinian days.

This speculation was enough to prompt Flaubert to write down what he could recall of a dream about monkeys which he had had some three weeks before.* Accompanied by his mother in the dream, he walked through a great forest filled with them. The farther they advanced, the more monkeys arrived. There were

---

*"J'ai rêvé, il y a environ trois semaines, que j'étais dans une grande forêt toute remplie de singes; ma mère se promenait avec moi. Plus nous avancions, plus il en venait: il y en avait dans les branches, qui riaient et sautaient; il en venait beaucoup dans notre chemin, et de plus en plus grands, de plus en plus nombreux. Ils me regardaient tous, j'ai fini par avoir peur. Ils nous entouraient comme dans un cercle; un a voulu me caresser et m'a pris la main, je lui ai tiré un coup de fusil à l'épaule et je l'ai fait saigner; il a poussé des hurlements affreux. Ma mère m'a dit alors: "Pourquoi le blesses-tu, ton ami? qu'est-ce qu'il t'a fait? ne vois-tu pas qu'il t'aime? comme il te ressemble!" Et le singe me regardait. Cela m'a déchiré l'âme et je me suis réveillé ... me sentant de la même nature que les animaux et fraternisant avec eux d'une communion toute panthéistique et tendre" (*NDV*, I, 15).

some in the branches of the trees, laughing and leaping about. Many more arrived and got in the way of Flaubert and his mother. They were larger and more numerous. All were looking at Flaubert and at last he became frightened. They surrounded him and his mother in a sort of circle. One of them wished to pat him and took his hand. Flaubert shot him in the shoulder—there is no earlier mention of a gun—and the monkey bled and howled horrendously. His mother then asked him: "Why do you wound your friend? What did he do to you? Don't you see that he loves you? How much he resembles you?" And the monkey kept looking at him. Flaubert was brokenhearted and wakened . . . he left the dots in his Notebook to indicate the transition, for as conscious thought began to take over, he was aware of a deep sensation of being of the same nature as the animals and of fraternizing with them in a communion at once pantheistic and tender.

It is perhaps well to face down certain temptations at once and to decline to give in to them. The gun and its firing may well have sexual implications; they probably do—but they cannot be elucidated to the satisfaction of any but the analyst who offers the particular elucidation. Is it homosexuality? Or heterosexuality? Or both? Or does it refer to intercourse with animals? To each of these questions affirmative or negative answers have been given with no more foundation than the comfortable assurance that Flaubert is not about for verifications and further analysis of other dreams and reactions. But even if one sets aside the temptation to go beyond what can be known, one still may ask more generally what the dream means. To be sure, nothing in the available record allows guesses concerning what immediate events may have provoked its story-line. But the precise events are of little import compared to what the dream means specifically in relation to the story of Saint Julian.

In the legend Julian was the great hunter who killed a stag. Before the animal died he miraculously cursed Julian and foretold his murder of his own parents. Julian fled his home in an effort to avoid the dire prophecy. He prospered and made a rich marriage in a distant land. His parents, despairing of his return, set out in search of him but arrived at his castle in his absence. His wife made them welcome and put them in her bed for the night. Julian returned and found the two; mistaking them for his wife and a lover, he killed them. Upon learning his error, he fled again until he came to a dangerous river ford; he spent the remainder of his life ferrying people across it. On a certain evening, he heard a voice, rose, and went to perform his accustomed service. Before him he found a hideous leper who, after being ferried over, demanded hospitality as well and even insisted on warming himself in Julian's bed. Upon Julian's willing consent, the leper was transformed into an angel, who informed him that his repentance had been accepted by the Lord: shortly he would die and go to heaven, which he did.

Flaubert made certain important changes in the story.[2] Within what compass the short-story form allowed him, he analyzed closely Julian's interest in hunting, which he transformed into a psychopathic blood lust whose beginnings are detailed and whose development is what sets loose the mechanism of the story. The killing of the deer then came as the culmination of a succession of killings terminating in a great hunt which had been a long, hideous massacre of animals for the sadistic pleasure of killing. For a long time thereafter, as a penance and through fear, Julian refused to hunt at all. At last unable to resist any longer, he went out upon a second great hunt. But where as before he had killed with miraculous ease, now he could kill nothing. Wild with frustration, he returned longing to kill people . . . and murdered his parents.

Flaubert's dream involved animals crowding about—they do this in Julian's second hunt—and becoming menacing, which legitimized shooting one of them, although it was friendly. His mother offered reprimand; and he wakened feeling fraternal, at peace. His guilt had been erased. This much the dream itself contained. And, while Flaubert cannot be questioned in all the ways an analyst would wish, still he did unwittingly provide the answers to some questions. For instance, what about other dreams? While many that he reports do not bear any overt relationship to the monkey dream, he does mention an interesting one of 1838 in which he also walks with his mother, this time by a riverbank. She falls into the water, but he is absolutely unable to save her. Although she calls for help, he is attached to the ground by some invisible force. Full of rage and despair he can only listen to her cries rising from the river bottom.[3] His helplessness in his dream suggests some of the ambivalence toward his mother which is also apparent in his whole life and in the dream of 1845.

More useful is Flaubert's attitude toward animals in general as he reported it all through his youth and early manhood. He was convinced—and that is all that really matters—that he had a rather special understanding of them because he could enter their world; they knew it and were drawn to him. Significantly, he felt he had the same power over the insane.[4] Julian, in Flaubert's reworking of the legend, is psychopathic when he kills. Animals in general, who were Julian's victims, were close to Flaubert; but he felt an equal kinship with their slayer. In *Julian* he could pity the one and absolve the other.

Monkeys occupied for Flaubert a very special place, even amongst animals. The declaration in the dream that they were like him and his comment that they were man's ancestors have overtones which tended to recur whenever Flaubert discussed them. They were almost always lascivious in the contexts in which he placed them, but their caresses were cold and horrible. In 1877 the aging Flaubert was still listening with delight to lubricious tales of their repulsive and licentious behavior.[5]

In his dream Flaubert shot the monkey, making him bleed and setting him to howling horrendously. Enjoyment of blood and carnage goes far back in his works: the *Memoirs of a Madman* recounted a bloody dream;[6] and other early tales oozed with it. *Salammbô* had even been hurt in the eyes of some readers by its insistent gore; and Saint Anthony had still bathed deeply in it in the version of 1874.

Keeping only to long-term constants in Flaubert's makeup, in his dream he shot at and wounded a very lascivious animal. It bled, which was morbidly attractive to Flaubert. This animal was then pronounced, by his mother, to be very like him. The discovery made him very sad and led to the interruption of the dream by his wakening. He then felt at peace with all nature. Rephrasing only slightly, animality, and in particular sexuality, which seemed frightening and yet which appealed to Flaubert, he enjoyed destroying. But then his mother, toward whom his feelings were ambivalent, told him that sexuality was his own nature and should not have been destroyed; this saddened him. But he wakened having made his peace with it all and feeling at one with it. The dream occurred during the extremely complex period when he was about to abandon the total chastity he had perforce practiced following the onset of his epilepsy. Sexuality was of course troubling him as he came nearer to allowing it to enter his consciousness again.

Flaubert, then, perturbed by the problem of sexuality and connecting it with sadism and carnage, was this once moved to embody his conflicts in a dream story revolving about the wanton killing of animals; the killing induced a feeling of contrition when he understood his error; through an unexplained transition during the waking period he was forgiven by nature and received into communion with her.

Sexuality, sadism, blood lust, guilt, contrition, and the desire for absolution continued throughout Flaubert's life. In 1875, during another period of deep and nearly intolerable strain, he was led back into his early memories and again found it possible to give outlet to his tensions in a further mythic structure. This time it was a conscious elaboration of the same concerns around a folkloric theme. The culture had long embodied the notions of sin, repentance, and absolution in a number of themes. The Julian story was one elaboration, which also added man's relationship to animals. To its ready-made framework Flaubert added the specific sin of blood lust and emphasized the animal element. Making both the sin and the penance more hideous, he gave the story that psychical potential which he needed to work out his own tensions in the writing of it. Of course he felt better as the writing progressed and the tale began to take shape before his eyes.

Such concerns, going back into Flaubert's childhood and renewed by adolescence and the onset of epilepsy, must always have sought outlets. Old Julie, who used to tell him stories and legends, may even have told him the story of Julian. Rouen Cathedral had a stained-glass window which recounts the events of Julian's life; Jules of the first *Education* used to admire such windows, and in a draft for *Madame Bovary* Flaubert specifically mentioned this one in the cathedral.[7] Moreover, his friend Ernest Langlois had done a study of stained-glass windows in France and had published a drawing of this window. The actual idea of writing the story may go back as far as 1846, the year following the dream, as Maxime Du Camp says Flaubert got the idea when he saw a statue of Julian at Caudebec in that year. He also says that Flaubert was annotating *The Golden Legend* at this time as part of his preparations for *Saint Anthony:* he would have found the story here too.[8]

While Flaubert was writing *Madame Bovary* in the 1850's, one of the tales he dreamed of writing—in reaction against the subject matter of the *Bovary*—was a romance of chivalry introducing elements of terror and high poetry as well as great feudal hunts and pictures of medieval castle life.[9] The Julian story was what he turned to immediately upon finishing his long novel. He did some desultory reading for it, and took a few notes; but Saint Anthony was more pressing and ultimately crowded out the other saint.

By coincidence, one of Louise Colet's works contained a story of hunting deer and of the pathos of their death, which must have touched this familiar chord in Flaubert.[10] Also in Flaubert's own projected *Spiral* there was to be a hashish episode concerning the hero's arrival in a foreign country, his falling in love with the sultan's daughter, and his leading armies and reaching supreme power.[11] But it may be that the writing of *Salammbô* gave vent to so many of these tensions in Flaubert's nature that it provided adequate release. At any rate, the tale seems to sink from sight thereafter until 1874.

Flaubert's visit to Kaltbad Righi in that year was in many ways like the original Mediterranean trip. An exhausted, frustrated, sick man, broken by tensions he could no longer master, had taken a trip once again—this time expressly for his health. But on this occasion, unlike the previous one, he had no occupation: hence his days had to be filled by some conscious activity of his own choosing. Notes and reading for Julian were part of what he elected to do.

The following year was to be far worse, and in September Flaubert withdrew to Concarneau. The feeling that he must return to literature obsessed him, and soon he was writing to Caro that he must force himself to begin *Saint Julian.* The renewed tensions he had again externalized in a story based on the killing of animals; and once again the Julian legend imposed itself on him. Turgenev, informed of the project, was delighted that he had again set to work, and he urged that the tale be restricted to thirty pages. Gradually Flaubert began to have books sent to him in Brittany. The Middle Ages, as he read on, seemed an attractive world, as far removed in time from his current troubles as Brittany was in space.

During the writing, which went on into February of 1876, Flaubert referred to his tale most casually and in deprecatory fashion. It was a storylet, poetico-religious and medieval-rococo in tone; it was a foolish small thing, fit for little girls, an edifying work which would make people think he was turning devout. And much of the preparation and some of the final story are just that, a delightful plunge into the extraordinary world of medieval castle life with hunting dogs of sonorous names and falcons brought from far countries.

Gradually, however, the deeper concerns which were in fact finding their form here, began to dominate; and Flaubert could tell George Sand that he was writing in all the sincerity of his heart. It must have gladdened her. For now Julian was becoming a substitute for a guilt-ridden Flaubert; the saint's sin was taking shape and acquiring the threatening tones which Flaubert's dream had foretold.

At last it was done and Flaubert could read it to Madame Roger des Genettes. He wrote to her later of what profound good it had done him to watch her eyes, which were deep and lustrous, as he read it aloud. Zola, too, heard him and remembered the way his voice rose as he neared the end, till the ceiling seemed to tremble and the last words came out like a clap of thunder.[12]

The story was Flaubert's first attempt since adolescence to write in a short form. As always, he paid stricter attention to form than his predecessors had. For the first time in France a writer consciously undertook to manipulate his form from beginning to end to produce deliberate artistic effects. As a result *Saint Julian* inaugurates the short story as art form in France.[13] The tale is broken into three parts, and in addition there are a number of further divisions. These Flaubert used to bring out emphases or indicate lapse of time, especially necessary in a story blending the fantastic and legendary with the real and normal. He was convinced this mingling was possible: the miracles in the story would not really bother anyone, since people in the Western culture are brought up with these tales all about them.[14] Moreover, as with Saint Anthony, Julian was the sort of person who makes no distinction between the real and the fantastic: the miraculous would be natural in his world. Flaubert proposed to present the story directly, without intrusions on his part, so that the reader would be caught up in it. James Joyce found this to be perhaps his most perfect work.[15]

The tale opens, as so often in Flaubert, with a single-sentence paragraph: "Julian's father and mother lived in a chateau, in the midst of a wood, on the slope of a hill." The commas cut the sentence into the kind of triple rhythms he enjoyed, and the sentence itself, as almost always, serves to give the location. It avoids the bravura of *Salammbô* in the garden of Hamilcar Barca, precisely because it is a legend and its truthfulness must be established in a tone of the utmost normality.

From the beginning Flaubert subtly prepared the reader by uniting at every turn the suggestions of the saint and the knight. The stones of the castle courtyard were as clean as the flagging of a church; the archer on guard in the hot sun soon slept as soundly as a monk; Julian's mother kept the castle with the severe excellence of a monastery. Obscure references to heraldry and the symbolism of flowers bore the message in domains the reader cannot even comprehend.

The quiet, matter-of-fact description of the chateau establishes a picture which has been thus forever, unchanging and unchangeable. The fortification walls, the gardens, the stables have the quiet clarity evoked by a manuscript illustration rather than arising from the querying glance of an onlooker, which Flaubert had learned to reproduce in his travel notes. Not only were the physical surroundings long unchanged, but also the good chatelain was already aged now: peace was everywhere, and no one could remember anything else: the defense works were worthless from disuse. As Julian's father walked quietly about, he was always clad in a fox fur. No new event had taken place since, long before, he had married, the first time in the story that Flaubert used anything but an imperfect tense.

Then into this timeless world there eventually came a further event: the birth of Julian, long prayed for by the couple.[16] In turn it set off a succession of events beginning with a feast lasting three days and four nights. Flaubert already enjoyed the idea of describing it when he was working on the tale in the summer of 1856. In dim, half-lit surroundings strange figures made incomprehensible predictions concerning Julian: he would be a saint; there would be much blood; he would belong to the family of an emperor. They concord, for the reader, with the couplings of saint and knight earlier.

The predictions are an addition of Flaubert's to the medieval legend, serving to bring in the element of blood lust, which will make the hunting a sin requiring penance. Flaubert developed Julian's pathological urge slowly. First he killed a mouse in a church, then a number of birds with a peashooter, and finally a pigeon with his bare hands. As he strangled it, the convulsions of the bird made his heart beat faster and filled him with a savage, wild voluptuousness such that he almost fainted as the bird stiffened and became motionless. Hamilcar Barca's child, Hannibal, had given signs of a similar joy in killing, which had filled his father with pride.

When Julian became old enough to hunt, he showed great aptitude, and his father purchased for him every kind of hunting dog, falcon, or other beast of prey that he could find. Enumerating them, too, had been one of Flaubert's anticipated joys in writing the story. Strange and resonant names paraded across his pages, each discreetly explained by a word or through its context, with a mastery in striking contrast to the crudity of some of the explanations in *Salammbô*.

Julian rejoiced in the ferocity of his falcon or the moaning of the deer under the teeth of his hunting pack. He was off with the first light and returned late at night covered with mud and gore and smelling of wild animals, for his joy was in killing them with his own hands or at close quarters with dagger or axe.

Flaubert had the printer skip a line before beginning the account of the great hunt which was to lead to the curse. Julian left one morning long before dawn, just as Charles Bovary had set out for Old Man Rouault's farm where he would meet Emma.[17] Like Charles, Julian noticed the motionless, nearly frozen birds on the branches. With a single stroke of his sword, he sliced through their legs and passed on, not even pausing to pick them up. Time indications accompany the actions closely: dawn began to whiten the sky . . . soon Julian entered a wood . . . three hours later he was atop a mountain. And then, imperceptibly, all sense of time slips away from him and from the reader.

With random brutality, akin to Flaubert's in the dream, Julian slew uncounted animals in a strange, mist-filled land. Again as in the dream, mysteriously they crowded around him, making the slaughter easy. Tirelessly he killed them with bow and arrow, sword or cutlass, "thinking of nothing at all, remembering nothing. He seemed to himself to have been in an indeterminate land for an indefinite time, by the sole effect of his own existence, everything taking place with that ease one experiences in dreams."*

The familiar reference to the facility with which dreamers accomplish their actions here links the sleeper's dream to the hallucination of the man possessed, moving from Flaubert's experience to literature and back to the dream again. It revives his earlier preoccupation with this mysterious state in the *Sentimental Education* of 1869 and in *Salammbô* as well as long before them in the earlier *Sentimental Education* of 1843-45, perhaps his first reference to it.[18]

After the massacre Julian paused. Before him he suddenly found a huge herd of deer, trapped in a valley; like the barbarian mercenaries of *Salammbô* in the Pass of the Axe, they could not escape. The thought of the carnage ahead of him took his breath away. Dismounting and rolling up his sleeves, he shot them all. Finally nothing moved.

Julian's blood lust had reached its paroxysm. With uncomprehending eye, he contemplated the enormity of his massacre . . .

*"Il était en chasse dans un pays quelconque, depuis un temps indéterminé, par le fait seul de sa propre existence, tout s'accomplissant avec la facilité que l'on éprouve dans les rêves" (*TC*, p. 91).

until he noticed on the far side of the valley a gigantic stag with a doe and fawn the color of dead leaves. When his arrow felled the fawn, the doe lamented, belling in a deep, heart-rending, human voice. He felled her, too, and shot his last arrow at the great stag, in whose forehead it remained planted.

Seeming not to feel the arrow, the stag advanced toward Julian and was about to kill him when he stopped, eyes aflame, with the solemn air of a patriarch. While a bell tolled in the distance, he cursed Julian three times and foretold his murder of his father and mother. Then falling to the ground and gently closing his eyes, he died.

Julian was stupefied, overcome with fatigue, and filled with disgust and an immense sadness. His forehead in his hands, he wept: it was the opposite of Flaubert's wakening from his dream, for Julian was overwhelmed with a guilty awareness of what he had done and a foreboding of what was to come. He was alone, his horse and dogs had disappeared; the enveloping solitude seemed full of threats, as it had in Flaubert's dream. Terrified, he set out at random and was almost at once in front of his chateau. The whole hunt, which had been attended by miracle and magic, ended on the same note, returning the reader at last to that solid normality from which he had departed when Julian's time sense slipped from him.

Julian was filled with remorse and fear as he meditated on the dire prediction. Then, like Anthony before him, he came to wonder if perhaps he might want to murder his parents. The subtle, embracing attraction of evil, which first intrigued Flaubert as he began to imagine creating Anthony, now found a moral context in the guilt patterns Julian wove about himself. But he was not yet repentant. Then two narrow escapes in which he almost killed first his father and then his mother assured him the curse was not in vain. He fled as Part One closes.

Julian now joins the long succession of men like Orestes and Oedipus, who are fated to kill their parents but must pay for their crime. Like his precursors, he will seek to evade the curse by flight, but to no avail: his own free actions will bring him to the dreaded deed. Unfortunately, Flaubert's taste failed him in recounting Julian's adventures during his travels, as it had failed him in describing the monsters Anthony saw. The reader, who will in fact accept miracle in a religious framework, will stubbornly refuse to believe fabulous adventures when no element of miracle may be postulated. Flaubert, of course, had medieval (and classical) precedent for writing that Julian traversed regions where the sun was so hot men's hair caught fire. But the reader's willing suspension of disbelief cannot be pushed that far. He may smile indulgently, remembering the odd beliefs of ancient times concerning distant lands. He will, however, lend them no credence himself, and the interest of the story drops off to mere antiquarianism. To be sure, this was what had intrigued Flaubert at a certain stage of his interest in the story; but he had so far surpassed it that its retention here is a shock and a disappointment. It is well that the material lasts only a few pages.

Julian's successes brought him the customary beautiful princess as bride. A period of rest and happiness began for him, spoiled only by his recurrent, obsessive desires (like Flaubert's) to travel to distant lands and to hunt in magic fashion, killing everything before him infallibly, as in Flaubert's dream. But, understanding dimly that hunting would be his undoing, he remained quietly at home.

At last one night Julian gave in and set out on the second hunt. While he was away, his parents appeared, were welcomed by his wife, and eventually went to sleep in her bed. Meanwhile Julian had been living a hideous, infuriating, ironic parallel to his first hunt. The second one, too, is preceded by a blank line on the page. Unlike the earlier one, however, this hunt had no basis in the medieval legend: it was added by Flaubert to make an esthetic —and therefore moral—parallel.

Here, as before, what is real, what is hallucination, and what is wholly unreal become so inextricably confused that the reader, like Julian, must abandon hope of untangling them. Once again precision disappeared from Julian's ken as the softness of the grass, the gentleness of the air, the shadows of night, and the melting perfume became the indistinct world in which he lived. Illusory puddles turned out not to be there or what seemed grass was a pond. Silence was all about him, bringing overwhelming malaise;

his feet sank into the dead leaves, he had to pause to catch his breath.

Miraculously, and ironically, Julian was unable to kill any creature. Soon he was in an indeterminate land, as he had been on the first hunt. Ruins, bones, and rotting crosses abounded. Then hyenas surrounded him but fled before he could strike at them. It was thus with everything he tried: a power greater than his own was making him helpless. He sought to return to his castle.

A host of animals crowded about the powerless Julian in a scene which came directly from Flaubert's dream. It held fascination for him: he had put a similar one into the draft on Saint Anthony which he wrote in 1856 after setting Julian aside. There, however, while the fabulous animals crowded about on every hand, they did not climb upon or touch Anthony. In 1872, as he was finishing the final version of *The Temptation* and its last pages were approaching their tremendous, pantheistic conclusion, he reused the scene; but this time a terrified Anthony did feel their cold, moist, or sticky contact from every direction.[19] This Julian now experienced. Helpless, his weapons of no avail, he cursed and raged, breathless with fury. Eyes closed, suffocated by the stinking breath of the animals, his arms outstretched, and, lacking even the strength to cry out for mercy, he staggered forward. Suddenly a cock crowed, and others answered. Like Anthony, he was delivered by the coming of morning: he was within sight of his palace.

At the edge of a field Julian discovered some partridges. He threw his cloak over them . . . only to find they had now become a single bird, long dead, and rotted. His rage reached paroxysms once again; unable to kill animals, he would have liked to massacre humans. He returned and killed his parents.

The murder Julian accomplished in a blind fury. As the death rattles of his parents died slowly away, another, far-distant one seemed to pick up and continue them. The sound approached, grew stronger, and became cruel; terrified, Julian recognized the belling of the great black stag. His original crime had not been enough to stop him; he had pursued his sin in a second hunt. Now, as the belling resounded in his ears, he turned, saw his wife in the doorway, and knew what he had done. Abandoning her, he took flight once more as Part Two closes.

Again Flaubert's hand faltered momentarily. Like all of his heroes, Julian had been a transposed Flaubert. Up to this point, however, the transposition had, for the most part, been complete and hence successful. Now, however, Julian was revolted by the bestiality of human faces, the noise of artisans' looms, and the total lack of interest in people's conversation: he was the recluse of Croisset suffering the torments of a hypersensitive nineteenth-century neurotic. The anachronism breaks the reader's illusion. But acceptance returns when Julian comes to feel the love of nature which for long years Flaubert had known and which was welling up within him again now. His later pantheism was thus rejoining the earlier reactions which had formed the conclusion of his dream and also of the last *Temptation*. Colts racing about the pasture, birds in their nests, and insects resting upon flowers all drew bursts of affection from Julian. Where murdering had been his passion, now life in all its forms aroused his love.

Despite his despair, Julian did not revolt against God but rather confessed his sin. He sought to save others in moments of danger, hoping thereby to find his own death. Finally, only suicide seemed to offer peace. Leaning over a stream bank one day, however, he perceived his own face and recognized his father's lineaments in it. He uttered a cry and put thoughts of a further murder out of his mind, as Flaubert seems not to have thought of suicide after 1870.

It occurred to Julian to spend his life in the service of others. He thus started on the road to salvation by seeking to be at one with his fellow man. In the original dream Flaubert reached this communion without knowing how, during the moment of waking: it was the wish the dream fulfilled for him and which life itself then offered no prospect of providing. Thirty years of further living were needed before he gained the wisdom to seek this communion. Its consummation was, of course, the path he had just followed—for the first time—in helping his niece.

Julian took to ferrying travelers across a river. There was a ferry across the Seine near Croisset, and Flaubert knew the man who operated it. With his return to swimming, he must have been reminded of it almost daily. Moreover, on the far side of the river, just a little upstream, was a prison which had previously been an asylum for lepers founded in 1160 and dedicated to Saint Julian.

Julian established himself in a small hut and spent his days at his appointed service. One night in the midst of a heavy storm a voice from the distant bank called him, easily traversing the long distance. It called three times, the mystic number which the great stag had also used; the voice had the intonations of a church bell. Mystery and miracle accompanied the entire episode. Under the prodigious weight of the leper, the boat almost sank; the waters, on the other hand, suddenly quieted. Julian bent to his task, understanding it was a matter of the highest importance.

The leper was revolting. For his description Flaubert drew on his experience at the leper's colony in Damascus in 1850 and on his own account of Hannon in *Salammbô*. As with Hannon, the great hole where the leper's nose had been was hideous, his breath was nauseating, and his eyes burned like coals. They were like those of the great stag or Julian's father on his death bed.

When they reached the bank, Julian took the leper to his cabin. The tremendous ending came rapidly. The leper, hungry, thirsty, and cold, demanded of Julian his food, his drink, and his bed. Then, still shivering, he insisted Julian get in, too, and embrace him, body against body, lips against lips. Julian felt the leper's skin, cooler than a serpent's, on his thigh: it was the sensation Salammbô had dreaded as she prepared to embrace her serpent before going to Mâtho's tent.

The leper then changed into the figure of Jesus Christ. His breath was perfumed with the scent of roses, and his eyes had the brilliance of the stars as he rose to heaven with Julian in his arms. The saint felt an abundance of delight and a superhuman joy: he fainted in ecstasy. The embrace, the resplendent glance, and the perfume of roses gave a meaning Flaubert had not previously suspected was there to his earlier concept of complete love as the union of physical and religious love. To be sure, the brilliant eyes and the rose-scented breath he had already depicted in Madame Renaud as she was seducing Henry in the first *Sentimental Education*;[20] but now the physical aspects were purged of any erotic meaning. And the religious ecstasy, which was what made Julian faint, had been won at the price of sacrifices Flaubert had not known existed—though he had seen them about him all his life—until the threat to his beloved niece had made him realize that self-sacrifice was more beautiful than self-aggrandizement, even in the name of art.

Flaubert closed the tale of his own temptations, his own sins, and his own salvation with a further blank line and a final one-sentence paragraph: "And that, more or less, is the story of Saint Julian the Hospitaller, as it is told, in a stained-glass window, in a church in my part of the country."* Once again the commas—as unusual in French as in English—pace the sentence and slow the reader. The tale slips quietly from his grasp, as Flaubert had long ago told Louise Colet she must end a tale of hers.

A Simple Heart

> The work of art which a man produces is nothing other than the long journey to rediscover through the byways of art the two or three simple and grandiose images upon which for the first time his heart opened.
>
> Albert Camus, Preface to *L'Envers et l'endroit* (1957)

In *Saint Julian* Flaubert had given to the short story dimensions and resonances which none of his predecessors in France had yet imagined. He had also stirred up the long fund of accumulated memories and tensions that the years had buried behind him. Neither form nor content had been exhausted; both clamored for further outlet. Immediately upon finishing *Saint Julian* in February of 1876, Flaubert started a new short story.

It was to be called "The Parrot."[21] Mademoiselle Félicité, a servant, was to own a parrot brought her by a seafaring nephew. When her masters died and, eventually, the parrot died too, she was to have him stuffed and would make of him her confidant. When a religious procession was being organized she would ask

---

*"Et voilà l'histoire de saint Julien l'Hospitalier, telle à peu près qu'on la trouve, sur un vitrail d'église, dans mon pays" (*TC*, p. 125).

the priest's permission to place him in one of the beflowered altars as part of the decoration. Seeing him there was to produce in her too great an emotion; and she would have an attack and have to be taken to the poorhouse. There she would have a mystic vision in which her parrot would replace the dove of the Holy Ghost. She worried over confusing the rattle of the chains holding the swinging censers with those of her parrot, but the priest would assure her that this was not a sin. She would expire in an odor of sanctity. Turgenev must have been apprised of this version of *A Simple Heart*, for six months later, in August of 1876, he still referred to it by its original name; but by then this title no longer properly described the tale.[22]

Just as *Saint Julian* had moved from being a tale with medieval trappings to an account of sin, suffering, and salvation, so "The Parrot" took on a deeper meaning as soon as Flaubert discovered how readily it would bear it. As he came toward the end of writing *Julian*, George Sand was making a supreme effort to persuade her solitary and unhappy friend to open his heart to his readers. She wanted him to expound directly the highest concept of morality which he knew and make no mystery of the moral sense of his writing. At long last—it had been ten years—her plea made sense to him, unconsciously if not consciously. This, and no doubt the example of Turgenev's own works, which he much admired,[23] led him to break through all his previous inhibitions to write what he at least later knew to be a work intended personally for George Sand.[24] It was what came out as he worked over his ironic tale about an idiot servant and a parrot idol.

As Flaubert revised his tale, it became the full account of a pure heart, a woman innocent to the point of harboring no evil within her and living all of her life with that total selflessness to which Julian came only toward the end of his existence Félicité's childhood was lonely and barren; her love life had been only brief, ironic disappointment. She turned her affections upon her new mistress, a cold, self-absorbed widow, and upon the two children of the house. The boy grew up to be a worthless gambler; the daughter died in her teens. When Madame was given a parrot, he became Félicité's uncomplaining companion, and she lavished her love upon him. After his death, she had him stuffed and kept him in her room, retaining him and the room even after Madame's death. Slowly, age narrowing her small circle of ideas, her only absorptions were her parrot and her prayers, and even the latter were confused. Upon her deathbed, she imagined that it was a parrot who received her soul into heaven. It sounds ironic; but as Flaubert told a friend, it was in no way so, being rather a tender tale of simple pathos and, no doubt, the most moving prose he ever wrote.[25]

Like *Julian*, *A Simple Heart* draws nourishment from roots which plunge far back into Flaubert's childhood. Félicité is an elaboration of his Flemish virgin living out her whole life in the provinces in a state of mystic devotion as Flaubert had imagined her in 1850. But now he understood such a love directly rather than ironically. When he first thought of the Flemish virgin, he was in the Holy Land. He had gone there, as he put it, in the simplicity of his heart; but he had found only disappointment. The simplicity he missed in Jerusalem he had experienced in Brittany in 1847 in the direct and uncomplicated devotion of the Breton peasants. There are even prototypes of it in his juvenile works of the late 1830's. Félicité's indifference to the world beyond her village also had forebears in Flaubert's experience. In 1853 he had been charmed to find that his cook, a simple woman, still did not know—or care—that there had been a revolution five years before and that there had been a succession of governments since then. She still believed Louis Philippe was king, since, as she said, "that sort of thing did not interest her." Such contempt for contemptible things made Flaubert realize that compared to her he was a triple fool, for he could not help but pay attention. In the 1850's, too, he had written his first sketch for Félicité, the Catherine Leroux episode in *Madame Bovary*.

Julian had had Flaubert's unconscious concerns of long standing for its base: *A Simple Heart* would use his conscious recollections. When George Sand succeeded in convincing him to change his manner, he realized he had hosts of unbidden memories which had tortured him over the preceding months of misery. Now he could give them outlet. There had been a time in the 1850's when such a return into memory had been his dream; but after he had made his great Trouville visit in 1853, he abandoned, he thought forever, the notion of writing his memoirs.[26] Now, if not his memoirs, he would write at least his memories, revisiting, as he had then put it, his old dreams.

"Félicité and her parrot really lived," wrote Caroline.[27] As a matter of fact, much if not most of the story had its living counterpart somewhere in Flaubert's background, while for this once he consciously and steadily allowed himself the enjoyment of writing of himself in fictional guise. In 1845, quite near the time when he had the dream about monkeys, he also met a man traveling with a sick parakeet carefully balanced on the mudguard of the light cart in which he traveled. At dinner the cage was brought in and set on the mantle, where the bird complained softly. Flaubert noted it was a strange affection that linked the man and the bird.[28] Furthermore, Félicité's parrot in particular, and much of Félicité herself, seemed to come from the household of a sea captain, Pierre Barbey, whom he had known at Trouville many years before and whom he mentioned in *Bouvard and Pécuchet.*[29]

A Simple Heart goes much further back, too, into Flaubert's childhood, for Félicité's unswerving devotion was a reflection of that of Old Julie for her master, Gustave. Moreover, the two children in the house, a brother and a sister three years younger, recreated Gustave and his sister Caroline, particularly when they played together at Trouville. And when Virginie died young, it was in part Caroline who posed again for Flaubert.

The decision to write *A Simple Heart* came at once as the writing of *Julian* was ending. By March 1, 1876, the plan was already established and Flaubert was beginning his search for documents. The story was to take place in Pont-l'Evêque, whence his mother had come and where he had himself often been, the more so as it was on the road between Rouen and Trouville, only a short distance from the coastal town. He had suffered his first attack of epilepsy near there. Despite all this, the scrupulous Flaubert felt that he must return to make notes on the precise disposition of its various elements and particularly the church; he also made a sketch of its bell tower. Not yet content, he then read about it in various guidebooks, even transcribing the fact that it was at the confluence of two rivers by the banks of which he must often have played as a child. He also went on to Harfleur, which he knew well.[30]

Flaubert was hesitant to start writing. By the middle of March, however, he was ready; the story was now entitled *A Simple Heart*. Sixteen hours of work on a first day and most of the following one finally produced the first page. In midsummer everything was going well, and Flaubert was immensely excited by his tale, returning to prune away excesses in his early pages. Now, moving more slowly again, in three weeks he produced only seven pages; but they seemed good.

Documentation was often a problem. The parrot occupied an important place in the story and had to be fully understood. Conferences with zoologists helped; then Flaubert began to read extensively. He gathered far more data than he could ever use, but that was not quite the point or purpose. He sought to master all one might know about parrots so as to be able—when the time came—to select the single, most telling fact for the place where he needed it within the short compass of a tale, for no word could be wasted. In late July the Rouen Museum lent him a stuffed parrot which sat on his desk for days staring with large, unblinking glass eyes. The bird's motionless stance and gaze began eventually to annoy him; but his eye and mind needed to be filled with parrot.

In August, working madly, sometimes as many as eighteen hours a day, Flaubert finished his tale, and just in time. His excesses were beginning to tell and his headache was almost constant. He knew he had written what George Sand had wanted. The story showed his sensitivities, and he was happy over this. It was serious and sad, and would even make some people weep. He looked forward to reading the manuscript to Madame Roger des Genettes. That he would enjoy, yet it could not be all he wished, which would have been to read it to George Sand. She had died a few weeks before, on June 8.

Once again the story opened—on that page which had given Flaubert so much trouble—with a single-sentence paragraph localizing the scene and giving one initial fact to set the story off: "For half a century the housewives of Pont-l'Evêque envied Madame

Aubain her servant Félicité."* The tone was established, and he could set about recounting fifty years of service, which he had been forced merely to mention in passing for Catherine Leroux in *Madame Bovary*.

Félicité did everything and, despite her mistress' frigid character, remained faithful to her as well. The widowed Madame Aubain was based in part on an aunt of Flaubert's; it amused him to give Madame Aubain one of his own farms.[31] As in so many Balzac novels, the reader now visits the house at Pont-l'Evêque in close detail. Here year after year Félicité rose at dawn and worked until bedtime. To save her mistress money, she ate slowly and took care not to waste even a breadcrumb. Her face was thin, her voice high; at twenty-five she looked forty; at fifty she no longer had any age. Always silent, her back rigid and her gestures measured, she seemed almost a wooden automaton.

The Introduction described the endless repetition of Félicité's days, as unchanging and timeless as the chateau of Julian's parents for long years. Flaubert then turned back to recapitulate her past: this is Part Two. Like everyone, he said, she had had her love story. And then he recounted the callous, unfeeling efforts of a farm boy first to seduce her, then to marry her . . . only to end by taking instead a rich widow who could keep him out of the army. Félicité, who had given her whole heart to him, wept the night through, then left the farm where she worked, and began her service with Madame Aubain. It was the end of living for herself in any way.

Beyond a basic faithfulness to her mistress, Félicité found a new outlet in devotion to Madame Aubain's children, Paul and Virginie, who seemed of more than human flesh to her. Her mistress—like Madame Flaubert with Gustave—had to order her not to keep kissing them constantly. Her affections now constitute the only events of the story: aside from them life repeats a comforting monotony, marked only by minor and manageable ceremonies such as occasional visits. Her days unroll smoothly before the reader, unscarred by the irony which had seared the presentation

---

*"Pendant un demi-siècle, les bourgeoises de Pont-l'Evêque envièrent à Mme Aubain sa servante Félicité" (*TC*, p. 3).

of village life in *Madame Bovary*. Flaubert's bitterness appears only at intervals and then only to touch the few bourgeois who cross her path.

Her formal education was what she gleaned in passing from the children's, for her life was other in its simple and direct devotion. When the family visited their farm and she risked her life to save Paul and Virginie from an angered bull, she was doing only what her affections told her to do; and it was Flaubert, not Félicité, who knew that she had been heroic.

After the narrow escape from the bull, Virginie was troubled by a nervous ailment. The doctor suggested she try sea bathing at Trouville, as Harriet Collier had earlier. The family moved there for the summer, not without pausing at another farm Madame Aubain owned to have another of those gigantic meals Flaubert so enjoyed depicting. At Trouville they put up at the *Agneau d'or*, where Flaubert and Du Camp had come at the end of their Breton trip and where Gustave had been so disappointed at not being recognized.[32] For Madame Aubain's children, as for Gustave and Caroline, the principal diversion was watching the fishing fleet return, just as Flaubert had been reminded of it recently at Concarneau.

Part Three is entirely taken up with Félicité's love for the two children and for her nephew Victor. Catechism classes and Virginie's first communion gave Félicité her first real taste of religion as she escorted the child. Félicité sat apart, quietly looking at the stained-glass windows of the apse. In one the Virgin appeared, dominated by the dove representing the Holy Ghost; in another she knelt before the Christ Child. Behind the tabernacle was a statue of Saint Michael with the dragon. Félicité's church is like Proust's at Combray, which was eventually destroyed in the story and lived on only in the memory and the descriptions of the narrator. For while there were once such windows and such a piece of sculpture as Félicité saw at Pont-l'Evêque, the village was badly damaged during the Second World War; bombs destroyed the nave vault and tumbled most of the apse into ruins. It has now been rebuilt, and the vault and apse stand once again much as Flaubert saw them when he made the notes from which his description stemmed. But stained glass cannot be replaced when it is gone; and today the windows are barren of color except in the mind of his readers.

Félicité listened to the religious instruction of Virginie and the other children preparing for their first communion. Flaubert, hearing only what Félicité could comprehend, had no need to balk. Since the ill-tutored servant could indulge in no theological debate and had no concern for dialectical subleties, she could not seek to know more of God than man can. What did lie fully within her compass was what Flaubert sought when he went to Jerusalem. What he could not find, because his heart was not simple but complex, Félicité could not fail to find, for hers was pure.

The God of the Old Testament inspired in Félicité an overwhelming respect and a fear of His wrath. Bouvard and Pécuchet, more learnedly, would come to the same conclusion a few years later when Flaubert wrote to them.[33] But Félicité's real devotion was for the Christ of the New Testament. She wept on hearing of His Passion and found all the humble things of her daily life recurring in His story and sanctified by His presence. The effort to understand what his person was like she abandoned wholly, contenting herself with the basis in superstition which was open to her simplicity: it was perhaps He who flickered over the swamps at night in the will-o'-the-wisp. She paid no attention to dogma whatsoever, for it was beyond her comprehension; she dozed quietly while the priest expounded it and wakened only in time to take Virginie home.

As Virginie was about to take her first communion, Félicité leaned forward to see her. It was as though she were this girl; her face, her robe, her heart became Virginie's. When the child opened her mouth to receive the wafer, Félicité almost fainted. Next day she herself took communion, but no longer tasted the same delights. Imagining is always greater than experiencing, Flaubert had long been urging. But now he was saying it gently, and Félicité's imagination was primed by love. He had retraced the long path back to the time before his cynicism, to 1840 or so, when he had experienced a brief period of greater religious peace and had written that the first communion was something naïvely good and that those who wept at it should not be mocked.[34]

Shortly it was time for Virginie to go away to school. Félicité resigned herself to losing her because she was sure Madame knew best. Fortunately, at this time she came to know her nephew, Victor; she became immensely proud of him. On Sundays she would ply him with good food, let him nap awhile, and then take his arm to attend vesper services. As he grew older, he had to go off on voyages which grew longer until at last he left for a two-year journey to Havana. Félicité walked the dozen miles or so from Pont-l'Evêque to Honfleur to see him sail; but she lost her way in the unfamiliar wharf area and had barely time to wave him off. Thereafter in each storm she trembled for his safety, and under each hot sun was parched for him.

Eventually word came that Victor had died of yellow fever in Havana. It was another old recollection of Flaubert's, for he had already referred to a similar event in his first *Sentimental Education*.[35] Taking her laundry down to the stream, Félicité pounded out her grief on it as she looked out across the empty meadows or beneath the surface of the river at the reeds waving like drowned men's hair. Until evening she was brave but then, alone in her room and flat upon her mattress, she let her grief have sway.

Virginie's health had never improved; soon she, too, was dying. Félicité reached the school only after her death. For two nights she did not leave the bedside, living Flaubert's vigil for Caroline. She noted as death wrought its changes, but kissed the child at intervals and would not have been surprised to see her resuscitate. For such people, Flaubert wrote, accepting the supernatural is quite simple. He had already made use of this trait in *Saint Anthony* and *Julian*. Before the casket was closed, Félicité cut a long lock of Virginie's hair as Flaubert had with Caroline; she resolved never to part with it.

Madame Aubain's grief was boundless; dreams of her dead husband and her daughter obsessed her. Once she came in precipitately from the garden: she had clearly seen the two standing there, motionless and looking at her. It was the hallucinatory power of imagination which Flaubert himself had experienced and which he had so often explored. Madame Aubain and Félicité one day got out Virginie's things, much as Flaubert liked to examine his relics of Caroline and his mother. When Félicité asked to have a vermin-eaten hat which had been Virginie's, Madame Aubain opened her arms and the two women embraced.

"His name was Loulou" is the opening sentence of Part Three, which the parrot dominates. Flaubert, who always invented pet names for those he loved, had often used this for his niece. A neighbor of Madame Aubain's who was leaving had been delighted to get rid of the bird; thus Loulou entered Félicité's life. As deafness slowly shut her off from the world, his was the only voice she could still hear. They would sit and converse, he repeating the few phrases he knew, she mumbling endearments to him. When he died, Madame suggested Félicité have him stuffed; she set out on foot for Honfleur to deliver him herself. She was, however, too deaf to hear the stagecoach as it bore down on her. The driver swerved to avoid her, making his vehicle lurch violently. In his fury, as he passed the old woman, he gave her a terrible lash across the face with his whip. It must have occurred about where Flaubert had his first epileptic seizure.[36] Fortunately Loulou was uninjured. Félicité pursued her way toward Honfleur, arriving at last on the heights above the city, whence she could see its lights. She paused a moment, as Emma had outside the convent, overcome with weakness: the past flooded across her. The wretchedness of her childhood, the disillusionment of her first love, the loss of her nephew, and the death of Virginie welled up and suffocated her. It was like the memories of the past which had been weighing down upon Flaubert during the past months, or like one of his attacks.

When Loulou at last returned, resplendent and with a large glass eye, Félicité placed him in a position of honor in her room near a print of the baptism of Christ. The dove descending upon the Lord in this picture or the one in the window of the church were like Loulou. Moreover, the idea of the dove became clearer in her mind through the parrot, and she decided the Father could not have chosen a dove—they cannot speak—but must instead have sent an ancestor of her bird. Flaubert's friends who heard the story before the manuscript went to the printer objected that this was too sophisticated a thought for her. But he refused to delete the passage: removing it would upset the structure of the story.

His decision was perhaps unfortunate, as even the first reviewer complained of improbability here.[37]

Time had long before this become paced only by Félicité's affections. Now that there were no more affections, it disappeared into the immutable round of her days. At last she caught pneumonia; death was near. It was a summer's day; the Corpus Christi Procession was about to begin. She and Virginie had once helped to prepare a street altar for it. One was being set up this time in her yard. The warm, grass-scented air of summer penetrated the room; flies buzzed; the sun made the river glisten; the tile roof grew hotter. A neighbor keeping watch over her dozed.

Félicité's death is orchestrated with the arrival of the procession in one of those complex unions across space which Flaubert had so successfully developed in the Agricultural Fair; but here there was no need for irony. Félicité had lent Loulou to decorate the altar, so that she was now alone except for her neighbor. As the blue vapors of the incense rose to her attic room, she opened her nostrils wide to breathe it in with mystic sensuality but with a purity unknown to Emma. She closed her eyes, a smile on her lips. Her heart beat slower, more vaguely and gently, as a fountain runs dry or an echo disappears. And, as she drew her last breath, she thought she saw in the half-opened heavens above her a gigantic parrot soaring over her head.

George Sand would have liked *A Simple Heart*. While some have seen bitter irony in the tale (and there are occasional, incidental paragraphs which do show this), or Flaubert's disgust for the monotony of life, on the whole most readers have taken the story at face value and are not surprised to find that Flaubert thought he was displaying his warm sympathy directly. He wrote Gertrude Collier Tennant that it was a tender story. To those who live lives of simple self-abnegation, his heart and his respect went out. He admired Félicité and asked his reader to join him in believing that those who are pure in heart will see God. Félicité did.

Félicité's solitude matches that of the aging bachelor Flaubert; and she found her outlet and salvation in love, as Flaubert had learned through his self-sacrifice for his niece. All those characters in the tale who do not love, live lives of total isolation like that of Flaubert for so many years. But Félicité from the start cared more for others than for herself and lived for them; hence she was never alone.) And hence as the reader comes to the end of her life, he knows that it has, as much as Julian's, been a good life; Félicité's world has been the better for her living in it.

The Sermon on the Mount declared to Flaubert that the poor in spirit are blessed, for theirs is the kingdom of heaven; and the pure of heart shall see God. Félicité was, then, as blessed as Julian, and her name was not ironic. But the question is complex, for she and Julian are not blessed, if that term will do, in identical ways. Religion and morality, as Hegel points out, are universal essences and may be fully present in each individual, although in a limited soul perhaps not in all their elaborate completion. The religiousness and morality of a limited life—Hegel suggests a shepherd or a peasant—although confined to a few simple circumstances, still has infinite value, and this religiousness and morality are of the same value as those of a trained intellect and a rich existence.

Let Félicité then be granted morality: she is good. But there are different ways to be good, which it is well to differentiate. Flaubert had read Hegel, as all his generation did. But he was also nurtured on Montaigne, who makes the distinction nicely, urging that there are people who, though sorely tempted, wage an arduous but victorious battle against their temptations, while others, who are but little tempted, at once overcome their inclination to vice. A third sort may exist, in whom evil seems to have not the slightest foothold and who are always and effortlessly good. The first two, as well, are also undeniably good; but somehow a distinction must be allowed. Montaigne suggests that the third sort, of whom Félicité is one, are to be termed innocent; the other two are virtuous; all three are good.[38]

The notion of virtue involves some suggestion of a struggle, however slight, some indication of a victory won. Félicité attains effortlessly and always to that sanctity which Julian accomplished only with unbearable pains. She is innocent. Would one wish her to have a struggle? It would add another and a different sort of interest to the story; but Félicité would no longer be herself and would become instead more like Françoise in Proust, who so much resembles her anyway. And literature would have lost, for as (she is, unique and innocent, she convinces, moves, and conquers the reader.)

Herodias

To be clear and lively with such complicated elements presents *gigantic* difficulties. But if there weren't any difficulties, what fun would there be in it?

Letter to Turgenev, October 28, 1876

By April, 1876, before he had more than half finished *A Simple Heart*, Flaubert had already thought of a third subject, Herodias, wife of Herod and mother of Salome. Salome's dancing won for Herodias the head of John the Baptist. It was a period and a milieu which had long attracted him. The ferociousness of Herodias excited him: he saw her as a combination of Cleopatra and Madame de Maintenon. Then there was Herod, a real prefect: Flaubert had often thought of writing a novel with that title satirizing the contemporary scene. Herod would be cowardly like so many people in *A Sentimental Education*, but still attracted to his wife. The essential issue, however, would be the confrontation of the two races, the Latin and the Semitic. Religion would not be involved.

Herodias, just like *Julian* and *A Simple Heart*, started out as a relatively superficial piece of amusement for its author. In early letters he called it his "little Jewish foolishness." On August 17, with his previous story finished only the night before, he could already see Herod and his wife standing on a balcony of their palace watching as the sun made the Dead Sea glitter and the gilded tiles of the temple sparkled: he had already found his opening scene. Within the week he had begun his readings. They were to require much time, for the subject was, like *Salammbô*, first a matter of archeology. Fortunately, Renan could be of great help; many of the books Flaubert needed came from Renan's private library. As before, he also made use of various specialists, many of whom were proud to collaborate with the famous novelist. He even made notes on his own travel notes from the Holy Land.[39] By October his documentation and plan were ready. He finished writing the story some four months later, jotting down on the manuscript that it was ten minutes after ten in the evening of January 31, 1877.

Even in the early stages Flaubert knew his third story presented major problems. There was, for instance, the constant shadow of *Salammbô*, from the same Semitic milieu and with many of the same effects. Moreover, as with the earlier work, many details would not be clear to the average reader and were going to have to be explained. As *Salammbô* had had as its first titles "Carthage" and "The Mercenaries," so, although *Herodias* started and ended with the same title, for several months during the period of writing, Flaubert always referred to it as "Saint John," or "Iaokanann," the Semitic form which it amused him to use. Such shifts were as significant as his inability to give a title to the multiform *Sentimental Education*. The whole prospect of writing it frightened but challenged him. As it was drawing to a close, he once more worked himself into a paroxysm, putting all his days and much of his nights into it; in eight days he was proud he had needed only ten hours of sleep! Nevertheless he knew *Herodias* contained many difficulties he had not been able to resolve. It is, for almost all readers, inferior to the other two tales and arouses less interest.

Herodias is the least broken of the *Three Tales;* its action moves rapidly from an initial view of the Holy Land through three tightly organized parts to the execution of John. The opening description of the view from Herod's fortress at Machaerous, despite Flaubert's efforts, does recall *Salammbô*. Here, too, it is dawn, and the view opens before Herod as the early sun tears asunder the fog hiding the Dead Sea and the mountains beyond. The familiar biblical names, Engedi, Hebron, Carmel, Jericho, and half a dozen more, establish not only a landscape but also the tone and sonorities of the New Testament as they do in the poetry of Vigny or Hugo. Flaubert even sought out from experts two-syllable place-names to build the rhythms. Remembering his trip through Palestine, he was trying to suggest by his prose the living experience of the special bibical quality in the shapes of the hills and their rough surfaces. This opening description is one of his most successful.

Herod and his problems, political and familial, give way almost at once to the second center of interest, John the Baptist, who was imprisoned at Machaerous but continued nonetheless to rail at Herod and Herodias and to prophecy the immediate coming of the Messiah. To his followers the Baptist repeated his mysterious prophecy: "For Him to increase, I must decrease." It was a reference—as the reader knows, but Herod could not—to the beginning of Christ's mission, with which John's own death had to coincide. Flaubert introduced the statement into the opening pages of the story and repeated it at the end. The tale had originated in his interest in the racial conflict in Jewish Palestine under Latin Rome and was to portray the relationship between Herod and his wife. But as the Baptist came more to the forefront, the story became also a profoundly religious account of John's ready acceptance of his own sacrifice. It bore a direct relationship to Flaubert's, and he could now put into words why he had wished to make the sacrifice: it was necessary to another's gain. *Herodias* could, then, make explicit what had underlain all three tales and what all three had portrayed: Julian had submitted himself to the needs of the leper; Félicité had subordinated herself to the needs of all those about her. John phrased the reason for these sacrifices, for Julian, for Félicité, and for Flaubert: in them all four had found salvation.

The political situation of Herod as prefect required elucidation, too. Flaubert sought to condense his explanations, no doubt so as to maintain the pace of his story. But he pushed this so far that the tale cannot be understood in detail except with the aid of extended footnotes. Thus, the two principal Romans are Lucius Vitellius and Aulus Vitellius. Flaubert refers to one of them, but only one, as "Vitellius." By the time the reader has discovered which it is, the tale is half over. Moreover, as early as *Salammbô*, and growing steadily thereafter, Flaubert had abused the pronoun to the point where its reference was frequently difficult to determine. In *Herodias*, it is impossible at times.

The two earlier tales had arisen in part from Flaubert's need to return into his past. Herodias is also a return to what he had written before, in particular to *Salammbô*. Despite his disclaimers, this was much of why he enjoyed it and had selected it. Hamilcar Barca in the Carthaginian novel had visited his treasures. Herod will make a similar, though more rapid one. Both cases allowed Flaubert free rein in describing the goods and chattels of the ancient world; but in both the interest lags badly for the reader. The historian and critic Taine was one of the few to compliment Flaubert on the passage.[40]

Flaubert also looked forward to writing *Herodias* because it would let him describe a Roman orgy, the Birthday Feast of Herod, which is mentioned in the biblical story. Meat and drink, slaves and guests, perfumes and costumes, conversations and vomiting pass before the fascinated eye of Flaubert and then of the overwhelmed reader. Taine, who was intrigued with these ingeniously handled scenes, was here more like the generality of readers. Unknown customs and strange foods abound, but at every turn Flaubert is there to guide the reader almost imperceptibly through this "historical hashish," which—as Taine noted—he treated so much more deftly than he had the similar material in *Salammbô*. It was the more difficult as Flaubert was here giving way to one of his great temptations: the pleasures of the table. Not infrequently in the past this had led to bad writing, and almost every novel of his had depicted huge meals. The Wedding Feast in *Madame Bovary* and the Feast of the Mercenaries in *Salammbô* were both excellent. But *A Sentimental Education* had a number of major dinners and in *Julian* there had been a feast for the saint's birth; in *A Pure Heart* there was a huge meal on the way to Trouville. *Bouvard and Pécuchet* would shortly have a dinner for all their neighbors. In none of these was the description of the eating a major contribution to the work, as it was in *Herodias*.

In detailing the feast of Herod, Flaubert could describe that interracial hatred which had initially interested him in the milieu; and he could also write philosophical and theological discussions around the coming of the Messiah, akin to those in *Saint Anthony*. He handled them rapidly, using directly reported dialogue with his customary sense for the great emphasis that it can give if sparingly used.

The feast is the background for Salome. The prospect of describing her dance terrified Flaubert. Through the bluish veil which covered her head and breast, he wrote,* one could make out

---

*"Sous un voile bleuâtre lui cachant la poitrine et la tête, on distinguait les arcs de ses yeux, les calcédoines de ses oreilles, la blancheur de sa peau ...
Ses caleçons noirs étaient semés de mandragores, et d'une manière indolente elle faisait claquer de petites pantoufles en duvet de colibri.
"Sur le haut de l'estrade, elle retira son voile. ... Puis, elle se mit à danser" (*TC*, p. 184).

her arched eyebrows, her earrings, and the whiteness of her skin. She wore black tights and indolently let her downy slippers slap against the floor. She removed her veil and began to dance.

First Salome did a pantomime to the rhythm of a flute and a pair of castanets.* She seemed to be pleading with someone who was always just beyond her grasp; like a wandering soul almost ready to take flight, she seemed to be pursuing him. It was one of Kuchiuk-Hânem's dances that Salome performed here, with something of the excellent pantomime Flaubert had admired in the male dancer, Hassan-el-Bilbesi, in Cairo; and the Tunisian dancers, too, contributed to it.

Changing instruments and mood,† Salome then danced as though overcome. Her poses were sighs, and her body suggested such languor that she seemed to be weeping for a god or dying under his caress. She was Anubis as, eyelids half closed, she writhed, moving her hips from side to side with the undulations of the sea; her breasts quivered while her face remained immobile and her feet moved ceaselessly.

As Herod lost himself in dreams, Herodias, who had brought up her daughter in a far away city and trained her for this moment, sent Salome into her third dance. It was the violence of aroused passion demanding to be satisfied. Drawing all of his memories together, Flaubert sought for the most savagely erotic dance he had ever seen: it was a night far up the Nile at Aswan, when he had watched the Nubian Azizeh. Salome danced, he wrote,‡ like the priestesses of India or the Nubian women of the cataracts. Once again like Hassan, she tipped her body from side to side like a flower in a storm. The light veils, her arms, her legs,

*"Ses bras arrondis appelaient quelqu'un, qui s'enfuyait toujours. Elle le poursuivait ... comme une âme vagabonde, et semblait prête à s'envoler" (*TC*, pp. 184-85).

†"L'accablement avait suivi l'espoir. Ses attitudes exprimaient des soupirs, et toute sa personne une telle langueur qu'on ne savait pas si elle pleurait un dieu, ou se mourait dans sa caresse. Les paupières entre-closes, elle se tordait la taille, balançait son ventre avec des ondulations de houle, faisait trembler ses deux seins, et son visage demeurait immobile, et ses pieds n'arrêtaient pas" (*TC*, p. 185).

‡"Elle dansa comme les prêtresses des Indes, comme les Nubiennes des cataractes, comme les bacchantes de Lydie. Elle se renversait de tous les

her feet seemed to give off sparks which enflamed all the men watching her. A harp spoke out; there was applause. Bending forward but keeping her knees straight, she leaned down until her chin touched the floor. The nomads in the hall, accustomed to abstinence, the Roman soldiers expert in debauchery, the miserly publicans, and the aged priests embittered by disputes dilated their nostrils, palpitated with lust.

As Salome danced about the prefect's table in a frenzy, Herod's voice was choked with desire, and he stammered out his offer of half his kingdom to her. If she would but come to him, she might have anything she wished. She stood upon her hands, her feet in the air, as she appears on Rouen Cathedral, and moved about the raised stand where Herod reclined. Suddenly stopping before him, her neck and her back making a right angle, she stared straight into his eyes like a sphinx, as Saint-Saens later wrote to Flaubert.[41] Herodias snapped her fingers, the dancer went to her and returned to lisp out her dread request for the head of John the Baptist.

After some delay the head was brought in, placed on a platter, and shown to all. The half-closed eyes burned like coals as the leper's had or Julian's father's or the great stag's. When they met the drunken gaze of the Romans, something seemed to pass between as the two races clashed. And then the platter was placed before Herod, whose cheeks ran with tears. The torches went out one by one, and the guests departed, leaving him, his forehead supported on his hands as he looked fixedly at the decapitated head in the same pose as Julian after his massacre of the deer. When the messengers returned with the word that Christ had begun His mission, John's followers understood at last what it was he had waited for.

---

côtés, pareille à une fleur que la tempête agite. ... de ses bras, de ses pieds, de ses vêtements jaillissaient d'invisibles étincelles qui enflammaient les hommes. Une harpe chanta; la multitude y répondit par des acclamations. Sans fléchir ses genoux en écartant les jambes, elle se courba si bien que son menton frôlait le plancher; et les nomades habitués à l'abstinence, les soldats de Rome experts en débauches, les avares publicains, les vieux prêtres aigris par les disputes, tous, dilatant leurs narines, palpitaient de convoitise" (*TC*, pp. 185-86).

Herodias was a remarkably successful realization of an impossible project. It sought to blend two separate subjects, the story of John the Baptist and the clash between Roman and Jew. In addition it strove to be an adequate historical resurrection which the reader would not so much comprehend as experience. Within the larger compass of the novel, *Salammbô* at least allowed hope of resolving the problems. *Herodias*, instead, had to be so tightly written that it has confused readers ever since. But Taine, who does allow that something of this is true, was also relieved, for he had feared his friends' tendency toward history was leading him to a position in which fiction would be impossible. Instead, in this tale he found what only the novelist's art could evoke, the intimate feeling a culture produced.[42]

The *Three Tales* were now complete and formed, as Flaubert had hoped, a solid unity. He had had his chance to work out the meaning of his own destiny through those of his three characters, as they rose to grandeur through the acceptance of life by a voluntary sacrifice of themselves in the name of a love that was larger.

Despite Flaubert's disclaimers and his minimizing comments, all three stories were very close to his heart, and in all three religion, or at least the religious feeling, was deeply interwoven. In one it was the spirit of the humble; in another, of the age of fable; in the last, of the age of Christ. The church as Flaubert abominated it, the institution of dogma and doctrine, of definition and prescription and prohibition, was either absent or seen only through the simple eyes of Félicité which were unaware of all of this and penetrated behind the outward signs to the incandescent reality. These are three tales of those who saw God: a simple servant woman, a medieval saint, and the great precursor of Christ himself. If neither Flaubert nor his reader could hope to live any of these lives, that was the tragedy Flaubert saw in life and which he had striven to portray. It remained only to hope for readers who could meet the demands of his exacting concept of esthetics as a higher justice. If his book were not false, then he might hope, too—to use his own terms—for readers who would not be fools.

25

The Final Years (1877-80)

The Publication of the *Three Tales* (1877)

On April 16 next my little volume will brighten the world.
Letter to Madame Brainne, February 15, 1877

As Flaubert was nearing the end of *Saint Julian* in January, 1876, he was already thinking of publishing it, perhaps even in *Le Figaro*, for, although he hated the paper, it paid the best rates. With a little more time and thought, however, he realized he could not stomach the idea of publishing in a newspaper, both because journalistic standards revolted him and because he could not bring himself, much as he needed money, to do anything so obviously intended only to earn it.[1] Moreover, by now it was already February, and he had the basic idea for *A Simple Heart*; the two would perhaps make a slim volume. Turgenev had arranged to have *Saint Julian* published in Russia and volunteered to do the translation himself. Flaubert, who was to receive fourteen hundred francs for it, asked him also to find someone to translate *A Simple Heart*.

As autumn began, his friend Raoul-Duval was interesting himself in a new periodical, *La Nation*, and asked Flaubert for a story to use in the opening number. He would have been happy to help Raoul-Duval, if only because he had helped in saving Caroline; but Flaubert had overcome his distaste for periodicals and had already promised *Julian* to *Le Bien Public* and *A Simple Heart* to *Le Siècle*. Raoul-Duval could have *Herodias* if he wished it, when it was completed; but it could not be ready for the opening number. Flaubert pressed Turgenev to arrange the Russian translation of *A Simple Heart*[2] and was corresponding with Gertrude Collier Tennant about doing illustrations for it, a radical departure he had never imagined making in earlier days. A translator had also to be found for the Russian version of *Herodias*, as soon as it should be finished, for Flaubert was in frantic need of the money. He read his manuscripts to several people. *A Simple Heart* was well received, but Edmond de Goncourt was disturbed on hearing Flaubert read *Herodias* to Princess Mathilde: it would not be the financial success he knew his friend needed.[3]

Toward the end of February, 1877, luck seemed really to be with Flaubert. The Russian translations were all arranged. Then, conveniently, the publishing schedule of the relatively poor *Siècle* became so crowded that it had to release its right to *A Simple Heart*, and Raoul-Duval left *La Nation*, releasing Flaubert from his obligation to give *Herodias* to it. He was free to sell these tales to the prosperous *Moniteur* for a thousand francs each.[4] *Julian* remained with *Le Bien public*. He felt like a successful businessman and was inordinately proud of himself.

The *Three Tales* appeared in periodicals during March. Toward the end of the month Flaubert presented to his faithful friend Laporte the autograph manuscript of his *Tales* bound in red morocco. Laporte had been, he wrote, his only consolation over the two years of writing them. After the usual delays, on April 24 Charpentier put them on sale in book form with *A Simple Heart* first as perhaps the easiest introduction for the reader.

Critical opinion was in general favorable to the first two tales and hostile to the third.[5] Sales began well, and author and publisher looked forward to a considerable success. Unfortunately sales were then cut off completely—for the moment at least—by France's political crisis of the Sixteenth of May, 1877, the first of a long series which were to dog the Third Republic and justify in some measure Flaubert's contempt for it. He had learned to accustom himself to financial disappointment, however, and could console himself with the praise coming to him on every hand. Daudet spoke of how proud and happy he must be and how lucky Charpentier was. Madame Roger des Genettes wrote that she embraced the victor and sent tender affection to the old friend.[6]

A MEMBER OF THE OLD GUARD

No one loves art any longer, I mean for its own sake.
Where can you find anyone today to delight in a beautiful
sentence? This aristocratic joy belongs to the dim past now.

Letter to Madame Roger des Genettes,
May 28, 1878

As if to signal Flaubert's return to success, at least with the critics,
there were a number of manifestations for him around the time of
the publication of the *Three Tales*. One of these was a dinner
organized at the Restaurant Trapp by a group of younger writers
including Maupassant and Huysmans. In fact it was as much to
bring themselves to public notice as to serve their ostensible purpose of honoring Flaubert, Goncourt, and Zola. The meal began
with a Potage Bovary, went through other courses named for
their guests' fictional characters, and ended with Naturalist Ice. It
was a pleasant affair, enlivened by Flaubert's good humor, which
soon infected them all.[7] Then, three days after his *Tales* went on
sale, Flaubert had an especial triumph. The popular critic Sarcey
gave a public lecture on the new work. While he shared the general impression that *Herodias* was inferior to the other two, he
had words of high praise for *Julian* and *A Simple Heart* and compared Flaubert's talent to Goya's. The essentials of the lecture
were reproduced in the influential *Moniteur*, which had published
the two tales Sarcey liked. Flaubert called it a stupid but kindly
critique.

More wholly to Flaubert's liking was the first of a succession
of annual celebrations in honor of Saint Polycarp, a convenient
excuse for a party honoring Flaubert. For many years he had been
wont to refer to himself as a reincarnation of the Saint, who had
been an early bishop of Smyrna perhaps most famous for his reiterated exclamation: "My God, my God, what a century you have
placed me in!" Flaubert once discovered a print showing the
Saint, his beard flying in the wind and his lamentation inscribed
beneath, which he had shown to Madame Brainne. She and his
other Angels knew of his delight in this ascetic and conceived the

idea of celebrating Saint Polycarp's Day. It took place late in April, usually on the twenty-seventh; a part of the ritual was the reading of verses in praise of Flaubert.[8]

Three weeks later, on May 19, 1877, there was a further showing of Maupassant's obscene play, to which Flaubert invited a number of his friends. Once again it amused him hugely. Edmond de Goncourt—and the ladies who were present—found it less entertaining. Not even Suzanne Lagier stayed for the end. Talking about the play with Goncourt the next day, Flaubert called it refreshing.[9]

These and similar activities seemed to devour all Flaubert's energies when he stayed in Paris for any length of time now. Shorter visits to the city were far better, enough time to see a small group of friends but not long enough to become tired. The social world was becoming intolerable to him: it had so little concern with justice, literature, or knowledge. He took to making up excuses and was rather proud of his inventions, for which he claimed his novelist's training was useful.[10]

Flaubert's language and general violence displeased some, including Edmond de Goncourt, as they always had, as did his eagerness to meet celebrities. When Flaubert monopolized Gambetta, the political hero of the day, at a dinner party, Goncourt was sure that shortly Flaubert would be calling him an intimate friend. Though perhaps severe, he was right: two weeks later Flaubert did indeed say that after twenty minutes he and Gambetta felt as though they had known each other all their lives.

In similar fashion Flaubert's reiterated statements on love no longer impressed Goncourt, who was convinced that neither Flaubert nor Zola nor he himself had ever really been in love or was even capable of depicting it in writing. On the other hand, as Flaubert's time in Paris drew to a close one spring, Goncourt noted sadly the last of his friend's Sundays. He always knew in one part of himself that, if one accepted Flaubert's insistence upon the leading role, he was a most agreeable companion with a fine gaiety, the contagious laugh of a child, and an affectionate nature which carried everything before it.[11]

Flaubert enjoyed Goncourt's company and saw much of him, but he reserved a higher admiration still for Victor Hugo, who continued to be most amicable and hospitable. Hugo did constantly insist that Flaubert present himself for election to the French Academy; but in this he was far from alone, and Flaubert's friends, Taine, Renan, and Du Camp, among others, all became members.

Fleeing Paris, Flaubert enjoyed Croisset more and more as a haven of peace where he was not at the mercy of a social world he disliked. He rejoiced in the countryside about him nowadays, and when the weather was warm, he swam daily in the Seine and walked in the garden looking at the flowers and listening to the birds. Autumn once again charmed him like a memory of a long-dead love, bringing all the languors of the season's end. It did him good to fill his lungs full of the cool air fresh with the smell of the fields.

Because he had no money, because he wanted to work, and because he was better at Croisset than anywhere else, Flaubert remained there all through the cold, rigorous winter of 1878-79 and again the following winter, even spending Christmas Day in complete solitude over his worktable. During the long days, his only distractions were chats with Old Julie, who used to come in to him after dinner to talk of bygone days. When spring began finally to come on in March, the spectacle about him seemed so voluptuous that it revived his flagging spirits just to look at the sun beating down on the river and to hear the clucking of the hens and smell the good odor of the garden. Flowers were beginning to come out; the sky was blue overhead.

His younger friends in Paris did not completely forget the lonely man in Croisset. Alphonse Daudet, with the warmth of his southern temperament, was particularly careful to remember him on New Year's Day, writing that nothing seemed right with him away; since there were no more Sundays to look forward to, no one saw anyone any more. Daudet reassured him that he was not merely the greatest of them all but also the best and the most human. He must return at once.[12] It touched Flaubert, who thought often of his friends there, particularly his young protégé Maupassant. He followed his career in the Ministry of the Navy and then helped him transfer to the Ministry of Education. He worried over his health, offered him counsel on writing and women, and delighted at his literary successes, even scolding Caro for failing to attend a first night to represent her uncle.

Turgenev continued to be a good friend, pleasing Flaubert by the gift of a dressing gown or in turn receiving gratefully Flaubert's letter of sympathy when his fortune was seriously reduced and he had to sell his collection of paintings. But when the Russian at last proposed to come for a visit in December of 1878, Flaubert had to refuse him: he was too short of money to afford a guest. On the other hand, and without being entirely logical, he was furious and hurt when Turgenev continued to promise visits he did not actually make.

One of the principal reasons for Flaubert's remaining in Croisset was his declining health. The long hours of work carried out for months during the writing of the *Three Tales* had seriously weakened him. His heart was slightly upset, and he was subject to fits of trembling which were annoying. Giving up coffee, however, and a return to dosing with potassium bromide did allow him to return to overworking, but it became increasingly hard for him to sleep as his excitement grew. Then he had bouts with grippe, he had troubles with his eyes, he thought he had jaundice, he suffered from lumbago and rheumatism: finally his doctor told him quite flatly that he was again behaving like a hysterical girl. It pleased him so much that he promptly wrote the diagnosis to Caro and several others. There was, he admitted, a feminine aspect to his temperament.

Into the midst of all these ailments, partly psychosomatic, partly ills that aging flesh is heir to, partly perhaps syphilitic manifestations, came a real and painful broken leg. On January 25, 1879, he received a letter from Turgenev with the very sound advice that he should get out and walk about more for the sake of his health. He went out—fortunately not specifically because of his friend's advice—slipped on the ice, fractured a fibula, and sprained one whole leg badly. For forty-eight hours he watched to see if the blood would begin to resorb, as—doctor's son that he was—he knew the alternatives in his day were an amputation or death from gangrene. It was his old friend and neighbor, the health officer Doctor Fortin, who diagnosed and treated him after several better trained men had failed to recognize his fracture.

Flaubert was able to keep the local Rouen papers from reporting his accident; Paris was another matter, and *Le Figaro* inserted an item on January 28, 1879, three days after the event. It always irritated Flaubert to have the public pry into his private life: his books and not his person were what he wished to give them. Moreover, the news item meant complications at once. His brother Achille, vacationing on the Mediterranean at Nice, had an anxious wait while the telegraph was out of commission and he could get no word of the seriousness of the affair. Then letters began to pour in, fifteen the first day, a dozen the second, and keeping on at the rate of eight to ten a day until by the fifth or sixth of February there had been sixty-three to which he had had to write answers. It was a major fatigue, and the stamps were an expense he could not afford. On the other hand the outpouring of affection must have done him good, and Du Camp's reminder of the time on the Nile when they had set a leg for one of their crew brought back memories of the trip to comfort him.[13] Laporte hardly left Flaubert's bedside except for indispensable trips to keep in touch with the factory he managed. Flaubert took to calling him his "Sister of Charity."

Some five days after the accident, the prognosis was that Flaubert would be able to move about in two weeks, although he would not walk easily for three or four months; his morale, thanks to all the care he was receiving, remained excellent. But neither his temperament nor his numerous financial worries prepared him for putting up with an extended ailment: by the ninth of February, although his skin showed no sign of trouble, he was tortured with itching all over his body, a nervous attack his doctor said, no doubt correctly. On the tenth his leg was put in a cast, but it became painful at once and had to be altered. On the eleventh they tried to have him walk about with crutches, but he resolutely declined them in fright. He got about by placing his leg on a chair, which he pushed about before him.

Flaubert's only distractions were watching his dog sleep before the fire or observing the masts of ships as they went by on the river. He read a bit; but for the rest of the time, he sat and moped. By the twenty-second of February, when his fall was a month behind him, his morale gave way completely. He now knew that he could not possibly recover in time to go to Paris that winter; he lacked the energy to return to writing; the itching was abominable; he could not sleep; and the single tooth he had left on his upper jaw ached. It was more than he thought he could stand.

Then, as such matters will, things took a turn for the better. Achille and his family returned from the south and made a fuss over the patient, who was not outwardly as grateful as he might have been, but who was probably pleased. In early March his cast was removed. His first steps caused the joint to swell again, but in late April he was able to attend another Saint Polycarp celebration. Although the movement of the carriage hurt him on the way in to Rouen, the sight of all his friends costumed for the occasion, the flowers about his place, and the poem in his honor warmed and pleased him. He could even forgive his hosts for their shrimp, which were not quite fresh. By June, when Goncourt saw him, he was becoming his old self again.

Even before his accident Flaubert had been unhappily aware of his advancing years; thereafter the feeling became even stronger, as did his habit of reliving the past in his memory. He could honestly say that he did not wish to return to the years of his youth; but there were so many later moments that he did long to recapture and which small events of daily living kept bringing to mind. Letting the past thus blot out the present was, he confessed, a vice with him. Madame Roger des Genettes continued to be a link with Louise Colet's salon; he would, on occasion, recall its various guests.[14] He learned that Louise's daughter, now married, was much seen in Parisian social life, but he did not see her himself and probably never knew that she had burned all of her mother's letters to him.

The death of Hamard, his brother-in-law, brought back longings for his sister Caroline; she was again in his mind as Laure de Maupassant became seriously ill and he went to visit her. Writing to Princess Mathilde recalled the world of the previous decade and the many deaths since then. And whenever he thought of the world outside, he would recall Jules Duplan, who had always kept watch over the newspapers so as to clip and send him anything that concerned him. Now he no longer knew what was happening.

As he studied the Revolution of 1848 for *Bouvard and Pécuchet*, Flaubert relived it for himself, wondering if it had not been perhaps the most wonderful year of his life. As he remembered it, he had been so gay and strong. He was forgetting perhaps that this was when his syphilis had become so dangerous his doctor had ordered him to warmer climates as soon as he could get there.

From those bygone days only Du Camp remained, now perhaps not an intimate friend, but almost the only living man he had known that long and the only living one to whom he had been so close earlier. Du Camp sent him a book he had published; Flaubert replied with a critique; Du Camp thanked him. The exchanges were not affectionate until Du Camp confessed how much the past meant to him. Flaubert replied at once telling how often in his solitude he himself thought of it and, consequently, of Maxime. He was submerged, he said, in the ocean of his memories, drowning even.

There were also minor, passing events, too, to bring back the past. The annual Saint Romain Fair had to be attended. Exhibits of sculpture could lead Flaubert down long reveries like those of Jules in the first *Sentimental Education*. Or Madame Brainne's trip to Rome reminded him of Italy, and he urged her to see the Roman campagna, Ostia, Naples, Perugia, Lake Trasimeno, everything that he had loved. The Mediterranean trip came back, too, when Camille Rogier, whom he had met in Beirut in 1850 and seen once again in Paris in 1857, suddenly appeared at his door one day.

Perhaps most lugubrious was a solemn ceremony Flaubert and Du Camp had to carry out. It arose because of the publication of the correspondence of Prosper Mérimée. Du Camp realized that, if they did not burn their letters to each other, there would come a time when they would get into the hands of unscrupulous people who would publish them; the idea worried Max. He proposed to Gustave that they destroy them; he agreed. Flaubert reread Du Camp's before burning them, and all his young manhood passed before him. They had been naïve, perhaps, but lovable. And what romantic temperaments! Their letters seemed to touch on nothing but art and women. They made him laugh once or twice and weep a bit, too, for the contrast with the present was sad. Reading the letters was like watching a procession of phantoms. Flaubert kept only a few of Du Camp's which he could not bear to destroy and a few more which he wanted as documents, nineteen in all. Du Camp kept none of Flaubert's apparently. But Flaubert had perhaps forgotten he had made copies of many of his letters to his friend. His niece found and published them a few years after his death.[15]

Raging against the inhabitants of Rouen sustained him in these difficult years, as it always had. He longed to give his feelings outlet in a book which would be a dissection, even a vivisection, of one of their notable families. Hatred of such people was, he averred, the beginning of taste. A day in their city reduced him to jelly; so much physical ugliness covered so few moral beauties. The company on the boat returning to Croisset then added the final blows.[16] He could be funny in his rages, and he knew it: he threatened to throw his inkwell at a childhood friend who roused his ire. Or he could be violent and unforgiving, rejoicing upon learning that his old enemy, the editor of *Le Figaro*, had died. Too much of *Bouvard and Pécuchet* was a distillation of all these hatreds.

The political scene, too, enraged Flaubert. All alone in the silence of his room, he would sit and think about it. Five minutes of reflection on President MacMahon sufficed to bring him to a paroxysm of fury; then he felt better and calmer. The Crisis of May Sixteenth had cut deeply into the sale of his *Three Tales;* but his anger had a less personal basis. MacMahon, the standard-bearer for the old-line Conservative party, had forced a parliamentary battle over an issue he could hardly win. It took the better part of the remainder of 1877 to settle the matter. MacMahon's defeat ended the effort to restore the powers of the executive arm of the government as Louis-Napoleon had enjoyed them. Flaubert noted wryly that he was no rabid republican but that the Conservatives had been disgustingly inept. He was, however, quite clear-headed enough to realize something of what was at stake, to understand that it was touch and go for months, and that the fate of France hung on the outcome. Lastly, unlike most of his contemporaries, he well knew that neither outcome could be good. While the defeat of the personal power of MacMahon was the better alternative, the sorry history of the Third Republic was even more surely fated when the president was rendered powerless.

Rages were not Flaubert's only emotional staple: he also had a number of warm affections. Quite a few women were very important to him. Princess Mathilde was a faithful correspondent, and she even came to Croisset once for lunch. This time he had enough money to receive her. Madame Pelouze, one of the very wealthy women of the age and the restorer of the chateau of Chenonceaux, received him there. It was a literary and artistic milieu where Ronsard's poems could be brought to the dinner table and Flaubert read aloud Bouilhet's *Melaenis*. Madame Pelouze even consulted him about her architectural plans for the chateau. Another patroness of letters, Madame Juliette Adam, a powerful figure under the Third Republic, also took it upon herself to help Flaubert, trying to get him to write for her *Nouvelle Revue* and watching out for his interests.

Flaubert realized now how much he missed tenderness in his life. He found it above all in the daily company of his old servant Julie. She wore an old dress of his mother's about the house, and he would watch her and think of the dead woman until his throat tightened and the tears came. His Three Angels, too, were as affectionate and solicitous as before. But all of them, like Flaubert, were aging. Madame Pasca and Madame Lapierre visited him one Sunday for lunch; both ladies dozed off quietly after the meal, while Flaubert returned to his worktable.

For Madame Brainne, whom he called "his dear, his true friend," Flaubert continued to feel a more than comradely affection. Still protected by the safe distance of a letter, he became even more daring in these years and complimented her not only on her bosom, as before, but also on her attractive legs and on everything in fact except her maid Nathalie, whose presence kept him within bounds during visits. He enjoyed thinking of her in the water: how nice to swim with her at some solitary beach or in vast baths with high Moorish vaults and a great pool in the middle. She would appear on the edge dressed in a flowing yellow silk robe and would test the water with her bare toe. Then off would come the robe and they would swim side by side, but not for long, as there would be a convenient divan in a welcoming corner where she would lie and, to the accompaniment of the plashing water from the fountain, . . . they would spend a nice quarter-hour. Eulalie Foucaud at Marseilles lived in his memory.

There were other women to whom he enjoyed being gallant, but the tone was different. He told Jeanne de Tourbey she was still adorable and could turn his head effortlessly; she made him feel eighteen again. Suzanne Lagier, now grotesquely fat, could still be sent lascivious messages through Maupassant, who was commissioned to do what absence made impossible for Flaubert. But for the most part these were words doing duty for action, habit, far more than serious reaction.

Gertrude Collier Tennant, who was "his dear Gertrude, his old friend, his youth," sent Flaubert a portrait of her daughter. It set him to dreaming of Trouville, the Rond-Point of the Champs Elysées where she had lived, and her stay in the hotel at Rouen. She was in France in the autumn of 1878, and Flaubert several times urged her to visit him in Croisset. She returned to France again in 1879, and he was sure she shared his need to talk of the old days. She spent a considerable time in Paris that year; he provided her an introduction to Alphonse Daudet. Each liked the other immensely. But financial worries, ill health, and the desire to press on with his book kept Flaubert tied to Croisset. He hoped she would return in the spring: he was sure he would be free then. It was not to be.

One of the reasons why Flaubert could not see Gertrude more easily—but hardly one he could tell her—was almost certainly that he was with Juliet Herbert in Paris. As with so many matters concerning Juliet, it is not clear. But during these years, and secretly as before, Flaubert went to Paris each September for what was at any rate a wild sexual orgy. His intimate friend Laporte was almost the only person who knew in fact where he was and what he was doing. Others, like Edmond de Goncourt, who in one way or another stumbled upon the fact of his presence in Paris when he was supposed to be elsewhere, were left to guess at his occupations.[17]

Even less than before could Flaubert's relations with women have any normal outlet in marriage and children. But now he knew that he had been wrong: over and over he reiterated to his married friends how much he adored children and his conviction that he would have been an excellent father. He would ask his correspondents to give their children a warm embrace from him. They had chosen the right path and he the wrong, but fate and literature, he said, had really chosen for him. One day when he and Caro were out for a walk, they stopped at the home of a friend whose baby was in the room: all the way back to Croisset he kept repeating to her that to have such a little being in a house was the most important thing in the world.[18] On the other hand the fussy bachelor had long since lost the adaptability necessary to having a child around. When one was with him for any length of time, the bursts of energy and the noise irritated his hypersensitive nerves beyond endurance: he was glad when the child was removed.

THE WORLD OF BOOKS

Poetry, like the sun, puts a covering of gold upon manure. Too bad for those who cannot see it.
            Open letter to Guy de Maupassant, February 19, 1880

Flaubert entered upon his last years as the successful author of the *Three Tales*. It delighted him that his volume was even on a list of books particularly recommended for Catholic reading. During the autumn of 1878, when it had been out for a year and a half, he tried to persuade Charpentier to publish a de luxe edition of *Saint Julian* to be sold as New Year's gifts. He hoped to make some much-needed money from it and was most annoyed when the project fell through. Charpentier wanted illustrations for it. To mollify Flaubert, who was furious, he offered to try to find a painter who would prepare original ones.[19] Flaubert, whose oppositions to all illustrations had grown if anything more violent with the passing years, replied haughtily that the only illustration he wished was a line drawing of the Saint Julian window in the cathedral at Rouen, which appeared as a frontispiece to Langlois's book on stained glass; the reproduction was to be colored. Flaubert added that while he still lived, no work of his would appear with illustrations. He told his friends that the point of including the Langlois drawing was to bewilder the bourgeois, who was to wonder how the author had drawn the story from it. Badly as he needed money, he rejected the adjurations of his more knowledgeable friends and refused what would presumably have been a lucrative possibility.[20]

His publisher Charpentier, mixing good business sense with a kindly affection for Flaubert, brought out ·a new edition of *A Sentimental Education* in 1879. Its failure ten years before still weighed on Flaubert's heart, and he urged Charpentier to arrange for favorable reviews to launch it. Turgenev reread it and sent a word of appreciation. Zola pronounced his high regard for Flaubert in a review which Madame Roger des Genettes, as faithful as ever in watching over her friend, copied and sent to him. He wrote to Zola that there was no point in pretending he had not seen it when in fact he had read it three times over and only modesty was keeping him from rushing down to show it to his cook. Zola's flattering opinion was a revenge for his earlier disappointment, and he was happy that this volume, which he preferred to *Madame Bovary*, was having its chance again. He almost came to wish he had never written the earlier novel so he would not endlessly have to hear about it. It did delight him, however, that the imperial prosecutor Pinard, who had conducted the attack on *Madame Bovary*, was identified as the author of pornographic verses. Flaubert fancifully suggested that all magistrates were naturally obscene: it was the result of wearing those long robes all day. His other novels preoccupied him but little, and he realized he would not seriously try the theater again, although for a brief moment he did think of attempting to stage *The Castle of Hearts* and at least persuaded Charpentier to publish it in a periodical he owned. When Anatole France saw Flaubert in March, 1879, he wrote him that he considered him the happiest of mortals, for he had written what he wanted to.[21]

Flaubert was excited over what he would write next, after finishing *Bouvard and Pécuchet*.[22] For the most part he was taken up with ideas for books he had been longing to write ever since the 1860's or earlier. There was the novel on the Near East with —as so often—two heroes, a barbarian who was becoming civilized and a civilized man becoming a barbarian. Each was to lose by the change; it was an idea that went back to the trip to the Levant. And there were the novels on life under the Second Empire, *Napoleon the Third* and *The Prefect*. Finally, in his last years he began to imagine a way to combine all of them in a novel to be called *A Parisian Household*. It would deal with a high official under Napoleon III and would treat not only the politics of the empire but also its social life, and in particular the Greek and Near Eastern groups who had been relatively common in Paris then. The husband would do everything to attain power, even capitalizing on the charms of his wife, but ultimately he would recognize the vanity of it all. They would end their lives in quiet disillusionment.

There was one project above all others that dominated Flaubert's last months, the story of the Battle of Thermopylae. The idea was an old one, for in 1871 or so he had added a line on the battle to his final version of *Saint Anthony*. He returned to it in April of 1877 as he was finishing the *Three Tales*, and he was still dreaming of a trip to see the site again when death overtook him. He intended to go with Georges Pouchet, who had been his companion at Concarneau during the writing of *Saint Julian*. He envisaged starting his tale off with the soldiers in Sparta and following them casually along their way to the pass. There he would recount the battle and their death. The trip to Greece and then the writing would, he hoped, revive his flagging spirits. It was only a dream and it was never realized, but he spent fifteen years explaining to his countrymen that dreams were always better than reality.

Flaubert followed much of the literary life of his day, rejoicing in the publication of Berlioz's correspondence for its permanent state of rage, reading and rereading Leconte de Lisle's *Sophocles*, and enjoying or objecting to Du Camp's successive works. The concept of pure art, to which he had dedicated his life, was now dead to others, a relic of bygone ages, except perhaps in the new poetry which it was wholly beyond him to read or understand. But with extraordinary good will he did read and criticize the stream of novels younger writers sent him. He felt one must never discourage a beginning talent, although he did not really like any of the productions of the young naturalists, Huysmans, Hennique, or Alexis, and he strove to wean them from attachment to a school. Their emphasis on sex seemed obsessive, except as Zola handled it in *Nana,* a book which pleased him immensely. Flaubert found it an epic work, a colossus, albeit with dirty feet. It succeeded in being mythic without losing touch with reality.

Flaubert read widely in philosophy and theology for *Bouvard and Pécuchet* and for his own edification. He leaned nearer to the Church in his last years, thinking seriously of having a Mass said for a dead friend and abstaining from meat on Good Friday. But the Christian authors whom he read for his writing confirmed his opposition to theology and to metaphysics. They were in the same category with those who wrote on magnetism, and it was perhaps only for the sake of the irony that he had allowed his clerks to be disillusioned in their religion and successful in curing patients this way.

The death of Pius IX in 1878 Flaubert proclaimed of less significance than that of Claude Bernard; he had been a part of the public procession accompanying the scientist's bier and felt that the crowd had sensed Bernard's importance, too. Science and organized religion were as hostile as ever in his view. The quiet, moderate positivism of Herbert Spencer, or the skepticism of Spinoza, to which he returned once more now, appeared to him the only tenable positions. Neither France nor Germany seemed to have anything to equal these men in his day.

For his own writing Flaubert continued to explore the relationship between art and reality; more and more he knew that all art was choice and hence ultimately idealistic. Art was not nature, but rather always a transformation, which gave the work of art its character. The artist must then have integrity as he made these changes. If he succeeded in his transformation and achieved beauty, then his work would be good. For Flaubert could now state with total simplicity: "What is beautiful is moral."

Art was still style, and style was still a way of seeing things; but now it was the only reality. External, objective truth did not exist, and the photograph was as false as the painting—or as true. If the reality of objects could never be determined, then only their relationship to the observer, only his mode of perceiving them, could have reality. And the illusory world of objects could never be more than a springboard, the material basis from which to rise to art. His Carthage had not been real but ideal. The discovery that every word in Tacitus was false would hurt Tacitus not a whit: there would then be two realities, that of history and that of Tacitus. And he sat long in thought over a phrase he picked up in his reading: "the sacred fear of Form." It had been his constant religion.

THE WRITING OF *Bouvard and Pécuchet*

The tortures of literature I will really have known.
Letter to Caroline, June 6-7, 1877

By October of 1876 Flaubert already knew that he was enough recovered to attack *Bouvard and Pécuchet* again as soon as he had finished *Herodias*. When he had completed the tale and a further stupid month of errands, dinners, and other wasted efforts during February of 1877, he got out his notes and returned to the work he had abandoned nearly two years before. From then until his death, steadily and almost unremittingly, he labored at it. In all of the last three months of 1877 he allowed himself only one after-noon off from his appointed task; nothing, not even his financial problems or his broken fibula, turned him aside. Month after month the pile of pages grew.

Fortunately several trips became necessary for the work. One, to the environs of Falaise, was for Bouvard and Pécuchet's study of geology and archeology. Laporte joined him and watched over him as Du Camp had thirty years before. They rose at six; all day long they traveled about under the sun or in the rain; by nine in the evening they were asleep. Their only debauchery was eating seafood or writing insulting phrases about current politics on walls. It was good for Flaubert thus to get out into the fresh air, good for his health and good for his writing.

Flaubert's friends were alarmed over how bookish all his sources were becoming: the written word was replacing the living experience.[23] He read and read, more than a hundred volumes for his chapter on medicine and equally widely for each of the others. What he could not track down himself he sent Laporte to read for him, or he wrote to specialist friends and acquaintances. He had always done this in the past; but now there was a new danger, for he was reading not for knowledge or vicarious experience (as he had done up to now), but only to confirm or elaborate his preconceptions or his prejudices. He hoped that his aim would come clear for the reader, not through any isolated part of what he then wrote, perhaps, but from its totality. Yet that totality was only a sum of readings, not a unified experience, except of hate. The reader would be staggered by what he found, Flaubert believed, that is, he added ingenuously, if he did not go to sleep over it instead. Toward the end of his writing, he defined his aim as displaying the defect in the scientific method. But even that, though it had a philosophic breadth adequate to underpinning his work, was still a bookish fount and not the clear, vigorous spirit of lived experience.

Flaubert was aware he was writing for only a small number of readers, a restriction he came regretfully to accept as the work progressed. The staggering range of his concept for the work dazzled him; but he knew that executing it was another matter and that instead of being sublime it might be no more than silly. As with *Salammbô* and *A Sentimental Education*, the deeper he got into his work, the more doubts he had about its underlying conception and the more he realized he was working out a mania, a type of lucid insanity. He struggled on.

In August of 1879 he looked ahead and hoped to have finished the final chapter of his first volume by the following March or April; he decided to remain at Croisset throughout the winter to complete it. But in November, he said—and not entirely in jest—that he was afraid he might be finished before his novel was.

A WORLD BASED ON MONEY

How all this infuriates me, dear God! What a nuisance!
What degradation!

Letter to Madame Roger des Genettes,
July 16, 1879

When Flaubert considered the long future, he had been wont for
many years to imagine a disagreeable world in which people
would all have to spend their time thinking about money; it would
be like America and he was grateful that he would not live to see
it. Now this was his world and, worse yet, the world of his niece.

As 1877 opened, Ernest was, as so often, sure that more hopeful times lay just ahead. He was, as always, mistaken. By the end
of March his situation was again desperate, and Flaubert was
forced again to urge Laporte on to even more devoted efforts to
get help from friends in Paris. Similarly Flaubert himself pressed
Charpentier to get out the edition of his *Three Tales* quickly in
order to catch the upswing of popularity from the separate periodical publication of the tales. If only he could write one such
book a year, he lamented, then he could be surer of being able to
live out his days in Croisset. It was in May, with matters becoming
even worse, that he began to talk with Charpentier about the de
luxe edition of *Saint Julian*.

During that month Flaubert, who usually kept such affairs at
arm's length, decided to intervene directly to help Ernest instead
of working through friends like Laporte. When he went to
Chenonceaux in the spring for what was becoming an annual
affair, he asked Madame Pelouze to interest herself in his nephew
and to take a prominent part in helping raise new capital for him.
He returned from the Loire convinced that matters were well
under way.[24] He then had conversations with Lapierre and Raoul-
Duval; on the strength of his representations, his old friends
agreed to lend their support again. He noticed the powerful effect
Madame Pelouze's name had in these financial circles. As June
wore along, there were constant delays in arranging meetings with

her, but he busied himself with his other subscribers. At last on the twenty-first she agreed to put up fifty thousand francs toward founding a stock company. Flaubert, much relieved, was privately sure he had saved his nephew's finances.

To be a little more accurate, of the four hundred thousand francs he needed, Commanville now had promises of one hundred fifty to two hundred thousand. Flaubert set about trying to find the rest of the money, as did Ernest. A month later, at the end of July, the additional funds had still not been raised, and Ernest himself was beginning to confess that they might not be forthcoming. Moreover, the sawmill was in Dieppe, a long way from Paris and the money market: investors declined to go inspect the property. Flaubert even tried writing Madame Husson, who was reputed to know financiers. By mid-August, Caroline, pushed almost beyond endurance, was suffering unremitting headaches. The weeks dragged by, and there was no change in their finances. Flaubert pressed Charpentier again to get out his special edition of *Saint Julian:* it was his only hope for further revenue. Meanwhile business activities in France slowed, awaiting the outcome of the political struggles which developed after the Crisis of May Sixteenth. They had to await a calming of the political scene to bring about the revival Flaubert needed in order to raise more money for his nephew.

Hope dimmed for Flaubert as the winter of 1877-78 began. Only Madame Pelouze's name seemed to be keeping his nephew afloat. Then trouble loomed in two new directions. There were serious problems with their landlord, and the factory Laporte managed for a living began to have major financial difficulties. The consequences for Laporte were to be disastrous. Flaubert sought to help by appealing to his friend Senator Bardoux; perhaps some post could be found for Laporte in the sprawling French bureaucracy.

The following spring, the summer, and then the autumn of 1878 were almost unrelieved gloom. Flaubert's nerves were badly on edge, and his whole body trembled. Madame Pelouze was trying to help raise money among her friends, and she did provide the fifty thousand francs of ready cash she had promised. But there were notes that had been signed and which required repayment; Laporte had no job; and people were losing patience with Commanville. By September it was clear he could not get the capital to start up his sawmill again. Caro initiated the moves to try to break her lease and thereby save at least that money: his nephew, his niece, and Flaubert would try to share the same apartment in Paris, taking turns living there. But every unexpected bill was a new disaster, and Flaubert kept asking when the last blow would have been dealt him. He was submerged in business, he loathed it, and it was a constant source of humiliation.

There seemed no real solution to Flaubert's woes. He pressed friends and editors during September, hoping for republication of his older works or a chance to sell *The Castle of Hearts* to someone; perhaps Charpentier would now put out the *Saint Julian*. Caroline, however, was as unable to sublet her apartment as she was to pay for it. Nevertheless Flaubert began making plans for the arrangement of their furniture when she and her husband moved into his apartment: his leather furniture, he insisted, must remain in his study. For the rest, he did not care. In October, he gave up for the moment the idea of coming in to Paris.

Word of Flaubert's situation was getting around, though fortunately he did not know it. Edmond de Goncourt heard about it all, including heart-rending details he had not known before. Caroline and her husband were complaining publicly about Flaubert's insistence on continuing to smoke cigars. And his niece had been heard to observe that he was indeed a strange man: he did not know how to meet adversity.[25]

By December of 1878 disaster could be staved off no longer: the sawmill at Dieppe had to be sold for whatever it would bring. Capital could not be found to get it running again, despite the contributions of Madame Pelouze and others. Commanville's many creditors were pressing for their money, but there was going to be almost none. The future was bleak; Flaubert, who had by now plunged his hands deeply into business affairs to no avail, felt himself soiled. Several of his friends, Senator Bardoux and Madame Brainne among them, raised with him the question of seeking some sort of government post. He replied honestly that, with his temperament, he would get himself dismissed within a week. What was there that he was capable of doing in return for a salary? He was not constitutionally adapted to living; he knew it and admitted it had cost him many a tear.

Flaubert could only wait. He hoped at first that the sale of the sawmill would take place in January, then in February. It would not be pleasant, but at least the waiting would be over and he would know where he stood. He had piloted his boat badly through life, and he was aware of it; he had been excessively idealistic and he was being punished for it. In January, with the sale being put off yet another time, he comforted himself that he would still have a few thousand francs a year; this would let him finish *Bouvard and Pécuchet*. He was having trouble sleeping, however, and had persistent headaches; but he was working hard at his book and enjoying the moonlight on the winter scene about him. Yet the waiting was becoming anguish. While it was futile to complain, it was equally futile to go on living. He was all alone; and when he did go in to Paris, Caro and her husband would have to come out to Croisset so there would be room in the apartment. Hence he would not be able to see her there.

Slowly what little reserve of money was left began to disappear. His servant required cash to buy provisions; the gardener, too, must be paid. He would then have sixty francs left. He forebore drawing any moral, but he did ask his niece to descend into her conscience and examine the situation into which she had put him. By the eighteenth of January, his mental state was serious; the next day he sent a telegram to Turgenev begging him to come see him. There were problems about breaking Caroline's lease, and Flaubert did not understand them. Caroline and Ernest told him what to write to their landlord, and he did as he was told: but why could they not have seen him themselves and have spared their uncle? Moreover, their landlord was in the right in objecting to Caroline's subletting. Why did they then insist Flaubert send him an insulting letter? He would stop his letter to her, he said, before he wrote more than he meant to; but it was odd that she and her husband always found others had obligations and they had only rights. He was rolling in anguish. He could only demand that, after the sale, they settle the whole matter and let him be free of all of this for just four years. That he insisted upon and would not compromise. But then the sale was put off again. It was at that moment that Flaubert slipped on the ice and broke his leg.

FRIENDS INTERVENE

What did you mean by this sentence: "I have been busy over your affairs . . . although with the proper discretion"?
Letter to Edmond de Goncourt, January 3, 1879

Flaubert's friends had long been alarmed. Better informed and more clear headed than he, they knew or suspected his nephew would never extricate himself from his financial tangles. Toward the end of 1878 they began secretly to seek out what might be done to help him. Princess Mathilde and Madame Brainne were among the first to begin casting about; soon Goncourt, Taine, Madame Adam, Senator Cordier, and Senator Bardoux (who was Minister of Education), Turgenev, and others were all working quietly but quickly to bring aid to their friend. It had, however, to be a conspiracy of silence, for even the mild suggestions of the Princess and Madame Brainne had already brought forth refusals from Croisset.

By early January of 1879 Flaubert's suspicions were sufficiently aroused and his friends' plans were sufficiently advanced for it to seem well to broach the matter directly with him. Taine was selected. He wrote Flaubert that the largely honorary post of librarian at the Mazarine Library was about to become vacant through the demise of the current occupant, who was already on his deathbed. It paid three thousand francs and provided a nice apartment in the Institute of France with windows overlooking the quay; the work was negligible. Would Flaubert accept? Flaubert, alas, felt that the requirement that he live in Paris would so add to his expenses that he could not afford the post; moreover he disliked the idea of having any job whatsoever. And besides, he remembered the letters he had had from the Princess and Madame Brainne: no doubt they had something better in mind.

Then came Flaubert's near breakdown in mid-January, his telegraphed appeal to Turgenev to come visit him, and finally his broken fibula. His friends decided that the moment had come to bring real pressure to bear. Turgenev seemed most able to act; he telegraphed Flaubert on the thirtieth that he would be there the next day. Disregarding Flaubert's reply not to come, he arrived in Croisset on February 3.[26]

Waiting until Caro and her husband had left, Turgenev told Flaubert the post was his for the asking and that the salary was eight thousand francs. There must be an immediate reply. All night Flaubert tossed and turned trying to make up his mind. It was, however, a way not to be a burden on Caro and her husband; he accepted. Turgenev returned happily to Paris to continue his campaign; unfortunately he had to report almost at once that the salary was only six thousand. But by then Flaubert had decided he really wanted the post; he even declined to withdraw when his old friend Baudry became his competitor for it. He was forgetting that the scholar Baudry's whole career had earned him a position like this. Moreover, Baudry had generously stepped aside ten years before to be sure that Bouilhet was named to the Rouen library. But Flaubert was a sick man and desperate.

He now put pressure on every friend he could reach. He told Turgenev how to approach Madame Pelouze, since he could not do so himself because of his nephew's loans; and he welcomed a visit from his old friend Senator Cordier. The promised salary dropped to three thousand, but Cordier was encouraging about Flaubert's chances. The senator wrote a day or so later: the previous government had fallen and Bardoux was no longer Minister of Education, but the new Minister was receptive to the idea. He did, however, fear there might be other promises involved. Additional powerful senators backed Cordier's efforts; Hugo, approached by him, had given his support at once. Matters looked hopeful . . . except that the new government owed favors to Sénard, the lawyer who had defended *Madame Bovary*, and Baudry was Sénard's son-in-law. Everything depended upon Gambetta, the man of the hour in the ministerial crisis.[27] Flaubert, who clearly remembered their meeting the year before, began to urge his friends to work on the powerful politician.

Flaubert's affairs were continuing to be unbearable throughout all these days, and the hours dragged miserably. On the tenth of February it was time to try to put the cast on his leg. Caro, hoping perhaps to press her uncle into accepting the post, was more than usually frank about the extent of the disaster ahead. Flaubert in turn pressed Ernest to accept a job at eight thousand francs. Caroline was being most courageous, but this in no wise affected the painful fact that Ernest's collapse was now going to involve Raoul-Duval because he had helped them earlier by cosigning her notes. As Flaubert sat on February 13 worrying about their financial disaster, he realized that it was far more painful to him than his sore leg or waiting for news of his own post.

Although poor Flaubert did not know it, his fate had already been played out. Turgenev and all his other friends had counted too heavily on the weight they would carry with Gambetta. The new government cared little about Flaubert and had many political debts to pay. When Turgenev approached Gambetta for the crucial request, he was refused. He wired Flaubert on the thirteenth. Facing matters stoically, Flaubert at once asked his friends to bring all their efforts to a halt. He was annoyed only with Baudry. The episode was, he thought, at an end.

Unfortunately, *Le Figaro* had got wind of it and, on the fifteenth, published a piquant version of it. Flaubert's penury, his sacrifice for his relatives, the efforts of his friends, Turgenev's request of Gambetta, and the latter's haughty refusal were all detailed for the enjoyment of readers. Flaubert wept for shame.

On February 17, Flaubert reached the lowest point he had ever known. He received a letter from Baudry concerning his own efforts over the years to obtain the post; it would not suit Flaubert at all, Baudry assured him. Flaubert, furious, was sure the letter was entirely hypocritical. In fact, given the actual salary, the post was not really a good one for Flaubert. And much may surely be forgiven Baudry if he felt the career man's annoyance when political favoritism threatened to rob him of his just reward for the work of a lifetime.

Baudry was not Flaubert's only problem. He also received a letter from his landlord in Paris raising questions about the lease: Ernest had written him in insulting terms, too. Flaubert was too exhausted and too trembling to write, he said. They were killing him. He wished that he did not have to afflict Caro still further, but he could stand no more. It was too much. Flaubert begged his niece to go see their landlord and bring peace. He had not slept for several nights because of the itching all over his body. He signed his letter with affection but then turned back to the top, where a bit of space remained, to add: "My strength has run out. All I can do is weep."*

Up to this point Flaubert had not fully explained the matter of his post to his niece for fear of wounding her. Now, however, she had read the story in *Le Figaro*, and he knew the account must be circulating all over the city; there was nothing for it but to give her a detailed explanation. He wrote on February 22. His fault lay, he said, in having trusted other people instead of his own judgment. And he told her everything he knew about the affair; he added he was sure Baudry would be nominated (as in fact he already had been). All the dignity of his long life of sacrifice was thrown away, he felt, by his soiled relations with the bankers and with their landlord and by the *Figaro* story. Nor was this all: Commanville was deeply indebted to Baudry's brother and could ill afford to have him annoyed. Suppose Flaubert were appointed! Of course Baudry would excite his brother against Commanville to get revenge. And all of this aspect Flaubert was only just beginning to learn from Caro; he had thought the matter with Baudry's brother long settled. Why could not Ernest deign to keep him informed? But perhaps it was better this way; at least his nephew's silence spared him a few moments of thinking about business.

Flaubert set his friends to work at finding out what had happened; he learned Madame Charpentier had set the whole thing off, but too late, with Gambetta.[28] In fact the post had already been promised to Baudry when Turgenev, unaware of this, approached the Minister and was refused. Baudry, meanwhile, was glorying. There was talk of appointing Flaubert as an additional librarian under him, and he was assuming the pose of generous

---

*"Mes forces sont épuisées, je ne peux plus que pleurer" (SUPPL, IV, 174).

friend in hoping he would not have to instruct Flaubert to do certain tasks. But having had his moment of triumph, Baudry—with real generosity—then wrote to Flaubert to propose that his friends seek to have him appointed an honorary librarian, with the title and an income but no duties; he would even work toward that end himself, he promised. Flaubert was too deeply wounded in his pride to understand his friend's gesture and looked forward to writing a stinging reply in a few days.

There was worse ahead. By the first of March, with the sale of the sawmill only days away, Caro and her husband finally had to tell Flaubert the facts of their situation more clearly than they had yet been driven to. While he had been partially warned much earlier, he had also been told the sawmill was worth six hundred thousand francs, enough to cover everything. Now he was allowed to learn that it would not bring more than two hundred thousand and that, although he was the largest single creditor, his mortgage was the latest in date and hence he would receive nothing at all. This alone terrified him. But what about their friends who had lent money to Ernest on the strength of that friendship? At least, he hoped, they could all be repaid. He wrote to Caro for reassurance about this; and he prepared himself for the inevitable in regard to his own future. He would once and for all give up the idea of having a place in Paris and would live as cheaply as possible at Croisset on what he could earn and what his nephew could send him. In addition, though it was acutely humiliating, he would ask his brother Achille for a small allowance to help make ends meet. Bad as it was, however, this ignominy was better than living at public expense in a post to which he had no right. He would sacrifice himself.

It was just as well that Flaubert waited to write Baudry until he was more calm. When he did write, he thanked him for his letter, declined its suggestions, and asked him to take no further steps: he could not accept such an honorary post and pension without doing injustice to the real librarians. It was not an unpleasant letter. On the same day he wrote again to his niece that their friends must be paid off at all cost; and he added that Laporte had a good chance of a job. That would at least take this worry off Flaubert's mind, for Laporte, too, had signed Caroline's notes. But how, he wondered, were he, Caro, and Ernest to live with no income? It was frightening.

The days dragged slowly by for the invalid at Croisset. There were more legal papers to be signed with the bankers, and he did not understand them; the terms of the mortgages and sale of the sawmill seemed steadily more puzzling. And what was going to happen to the money of their friends?

Flaubert's friends in Paris knew far more than he realized of his situation and were determined to save him. Their problem was not how to get him money from the government: that they could easily arrange through various political connections. The difficulty lay in finding a guise in which to offer it that Flaubert would find acceptable. The form, he had always insisted, was a part of the content; and he was not abandoning his stand. He had, after all, just paid bitterly for forgetting it momentarily.

This time it was Maupassant who undertook to persuade Flaubert. Everyone, he wrote, and he underlined and repeated it, everyone considered the offer of a pension to an author by the Ministry a completely natural thing. It was no more than an official testimony of esteem. Through all the ages princes had given them to the great men of their day: why could not the Republic do the same? Why was what had always been thought of as an honor (and again he underlined) so painful and humiliating to Flaubert alone? The Minister of Public Education wanted (and another underline) to do something. If Flaubert insisted on rejecting an honorific title, very well; it would be a pension which no one else knew of. Renan . . . he started to write and then he crossed out the rest so carefully that it is illegible. All that is decipherable is the crucial: "and no one says anything about that." Four people and only four would ever know, and then the document would be filed away in the archives. All Flaubert had to do was to say "yes." He must do so. Confidentially he also told him that he thought the figure would perhaps be five thousand francs; Flaubert must not speak of it as a loan or a sum to be repaid as it would hurt the feelings of the Minister. It was a homage, not a pension.[29]

On March 9, with the sale of the sawmill now only a day away, Flaubert knew he could no longer refuse. With deep humiliation he resigned himself and wrote his acceptance to Maupassant. But the secrecy must be total, absolute; not even the Commanvilles were to be told until he decided so himself. It worried him two days later that his niece could write about plans for him which she thought were wise and which she hoped he would accept. He wrote himself shortly to tell her about his acceptance: though it humiliated him hideously, it seemed the only way in which he could await his death in some peace.

If only he could have peace! But there were still all his friends who were involved in Commanville's disaster. Laporte had pledged large sums and was now unable to pay them without mortgaging his own home, which he desperately did not wish to do. And what of Madame Pelouze? Her money had been lent to help form a stock company; instead it had been used to pay current debts and now no stock company existed or could exist. Flaubert grew steadily more confused and alarmed. On March 24 the property around the sawmill was sold and for a higher price than Caro had expected. But still their personal friends could not be paid off, she wrote. How was this possible?

As the month of anguish drew to its close, Caro was pressing him to reconsider his stand on accepting an honorary but public post at the Mazarine Library, for she knew, as he did not, that she and her husband could not then or probably ever pay him anything of what they owed him. He still declined and even scolded her for stirring up Madame Charpentier once again to approach Gambetta.

Flaubert was still hoping that Maupassant could arrange a secret pension for him. By late April arrangements were well under way, and Maupassant reported that his friend could count on five thousand francs, that there was nothing disgraceful about it as there were six hundred such pensions, many of them being paid to people with incomes over fifty thousand francs a year. It would, however, take time, and the difficulty was that there was no time left.[30] Flaubert had been trying to get some honest and complete statement from Caroline; but to no avail. He did not know how much was owed or to whom. Meanwhile he learned that Laporte's efforts to get a government job had failed and that he was having to mortgage his home in order to cover a payment due on Commanville's loans. Flaubert wrote Caro that he no longer had the physical strength to become irritated but that his vitality was slipping slowly away from him through this infected wound. How, he asked could he hope to write under such conditions? On April 30 he spent the last three hundred francs he had in the world; they were what he owed at that moment for his share in Bouilhet's monument. His servant was unpaid and he had no household money left.

There was a thoroughly real possibility that Flaubert would starve. His friends could not allow matters to continue thus. In due course there would be a pension, but it could not be arranged quickly. A considerable number of people worked together upon the only plan which could be put into action at once, which was still the honorary post at the Mazarine Library. Maupassant and the writer Edmond About joined forces: Baudry must write to present the idea once again to Flaubert. It would be an honorific appointment with no duties whatsoever and would carry a salary of three thousand francs. Two thousand additional francs could be found later from the pension funds. A letter embodying this must go to Flaubert immediately; About undertook to see that it was sent.

It was fated that Flaubert, like Julian, should have to drink his cup to the dregs. Edmond About, whose kindliness was not in doubt but who really did not know the details of the matter at all, went, not to Frédéric Baudry at the Mazarine, but to the painter Paul Baudry. The artist must have understood little or nothing of what was wanted of him. His only really direct connection with Flaubert had been a letter to the Rouen municipal council urging them not to erect a monument to Bouilhet, a letter of which Flaubert had a copy. However, he obediently wrote Flaubert.[31]

Totally bewildered, Flaubert wrote Maupassant, who alone might have the key to what had happened. He could not accept the post if it were to be public, he said; but could it be kept secret? He was beyond being able to be proud and refuse totally, though he knew that it was only disguised charity. On May 11 he decided that he must go to Paris himself to see the Minister. It was not, however, clear either how he would pay his railroad fare or where he could stay if he got there.

In Paris, and probably for the first time, Flaubert and his niece had an unpleasant scene. He was himself filled with remorse when it was over, and upon his return to Croisset at once wrote his excuses for having been so egotistical. He also saw the Minister, who was very kind, and shortly thereafter his brother Achille, who agreed at once to give him three thousand a year. Unfortunately Achille was a seriously ill man and not always of sound mind. He might forget. But on the seventeenth, Laporte had better news: he had a job. Flaubert wrote, almost hopefully, to ask if he thought perhaps fortune were changing for them all and better days lay ahead.

A pleasant letter from the right Baudry closed the matter. But swallowing the three thousand francs would, Flaubert wrote, choke him, whatever name they were called by. He had lost his integrity and could no longer hold his head high. A letter from Madame Adam confirmed Flaubert's suspicions that all was not as secret as Maupassant had promised. It helped that Maupassant soon wrote his nomination to the post had been signed and he could have 750 francs on arrival in Paris.[32] Flaubert wrote to Baudry accepting, because he was about to starve.

He went to Paris in June, where he saw the Minister of Education and the Premier, too, who had been instrumental in the whole affair. He accepted the money, but only in the hope of being able to return it, upon his death, from what he would inherit from his brother and others. Since it was so widely known, he also told it to Goncourt. And Zola as well heard of it as a disguised pension.[33] Flaubert still did not dare to speak his mind on the subject to Baudry, as he could get no answer from Caroline concerning the terms upon which her husband and Baudry's brother now were.

There were interminable delays in getting the money to Flaubert and uncertainties about when and how much. Eventually all hope of making it a secret pension instead of a public post disappeared when the budget for such funds was badly cut. But by that time the fatal word was out, and Flaubert had accepted the post. It was made easier for him when his old friend Cordier told him that the principal agent had been Victor Hugo.[34]

Flaubert spent the summer making arrangements for having *Salammbô* at last put on as an opera, for reprinting *A Sentimental Education*, and for the publication of *The Castle of Hearts* in Charpentier's periodical, *La Vie moderne*. All were means to make money from his writing. The late summer and early autumn looked far better, and a tired Flaubert began to take new hope.

He was mistaken. In October, pushed to the wall again, Caroline and her husband took from her uncle the only thing he had left of which they had not yet despoiled him: his friendship with Laporte. Unlike Flaubert, Laporte was a businessman, had the necessary connections to know what Ernest was really doing, and could no longer allow himself to be victimized. Although his nephew had readily fooled Flaubert about his situation, it was in fact as shoddy as ever, and a day of reckoning was at hand. For the young couple the problem was whether they could force Laporte, through his friendship for Flaubert, to allow the use of his signature once more. After all, despite their dilapidations, he still had a considerable capital in his house. Realizing that there would be no end to their maneuvers until he refused them, Laporte declined to be pillaged again when new notes fell due in October. Flaubert, knowing only what his niece and nephew told him, wrote to Laporte begging his acquiescence: they so needed his help and it was only a signature, no more than he had done before. With great dignity and restraint, Laporte replied that he could not allow a matter of dispute between himself and Commanville to be judged by Flaubert, who would thus have to choose between hurting a nephew or a dear friend. He begged Flaubert to let Commanville and himself settle the matter between themselves.[35]

This Caroline and her husband could not allow. If they could not extort more money from Laporte, at any rate he must not be permitted ever to reach their uncle with his side of the story. To a helpless Flaubert who could never possibly untangle the truth, they spoke of the gross callousness of his pretended friend and effectively separated from him the most devoted companion he had had over the last years, all through the time of trouble and anguish. They did not meet again, for Flaubert believed his old friend had been guilty of deserting him when the path became steep. It broke his heart.

The rest of the year was not easy. There were more promissory notes to worry over; Flaubert feared to go to Rouen lest he meet Laporte; Charpentier, whom he was harrassing for payments of royalties, was himself in financial difficulties and could not send what was owing. December saw gloom settling again upon a helpless old man.

THE LAST MONTHS

> This permanent incertainty is reducing me to desperation.
> Despite heroic efforts on my part, I can feel myself succumbing to this anguish.
>
> Letter to his niece Caroline, January 9, 1879

As 1880 began, Flaubert had four more months to live. The year opened sadly with the receipt of a New Year's greeting from Laporte. It was quiet, dignified, and affectionate. Laporte addressed himself to his old friend and assured him that, despite whatever feelings others had inspired in Flaubert toward him, he did not wish the new year to begin without sending his affection and his good wishes. He told Flaubert to accept them without fear, for they came from perhaps his dearest friend. He closed with formal regards to Madame Commanville. Reporting on it to Caroline, Flaubert assured her he would of course do nothing about it.[36] The mail also brought the customary unpaid bills to infuriate him. He had spent the last month or so alone and would be alone for most of the time to come, seeing no one and perhaps better off thus, for at least he had no stupidities to face that way, he said. He admitted he was hypersensitive and almost sick now from exasperation. At intervals he had brief visits from Ernest, in Rouen on business.

On January 10 he finished the next to the last chapter of *Bouvard and Pécuchet* and started at once on the final documentation for the closing chapter of Volume One. As it dealt with education, he was sure Maupassant could help him with information from the Ministry. Caroline, too, provided him materials, especially on drawing lessons; and he arranged for the loan of a pair of peacocks so that he might study their amours. There were also books to read; in all, he noted later in the month, he had read more than fifteen hundred works to write his single volume. At least his labors had made it possible for him to let the reader pass easily through difficult materials.

Sometimes his readings were more agreeable. Turgenev sent him a translation of *War and Peace*, of which he found the first two volumes outstanding. Nature and humanity appeared in almost Shakespearean terms. He asked Turgenev to tell him about the author. In his reading these days he found himself more emotional than heretofore; he even had to wipe away a tear now and then. Once he signed himself "The Last Doddering Fool of Romanticism."

After all these years *The Castle of Hearts* began to appear in print. Flaubert had waited almost two decades for this moment. For long he had hoped to see it staged, but now at least he could see it with illustrations to suggest the theater. Unfortunately, when he saw them, they horrified him: he found them in bad taste and contrary to the spirit of the text, which they interrupted abominably. He howled in protest. But he wrote to ask Caro to keep her copies of *La Vie moderne*, in which it was appearing serially, for he would be sending his to Juliet Herbert. It seems to be the last time her name appears in Flaubert's hand.[37] Mademoiselle Julie, too, was impressed by the publication: she had never before known her master was a famous author. She was partially deaf, blind, and halt; but she had heard of his fame at the grocer's and reported it to him. He wrote at once to several people to confess how moved he was.

The naturalist group was about to publish a volume of stories together. Critical opinion ever since has been unanimous that Maupassant's contribution was outstanding. Flaubert, who saw it in proof, found its concept original and the story told in excellent style. He was charmed by it and laughed out loud several times reading it. He wrote Guy he had produced a masterpiece.

There were contacts, too, with time long past. Gertrude Collier Tennant wrote to tell of her departure from Paris; she enclosed a letter from her daughter assuring Flaubert she had known him ages before her mother . . . in a prior existence. From Maupassant he learned Guy's mother Laure was much improved after serious illness; he replied urging the two to come spend time with him at Croisset during the summer. And, at Maurice Sand's request, he sent him the letters he had carefully preserved from George Sand; they were to be published along with his to her.

February was punctuated with money problems. Flaubert was still unable to get from Charpentier all that was owing to him. There were the eternal bills and notes. Was it not enough, he complained, that he was ruined? Did he in addition have to spend his days paying attention to these matters of which he understood not one word?

And then from Laporte there was a formal demand for repayment of thirteen thousand francs. Flaubert, helpless and deeply worried, wrote to Ernest for a clarification and some explanation of what his nephew proposed to do. It revived Flaubert's suffering. But as time went by, hope returned; he began to plan for a trip to Paris in early May and he even dreamed of a journey to the Near East. Mademoiselle Julie kept driving him back to his work again now that she knew he was an author: he began the final chapter of his novel.

Another worry loomed and disappeared: Guy de Maupassant was threatened with prosecution for obscenity in some verses he had published. Flaubert interrupted work long enough to write Raoul-Duval for help and to send a magisterial open letter to the newspapers. It aided in stopping the law suit.

Quite suddenly Ernest got a new start, finding the capital to begin another sawmill; he left almost at once for Odessa to buy wood. Flaubert asked Turgenev to look into possibilities for him; he believed now that real poverty could be averted. Nature seemed suddenly serene again and splendid under the oncoming spring. As if in celebration, too, the ten-year struggle to get the fountain erected for Bouilhet came to a final and successful end: permission was granted. It was in fact inaugurated some two and one-half years later and remains there today, decorated with a bust of Bouilhet, which looks, as he did, enough like Flaubert to be deceptive at a hundred paces. A happy Flaubert could write imperiously to his niece about how he wished his apartment rearranged for his arrival in a month or two. He looked forward to being unencumbered as he walked about the room. No longer would he bump into his enemy the piano or crash his head against an overhead lamp.

Du Camp in these months at last realized his ambition of being elected to the French Academy. It made Flaubert smile and set him again to thinking of all the years he had known him. Du Camp very nicely sent him personal word of it, too; they exchanged several letters. Oddly, in March, they had differences of opinion again. Caroline wrote that he had been rude to her; and he himself mailed to Flaubert a collection of papers which, he said, were the sad but perfectly real relics and proofs of his excesses. He urged Flaubert to read them, to blush, and to repent.[38] It was perhaps their last contact and may explain the covert but damaging tone of so much of Du Camp's memoirs concerning Flaubert.

Bouvard and Pécuchet provided problems in March. Flaubert was, as always, attempting in each discipline to find exceptions to the general rules. His correspondents were quite unable to accept the logical framework from which he started, and so he had difficulties with them. Pouchet and Baudry were failing him, he complained.

For Easter weekend, Flaubert had as house guests Daudet and Maupassant, Zola and Goncourt, and his publisher Charpentier. Maupassant preceded them; the others, who took the train to Rouen, were as happy as a group of boys unexpectedly let out of school. Maupassant was at the station with a cab and took them to Croisset, where Flaubert, an Italian hat on his head, met them affectionately. Goncourt had forgotten how beautiful the property was with its great trees shading the walks on the long terrace: it was the proper dwelling place for a man of letters.

The dinner was very good and the wines excellent and plentiful. The whole evening went to telling hearty jokes at which Flaubert roared with childish glee. He refused to read them sections of the new novel; finally they all went off to their rooms, which were chilly and peopled with family busts. Everyone slept late. Next morning they stayed indoors talking until time to leave, as Flaubert declared walking out of doors an unnecessary waste of energy. When the moment came to bid them adieu, Flaubert had a tear in his eye on embracing his parting guests.[39] It was the last time any of them were to see him.

April should have been without financial worries, now that Ernest had a new business; but it was not to be so. Threatening letters and announcements of law suits continued to rain in upon Flaubert, including even a threat to seize his property for his debts, a shock his heroines had so often experienced, from Emma Bovary to Madame Arnoux. He had no money, Ernest having borrowed what little Flaubert had received from Charpentier; his resources of nervous energy were gone; he was even beyond demanding explanations. All he asked was peace and that this persecution cease.

As if in answer to this reiterated prayer, Flaubert's last days were very happy. An Englishman wrote to say he wished to stage *The Castle of Hearts:* at last Flaubert would see it in a theater with real actors. Ernest wrote hopefully of his Russian trip; and disciples continued to come pay homage to the master. April 27 was Saint Polycarp Day. There were more than thirty letters written in his praise, and three telegrams arrived during the dinner. The Archbishop of Rouen sent his compliments, as did Italian cardinals. There were a number of gifts, including a tooth alleged to be a relic of the saint, and a whole case of flowers was on its way from Nice. Maupassant was behind much of it, Flaubert was sure. He was deeply touched. The only lugubrious note came when he attempted to place the crown on his head; it was too large and dropped onto his shoulders, leading him to comment that he felt as though he were in a tomb.

As April slipped away, he was looking forward to going to Paris. It would be so good to see his niece again and go to the expositions with her! He expected to arrive on May 10 and to remain until about the end of June before returning to Croisset to prepare the copy for his second volume. In September he would return to Paris and not stir again for a long time.

On May 2 he was overjoyed: Guy de Maupassant had been able to find precisely the piece of botanical information which

Pouchet and Baudry had denied existed. Flaubert was sure he had been right because esthetics is the truth, and at a certain level of intellectuality, one does not err if one is careful. Reality, he affirmed, does not bend itself to the ideal but rather confirms it. It was what he had always believed.

On Monday, May 3, he wrote his last known letter. It was to Maupassant and closed: "You will see me at the start of next week."

DEATH

> I am tempted to congratulate him on having enjoyed the gentlest death which it can fall to a mortal to have. It is you whom I pity, you and myself, to whom is left only the care of his memory.
>
> Letter from Frédéric Baudry to Caroline, May 10, 1880

On Sunday, May 9, Flaubert expected, as he had written Maupassant, to go in to Paris.[40] The preceding Friday, the seventh, he invited his doctor and friend, Fortin, to dine with him. When the table was cleared, he declaimed Corneille to him at length.

On the morning of the eighth he slept until about eight-thirty. Then, as was his wont, he took a very hot bath, in which he remained a long time. Thereafter, going to his study, he ran through the morning mail while smoking several pipes. Around ten-thirty, feeling uncomfortable, he called his servant several times. When she answered, he sent her for Fortin, who had unfortunately left moments before. Upon the servant's return, she found Flaubert dazed but still in control of himself and able to stand up. He thought he was about to have another epileptic attack. Very gently, he lay down on his divan, rubbing his temples with Eau de Cologne; his speech became thick and indistinct; he slipped back, his hands clamping closed; his face swelled and began to blacken. In this state he must have slipped into unconsciousness. It was the peace for which he so yearned and it can only have been relief.

A Rouen doctor, who was called in haste, arrived at noon. The congested face and almost imperceptible breathing were what had alarmed his servants. Now his heart was barely beating. A moment later it was over. The doctor diagnosed a ventricular hemorrhage of the brain; it may well have been caused by tertiary syphilis.

His niece and nephew and Maupassant were summoned at once and left Paris together at six in the evening. Flaubert had been placed upon his bed, a black swelling showing about the neck. For three days Maupassant stood vigil by his side. Then he and Pouchet prepared the body for burial.

Sunday morning, Edmond de Goncourt's maid asked if her master intended to see Flaubert that day, as she placed a telegram on his desk. It read: "Flaubert dead." All day long it seemed to Goncourt that something deep within himself was dislocated: he did not know where he was or what he was doing. It was as though an inextricable bond tied him secretly to the dead man. He remembered the tear in Flaubert's eye as they parted a month before. He was now alone.[41]

The preparations for the departure of the funeral procession were heart-breaking.[42] Commanville was unbearable: he had pocketed twenty francs Flaubert had given him to pay the gardener and was playing card games and cheating at them. Maupassant, with whom Goncourt talked, was unable to tell whether Caroline was as dishonest as her husband or merely in his power. Commanville was fascinated by calculations of what money he could make from his uncle's works and particularly from the sale of his love letters. Goncourt, by now furious with him, wondered if he were intending to blackmail the women. Caroline, for her part, seemed to be trying to seduce the poet Hérédia. She announced she would sell the property at once; less than a week later, she did. The house was torn down and the land used as the site of a distillery.

Around ten o'clock the procession set out. Du Camp was unable to come because of rheumatism; Hugo and Dumas and Taine were not present. Princess Mathilde was represented by one of her close friends. Laporte was not even allowed to see the body. There were eight people from Rouen.

The convoy set out up the dusty road from Croisset to the church at Canteleu high above on the bluff, the sort of little church, wrote Goncourt, where Emma Bovary had gone to confess her sins on an earlier spring day and where one of the youngsters scolded by Bournisien was even now walking along the top of the cemetery hill.

On the way the journalists and others revolted Goncourt by their conversations over where they would have dinner and the brothel they would go to later. He withdrew within himself.

Zola, arriving late, caught up with the procession as it neared the church, the horses moving at a slow walk, the bier swaying gently from side to side. When it came fully into his view, a chill ran down Zola's spine. Fields spread out on either side, the hedges cutting them into parcels; poplars blocked the view as the procession advanced toward him. In a pasture on one side, a cow put her muzzle across the hedge and began gently to low. The sounds, soft and prolonged in the silence of the people and with the beat of the horses' hooves and the muffled steps of those in the procession, seemed like the adieu of this countryside he had loved.

At last they reached the cemetery, full of the smell of hawthorn, dominating Rouen, which was enveloped in purple shadow, looking like a city of slate. Daudet, Zola, and Goncourt, abandoning the others, walked quietly away, speaking reverently of the dead man.

A Note on Sources

There are two principal sources for this volume. First are the works by Flaubert in the Conard Edition (Paris, 1910-54), with these abbreviated in the notes as follows:

ODJ	*Oeuvres de jeunesse inédites*, 3 vols.
NDV	*Notes de voyages*, 2 vols.
PLC	*Par les champs et par les grèves* [*Across Field and Strand*]
TENT-49	*La Tentation de Saint-Antoine,*
TENT-56	three successive versions
TENT-74	published in one vol. by Conard
BOV	*Madame Bovary*
SAL	*Salammbô*
TH	*Théâtre*
ES	*L'Education sentimentale* (version of 1869)
TC	*Trois Contes* [*Three Tales*]
BP	*Bouvard et Pécuchet*
CORR	*Correspondance de Gustave Flaubert* (9 vols., 1926-33)
SUPPL	*Supplément à la Correspondance* (4 vols., 1954)

Second, there are the manuscript sources. The Bibliothèque nationale in Paris (abbreviated: Bib. nat.) has the manuscripts of a number of Flaubert's works: most of *ODJ;* the three versions of *TENT;* the drafts and final version of *SAL* and *TC;* and, in the Fonds Descharmes, certain autograph letters from Flaubert, especially to Louise Colet, typed copies of most of the letters from Flaubert to her (important because they contain much material excised from the printed versions), and a number of miscellaneous items of Flaubertiana. All of these are in the Nouvelles Acquisitions françaises (abbreviated N.A.F.).

The Bibliothèque historique de la Ville de Paris (abbreviated: BHVP) contains the final autograph manuscript and the copyist's manuscript of *ES* and two series of Flaubert's Notebooks: the *Carnets de voyages* and the *Carnets de lectures,* the somewhat improperly titled Notes on various subjects, including his readings.

The Collection Lovenjoul (abbreviated: LOV) in Chantilly contains three series of autograph Flaubert letters:

Series A   Letters from Flaubert to various recipients. The letters are grouped according to recipient and are arranged chronologically within the group.

Series B   Letters to Flaubert from various correspondents. The letters are grouped according to writer and are arranged chronologically.

Series C   Letters to Flaubert from Louis Bouilhet, arranged chronologically.

The Bibliothèque municipale in Rouen contains a large number of Flaubert manuscripts including the drafts, final autograph manuscript and copyist's manuscript of *BOV*, the autograph manuscript and drafts of *BP* and materials for the preparation of this volume and the second *Education sentimentale*, and the autograph manuscript of the *Dictionnaire des idées reçues*, as well as thousand of items, autograph and other, from Flaubert's private papers.

All other sources are fully indicated on their first appearance in these notes.

The text of the Conard edition, although usually the best available, is frequently unreliable. Where I have been able to consult the originals and the printed text is seriously misleading or omits material, I have cited the manuscript source as well as the Conard page reference in the form, e.g., *CORR*, II, 240 + LOV, Where this would not suffice for immediate reference, I have given all necessary details.

One further source requires discussion. Maxime Du Camp's *Souvenirs littéraires*, 2 vols. (Paris: Hachette, 1892), gives a great deal of information on Flaubert, but I have used it only sparingly and with the greatest caution. In an article, "Is Maxime Du Camp a Reliable Witness?" *Modern Language Review*, Vol. XLVIII (1953), 17-25, I have shown, with substantiating documents, that Du Camp alters the facts at will and very frequently in places where the reader has no possible way to suppose that he has done so, or even, knowing it, to imagine why he made the alteration. Under the circumstances it has seemed to me preferable—though here I differ from certain other students of Flaubert—in general not to give weight to what Du Camp says, since the true cannot be distinguished from the false.

The notes which follow consist largely of bibliographical references and of acknowledgments when I have adopted judgments or discoveries of other scholars.

The notes give references for the following classes of material:
(1) Secondary sources
(2) Unpublished manuscripts
(3) Published works of Flaubert not in the Conard Edition
(4) Published works or letters of Flaubert not coming from the work or period under discussion

Where the materials do come from the specific published work of Flaubert under discussion or from his published letters written during the period in question, I have not indicated the page reference. To have done so in a study frequently made up of a mosaic of paraphrases from his published works would have increased the notes tenfold and so encumbered the text as to make it unreadable. On the other hand, for many sections throughout this study there do exist fully annotated articles or books which provide all these references; I have indicated them in my notes. I offer apologies for listing among these certain of my own prior publications: by doing so I have been able to reduce very considerably the number of notes otherwise necessary.

I have also, occasionally, indicated where the reader may find a fuller treatment or a different understanding of certain aspects of Flaubert.

Notes to Part I: To *Madame Bovary*

1. Growing Up in the Hôtel-Dieu (1821-35)

1. *BOV*, pp. 363-64.

2. I have drawn on the resources of the Musée des Arts et Traditions populaires in Paris for this account of Rouen, including a number of contemporary prints and several contemporary guidebooks, particularly A. Hugo, *La France pittoresque* (Paris: Delloye, 1835), III, 137-38, and L. N. A. and C. T. [*sic*], *Les Jeunes Voyageurs* . . . (Paris: Lelong, 1821), II, 200.

3. *CORR*, III, 269.

4. In addition to the letters of Flaubert's youth, see: R. Descharmes, *Flaubert . . . avant 1857* (Paris: Ferroud, 1909); Gérard-Gailly, *Le Grand Amour de Flaubert* (Paris: Aubier, 1944); R. Dumesnil, *Gustave Flaubert*, 3rd Ed. (Paris: Desclée de Brouwer, 1947); J. Bruneau, *Les Débuts littéraires de Gustave Flaubert* (1831-45) (Paris: Colin, 1963). Also *CORR*, I, 355, and *NDV*, II, 63.

5. *BOV*, pp. 441-42.

6. Docteur Galérant, "Le Docteur Achille Cléophas Flaubert," *Les Amis de Flaubert*, Vol. VII (1955), 25-32.

7. E. and J. de Goncourt, *Journal*, edited by R. Ricatte (Monaco: Imprimerie nationale, 1956), X, 160.

8. P. Spencer, "New Light on Flaubert's Youth," *French Studies*, Vol. VIII (1954), 97-108.

9. See the sources cited in note 4.

10. Spencer, *loc. cit.*

11. Lucie Chevalley-Sabatier, "Correspondance de Gustave Flaubert et sa soeur Caroline," *La Revue hebdomadaire*, Dec. 12, 1936, p. 176, note 1.

12. For Ernest Chevalier, see Descharmes, *Flaubert*, and Dumesnil, *Gustave Flaubert*, p. 60, note 2.

13. For Alfred Le Poittevin, see especially Bruneau, *Les Débuts*, also Descharmes, *ibid.*; Dumesnil, *ibid.*; and A. Thibaudet, *Gustave Flaubert* (Paris: Gallimard, 1935).

14. Bruneau, *ibid.*, *passim*, offers a sound, conservative view of the matter.

15. *CORR*, I, 354-55.

16. *Ibid.*, II, 141.

17. *Ibid.*, I, 383.

18. Caroline Commanville, "Souvenirs intimes," published as a preface to *ibid.*, x-xi.

19. Goncourt, *Journal*, XI, 89-90.

20. See Commanville, *CORR*, I, x-xi; Gérard-Gailly, *Le Grand Amour;* Descharmes, *Flaubert;* Dumesnil, *Gustave Flaubert.*

21. *CORR*, VII, 383.

22. Descharmes, *Flaubert*, gives an excellent account of the atmosphere here.

23. Commanville, *CORR*, I, x; Goncourt, *Journal*, VI, 8.

24. Bruneau, *Les Débuts*, pp. 150-56, reviews all the data.

25. This evaluation, which is Bruneau's (see *ibid.*), is especially perceptive.

26. Letter of Caroline to Gustave, Sept. 23, 1840, quoted in Chevalley-Savatier, *loc. cit.*

27. It is the opening sentence of the second known letter of Flaubert's *CORR*, I, 1.

28. They are preserved in the Bibliothèque municipale of Rouen.

29. *CORR*, I, 1.

30. The best analysis of these early works is in Bruneau, *Les Débuts*.

31. A. Hugo, *La France*, III, 140.

2. ADOLESCENCE UNDER ROMANTICISM (1836-37)

1. The story is recounted in *ODJ*, I, 504-15, 524-25, 537-42.

2. The story of Elisa Schlésinger was first ferreted out by Gérard-Gailly *(Le Grand Amour)*. His extraordinary piece of detective work around the events of this summer is marred only by an effort to see in this adolescent infatuation a passion which lasted a lifetime. He is entirely reliable for the events concerning Elisa and her life up to about 1840, and these were wholly his discoveries.

3. The *Memoirs of a Madman*, which I have been following, were written in the autumn of 1838 (see Bruneau, *Les Débuts*, pp. 239-42).

4. *ODJ*, I, 524-25; II, 192; Goncourt, *Journal*, III, 227.

5. *ES*, 6ff.

6. Goncourt, *Journal*, X, 152.

7. *CORR*, IV, 127.

8. *Ibid.*, III, 386.

9. *Ibid*, 145.

10. Much of the documentation for this chapter can be found in E. Maynial, *La Jeunesse de Flaubert* (Paris: Mercure de France, 1915), in A. Y. Naaman, *Les Débuts de Gustave Flaubert* (Paris: Nizet, 1962), and in Descharmes, *Flaubert;* Dumesnil, *Gustave Flaubert;* and Bruneau, *Les Débuts*.

11. Commanville, *CORR*, I, xiii.

12. Benjamin F. Bart, "Flaubert, Plagiarist of Chateaubriand," *Modern Language Notes*, Vol. LXV (1950), 336-39, corrected and amplified by Bruneau, *Les Débuts*, 81-82.

13. This unusual view is fully documented in Bruneau, *ibid.*, 72ff.

14. *CORR*, II, 327; IV, 389; VI, 474-75; Goncourt, *Journal*, III, 214.

15. *ODJ*, II, 164.

16. *CORR*, III, 130.

17. Commanville, *ibid.*, I, xiii.

18. E.g., *Mémoires d'Outre-tombe* (Paris: Flammarion, 1948), II, 43-44.

19. Most are printed, with many inaccuracies, in *ODJ*, I and II. Bruneau, *Les Débuts*, offers many corrections and publishes a number of additional works for the first time.

20. E.g., *ODJ*, I, 157-58.

21. *ODJ*, I, 409-11.

22. *Ibid.*, 219-30; III, 78-84; *NDV*, II, 161; *CORR*, II, 177, 405-06. See S. Cigada, "Uno Scritto autobiografico di Flaubert . . .," *Aevum*, Vol. XXX (1956), 505-24.

23. *BOV*, 63-77.

24. *ODJ*, I, 241-75.

3. Maturing (1838-39)

1. *CORR*, III, 145.
2. Benjamin F. Bart, "Lettres inédites de Gustave Flaubert à Sainte-Beuve," *Revue d'histoire littéraire de la France*, Vol. LXIV (1964), 427-35.
3. *CORR*, I, 39.
4. *ODJ*, II, 272-73.
5. *Ibid.*, I, 217, 276-464.
6. *ES*, 610-12.
7. *Mémoires d'un fou, passim* and esp. *ODJ*, I, 525.
8. Auriant (ed.), *Gustave Flaubert, Lettres inédites* . . . (Sceaux: Palimugre, 1948) gives a better version of certain Flaubert letters than that contained in *CORR*. In this case, see p. 30 correcting and completing *CORR*, II, 85. See also a number of references in letters to Bouilhet in LOV, A-V.
9. *CORR*, III, 379.
10. Maxime Du Camp, *Souvenirs littéraires*, 2 vols. (Paris: Hachette, 1892), I, 219, speaks of its preponderant influence on Flaubert. While this is certainly exaggerated, Flaubert no doubt read it. See Bruneau, *Les Débuts*, 22.
11. *ODJ*, I, 483-542. The discussions in Bruneau (*Les Débuts*) are excellent; see his Index.
12. *Ibid.*, 490-91.
13. *Ibid.*, 489.
14. *Ibid.*, 541-42.
15. *Ibid.*, 488, 501, 528; and *CORR*, I, 35.
16. *ODJ*, I, 504-15.
17. *Ibid.*, 538-39.
18. *CORR*, I, 29.
19. *ODJ*, I, 508-509.
20. *Ibid.*, 532-33.
21. *Ibid.*, 540.
22. Most of the material for this section comes from Flaubert's letters for this year in *CORR* and *SUPPL*. All other sources are noted here.
23. *ODJ*, I, 492; II, 279-81.
24. *Ibid.*, I, 147, 577.
25. Bruneau's discussion (*Les Débuts*) of this matter is excellent.
26. *ODJ*, II, 8-12.
27. I am here following Bruneau, *Les Débuts*.
28. *CORR*, I, 61.
29. Labracherie, "L'Eleve Gustave Flaubert . . . ," *Les Amis de Flaubert*, Vol. X (1957), 2-10.
30. *Les Amis de Flaubert*, Vol. VIII (1956), 4-5.
31. *ODJ*, II, 157-61.
32. Reprinted in *PLC*, 343-478. The location of the manuscript is unknown.
33. In addition to *ibid.*, 406-408, see *CORR*, I, 116, 221, 354; LOV, B-V, fol. 40 verso; Goncourt, *Journal*, III, 227; and Benjamin F. Bart, "New Flaubertiana, 1850-1860," *Symposium*, Vol. XV (1961), 5-11.
34. Quoted in Bruneau, *Les Débuts*, 285.
35. *NDV*, II, 183.
36. See Gustave Flaubert, *Souvenirs, notes, et pensées intimes* (Paris: Buchet/Chastel, 1965), pp. 77-86.
37. *Ibid.*, I, 72; *SUPPL*, I, 44; and Bruneau, *Les Débuts*, 282.

4. FALSE STARTS (1840-44)

1. *CORR*, II, 270.
2. *Ibid.*, I, 336; III, 379.
3. *Ibid.*, I, 123-24, 135-36; *ODJ*, III, 5.
4. *CORR*, III, 76-77.
5. *Ibid.*, 287.
6. Spencer, "New Light on Flaubert's Youth," *French Studies*, Vol. VII (1954), 97-108; *Les Amis de Flaubert*, Vol. VIII (1956), 12.
7. *SUPPL*, I, 156, 158-59.
8. Rouen, Bibliothèque municipale, Ms g 226⁸, fols. 198-99.
9. Paris, Bib. nat., N.A.F. 23,825 fol. 84 recto.
10. *ODJ*, II, 162-256. The best discussion is by Bruneau, *Les Débuts*.
11. *CORR*, I, 47; *ODJ*, II, 175.
12. Goncourt, *Journal*, VI, 143.
13. *BOV*, 392-93.
14. BHVP, *Carnet de lectures*, II, fol. 186 recto, of 1862; reproduced in *NDV*, II, 361, without date.
15. Goncourt, *Journal*, XI, 17.
16. *CORR*, VIII, 116.
17. Gustave's letters to his sister Caroline, a most useful source for this period, are reproduced in *Les Amis de Flaubert*, Vol. VIII (1956), 2-15, and IX (1956), 2-14. The Fonds Descharmes in the Bib. nat. in Paris contains copies of Alfred Le Poittevin's letters to Flaubert. The tone of the letters and the matters discussed are such that very little of them can ever be published. I have, however, drawn on them for many of my statements. On the other hand, I have made little use of Du Camp, *Souvenirs littéraires*.
18. *CORR*, VIII, 111.
19. LOV, A-1, fol. 191 verso.
20. *CORR*, III, 387.
21. Gérard-Gailly *(Le Grand Amour)* gives the fullest account.
22. Auguste Préault, cited by Du Camp, *Souvenirs littéraires*, I, 243-44.
23. Du Camp, *ibid.*, 161.
24. *SUPPL*, I, 143, 155.
25. *CORR*, I, 373-74. The Descharmes copy of this letter (N.A.F. 23,830, fol. 80) for "une bonne, belle, et grande nature" has "une bonne tête et grande nature." I have followed Descharmes.
26. Du Camp's letters to Flaubert are in LOV, B-11. In considerable measure, like those of Le Poittevin, they cannot be cited directly; but I have made use of their substance repeatedly.

5. ILLNESS AND WITHDRAWAL (1844-45)

1. I am indebted to a number of doctors over a number of years for suggesting what sorts of symptoms I should look for in developing a picture of what happened to Flaubert so that a diagnosis might be made. When I had pieced

together an account of the crucial events and symptoms, Dr. Arthur Ecker, clinical professor of neurological surgery at The Upstate Medical Center, Syracuse, New York, provided the diagnosis which I give in this section. Independently, a French doctor, Pierre Gallet, came to somewhat similar conclusions in his monograph, *Quel Diagnostic aurions-nous fait si nous avions soigné Flaubert?* (Paris: Foulon, 1960). The differences between his diagnosis and Dr. Ecker's depend in part on the fact that only some of the data were available to Dr. Gallet and in part on a slight difference in interpretation. The elucidation of these matters cannot be carried out here; I hope to do so elsewhere. Suffice it for present purposes that we are in substantial agreement. For a current medical study of the disorder, see W. G. Lennox *et al.*, *Epilepsy and Related Disorders*, 2 vols. (New York: Little, Brown, 1960). Flaubert's principal statements are in *CORR* I, 147-148, 150; III, 77, 270, 331; *SUPPL*, II, 94-96. Du Camp, *Souvenirs littéraires*, provides a great deal of information, but as always his statements must be accepted cautiously.

2. *CORR*, I, 159; II, 12; *Les Amis de Flaubert*, Vol. IX (1956), 37.

3. Letter from Achille Flaubert to an unknown recipient in LOV, A-VI, dated Jan. 17, 1860.

4. Du Camp's account is in *Souvenirs littéraires*, I, 181-82. Raoul-Duval's letter to him is LOV B-VI, fols. 435 recto-438 recto.

5. Dr. Gallet provides this information on standard treatment in the period.

6. Caroline's migraines are mentioned frequently in Flaubert's letters, e.g., *CORR*, VI, 260 and 424.

7. Commanville, *CORR*, I, x-xi; Goncourt, *Journal*, VI, 6.

8. See sources cited in note 4 above.

9. Lennox, *Epilepsy*, II, 7; *CORR*, I, 305-06.

10. Lennox, *ibid.*, offers an even stronger view; see the opening pages of his second volume.

11. *CORR*, II, 461; III, 146; IV, 169; *SUPPL*, I, 85.

12. *CORR*, II, 463; III, 22, 146, 270; IV, 180-81.

13. *Ibid.*, III, 11, 76-77; LOV, A-V, fol. 40 verso; A-VI, fols. 22 recto and verso.

14. *CORR.* I, 277-78.

15. *Les Amis de Flaubert*, Vol. IX (1956), 13.

16. Du Camp's letters are in LOV, B-II.

17. Commanville, *CORR*, I, xxv-xxvii.

18. LOV, A-VI, fol. 27 recto; B-II, 140 verso, 151 verso.

19. Printed in *ODJ*, II. Bruneau's discussion is excellent.

20. *ODJ*, III, 312-13.

21. Bruneau, *Les Débuts*, casts doubt on this.

22. *CORR*, II, 343.

23. *ODJ*, II, 250-51.

24. A. Coleman, *Flaubert's Literary Development in the Light of his "Mémoires d'un fou," "Novembre," and "Education sentimentale"* (Version of 1845) (Baltimore: Johns Hopkins Press, and Paris: Champion, 1914) is excellent on this. See particularly 146ff.

25. Bruneau, *Les Débuts*, 445ff.

26. For other interpretations, see M. Bonwit, "The Significance of the Dog in Flaubert's *Education sentimentale*," *PMLA*, Vol. LXII (1947), 517-24; and Bruneau, *ibid.*, 425-30.

6. THE ROAD BACK (1845-46)

1. Letters of period and *CORR*, II, 363; III, 58; IV, 233.
2. Fonds Descharmes, Bib. nat. N.A.F. 23, 825.
3. Letters of period; *NDV*, I, 3-61; BHVP, *Carnet* I (the manuscript). See also Jean Bruneau, "Les Deux Voyages de Gustave Flaubert en Italie," *Connaissance de l'Etranger. Mélanges offerts à la mémoire de Jean-Marie Carré* (Paris: Didier, 1964), 164-80.
4. LOV, A-VI, 12 recto and verso; BHVP, *Carnet* I, fols. 3 verso-4 recto.
5. *CORR*, I, 161-63 + LOV, A-VI, fols. 11 verso-13 recto.
6. BHVP, *Carnet* I, fol. 4 verso.
7. *CORR*, I, 163, 166, 169 + LOV, A-VI, fols. 12 recto and verso; BHVP, *Carnet* I, fols. 9 verso-10 verso.
8. LOV, A-VI, fols. 22 recto and verso; *CORR*, II, 172-73.
9. BHVP, *Carnet* I, fol. 7 verso.
10. *Ibid.*, fols. 7 verso, 9 recto and verso, 27 recto and verso.
11. G. Leleu and J. Pommier, *Madame Bovary. Nouvelle Version* . . . (Paris: Corti, 1949), 21.
12. BHVP, *Carnet* I, fol. 23 verso.
13. *PLC*, p. 34.
14. Letters of period and *CORR*, I, 332-33.
15. Spencer, "New Light on Flaubert's Youth," *French Studies*, Vol. VIII (1954), 97-108; and Goncourt, *Journal* for Oct. 29, 1863.
16. LOV, A-VI, fol. 19 verso.
17. BHVP, *Carnet* I, fols. 53 recto and verso, notes made at the end of the trip to Italy, reproduced without date in *NDV*, II, 366 and 367.
18. J. Bruneau, who has studied the "Conte oriental," kindly allowed me to see his typescript of the text. In due course it will be published.
19. While the printed text of *NDV* does not make this clear, the *Carnet* does.
20. *NDV*, I, 15.
21. *Ibid.*, 67; Concourt, *Journal*, X, 70.
22. *CORR*, IV, 426; VI, 48.
23. The material for Caroline's death is to be found in the published letters, those to Du Camp being better consulted in Auriant, *Gustave Flaubert*.
24. *CORR*, III, 35.
25. *Ibid.*, II, 1-3; III, 269.
26. See Gérard-Gailly, *Le Grand Amour*.
27. *CORR*, II, 430.
28. *Les Amis de Flaubert*, Vol. III, 16.
29. Léon Letellier, *Louis Bouilhet* . . . (Paris: Hachette, 1919). Bouilhet gives some of the data in a letter, LOV C, fol. 474 recto.
30. Benjamin F. Bart, "Louis Bouilhet, Flaubert's 'Accoucheur,'" *Symposium*, Vol. XVII (1963), 183-201.
31. *ODJ*, III, 339-65.
32. *CORR*, V, 72, and *SUPPL*, I, 59.

7. Louise Colet (1846-47)

1. The chronology of the events here can be pieced together from *CORR*, I, 211-63, 273, 378, 400, 403, 406; and *PLC*, 339.

In a forthcoming publication by M. Jacques Nebout, hitherto unknown private papers of Louise Colet will become available. They will add materially to what is known of the complex story of the relationship between Flaubert and Louise. In the meantime, Monsieur Nebout has kindly read my manuscript and has verified its accuracy in the light of his materials.

2. See Descharmes, *Flaubert*, and Gérard-Gailly, *Les Véhémences de Louise Colet* (Paris: Mercure de France, 1934).

3. LOV, B-VI, fol. 390 recto.

4. Rouen, Bibliothèque municipale, Ms g 226⁸, fols. 134-36.

5. *PLC*, p. 34.

6. Louise Colet, *Lui* (Paris: Librairie nouvelle, 1860).

7. The material on Louise's possible pregnancies is in the materials excised from the *CORR* but reproduced in the typed copies of these letters in Paris, Bib. nat., Fonds Descharmes, N.A.F., 23,830.

8. See the letters of the period and Louise Colet's poem, "Souvenir," in her handwriting in BHVP, *Carnet de Lectures* V.

9. *CORR*, III, 413.

10. LOV, B-II, fol. 168 recto.

11. From the typed copy, Bib. nat., Fonds Descharmes, N.A.F. 23,830, fol. 134 recto.

12. The materials for this visit and the break later are from letters in the Fonds Descharmes, Bib. nat. N.A.F. 23,825.

8. Brittany (1847-48)

1. The text is given, rather accurately, in *PLC*, although there is some dispute over certain portions. Flaubert's summaries, presumably made en route, are in BHVP, *Carnet* III. There is further material in the letters from the period. I have made little use of the account of Du Camp.

2. *CORR*, I, 325.

3. *Ibid.*, II, 28.

4. BHVP, *Carnet* III, fols. 31-32.

5. LOV, B-II, fols. 183ff.

6. BHVP, *Carnet* III, fol. 47 recto.

7. *Ibid.*, fol. 87 recto.

8. The text is *PLC*; again I have made little use of Du Camp.

9. *CORR*, II, 409; III, 260.

10. Du Camp, *Souvenirs littéraires*, II, 257-58.

11. As usual, Auriant, *Lettres inédites* (see pp. 25-32) gives better texts for the letters to Du Camp than does *CORR*.

12. Bib. nat., Fonds Descharmes, N.A.F. 28,831, document 332.

13. LOV, B-II, fols. 189, 199-200.

14. M.-J. Durry, *Flaubert et ses projets inédits* (Paris: Nizet, 1950), 403-04.

9. *The Temptation of Saint Anthony* (1849)

1. The text is printed in *TENT*, 205-496. The most useful studies are A. Lombard, *Flaubert et Saint Antoine* (Paris: Attinger, 1934); J. Seznec, *Les Sources de l'épisode des Dieux dans la Tentation de Saint Antoine* (*Première version,* 1849) (Paris: Vrin, 1940); and *Nouvelles Etudes sur la Tentation de Saint Antoine* (London: Warburg Institute and University of London, 1949).

2. See Maynial, *La Jeunesse, passim.*

3. *PLC*, 130-31.

4. *Ibid.,* 294-95, 424-25; *ODJ*, II, 190-91; *CORR*, II, 3.

5. Seznec, *Les Sources;* and Bart, "New Flaubertiana, 1850-1860," *Symposium,* Vol. XV (1961), 6-7.

6. *CORR*, II, 461-62.

7. *PLC*, 196-97.

8. BHVP, *Carnet* III, fols. 81 verso and 82 recto.

9. Cf. *PLC*, 247-49.

10. *ODJ*, III, 263 and 265.

11. *PLC*, 59-60.

12. BHVP, *Carnet* III, fols. 81 verso and 82 recto.

13. Goncourt, *Journal*, V, 115. Du Camp's report seems seriously exaggerated and embellished.

10. AROUND THE EASTERN MEDITERRANEAN (1849-51)

1. The principal sources for the trip are: *NDV*, I and II; the *Carnets de Voyages* in BHVP; and Flaubert's letters from the period. Benjamin F. Bart, *Flaubert's Landscape Descriptions* (Ann Arbor, Michigan: University of Michigan Press, 1956) contains considerable documentation.

2. *ODJ*, III, 178.

3. *NDV*, I, 51.

4. *SUPPL*, I, 26.

5. Du Camp, *Souvenirs littéraires*, I, 372-73, gives another account, which the facts will not substantiate.

6. *CORR*, II, 354.

7. *SAL*, 379.

8. Du Camp, *Souvenirs littéraires*, I, 384-85, is obviously inaccurate in asserting that Flaubert showed no curiosity until he reached Greece.

9. BHVP, *Carnet de voyages*, IV, contains a list at the end of the notebook.

10. Cf. Rouen, Bibliothèque municipale, Ms g 226⁴, fol. 221 recto, notes on Arabic poetry.

11. *NDV*, I, 211 + *Carnet.*

12. Du Camp, again, *Souvenirs littéraires*, I, 358-61, has an improbable account of this trip.

13. *NDV*, II, 290. The mention of the cigarette is an interlinear addition in *Carnet* V.

14. There are sketches in the *Carnet*.

15. The outlines for these works, in certain of the *Carnets* in BHVP, are printed and discussed in Durry, *Flaubert et ses projets inédits*.

16. For the details, see Benjamin F. Bart, "Flaubert's Itinerary in Greece," *PMLA*, Vol. LXV (1950), 371-87.

17. *CORR*, II, 55.

18. Preface to P. Morand, *Tendres Stocks* (Paris: NRF, 1921).

19. *CORR*, VII, 294.

20. *Ibid.*, II, 390; III, 312; IV, 35.

21. See Note 16 and also Benjamin F. Bart, "Is Maxime Du Camp a Reliable Witness?" *Modern Language Review*, Vol. XLVIII (1953), 17-25.

22. *NDV*, I, 39-40.

23. *CORR*, II, 343.

24. *Ibid.*, II, 295 + LOV.

25. In addition to the material noted earlier see also Jean Bruneau, "Les Deux Voyages de Gustave Flaubert en Italie," *Connaissance de l'Etranger. Mélanges offerts à la mémoire de Jean-Marie Carré* (Paris: Didier, 1964), 164-80.

26. BHVP, *Carnet* VIII, fol. 39 verso.

27. J. Pommier, "Les Maladies de Flaubert," *Le Progrès médical*, Aug. 10-24, 1947, Nos. 15-16, pp. 408-16, first discovered and published this material.

28. *TENT-49*, 479.

29. *CORR*, III, 217.

30. *NDV*, I, 327 + *Carnet*.

31. *CORR*, II, 240 + LOV.

32. The *NDV* and *CORR* for this section of the trip are heavily censored. I have completed them from BHVP and, for the crucial letters to Bouilhet, from LOV.

33. Letter from Du Camp to Flaubert reporting a conversation with Achille, LOV B-III, fols. 213 verso-214 recto.

34. The censoring of *NDV* and *CORR* is particularly heavy here. See also *CORR*, III, 135.

35. *NDV* and letters for the period plus *CORR*, III, 135-36.

36. *TC*, 185.

37. *CORR*, II, 140 + LOV, A-IV, fols. 10 verso and 11 recto.

38. *Ibid.*, 202ff, + LOV, B-V, fol. 25 verso.

39. E. Zola, *Les Romanciers naturalistes* (Paris: Bernouard, 1928), 182-83; *ODJ*, II, 182; Fonds Descharmes in Bib. nat., letters from Alfred Le Poittevin to Flaubert; *PLC*, 148, 186; *CORR*, IV, 256 + LOV, A-V, fol. 228 verso; V, 256; LOV: Letters from Du Camp in Series B and from Bouilhet in Series C.

40. *CORR*, II, 227-32 + LOV, A-V, fol. 33 verso; II, 121 + LOV, A-V, fol. 4 recto.

41. *CORR*, II, 169 + LOV, A-V, fol. 14 recto; *NDV*, I, 184 + *Carnet* V, fol. 10 verso.

42. BHVP, *Carnet* V, fols. 80 verso and 80 recto, omitted from *NDV*.

43. In addition to *NDV* and *CORR* for the period, see *CORR*, III, 136 and *NDV*, II, 34 + *Carnet*.

44. See his *Chants modernes* (Paris, 1855).

45. From the *Complément*, p. 5, published at the start of later printings of *SUPPL*, I.

46. See J. Pommier and G. Leleu, "Du Nouveau sur *Madame Bovary*," *Revue d'histoire littéraire*, Vol. XLVII (1947), 211-26; *CORR*, II, 253-54 + LOV; BHVP, *Carnet de lectures*, III, fol. 33 verso.

47. *PLC*, 11.

48. A. Singer, "Flaubert's *Une Nuit de Don Juan*," *Modern Language Notes*, Vol. LV (1940), 516-20.

49. The manuscripts are currently in the Houghton Library of Harvard University.

50. *CORR*, VII, 374.

51. LOV, A-V, fols. 64 recto and verso.

11. The Years of the *Bovary* (1851-56)

1. *NDV*, II, 84; LOV, B-II, fol. 214 recto.

2. E. Roger des Genettes, "Une Correspondante de Flaubert," *Le Figaro*, October 14, 1893.

3. A rather futile controversy has raged over this whole matter. For recent statements, see R. Herval, *Les Véritables Origines de Madame Bovary* (Paris: Nizet, 1957) and G. Venzac, *Au Pays de Madame Bovary* (Paris and Geneva: La Palatine, 1957).

4. E.g., in his *Génie du christianisme*, II, 2, xi.

5. This much at any rate of Du Camp's story is no doubt accurate (*Souvenirs littéraires*, II, 312-18).

6. *SUPPL*, I, 91, and J. Seznec, *Flaubert à l'Exposition de 1851* (Oxford: Clarendon Press, 1951).

7. Commanville, *CORR*, I, xxiv, LOV, B-II; fol. 241 verso; *SUPPL*, I, 143-44.

8. *CORR*, IV, 87; *SUPPL*, I, 149-50, 152-53, 155-56, 158-59, 167.

9. LOV, B-II, fol. 229 verso.

10. Auriant, *Lettres inédites*, 38ff.

11. LOV, B-II, fols. 238 recto-241 recto.

12. LOV, A-V, fols. 99 recto, 105 verso, 108 verso, omitted from the Conard Edition. See also, G. Normandy, ed., *Gustave Flaubert, Lettres inédites à Raoul-Duval* (Paris: Michel, 1950), 299ff.

13. Commanville, *CORR*, I, xxivff.

14. LOV, A-V, fol. 268 recto.

15. Bart, "Louis Bouilhet, Flaubert's 'Accoucheur,'" *Symposium*, Vol. XVII (1963), 183-201.

16. *SUPPL*, I, 189.

17. Bib. nat., Fonds Descharmes, N.A.F. 23,825, fols. 9 recto-12 verso.

18. *Ibid*, fols. 13 recto-14 recto. Gérard-Gailly, who did not know of the existence of this letter, has, however, put together the rest of the story in his *Grand Amour de Flaubert*.

19. Additions from the typed copies in the Fonds Descharmes to *CORR*, II, 386, and III, 56 and 65.

20. LOV, B-II, fol. 245 verso.

21. *Ibid*., A-V, fols. 79 recto and 84 verso.

22. *CORR*, III, 317 + LOV A-V, fol. 80 recto.

23. Louise Colet recounts her version in her *Histoire d'un soldat* (Paris: Cadot, 1856), 129-31.

24. LOV, A-V, fol. 84 verso.

25. I am summarizing here the published letters and those in the Fonds Descharmes.

26. LOV, C-I, fol. 8 verso.

27. Published letters and LOV, A-V, fol. 117 verso.

28. E.g., LOV, B-V, fol. 108 verso.

12. The Story Evolves

1. The basic documents are almost all in the Bibliothèque municipale in Rouen. Many of them have been published. See the Notes to the Conard Edition of *BOV*; G. Leleu, *Madame Bovary. Ebauches et fragments inédits* (Paris: Conard, 1936): Leleu and Pommier, *Madame Bovary*.

2. *BOV*, 495.

3. Rouen, Bibliothèque municipale, Ms g 226⁴, fols. 233ff., first studied by Pommier and Leleu, "Du Nouveau sur *Madame Bovary*," *Revue d'histoire littéraire*, Vol. XLVII (1947), 216-26.

4. *ODJ*, I, 241-75.

5. *CORR*, IV, 169; Goncourt, *Journal*, IV, 167.

6. BHVP, *Carnet de lectures*, III, final page.

7. *ODJ*, III, 321-25.

8. R. Dumesnil, Introduction to his edition of *Madame Bovary* (Paris: Les Belles Lettres, 1945), cvii.

9. *PLC*, 7.

10. *Ibid.*, 18.

11. *Ibid.*, 11.

12. R. Herval, *Les Véritables Origines*, 179ff.

13. *CORR*, III, 342-43.

14. *ODJ*, I, 409-11.

15. Baudelaire made his comments in his review of *Madame Bovary*.

16. Jules Troubat, "Sainte-Beuve et Gustave Flaubert," *Le Temps*, April 16, 1912.

17. *ODJ*, III, 171; *CORR*, I, 366; III, 295, 339, 356, etc.

18. G. Mason, "Les Deux Clairs de lune de Madame Bovary," *French Studies*, Vol. VIII (1954), 250-61.

19. Leleu and Pommier, *Madame Bovary*, 78; *NDV*, II, 271.

20. S. Cigada, "Genesi e struttura tematica di Emma Bovary," *Pubblicazioni dell' Università Cattolica del Sacro Cuore* (Milan), Nuova Serie, Vol. LXII, 218-19; *ODJ*, II, 202-203.

21. LOV, C, fols. 13 recto-14 recto.

22. The connection was first pointed out by J. Lapp, "Art and Hallucination in Flaubert," *French Studies*, Vol. X (1956), 322-34.

23. The materials for this paragraph come from articles by J. Pommier and conversations with him.

24. I have analyzed this more fully in my "Aesthetic Distance in Madame Bovary," *PMLA*, Vol. LXIX (1954), 1112-26.

25. G. Mason, "La Veillée et l'enterrement d'Emma Bovary," *French Studies*, Vol. XIII (1959), 125-34.

26. Bib. nat., Fonds Descharmes, N.A.F. 23,825, fol. 22 verso.

13. THE SIGNIFICANCE OF EMMA

1. For this section see especially Baudelaire's review of *Madame Bovary;* Levin, *Gates of Horn,* chapter on Flaubert, especially pp. 246-69; A. Thibaudet, *Gustave Flaubert,* especially chap. 5; P. Spencer, *Flaubert* (New York: Grove Press, 1952), chap. 8; and Flaubert's letters of the period. For further discussions of Emma, see my *Madame Bovary and the Critics* (New York University Press, 1966), which gathers together a number of essays in English on *Madame Bovary.*

2. *CORR*, IV, 71 and 474.

3. The point is made by Thibaudet, *Gustave Flaubert.*

4. S. David, "Carol Kennicott de Main Street et sa lignée européenne: Emma Bovary . . . ," *Revue de la littérature comparée,* Vol. XIX (1939), 407-16.

5. See Thibaudet, *Gustave Flaubert;* and Spencer, *Flaubert.*

6. J. Pommier suggests the antecedents in his article, " 'La Muse du Département' et le thème de la femme mal mariée chez Balzac, Mérimée et Flaubert," *L'Année balzacienne* (1961).

7. Zola, *Les Romanciers naturalistes,* 107, 120.

8. For a harsher view, see Thibaudet, *Gustave Flaubert.*

9. Levin, *Gates of Horn,* 263.

10. Thibaudet, *Gustave Flaubert,* 114.

14. THE NOVEL AS ART

1. The principal source is Flaubert's letters of the period, particularly those to Louise Colet. I have treated the same topic but in another framework and with full documentation in "Flaubert's Concept of the Novel," *PMLA*, Vol. LXXX (1965), 84-89.

2. Descharmes, *Le Grand Amour,* makes the point.

3. *CORR*, V, 164-65.

4. Thibaudet, *Gustave Flaubert,* chapter on *Madame Bovary.*

5. *CORR*, IV, 183.

6. LOV, C, fol. 29 recto, letter from Bouilhet to Flaubert.

7. Spencer, *Flaubert,* chapter on *Madame Bovary.*

8. *CORR*, IV, 211-12; Bib. nat., Fonds Descharmes, N.A.F. 23,825, fol. 34 verso.

9. *CORR*, IV, 292; Bib. nat., Fonds Descharmes, N.A.F. 23,825, fol. 22 verso.

10. *CORR*, V, 165.

11. Bib. nat., Fonds Descharmes, N.A.F. 23,825 fol. 23 recto.

12. *CORR*, IV, 135-36, 171, 182.

13. Benjamin F. Bart, "Madame Bovary after a Century," *French Review*, Vol. XXXI (1957), 203-10.

14. Benjamin F. Bart, "Balzac and Flaubert, Energy versus Art," *Romanic Review*, Vol. XLII (1951), 198-204.

15. The point is made by Thibaudet, *Gustave Flaubert*.

16. Bart, "Louis Bouilhet, Flaubert's 'Accoucheur,'" *Symposium*, Vol. XVII (1963), 191.

17. See W. Wasserstrom, *The Time of the Dial* (Syracuse, N.Y.: Syracuse University Press, 1963).

18. For further considerations, see H. Meyerhoff, *Time in Literature* (Berkeley and Los Angeles: University of California Press, 1960), 102; E. Auerbach, *Mimesis*, 258-79; Levin, *Gates of Horn*, *passim*.

19. Levin, *ibid.*, 252.

20. Bart, "Aesthetic Distance . . . ," *PMLA*, Vol. LXIX (1954), 1112-26; S. Ullmann, *Style in the French Novel* (Cambridge: Cambridge University Press, 1957), chap. 2.

21. Adam A. Mendilow, *Time and the Novel* (London and New York: P. Nevil, 1952), 112.

22. Bib. nat., Fonds Descharmes, N.A.F. 23,825, fol. 26 recto.

23. A. Gide, *Si le grain ne meurt* (Paris: NRF, 1928), 246.

24. LOV, B-II, fol. 386 verso.

25. *The Dial*, LXIII, 33 (September, 1922).

26. In his *Appreciations, with an Essay on Style*, first published in 1889.

27. H. Block, "Theory of Language in Gustave Flaubert and James Joyce," *Revue de la littérature comparée*, Vol. XXXV (1961), 197-206.

28. Levin, *Gates of Horn*, 253.

29. Bib. nat., Fonds Descharmes, N.A.F. 23,825, fol. 19 verso.

30. Bart, "Louis Bouilhet, Flaubert's 'Accoucheur,'" *Symposium*, Vol. XVII (1963), 191-92.

31. Thibaudet, *Gustave Flaubert*, 221-25.

15. The Trial of *Madame Bovary* (1856-57)

1. Much of the information is contained in the letters of the period. The data are assembled by R. Dumesnil in his Introduction to his edition of *Madame Bovary*.

2. *CORR*, V, 155.

3. LOV, B-II, fols. 250 and 251.

4. Rouen, Bibliothèque municipale, Ms g 226⁵, fol. 214.

5. LOV, B-I, fols. 118 recto-119 recto.

6. *Complément*, 13ff., published at the start of later printings if *SUPPL*, I.

7. LOV, B-II, fol. 263 recto.

8. The story, while not fully supported, is widely reported. See Du Camp, *Souvenirs littéraires*, II, 148. Dumesnil discusses it in his edition (see Note 1), cxl-cxli. See also *CORR*, VI, 5.

9. Du Camp, *ibid*.

10. See the letters for the period. J. Suffel, *Flaubert* (Paris: Presses universitaires, 1958), corrects certain dates; I have followed him here.

11. LOV, B-I, fol. 443 recto.

12. LOV, B-II, fol. 275 recto.

13. The speeches at the trial are published as an appendix to many editions of *Madame Bovary*.

14. CORR, VIII, 57.

15. Dumesnil's Introduction to his edition of *Madame Bovary* has many of the details of the preparation and publication of this first edition.

16. CORR, IX, 28.

17. Goncourt, *Journal*, III, 205.

18. Thibaudet, *Gustave Flaubert*, has a good discussion.

19. Bart, "Lettres inédites de Gustave Flaubert à Sainte-Beuve," *Revue d'histoire littéraire*, Vol. LXIV (1964), 427-35.

20. CORR, VI, 107.

21. The article appeared in *Le Figaro*, Aug. 9, 1857. Bouilhet's letter drawing it to Flaubert's attention is LOV, C, fol. 47 recto.

22. *Complément*, 17-18, published at the start if later printings of *SUPPL*, I.

23. Zola, *Les Romanciers naturalistes*, 107.

Notes to Part II: Mid-Passage

16. A Noted Author (1857-62)

1. The text is published in *TENT*, 497-651. See the letters of the period, the studies listed in connection with the version of 1849, and E. Maynial, *La Jeunesse de Flaubert* (Paris: Mercure de France, 1913).

2. Commanville, "Souvenirs intimes," *CORR*, I, xxxi-xxxii, and LOV, C, fols. 382 verso, 383 recto, 386 recto, etc.

3. Goncourt, *Journal*, V, 17, and XX, 216-17.

4. LOV, C, fol. 68 recto.

5. LOV, A-VI, letter from Achille Flaubert, and C, fols. 234 recto *et* ff.

6. *Le Figaro*, December 3, 1862.

7. Nadar, *Mémoires du géant* (Paris: Dentu, 1865), 105, and *CORR*, VI, 346-47.

8. Commanville, "Souvenirs intimes," *CORR*, I, xix; H. Taine, *Sa Vie et sa correspondance* (Paris: Hachette, 1904), II, 234; Goncourt, *Journal*, III, 208; IV, 176-77; V, 106, 108.

9. Judith Gautier, *Souvenirs de ma vie* (Paris: Juven, n.d.), II, 266; Goncourt, *Journal*, V, 84; XI, 210; Zola, *Les Romanciers naturalistes*, 158.

10. LOV, C, 176 verso.

11. See the letters from Louis Bouilhet to Flaubert, LOV, C; LOV, B, letters from Du Camp; Auriant, ed., *Lettres inédites*, 42-43.

12. Goncourt, *Journal*, III, 120; IV, 25; XX, 173; *Charles Demailly* (Paris: Charpentier, 1877), 161.

13. *CORR*, IV, 116 + LOV, A-V, fol. 195 recto.

14. LOV, C, fols. 222 recto-223 recto.

15. LOV, C, 87 verso, 319 verso, 320 recto.

16. Goncourt, *Journal*, 232; BHVP, *Carnet de lectures*, II, fol. 6 verso; reproduced in *NDV*, II, 359.

17. Zola, *Les Romanciers naturalistes*, chapter on Flaubert; Goncourt, *Journal*, entries for May 9, 1865, and May 5, 1877.

18. BHVP, *Carnet de lectures*, II, fol. 7 recto; also fol. 14 recto, reproduced in *NDV*, II, 361.

19. Gérard-Gailly, *Les Véhémences de Louise Colet* (Paris: Mercure de France, 1934), *passim*.

20. *CORR*, IV, 190; *SUPPL*, I, 242; LOV, C, fols. 40 and 175 recto.

21. Du Camp, *Souvenirs littéraires*, chap. 22; LOV, B-II, fol. 280 recto; LOV, C, 368 verso; and letters of period.

22. *CORR*, IV, 351-52.

23. Letters of the period and C. Bauchard, "Sur les traces de Gustave Flaubert et de Madame Schlésinger," *Revue d'histoire littéraire de la France*, Vol. LIII (1953), 39; for Bouilhet, LOV, C.

24. Goncourt, *Journal* (see its Index under Lagier); LOV, C, *passim*.

25. LOV, C, fol. 408 recto.

26. LOV, A-V, fol. 243 verso; C, fols. 244 recto and 254 recto.

27. Dumesnil, *Flaubert; CORR*, IV, 350, note.

28. E. Roger des Genettes, *loc. cit.*

29. Flaubert's letters to Mademoiselle Leroyer de Chantepie are printed in *CORR*. Typed copies of her letters to him are preserved in the Fonds Descharmes of the Bib. nat.

30. Most of the data on Juliet Herbert come from suppressions from *CORR* ascertainable in the LOV copies, from *SUPPL*, and from Bouilhet's letters to Flaubert in LOV, C.

31. Letters of the period, especially to Bouilhet, and LOV, A-V, fols. 114 verso, 152 recto, etc.

32. LOV, C, fol. 52 recto; *Catalogue de la Vente Franklin-Grout, Antibes, les 28, 29, 30 avril 1931*, p. 5, No. 15.

33. Letters of period and Goncourt, *Journal*, III, 203-204; V, 54.

34. Bart, "Louis Bouilhet . . . ," *Symposium*, Vol. XVII (1963), 183-201.

17. *Salammbô* (1862)

1. Goncourt, *Journal*, IV, 166-67.

2. *ODJ*, II, 4.

3. LOV, B-II, 396 recto.

4. Most of the drafts are preserved in the Bib. nat.; almost none have been published.

5. A. Camus, Preface to his *L'Envers et l'endroit* (Paris: Gallimard, 1957).

6. LOV, C, letters of this date.

7. *CORR*, IV, 250, 251; LOV, C, fols. 78 recto and 91 recto.

8. *NDV*, II, 289-347 completed from BHVP, *Carnet de voyages*, X; also the letters from the period.

9. *NDV*, II, 330 + *Carnet*.

10. Léon Deffoux, "Le Pupitre de Flaubert," *L'Oeuvre*, November 20, 1931.

11. *ODJ*, III, 55; *TC*, 91.

12. For criticism of *Salammbô*, see L. Benedetto, *Le Origini di "Salammbô"* (Florence: Bemporad, 1920); Sainte-Beuve, *Lundis* for December, 1862, and Flaubert's reply and his other letters of the period; Chateaubriand Notes and Prefaces, especially to his *Itinéraire* and *Les Martyrs;* L. Albalat, *Le Mal d'écrire* (Paris: Flammarion, 1895), 62ff.; L. Bertrand, *Gustave Flaubert* (Paris: Ollendorf, 1923), 150-51; J. Lemaître, *Les Contemporains* (Paris: Boivin, n.d.), 5ᵉ Série, 95-96.

13. Taine, *Sa Vie*, II, 232.

14. *SAL*, 235 and 240; *BOV*, 432.

15. G. R. Ridge, "The 'Femme fatale' in French Decadence," *French Review*, Vol. XXXIV (1961), 352-60.

16. BHVP, *Carnet de lectures*, II, fol. 5 recto, partially reproduced in *NDV*, II, 358.

17. *SAL*, 259-63; *ODJ*, I, 504, 538-39; II, 237; *SUPPL*, I, 239-40.

18. *SAL*, 267; *BOV*, 432; G. Leleu, ed., *Madame Bovary*, II, 500.

19. Flaubert, *Souvenirs*, 73-74.

20. In addition to the earlier references, see Thibaudet, *Flaubert*, and D. Demorest, *L'Expression figurée et symbolique dans l'oeuvre de Gustave Flaubert* (Paris: Presses universitaires, 1931).

21. E.g., Cuvillier-Fleury in *Le Journal des Débats*, December 13, 1862.

22. BHVP, *Carnet de lectures*, II, 47 recto; reproduced in *NDV*, II, 364; Taine, *Sa Vie*, II, 232.

23. A. Thorlby, *Gustave Flaubert and the Art of Realism* (New Haven: Yale University Press, 1957), 30.

24. *CORR*, I, 210, 218.

25. Goncourt, *Demailly*, 161.

26. Taine, *Sa Vie*, II, 231.

27. E.g., LOV, B-I, 126 verso-127 recto.

28. The point is elaborated in Bertrand, *Flaubert*.

29. A. Thibaudet, *Réflexions sur la critique*, 4th ed. (Paris: Gallimard, 1939), 37-38.

30. LOV, C, fol. 253 recto; reprinted in *SAL*, 472-73.

31. E.g., Goncourt, *Journal*, IV, 181.

32. See Thibaudet, *Flaubert*, chapter on *Salammbô*.

33. Thorlby, *Gustave Flaubert*, 29.

34. Bib. nat., N.A.F. 23662, fol. 200 recto.

35. BHVP, *Carnet de lectures*, II, fol. 5 verso; reproduced in *NDV*, II, 358; *CORR*, IV, 357-58 and 361.

36. BHVP, *Carnet de lectures*, XV, fol. 11 verso; reproduced in *NDV*, II, 355.

37. Sainte-Beuve, *Lundis;* Goncourt, *Journal*, III, 72-73; IV, 178-79.

38. *NDV*, I, 345; *CORR*, II, 241; V, 58.

39. BHVP, *Carnet de voyages*, I, 53 verso; reproduced in *NDV*, II, 367; *NDV*, I, 190-91; *PLC*, 175.

40. Goncourt, *Journal*, V, 15-16.

41. BHVP, *Carnet de lectures*, II, fols. 4 recto and 6 verso; reproduced in *NDV*, II, 359.

42. Goncourt, *Journal*, II, 94; III, 204-205; IV, 181-82, 177; V, 67-68, 230.

43. Thibaudet, *Gustave Flaubert*; Levin, *Gates*, 277-78; Martin Turnell, *The Novel in France* (New York: New Directions, 1951), 21.

44. See Bart, *Flaubert's Landscape Descriptions*, 42ff.

45. *NDV*, II, 92.

46. LOV, B-II, fols. 295 verso-296 recto.

47. Letters of the period; LOV, B-III, 3 recto-43 recto; C, 481 recto and 492 recto.

48. Commanville, "Souvenirs," *CORR*, I, xxxiii.

49. Goncourt, *Journal*, V, 179.

50. Letters of the period; Sainte-Beuve, *Lundis*; Bart, ed., "Lettres inédites à Sainte-Beuve," *Revue d'histoire littéraire*, Vol. LXIV (1964), 427-35.

51. Gérard-Gailly, *Les Véhémences*.

52. LOV, B-I, fol. 340 recto and verso.

53. LOV, B-V, fol. 266 recto and verso.

54. Goncourt, *Journal* for December, 1862.

55. *Ibid.*, V. 216.

56. Bart, "Flaubert's Letter Concerning Froehner: The Background," *Symposium*, Vol. XVI (1962), 148-50.

57. Taine, *Sa Vie*, II, 234.

58. Goncourt, *Journal*, numerous entries in 1861-62.

59. BHVP, *Carnet de lectures*, II, fol. 16 verso; reproduced in NDV, II, 361.

18. Facing the Mid-Forties (1863-69)

1. Bart, "Louis Bouilhet . . . ," *Symposium*, Vol. XVII (1963), 183-201.

2. LOV, C, fols. 201 verso and 293 recto.

3. Goncourt, *Journal*, III, 202-203.

4. Letters of the period and those from Bouilhet in LOV, C.

5. The text is printed in *TH*, 157-350. For the influence of Aristophanes, see Jean Canu, *Flaubert, auteur dramatique* (Paris: Les Ecrits de France, 1946), 18.

6. Durry, *Flaubert, passim*.

7. *CORR*, V, 242, 249; VI, 47-48 (misdated there: the letter is of March 24 or 31, 1863).

8. *Ibid.*, IV, 318 and 442.

9. BHVP, *Carnet de lectures*, II, fol. 48 verso; reproduced in *NDV*, II, 364.

10. LOV, C, fol. 514 recto.

11. *Ibid.*, C, fols. 535 recto-536 recto.

12. Goncourt, *Journal*, VI, 141-43.

13. Letters of the period and LOV, B-II, fols. 337-38.

14. Letters of the period and LOV, C, of the period.

15. Letters of the period and Suffel, *Flaubert*, 142.

16. See Gérard-Gailly, *Le Grand Amour,* and Spencer, *Flaubert.*

17. LOV, B-II, fol. 318 recto.

18. LOV, B-II, fols. 302 recto and verso, 314 recto; C, 688 recto, 695 recto, 718 recto, and 803 recto; *SUPPL,* II, 104.

19. LOV, A-II, 111 recto.

20. Goncourt, *Journal,* III, 121.

21. Spencer, *Flaubert,* esp. p. 168.

22. Taine, *Sa Vie,* II, 229-34.

23. LOV, B-II, fol. 102 recto and verso; J. Kühn, *La Princesse Mathilde* (Paris: Plon, 1935), 241ff. *et passim;* Goncourt, *Journal,* VI, 13.

24. Goncourt, *Journal,* XVII, 107.

25. *Ibid.,* VI, 19; VIII, 130.

26. LOV, C, fols. 731 verso and 733 recto.

27. Letters of the period and LOV, B-III, fol. 349 recto; C, fol. 753 recto.

28. The details are in LOV, A, letters of the period.

29. Bart, "Louis Bouilhet . . . ," *Symposium,* XVII (1963), 183-201.

30. LOV, B-II, letters from Du Camp of the period.

31. Goncourt, *Journal:* see its Index for the period, and esp. VI, 141-45.

32. *Ibid.,* XV, 42.

33. Normandy, ed., *Lettres inédites.*

34. Letters of the period in *SUPPL* and originals of *CORR* in LOV.

35. Goncourt, *Journal,* VI, 172-73.

36. BHVP, *Carnet de lectures,* II, fol. 28 verso; reproduced in *NDV,* II, 363.

37. LOV, B-II, 308 recto.

38. LOV, C-II, many allusions. See also LOV, B-VI, fols. 79 recto-80 verso; Goncourt, *Journal,* XX, 99; Bibliothèque municipale de Rouen, Ms g 226⁴ fols. 80 recto and 81 recto.

39. LOV, B-II, fols. 310 verso, 313 recto, and 314 recto.

40. Letters of the period and *SUPPL,* II, 37-38; LOV, B-II, fols. 337 and 338; C, fols. 844 verso, 850 recto, 870 verso, and 874 recto.

41. BHVP, *Carnet de voyages,* XIII; partially published in Bart, "New Flaubertina, 1850-60," *Symposium,* Vol. XV (1961), 5-11.

42. LOV, C, fol. 706 recto.

43. *Bulletin de la Société des Amis de Flaubert,* Vol. V (1954), 36.

44. A. Maurois, *Lélia* (New York: Harper and Row, 1953).

45. *PLC,* 34.

46. Maurois, *Lélia; Correspondance entre George Sand et Gustave Flaubert* (Paris: Calmann-Lévy, n.d.); A.-F.-J. Jacobs, "George Sand à Croisset et Flaubert à Nohant," *Bulletin de la Société des Amis de Flaubert,* Vol. VIII (1956), 23-33.

47. *CORR,* V, 247ff. + LOV.

48. LOV, A-I, fols. 252 verso-253 verso.

49. BHVP, *Carnet de lectures,* II, fol. 36 recto, dated sometime after 1862.

50. *Ibid.,* fol. 24 recto; reproduced *NDV,* II, 362.

51. *Ibid.,* fol. 7; reproduced in *NDV,* II, 359.

52. *CORR* has been seriously abridged here; I am completing from LOV; also BHVP, *Carnet de lectures,* XV, reproduced in *NDV,* II, 355.

53. *CORR,* V, 249 + LOV.

54. BHVP, *Carnet de lectures,* II, fol. 19 recto; reproduced in *NDV,* II, 362.

55. E.g., Goncourt, *Journal*, VI, 69 and 159.

56. BHVP, *Carnet de lectures*, XIX, fol. 14.

57. Goncourt, *Journal*, VI, 145; Taine, *Sa Vie*, II, 232; BHVP, *Carnets de Lectures*, II, fol. 28; reproduced in *NDV*, II, 363.

58. CORR (Flaubert is quoting his friend Chesneau); Goncourt, VI, 157-58.

59. BHVP, *Carnet de lectures*, XV, 13 recto.

60. *Ibid.*, II, fol. 37 recto; reproduced in *NDV*, II, 363.

19. *A Sentimental Education*

1. See Thibaudet, *Gustave Flaubert;* Levin, *Gates;* Dumesnil, ed., *L'Education sentimentale* (Paris: Les Belles Lettres, 1958).

2. This and subsequent indications of the initial sketches all come from Durry, *Flaubert.*

3. LOV, C, fol. 668 recto.

4. *CORR*, III, 255.

5. Levin, *Gates*, 225.

6. Bart, ed., "Lettres inédites à Sainte-Beuve," *Revue de l'histoire littéraire*, Vol. LXIV (1964), 427-35.

7. A. Vial, "De 'Volupté' à 'L'Education sentimentale,'" *Revue de l'histoire littéraire*, Vol. LVII (1957), 45-65, 178-216.

8. *CORR*, I, 333.

9. Bib. nat., Fonds Descharmes, Lettres d'Alfred Le Poittevin à Flaubert.

10. *CORR*, III, 257.

11. A. Vial, *loc. cit.*

12. Flaubert, *Souvenirs*, 68-69.

13. H. James, *The House of Fiction* (London: Hart-Davis, 1957), 202-203.

14. LOV, B-II, fol. 380 recto.

15. Cited in Suffel, *Flaubert*, 79.

16. Goncourt, *Journal*, XIV, 144.

17. BHVP, *Carnet de lectures*, II, fol. 17 recto; cited in Durry, *Flaubert*, 16.

18. *CORR*, I, 250.

19. Zola, *Les Romanciers naturalistes*, 112.

20. *CORR*, III, 332.

21. Marcel Proust, *loc. cit.*

22. Bart, "An Unsuspected Adviser on Flaubert's 'Education sentimentale,'" *French Review*, Vol. XXXVI (1962), 37-43.

23. His notes are preserved in BHVP, *Carnets de voyages.*

24. BHVP, *Carnet de lectures*, XX, fol. 70; reproduced in Durry, *Flaubert*, 361.

25. BHVP, *Carnet de lectures*, XIX, fol. 33; reproduced in Durry, *Flaubert*, 124-25.

26. LOV, B-III, fol. 271 recto.

27. *CORR*, II, 256-57.

28. *Ibid.*, II, 78-79.

29. Alexis François, "Gustave Flaubert, Maxime Du Camp et la Révolution de 1848," *Revue d'histoire littéraire*, Vol. LIII (1953), 44-56.

30. LOV, C, fol. 634 verso.

31. *CORR*, II, 238-39.

32. A. Camus, "L'Intelligence ou l'échafaud," in Jean Prévost, *Problèmes du roman* (Paris: Confluences, 1943), 223.

33. BHVP, *Carnet de lectures*, II, fol. 37 recto; reproduced in *NDV*, II, 364.

34. Letters of the period and *CORR*, VIII, 224.

35. Letter reproduced in *ES*, 703.

36. Maupassant, "Etude," in *BOV*, 551.

37. A. Robbe-Grillet, *La Revue de Paris*, Vol. LXVIII (1961), 115-21.

38. Zola, *Les Romanciers naturalistes*, 173-74.

39. Du Camp's notes are in BHVP.

40. Bart, "An Unsuspected Adviser . . . ," *French Review*, Vol. XXXVI (1962), 37-43.

41. Zola, *Les Romanciers naturalistes*, 177; Kühn, *Princesse Mathilde*, 300.

42. LOV, B-II, fols. 380-87.

43. Du Camp, *Souvenirs littéraires*, II, 339.

44. Much of this material is printed in *ES*. The LOV has further letters. See also *Correspondance George Sand-Gustave Flaubert*, p. 195.

45. Henry Céard, quoted in Dumesnil, *Flaubert*.

46. LOV, 502 quinque, fol. 54 recto.

Notes to Part III: Tribulation

20. The Old Order Passes (1869-72)

1. Letters of period in *CORR, SUPPL,* and LOV, C (from Bouilhet to Flaubert).

2. LOV, C, fol. 968 recto.

3. Goncourt, *Journal*, VIII, 213.

4. Zola, *Les Romanciers naturalistes*, 145, 153.

5. BHVP, *Carnet de lectures*, XX, fols. 4, 6, and 7; reproduced in *NDV*, II, 365-66; *Carnet de lectures*, XVI, fol. 34 verso.

6. BHVP, *Carnet de lectures*, XV, fol. 20 recto; reproduced in *NDV*, II, 356.

7. Goncourt, *Journal*, XV, 81.

8. Jacob, *loc. cit.*

9. BHVP, *Carnet de lectures*, XX, fols. 11 recto and 32 recto; discussed in Durry, *Flaubert*.

10. *Ibid.*, fol. 4 recto; reproduced in *NDV*, II, 365, and Durry, *Flaubert*; *CORR*, VI, 126.

11. *CORR*, V. 90-91.

12. *Ibid.*, VI, 154 + LOV, 158 + LOV, and 163 + LOV.
13. Letters in LOV from Du Camp at this time, esp. B-II, fols. 400-403; Auriant, *Lettres inédites*, 101.
14. *CORR*, VI, 211 + LOV.
15. See letters of this period in *Correspondance George Sand-Gustave Flaubert.*
16. BHVP, *Carnet de lectures*, XV, fol. 20 recto; reproduced in *NDV*, II, 356.
17. Zola, *Les Romanciers naturalistes*, 152.
18. LOV, B-II, fols. 390-394.
19. *CORR*, VI, 347 + LOV and 352 + LOV.
20. *Ibid.*, VII, 338-39.
21. *Ibid.*, 341-42.
22. The letter is of early January, 1872; it is reprinted in *CORR*, VI, 463-72.
23. See Jacques Suffel, ed., *Lettres inédites de Gustave Flaubert à son éditeur Michel Lévy* (Paris: Calmann-Lévy, 1965); letters to George Sand and others + LOV.
24. Maupassant, Preface to his *Pierre et Jean*, reprinted in his *Boule de suif* (Paris: Conard, 1910); Goncourt, *Journal*, XX, 20.
25. Zola, *Les Romanciers naturalistes*, 152; Maupassant, "Etude," in *BOV*, 554.
26. Letters of the period; *Correspondance George Sand-Gustave Flaubert*, 307.
27. LOV, B-III, fols. 138 recto-140 recto.
28. Goncourt, *Journal*, XVII, 133-34.
29. *Ibid.*, X, 48-49.
30. Many entries in BHVP, *Carnet de lectures*, XV, of this date are of this cast.
31. *CORR*, VI, 133-34 + LOV.
32. Zola, *Les Romanciers naturalistes*, chapter on Flaubert; Maupassant, "Etude," in *BOV*, 544.
33. BHVP, *Carnet de lectures*, XV, fol. 48 recto.

21. *The Temptation of Saint Anthony* (1874)

1. See the works listed for the earlier versions; in addition, Claude Digeon, *Le Dernier Visage de Flaubert* (Paris: Aubier, 1946); Levin, *Gates.*
2. Letters of the period; Commanville, "Souvenirs intimes," *CORR*, I, xxxv.
3. Bart, *Flaubert's Landscape Descriptions*, Appendix A.
4. Reprinted *TENT*, 683.
5. BHVP, *Carnet de lectures*, XIX, fol. 7; reprinted and discussed in Durry, *Flaubert*, 73-74.
6. Reprinted *TENT*, 683.
7. BHVP, *Carnet de lectures*, XX, fol. 7; partially reprinted in *NDV*, II, 366.
8. See LOV, B.
9. Goncourt, *Journal*, X, 43.
10. BHVP, *Carnet de lectures*, XV, fol. 18 recto; reproduced in *NDV*, II, 366.
11. *CORR*, III, 271.
12. *Ibid.*, VI, 12.
13. Reprinted *TENT*, 683.

22. *Bouvard and Pécuchet*

1. The recent edition of *Bouvard et Pécuchet* by Alberto Cento (Paris: Nizet, 1964) has displaced all earlier scholarship. I have adopted the conclusions suggested there. For additional data, see Cento's bibliographical indications; Index to *CORR;* G. Bollème, ed., *Gustave Flaubert; Le Second Volume de Bouvard et Pécuchet.* (Paris: Denoël, 1966).

2. See Cento, *Bouvard;* Goncourt, *Journal*, XIV, 219 and note; XVII, 149.

3. See Marie-Jeanne Durry and Jean Bruneau, "Lectures de Flaubert et de Bouvard et Pécuchet," *Rivista di letterature moderne e comparate*, Vol. XV (1962), 5-45.

4. L. Rossi, "The Structure of Flaubert's *Bouvard et Pécuchet*," *Modern Language Quarterly*, Vol. XIV (1953), 102-11.

5. *CORR*, VII, 287 + LOV.

6. I am particularly indebted to Cento here.

7. Cento, *Bouvard*, I, 153.

8. E.g., *CORR*, VI, 484.

9. Thorlby, *Realism*, 49-51.

10. As Cento amply demonstrates, no edition prior to his own is accurate. I have however, continued to cite from the Conard edition as it is more readily available.

11. Maupassant, *Etudes*, (Paris: Conard, 1938), 114.

12. E. Pound, "Joyce and Pécuchet," *The Dial*, Vol. LXII (1922), 623-29.

23. OLD AGE BEGINS (1872-77)

1. The text is in *TH*, 351-507.

2. Goncourt, *Journal*, XVII, 149.

3. *Ibid.*, X, 168-69 for the entire following account.

4. See the letters of the period; they have been heavily censored; also Suffel, *Lettres inédites*, and *Gustave Flaubert; CORR*, VI, 454-55 + LOV; VII, 7 + LOV.

5. The data are confusing. See *CORR*, VII, 11 + LOV, 70, and 240; Goncourt, *Journal*, XI, 18; Zola, *Les Romanciers naturalistes*, 180-81.

6. *CORR*, VII, 107-108 + LOV, 118 +LOV.

7. See Dumesnil, *Flaubert*.

8. Goncourt, *Journal*, X, 170; *TENT*, 683; Zola, *Les Romanciers naturalistes*, 132, 203.

9. E. Pound, *loc. cit.*

10. Letters of the period; Maupassant, "Etude," in *BOV*, esp. 546ff.

11. Zola, *Les Romanciers naturalistes*, 160.

12. This can be followed from the entries in the *Journal*.

13. The details are summarized in *SUPPL*, III, 167, note 1.

14. Goncourt, *Journal*, XI, 91.

15. Goncourt, *Journal*, XI, 78.

16. *Correspondance George Sand-Gustave Flaubert*, 312ff.

17. Jacob, *loc. cit.*

18. *Correspondance George Sand-Gustave Flaubert*, 413.

19. *CORR*, VI, 450 + LOV.
20. *Ibid.*, VII, 255 + LOV.
21. *Ibid.*, VI, 404 + LOV.
22. *Ibid.*, VI, 406-21 + LOV.
23. *SUPPL*, III, 143 +LOV.
24. Letters of the period and Goncourt, *Journal*, XIV, 130.
25. Goncourt, *Journal*, XI, 43.
26. *CORR*, VII, 234 + LOV.
27. Maupassant, *Etudes*, 105.
28. *CORR*, VII, 279 + LOV.
29. Cited in Digeon, *Le Dernier Visage*, 14-15.
30. The inscribed copy is with Flaubert's other books in the Mairie at Croisset.
31. *CORR*, VII, 70 and 296 + LOV.
32. *CORR* has been heavily censored here; I am completing from LOV, especially the letters to Madame Roger des Genettes.
33. *Correspondence George Sand-Gustave Flaubert*, 432-33.
34. *CORR*, VI, 336-37 + LOV.
35. *Ibid.*, VI, 342 + LOV.
36. Letters to Caroline of the period + LOV.
37. BHVP, *Carnet de lectures*, XVII, fol. 4 recto.
38. *CORR*, VIII, 3 + LOV.
39. Most of the letters of this period have been heavily censored; I am completing from LOV.
40. For the whole section, Maupassant, "Etude" in *BOV*, 540-55; Zola, *Les Romanciers naturalistes*, chapter on Flaubert; *SUPPL, I*, "Complément," 31.
41. F. Coppée, *Souvenirs d'un Parisien* (Paris: Lemerre, 1910), 113.
42. *Correspondance George Sand-Gustave Flaubert, passim.*
43. *CORR*, VII, 282 + LOV.
44. Zola, *Les Romanciers naturalistes*, 113.
45. Maupassant, "Etude," in *BOV*, 548-49.
46. *Ibid.*, 546.

24. *Three Tales* (1877)

1. *NDV*, I, 15.
2. I have considered the import of these changes in my "The Moral of Flaubert's *Saint-Julien*," *Romanic Review*, Vol. XXXVIII (1947), 23-33.
3. *ODJ*, I, 495.
4. *NDV*, I, 50; *CORR*, I, 178, 218, 402,403, etc.
5. *ODJ*, I, 220-223, 252, 513; *CORR*, VIII, 97.
6. *ODJ*, I, 493-94.
7. *Ibid.*, III, 163; Leleu, *Madame Bovary*, II, 294.
8. Du Camp, *Souvenirs littéraires*, I, 140.
9. *CORR*, III, 245 and 350.
10. Louise Colet, *Lui* (Paris: Librairie nouvelle, 1860), 100.
11. E. Fischer, *Etudes sur Flaubert inédit* (Leipzig: Zeitler, 1908), 126-27.
12. Zola, *Les Romanciers naturalistes*, 177.

13. A. J. George, *Short Fiction in France*, 1800-1850 (Syracuse, Syracuse University Press, 1964).

14. *BP*, 300.

15. R. Ellmann, *James Joyce* (Oxford: Oxford University Press, 1959), 78.

16. See a forthcoming study by Heidi C. and B. F. Bart, "Time, Space, and Reality in Flaubert's *Saint-Julien*," *Romanic Review*.

17. *BOV*, 16.

18. *ODJ*, III, 55; *SAL*, 102; *ES*, 70, 287, and 327.

19. *TENT*, 198 and 599-600.

20. *ODJ*, III, 113.

21. Bibliothèque municipale de Rouen, Ms 226⁸, fol. 195.

22. Gérard-Gailly, ed., Gustave Flaubert, *Lettres inédites à Tourgueneff* (Monaco: Editions du Rocher, 1946), 109.

23. The complex data may be found in *CORR*, VII, 287 + LOV and LOV, A-IV, fol. 393.

24. *CORR*, VIII, 65.

25. A considerable volume of recent scholarship, particularly in *French Review*, has opposed this view, preferring to see irony dominant in the tale.

26. *CORR*, III, 130 and 189.

27. Commanville, "Souvenirs intimes," *CORR*, I, xxii.

28. *NDV*, I, 17.

29. See Gérard-Gailly, *Le Grand Amour*, and *BP*, 251.

30. BHVP, *Carnet de lectures*, XVI.

31. Gérard-Gailly gives all the personal details: *Le Grand Amour*.

32. *PLC*, 336.

33. *BP*, 300.

34. Flaubert, *Souvenirs*, 34.

35. *ODJ*, III, 185. See Gérard-Gailly, *Le Grand Amour*, 201.

36. See Gérard-Gailly, *Le Grand Amour*.

37. Zola, *Les Romanciers naturalistes*, 177; Maupassant, *Etudes* 131; *TC*, 236-37.

38. Montaigne, *Essais*, Bk. II, chap. 11, "De la Cruauté."

39. The notes and drafts are in the Bib. nat.

40. *TC*, 227.

41. LOV, B-V, 444 recto-445 recto.

42. *CORR*, IV, 450; *TC*, 242, 247; Digeon, *Le Dernier Visage*, 68.

25. THE FINAL YEARS (1877-80)

1. *CORR*, VII, 286 and 287 + LOV.

2. Letters to Turgenev and his replies in LOV, B-VI.

3. Goncourt, *Journal*, XI, 127.

4. The letters are in LOV, A and B, for the period.

5. Reprinted in *TC*.

6. LOV, B-II, fols. 19 recto and 368 recto and verso.

7. The best account is in R. Baldick, *The Life of J.-K. Huysmans* (Oxford: The Clarendon Press, 1955), 38-39; see also Goncourt, *Journal* entries for the period.

8. Charles Lapierre, *Les Environs de Rouen* (Rouen: Augé, 1890), 23-32.

9. Goncourt, *Journal*, XI, 145.

10. *Ibid.*, XII, 47.

11. *Ibid.*, XI, 131, 143, 160, 178, 187, 212-13; XII, 32, 47, and 57.

12. Cited in R. Dumesnil and R. Demorest, *Autour de Flaubert* (Paris: Giraud-Bodin, 1937).

13. LOV, B-II, 410ff.

14. *CORR*, VIII 140.

15. Goncourt, *Journal*, XVI, 51.

16. *Ibid.*, XII, 48; *SUPPL*, IV, 280.

17. E.g., LOV, B-III, fol. 290.

18. Goncourt, *Journal*, XII, 74.

19. LOV, B-I, fols. 314 recto-315 verso.

20. Goncourt, *Journal*, XII, 29.

21. *CORR*, VIII, 56 + LOV; LOV, B-III, 209 recto.

22. The various projects are discussed in Durry, *Flaubert*. See also letters of the period; Maupassant, *Etudes*, 127-28; Zola, *Les Romanciers naturalistes*, 170-71.

23. Goncourt, *Journal*, XI, 125-26.

24. *CORR*, VIII, 44 + LOV. There is a considerable amount of suppressed material here which I have drawn from LOV.

25. Goncourt, *Journal*, XI, 231.

26. This complex matter can be elucidated from Gérard-Gailly, ed., *Lettres à Tourgueneff*, 179-81; *SUPPL*, IV, 161, note 1; and the letters of the period, particularly those in LOV.

27. The exchanges of letters are in LOV.

28. See esp. LOV, B-IV, 335 recto, letter from Maupassant to Flaubert of February 26, 1879.

29. LOV, B-IV, fols. 357 recto-362 verso.

30. LOV, B-IV, fol. 363 recto and verso.

31. The story can be pieced together from the materials in LOV, B, and the letters of the period by Flaubert. See esp. letter from Maupassant to Flaubert, LOV, B-IV, fols. 365 recto-366 recto; also BHVP, *Carnet de lectures*, XX, fol. 56, reprinted in Durry, *Flaubert*, 359.

32. Again, the materials can be pieced together from the letters in LOV.

33. Goncourt, *Journal*, XII, 26; Zola, *Les Romanciers naturalistes*, 197.

34. LOV, B-I, fol. 432 recto and verso.

35. The essential material is in *SUPPL*, IV, 266-68 and notes.

36. *CORR*, VIII, 341 + LOV; LOV, B-III, fols. 431 verso and 433 recto.

37. *CORR*, VIII, 355 + LOV.

38. LOV, B-II, 418 recto.

39. Goncourt, *Journal*, XII, 69-71, 73.

40. Many of the details surrounding Flaubert's death are in dispute. The best accounts are: Dumesnil, *Flaubert*, 490-91; Gérard-Gailly, *Lettres à Tourgueneff*, 224-27; Normandy, *Lettres à Raoul-Duval*, 251ff.

41. Goncourt, *Journal*, XII, 73.

42. *Ibid.*, 74-77; Zola, *Les Romanciers naturalistes*, 139-41; Suffel, *Flaubert*, 117-19; Normandy, *Lettres à Raoul-Duval*, 309ff; Auriant, *Lettres inédites*, 119-21.

Index

About, Edmond: efforts on Flaubert's behalf, 734

Across Field and Stream: written in alternate chapters, 164; descriptive passages in, 165; pantheistic vision in, 173-75; mockery of vapid reading in, 275

Adam, Madame Juliette, interest in Flaubert, 715

Adams, Henry, *The Education of Henry Adams:* a record of futile will-lessness, 488

Agonies, priest in prefiguration of Bournisien, 285

Agricultural Fair of Yonville: account of, 287-88; irony in story of, 333

Ahasvérus, 42

Alexis, Paul, 720

Alhambra, dance hall in *Sentimental Education,* 509

Anna Karenina, 310

Anna Maria, nun in *Don Juan,* 269

Anthony, *See Temptation of Saint Anthony*

"Anubis, " 235, 369

Arnoux, Jacques, in *Sentimental Education:* patterned after Maurice Schlésinger, 27; characterized, 496; mentioned, 482

Arnoux, Madame Marie, in *Sentimental Education,* 26, 482-98 *passim*

Aupick, General, 204

Azizeh, Nubian dancer, 224

Balzac, Honoré de: influence on Flaubert, 20; "Chateaubrianized Balzac," 342; on the psychology of love, 480; Flaubert's criticism of, 664-65; mentioned, 69, 116, 319, 322, 328, 338, 363, 463, 494, 513, 664

Bambeh, Egyptian courtesan, 222

Banville, Théodore de: description of Louise Colet by, 143; favorable review of *Sentimental Education* by, 539; reaction of to *Saint Anthony,* 627-28

Barbey, Pierre, 689

Bardoux, Senator, 724

Baty, Gaston, 394

Baudelaire, Charles P.: interpretation of episode in *Madame Bovary,* 293; belief that a work of art needs no moral structure, 331; *Flowers of Evil,* 331; opposition to realists, 333; favorable criticism of *Madame Bovary,* 365; mentioned, 18, 22, 43, 49, 70, 72, 117, 204, 250, 318, 337, 341, 342, 349, 358, 381, 390, 438, 447

Baudry, Frédéric, competitor against Flaubert for library post, 728, 729, 731, 734; mentioned, 356, 417, 630, 736

Baudry, Paul, 734

Beauséant, Countess de, character in Balzac's *Père Goriot,* 495

Béranger, Pierre Jean de, 472, 664

Berenson, Bernhard, 216-17

Berlioz, Hector: interested in *Salammbô* for an opera, 436; correspondence with Flaubert, 719

Bernard, Claude, 251, 720

Bernhardt, Sarah, 634

Berry, Duchesse de, 14

Berthelot, Marcellin, 632

Bethlehem, favorable impression of, 203

Binet, tax collector of Yonville, 281

Bismarck, Otto von, 454

Boileau-Despreaux, Nicolas, 336

Bonaparte, Louis-Napoléon, 232, 250, 451

Bosquet, Amélie, 390-91, 462, 465, 539

Bouilhet, Louis: beginning of long friendship with Flaubert, 138, 139; visits to Croisset, 168, 252; opinion of *Saint Anthony*, 183; with Flaubert in the Louvre, 187; poem *Mélaenis*, 253, 715; move to Paris, 254; dedication of *Madame Bovary* to, 255; hallucination involving, 317; play *Madame de Montarcy*, 357; Flaubert introduced to theatrical world by, 383-84; changes in *Bovary* suggested by, 395; alarmed over *Salammbô*, 398; aid on structure of *Salammbô*, 403; collaboration with Flaubert on fairy tale, 438; disapproval of Flaubert's social life, 452-53; appointed librarian at Rouen, 455; illness, 455; illness and death, 543-44; memorial to completed, 739; mentioned, 30, 140, 169, 176, 196, 201, 226, 245, 263, 282, 331, 351, 370, 376, 385, 387, 392, 419, 435, 443, 522

Bournisien, curate in *Madame Bovary*, 136, 281, 300, 311, 318, 325, 339

Bouvard and Pécuchet: framework, 587; various disciplines explored, 589; inclusive character, 590; satirical character, 592; illusions, 593; critical opinion on, 594; good opening, 595; agricultural experiences in, 598; succession of errors, 599; not a novel, 602; arid stretches, 602; and Balzac, 603; autobiographical features, 604; cults explored, 605; love life of the two clerks, 605; philosophy explored, 605-606; religious experiences in, 606; confusion for reader, 607; education experiment, 608; comparison of the clerks with other Flaubert characters, 611-12; secondary characters, 612; stupidity of masses blamed, 615; humor, 616-17; marred by pedantry, 618; unsuccessful, 620; set aside, 622, 670; progress on, 737-38; problems with, 740; mentioned, 18, 35, 440, 586, 587, 609-10, 613, 619, 718-19, 721, 722

Bovary, Berthe, child of Charles and Emma in *Madame Bovary*, 314

Bovary, Charles, husband of Emma: first marriage, 272; school life of, 272; medical practice begun, 272; marriage to Emma, 273; changes in appearance, 278; failure of operation by, 292-93; dreams of Berthe's future, 296; mistakes of, 300-301; at deathbed of Emma, 307; growth in stature, 312; later life and death, 313-14; failure as husband, 319; virtues and weaknesses, 320

Bovary, Emma: evolution of character of, 17; and Flaubert's ball experience, 37; connection with the first *Sentimental Education*, 109; drawn from Flaubert's experience, 186; sad destiny of, 244; emotional terrors of, 249; successive liaisons of, 266; need of luxury, 268, 277, 319; suicide planned, 268; convent experience of, 270, 304; and Rodolphe, 290, 291, 292, 293, 294, 297, 299, 306; and Lheureux, 286-87; and the operation by Charles, 293; new interest in religion, 299; attracted to Lagardy, 301; and Léon, 302, 303, 305; epileptic attack, 306; suicide and death, 307-309; funeral, 312; gave form to Flaubert's hallucinations, 316; desire for a son, 318; fate determined by surroundings, 318; sensuality of, 318, 319; sympathy for, 325; as embodiment of Flaubert's romanticism, 346; compared to Salammbô, 407; mentioned, 111, 126, 204, 216, 242, 315, 317, 322

Bovary, Madame: description of Rouen in, 3; portrait of Dr. Flaubert in, 6; a satire in form of a novel, 12; drawn from early experiences, 36; likeness to first *Sentimental Education*, 106, 109; corrections in, 165; reluctance to publish, 245; early drafts of, 248; work on at Croisset, 251; serialized in *Revue de Paris*, 253; variations on earlier themes, 270; drawn from many sources, 271; opening of, 272; flaws in conclusion of, 310; shows Flaubert's bitterness, 314; not excessive, 335; classicism of, 336; and Flaubert's religion of art, 337; place in literature, 338; inferior over-all plan, 339; vulgarity in, 341; early stream of consciousness technique, 344; completion of, 354; first installment of, 356; trial of 358-63, 396-97; increased demand for, 362; lasting success, 365, 426; dramatization, 394; new edition, 627; mentioned, 17, 22, 31, 32, 36, 38, 51, 131, 154, 170, 184, 186, 235, 242, 262, 267, 268, 271, 277, 281, 295, 315, 317, 318, 322, 327, 329, 331, 353, 354, 355, 366, 369, 373, 430, 477, 502, 718. *See also* Emma Bovary, Charles Bovary, Léon, Rodolphe

Breughel, Pieter: picture of Saint Anthony and Flaubert's book, 131, 159, 172, 181

Brianne, Madame: friendship with Flaubert, 569, 715; admiration for *Saint Anthony*, 628; and the Saint Polycarp celebration, 707; mentioned, 637, 638, 639, 640, 713, 725, 727

Brittany trip: planned itinerary, 159

Bruyère, J. de, 101, 348

Byron, George: read by youthful Flaubert, 21; Don Juan as a model, 32, 71; effect of death of, 48; mentioned, 172

Busnach, 394

Camus, Albert, 34, 438, 525

Candidate, The, 624-25

Candide: satiric high point of picaresque novel, 478

Carthage: long attraction for Flaubert, 396

Carvalho, and *The Weaker Sex,* 621, 622; work on *The Candidate,* 623

Castle of Hearts, The, hope of staging in England, 741

Catholic church, 423, 468-69, 720

Catoblepas, monster in *Saint Anthony,* 180-81

Céard, 630

Cervantes, Saavedra Miguel de, discovered by Flaubert, 18

Champfleury, Jules: and *Bovary,* 363; affair with Louise Colet, 386; mentioned, 241, 264

Charcot, Jean Martin, 326

Charles Demailly, hero of, modeled after Flaubert, 382

Charpentier, Georges: publication of *Three Tales* by, 706; publication of *The Castle of Hearts,* 718; mentioned, 626, 706, 717, 723, 739, 740

Charpentier, Madame Georges, 730

Chateaubriand, François René de: romanticism of, 20, 32; influence on Flaubert, 21, 31, 323, 664; effect of *René*, 32, 33-34, 110-11; skepticism of, 42; *The Martyrs*, 160, 417, 434; tomb of, 161; "Chateaubrianized Balzac," 342; symbolism in *Atala*, 422; mentioned, 40, 44, 49, 71, 168, 206, 230, 242, 274, 276, 346, 355, 583, 598, 664

Chateau du Héron, 37

Cheruel, Pierre Adolphe: influence on Flaubert, 30; pupil of Michelet, 415

Chevalier, Ernest: boyhood friendship with Flaubert, 10-11, 18; marriage, 238; apostasy of, 325; praise of *Salammbô*, 434; mentioned, 14, 22, 40, 46, 63, 64, 133, 252, 305, 448

Chevalier, Madame, 10

Classicism, 54, 118-19

Cleves, Princess de, 479

Colet, Louise: first meeting with Flaubert, 141; childhood, education, marriage, 142, recognition as a poet, 142, 143; appearance, 143-44; liaison with Flaubert, 145, 153, 154, 155, 240-41, 244, 255; as model for Emma Bovary, 156; dissatisfaction with Flaubert, 157, 159, 163, 256, 263; attacks on Flaubert in novels, 264; publication of relationship with Flaubert in *Lui*, 387; favorable reaction to *Salammbô*, 434; in *Le Figaro*, 459-60; death, 656; letters to Flaubert destroyed, 712; private papers of, 755 n1; mentioned, 150, 205, 242, 255, 274, 283, 295, 299, 302, 350, 363, 569, 583, 612, 634, 676

Collier, Captain: contempt for the French, 67

Collier family: in Trouville, 67; in Paris, 81

Collier, Gertrude: pursuit of Flaubert, 84; inscribed copy of *Bovary* sent to, 363; mentioned, 67, 123, 243, 389, 551. *See also* Gertrude Collier Tennant

Collier, Harriet: nature of invalidism,. 67; early association with Flaubert, 83; evidence of love for Flaubert, 128; with Flaubert in London, 243; marriage, 244; likeness to Louise Roque in *Sentimental Education*, 501; mentioned, 78, 84, 112, 123-24, 162, 259, 283, 389, 551-692

Collier, Herbert, 67

Commanville, Caroline: share in financial failure uncertain, 743; mentioned, 556, 628, 646. *See also* Caroline Hamard

Commanville, Ernest: background, 444; marriage to Caroline Hamard, niece of Flaubert, 445-46; financial difficulties of, 647, 649; and Flaubert's finances, 649, 723, 725; at Flaubert's funeral, 743

Conrad, Joseph, *Nigger of the Narcissus*, 413

Coppée, François, 664

Cordier, Senator, 728, 736

Corneille, Pierre, 59

Corsica, 57-58

Courbet, Gustave, 346

Cousin, Victor: philosophy of and Flaubert, 48, 49; sponsorship of Louise Colet, 142; mentioned, 117, 241

Couturier, Delphine, 242

Croce, Benedetto, 469

Croisset: Flaubert's lifelong home there, 4; description of, 102; family routine at, 251; advantages of, 373; Flaubert's later life there, 629-30; source of peace to Flaubert, 660, 709; sold after Flaubert's death, 743

Dambreuse, Madame, character in *Sentimental Education*, 483, 496, 510, 511

Daudet, Alphonse: at Flaubert's Sundays, 630; characterized Flaubert, 633; dedicated a novel to Flaubert, 656; praise for *Three Tales*, 706; at Flaubert's funeral, 744; mentioned, 588, 646, 709, 716, 740

Death of Louis XI, The, 18

Degas, Ernest, 251

Delamare, D e l p h i n e : connection with the story of Emma Bovary, 131, 266; mentioned, 314

Delamare, Eugène, 242, 272

Delavigne, Casimir: insulted by Flaubert, 664

Delessert, Edward, 204

Delessert, Valentine, prototype of Madame Dambreuse in *Sentimental Education*, 495

Démonassa, Athenian courtesan in *Saint Anthony*, 179

Deslauriers, character in *Sentimental Education*, 483, 523

Dial, The: vehicle for Joyce and Pound, 342

Dictionary of Accepted Ideas, 234, 286, 369, 506, 587, 588, 589, 596, 610

Dictionary of French Institutions, 31

Diderot, Denis, 327, 330

Donatello: scorned by Du Camp, 86

Don Juan, 234, 236, 242, 268-69, 340

Don Quixote: effect on Flaubert, 10; fusion of reality and illusion in, 318

Dorval, Marie, 186

Dryden, John, 119

Drouet, Juliette, 141

Du Camp, Baron Maxime: close friendship with Flaubert, 84; appearance of, 85; interest in art, 86; description of Flaubert's epilepsy, 93, 100; letters to Flaubert, 100; comment that Flaubert substituted art for life, 103; and Flaubert's relations to Louise Colet, 143-44, 154, 155, 170, 388; hiking trip with Flaubert, 158-62, 449; at Croisset, 164-65; and pantheism, 173; unfavorable opinion of *Saint Anthony*, 183; use of camera on Eastern trip, 190; tendency to homosexuality, 225, 226; interest in Utopian Socialism, 231; relations with Ludovica, 240; approval of *Madame Bovary* as a subject, 242; acquired *Revue de Paris*, 244-45; break with Flaubert, 246, 247; correspondence of, 252-53; purchase of *Bovary* for *Revue de Paris*, 354; fear of action against *Bovary*, 356; demands for deletions, 357; c r i t i c i s m of *Salammbô*, 432; rapprochement with Flaubert, 455; cynicism of, 459; characters in *Sentimental Education* borrowed from, 498; reaction to *Sentimental Education*, 533, 537-38; deep trouble of, 559; source of Julian story suggested by, 676; agreed on burning of correspondence with Flaubert, 713-14; works reread by Flaubert, 719; differences with Flaubert, 740; election to French Academy, 740; mentioned, 95, 113, 136, 139, 140, 147, 148, 152, 163, 168, 186-87, 209, 221, 380, 401, 446, 495, 519, 520, 522, 544, 709

Du Locle, librettist for opera *Salammbô*, 436

Dumas, Alexandre: read by youthful Flaubert, 21, 32; work of pub-

Dumas, Alexandre—*Cont.*
lished by Schlésinger, 27; mentioned, 381, 657
Dumas, Alexandre, *fils,* 558
Duplan, Jules: kindness to Flaubert, 381; collaboration with, 588; mentioned, 401, 435, 458, 509, 544, 712
Duranty, editor of *Réalisme:* critical comment on *Bovary,* 363

Eastern trip: duration and cost, 188, 189
Ecker, Dr. Arthur: diagnosis of Flaubert's seizures, 753 n1
Eliot, T. S.: objection to Flaubert's view of mankind, 337-38; his character, Prufrock, compared to Frédéric, 488
Epilepsy, uses in works: in *Bovary,* 306-307; in *Saint Julian,* 680; in *Salammbô,* 409, 412-13; in *Sentimental Education,* 534-36, in *Temptation of Saint Anthony,* 575, 576, 579, 583-85. *See also* Gustave Flaubert, Health
Eschmoûn, 430
Eugénie, Empress: Flaubert favored by, 359
Eugénie Grandet, 20

Fanny, 427
Faulkner, William: debt to Flaubert, 345; mentioned, 617
Faust, 110, 117
Félicité, heroine of *A Simple Heart,* 688, 689
Feuillet, Octave, 513
Feydeau, Ernest: friendship with Flaubert, 380, 631; copying Flaubert by, 381; on importance of style, 427; aided by Flaubert, 557; mentioned, 401
Flandrin, Jean Hippolyte, fresco *Entry Into Jerusalem,* 187-88; mentioned, 201

Flaubert, Dr. Achille, brother of Gustave: marriage, 46; fear for Gustave's health, 377, 711; financial aid to Gustave, 735; mentioned, 8, 90, 252, 374, 443, 544
Flaubert, Dr. Achille-Cléophas, father of Gustave: hospital at Rouen, 5; career of, 7; business success of, 65; care of Harriet Collier, 79; and Gustave's first attack of epilepsy, 91, 93, 99; purchase of home at Croisset, 102; illness and death, 132; mentioned, 9, 14, 56, 88, 127
Flaubert, Caroline, sister of Gustave: relations with her brother, 9-10, 17-18, 80, 83, 99; at Trouville, 67; maturity, 80; migraine headaches, 94; engagement to Hamard, 105; marriage, 122; pregnancy, 127; death, 133; funeral, 135; mentioned, 6, 8, 14, 55, 88, 112, 309
Flaubert children, 8
Flaubert, Gustave
Art, reactions to: admiration of Vatican "Torso," 215; calmness of Flaubert effected by, 332; Canova's statuary, 126; disapproval of conclusions by artists, 330; critic of painting, 216; escape from life through, 467; esthetics of, 49, 114, 527, 668; exaggeration in, 233; Fra Angelico, supremacy of, 216; as goal of writing, 328; impersonal, 470; life lived for sake of, 120; Michelangelo's "Last Judgment" supreme, 216; Murillo's "Virgin and Child," 217; museum studies in Rome, 215; power to move people, 604; relation to reality, 720; science and art, relations of, 330, 333; seeks truth, 334; task of, 334
As author: characteristics of early writing, 18-19, 32-33,

34, 35; convinced of ability to write, 184; debt to Voltaire, 102; decision on new work, 235, 370, 440, 550; description as opposed to criticism, 232; difficulty in writing, 165; French prose, admiration for, 667; freedom of choice in subject matter, 69; historical sources, use of, 175-76, 469, 719; illustrations, opposition to, 717; living habits while writing, 323-24; methods for depicting violence, 411; novelist, conception of work of, 110; planning for work, 64, 130, 234; points of view, 343; publication, problem of, 245; ranking of self below geniuses, 338; reading in relation to writing, 101, 130, 137, 578; types substituted for individuals, 612. *See also* Style, *Madame Bovary*, and other book titles

Characteristics: admirations for Nero, 47, Hamlet, 487; adult traits evident in boyhood, 31; death, thoughts of, 41; emotionalism, 230; ennui, 71; equilibrium achieved by, 130; excess, belief in, 582; fantasies, childhood, 16, in later work, 110; fatalism, 14, 73, 74, 337; hallucinations, 200, 533-34, 545; hatreds, 333, 665; illusion, persistent, 573, 607; impassive, impersonal, 329; intolerance of disagreement, 631, of stupidity, 18; lacks detachment, 324, humor, 17, judgment, 449; meaninglessness of life felt by, 182; melancholy of, 74, 90, 158, 375, 641, 644; opposition to inhibitions, 469; pessimism, 40, 571; rages of, 16, 592, 714; retreat into self, 136; skepticism, 614; solitude,

641; suicide considered, 551-52; unhappiness at a ball, 37; valued men friends, 589, 648, 733, 740

Classicism, interest in: antiromanticism of, 335; Athenian, vigorous and natural, 207; beyond classicists the goal, 336; boyhood reading of, 19; devotion to continued, 471; Greek sources of, 335-36, 414, 415; interest in renewed, 54; *Odyssey* and *Iliad*, 196; Platonic reverence for idea, 326-27; study of Plautus, 87; Spanish trip increased interest in, 58

Croisset: fear of loss of, 650; Prussians in, 558; returns to, 129, 146, 384, 649; study at, 442; summer life at, 374

Education: early, 30, 53-54, 56; in law school, 63, 64, 65, 66, 82, 84, 87

Family relations: childhood, 8, 13; with father, 6, 7; with Julie, servant, 14, 637, 659, 675, 709, 715, 738; with mother, 9, 137-38, 151, 185-86, 195-96, 564, 566; with sister Caroline, 8, 62, 133-34; with niece Caroline, 444, 446, 547, 557, 564, 637, 735. *See also* Dr. Achille Flaubert, Dr. Achille-Cléophas Flaubert, Caroline Flaubert, Madame Flaubert

Financial problems: attitude toward bankruptcy, 650; crisis in, 662; Commanville, funds entrusted to, 647, 723; difficulties, 549, 550; fluctuations, 656, 739; loss of entire fortune, 653, 731, 734; pension proposed, 733, delayed, 734; plan to share apartment, 725; proposal for government post, 725; public post accepted, 735-36; search for sine-

Financial problems—*Cont.*
cure, 652; spendthrift tendencies, 454, 646; unwillingness to receive help, 732; view of life resulting from, 655

Health: emotional instability, 93, 97, 446, 570; epilepsy, first attack, 90-91, progress of, 92, 96, control of seizures, 92, diagnosis of, 95, 752-53 n1, flow of words affected by, 95, treatment for, 97; his description of attacks, 536, 583, 584; periodic bad health, 168, 248-49, 643, 645, 670, 710; venereal diseases, 218, 220; death, 742-43, 773 n40; funeral, 743-44. *See also* Epilepsy

Literary style: concept of the historical novel, 417; development of style, 69, 529; devices used to promote ideas, 530; difficulty of impersonal presentation, 343; distaste for the new poetry, 656; flamboyance, 332; image natural to the character, 351; importance of form, 119, 339, 340, 473; indirect discourse used, 318, 344, 350; influence on American and English novelists, 328; interest aroused by ideas, 346; lapses in grammatical structure, 532-33; levels of fantasy, 575; manipulation of time in a novel, 345; matter of composite whole, 348; means of achieving, 343; overuse of imagery, 350; precision of language, 348; preference for short story form, 340; rhythm important, 427; subject basis for, 347, 427; stream of consciousness foreshadowed, 536; touch of preciosity, 531; transitions, 532; use of metaphor, 349-50, 352; use of words, 346

Paris, life in: apartments, 79, 255, 373-74, 378, 549-50; acquaintances, 381; imperial court affairs, 451, 452, 453; lascivious life, 83, 377, 383; limitations felt, 65-66; misadventures, 465-66; parade on the Champs Elysées, 551; Sunday affairs attended by writers and artists, 379; visits to, 64, 79, 88, 91, 560; work schedule, 81

Physical appearance: at fifteen, 29; between sixteen and nineteen, 39-40; at seventeen, 53; dress, 630; changes in, 213; self-portrait, 70; mentioned, 67, 82

Political views: attacks on liberals, 529; boredom with the Second Empire, 250; distaste for Socialists, 468, 523; dissatisfaction, 641; military service, 62, 556, 557; misinterpretation of Prussian menace, 454; opposition to the Republic, 555, 556, 714; progress by aristocracy or monarchy, 524; revolt against contemporary society, 86; revulsion toward masses, 45, 70, 325, 449, 468, 528

Religion and philosophy: alliance of religion, sexuality, and art, 217; appeal of esthetic Christianity, 40; attitude toward humanitarianism, 231; attracted by piety, 422; Buddhist works read, 136; on the Catholic church, 468; early religious doubts, 36; enduring religion of art, 167; Midnight Mass attended, 661; opposition of science and Catholicism, 422; organized religion a travesty, 202; pantheistic tendencies, 75, 173, 174, 211, 327, 430, 572, 653; philosophy of antiromanticism, 332;

problem of terrestrial and spiritual love, 315; reading in philosophy and theology, 720; religion a philosophy in form of art, 583; relationship between religion and sexuality, 421; romanticism, 98, 440; tranquility found, 660, 669; ultimate hope of, 327; unable to accept faith, 180

Rouen: boyhood in, 3, 4-5, 21, 29; return to, 91

Sex life: actresses in Paris, 384; assignations c o n t i n u e d , 458; adolescent eroticism, 42; carnal love described, 72; change from debauchery to asceticism, 97-98; excessive sexual life, 82-83; first experience of sex, 25; homosexual tendency, 225, 226; interest in abnormal sex, 384; mistresses, on having two, 164; orgiastic dreams, 113; orgies, 716; Parisian brothels, 64; prostitution, use of, 41, 42, 218, 220; revived problem of sex, 173; sexuality on Eastern trip, 207, 218

Terrestrial and spiritual love, 270, 315, 397, 406-407, 410, 411-13, 421

Theatrical experiences: Bouilhet's play Aïsse produced, 545, 565; Bouilhet's play The Weaker Sex worked on, 621, 622; The Candidate, production and failure of, 623, 624; Castle of Hearts rejected, 438, 550; effect of theater on early writing, 21; interest in theater, 438; Maupassant play, 708; offers to dramatize Bovary, 394; revival of classicism in the theater, 55; scenarios in papers of, 51; tragedienne Rachel, 55

Travel: love of travel, 60-61; observations on, 192; use of experiences, 190, 198, 206, 295; in Africa, 399-401; in Brittany, 159-160, 166-67; in Egypt, 189-98; effect of, 227; in Greece, 205-10; in Italy, first trip, 59, 122-27, return to, 213-18; in the Near East, 184, 188, 199-204; in Spain, 56, 58

Women, attitude toward: changes in, 633; contempt for, 257, 386, 477; diatribe on rearing girls, 273; dismissal of a mistress, 287; general, 458 59; marriage, fear of, 237, 385; presents from, 278. See also Harriet Collier, Louise Colet, Eulalie Foucaud, Juliet Herbert, Kuchiuk-Hânem, Suzanne Lagier, "Ludovica," Princess Mathilde, George Sand, Elisa Schlésinger, Jeanne de Tourbey

Flaubert, Madame, mother of Gustave: character and appearance, 8-9; victim of migraines, 94; reaction to family deaths, 135; Gustave's attachment to, 151, 152, 153-54; and Gustave's Brittany trip, 159; with Gustave in Italy, 215, 221; hope for marriage of Gustave, 237; in London, 243; aging difficulties, 252, 442-43; chagrin at Gustave's African trip, 399; at Vichy with Gustave, 433; concern for Gustave's extravagance, 454; and George Sand, 463; last days, 562; death and will, 563; mentioned, 23, 163, 184, 363, 377, 385, 444, 487, 547

Fontainebleau: in Sentimental Education, 514-17

Fortin, Dr.: in attendance on Flaubert, 710, 742

Foucaud, Eulalie: association with Flaubert, 56, 76, 125, 134, 145, 189, 298, 399, 501, 716

Fourier, François, Socialist, 468
France, Anatole: influence of *Saint Anthony* on *Thais*, 628; estimate of Flaubert, 631; mentioned, 718
Franco-Prussian War, 554-59
Freud, Sigmund, 167, 326
Froehner, German archeologist, 435

Gabrielle, play by Emile Augier, 229, 276
Gambetta, Leon, 708, 728-29
Gautier, Théophile: effect on young Flaubert, 43, 72, 108; publication of parts of *Saint Anthony* in *L'Artiste,* 372; death and funeral, 640-41; mentioned, 49, 111, 119, 172, 189, 379, 380, 390, 401, 540, 563, 665
Gazette musicale, 26
Genettes, Madame Roger des: intimacy with Flaubert, 391, 462; interest in *Saint Julian,* 677; pleased with *Three Tales,* 706; mentioned, 253, 638, 657, 690, 712, 718
"Giaffar," 269
Gide, André, 348
Gil Blas: example of picaresque novel, 478
Girardin, Emile, publisher, 241
Giraud, court painter: portrait of Flaubert, 452-53
Gleyre, Charles Gabriel: advice on Eastern trip, 189
Goethe, Johann Wolfgang von: read by Flaubert, 21, 32; influence on Flaubert's works, 111, 172; debt to, 331-32; mentioned, 71
Goncourt, de, brothers: criticism of Flaubert by, 382-83, 433, 435-36; visits to Croisset, 441-42, 456; mentioned, 72, 394, 424, 447, 452, 457, 470, 479, 544
Goncourt, Edmond de: and Flaubert's Sundays, 550; reaction to *Saint Anthony,* 582, 628; plagia-rism suggested by, 588; adverse opinion of Flaubert by, 632; critical of *Heriodias,* 706; news of Flaubert's death, 743; at Flaubert's funeral, 744; mentioned, 382, 452, 498, 518, 567, 570, 571, 624, 630, 631, 642, 645, 666, 708, 716, 740
Goncourt, Jules de: friendship for Flaubert, 382; death of, 546
Greece: Flaubert's visit in 1850, 205-13

Hamard, husband of Caroline Flaubert: friend of Gustave, 79; engagement to Caroline, 80, 105; mental illness of, 169; death of, 712
Hamard, Caroline, niece of Gustave Flaubert: birth of, 133; baptism, 135-36; English governesses for, 243; taught by uncle, 251; mutual devotion, 377, 384; life at Croisset, 441-42; marriage, 445; mentioned, 392, 433. *See also* Caroline Commanville
Hamard, Caroline, sister of Gustave. *See* Caroline Flaubert
Hamilcar Barca, Carthaginian leader: hero of *Salammbô,* 397, 403, 404, 405, 406
Hannibal, 404, 679
Haussman, Georges Eugene, Baron, 596
Hegel, Georg, 48, 117, 697
Hennique, Léon, 630, 720
Herbert, Juliet, English governess in Flaubert home: relations with Gustave, 391, 392, 460-61, 639-40; mentioned, 462, 546, 557, 559, 633, 638, 645, 716, 738
Hérédia, José Maria de, 630
Herodias, third of the *Three Tales:* mentioned, 198, 698, 699, 701-702, 704
Herodotus, 228

Hilarion, character in *Saint Anthony*, 575, 577, 578

Homais, pharmacist in *Madame Bovary*, 249, 282, 302, 311, 312, 314, 319, 323, 325, 331, 334, 339, 488, 497, 587

Homer, 19, 64

Honfleur, 28

Hôtel-Dieu, or Hospital, of Rouen, 5

Howells, William Dean, 56

Hugo, Victor: and romanticism, 19; read by the young Flaubert, 21; philhellenism of, 48; first meeting with Flaubert, 82; opposed Second Empire, 250; *Les Contemplations*, 335; comment on *Bovary*, 363; *Les Miserables*, 402; *Notre-Dame de Paris*, 417; urged Flaubert's election to French Academy, 709; support of Flaubert for government post, 728, 736; mentioned, 49, 69, 82, 141, 206, 510, 539, 567, 645, 656, 664, 669

Husson, Adèle, 634

Huysmans, Joris Karl: approval of *Saint Anthony*, 628; at Flaubert's Sundays, 630; estimate of Flaubert, 631; mentioned, 349, 488, 707, 720

Iliad, 196

James, Henry: on Flaubert's place in literature, 328-29; on *Bovary*, 342; on *Sentimental Education*, 492-93

"Jenner, or the Discovery of Vaccine," incomplete satire by Bouilhet and Flaubert, 139

Jerusalem: disappointment in, 201-203, 205

Jeufroy, Abbé, 608

Journey to Hell, first of series of tales of flight through space, 49, 50

Joyce, James: praise for Flaubert's work, 328, 329, 619-20, 628, 678; use of indirect discourse, 344; shared Flaubert's convictions, 349; mentioned, 345, 520

Justin, character in *Madame Bovary*, 287, 294, 303, 307, 312, 331

Karr, Alphonse, 142-43

Kuchiuk-Hânem, Egyptian courtesan: erotic dancing by, 224; mentioned, 222-23, 237, 256, 333, 411, 520, 701

Lagier, Suzanne, actress friend of Flaubert, 375, 389, 459, 516, 550, 634, 708, 716

Lamartine, Alphonse de, 19, 20, 49, 302, 360, 516, 594

Lambert, Charles, prophet of Utopian Socialism, 231

Langlois, Ernest, 675, 718

Lapierre, Charles, editor of *Nouvelliste de Rouen*, 457

Lapierre, Madame, 569, 640, 715

Laporte, Edmond: close friendship with Flaubert, 458, 567, 628, 633; Normandy trip with Flaubert, 643; financial involvement with Commanville, 652, 723, 724, 736; mentioned, 637, 645, 649, 706, 713, 732

Larivière, Dr.: prototype of Dr. Flaubert in *Bovary*, 307, 331

La Vaubyessard, chateau in *Bovary*, 276

La Vie moderne: publication of *The Castle of Hearts*, 738

Lawrence, D. H., 290

Le Bien Public: and the publication of *Saint Julian*, 705, 706

Le Colibri, biweekly Rouen journal, 35

Le Conte de Lisle, Charles, 241, 250, 657, 719

Le Figaro, 705, 711, 729

Le Garçon, imaginary character of Flaubert's childhood, 16-17

Legend of Saint Julian, The. See Saint Julian, The Legend of

Léon, Emma's lover in Bovary, 266-67, 282, 283, 284, 285-86, 301-302, 303, 305, 306, 318, 322

Le Pere Goriot, 20, 495

Leporello, servant of Don Juan, 321

Leroux, Catherine, 289, 688

Leroyer de Chantepie, Mademoiselle: correspondence with Flaubert, 391; review of Sentimental Education, 539; mentioned, 408, 422, 634

Le Sage, 101

Le Siècle: and the publication of A Simple Heart, 705, 706

Lestiboudois, gravedigger in Bovary, 281

Lévy, Michel: purchase of printing rights to Bovary, 361, 362; new edition of Bovary, 394; purchase of Salammbô, 432; bargaining for Sentimental Education, 549; break with Flaubert, 566, 626; mentioned, 454, 538, 545

Lewis, Sinclair, 318, 343

Lheureux, merchant and money lender in Bovary, 282, 284, 289, 294-95, 302, 304-305, 318, 319, 331, 488

"Little Bourgeois Comedy": analysis of, 51

London Exposition, 243

Louis-Philippe: abdication in background of Sentimental Education, 521

Lucia di Lammermoor, 204, 300

"Ludovica" (Louise Pradier), 124, 156, 163-64, 170, 187, 258, 259, 261, 267, 268, 272, 286, 303-304, 306, 435, 459

MacMahon, President Marie Edmé, 214

Mallarmé, Stéphane, Afternoon of a Faun, 656

Mallet, Flaubert's philosophy teacher, 48, 117

Manet, Edward, 251

Mann, Thomas, 467

Mathilde, Princess: appreciation of Bovary, 451; on Flaubert's character, 451; visit from Flaubert, 559; correspondence with Flaubert, 715; mentioned, 453, 460, 479, 537, 556, 568, 631, 634, 638, 639-40, 643, 656, 659, 706, 712, 727

Mâtho, hero of Salammbô, 397, 403, 404, 407, 409-10, 421, 422, 424, 429, 479

Maupassant, Guy de: friendship for Flaubert, 11, 567, 629, 707, 732, 735; distaste for Sentimental Education, 526-27; view of Bouvard and Pécuchet, 616; threat of prosecution for obscenity, 739; mentioned, 236, 528, 631, 667, 738, 740, 741, 742, 743

Maupassant, Laure de, 712, 739. See also Laure Le Poittevin

Maury, 326, 417, 457, 547

Memoirs of a Madman, The, 42-43, 46, 47, 50, 282, 302, 477, 490, 674

Mendès, Catulle, 630

Mérimée, Prosper, 319, 387, 495, 713

Meyerbeer, Giacomo, The Prophet, 187

Michelangelo, 86, 216

Michelet, Jules: influence on Flaubert, 21, 137, 415; copy of Bovary sent to, 363; mentioned, 30-31, 381, 427, 457, 469

Mignot (père), 10

Milhaud, Darius, 394

Minister of Fine Arts: defense of Flaubert, 359

Molière, 45, 59, 330, 336

Moloch, sun god, 397, 405, 421, 423, 577

Moniteur: purchase of publication rights to *A Simple Heart* and *Herodias*, 706

Monnier, Henry, offer to dramatize *Madame Bovary*, 394

Montaigne, Michel de, 19, 42, 43, 101, 110, 116, 120, 134, 325, 422, 478, 557, 614, 697

Moreau, Frédéric, hero of *Sentimental Education*, 87-88, 479

Mozart, Wolfgang, *Don Giovanni*, 236

Murillo, "Virgin and Child," 512

Musset, Alfred de, 19, 241, 256, 387

Mycerinus, king of Egypt, 228

Nadar, photographer, 378

Narcisse, servant to Flaubert at Croisset, 375

Narr'Havas, barbarian chief in *Salammbô*, 403, 405, 409

Nebuchadnezzar, 575

Nero: Flaubert's enthusiasm for, 416

New Year's Day celebration, 15, 661

Nogent, 21

November: highly personal character of, 70, 75-76; mentioned, 68, 77, 109, 110, 112, 115, 125, 148, 162, 225, 236, 250, 268, 269, 278, 302, 370, 456

Oedipus, 681

Oedipus complex: Flaubert victim of, 459

Orestes, 681

Pantheon, 334

Parmigiano, 217

Parthenon: Flaubert's deep appreciation for, 207

Pasca, Madame, 569, 715

Pascal, Blaise, 40

Passion and Virtue, forerunner of *Bovary*, 37, 268

Pasteur, Louis, 251

Pater, Walter: estimate of Flaubert by, 328-29; mentioned, 349

Pelouze, Madame: involvement in the Commanville finances, 723, 724; mentioned, 715

Person, Beatrix, 265, 389, 401

Phidias, 210

Pierre, Flaubert family servant, 14

Pinard, imperial prosecutor in Flaubert trial, 360, 372, 627, 718

Plato, 48, 117

Plautus, 401

Poe, Edgar Allan, 438

Poiters, Diane de, 514

Poittevin, Alfred le, devoted friend of Flaubert, 11; obsession with sexuality, 82; hatred of Du Camp, 86, 104; bad influence on Flaubert, 104; letters from Flaubert, 128, 752 n14; marriage, 139; pantheistic belief, 173; death of, 309; dedication of *Saint Anthony* to, 581; mentioned, 12-13, 14, 22, 35, 40, 68, 72, 81, 116, 123, 124, 132, 138, 169, 170, 226, 263, 322, 376

Poittevin, le, family, 172, 448

Poittevin, Laure le, 11, 14, 170, 448, 567. *See also* Laure de Maupassant

Poittevin, Madame le, 23

Polybius, 414

Pomereu, Marquis de, 61

Pont-l'Evêque, home of Madame Flaubert, 9, 23, 689, 690, 691, 694

Pope, Alexander, 119

Pouchet, Dr. Felix: friendship with Flaubert, 457

Pouchet, Georges, 652-53, 670, 719

Pound, Ezra: estimate of Flaubert's work by, 328-29, 349, 619-20

Pradier, James, sculptor, 82, 129, 133, 141, 145, 146, 241

Pradier, Louise. See "Ludovica"

Praxiteles, 210

Proudhon, Pierre Joseph, 468

Proust, Marcel, 25, 78, 206, 428, 485, 613

Quinet, Edgar, 42, 172

Rabelais, François, 44, 101, 116, 324, 334

Rachel, Madame, tragedienne, 55, 56, 335

Racine, Jean, 59, 118

Raoul-Duval, p u b l i c prosecutor, 458, 652, 705, 739

Régnier, Mathurin, 101

Renan, Edgar Ernest, 219, 326, 417, 457, 547, 552, 578, 582, 614, 657, 668, 709

René, 161

Renoir, Pierre: directed musical version of Bovary, 394

Revolution of 1848, 170-71, 478, 713

Revue de Paris, 244-46, 354-59, 388

Revue des Deux Mondes: published Louise Colet's verse, 142

Reyer, Ernest, composer of opera Salammbô, 436

Ricord, Dr., 249

Rimbaud, Jean Arthur, 656

Robbe-Grillet, Alain, 529

Rodolphe, Emma's lover in Bovary, 266, 287, 288-90, 295, 298, 313, 318, 321

Rogier, Camille, 713

Romanticism: effect on Flaubert, 19, 28, 32, 54

Ronsard, Pierre de, 87, 370, 715

Roque, Louise: in Sentimental Education, 483, 489

Rosanette, lorette in Sentimental Education, 482-538 passim

Rosembourg, Nelly, 400

Rossini's Stabat Mater, 26

Rousseau, Jean Jacques, imitated by Flaubert, 43

Rubens, 217

Sabatier, Madame, 389-90, 393, 474, 482

Sade, Marquis de: effect of on Flaubert, 45, 379, 413, 424, 539

Sadism: in Saint Julian, 674-75, 679-81; in Salammbô, 413-14, 423-26. See also Marquis de Sade

Saint Julian, The Legend of: dream of Flaubert basis of story, 67; summary of, 673, 678; Flaubert's reading for, 676; three parts of, 677; beginning of modern short story form, 677, 686; killing of animals in, 677; two hunts, 679, 682; murder of parents, 683; the black stag, 683; self-portrait of Flaubert in, 684, 686; expiation in service, theme of, 684; leper in, 685; mentioned, 5, 131, 370, 658, 672, 673, 675, 677, 681, 684

Saint Polycarp's Day, celebration in Flaubert's honor, 707-708, 741

Saint Romain Fair: marionette show at, 31

Saint-Simon, Utopian Socialist, 468

Saint-Victor, Paul de: offended Flaubert, 571

Sainte-Beuve, C h a r l e s Augustin: effect on Flaubert, 20; comments on Madame Bovary, 363, 364; attacked in Lui, 387; criticism of Salammbô, 433; started Restaurant Magny dinners, 457; death, 545-46; mentioned, 40, 52, 251, 381, 401, 418, 424, 426, 440, 480, 487, 523, 546

Salammbô: daughter of Hamilcar Barca, 397; and the zaïmph

(veil), 405, 408; desires for religion and love, 407; analysis of her character, 409; dance with the python, 411

Salammbô, foreshadowed by *Smarh*, 50; hallucinations in, 77, 412; effect of Flaubert's trip to Egypt on, 198; exaggeration in, 233, 335; aspiration toward love theme of, 383; five years in the writing of, 393; choice of subject and characters, 396, 397; study for, 398; main hazards in story, 402; Feast of the Mercenaries, 403; sieges in, 404; epileptic seizures in, 409; sadism in, 413, 419, 423, 425, 674, 680; and classical concepts, 414, 415; new dimension given to French literature by, 414; use of sources, 417, 418; overly detailed, 418; erudition and fabrication, 418-19; use of symbols, 420; repulsiveness, 424, 425-26; metaphor displaced by direct adjective, 428; terms of sale, 433; reception, 433; opera form, 436; mentioned, 109, 137, 215, 235, 372-73, 375, 381, 395, 399, 401, 402, 403, 420, 423, 429-30, 431-32, 477, 479, 577, 676, 680, 699

Salomé: dance of patterned after Azizeh, 224

Sand, George: inscribed copy of *Bovary* for, 363; attacked in *Lui*, 387; friendly relationship with Flaubert, 391, 462-63, 464-65, 466, 551, 568, 634, 635, 658; visit to Croisset, 463-64; concern with Flaubert's v i o l e n c e, 561, 687; death, 657, 690; place in literature, 658; criticism of Flaubert, 665; correspondence with Flaubert, 739; mentioned, 31, 49, 148, 447, 453, 481, 523, 539, 546, 548, 549, 562, 612, 624, 625, 634, 648, 651, 654, 677

Sand, Maurice, 580, 636, 657

Sarcey, Francisque, 707

Schahabarim, high priest of Tanit in *Salammbô*, 405, 407, 408

Schlésinger, Elisa: first meeting with Flaubert, 24-25; story of her life, 27-28; effect on Flaubert, 44-45; in first and final *Sentimental Education*, 108, 474, 475, 494; resemblance to Murillo's "Virgin," 217; copy of *Bovary* sent to, 363; illness and death, 639; mentioned, 77, 88, 146, 258, 260, 294, 388-89, 412, 460, 477, 562, 569, 586, 750 n2

Schlésinger, Maurice, 26-27, 28, 81-82, 108, 116, 185, 284, 559

School of Common Sense, 32

Scott, Sir Walter, 603

Sénard: defense lawyer in Flaubert trial, 358, 361; mentioned, 356, 362, 627, 728

Sentimental Education, A (the first form): as a satire, 12; autobiographical features of, 41, 108; plot, characters, theme, 106; criticism, 106; suicide, 108; derivation, 110-11; in New York, 112; Negro in, 113; tale of the mangy dog, 117-18; mentioned, 26, 27, 107, 109, 137, 172, 175, 295, 298, 340, 479

Sentimental Education, A (final form): story of Elisa Schlésinger, 460; material for on trip to England, 462; attack on apathy of the day, 470; early sketch, 474; picture of youth, 478-79; purpose, 479; bourgeois character, 480; influence of Balzac, 480; difficulty in development, 481; autobiographical features, 493, 499, 500, 526; characters, 475, 482-83, 495, 498; general outline, 483-85; meaning and unity, 486; fusion of fact and fiction, 521; aphorisms and observations, 528-29; criticisms,

Sentimental Education—Cont.
538, 539; h a l l u c i n a t i o n and
dreams, 680; second edition, 718;
mentioned, 441, 449, 453, 455, 477,
481, 489, 499, 501-507 *passim*, 509,
510, 513, 522, 523, 525
Seven Capital Sins, 574
Seven Deadly Sins, 173, 177, 178
Sévigné, Madame de, 148
"Sheik, The," 18, 191
Simple Heart, A, written for
George Sand, 660, 687, 696; plan,
687; religious aspect, 692-93; the
parrot, 695; death of Félicité, 696;
reception of, 706; mentioned, 9,
15, 688, 689, 690
Smarh: sources of the tale, 49; idea
of God, 50; loose structure, 51;
mentioned, 158, 172, 279
Smith, Adam: and *Economic Man*,
19
Spencer, Herbert, 720
Spendius, Greek slave of Hamilcar
Barca, 403, 429
Sphinx and Chimera, 180, 579
Spinoza, Benedictus de, 48, 117, 173,
720
Staël, Madame de, 127, 148
Sterne, *Sentimental Journey*, 106
Switzerland, Flaubert's visit to, 127,
643-45

Tacitus, 64
Taine, Hippolyte: correspondence
of with Flaubert, 472-73; comment on *Sentimental Education*,
488, 539; approved of use of hallucinations, 583; reaction to *Saint
Anthony*, 628; at Flaubert's Sundays, 630; comments on *Herodias*,
704; suggested library post for
Flaubert, 727; mentioned, 326, 416,
450-51, 457, 479, 575, 576, 664, 709
Temptation of Saint Anthony, The:
early interest in Saint Anthony
story, 31; Breughel picture, 131;
effect of Brittany trip on idea,
158, 166; dedication, 170; completion, 171; reading for, 173; Seven
Deadly Sins in, 173, 177, 178; and
Flaubert's temptations, 176, 179;
literary device used for, 177, failure of metaphysics in, 331; adverse judgment of Du Camp and
Bouilhet, 371; publication delayed,
566; illusion, 573-74, 579; outline,
574; A n t h o n y 's trance, 575;
Queen of Sheba, 575; Procession
of Heresies, 575-76; Procession of
Gods, 576, 577; Procession from
the Parthenon, 577; the Devil, 578-
79; Procession of Fabulous Monsters, 580; closing version, 581;
Flaubert's favorite work, 581; attacks by critics, 627; publication
authorized, 627; sale in Russia refused, 627; mentioned, 31, 36, 38,
49, 172, 181-83, 198, 276, 370, 371,
552-53, 573, 574, 575, 577, 581-82
Tennant, Gertrude Collier: visits to
Flaubert, 660, 661, 716; illustrations for *A Simple Heart*, 705;
mentioned, 696, 739. *See also* Gertrude Collier
Thebes and Karnak, 196-97
Thiers, Louis: Flaubert's antagon-
ism to, 527
Third Republic: Flaubert's opposition to, 561
"Three Angels," 569, 637, 662
Three Tales: frame of mind in
writing, 663; religious feeling,
704; success, 717; mentioned, 666,
686, 700. *See also The Legend of
Saint Julian, A Simple Heart,
Herodias*
Tourbey, Jeanne de, 390, 400, 401,
402, 435, 452, 460, 716
Trouville, 23, 66-67, 162, 259, 260,
262, 448

Troyes, Chrétien de, 480

Turgenev, Ivan S e r g e y e v i c h : friendship with Flaubert, 457, 471-72; efforts to secure Russian edition of *Saint Anthony*, 627; at Flaubert's Sundays, 630; encouraged short story idea, 677; translation of *Saint Julian* into Russian, 705; further Russian translations, 705; gift to Flaubert, 710; favorable comment on *Sentimental Education*, 718; visit to Croisset, 728; efforts to help Flaubert, 730, mentioned, 548, 558, 567, 631, 635, 645, 651, 687, 738, 739

Verlaine, Paul, 656

Viardot, Madame, 187, 567, 635

Vigny, Alfred de, 19, 20, 387, 699

Villemain, Abel François, 241

Voltaire, F. M. Arouet de, 19, 102, 330, 422, 551

Volupté, 40, 52

Wordsworth, William, 327

Yuk, servant of Satan in *Smarh*, 50, 51, 158

Zola, Emile: on *Madame Bovary*, 320, 366, 547; explains Flaubert's relations with women, 385; opinion of Flaubert, 547; criticism of *Saint Anthony*, 628; at Flaubert's Sundays, 630; review of *Sentimental Education*, 718; his *Nana* enjoyed by Flaubert, 720; at Flaubert's funeral, 744; mentioned, 66, 394, 471, 561-62, 631, 661, 664, 666, 677, 708, 740